THE BISHOP-ELECT

the Bishop-elect

A STUDY IN MEDIEVAL ECCLESIASTICAL OFFICE

BY ROBERT L. BENSON

PRINCETON, NEW JERSEY

PRINCETON UNIVERSITY PRESS

1968

in memoriam
Ernesti Kantorowicz

Behind this study stands an assumption: Like most societies (including our own), medieval Latin Christendom
devised an elaborate network of ideas to justify and control
the exercise of power. On their most general level, these
doctrines reflect the conception of a right social and even
cosmic order. More concretely, however, these ideas are manifest through the different ways in which medieval men conceived the highest governing offices—emperor, king, pope,
archbishop, bishop—and through the public law defining
their authority. But to understand these offices, one must
examine the theories and acts surrounding the bestowal of
power.

This study devotes its principal attention to the office of
the medieval bishop. In its beginnings, the interest which
eventually led to this book had little to do with the episcopate.
My original inquiry concerned the juristic doctrines on the
office of emperor during the High Middle Ages. As I soon
discovered, however, the Church's jurists constructed their
theories of the imperial office by borrowing from Roman law,
from theology, and above all from the legal definitions of
ecclesiastical office. When I could not find a systematic
account of those aspects of the Church's administrative law
which, in terminology and substance, most deeply affected
the theories of the imperial office, I began to explore. Soon
this expanded inquiry created an independent interest and
acquired a shape of its own. The present study is the product
of this new inquiry into the development of the Church's
constitution. Nonetheless, the initial impulse remains occa-

sionally visible where I have tried to point out political consequences emerging from the canonists' ideas of office.

Specifically, this study focuses on the constitutional status
of the bishop-elect both within the Church and in his relation
to the secular monarch. To explain this twofold topic, several
chapters concentrate on the effects of a new principle within
the Church's constitution: the doctrine asserting that for
most prelates, electoral confirmation is prerequisite to the
exercise of jurisdiction. Tracing various threads in the history
of ecclesiastical office from the eleventh century to the thirteenth, I have relied heavily on the writings of the canon
lawyers during the crucial period from Gratian's *Decretum*
to the Fourth Lateran Council. For through their close familiarity with the machinery of Church government, the canonists' treatises and commentaries both illuminate and illustrate
the new technical language of office and jurisdiction, as this
new idiom crystallized in the twelfth and early thirteenth
centuries.

Delacroix once remarked, "To finish requires a heart of
steel. . . . How many incomplete or uncompletable passages
there are, in what a man calls a finished or complete work!"
This essay touches upon many topics which necessarily could
only be treated in fragmentary fashion: the theory and practice of election, the ideas of office and jurisdiction, the growth
of papal primacy, investiture and the *regalia*, and so forth.
To have dealt with any of these systematically would have
required a radically different or much larger book. In any
case, this essay does not aspire to an unattainable completeness, either in its selection and discussion of topics, or in its
presentation of canonistic texts, or in the list of scholarly
works consulted. Sometimes I have indicated particular problems which deserve a more extended analysis than would be
appropriate in this study. It is better to open doors than to
close them.

*

In my studies and in the writing of this book, I have contracted a larger indebtedness than I can repay in the book's footnotes—or, for that matter, in this Preface.

The research for this book has been generously subsidized through a Fulbright Fellowship in Munich, through a Fellowship from the American Council of Learned Societies, and through grants from the Danforth Foundation funds administered by Wesleyan University, and from the Columbia University Council for Research in the Social Sciences. I am also grateful for hospitality and help from the officials of many libraries and research institutes, in Europe as well as in the United States.

Like all of their students, I owe much to Professor Joseph R. Strayer and to the late Professor Theodor E. Mommsen. At various stages in the writing of this book, other colleagues and friends have also read parts of it. For their criticism and suggestions, my warm thanks go to Professors Herbert A. Arnold, John F. Benton, Gerard E. Caspary, Horst Fuhrmann, Hartmut Hoffmann, John H. Mundy, Glenn Olsen, Brian Tierney, and Kennerly M. Woody.

The two largest debts incurred in the making of this book have not yet been mentioned. First, to Professor Stephan Kuttner: All medievalists—and especially those who have studied medieval law—owe much to his achievements as scholar, as editor, and as founder and director of the Institute of Medieval Canon Law. My own obligation goes far beyond this. His friendship has been a constant support. With unfailing generosity, he has placed at my disposal both the facilities of the Institute and, in countless conversations, his magisterial knowledge of legal history. His comments and criticisms have prevented some of the errors that are inevitable for an amateur venturing into the technical arcana of the professional lawyer.

In September 1963, the death of Professor Ernst H. Kantorowicz deprived this book of its ideal reader, and its author of the chance to repay an enormous debt. At the Uni-

Preface

versity of California, his lectures and seminars first revealed to me the excitement of the historian's inquiry, and his subsequent guidance inspirited my studies. His friends, colleagues, and students can fully understand the measure of this indebtedness. Indeed, his interest and his criticism would have been the author's best reward for the labors of this book.

In the preface to *The King's Two Bodies*, Professor Kantorowicz regretted that he had not devoted a special chapter to "the dualities present in ecclesiastical offices," which "would have been a subject in its own right." Of course, that monumental book provides rich insights into the complexities of ecclesiastical office—and I have not hesitated to borrow from his account. Nonetheless, only after most of these chapters had been written did I realize that this study might properly be regarded as an attempt to trace those "dualities," and thus as a modest supplement to *The King's Two Bodies*. It is therefore doubly appropriate that this book be dedicated to his memory.

RLB

Portland, Connecticut
15 January 1968

CONTENTS

Contents

PART II

The Bishop-Elect Between Church and Monarchy

Contents

ABBREVIATIONS

ABBREVIATIONS IN CITATION OF PRINTED WORKS

Abh.	*Abhandlungen* (usually, Abhandlungen of the learned society indicated by the name of a city following, such as: Abh.Göttingen = Abhandlungen der Gesellschaft der Wissenschaften in Göttingen, philologisch-historische Klasse)
AKKR	*Archiv für katholisches Kirchenrecht*
AUF	*Archiv für Urkundenforschung*
CHR	*The Catholic Historical Review*
CIC	*Codex iuris canonici*
DA	*Deutsches Archiv für Erforschung des Mittelalters*
DDC	*Dictionnaire de droit canonique*
DThC	*Dictionnaire de théologie catholique*
EHR	*The English Historical Review*
FDG	*Forschungen zur deutschen Geschichte*
Gall.Chr.	*Gallia Christiana in provinciis ecclesiasticis distribuata*
HZ	*Historische Zeitschrift*
Jaffé, *Bibl.*	P. Jaffé, *Bibliotheca rerum Germanicarum* (6 vols. Berlin 1864-73)
JK, JE, JL	P. Jaffé, *Regesta pontificum Romanorum ab condita ecclesia ad annum post Christum natum MCXCVIII*, 2nd ed. rev. F. Kaltenbrunner (to 590), P. Ewald (590-882), S. Loewenfeld (882-1198) (2 vols. Berlin 1885-88)

Abbreviations

KG	*Kirchengeschichte*
KR	*Kirchenrecht*
Mansi	J. D. Mansi, *Sacrorum conciliorum nova et amplissima collectio*
MGH	*Monumenta Germaniae historica*
Const	*Constitutiones et acta publica imperatorum et regum*
DD	*Diplomata*
Ep.saec.XIII	*Epistolae saeculi XIII a Regestis pontificum Romanorum selectae*
LdL	*Libelli de lite imperatorum et pontificum*
SS	*Scriptores* (folio)
SS.rer.Germ.	Scriptores rerum Germanicarum in usum scholarum
MIÖG	*Mitteilungen des Instituts für österreichische Geschichtsforschung*
NA	*Neues Archiv der Gesellschaft für ältere deutsche Geschichtskunde*
PBA	*Proceedings of the British Academy*
PL	J. P. Migne, *Patrologia latina*
Po.	A. Potthast, *Regesta pontificum Romanorum* (2 vols. Berlin 1874-75)
PU	*Papsturkunden in [Frankreich, England, etc.]*
Reg.	*Register, Registre, Registrum*
Reg.imp.	*Regesta imperii*, ed. J. F. Böhmer et al., (2nd ed. Innsbruck 1877ff)
RG	*Rechtsgeschichte*
RNI	*Regestum Innocentii III papae super negotio Romani imperii*, ed. Friedrich Kempf (Miscellanea Historiae Pontificiae 12: Rome 1947)
RQSchr	*Römische Quartalschrift für christliche Altertumskunde und Kirchengeschichte*
SB	*Sitzungsberichte* of the learned society indicated by the name of a city following, such

Abbreviations

as: *SB Wien = Sitzungsberichte der kaiserlichen Akademie der Wissenschaften zu
Wien*, philosophisch-historische Klasse

SGrat   *Studia Gratiana*
SGreg   *Studi Gregoriani*
UB   *Urkundenbuch*
ZKG   *Zeitschrift für Kirchengeschichte*
ZRG   *Zeitschrift der Savigny-Stiftung für Rechts-
geschichte*
GA   germanistische Abteilung
KA   kanonistische Abteilung

MANUSCRIPT ABBREVIATIONS

Where there is no possibility of confusion, manuscripts are cited simply by the place of their repository (for example: Rouen = Rouen, Bibliothèque municipale) and by their number. In other cases, an abbreviated indication of the particular library or fond has also been provided. For full information, see the list of "Manuscripts Cited" in the Bibliography. In addition, the following abbreviations are used:

BM   London, British Museum
BN   Paris, Bibliothèque nationale, Manuscrits latins
BN n.a.   —, —, Nouvelles acquisitions latines
Clm   München, Staatsbibliothek, Codex latinus monacensis
Vat.   Città del Vaticano, Biblioteca Apostolica Vaticana, Codices latini
Vat.Arch.   —, Archivio della Basilica di San Pietro (MSS now in the Biblioteca Apostolica Vaticana)
Vat.Pal.   —, —, Codices Palatini latini
Vat.Reg.   —, —, Codices Reginenses

xvii

Abbreviations

The standard editions of the basic legal sources are used throughout:

E. Friedberg, ed., *Corpus iuris canonici* I: *Decretum magistri Gratiani* (Leipzig 1879), and II: *Decretalium collectiones* (Leipzig 1881)

E. Friedberg, ed., *Quinque compilationes antiquae* (Leipzig 1882)

P. Krueger, T. Mommsen, R. Schoell and W. Kroll, eds., *Corpus iuris civilis* (3 vols. Berlin 1877)

For those medieval legal works which were repeatedly republished in the fifteenth and sixteenth centuries, several editions have been consulted, and the citation of page (or folio) numbers has consequently been omitted. The old glossed editions of the *Corpus iuris canonici* contain, in the margins, the commentaries of Johannes Teutonicus (*Glossa ordinaria* on the *Decretum*) and Bernard of Parma (*Glossa ordinaria* on the *Liber extra*).

In legal citations throughout, the first number in each citation refers to the largest unit, and thereafter in the order of size, with the last number referring to the smallest unit.

C.	Causa (*Decreti* pars secunda)
c.	capitulum
Clem.	*Clementinae*
Cod.	*Codex Iustinianus*
Comp.I (*II*, etc.)	*Compilatio prima* (*secunda*, etc.)
D.	Distinctio (*Decreti* pars prima; De poen.; De cons.)
De cons.	De consecratione (*Decreti* pars tertia)
De poen.	Tractatus de penitentia (= C.33 q.3)
dict.p.c.	dictum Gratiani post capitulum
Dig.	*Digesta*
Extrav. com.	*Extravagantes communes*
Extrav. Jo. XXII	*Extravagantes Joannis XXII*

Abbreviations

gl.	gloss, glossa
Gl.ord.	*Glossa ordinaria*
Inst.	*Institutiones*
Nov.	*Novellae*
pr.	principium
q.	quaestio
rubr.	rubrica
VI	*Liber sextus*
X	*Liber extra* (= *Decretales Gregorii IX*)

THE BISHOP-ELECT

CHAPTER I

THE DIMENSIONS OF THE PROBLEM:
AN INTRODUCTION

ᴆuʀɪɴɢ ᴄʜᴇ High Middle Ages the episcopate was, like
monarchy, a universal governing institution throughout Latin
Christendom. The double role—ecclesiastical and secular—
of most bishops heightened the historical importance of epis-
copacy and the episcopate. Every bishop was a successor of
the Apostles and a prince of the Church, possessing both
sacramental and jurisdictional powers, and with a solemn
responsibility for the salvation of Christian souls. Moreover,
most bishops were also princes of this world, whose duties
demanded the combined talents of a politician, an administrator, and even sometimes (at least until the twelfth century)
a soldier. Many bishops bore the rank and title of prince or
baron, and their bishoprics held vast lands and far-reaching
powers of secular jurisdiction. The monarchy's highest officials
and advisers were often drawn from the episcopate. Bishops
governed for the ruler, furnished much of his army, and provided indispensable support. In short, the episcopate was
inextricably enmeshed in the machinery of monarchical government, and a history of the medieval episcopate would
necessarily include a large part of medieval Europe's political
history. As an imperial bishop lucidly explained to the
emperor in the mid-eleventh century, the bishop's twofold
status created a double obligation:

To the Supreme Pontiff, we owe obedience. To you, how-

3

ever, we owe fealty. To you, we are accountable for secular matters, to him for those things which seem to concern the divine office.[1]

Belonging simultaneously to two governmental hierarchies, the bishop derived a portion of his jurisdictional and administrative powers from his monarch, although a portion of his powers was inherent within his ecclesiastical office. In other words, some of these powers were sanctioned by the monarchy, some by the Church. Though usage varied from realm to realm and sometimes even from one decade to the next, these governmental powers were commonly bestowed on bishops-elect, that is, were conferred prior to the episcopal consecration.

During the Middle Ages a wide variety of ceremonial and administrative enactments contributed to the making of a bishop, and within these complex proceedings the different acts fell into categories. Some acts were *prerequisite*, merely guaranteeing eligibility; for example, a candidate for the episcopal office normally had to have received the orders of a priest or deacon.[2] Other acts, such as election, were *designative* and served the function of selecting the candidate. There were acts which were truly *constitutive*, that is, which effectively conveyed powers and status to the candidate and which were therefore operative in moving him significantly closer to the full possession of his office.[3] *Consentaneous* acts expressed approval of the candidate's promotion. Finally, a few acts were purely *declarative*, since they recorded, solemnized, or publicized the previous proceedings. As one might expect, in the Middle Ages these categories were not

---

[1] Wazo of Liège to Henry III, quoted by Anselm, *Gesta episcoporum Leodiensium* c.58, *MGH SS* VII 224 (below, Ch. VIIA n.12 [= Chapter VII Section 1 note 12: form used throughout for cross-references]).

[2] One might further distinguish prerequisite *acts* from prerequisite *conditions* or *characteristics*, such as legitimate birth, minimum age, sufficient knowledge, personal virtue, and so forth.

[3] In modern philosophy, an analogue of the "constitutive act" is the "performative utterance"; on this, see the illuminating and amusing discussion by J. L. Austin, *Philosophical Papers*, ed. J. O. Urmson and G. J. Warnock (Oxford 1961) 220-39.

always exclusive, and a single act could fulfill several functions simultaneously.

These reflections lead to a series of interlocking questions which have never been systematically examined.[4] In constitutional law and theory, what regulations determined the bishop-elect's accession to his powers over men and property? And in practice, at what moments did he gain the different segments of these powers? What ceremonies and formalities signalized this accession? Which powers were sanctioned by the Church, which by the monarchy? Finally, what do these various regulations reveal about the constitutions of Church and monarchy, and about the long competition between them over control of the episcopate?

By the first quarter of the twelfth century, Church and monarchy had just begun to be aware of these questions. By the first quarter of the thirteenth century, however, the questions had been subtly formulated, and differing answers had been proposed. Both ecclesiastical and secular law had established separate requirements for the bishop-elect's exercise of his powers. Indeed, throughout the thirteenth century there was an unmistakable tension between the secular and the ecclesiastical norms for the bishop-elect. To sum up the problem: What were the various constitutive acts in the making of a bishop, and what was their significance?

This is, then, a study of the changing constitutional status of the bishop-elect in the twelfth and thirteenth centuries. Within the Church during these two centuries, Roman— that is, Curial—and Bolognese conceptions of canonical procedure were spreading to every part of Latin Christendom. So far as the Church's norms and practices are concerned, therefore, the evidence and the conclusions of this study represent the entire Latin world. In tracing the monarchical regulations for the bishop-elect, however, this study concen-

4 Needless to say, historians of the medieval Church's constitution have regularly noted most of these questions; consult, for example, the classic and still indispensable work by Paul Hinschius, *Das Kirchenrecht der Katholiken und Protestanten* (6 vols. Berlin 1869-97).

trates mainly on Germany, with an occasional comparative glance at other lands, most frequently at France.

1. The Powers of an *Electus*

27 May 1917: By decree of pope Benedict XV, the *Codex iuris canonici* became the official legal code of the Roman Catholic Church.[1] The *Codex* thus superseded all of the great monuments from the classical period of canon law. Especially, it replaced those official collections of Church law which form part of the *Corpus iuris canonici*: the *Decretales* (1234), the *Liber sextus* (1298), and the *Clementinae* (1312-17).[2] Similarly discarded were all but a few of the great mass of uncodified decretals issued during the six centuries between 1298 and 1917, and except under the most extraordinary circumstances, in case of conflict the *Codex* overrides customary law. That enormous body of outdated law, no longer of immediate interest to the jurist, passed uncontested into the historian's hands.

Everything which touches the complex life of the Church is regulated within the new codification. Of course, long before 1917, election had ceased to be the normal mode of selecting bishops, and the *Codex* stipulates that "the Roman pontiff appoints them freely."[3] Nonetheless, in some places various modes of promotion—including election—continue to exist by concordat with secular states. As one would expect of a systematic codification, the *Codex* offers a detailed discussion of election, as well as other methods of promoting to an ecclesiastical office, with special provision for the election of bishops.[4] Since the High Middle Ages the Church has sought

[1] Since 1917 the *Codex* has been frequently reprinted. In general, see Hans Erich Feine, *Kirchliche Rechtsgeschichte* I: *Die Katholische Kirche* (2nd ed. Weimar 1954) 637ff; Alfons M. Stickler, *Historia iuris canonici latini* I: *Historia fontium* (Turin 1950) 371ff.

[2] Stickler, *op.cit.* I 197ff and esp. 237ff; also, Feine, *RG* I 254ff.

[3] *CIC* can.329 §2.

[4] *CIC* can.160-78, 329 §3, 321; Anscar Parsons, *Canonical Elections* (Washington, D.C. 1939) chs. 7-12. On *postulatio* as an alternative method, cf. *CIC* can.179-82.

The Dimensions of the Problem

to widen the gulf between the clerical and the lay spheres of
action and, so far as possible, to deprive the laity of an active
role in Church affairs. In its canons on election the *Codex*
reexpresses this tendency. The layman is strictly excluded
from ecclesiastical elections; if lay influence interferes with
an election in any way, the election itself is invalid.[5] On the
other hand, the twofold status of the bishop has vanished as
an anachronism in the twentieth century, and the death of
that world in which bishops were also secular princes is now
officially recognized and certified. In 1951 pope Pius XII
issued a consistorial decree forbidding bishops and all other
ordinaries to use the titles and emblems of nobility, "even if
these are connected to an episcopal or archiepiscopal see."[6]

In characteristically precise terms the *Codex* defines the
constitutional status of an elected but not yet consecrated
prelate, that is, of an *electus*: If an ecclesiastical election has
been accepted and does not need the confirmation of a
superior, the *electus* immediately has full administrative rights
in his office.[7] The most obvious example of this kind of office
is the papacy, for properly elected and having accepted the
election, the Roman pontiff-elect (who of course has no
superior) immediately obtains his full powers.[8] In 1904
Pius X had already stressed the same point in a constitution
which retained its validity after 1917 as an appendix to the
Codex, and though his constitution was superseded by a
constitution of Pius XII in 1945, Pius XII repeated this statement verbatim:

When his consent has been given . . . , the pontiff-elect is

5 *CIC* can.166, 2390 §2.
6 *Acta Apostolicae Sedis* 43 (1951) 480; Leo Santifaller, *Zur Geschichte
des ottonisch-salischen Reichskirchensystems* (Vienna 1954-55) 110-18,
137-41. In 1644 Innocent X decreed the same prohibition for the cardinals;
in 1915 Benedict XV extended the prohibition to patriarchs, archbishops,
and bishops—"unless perhaps a certain secular dignity is connected to the
episcopal or archiepiscopal see."
7 *CIC* can.176 §2: "Acceptatione electionis electus, si confirmatione non
egeat, plenum ius statim obtinet; secus, non acquirit nisi ius ad rem."
8 *CIC* can.219.

7

the true pope, and he receives and can exercise in action a full and absolute jurisdiction over the entire world.[9]

Yet for most other prelates, a different body of regulations governs the accession. If the election needs confirmation, soon after he has accepted the election, the elected official must request its confirmation from the competent superior.[10] Under no circumstances may the *electus* administer his office before he has received and shown the written confirmation of his election, and the *Codex* provides severe penalties for unauthorized administration.[11] An accepted election merely confers a claim upon the office and upon its powers (*ius ad rem*), but "unless something else is stipulated in law," the confirmation entitles the prelate-elect to exercise his full jurisdictional powers of office (*plenum ius in officio*).[12] The bishop-elect is a special case, however, since confirmation is not the only prerequisite to the exercise of his powers: before he is entitled to govern his diocese in any way, he must, either personally or through a proctor, "canonically take possession" of it.[13]

Within the *Codex*, the canons relevant to the episcopal office presuppose a fundamental distinction between two different areas of activity: the powers of a bishop in his

---

[9] Pius X, *Vacante Sede Apostolica* §88 (*CIC* Documenta no.1); Pius XII, *Vacantis Apostolicae Sedis* §101 (*Acta Apostolicae Sedis* 38 [1946] 97 = *Apollinaris* 19 [1946] 173).

[10] *CIC* can.177 §1.

[11] *CIC* can.176 §3: "Ante acceptam confirmationem ipsi praetextu electionis non licet sese immiscere administrationi officii sive in spiritualibus sive in temporalibus, et actus ab eo forte positi nulli sunt." Also, *CIC* can.2394.

[12] The *ius ad rem* appears in *CIC* can.176 §2 (above, n.7). Also, cf. *CIC* can.177 §4: "Recepta confirmatione, electus obtinet plenum ius in officio, nisi aliud in iure caveatur." In these two canons, the *Codex* was echoing the technical terminology of 13th-century administrative law, which similarly contrasted a simple claim upon an office (*ius ad rem petendam*) with a fully effective right to the office (*ius in re*). On this medieval duality, see Carl Gross, *Das Recht an der Pfründe* (Graz 1887); Franz Gillmann, "Zum Problem vom Ursprung des ius ad rem," *AKKR* 113 (1933) 463-85.

[13] *CIC* can.334 §2. Similarly, a parish priest receives his *cura animarum* at "the moment of taking possession" (*CIC* can.461). In general, on the *missio in possessionem*, see *CIC* can.1443-46.

capacity as priest, and those in his capacity as leader of a community.[14] On the one hand, through the "power of his orders" (*potestas ordinis*), the bishop has the sacramental competencies of any priest; he can, for instance, say mass. In addition, however, he has sacramental powers which derive solely from his episcopal consecration. Above all, only a bishop can consecrate another bishop, ordain priests, and prepare the oils and chrisms used in ecclesiastical ceremonies. Though normally episcopal, certain other powers can, by command of the pope, be delegated to a priest: bestowal of the sacrament of confirmation, ordination to minor orders, and the consecration of altars and liturgical objects.[15] On the other hand, through his "power of jurisdiction" (*potestas iurisdictionis*), the bishop holds—subject to the Roman pontiff—the supreme judicial, legislative, and governmental authority within his diocese. To the bishop alone pertain such rights as the calling of a synod, the filling of offices, the higher disciplinary powers. By virtue of the proprietary rights annexed to his "power of jurisdiction," he also administers the revenues and properties of the diocese. The various elements of the *potestas iurisdictionis* are, of course, purely ecclesiastical: they derive none of their authority from any civil power.[16]

As set forth in the *Codex*, the regulations on the status of prelates-elect belong to a systematic body of administrative and constitutional law. Without glancing at cardinal Gasparri's useful notes to the *Codex*, one might easily be unaware that these provisions have a history, and that they were once an object of uncertainty and disagreement.[17] As cardinal Gas-

[14] Feine, *RG* I 37f, 191f, 323, and the literature cited there; see especially Hinschius, *KR* II 40ff.

[15] The right of consecrating kings was formerly reckoned among those powers which are normally episcopal, but it is not mentioned in the *Codex*.

[16] The *Codex* asserts, for example, that the Church's *potestas coactiva* is "independens a qualibet humana auctoritate" (can.2214 §1).

[17] Not all editions of the *Codex* contain cardinal Gasparri's historical notes. And even these valuable notes give no reminder of the medieval monarchical regulations for prelates-elect.

parri's notes reveal, however, the *Codex* commonly drew its content—often even its wording—from Gratian's *Decretum* and especially from the decretals and constitutions issued since the mid-twelfth century. Crucial concepts, such as the idea of jurisdiction, first acquired precision in the later twelfth and early thirteenth centuries, when the Bolognese canonists elaborated new constitutional theories and a new constitutional terminology. Indeed, in those essential elements which concern the papal, archiepiscopal, and episcopal offices, the Church's constitutional structure gained most of its present form during the High Middle Ages. Largely complete by 1300, those portions of the structure were created mainly by canon lawyers and by canonistically trained popes. Before one can trace the changing status of the bishop-elect, therefore, the next task is to survey the achievements of these canonists.

2. *Dramatis personae*: The Canonists[1]

It is appropriate to begin a discussion of medieval canon law with Gratian's *Decretum*, which marks the end of an era in legal history and the beginning of a new age. Before

[1] Within the scope of a specialized study on the Church's constitution one cannot furnish a general introductory history of medieval canon law. The rest of this chapter has a far more modest aim: to identify the canonists briefly, to sketch broadly a few features of their work, and to suggest their importance. That is to say, the following pages are intended merely to indicate a context and perspective in which to view the canonists' achievement. Of course, any scholar who has studied the medieval canon lawyers will need neither a proof of their importance, nor a key to their technical language, nor a guide to the growing scholarly literature about them. For the unfamiliar reader, however, the complexity of medieval canon law creates formidable obstacles, and requires a more extensive introduction than the next few pages can offer:

On the growth of canon law from Gratian to Gregory IX see Stephan Kuttner, *Repertorium der Kanonistik 1140-1234* (Vatican City 1937), an indispensable reference work. (Throughout the present study, even where it has not been cited in footnotes, his book should be presupposed as the basic authority for statements on canonistica during this period; Professor Kuttner is now preparing a second edition.) On canon law before Gratian consult Paul Fournier and Gabriel LeBras, *Histoire des collections canoniques en Occident depuis les fausses décrétales jusqu'au Décret de Gratien* (2 vols. Paris 1931-32); for the period after 1234 one must rely, at least

The Dimensions of the Problem

Gratian's work, canon law was considered a branch of theology, and master Gratian was, in fact, a Camaldolese monk who taught theology at Bologna. But after the appearance of his *Decretum* around 1140, canon law became an independent and enormously influential discipline; it became a system and a science. The *Decretum* is a compilation of texts rather than a treatise of single authorship. For his sources Gratian incorporated passages from the older canon law, and he included materials from almost every other corner of medieval life. In its final revision the *Decretum* includes papal and conciliar decrees, patristic writings, Roman and Germanic law, royal and imperial documents, collections of letters, and selections from historical, theological, and liturgical works, as well as from works which practically defy categories (or which are at least *sui generis*), like the philological encyclopedia of Isidore of Seville. The variousness of Gratian's sources is important, for this diversity gave to the new discipline a breadth and scope unequalled by any other area of medieval learning. This was decisive in the formation of canonistic doctrine on controversial questions, since the canon lawyers could thus assemble superb arsenals of authoritative texts supporting widely divergent interpretations.

In the *Decretum* Gratian had sought to reconcile the conflicts in the inherited body of law, custom, precedent, and precept, to resolve the contradictions and to create a *Concordia discordantium canonum*—as his own title for the work tells us. For the half-century following its publication, as their principal task the canon lawyers tried to fulfill Gratian's purpose by the elucidation of his formidable book. The main tradition of these efforts by the decretists—glosses, summa-

partially, on the older work by Johann Friedrich von Schulte, *Die Geschichte der Quellen und Literatur des canonischen Rechts von Gratian bis auf die Gegenwart* (3 vols. Stuttgart 1875-80) II.

Since the publication of Professor Kuttner's *Repertorium* in 1937, and especially since the end of World War II, 12th- and 13th-century canon law has been studied intensively. Appendix 1 provides an introductory guide to the recent works on this subject.

ries, commentaries, treatises, abridgments, and rearrangements—stretches from the early and relatively primitive *Summa* by Gratian's pupil Paucapalea, to the authoritative commentary on the *Decretum*, the *Glossa ordinaria* by Johannes Teutonicus (1210-15), and beyond. Beginning with Gratian, the school of Bologna became and remained the center of canonistic studies, but canon law was soon taught in a French school at Paris, in the Anglo-Norman school at Oxford, and in a Rhenish school at Cologne.

The aim of Gratian and the decretists was to mold a consistent body of law which would be equally applicable everywhere in the entire Church—in short, to create a Common Law for the Church. By itself, the work of the schools could never have achieved this end. However, in 1159 a professional canonist, master Roland Bandinelli, was elevated as Alexander III to the throne of Peter. Apart from its considerable importance in other ways, his long pontificate (1159-81) was a period of prodigious legal activity. More than seven hundred of Alexander's decretals have been preserved. This impressive mass of decretals regulated every aspect of the Church's life in every part of Europe. A decretal was not necessarily, *per se*, universally binding and valid law, just as the *Decretum* was not—and never became—an authentic book of Church law. The decretals were simply letters in which the pope, either alone or with the consultation of the cardinals, answered the various questions which had been referred to the papal Curia, chiefly questions on legal and administrative problems. But like the *Decretum*, the decretals had the highest authority as a repository for legal doctrine and theory, as an inexhaustible quarry for legal cases and precedents, and as a chief source from which the law was formed and justified.

As the mass of decretals grew in the second half of the twelfth century, there arose the urgent problem, almost immediately recognized by contemporary canonists, of reconciling the *Decretum* with the newer material embodied in these papal decisions. The canonists undertook this task in three ways. First, even before the Third Lateran Council, in the various decretistic commentaries, they began the process of incorporating the decretals by citing them in the proofs of their arguments and in their interpretations of the *Decretum*. Second, they also undertook the long job of collecting and systematizing the decretals—at first simply by appending some decretals to a text of the *Decretum*, later by making separate collections of decretals, and finally by systematically arranging their decretal collections in categories (*tituli*) according to subject matter. Third, in the last decade of the twelfth century, canonists began to compose glosses, summaries, and commentaries on these systematic collections.

This long development culminated in the brilliant pontificate of Innocent III (1198-1216), who had studied canon law at Bologna under master Huguccio, the greatest of the decretists. For eighteen years new decretals poured forth, and the preliminary work of studying, collecting, and organizing the new and old decretals went steadily forward. During his pontificate five major systematic collections were prepared. By 1220 decretalists had written more than a dozen commentaries to explicate the three most important collections—the first three of the *Compilationes antiquae*. It is unnecessary here to trace the steps which led to the promulgation in 1234 of the *Liber extra vagantium*, commissioned by Gregory IX and edited by Raymond of Peñafort. The *Liber extra* (or *Decretales*, to use its other name) was an official papal collection superseding all previous compilations. It was, moreover, exclusive: since Gregory's bull of promulgation decreed that no other collection might be made nor any other used in school or court, it created a papal monopoly on the collecting and editing of decretals. For the rest of the thirteenth century the major task confronting the canon lawyers was the interpretation and elucidation of this immense corpus.

The canonists of the twelfth and thirteenth centuries were scholars and also, for the most part, teachers. Still, the ideas and events which we shall examine appeared on a larger stage than any classroom or library affords. Indeed, the canonists played a role which crucially affected the transformation of the Church's structure, the relations between Church and monarchy, and ultimately the lives of Latin Christians on all levels of society. How, then, could these scholar-teachers affect the history of their age?

The Middle Ages, it is customarily said, was a law-centered period. On the simplest level, this means that the medieval ruler, far from being an arbitrary despot, was considered subject to the restraints of law; it means that customary and positive law prescribed the proper relations between individual and individual, between group and group. More important for the political and constitutional development of the twelfth and thirteenth centuries, however, was the emergence of a new scientific jurisprudence around 1100, as men began, once again, to study intensively and systematically the sources of ancient Roman law. Within the same generation, the inherited tradition of Church law was receiving a fresh critical scrutiny. As the sacramental character of kingship, which had been a dominant idea in the Early Middle Ages, receded in the twelfth century, it was supplanted by a new, primarily juridical conception of the royal office. To contemporaries, there was nothing improbable in the famous tale about emperor Frederick Barbarossa, who asked two distinguished Roman lawyers of Bologna whether as "lord of the world" (*dominus mundi*) he had absolute property rights or simply a worldwide jurisdiction. Correspondingly, Innocent III found a place for his decretal *Venerabilem*, which discussed the imperial election and the imperial office, in the *Compilatio tertia* under the title "On election and on the power of an elected official" (*De electione et electi potestate*); again, the political problem could be subsumed under a legal category. Indeed, the idea of the State, in its modern sense, first began to emerge as a juridical concept in the twelfth century under the influence of Romano-canonical public and private law. For the High Middle Ages, in short, political power and institutions were *legally* definable. Forcefully and to great effect, the professional Roman and canon lawyers defined the origins and nature of political authority within both *regnum* and *ecclesia*. Politics was, so to speak, a branch of scientific jurisprudence. It should be no surprise that canon law embraced the realm of political values and political theory, for the canonists inherited from the *Decretum* a wider range of professional interests and information than could be found among their contemporaries in other fields of knowledge—indeed, wider than one would usually find among the lawyers of our own century. Through their concern with divine law and natural law, they had a share in the theological speculations of their time, and it was not at all foreign to the spirit of canonistic science that the first *titulus* in the *Liber extra* consists of two long decretals "On the Supreme Trinity and the Catholic Faith" (*De summa trinitate et fide catholica*). Theological literature was also directly enriched by the canonists; as examples of twelfth-century canonist-theologians, both master Gandulph and master Roland (Alexander III) wrote *Sententiae*, and a number of shorter theological works were composed by cardinal Laborans and by Omnebene, the editor of an *Abbreviatio decreti*. Roman law, as well as theology, lay within the canonists' province. Most canonists enjoyed a substantial working acquaintance with the corpus of Roman law, many had studied under professional Roman lawyers, and some—like Laurentius Hispanus, Gerard Pucelle, and others —were masters of both laws. This intellectual versatility sometimes extended even further: master Huguccio was also a grammarian and lexicographer, and, as another example, besides his *Summa* on the *Decretum*, Sicard of Cremona wrote a chronicle, a liturgical treatise, and a *Liber mythologiarum*.

To some extent, nonspecialization can be considered characteristic of the European intellectual community in the High Middle Ages, and the canonists' versatility may well have been a reflection of this; but even more, versatility was, one might say, an obvious requirement arising from the all-inclusiveness of canon law. For in the High Middle Ages ecclesiastical courts were competent to treat practically all of the cases which now appear before civil tribunals, as well as some cases (like heresy) which have no official place in the modern codes of civil and criminal law. At all times theology and Roman law were surely instructive for the canonist, especially when he was confronted by a theoretical problem or a question of private law (as we should say: civil law). But at any moment the professional canonist might have to deal with matters of sacramental doctrine, liturgical practice, procedural law in the courtroom, administrative law for the various offices in the Church, contractual law, usury and business ethics, marriage, and various other legal or moral problems in the daily life of ordinary Christians. Or he might be called upon to discuss the nature of temporal power, especially in its relation to the Church.

Between the mid-eleventh and the mid-fourteenth century, the structure and government of the Church were decisively transformed, rationalized, and centralized. Even more narrowly, one can regard the span from the mid-twelfth century to the mid-thirteenth as the crucially formative period in the development of the Church's constitution. In this respect, the topic of the present study—the changing position of the bishop-elect—was merely one part of a vast process which remade the medieval Church. It is no coincidence that the key period in this transformation overlapped with the most brilliant phase in the growth of canon law, that is, with the great century stretching from Gratian's *Decretum* to Gregory IX's *Decretales*. Needless to say, the canonists accurately reflected the changes in the Church's structure. But they did more than this. Administrative and (as we should say) constitutional law were major concerns for the canonists. Understandably, therefore, canonistically formed concepts lay at the center of these new developments within the Church. Since theories of election, office, and jurisdiction belonged to the canonist's stock in trade, a constitutional study of the bishop-elect—like any study of the Church's constitution in the High Middle Ages—must place special emphasis on the canonistic contribution to the transformation of the Church.

Like the Church itself, canon law was never the province of a single nation. Rather, it was a European phenomenon. The law of the Church was, in fact, achieving the universality which the civilian glossators claimed theoretically for Roman law. Increasingly, as a result of the canonists' efforts, a uniform law was practiced and used in the ecclesiastical courts and chanceries of Europe. From every part of Latin Christendom clerics streamed toward Bologna, Paris, and the other canonistic centers. Within these schools the scholars and teachers whose writings they studied and whose lectures they heard were an international group. The Italians included: Paucapalea, Roland, Simon, Sicard, Huguccio, and Tancred. From France: Stephen of Tournai, Evrard of Ypres, and Peter of Blois. England, Ireland, and Wales could boast a large contingent: Odo of Dover, Honorius, John of Tynemouth, Robert of Flamesbury, John of Fintona, Gilbertus, Ricardus, Alanus, and Johannes Galensis. From Hungary: Paulus Ungarus and Damasus. From Germany: Johannes Teutonicus and the authors of the *Summa Inperatorie maiestati* and the *Summa Elegantius in iure divino.* Spain and Portugal contributed heavily: Petrus Hispanus and (for the sake of confusion) Petrus Hispanus-Portugalensis, Melendus, John of Petesella, Bernard of Compostella, Laurentius, Vincentius, and Raymond of Peñafort. The canonists moved freely and frequently from place to place, and the mobility of their cosmopolitan world was important for the diffusion of canonistic doctrine. At the same time, the local peculiarities of customary law, as practiced in their homelands or in the countries where they studied, modified their legal conceptions. Similarly, national origin was an element in the formation of the canonists' political opinions: Vincentius Hispanus and Alanus Anglicus were nationalists, vigorously asserting the sovereignty of the national monarchies, while Johannes

Teutonicus was a passionate imperialist who regarded the German emperor as the *dominus mundi.*

During the hundred and fifty years from the mid-twelfth century to 1300, a revolution took place in central Europe. Around 1150 the empire was a power of the first magnitude in the European constellation, and the papacy was in the ascendant. A hundred and fifty years later the papacy had achieved, like the national monarchies, an extraordinary degree of centralization, it seemed at the height of its power, and it was still extending its claims under the aggressive leadership of Boniface VIII. After a century of struggle between empire and papacy the Hohenstaufen dynasty had been finally exterminated, and in the jubilee year 1300 the imperial throne had been officially empty for fifty-five years. To leap from 1150 to 1300, however, is to cross the distance from Gratian and Alexander III to Boniface VIII—in short, the great age of the canon lawyers as well as the high tide of medieval papalism. During that period, the papacy and the Church at large—indeed, the entire history of Western Europe —were profoundly altered by the work of the canonists, for it is surely apparent that the papacy itself stood at the very center of the development of canon law, where it guided that movement and was at the same time transformed by it. Several popes in that age were themselves professional canon lawyers, Bolognese masters, like Alexander III and like the distinguished glossator, master Albert of Benevento, who ascended the papal throne in 1187 as Gregory VIII and who issued a number of important decretals during his brief pontificate. More typical for the background of the thirteenth-century popes, however, was the study of canon law as a general preparation for an administrative career within the Church. Canonistically trained administrators were entrusted with the great legatine commissions which did so much to consolidate the powerful position of the papacy throughout Europe. Of course, Bologna could offer no infallible recipe for a brilliant career, but the canonist's prospects were good.

The Dimensions of the Problem

One might, for example, look at a list of canonists between the mid-twelfth and the mid-thirteenth century who held high Church office—archbishops, bishops, and archdeacons: Rufinus, Stephen of Tournai, Sicard of Cremona, Gerard Pucelle, Huguccio, Bernard of Pavia, Laurentius, Vincentius, Tancred, and others. Equally impressive would be a roster of the Sacred College from the same period, which would show a number of distinguished canonists among the cardinals: the glossator Cardinalis, Laborans, master Peter of Benevento, Godfrey of Trani (who wrote the first *Summa* on the *Liber extra*), and the great Hostiensis.

In that legal age canon lawyers were, so to speak, the leading intellectuals, holding positions of power and influence within the Church. Among them were many of the most vital and original minds in Europe. They transformed the Church's institutions, and the papacy became increasingly a canonistic creation. Indeed, within the Church the jurisdictional primacy of the Roman bishop was most authoritatively defined by the canon lawyers. By their leadership and loyalty, as well as through the ideological weapons which they forged for the papal armory, the canonists, more than anyone else, brought the papacy to the preeminence which it had throughout the thirteenth century, with regard both to the Church and to the secular world. By their contributions to the Church's various struggles against the empire and the other monarchies, the canonists could claim much credit for the victories won. Moreover, contemporaries clearly recognized their part in these conflicts. The exiled Thomas Becket turned to the study of canon law in a search for arguments against Henry II, and the archbishop's friend John of Salisbury was fearful that canon law would stiffen Becket in his intransigent opposition to the king. And in the early fourteenth century, writing the *Monarchia*, his great vision of universal empire, Dante bitterly attacked and denounced the high papalism of the decretalists —reluctant homage to the effectiveness of their role in Europe's history. Even two centuries after Dante the memory

19

and the meaning of the canonists' achievements had not disappeared. After Philip Melanchthon and Martin Luther burned, among other works, the corpus of Church law, Luther explained that he had included the canon law "because it makes the pope a god on earth."

PART ONE

THE BISHOP-ELECT AND HIS
ECCLESIASTICAL JURISDICTION

CHAPTER II

CONSTITUTIONAL BACKGROUND:
GRATIAN'S *DECRETUM*

1. Episcopal and Papal Election

the chapters of the *Decretum* represent the accumulated production of ten centuries. These texts furnish an impressive sampling of the surviving evidence for the ecclesiastical history of the Early Middle Ages, and a close study of the *Decretum* illuminates not only the structure of Gratian's thought, but also its early medieval background. Indeed, since every canonist of the generations after 1140 was schooled in the *Decretum*, this great compilation is also an indispensable point of departure for any inquiry into the constitutional history of the Church in the later twelfth and thirteenth centuries.

Within the *Decretum*, master Gratian devoted three *distinctiones* almost entirely to an analysis of ecclesiasical election, and relevant materials are scattered at many other points.[1] Specifically on episcopal election, Gratian drew from the Council of Nicaea in 325, from the Second Lateran Council in 1139, and from every century between.[2] Consequently, different conceptions of election are visible side by side in the

[1] Mainly, D.61-63; further important texts can be found in D.64-65. Cf. also C.7-8, and elsewhere (e.g., D.23 c.2 §3; D.51 c.5 §1). The fundamental study of Gratian's electoral doctrine is by Johann Baptist Sägmüller, *Die Bischofswahl bei Gratian* (Cologne 1908). For shorter accounts see Parsons, *Canonical Elections* 47-51; Marcel Pacaut, *Louis VII et les élections épiscopales dans le royaume de France* (Paris 1957) 37-41.

[2] D.64 c.1 (325); D.63 c.35 (1139).

Decretum. Like the shards of a midden under the eye of an archaeologist, Gratian's *capitula* reveal the historical layers in the development of electoral theory and practice. To be sure, Gratian did not arrange his electoral chapters in chronological order, and the full meaning of their pattern becomes apparent only after one has grouped the various fragments into the historical periods of their origin, has sketched the sequence assigned to them by Gratian, and has examined Gratian's own remarks on the nature of ecclesiastical election.

From the Church councils of the fourth century until the *Decretum,* the Church regarded election and consecration as the two crucial acts in the making of a bishop.[3] Throughout most of this long period active participation in an episcopal election was not the prerogative of a closed body of electors, for both custom and opinion granted to everyone concerned a voice in the selection of a new bishop.[4] Though already formed by the fifth century, the main elements in the early medieval concept of election survived into the twelfth century. Indeed, a majority of the chapters in Gratian's electoral *distinctiones* derive from the fourth, fifth, and sixth centuries. The views of Celestine I, Leo the Great, and Gregory the Great were the typical expressions of this early age, and the letters of these three pontiffs are well represented in the *Decretum.*[5]

In fifth-century practice, the bishops of each province had primary responsibility for the election of a new colleague.[6]

[3] See, for example, D.40 c.8 (wrongly ascribed by Gratian to Isidore of Seville): ". . . electio et consecratio . . . faciunt episcopum . . ."; the same idea is repeated by Geoffrey of Vendôme, *Libelli* 2, 3, *MGH LdL* II 684, 687. Note also the implication in D.62 pr.: ". . . uidendum est, a quibus sunt eligendi et consecrandi. . . ."

[4] There is an enormous literature on episcopal election in the Early Middle Ages. For a brief summary with citation of recent scholarship, see Feine, *RG* I 109f, 224, 226 and passim; for a more detailed discussion, Hinschius, *KR* II 512-78.

[5] Of the 48 *capitula* in D.61-63, a total of 20 can be traced to these three popes.

[6] Feine, *RG* I 109f; a detailed account is given by François Louis Ganshof, "Note sur l'élection des évêques dans l'empire romain au IVe et pendant la première moitié du Ve siècle," *Revue internationale des droits de l'antiquité* 4 (1950) 467-98.

Nonetheless, their preference was not necessarily decisive, for others had to be consulted. A *dictum* of Celestine I expressed this basic assumption underlying electoral theory throughout the Early Middle Ages:

A bishop should not be given to those who are unwilling [to receive him]. The consent and the wishes of the clergy, the people, and the nobility are required.[7]

With words reminiscent of Roman political and legal maxims, Leo the Great succinctly restated this guiding principle: "He who governs all should be elected by all."[8] In the authoritative view of the fifth-century papacy, a bishop was chosen—to use the common early medieval formula—through "election by the clergy and the people." Not at all surprisingly, Leo insisted that "popular tumult" must never influence the choice of a bishop,[9] yet he maintained that proper election needs not only the will of the clergy, but also of the more eminent laymen and of the common people.[10] Moreover, imperial

[7] *Ep.* 4 c.5, *PL* 50 434: "Nullus invitis detur episcopus. Cleri, plebis et ordinis consensus ac desiderium requiratur" (D.61 c.13; D.63 c.26). The meaning of *ordo* in this context is explained by Hinschius, *KR* II 515 n.5, and by Ganshof, *op.cit.* 487, 495, who identifies them with the *decuriones*. Though the principle *Nullus invitis detur episcopus* found general acceptance, the Anglo-Norman Anonymous of 1100 argued against it; see his *Tractatus* xiiia, in Heinrich Böhmer, *Kirche und Staat in England und in der Normandie im XI. und XII. Jahrhundert* (Leipzig 1899) 463.

[8] *Ep.*10 c.4, *PL* 54 632: "Exspectarentur certe vota civium, testimonia populorum; quaereretur honoratorum arbitrium, electio clericorum, quae in sacerdotum solent ordinationibus ab his qui noverunt patrum regulas, custodiri"; c.6, *PL* 54 634: "Per pacem et quietem sacerdotes qui futuri sunt postulentur. Teneatur subscriptio clericorum, honoratorum testimonium, ordinis consensus et plebis. Qui praefuturus est omnibus, ab omnibus eligatur" (cf. D.63 c.27). Leo's concluding remark strongly suggests a statement by Pliny the Younger, *Panegyricus* 7.6: "imperaturus omnibus eligi debet ex omnibus." Cf. also the Roman law principle (*Cod.* 5.59.5 §2): "quod omnes similiter tangit, ab omnibus comprobetur"; Gaines Post, "A Romano-Canonical Maxim, *Quod omnes tangit*, in Bracton," *Traditio* 4 (1946) 197-251 (slightly augmented in his *Studies in Medieval Legal Thought* [Princeton 1964] 163-238). Similar assertions from the 5th century were frequently repeated: "ille [scil. archiepiscopus] qui preest ab omnibus episcopis quibus preest debet constitui" (D.66 c.1 §1; P. Hinschius, *Decretales Pseudo-Isidorianae* [Leipzig 1863] 120).

[9] *Ep.*12 c.1, *PL* 54 646 (D.61 c.5).

[10] Above, n.8; below, n.14.

approval of the election might be required,[11] and without alarm Gregory the Great recognized that bishops could be chosen "by the will of the most serene prince" as well as by ecclesiastics.[12] Finally, as Leo asserted, for the election of a metropolitan the bishops of the province act together with the clergy and citizens of the metropolis,[13] and following the election of any lesser bishop the metropolitan of the province has the right to judge and approve the bishop-elect.[14] Thus, in the selection of a bishop, the fifth century expected the participation of the diocesan clergy and laity and of the bishops of the province, as well as the consent of the metropolitan. These elements were inseparable, for each was necessary, and no single act was sufficient to create a bishop or even to convey his jurisdictional and administrative powers. In short, the elevation of a bishop was a protracted but indivisible process, and until the process was completed by the consecration, no individual stage in the process produced effects of its own.

All of these texts from the fourth, fifth, and sixth centuries found their way into the *Decretum*, where they contribute to a bewildering impression of obscurity and contradiction. But there are also other sources of confusion. From the sixth century to the late eleventh, the Latin Church was largely under the dominance of Germanic kings, and some of the chapters in the electoral *distinctiones* reflect these historical circumstances. For example, Gratian includes a canon of the Twelfth Council of Toledo, which mentions "the prince's free choice" of bishops (*libera principis electio*), and which adds that the archbishop of Toledo should promote to the episcopate "whomever the royal power chooses" (*quoscumque regalis potestas elegerit*), so long as the archbishop himself considers the candidates worthy.[15] Other *capitula* ascribe to the mon-

---

[11] Hinschius, *KR* II 513-15.   [12] D.63 c.9.

[13] *Ep.*14 c.6, *PL* 54 673 (D.63 c.19).

[14] *Ep.*167, *PL* 54 1203: "Nulla ratio sinit ut inter episcopos habeantur qui nec a clericis sunt electi, nec a plebibus sunt expetiti, nec a provincialibus episcopis cum metropolitani iudicio consecrati" (D.62 c.1).

[15] D.63 c.25 (681).

arch the right of approving and investing a bishop-elect before his consecration,[16] and the right of granting (or refusing) an episcopal church to a candidate for the episcopate.[17] Yet some of the chapters dating from the sixth to eleventh centuries restate the older ideal of election by "clergy and people." In this vein, the Fourth Council of Toledo insisted,

> He whom the clergy and people of his own city have not elected, and whom neither the authority of the metropolitan nor the assent of the provincial bishops has chosen—he shall not be a bishop.[18]

Undoubtedly such provisions often represented a conservative reaction against the misuse of princely power in ecclesiastical elections. In the eleventh century, "election by clergy and people" became a slogan of the reformers. At first the program behind this slogan implied no necessary attack on princely and lay rights, for it was originally a simple demand that clergy and people should be consulted in the selection of a bishop, and at least allowed to register their approval. During the third quarter of the century, however, reformers began to insist that the clergy should have the initiative in electing a bishop, and therewith the reformers' program was aiming toward the exclusion of all direct lay participation in ecclesiastical elections.[19] Yet to most people during the eleventh and early twelfth centuries, canonical election by the "clergy and people" implied the election or at least the consent of all concerned: canons of the cathedral chapter, cathedral and monastic clergy, nobility, *ministeriales*, and citizens.[20]

---

[16] D.63 cc.22, 23.   [17] D.63 c.16 (850-52).   [18] D.51 c.5 §1 (633).

[19] In general, see Paul Schmid, *Der Begriff der kanonischen Wahl in den Anfängen des Investiturstreits* (Stuttgart 1926), who, however, exaggerates the tendency to require papal approval of 11th-century episcopal elections. See also, Gerd Tellenbach, *Church, State, and Christian Society at the Time of the Investiture Contest*, trans. R. F. Bennett (Oxford 1940) 100f, and the interesting evidence assembled by R. W. and A. J. Carlyle, *A History of Mediaeval Political Theory in the West* (repr. 6 vols. Edinburgh 1950) IV 25-39, on the appointment of bishops from the 10th century to 1075.

[20] Hinschius, *KR* II 550.

In fact, Gratian devoted *Distinctio* 63 to the analysis and resolution of the principal tensions in the tradition of electoral theory and practice. Among the texts of this long *distinctio*, strong statements of lay rights and of royal prerogative jostle against equally strong assertions of the Church's freedom from all lay intervention in the elevation of bishops. In his rubrics, master Gratian abstracted the contents or implications of the *capitula*, and these rubrics reveal startling contradictions. For example, on the role of the *populus* in an election:

> Laymen should not take part in the election of bishops.[21]
>
> In the election of a bishop, the people must be present.[22]
>
> Clergy and people should take part in the election of a bishop.[23]

Some rubrics categorically deny the monarch's rights:

> The emperor must not take part in the election of bishops.[24]
>
> He who attains the episcopal eminence by royal appointment should not be accepted by the bishops of his province.[25]

Other rubrics disagree, however, apparently recognizing the ruler's right to participate or at least to approve:

> The will of the prince is needed in the appointment of a bishop.[26]
>
> A letter from the emperor is needed in confirmation of an election.[27]
>
> In the election of bishops, the consent of the prince is needed.[28]

As usual, Gratian's own views emerged from his attempts to harmonize the discords in the inherited tradition. *Distinctio*

[21] D.63 rubr.c.1; also, D.63 rubr.c.8.   [22] D.63 rubr.c.11.
[23] D.63 rubr.c.10; similarly, D.63 rubr.c.34.
[24] D.63 rubr.c.3; note also D.63 rubr.c.4.
[25] D.63 rubr.c.5; also, D.63 rubr.c.7.
[26] D.63 rubr.c.9.   [27] D.63 rubr.c.18.   [28] D.63 rubr.c.25.

63 offers, in fact, an excellent model of his dialectical method in operation. At the beginning of this *distinctio*, Gratian states the proposition which he will defend: "Laymen must in no way involve themselves in election."[29] Following this thesis, the first eight *capitula* oppose any participation by people or prince. After these chapters, Gratian observes:

> By all these authorities, laymen are excluded from the election of bishops, and the necessity of obedience, not the freedom of command, is enjoined upon them.[30]

Then follow seventeen *capitula* which defend various rights of ruler or people. Some of these chapters showed plainly that in earlier centuries emperors had held and exercised wide powers of supervision and approval in ecclesiastical elections, even in papal elections. Thereupon Gratian begins his resolution of the conflict in the texts:

> By these examples . . . , one concludes clearly that laymen should not be excluded from election, nor princes barred from the filling of [offices in] the churches. Yet . . . it is commanded that the people be summoned not to perform the election, but rather to give consent to the election. For election . . . belongs to the priests, and the duty of the faithful people is to consent humbly. . . .[31]

This "humble consent" should manifest itself in a popular acclamation of the newly elected bishop. After this *dictum*, Gratian provided a chapter from Celestine I and one from Leo the Great, each designed to suggest that the role of the people is limited to assent.[32] In a further *dictum*, Gratian explains that in both usage and law, because of the dangers of schism and heresy, emperors had formerly exercised extraordinary powers over ecclesiastical elections. For

---

[29] D.63 pr.
[30] D.63 dict.p.c.8: "His omnibus auctoritatibus laici excluduntur ab electione sacerdotum, atque iniungitur eis necessitas obediendi, non libertas inperandi."
[31] D.63 dict.p.c.25. [32] D.63 c.26 (above, n.7), c.27 (above, n.8).

although the emperor was a mere layman, he was nonetheless a chosen member of the *populus*, with the special duty of helping the Church and defending it against schism and heresy. Hence, earlier emperors could claim the right to be informed of ecclesiastical elections, and the right to give consent.[33] At this point, the next chapter justifies the emperor's right to be represented by legates at a papal consecration.[34] Thereafter, Gratian resumed his own argument, and in order to explain away the privileged position which earlier princes had enjoyed, he applied the principle of historical relativism. What is blameless in one period, he pointed out, may become a dangerous "error and superstition" in a later age—and if so, it must be destroyed.[35] Some emperors, he maintained, had not been satisfied with their right of consent, but had actually bestowed ecclesiastical offices. Moreover, these emperors had even lapsed into heresy and tried to disrupt the unity of the Church. Consequently, the Church had excluded the emperors from ecclesiastical elections. Thus, as Gratian admits, these imperial prerogatives had once been lawful, but because of the emperor's abuses, the Church had revoked these privileges.[36] In support of his view, Gratian furnishes several chapters illustrating the independence of papal elections from imperial influence, and the emperor's obligation to aid (but not to control) the Roman Church.[37] Concluding his argument, then, Gratian added that in any case, some pious emperors had renounced their former privileges.[38] Hence, he explains,

> From the foregoing authorities, it is clear to everyone that election belongs only to clerics.[39]

At the end of *Distinctio* 63, Gratian appended two *capitula* as an epilogue to his analysis of lay rights in ecclesiastical

---

[33] D.63 dict.p.c.27. [34] D.63 c.28.

[35] D.63 dict.p.c.28. Gratian drew this doctrine almost verbatim from Placidus of Nonantula, *De honore ecclesiae* c.69, *MGH LdL* II 597; Sägmüller, *Bischofswahl* 17f.

[36] D.63 dict.p.c.28. [37] D.63 cc.29, 30, 33.

[38] D.63 dict.p.c.34, also dict.p.c.28. [39] D.63 dict.p.c.34.

elections. First, in a constitution of the Second Lateran Council, the right of electing a bishop is restricted to the canons of the cathedral chapter, but the constitution insisted that other clerics of the diocese must have a consultative voice and the right of consent.[40] In this respect, Gratian regarded the canonical election of a pope by the cardinals as the appropriate model for episcopal elections, since the papal election decree of 1059 had stipulated that the electors, that is, the cardinal-bishops, should act together with the other cardinals, and that "the rest of the clergy and the people" should then give their consent to the election.[41] In Gratian's words:

> Just as the election of the Supreme Pontiff should be performed not only by the cardinals, but rather also by the other religious clerics . . . , similarly also the election of bishops should be performed not only by the canons, but also by the other religious clerics. . . .[42]

Finally, the last *capitulum* of *Distinctio* 63 repeats Leo the Great's decision that the metropolitan should settle a split election.[43]

In *Distinctio* 63, Gratian's main point was the contrast between the clergy's right to elect and the right of the people (including the prince) to approve the election. Needless to say, Gratian did not invent this distinction. At least on the level of semantics, the need for this distinction grew out of the ambiguities in the word *eligere*, which could serve, on the one hand, as a specific and technical term for the juridical act of election, and on the other hand, as a broad term indi-

40 D.63 c.35; on this development, Georg von Below, *Die Entstehung des ausschliesslichen Wahlrechts der Domkapitel* (Leipzig 1883).

41 D.23 c.1 §2.

42 D.63 dict.p.c.34: ". . . queritur, quorum sit ipsa electio, an clericorum maioris ecclesiae tantum, an etiam religiosorum aliorum, qui in eadem ciuitate fuerint? Sed . . . statutum est, ut ad eligendum episcopum sufficiat ecclesiae matricis arbitrium. Nunc autem sicut electio summi pontificis non a cardinalibus tantum, immo etiam ab aliis religiosis clericis auctoritate Nicolai papae est facienda, ita et episcoporum electio non a canonicis tantum, sed etiam ab aliis religiosis clericis. . . ."

43 D.63 c.36 (*Ep.*14 c.5, *PL* 54 673).

cating choice or approval.[44] Leo the Great had applied the verb *eligere* to the participation of clergy and laity alike,[45] but he could also distinguish between an "election" by the clergy (*eligere*) and a "request" by the people (*expetere*).[46] Indeed, Leo's terminology reflected fifth-century usage, for despite diversity arising from place and circumstances, the fifth century generally recognized the different character of the roles played by clergy and laity in the promotion of a bishop.[47] Backed by Leo's authority, the distinction between clerical "election" and popular "request" or "consent" re-appeared from time to time,[48] but in the mid-eleventh century it finally became stock in trade, when the reformers and the papacy sought to limit prince and people to mere approval of an election. Cardinal Humbert drew a sharp line between the clergy's "election" and the people's "request," for in his view of episcopal promotions, clerical election was the first act, followed by the popular request. In fact, Humbert's idea of the proper sequence required that the metropolitan should confirm the election by the clerics, and that the prince should then confirm the request by the nobility and the plebs.[49] In 1059 Nicholas II's papal election decree not only explicitly distinguished election from consent, but also quoted one of Leo's statements making the same point.[50] Like Leo's other texts on election, this statement was repeatedly republished in canonical collections from the mid-eleventh century to the early twelfth,[51] and Gratian assigned

44 This ambiguity is still evident in the *Codex iuris canonici*; Parsons, *Canonical Elections* 2.

45 *Ep*.10 c.6, *PL* 54 634 (above, n.8).

46 *Ep*.10 cc.4, 6, 167, *PL* 54 632, 634, 1203 (above, nn.8, 14).

47 Above, nn.7f, 14; see also Ganshof, *Rev. internat. des droits de l'ant.* 4 (1950) 480f, 486-98.

48 Ratherius of Verona, *Phrenesis* c.1, *PL* 136 366f; Parsons, *op.cit.* 43f. Also, Burchard of Worms, *Decretum* 1.10-12, *PL* 140 552f; Albert M. Koeniger, *Burchard I. von Worms und die deutsche Kirche seiner Zeit* (Munich 1905) 69.

49 *Adversus simoniacos* 1.5, *MGH LdL* I 108; also, *id.* 3.6, *ibid.* 205: ". . . summi pontifices . . . decreverint, ut metropolitani iudicio electio cleri, principis consensu expetitio plebis et ordinis confirmetur. . . ."

50 D.23 c.1 §3; for the quoted passage, see above, n.14.

51 See Friedberg's apparatus ad D.63 c.1 (n.2).

it a prominent place as the first *capitulum* of *Distinctio* 62, where it illustrated his fundamental principle: "Election belongs to clerics; consent, to the people."[52] Gratian's concept of election obviously represents a middle course, neither allowing prince and laity to play a dominant role, nor completely excluding them.

In the elaboration of his electoral doctrine, Gratian faced other difficulties besides the inconsistencies within the tradition. By demanding "freedom" for the Church, the Gregorian reformers had aimed at the abolition of lay control over ecclesiastical elections. Though clear enough in its negative aspects, this program was essentially vague. The Gregorians found it easy to recognize the major violations of the Church's *libertas*, but on its positive side their program was weak, for despite two generations of struggle to restore "canonical election," the reformers never achieved an adequately detailed definition of canonicity.[53] Gratian inherited this defect of Gregorian thought. Although his electoral *distinctiones* began the task of remedying this deficiency,[54] he added little to the tradition.[55] In short, it would be an exaggeration to claim that Gratian's electoral theory reveals a radical departure from the principles accepted in the fifth century and in the later eleventh. The continuity is unmistakable. Indeed, like the eleventh-century reformers, Gratian was a conservative relying heavily on the electoral doctrines drawn from Leo the Great and others in the fourth, fifth, and sixth centuries.[56]

[52] D.62 pr.: "Electio clericorum est, consensus plebis."

[53] Unfortunately, Paul Schmid's *Der Begriff der kanonischen Wahl* ends with an analysis of Gregory VII's idea of canonical election; a study on the later development of this concept would be desirable.

[54] Of course, these *distinctiones* furnished an indispensable foundation for the much more detailed discussions of election in decretistic works.

[55] The main elements of Gratian's views on episcopal election have been examined in the preceding pages, but a few more of his provisions should be mentioned for the sake of completeness: To be elected bishop, one must already be either a deacon or a priest (D.60 dict.p.cc.3, 4; D.61 dict.p.c.8), and ideally, a bishop should be elected from the clergy of the diocese which he will rule (D.61 dict.p.c.11). Moreover, the election decree must be solemnly undersigned by all (D.61 dict.p.c.10).

[56] Sägmüller, *Bischofswahl* 13.

Unlike most eleventh-century reformers, however, Gratian sharpened these early theories and further emphasized the gulf between the roles played by clergy and people in ecclesiastical elections.

In his main electoral *distinctiones*, with their preponderance of early texts, Gratian completely omitted the papal letters and conciliar decrees from the crucial years between the mid-eleventh century and 1122.[57] To be sure, Gregory VII constantly reiterated the slogan of election by the *clerus et populus* without distinguishing the people's consent from the more active function of the clergy.[58] Still, since other reformers of the eleventh and early twelfth centuries harped on this distinction and cited Leo the Great in defense of it,[59] Gratian could undoubtedly have found additional texts from the period of the Investiture Struggle, but his argument did not require them. Obviously, Gratian's preference for the earlier doctrines was far from mere antiquarianism, since the very antiquity of a text enhanced its authority.[60] In any case,

[57] It is ironic that in D.61-65, the only texts dating from the period 1050-1122 are an excerpt from the spurious decree of Hadrian I (D.63 c.22; *MGH Const* I 657-60 no.446) and one from the forged privilege of Leo VIII (D.63 c.23; *MGH Const* I 665-67 no.448), both dating from the 1080's. In D.60, however, there are two texts from Urban II (cc.1, 4).

[58] See the Index to Erich Caspar's edition of Gregory's *Registrum* (Berlin 1920-23) s.v. "electio"; also, Sägmüller, *op.cit.* 17, and Schmid, *Begriff der kanonischen Wahl* 171-99.

[59] Humbert, *Adv. simoniacos* 1.5, 3.5-6, *MGH LdL* I 108, 204f (above, n.49); Manegold of Lautenbach, *Ad Gebehardum* c.51, *MGH LdL* I 400f; Deusdedit, *Libellus contra invasores* 1.5, *MGH LdL* II 304; Placidus of Nonantula, *De honore ecclesiae* cc.23, 37, *MGH LdL* II 582, 585; Gerhoh of Reichersberg, *De edificio Dei* c.61, *MGH LdL* III 171.

[60] Cf. Sägmüller (*op.cit.* 17), who noted the absence of Gregory VII's letters and decrees in D.60-63 and concluded that Gratian left out these materials because Gregory had stressed election by *clerus et populus,* whereas Gratian himself wished to exclude the *populus* completely from election. As Sägmüller saw, Gratian was not totally prejudiced against Gregory, two of whose decrees against investiture are quoted in the *Decretum* (C.16 q.7 cc.12, 13); for a list of Gregorian texts in the *Decretum*, see Emil Friedberg's Prolegomena to his edition (cols.xxiv-xxv, xxxi). Of course, simple disagreement does not fully explain an omission, for in the *Decretum* Gratian included much to which he was opposed.

The relation between Gratian's thought and the Gregorian program is a complex question, which deserves a separate study but can only be briefly mentioned here. For understandable reasons, the central concerns of the

his synthesis was also fully up to date, for by republishing and explicating electoral decrees from the First and Second Lateran Councils, he took account of the most recent developments, such as the cathedral chapter's growing monopoly on the right to elect.[61] Thus, the achievement of Gratian's doctrine on election lay in his critical approach to tradition, in the lucidity with which he discriminated the valuable and the dangerous elements of the inherited tradition, in the solid comprehensiveness of his argument, and in the firmness of his stand. Because of these characteristics, the *Decretum* was, like the papal election decree of 1059 and like the Fourth Lateran Council, a major event in the history of ecclesiastical election.[62]

BISHOP-ELECT AND ROMAN PONTIFF-ELECT

Within the *Decretum*, what regulations governed the prelate-elect's acquisition of jurisdictional and administrative powers? Under the *Codex iuris canonici*, confirmation of the election will, in some cases, sanction the prelate-elect's exercise of these powers. One may well begin, therefore, by examining the *Decretum*'s testimony on the various forms of "consent" or "confirmation" needed in the promotion of a bishop.

Though Gratian recognized the consent of the people as a factor in the elevation of a bishop, it is not surprising that he ascribed no specific effects to this assent. In Gratian's view,

---

11th-century reformers received close attention in the *Decretum*: canonical election (D.61-63), clerical celibacy (D.27-33), simony and the validity of ordination by simoniac bishops (C.1 q.1), lay investiture (C.16 q.7), and the relations of Church and monarchy (D.96-97 and passim). Gratian was certainly not in complete agreement with Gregory's views on canonical election, on lay investiture (below, Ch.VIIA nn.47ff and Ch.IXB nn.3ff), and on relations between Church and monarchy (cf. Alfons M. Stickler, "Magistri Gratiani sententia de potestate Ecclesiae in Statum," *Apollinaris* 21 [1948] 36-111). It is consequently misleading to assert, as Sägmüller (*op.cit.* 19) and Schulte (*Geschichte der Quellen* I 92ff) have done, that Gratian was, in his electoral doctrine and elsewhere, an "ausgesprochener Gregorianer."

[61] D.60 c.2, D.62 c.3 (1123); D.60 c.3, D.63 c.35 (1139).
[62] Sägmüller, *op.cit.* 13.

the *populus* should express its consent by acclamations to the new bishop at his election or enthronement.[63] To be sure, in former times these acclamations had had constitutive power: the most famous example is the election of St Ambrose, an election "by inspiration" in which the act of election and the acclamation coincided completely.[64] Still, Gratian regarded the acclamations merely as the people's approval of the effective nomination by the clergy.

One of the oldest texts in the *Decretum* is a canon from the Council of Nicaea, stressing the importance of the metropolitan archbishop's approval as an element in the promotion of any bishop within his province.[65] For the period stretching from the fourth century to the mid-twelfth, this canon of Nicaea is typical, since it links the metropolitan's "confirmation" with the consent of the other bishops in the province. Characteristic of the *Decretum*'s texts is the fact that the approval of the metropolitan and of the other provincial

[63] D.63 dict.p.c.25: ". . . Tunc enim in ecclesia Dei rite preficietur antistes, cum populus pariter in eum acclamauerit, quem clerus communi uoto elegerit." Gratian may here be following Placidus of Nonantula, *De honore ecclesiae* c.73, *MGH LdL* II 599: ". . . electione clericorum et petitione seu acclamatione omnium populorum. . . ." In the 11th and 12th centuries, the verb *laudare* could mean "to approve" as well as "to chant the acclamations (*laudes*)."

[64] Paulinus, *Vita sancti Ambrosii* c.6, *PL* 14 31; in general, Ernst H. Kantorowicz, *Laudes regiae* (Berkeley 1946) 118-20. Gratian repeatedly mentioned Ambrose's election (D.61 dict.p.cc.8, 11; D.63 dict.p.cc.25, 27) but did not comment on this aspect.

In 1004 the *laudes* were chanted following the investiture of the bishop-elect of Halberstadt; Thietmar of Merseburg, *Chronicon* 5.41, ed. R. Holtzmann (2nd ed. MHG SS.rer.Germ. n.s.9: Berlin 1935) 268f, and Kantorowicz, *op.cit.* 120 n.27. In this instance, however, one may suspect that the investiture was constitutive, whereas the *laudes* were simply consentaneous.

[65] D.64 c.1 (Conc. Nic. c.4): "Episcopi ab omnibus, qui sunt in sua prouincia, debent ordinari. Si uero hoc difficile fuerit . . . , tres episcopi debent in unum congregari, ita ut ceterorum, qui absentes sunt, consensum litteris teneant. Potestas sane uel confirmatio pertinebit per singulas prouincias ad metropolitanum episcopum." In the canonical collections, this canon underwent many textual variations. Where *confirmatio* appears, often a different term (*firmamentum, firmans, ordinatio, firmitas*) was used; Cuthbert H. Turner, *Ecclesiae occidentalis monumenta iuris antiquissimi* I: *Nicaenum Concilium* (Oxford 1899-1930) 116f, 188f, 258. Gratian's version evidently derives from Pseudo-Isidore; cf. Hinschius, *Decr. Ps.-Isid.* 258.

bishops referred not to the election of the new bishop but to his consecration or, even more broadly, to the entire process of his elevation. In other words, this consent was regarded as the prerequisite to the consecration rather than as the fulfillment of the election. Indeed, the consent of metropolitan and bishops could even express itself through their participation in the consecration of a new episcopal colleague.[66] From the fifth through the seventh centuries, Church councils demanded the metropolitan's presence at or consent to the consecration of a bishop.[67] In a similar vein, Gratian insisted that the primate (if any) also had to have full knowledge and to give approval before a new bishop could be consecrated.[68] Since none of these regulations attributed any specific effects to the different forms of consent, the consent was not, in itself, legally constitutive.

At any time in the Middle Ages, however, there was a particular circumstance which required confirmation of the election, rather than consent to the consecration. In the words of Leo the Great:

> If it happens that the votes of the parties are divided in favor of a second person, *through the decision of the metropolitan* the one who is aided by greater zeal and merit should be given preference over the other.[69]

Here the metropolitan's confirmation effectively settles a disputed election. For such cases, Leo's opinion remained authoritative throughout the Early Middle Ages, and it was

[66] D.23 c.2 §3: "Cum . . . examinatus inuentus fuerit plene instructus, tunc cum consensu clericorum et laicorum et conuentu totius prouinciae episcoporum, maximeque metropolitani uel auctoritate uel presentia ordinetur episcopus." Also, D.62 c.1 (above, n.14); D.23 c.1 §3; D.64 cc.2-8; D.65 pr., cc.1-3.

[67] Mansi VIII 860; IX 114; X 539f; in general, see André Desprairies, *L'élection des évêques par les chapitres au XIIIe siècle: Théorie canonique* (Paris 1922) 52.

[68] D.65 dict.p.c.3, cc.4, 5.

[69] *Ep.*14 c.5, *PL* 54 673: "si in aliam forte personam partium se vota diviserint, metropolitani iudicio is alteri praeferatur qui maioribus et studiis iuvatur et meritis"; D.63 c.36 (minor differences in wording).

transmitted by at least seven canonical collections before Gratian republished it in the *Decretum*: the frequent reappearance of this pronouncement testifies to the importance of the problem and to the widespread acceptance of this solution.[70] Yet Leo's doctrine did not ascribe any other juridical effects to the metropolitan's confirmation, nor did Leo explain at what moment a bishop-elect receives his jurisdictional and administrative powers. It is clear that by the time of the *Decretum*, the metropolitan's "confirmation" had not yet become a precise technical term within the Church's administrative law.[71]

Of course, Gratian also took account of the emperor's "confirmation." Two of the texts in *Distinctio* 63 portray the papacy as having been in full agreement with this imperial "right." Though Gratian accredited these texts in good faith, they were, in fact, merely masquerading as papal documents, for they had been forged by imperialists at Ravenna during the 1080's. One of the documents states:

> Even though a bishop is elected . . . by the clergy and people, unless he is approved and invested by the king, he may be consecrated by no one.[72]

70 See Friedberg's apparatus ad D.63 c.36 (n.388). A similar rule was imposed by the Council of Arles in 451 (Mansi VII 879): ". . . Quod si inter partes aliqua nata fuerit dubitatio, maiori numero metropolitanus in electione consentiat"; cf. also Burchard of Worms, *Decretum* 1.27, *PL* 140 556.

71 It would be relatively easy to assemble a mass of evidence indicating that before the mid-12th century (and sometimes thereafter) confirmation by metropolitan or pope did not furnish the sanctions for a prelate's exercise of jurisdictional powers; documents from any volume of *Papsturkunden* will illustrate this fact. One should note that in a letter of Gregory I (JE 1774; *Comp.I* 1.4.11 [*X* 1.6.3]) apparently the term *confirmatio* simply indicated the episcopal consecration. See also the *Liber diurnus Romanorum pontificum* nos.2-5, ed. T.E.A. Sickel (Vienna 1889) 3-5, for episcopal election decrees in which the consecration is requested without any mention of confirmation or of administrative powers.

72 Decree of Pseudo-Hadrian I, *MGH Const* I 660 no.446 (cf. the text in D.63 c.22): "quamvis a clero et a populo . . . eligatur episcopus, nisi a rege laudetur et investiatur, a nemine consecretur"; almost verbatim, the charter of Pseudo-Leo VIII, *MGH Const* I 667 no.448 (D.63 c.23). Gratian apparently regarded both documents primarily as evidence that the "electio Romani pontificis ad ius pertinet inperatoris" (D.63 rubr.c.23). The main literature is cited below, Ch.VIIB n.18.

Constitutional Background

By juxtaposing royal approval and royal investiture of the bishop-elect, this text defends an imperial tradition reaching back to the time of Otto the Great. Within that tradition, assent and investiture were associated as twin requirements, mentioned together in chronicles and documents. Although the approval and the investiture were sometimes bestowed separately upon the bishop-elect, they were sometimes given together.[73] In the course of the later eleventh century the link between the consent and the investiture grew closer. Indeed, from the 1080's to the end of the Investiture Struggle the joining of consent and investiture was a deliberate element in imperial policy. Probably under Henry IV, and certainly under Henry V, the two acts fused, so that the investiture of a bishop-elect was considered identical with the grant of royal approval.[74] As an imperial propagandist pointed out, the monarch expresses his approval through the investiture.[75] Thus, early twelfth-century Germany was familiar with a typical procedure for the election of a bishop:

[73] Gerhard, *Vita sancti Oudalrici episcopi* c.1, *MGH SS* IV 387: "[supplicatum est] ut praefecto domino Oudalrico episcopalis potestas ab eo [scil.rege] concederetur. Rex . . . petitioni eorum assensum praebens, regio more in manus eum accepit munereque pontificatus honoravit." However, cf. *Gesta episcoporum Cameracensium* 1.90-92, *MGH SS* VII 438; and *Chronicon sancti Benigni Divionensis*, in *MGH SS* VII 236. On the relation between investiture and consent, see the important article by Ernst Bernheim, "Investitur und Bischofswahl im 11. und 12. Jahrhundert," *ZKG* 7 (1885) 306f.

[74] On Henry IV see the *Gesta Treverorum* Continuatio prima c.9, *MGH SS* VIII 182: ". . . adhibita regis adhuc pueri investitura et confirmatione . . ."; also, *Gesta episcoporum Cameracensium* Continuatio: *Gesta Gerardi II* c.1, *MGH SS* VII 497: ". . . omnium electione, cum assensu et dono regalis potentiae. . . ." On Henry V see below, n.76. The same idea is reflected in a gloss on the *Chronicon Ottenburanum*, in *MGH SS* XXIII 613: "Heinricus imperator: Omnis episcopus . . . electus regni nostri de partibus Teutonicis . . . regalia per ceptrum accipiat sicque confirmatus per nos et sublimatus dignitate principaliter exhinc pociatur"; for the interpretation of this text, note the warning by L. Weiland (*MGH Const* I 159). Note also the spurious charter of Charlemagne quoted in the *Chron. Ottenburanum*: "[abbas] regia sublimetur auctoritate et confirmetur." Through the 12th century the emperors continued to exercise a general right of "confirmation" in episcopal elections (Hinschius, *KR* II 561f); on these later developments, see below, Ch.VIIIᴮ and c.

[75] Gregory of Catino, *Orthodoxa defensio imperialis* c.3, *MGH LdL* II 537.

When the bishop of any church . . . has died, thereupon the
provost, the dean, [and] the master of scholars . . . do not
delay in setting off for the palace, and with them the more
distinguished and wiser persons from the city, bringing with
them the episcopal ring and staff. When they have conferred with the bishops, chancellor, and chaplains whom
they find in the palace near the emperor, the one to be
promoted is elected in accordance with the pleasure and
favor of the emperor . . . and [is] immediately confirmed
by the emperor with the grant of the bishopric.[76]

That is, the election was commonly held at court, where the
emperor and his advisers exerted a decisive influence upon
it, and after the election the emperor "confirmed" the prelate-
elect by investing him. It is obvious that such proceedings
could never be fully reconciled with the reformers' ideal of
free and canonical election. Although the reformers recognized the emperor's right of consent, they were likely to mini-
mize its importance by comparing it to the consent of the
plebs, and by explaining it as a general obligation to protect
ecclesiastical elections.[77] Appropriating both of these arguments, on this question Gratian followed the reformers' line
of thought.[78] As one would expect, Gratian stressed neither
the imperial "confirmation" nor the investiture, and he
assigned no specific juridical effects to the emperor's grants.

In short, within the *Decretum*, confirmation and consent
did not directly affect the prelate's acquisition of govern-

[76] *Vita Chuonradi archiepiscopi Salisburgensis* c.5, *MGH SS* XI 65:
"Chuonradus in palatio eligitur in episcopum. Forma vero electionis quae
tunc fiebat episcoporum . . . talis erat. Defuncto ecclesiae cuiuslibet episcopo . . . , mox ad palatium proficisci non differunt prepositus, decanus,
magister scolarium . . . et cum eis maiores et sanioris consilii personae de
civitate, anulum episcopalem secum portantes et baculum, communicatoque
consilio cum his quos in palatio circa imperatorem invenerint episcopis,
cancellario et capellanis, secundum beneplacitum et favorem imperatoris,
qui sustinendus erat, eligebatur. Iuxta hanc formam etiam is de quo sermo
agitur in palatio electus est et ab imperatore continuo concessione episcopatus confirmatus." Conrad's election took place in 1106.

[77] For example, Placidus of Nonantula, *De honore ecclesiae* c.37, *MGH
LdL* II 585.

[78] D.63 dict.p.cc.25, 27.

mental and administrative powers. Moreover, with one or two exceptions, Gratian's texts and comments furnished no regulations on the powers of the bishop-elect. Nonetheless, eleventh-century reformers had assumed that the episcopal consecration confers the right to administer ecclesiastical property. And almost two decades before the *Decretum* churchmen had already made a hesitant attempt to legislate upon this question. In 1123 the First Lateran Council decreed that a bishop-elect, even though he has been canonically elected, may not alienate his church's possessions, and that any such alienation is invalid. According to this canon, a crucial part of the bishop's administrative power—specifically, the right to dispose of property—derives from his episcopal consecration. Though Gratian took this law into the *Decretum*, he placed it in a group of canons which illustrated primarily the restrictions upon the alienation of property.[79] Within Gratian's thought, however, there is an analogue to this decree, for he believed that there is also another context in which a sacramental act can sanction the exercise of administrative power. As he explained, when a monk becomes a priest, ordination is a prerequisite to be acquired before the new priest may enjoy the income from his benefice.[80]

Obviously, Gratian himself did little to clarify the constitutional status of the bishop-elect. Characteristically, however, in theory as well as in practice, innovation often altered the papacy before it touched the rest of the episcopate. For the earliest attempt to define in precise terms the constitutive

---

[79] The consent of the cathedral clergy was apparently also required for any alienation. C.12 q.2 c.37: "Alienationes omnium per intrusionem, seu canonice electorum sub episcopi nomine . . . , alienationes quocumque modo factas, nec non personarum ordinationes ab eisdem sine communi consensu clericorum ecclesiae . . . factas, irritas iudicamus." The canon continues (§1) with a prohibition forbidding any cleric "to alienate his prebend or any ecclesiastical benefice." For other restrictions on alienation cf. C.12 q.2 cc.35, 36, 41, 42, and see Peter N. Riesenberg, *Inalienability of Sovereignty in Medieval Political Thought* (New York 1956) ch.3. The 11th-century reformers' view was stated by Peter Damian, *Ep.*1.13, *PL* 144 221: "licet ecclesiasticae facultatis mentio in ipsa manus impositione non fiat, is tamen qui consecratur, bonorum ecclesiae dispensator efficitur."
[80] C.16 q.1 dict.p.c.19 (quoted below, Ch.IIB n.36).

force of an ecclesiastical election, one must point to Nicholas
II's Roman synod of April 1059 and to its famous decree on
papal election. Probably not composed by any single person,
this decree should be regarded as the collective achievement
of the group of gifted reformers within the Roman Church:
that is, of Humbert of Silva Candida, Peter Damian, Hildebrand, and their colleagues. In fact, the decree was designed
not only to legalize the irregularities in Nicholas's election
but also, by establishing both the theory and the procedure
surrounding papal elections, to prevent such irregularities in
the future. The decree is long, and it articulated the first truly
detailed account of the proper way to elect a Roman pontiff.[81]
What matters here, however, is the decree's provision for the
eventuality of a crisis in the city of Rome. Specifically, it
stipulated that if a free election should be impossible in Rome,
the election might be held elsewhere.[82] In similar vein, the
decree then settled the procedure following an election:

> If a fierce disturbance . . . opposes, so that he who has been
> elected cannot be enthroned according to custom in the
> Apostolic See, nonetheless the pontiff-elect should possess
> the authority to rule the Holy Roman Church and to man-
> age all of its resources, just as if he were pope.[83]

[81] A critical text of the decree is given in *MGH Const* I 538-41 no.382;
note the variants transmitted in the *Decretum* (D.23 c.1). For a summary
of the older scholarly literature, see Feine, *RG* I 236f; recent studies include
the monograph by Hans-Georg Krause, *Das Papstwahldekret von 1059 und
seine Rolle im Investiturstreit* (Rome 1960), and the judicious essay by
Friedrich Kempf, "Pier Damiani und das Papstwahldekret von 1059,"
Archivum historiae pontificiae 2 (1964) 73-89. On authorship (against
A. Michel's ascription of the decree to Humbert) see Krause, *op.cit.* 116-25,
257-70. For our present purposes, the differences between the "papal" and
"imperial" versions can be ignored; cf. *MGH Const* I 541-46 (esp. p.543)
no.383.
[82] *MGH Const* I 540 no.382 §7 (D.23 c.1 §5).
[83] *Ibid.* §8 (D.23 c.1 §6): "Plane postquam electio fuerit facta, si bellica
tempestas vel qualiscunque hominum conatus malignitatis studio restiterit,
ut is qui electus est in apostolica sede iuxta consuetudinem intronizari non
valeat, electus tamen sicut papa auctoritatem obtineat regendi sanctam
Romanam ecclesiam et disponendi omnes facultates illius, quod beatum
Gregorium ante consecrationem suam fecisse cognoscimus." The concluding
remark on Gregory I is correct, for there was a gap of almost seven months
between his election and consecration, and he took over the duties of his
office immediately; Erich Caspar, *Geschichte des Papsttums von den
Anfängen bis zur Höhe der Weltherrschaft* (2 vols. Tübingen 1930-33)
II 374f.

A year later, again at a Roman synod, Nicholas summed up the decree of 1059 and promulgated this abstract as law. It is evident that he attached much value to his provisions in case of a "fierce disturbance," for they reappeared in this brief summary and, indeed, constituted almost half of it: If the election must be held outside of Rome, the pontiff-elect receives

> the authority to rule and to manage the properties and the welfare of the Holy Roman Church, . . . as if he were already fully enthroned.[84]

In the two election decrees, the "authority to rule and to manage" (*auctoritas regendi et disponendi*) represents the sum of those papal powers which were not purely priestly. The *auctoritas regendi* was a political or governmental form of jurisdiction, a juridical and administrative headship over the Church and the clergy, while the *auctoritas disponendi* was the stewardship of the Church's properties and possessions. As the emphasis on the enthronement clearly shows, before 1059 the enthronement had been the decisive moment which bestowed these jurisdictional powers upon the new pope.[85] Indeed, according to both decrees, *under normal circumstances* the enthronement should remain jurisdictionally constitutive.

The canonists of the late eleventh and early twelfth centuries recognized the importance of these two decrees. Anselm of Lucca, Ivo of Chartres, and the compiler of the *Caesaraugustana* quoted the decree of 1059 in part or in full. Probably because it was much shorter, the decree of 1060 was republished even more often in the canonical collections. Sometimes these canonists used one or both of the decrees simply for their relevance as documents illustrating certain principles of ecclesiastical election, but sometimes they

---

[84] *MGH Const* I 551 no.386 §4 (D.79 c.9).

[85] Franz Wasner, "De consecratione, inthronizatione, coronatione Summi Pontificis," *Apollinaris* 8 (1935) 86f, 256f.

quoted one of the decrees as specific evidence of the primacy and privileges of the Roman Church.[86] The decree of 1059 reappeared in the publicistic literature of the Investiture Struggle, for Hugh of Fleury reproduced its entire text.[87] Even a theologian like Hugh of St Victor, writing shortly before Gratian, could put the decree of 1059 to good use. When he analyzed the functions and prerogatives of the various offices within the Church, in order to describe the papal office he briefly summarized the decree of 1059, giving special prominence to its provision for the powers of a pontiff-elect who cannot be enthroned because of "violence" in Rome.[88] Gratian placed the decree of 1059 at the head of *Distinctio* 23, immediately following a *distinctio* devoted to the primacy of Rome and the relative rank of the other patriarchal sees, and he announced that *Distinctio* 23 would explain how each prelate is installed in his office, "beginning from the highest and going down to the lowest rank."[89] On the other hand, Gratian placed the decree of 1060 in a *distinctio* which is wholly concerned with papal election.[90] Neither decree appeared in his main electoral *distinctiones*, and he only once made a serious effort to apply the theoretical principles of

[86] Decree of 1059: (1) Anselm, *Collectio canonum* 6.12 (excerpt), ed. F. Thaner (Innsbruck 1906-15) 272; bk.vi is chiefly devoted to election. (2) Ivo, *Panormia* 3.1, *PL* 161 1127-29; bk.iii begins with papal election, then continues with episcopal election. (3) *Caesaraugustana* (2nd recension only); Fournier and LeBras, *Hist. des coll. can.* II 281.

Decree of 1060: (1) Anselm, *Coll. can.* 6.13, ed. Thaner 272f. (2) Bonizo of Sutri, *Liber ad amicum* 6, *MGH LdL* I 594. (3) Deusdedit, *Collectio canonum* 1.169, ed. Victor Wolf von Glanvell, *Die Kanonessammlung des Kardinals Deusdedit* (Paderborn 1905) 107; bk.i concerns the authority of the Roman See. (4) Ivo, *Decretum* 5.80, *PL* 161 352; bk.v is devoted to the higher offices, but the decree is surrounded by canons specifically directed against simony. Finally (5) cardinal Gregory of St Chrysogonus, *Polycarpus* 1.4.5 (bk.i treats the privileges of the Roman See, whereas bk.ii concerns election), and (6) *Caesaraugustana* 3.9 (bk.iii deals with election); for both, see Friedberg's apparatus ad D.79 c.9 (n.60), and Fournier and LeBras, *op.cit.* II 171, 271.

[87] *Tractatus de regia potestate et sacerdotali dignitate* 2.5, *MGH LdL* II 491f.

[88] *De sacramentis Christianae fidei* 2.3.15, *PL* 176 430f.

[89] D.23 pr.: ". . . Nunc a summo incipientes, et usque ad ultimum gradum descendentes, qualiter quisque eorum debeat ordinari, . . . ostendamus."

[90] D.79 c.9.

papal election to other ecclesiastical elections.[91] Yet in the subtlety and precision of their constitutional terminology, both decrees were, by eleventh-century standards, extraordinary documents, and both stressed the new regulation on the powers of a pontiff-elect. It is surely not surprising, therefore, that for the early commentators on the *Decretum*, these two decrees provided an occasion to discuss the constitutive moment of any accession, and the stages in the acquisition of full power by any prelate-elect.

2. Office and Jurisdiction

In the *Decretum*, the problems of governing the Church were, of course, a paramount concern. Many chapters discuss in general the governing authority inherent in the Church and its higher offices, and more specifically, many chapters treat the legislative, judicial, and coercive powers. Though the *Decretum* mirrored the thought of the entire Early Middle Ages, Gratian could find no precedent for a clear definition of ecclesiastical office, for an adequate analysis of ecclesiastical jurisdiction, or for a sharp distinction between "orders" and "jurisdiction."[1] Judged by the standards of the later twelfth century, Gratian himself sometimes confused the jurisdictional and sacramental spheres; to cite only one instance, he linked the power to baptize and the power to excommunicate as the joint effects of priestly ordination.[2] Since the mid-eleventh century, of course, the struggle for the reform of the Church had stimulated an intensive reexamina-

---

[91] Qualifying the electoral rights of the canons, Gratian cited the decree of 1059 to draw an analogy with the cardinals' role in a papal election; D.63 dict.p.c.34 (above, n.42).

---

[1] On Gratian's concepts of office and jurisdiction, see Martinien van de Kerckhove, "La notion de juridiction chez les Décretistes et les premiers Décrétalistes (1140-1250)," *Études franciscaines* 49 (1937) 420f, 425f, 440-43; Donald E. Heintschel, *The Mediaeval Concept of an Ecclesiastical Office* (Washington, D.C. 1956) esp. 16-25.

[2] C.24 q.1 dict.p.c.37 §1: "Cum ergo sacerdotalem unctionem utraque potestas, baptizandi uidelicet et excommunicandi, sequatur, a fide recedentes aut utramque retinebunt, aut utraque carebunt."

tion of ecclesiastical office, and by the end of that long conflict, the different powers and appurtenances of office had
been distinguished with heightened clarity. Nonetheless, in
the second quarter of the twelfth century, the continuing need
for a new doctrine of office was still fully apparent.

A new doctrine of ecclesiastical office could not be created
without a body of precise technical terms to describe the
functions and powers of office. Till the mid-twelfth century,
theorists of the Church's constitution were hampered by the
inadequacy of early medieval terminology. To be sure, in
many *capitula* within the *Decretum,* occasional terms and
phrases lucidly delineate various facets of office; the papal
election decree of 1059, for example, speaks of "the authority
to rule and to administer," thus distinguishing between power
over men and power over property.[3] Occasionally, Gratian
managed to mark a clear division between "orders" and
"jurisdiction"; for instance, by juxtaposing the *potestas gubernandi populum* and the *potestas spiritualia ministrandi,* he
indicated his awareness of the boundary between governing
and sacramental powers.[4] Usually, however, Gratian was
neither so explicit nor so precise. For Gratian and for the
early decretists, the difficulty arose more from a surfeit than
from a shortage of available terms; the task was to select the
most suitable expressions and, by giving them a narrowed
meaning, to transform them into technical terms. Of course,
Gratian appropriated his constitutional terminology largely
from the texts which he assembled. A few of his expressions
for various forms of jurisdiction will illustrate the problem
which he faced: he sometimes chose the term *iurisdictio* to
designate the Church's governing power in the broadest
sense,[5] but he also used the same word for purely judicial
power.[6] *Auctoritas* can refer to general governing authority,[7]

[3] D.23 c.1 §6: "auctoritatem obtineat regendi Romanam ecclesiam et
disponendi omnes facultates illius."
[4] C.16 q.2 dict.p.c.7 (below, n.43). [5] C.16 q.1 dict.p.c.47, rubr.c.52.
[6] C.13 q.2 dict.p.c.6. [7] D.96 rubr.c.10.

or specifically to legislative power,[8] or to administrative rights over property.[9] In his diction, the word *potestas* appears constantly, often without an explicit effort to specify its meaning, but sometimes accompanied by an explanatory phrase (for example: *regendi et iubendi potestas*, or *potestas gubernandi populum*).[10] Moreover, *potestas* could indicate governing authority in general,[11] or judicial power in particular,[12] or even power over property.[13] As the term itself suggests, *regimen* designated broad powers of rule.[14] Most commonly, *dispositio* and *dispensatio* referred to property rights.[15] In a single *quaestio*, Gratian used six different terms to indicate various aspects of jurisdictional and administrative power (*lex diocesiana, potestas, ordinatio, provisio, iudicium, dominium*), but it would be difficult to demonstrate that he varied the terms to fit the different contexts in which they were placed. Indeed, for Gratian, these six terms were practically interchangeable, and each acquires a measure of clarity only through its setting.[16]

Despite the obstacles posed by the terminology which he had inherited, Gratian made one notable contribution to the definition of ecclesiastical jurisdiction. In the famous text of *Matthew* 16.18-19, when Christ gave to St Peter "the keys of the kingdom of Heaven," He promised him the power to bind and to loose.[17] There was a scriptural basis for the interpreta-

---

8 D.17 pr., rubr.cc. 1, 2, 4, 5.
9 C.16 q.7 pr.; cf. D.23 c.1 §6 (*auctoritas disponendi*).
10 D.21 dict.p.c.3; C.16 q.2 dict.p.c.7.
11 C.16 q.7 pr.; also, above, preceding note.   12 D.20 pr. §1.
13 C.10 q.1 rubr.cc.2, 5, 6; C.10 q.2 pr.   14 C.7 q.1 dict.p.c.16.
15 C.10 pr.; D.23 c.1 §6; C.10 q.2 pr.; C.16 q.7 dict.p.c.30.
16 C.10 q.1 rubr.cc.1, 2, 3, 4, 5, 6, 15, dict.p.c.15.
17 "Tu es Petrus . . . et tibi dabo claves regni caelorum, et quodcumque ligaveris super terram, erit ligatum in caelis et quodcumque solveris super terram, erit solutum et in caelis." On Gratian's interpretation of this passage, see van de Kerckhove, *Études franciscaines* 49 (1937) 440-43; Paul Anciaux, *La théologie du sacrement de pénitence au XIIe siècle* (Louvain 1949) 547; and, above all, the brilliant analysis by Brian Tierney, *Foundations of the Conciliar Theory* (Cambridge 1955) 30-33. For a more recent and extended discussion of the *claves*, see Ludwig Hödl, *Die Geschichte der scholastischen Literatur und der Theologie der Schlüsselgewalt* I (Münster 1960) 155-75 (on Gratian), 175-86 (early decretists).

tion of this gift as the power to remit sins.[18] In this sense, the "power of binding and loosing" was an essentially sacramental prerogative belonging to any priest. Gratian accepted this traditional explanation referring the *potestas ligandi et solvendi* to the remission of sins—that is, to the sacrament of penance administered in the Church's *forum internum*.[19] Discussing the preeminent authority of papal decretals, however, he formulated an alternative interpretation of the *potestas ligandi et solvendi*. Gratian first asked whether the writings of learned theologians should be preferred to the decisions of the Roman pontiffs, and then he remarked:

> But it is one thing to pass judgment in law-cases, it is something else to expound Holy Scripture carefully. In deciding cases, not only knowledge (*scientia*) is necessary, but also power (*potestas*).[20]

Then, after citing Christ's promise to Peter, Gratian explained that the "keys" are indispensable for the exercise of "the power of binding and loosing": The first "key" consists of the "knowledge" needed for the judgment of those crimes which are tried in an ecclesiastical court. The second "key," however, is "power," including the power to excommunicate or to reconcile, as well as the power to decide certain criminal cases.[21] Thus, in Gratian's thought the "power of binding and loosing" acquired a new meaning: the judicial authority of the

18 *Ioan.* 20.22-23: "dixit eis: Accipite Spiritum sanctum: quorum remiseritis peccata, remittuntur eis; et quorum retinueritis, retenta sunt."

19 C.24 q.1 dict.p.c.4; Tierney, *op.cit.* 31.

20 D.20 pr. §1: "Sed aliud est causis terminum imponere, aliud scripturas sacras diligenter exponere. Negotiis diffiniendis non solum est necessaria scientia, sed etiam potestas. Unde Christus dicturus Petro: 'Quodcumque ligaueris . . . ,' prius dedit sibi claues regni celorum: in altera dans ei scientiam discernendi inter lepram et lepram, in altera dans sibi potestatem eiciendi aliquos ab ecclesia, uel recipiendi. Cum ergo quelibet negotia finem accipiant uel in absolutione innocentium, uel in condempnatione delinquentium, absolutio uero uel condempnatio non scientiam tantum, sed etiam potestatem presidentium desiderant. . . ."

21 Elsewhere, Gratian contradicts himself by linking excommunication to the priest's sacramental power. See C.24 q.1 dict.p.cc.4, 37 (above, n.2); Peter Huizing, "The Earliest Development of *excommunicatio latae sententiae* by Gratian," *SGrat* 3 (1955) 285.

ecclesiastical tribunals over the Church as a society.[22] In modern terminology, the *forum externum* of the Church's courts was thereby distinguished from the sacramental *forum internum* of penance.[23] It is not surprising that a few later canonists, commenting on Gratian's statement, glossed the word *potestas* simply as "jurisdiction."[24] Indeed, Gratian's perception of the judicial elements in the *potestas ligandi et solvendi* was a considerable step toward a clear demarcation of the boundary between "orders" and "jurisdiction."

Until the twelfth century, the Church focused its attention primarily on the sacramental sphere. Correspondingly, as viewed by the Early Middle Ages, the central element in any ecclesiastical office was the sacramental power of its incumbent. Gratian followed early medieval usage in applying the term *officium* itself mainly to the sacramental sphere of one possessing holy orders, major or minor.[25] Moreover, like his predecessors, Gratian was more adroit in analyzing sacramental competence than in defining ecclesiastical jurisdiction.

Gratian's most trenchant analysis of "office" derived ultimately from St Augustine. In the fourth century the Donatist controversy had given rise to an urgent question: Are sacraments administered by schismatic or heretical clerics valid,

[22] In this passage Gratian's claim refers exclusively to the supreme judicial power of the pope; Tierney, *op.cit.* 31-33. But in another *dictum*, Gratian observed that in receiving the keys, Peter stood for the entire Church; C.24 q.1 dict.p.c.4: ". . . ab unitate ecclesiae que per Petrum intelligitur. . . ." Moreover, since the argument was obviously applicable *mutatis mutandis* to lesser prelates and even to simple priests, the decretists interpreted it in this extended sense; see the texts quoted by Anciaux, *op.cit.* 548f, and by Tierney, *op.cit.* 32 n.2.

[23] Of course, since the remission of sins entails judgment and the imposition of penance, the *forum internum* presupposes that the priest has at least a limited jurisdiction. Gratian himself was probably not aware of this point, but cf. the remarks in the *Apparatus Ecce uicit leo* on D.20 pr. and on C.24 q.1 c.6: "non dantur [sacerdotibus] claues in ordinatione set tantum in iurisdictione" (Tierney, *op.cit.* 32 n.2).

[24] Huguccio, *Summa* on D.20 pr. v. *potestas*: "id est iurisdictio" (Anciaux, *op.cit.* 549). *Glossa Palatina* ad loc. v. *claues*: ". . . credo clauem esse iurisdictionem" (Anciaux, *loc.cit.*).

[25] For his use of *officium* see: D.23 pr.; D.25 rubr.c.1, dict.p.c.1; D.50 rubr.cc.4, 6, 7, 19, 69, dict.p.c.52; D.51 rubr.c.3; D.55 rubr.c.1; D.56 pr.; and often. In general, Heintschel, *op.cit.* 17-23.

49

and especially, can a schismatic or heretical bishop effectively ordain clerics?[26] In response to the Donatist challenge, Augustine developed a new doctrine, distinguishing sacramental power (*sacramentum*) from the right to exercise such power (*usus sacramenti* or, more simply, *officium*). For as Augustine explained, when a cleric is deprived of his *officium*, he loses the authority to confer sacraments, but if he acts without this authority, the conferment is nonetheless effective, and the sacraments themselves are valid.[27] Indeed, if an unworthy minister bestows a sacrament, it is still a true sacrament, since it comes not from him but from God.[28] On this problem, as the debate continued during the following centuries, the Augustinian solution was largely forgotten. Hence, in the mid-eleventh century the bitter struggle against simony led the early reformers to an extreme position: that simoniac ordinations are invalid. Then Augustine's doctrine was rediscovered in the later eleventh century, and in the early twelfth Hugh of Amiens revived the Augustinian distinction between *sacramentum* and *officium*.[29] In this tradition, Gratian remarked:

> We should understand that the power of conferring holy orders is one thing, the exercise of that power is something else.[30]

[26] The classic study of this problem is by Louis Saltet, *Les réordinations: Étude sur le sacrement de l'ordre* (Paris 1907); also, Anton Michel, "Ordre," *DThC* XI (1932) esp. 1275-98.

[27] *De baptismo* 1.1.2, 6.1.1, *PL* 43 109, 197; *Contra epistolam Parmeniani* 2.28, *PL* 43 70; *De bono coniugali* 32, *PL* 40 394; in general, E. Portalié, "Augustin," *DThC* I (1909) 2416f, and Michel, *op.cit.* 1279f.

[28] Augustine, *Contra litteras Petiliani* 2.69, *PL* 43 281; *Contra Cresconium* 2.12, *PL* 43 473.

[29] Saltet, *op.cit.* chs.4-14; Michel, *op.cit.* 1280-93.

[30] C.1 q.1 dict.p.c.97 §3: ". . . intelligamus aliud esse potestatem distribuendi sacros ordines, aliud esse executionem illius potestatis. Qui intra unitatem catholicae ecclesiae constituti sacerdotalem uel episcopalem unctionem accipiunt, offitium et executionem sui offitii ex consecratione adipiscuntur. . . ." C.24 q.1 dict.p.c.37: "Sed aliud est potestas offitii, aliud executio. Plerumque offitii potestas uel accipitur, ueluti a monachis in sacerdotali unctione, uel accepta sine sui executione retinetur, ueluti a suspensis, quibus amministratio interdicitur, potestas non aufertur. . . ." Saltet, *op.cit.* 291-96; Michel, *op.cit.* 1293f.

Though both his terminology and his doctrine differ from Augustine's, Gratian has similarly distinguished the sacramental power (*officium* or *potestas* or *potestas officii*) from its lawful use and exercise (*executio officii* or *executio potestatis*). Despite doctrinal variations in their discussions of this problem, the early decretists adopted similar formulas. The *Summa Parisiensis* followed Gratian's diction closely.[31] In the same context, master Rufinus played off the power of orders (*veritas sacramenti* or *sacramentum ordinis*) against its use (*executio ordinis* or *executio officii*).[32] Elsewhere, however, Rufinus subtly distinguished four separate elements which justify the use of the priestly office: first, the sacramental power itself (*potestas aptitudinis*); second, the personal characteristics, such as virtue and knowledge, needed for the priest's functions (*potestas regularitatis*); third, the right to exercise sacramental power (*usus officii*); and finally, the possession of an office sanctioning the potential use of this power (*potestas habilitatis*). Nothing can remove a priest's *potestas aptitudinis* "so long as he lives," but a crime deprives him of his *potestas regularitatis*, suspension cancels his *usus officii*, and deposition destroys his *potestas habilitatis*.[33]

---

[31] *Summa Parisiensis* on C.1 q.1 cc.2, 17, dict.p.c.97, on C.24 q.1 dict. p.c.37, ed. T. P. McLaughlin (Toronto 1952) 80f, 88, 226f.

[32] *Summa* on D.70 pr., ed. H. Singer (Paderborn 1902) 161f: ". . . Sed sciendum quod, velut quidam sentiunt, ordinatio habetur irrita tribus modis: quoad sacramenti veritatem, quantum ad officii executionem, quantum ad beneficii perceptionem. . . . Nobis autem videtur quod duobus tantum modis ordinatio sit dicenda vacua: quippe, ex eo quod quis privatur sua culpa officio, privatus intelligitur et stipendio. . . . Unde . . . absoluta ordinatio [scil. sine beneficio] irrita est, non quoad veritatem sacramenti . . . sed quantum ad officii executionem. . . ." *Id.* on C.9 q.1 pr., ed. Singer 298: ". . . ordinatio dicitur . . . non habere vires duobus modis: quoad veritatem sacramenti et quantum ad executionem officii. . . ." See also *id.* on C.1 q.1 c.17, ed. Singer 206, where Rufinus contrasts the *sacramentum ordinis*, the *executio ordinis*, and the *virtus sacramenti*; the latter term refers to the sacramental grace acquired by proper ordination.

[33] *Id.* on C.1 q.1 c.30 v. *si iustus fuerit*, ed. Singer 210f. Cf. the discussion by M. J. Wilks, "Papa est nomen iurisdictionis," *Journal of Theological Studies* n.s.8 (1957) 79f, who rightly stresses the importance of Rufinus in the development of the ideas of office and jurisdiction. However, Wilks regards Rufinus's analysis here as the "fusion" of the old distinction between

Thus the problem of the schismatic or heretical prelate enriched the tradition of technical terms and concepts available for the analysis of ecclesiastical office. In the discussions of this problem, however, the distinctions between *ordo* and *executio* were not at all equivalent to the distinction between "orders" and "jurisdiction."[34] Yet Gratian applied the distinction between *ordo* and *executio* to a different question, and against this new background his familiar distinction foreshadowed the later differentiation of *ordo* and *iurisdictio*. The question was: Under what circumstances can monks fulfill priestly functions?[35] Obviously, as Gratian explained, priestly ordination is the first prerequisite, but monks need more than merely the *ordo* of a priest:

> They do not have the exercise of their power (*executio suae potestatis*), unless they have been elected by the people and ordained by the bishop with the abbot's consent.[36]

In short, before exercising his priestly *ordo*, the monk-priest must be assigned to a specific church. Behind Gratian's stipulation stood a much older requirement. Since the Council of Chalcedon, it was forbidden to ordain a cleric without giving him an appropriate ecclesiastical office, and in 1095 Urban II

---

ordo and *executio ordinis* with a newer distinction between *ordo* and *iurisdictio*. In fact, a separation of *ordo* and *iurisdictio* is certainly not explicit in Rufinus's text at this point.

[34] Cf. Wilks, *op.cit.* 74f.

[35] For a general view of this question, see Ursmer Berlière, "L'exercice du ministère paroissial par les moines dans le haut moyen-âge," *Revue bénédictine* 39 (1927) 227-50, 340-64; Gratian's interpretation is discussed by Anciaux, *Théologie* 309f.

[36] C.16 q.1 dict.p.c.19: ". . . Monachi autem, et si in dedicatione sui presbiteratus (sicut et ceteri sacerdotes) predicandi, baptizandi, penitenciam dandi, peccata remittendi, beneficiis ecclesiasticis perfruendi rite potestatem accipiant, ut amplius et perfectius agant ea, que sacerdotalis offitii esse . . . conprobantur: tamen executionem suae potestatis non habent, nisi a populo fuerint electi, et ab episcopo cum consensu abbatis ordinati. . . ." C.16 q.1 dict.p.c.25: ". . . monstratur, monachos posse penitenciam dare, baptizare, et cetera sacerdotalia offitia licite administrare. Quod uero populi electione, episcoporum institutione, et abbatis consensu potestatem suam exequi ualeant . . . probatur"; almost verbatim, C.16 q.1 dict.p.c.36. Also, C.16 q.1 dict.p.c.40 §§2-3; and C.24 q.1 dict.p.c.37 (above, n.30).

renewed this prohibition against ordination without provision of an office (*absoluta ordinatio* or *ordinatio sine titulo*).[37] According to Rufinus and Stephen of Tournai, such ordinations were effective "with regard to the validity of the sacrament" but were null and void "with regard to the exercise of the office."[38] Roland Bandinelli summed up the general principle succinctly:

> For the administration of the priestly dignity, two things are necessary: orders (*ordo*) and permission to use the orders (*licentia ordinis exequendi*).[39]

Yet master Roland drew a new implication: In his view, this "permission" was linked to a grant of jurisdiction, that is, of governing power over a parish.[40]

The Church's property raised problems which complicated the task of analyzing and defining ecclesiastical office. What was Gratian's concept of the relation between office and property? Of course, Gratian was writing in the aftermath of the Investiture Struggle, and it is not surprising that he assimilated the recent but fundamental distinction between the *regalia* (including secular jurisdiction as well as property)

---

[37] D.70 cc.1 (451), 2 (1095). In general, see Vincenz Fuchs, *Der Ordinationstitel von seiner Entstehung bis auf Innocenz III.* (Bonn 1930).

[38] For Rufinus's view see above, n.32; Stephen of Tournai, *Summa* on D.70 pr., ed. J. F. von Schulte (Giessen 1891) 95f: "qui ecclesiae attitulatus non est, exequi divina ministeria populo publice non potest."

[39] *Summa* on C.16 q.1, ed. F. Thaner (Innsbruck 1874) 37f: ". . . monachorum sacerdotum quidam habent populum sibi commissum, quidam non. Nulli ergo monachorum licebit missas publicas celebrare . . . atque alia sacerdotalia populis ministrare, nisi constiterit eum populum sibi subiectum habere. . . . Notandum est enim, quod ad sacerdotalis dignitatis amministrationem duo sunt necessaria: ordo et licentia ordinis exsequendi. . . ." See the view expressed by Stephen of Tournai, *Summa* on C.16 q.1 dict.p.c.19 v. *dedicatione*, ed. Schulte 222: ". . . Nec monachus nec alius sacerdos ex sola consecratione habet executionem docendi populum, nisi assignetur ab episcopo . . . "; Johannes Faventinus repeated this text (van de Kerckhove, *Études franciscaines* 49 [1937] 422). Cf. also *Summa Parisiensis* on C.16 q.1 dict.p.c.20, on C.24 q.1 dict.p.c.37, ed. McLaughlin 178, 226f.

[40] Such is the meaning of the phrase "populum sibi subiectum habere" (above, preceding note).

and the purely ecclesiastical properties.[41] As he clearly recognized, the prelate holding *regalia* owes service to the emperor.[42] At his best, Gratian could draw an even sharper distinction, for he believed that the property rights of a prelate may be separate from his governing power and sacramental competence.[43] Moreover, he was thoroughly familiar with the concept of an ecclesiastical benefice, which he regarded as the right to receive an income from the church properties attached to an ecclesiastical office.[44] Indeed, within the *Decretum* it was forbidden for a bishop-elect to alienate church property prior to his consecration, and for any cleric to enjoy the income from his benefice prior to his ordination.[45] In Gratian's view, possession of a *beneficium* was thus linked to, and even dependent upon, possession of the sacramental *officium*.

Summarizing the doctrine of the Reform papacy, Gratian maintained that any deacon, priest, or bishop who marries should be stripped of both his *officium* and his *beneficium*.[46] On the other hand, also in the context of penal regulations, Gratian could distinguish between *officium* and *beneficium*, for he conceded that a cleric who has unintentionally committed simony may keep his holy orders but must give up his benefice.[47] In contrast to this assertion, Gratian incorporated a ninth-century text depriving a criminal cleric of his

[41] As *regalia*, Gratian listed *predia, uillae, castella,* and *ciuitates* (C.23 q.8 dict.p.c.20; cf. C.11 q.1 dict.p.c.26); below, Ch.IXв n.9.

[42] Below, Ch.IXв.

[43] C.16 q.2 dict.p.c.7: "Tales [abbates], etsi ius territorii habeant, tamen potestatem gubernandi populum, et spiritualia ministrandi non habent." The *ius territorii* is discussed by Ulrich Stutz, "Gratian und die Eigenkirchen," *ZRG* KA 1 (1911) 18f.

[44] In general, G. Mollat, "Bénéfices ecclésiastiques en Occident," *DDC* II (1937) 407-49. On Gratian's thought, see Heintschel, *Mediaeval Concept* 6f, 19-22, and above all, Dominikus Lindner, "Das kirchliche Beneficium in Gratian's Dekret," *SGrat* 2 (1954) 377-86; most recently, Glenn Olsen, "The Definition of the Ecclesiastical Benefice in the Twelfth Century," *SGrat* 11 (1967) 431-46.

[45] C.12 q.2 c.37 (above, Ch.IIA n.79); C.16 q.1 dict.p.c.19 (above, n.36).

[46] See D.32 c.10 (Urban II), D.81 cc.16-18 (Alexander II), and Gratian's rubrics to these *capitula*.

[47] C.1 q.5 dict.p.c.2; here, Gratian contrasts the *sacri ordines* with the *fructus emptionis*.

office but allowing him to keep his benefice; yet it is significant that in his summary of this ninth-century *capitulum*, Gratian stressed the loss of the *officium* as a penalty, but did not comment on the cleric's retention of his *beneficium*.[48] Still, in general it remains true that Gratian recognized a close bond between *officium* and *beneficium,* for as he explained, ecclesiastical benefices, though distinct from the *spiritualia*, are "the temporalities annexed to them."[49] Consequently, he agreed with Guido of Arezzo's attack upon the simoniacs who claimed to be purchasing merely property (*res*), rather than sacramental powers (*consecrationes*). "He who buys ecclesiastical benefices," Gratian asserted, "is also buying churches."[50]

It is evident that Gratian improvised endlessly in the construction of terms and concepts applicable to the different aspects of office. His improvisation rarely achieved precision in the sphere of jurisdictional powers, but it was more often successful in discussions of sacramental functions and of ecclesiastical property. Though his treatment of office was subtle and lucid in these contexts, he nonetheless failed to create a systematic terminology and a conceptual scheme explaining the nature of ecclesiastical jurisdiction: its acquisition, its limits, and its proper exercise. This task awaited the decretists.

[48] D.50 c.39 (Nicholas I); D.50 rubr.c.39: "Perpetuo careat offitio presbiter, qui ira conmotus, licet extra animum, aliquem interfecerit."

[49] C.1 q.3 pr. §1: "Non solum qui spiritualia, sed etiam qui temporalia eis annexa precio accipiunt symoniaci iudicantur." The *temporalia spiritualibus annexa* refer to *beneficia* and *prebendae* (C.1 pr.; C.1 q.3 c.3, rubr.cc.2, 3, 4, 7, 15). In general, see also: C.1 q.4 dict.p.c. 10; C.16 q.1 c.22, rubr.c.22; C.17 pr., and C.17 q.2 c.1.

[50] Gratian republished Guido's attack in C.1 q.3 c.7 (incorrectly attributed by Gratian to "Pascalis papa" and not identified by Friedberg); see *MGH LdL* I 6 (below, Ch.VIIᴀ n.18). Also, C.1 q.3 rubr.c.7: "Qui ecclesiastica beneficia emunt, ecclesias quoque emere probantur."

CHAPTER III

MASTER RUFINUS:

AUCTORITAS AND *ADMINISTRATIO*

1. A New Doctrine of Election

BY 1133, when Innocent II granted a charter to Lothar III, the German monarchy had gained general acceptance for a juridical definition of investiture as an indispensable prerequisite to the German bishop-elect's administration of his *regalia*; this development will be discussed in a later chapter. By 1133, however, the Church had done little to define ecclesiastically the moment and the ceremonial act in which a prelate-elect receives his jurisdictional and administrative powers. Before the mid-twelfth century, in fact, of all the offices within the Church, only the papacy had explicit regulations dealing with this question. For the episcopate in general, moreover, the Church had scarcely even demonstrated an awareness of this problem until the early decretists began to explicate the *Decretum*'s chapters on office and election. The first strides toward this achievement can be found in master Rufinus's *Summa*, which appeared between 1157 and 1159.[1] Though he held positions of substantial importance—

[1] It has been edited by Heinrich Singer, *Die Summa decretorum des magister Rufinus* (Paderborn 1902); on his life and work, see Singer's excellent introduction to the edition (esp. pp.xlv-cxxvi), and for a shorter account with a bibliographical survey, my article "Rufin," *DDC* VII (1961) 779-84. The edition by Johann von Schulte, *Die Summa magistri Rufini zum Decretum Gratiani* (Giessen 1892), should never be used, since Schulte incorrectly ascribed to Rufinus the later *Summa Antiquitate et tempore* (Rhenish

a professorship of law at Bologna, the bishopric of Assisi, and finally the archbishopric of Sorrento—little is known about Rufinus's career. In 1179 he was singled out and honored with the responsible task of delivering the opening address to the Third Lateran Council. Judged for his most durable accomplishments and his historical influence, however, he was a pivotal figure in the development of canon law and canonistic thought. Indeed, a century after his death he was still justly remembered as "the first elegant commentator or interpreter of that golden book, the *Decretum*."[2]

The imagination, originality, and high juridical precision of master Rufinus's mind are nowhere more apparent than in his constitutional concepts and political ideas. His constitutional doctrines can perhaps be most easily approached through his commentary on Nicholas II's papal election decree of 1059, which Gratian had republished in the *Decretum*. Neither Paucapalea nor Roland Bandinelli—nor, so far as one can tell, any other decretist of the first generation after Gratian—had written about the constitutional problem in this decree.[3] Rufinus began his discussion of Nicholas's

---

school) and the *Summa Conditio ecclesiastice religionis* (French school), both of which were heavily influenced by Rufinus.

Rufinus's treatise *De bono pacis* is available in *PL* 150 1591-1638; see Francesco Di Capua, "Il canonista Rufino e il suo trattato 'De bono pacis,'" *Atti del III Congresso nazionale di studi romani* II (Bologna 1935) 89-99, and Yves M.-J. Congar, "Maître Rufin et son *De bono pacis*," *Revue des sciences philosophiques et théologiques* 41 (1957) 428-44. His sermons have been discovered and identified by Germain Morin, "Le discours d'ouverture du Concile général de Latran (1179) et l'oeuvre littéraire de maître Rufin, évêque d'Assise," *Atti della Pontificia accademia romana di archeologia* 3rd ser., *Memorie* 2 (1928) 113-33 (with the text of the address to the Lateran Council edited on pp. 116-20).

[2] Singer, *Summa* Einleitung p.xviii: "aurei uoluminis decretorum elegans apparator siue expositor primus." An anonymous scribe of the late 13th or early 14th century made this comment at the end of the Moulins MS.

[3] See D.23 in Paucapalea, *Summa*, ed. Schulte 22; Roland Bandinelli, *Summa*, ed. Thaner 6; and the *Summa Parisiensis*, ed. McLaughlin 23. Although perhaps composed as early as 1160 (that is, after Rufinus's *Summa*), the anonymous *Summa Parisiensis* shows no traces of Rufinian influence. Two fragmentary *summae* of the Bolognese school, the *Summa Wigorniensis* (Worcester Cathedral MS Q.70 fols.1-40v) and the *Summa Cantabrigiensis* (Cambridge University Library Addit. MS 3321 I fols.1-35v) antedate Rufinus in their use of extended criticism and commentary. How-

decree by remarking, "It is customarily asked . . ." (*Solet queri* . . .), and unless this phrase was a meaningless formula, clearly the constitutional questions in the election decree were already, even before Rufinus's *Summa*, a serious concern of the lawyers in the Bolognese school. Dealing with this text, Rufinus crystallized a new terminology and gave a lasting form to these constitutional problems:

> It is customarily asked whether one who has been con-
> firmed in an election possesses such full authority that he
> has the right, before his episcopal anointment, to depose
> clerics just like a consecrated bishop. We, however, say
> that he should have full power with respect to adminis-
> tration but not with respect to the authority of his dignity.
> And therefore, with the right of full administration, he
> can suspend others from the administration of offices or
> orders. . . . On the other hand, he who does not yet have
> the plenitude of authority—which certainly comes only
> from consecration—cannot depose.[4]

Here the question concerns the status of an elected but not yet consecrated bishop. (It could, conceivably, also refer to the status of an elected pope, who was however not a bishop prior to his election—a phenomenon which had indeed been the rule rather than the exception in the earlier Middle Ages.[5]) The terms "full authority" (*plena auctoritas*) and

---

ever, it has not yet been ascertained that they exerted any noticeable influence upon later canonists. An examination of these two MSS in microfilm
has convinced me that—at least in the sections preserved—they did not
contribute to the development of these constitutional ideas.

[4] Rufinus, *Summa* on D.23 c.1 v. *tamen sicut verus papa auctor. regnandi
optin. in ecclesia*, ed. Singer 52: "Solet queri, si in electione confirmatus ante
episcopalem unctionem usque adeo plenam auctoritatem possideat, ut
quemadmodum episcopus consecratus deponere clericos valeat. Sed dicimus
quod plenam potestatem habeat quoad administrationem non autem quoad
dignitatis auctoritatem, et ideo iure plene administrationis potest aliquos ab
administratione procurationum vel ordinum suspendere—quod tamen non
sine presentia capituli sui, cui capitulo episcopo mortuo licet itidem facere.
Deponere autem, id est exauctorare non potest qui plenitudinem auctoritatis
nondum habet, quam ex sola consecratione est certissimum evenire."

[5] Wasner, *Apollinaris* 8 (1935) 91ff.

"full power" (*plena potestas*) are by no means used inter-changeably and cannot be regarded as equivalent. On the other hand, "full power with respect to administration" (*plena potestas quoad administrationem*) is clearly to be identified with the "right of full administration" (*ius plene administrationis*), and it is inferior to the "plenitude of authority" (*plenitudo auctoritatis*), which derives only from the episcopal consecration. The power of administration is dependent upon the election, and it is merely the first step toward the acquisition of authority. Correspondingly, one might also describe the power of administration as a *part* of full authority, as included within it.

Master Rufinus's example, the suspension or deposition of clerics, is a happy choice for the purpose of showing the com-plexity of constitutional thought in this area. Gratian had not distinguished clearly between these two judicial acts.[6] Rufinus, however, drew a sharp line between them, for, as he explained, suspension merely removes the right to use an ecclesiastical office (*usus officii*), whereas by deposition a prelate loses the office itself and all powers within it (*dignitas officii* and *potestas habilitatis*) but retains the original sacra-ment of his holy orders (*sacramentum* and *potestas apti-tudinis*).[7] Obviously, both suspension and deposition involve judgment, and they engage the bishop in his role as judge. In this way, Rufinus exemplified the bishop's *administratio* in the judicial component of the episcopal *potestas iuris-dictionis*, to use the familiar terminology of a later period. But in Rufinus's view, a part of the bishop's judicial power belongs to his *auctoritas*, that is, to his *potestas ordinis*, and just as the bestowal of holy orders requires the episcopal *potestas ordinis*, which is achieved only in the episcopal con-secration, similarly deposition is one of the bishop's *iura*

---

[6] C.1 q.1 dict.p.c.97 (§2); Saltet, *Réordinations* 294.

[7] Rufinus, *Summa* on C.1 q.1 c.30 v. *si iustus*, and on D.18 c.9 v. *presby-ter*, ed. Singer 210f and 66; also, Saltet, *op.cit.* 310-15 and esp. 314f. Cf. above, Ch.IIB nn.33f.

ordinis reservata.[8] In this respect, if one measures master Rufinus by the standards of thirteenth-century canonists, he confused *ordo* and *iurisdictio* when he identified the jurisdictional power of deposition as a sacramental prerogative.

Despite the fact that this chapter in the *Decretum* (D.23 c.1) is concerned only with papal elections, Rufinus certainly did not wish to confine his discussion to this single case. Master Rufinus might have been referring to both papal and episcopal elections, since the pope is, after all, bishop of Rome. In this respect, there would be no constitutional difference between the bishop of Rome and any other bishop, since the basic constitutional issue is equally applicable to all bishops. In his commentary, however, Rufinus was primarily interested in episcopal elections, and therefore, a further point remains to be discussed: Rufinus was inquiring into the powers of "one who has been confirmed in an election" (*confirmatus in electione*). What sort of "confirmation" did Rufinus have in mind? Was he referring to a vaguely defined "consent," or was he referring to a necessary act with specific consequences and technical juridical significance? In other words, did Rufinus use the word *confirmare* in the sense common to the *Decretum* and to earlier writings, as a form of consent which was based on customary law but which created no new powers and no new rights for a prelate-elect? Or was he the first to use the term *confirmare* in the specific sense defined by the *Codex iuris canonici*, as a reference to the act through which the *electus* gains his jurisdictional and administrative powers? Since the expressions *confirmare* and *confirmatio* appeared conspicuously elsewhere in Rufinus's *Summa*, one need not look far for the answer to these questions.

For example, master Rufinus remarked that according to many canonical texts, the emperor should "confirm" a papal election.[9] With this assertion, however, Rufinus was merely

---

[8] Deposition and degradation were not universally regarded as *iura pontificalia* in the 12th century. Huguccio asserted that deposition belongs to the *potestas iurisdictionis*; see below, Ch.VA n.7.

[9] Rufinus, *Summa* on D.63 pr. v. *laici vero*, ed. Singer 155: ". . . Quod

echoing one of Gratian's rubrics, and, following Gratian in this respect too, Rufinus was quick to add that this *confirmatio*, as well as all other lay interference, should be excluded from ecclesiastical elections.[10] And insofar as confirmation pertains to a superior official, since no one—neither cleric nor emperor—stands above the pope, a papal election cannot receive a true confirmation.[11] In any case, within Rufinus's conception of the proper relations between emperor and pope, the emperor is markedly subordinate to the pontiff —hence, there could be no legitimate imperial jurisdiction over papal elections.

As defined in the *Codex*, electoral confirmation bestows full jurisdictional powers upon the *electus*, but only the hierarchical superior can sanction those powers by confirming the election. Also in this way, Rufinus's conception derived from the Early Middle Ages, for he regarded the "confirmation of the metropolitan and of the comprovincial bishops" as one of the factors in an episcopal election. It is immediately apparent that this Rufinian version of *confirmatio* differs from the more modern concept, for it includes the other bishops of the province as well as the competent superior, the metropolitan. The context clarifies Rufinus's idea:

> In the election of a bishop, these five things are especially to be considered: the wishes of the citizens, the testimony of the people, the choice of those in high positions and of the regular clergy, the election of the clerics, the confirmation of the metropolitan and of the comprovincial bishops.[12]

In this list Rufinus has specifically enumerated the various

---

sine principe non confirmetur electio [scil. papae], innumeris decretis exemplisque perpenditur. . . ."

[10] For Gratian's position, cf. D.63 dict.p.cc.25, 27, 28, 34.

[11] As later canonists clearly pointed out; see below, Ch.VIA.

[12] Rufinus, *Summa* on D.63 pr. v. *laici vero*, ed. Singer 155: ". . . Sciendum ergo quod in electione episcopi hec quinque maxime attenduntur: Vota civium, testimonium populorum, arbitrium onoratorum vel religiosorum, electio clericorum, confirmatio metropolitani et coepiscoporum. . . ." Following Rufinus almost verbatim, Stephen of Tournai listed the same factors (*Summa* on D.63 pr. v. *laici vero*, ed. Schulte 89).

parties with a rightful interest in episcopal elections—manifestly, these elements constitute the different parts of the *clerus et populus*, in other words, the traditional theory, far older than Gratian's *Decretum*. Moreover, the first four of these five factors were taken over directly by Rufinus, practically verbatim, from a chapter of the *Decretum* which derived from Leo the Great. Drawing on elements given in the early canons, however, Rufinus himself formulated the juridical term for the fifth factor, that is, the *confirmatio metropolitani et coepiscoporum*—note that it echoes the phrase in the Calixtinum, *metropolitani et conprovincialium consilio vel iudicio*.[13] This fifth factor represents Rufinus's summary of those chapters in the *Decretum* which insist upon the consent of the metropolitan and the comprovincial bishops to the installation of a new bishop.

Within the Rufinian constitutional system, electoral confirmation could have still another meaning, for through his diocesan jurisdiction a bishop had the right to carry out the installation (*institutio*) of an abbot-elect in his abbey—and Rufinus defined this *institutio* as a confirmation of the election held by the monks of the abbey.[14]

Thus, for Rufinus the meaning of electoral confirmation varied in different contexts, and certainly he was unwilling to emphasize it by giving it great juridical weight. In his thought it never became more than the normal last stage in the electoral process, for it was simply a form of consent and agreement. This consent might strengthen and complete an episcopal election, and it was an expected preliminary to the

---

[13] D.63 c.27 (Leo I; cf. above, Ch.IIA n.8): "Vota ciuium, testimonia populorum, honoratorum arbitrium, electio clericorum in ordinationibus sacerdotum constituantur. . . ." Cf. also D.23 c.2 §3 (above, Ch.IIA n.66). For the Calixtinum's text, see below, Ch.VIIB n.5. Similar phrases can occasionally be found in the earlier tradition; e.g., Bonizo of Sutri, *Liber de vita christiana* 2.23, ed. E. Perels (Berlin 1930) 43: "electione cleri et populi et assensu metropolitani et comprovincialium [episcopus] sit eligendus."

[14] Rufinus, *Summa* on C.18 q.2 pr. v. *secundam vero*, ed. Singer 377: ". . . abbas . . . est eligendus . . . per monachos; instituendus est autem, i.e., in electione confirmandus, per episcopum. . . ."

consecration, but the consent had no specific consequences above and beyond the effects of election and consecration. In other words, Rufinus's conception of *confirmatio* was still the old notion of assent as a right sanctioned by customary law.

Soon after Rufinus wrote his *Summa*, electoral confirmation emerged in a much more modern sense. Nonetheless, it is not surprising that master Rufinus, despite the subtlety and sharpness in his theories of office and jurisdiction, did not yet arrive at a precise definition of the newer concept of electoral confirmation, for the early medieval idea of consent died slowly. Indeed, one might say that even in the twentieth century, within the *Codex iuris canonici*, the earlier and less concrete meaning of *confirmatio* is still alive, as an act which "strengthens" the already acquired powers of office, rather than sanctioning their effective beginning.[15] And *a fortiori*, two or three decades after Rufinus's *Summa*, the early medieval idea of consent was still vigorous—partly, perhaps, because it was embedded in the *Decretum*, but chiefly because it had survived in canonical practice. Because the term *confirmatio* could be used for both, it was easy to confuse the early medieval notion of consent with the post-Rufinian idea of electoral confirmation. Moreover, even the finest canonistic minds were capable of this confusion; around 1190 master Huguccio wrote:

> In some places . . . [the elections of] metropolitans . . . are confirmed . . . by their own suffragan bishops . . . even when the pope has not been consulted. . . .[16]

Huguccio was fully familiar with electoral *confirmatio* as a

---

15 Klaus Mörsdorf, *Die Rechtssprache des Codex iuris canonici* (Görres-Gesellschaft, Veröffentlichungen der Sektion für Rechts- und Staatswissenschaft 74: Paderborn 1937) 85f, 196f, has pointed out that in its meaning as a juridical act, *confirmatio* can be either "rechtsbekräftigend" or "rechtsbegründend."

16 Huguccio, *Summa* on D.63 c.9 v. *consentimus*: ". . . in quibusdam locis . . . metropolitani qui subsunt pape nullo medio . . . confirmantur et consecrantur a suis suffraganeis . . . etiam inconsulto papa" (Clm 10247 fol.69ra).

new technical term and as a jurisdictionally defined concept, but in this passage he was applying the verb *confirmare* to the suffragan bishops' ancient right of consent. A similar ambiguity is apparent in the remark by Simon of Bisignano (1177-79), that in some places "the confirmation of an election belongs to the prince"—a remark with which the twelfth-century emperors would have agreed.[17] On the whole, however, as we shall see, the canonists who followed Rufinus used the term *confirmatio* in its most precise juridical sense.

2. Ecclesiastical Office and Jurisdiction

Now to return to master Rufinus's idea of office: The duality *auctoritas* and *administratio*, as applied to the papal election decree, was a contribution to the theory of episcopal election and of episcopal jurisdiction; it described the functions or powers of a single official in different acts and at different moments. In any case, only one person is involved: the bishop. But Rufinus did not remain content with the theory embodied in his commentary on the election decree, essentially a clarification of the distinction between the bishop's *ordo* and his *iurisdictio*. When Rufinus extended the doctrine to other problems, he enhanced the importance of this dualism and elevated it to the level of a broad ecclesiastico-constitutional theory.

In a discussion of the prerequisites for promotion to different ecclesiastical offices, master Rufinus pointed out a curious inconsistency in the hierarchical system. According to the view held by Rufinus and definitively pronounced as law by Innocent III, the subdiaconate is one of the "holy orders." Among those with *sacri ordines*, however, the subdeacon has a markedly lower grade than the priest or deacon.[1]

---

[17] Simon of Bisignano, *Summa* on D.85 c.1 v. *ab omnibus fuerat electus* [sic]: ". . . hoc ibi forte obtinet, ubi confirmatio electionis ad principem pertinet, sicut in nonnullis prouinciis observatur" (Rouen 710 fol.72rb). Even a century earlier, the prince's investiture was conceived as a *confirmatio*; above, Ch.IIA nn.72-76.

[1] Rufinus, *Summa* on D.32 c.11 v. *Erubescant* etc., ed. Singer 75; Inno-

In one of Gratian's *distinctiones* on election, three *capitula* insist that to become an archdeacon, provost, or dean, a candidate had to be already either a deacon or a priest.[2] Then follows a *capitulum* which qualifies this principle by asserting that "when the occasion demands it" (*opportunitate exigente*), even a subdeacon can be elected bishop.[3] The archidiaconate, provostship, and decanate are important offices of the Church, but certainly far inferior to the episcopate— hence the relatively modest requirement for election to the episcopate must seem inconsistent with the stiffer prerequisite for election to the other three offices. To phrase this paradox in other terms, it is as though military law prescribed that a lieutenant can be directly promoted to a general's rank, but to become a colonel, one must first win the captain's bars. Gratian himself ignored the paradox, and simply regarded the possible election of a subdeacon to the episcopate as an exceptional act, requiring special permission and allowed only under urgent pressures:

> Otherwise, however [as Gratian explained], because of the dignity of the [episcopal] rank (*propter dignitatem ordinis*), only those in holy orders may be elected bishop or archbishop.[4]

Master Rufinus noted the apparent contradiction of these various *capitula*, and in order to explain it away, he once again drew the distinction between *auctoritas* and *administratio*, this time, however, quite differently:

> There is one ecclesiastical dignity of administration, another of authority. Similarly, there is one administration of spiritual things, another of secular things: an administration of spiritual things, such as belongs to . . . the dean, an administration of secular things, such as belongs to the archdeacon. The dignity of authority belongs to the bishop.[5]

cent's decretal establishing the subdiaconate among the *maiores ordines* is *X* 1.14.9 (1203); Feine, *RG* I 345.
[2] D.60 cc.1-3.   [3] D.60 c.4.   [4] D.60 dict.p.c.4.
[5] *Summa* on D.60 pr. v. *ecce ex parte* etc., ed. Singer 151f: ". . . Aperit

With respect to any bishop, Rufinus had ascribed both *auctoritas* and *administratio* to one individual. In this text, however, the duality is broken up, for only the bishop has *auctoritas*. Yet this *auctoritas*, one may assume, assimilated and incorporated the episcopal *administratio*. Here, however, the constitutional exercise of "administration" is the primary attribute of lesser officials, like the archdeacon and dean. Also, in this passage the idea of "administration" is different in another way, for in the commentary on the papal election decree, *administratio* was connected with those duties of a bishop which are *not* dependent on his *iura ordinis episcopalia*. That is to say, in Rufinus's electoral discussion, *administratio* was clearly separated from the *spiritualia* of the episcopal office. But in this text Rufinus has subdivided the concept of *administratio*, for one learns that there can be an "administration of spiritual things" as well as of "secular things."[6]

As Rufinus's distinction between the *administratio spiritualium* and the *administratio secularium* could be rephrased in a more modern terminology, on the intermediate level of the Church's hierarchy some offices pertain primarily to the *potestas iurisdictionis*, some primarily to the *potestas ordinis*. Within Rufinus's new terminology, the *administratio secularium* neatly summed up the actual prerogatives and duties of the archdeacon during the twelfth century, for the archdeacon had broad supervisory and disciplinary powers over

---

igitur ante omnia subiecta distinctione, ex quibus ordinibus aliqui in prepositum, decanum, archidiaconum, episcopum eligi valeant, dicens quod nullus est eligendus in archidiaconum, nisi sit diaconus; et nullus in decanum vel archipresbiterum, nisi sit presbiter vel diaconus; nullusque in prepositum, nisi sit presbiter vel diaconus. Nullus in episcopum vel archiepiscopum eligatur, nisi presbiter sit aut diaconus; opportunitate tamen exigente etiam subdiaconus in episcopum eligi poterit. Queritur autem hic, cum episcopalis dignitas longe maior sit archipresbiteratu vel archidiaconatu, cur ex inferioribus gradibus eligi valeat potius episcopus, quam archipresbiter vel archidiaconus. Ad quod est sciendum quod ecclesiastica dignitas alia est amministrationis, alia auctoritatis; item amministratio alia spiritualium, alia secularium: spiritualium amministratio, ut archipresbiteri et decani; secularium, ut archidiaconi. Dignitas auctoritatis est episcopi. . . ."

6 On the *administratio spiritualium*, see Hinschius, *KR* II 41.

the clergy of his archidiaconate, and administrative powers over the ecclesiastical buildings, possessions, and wealth within his jurisdiction. The archdeacon was often simultaneously provost of the cathedral chapter, and he thereby also administered the chapter's wealth.[7] The Rufinian term *administratio spiritualium* was correspondingly appropriate to the office of the dean (*decanus* or *archipresbyter*), who also had disciplinary powers, either as chapter dean within the cathedral chapter, or as rural dean within his decanate at large, where he was responsible for maintaining moral and religious standards. Although in many cases the dean assisted the archdeacon in the performance of his duties, the decanal office generally emphasized spiritual matters rather more than jurisdictional affairs, for the chapter dean was closely concerned with the proper performance of divine services in the cathedral; moreover, both the chapter dean and the rural dean were responsible for the spiritual welfare of the clergy within their spheres.[8] Describing his conception of the two kinds of *administratio*, Rufinus explained that for the archdeacon, the dean, and the others on their level of the hierarchy, the election immediately bestows the full rights of "administration." These offices, however, differ from the episcopate, which is fully realized only when the bishop is consecrated. But since these officials will not gain a higher *potestas ordinis* through an act of consecration, they must, in their previous offices, already have held a *potestas ordinis* sufficient to carry out their new duties. Hence, concluded Rufinus, a mere subdeacon can be elected to the episcopate.[9]

[7] *Ibid.* II 183ff; Albert Werminghoff, *Verfassungsgeschichte der deutschen Kirche im Mittelalter* (2nd ed. Leipzig 1913) 154ff.

[8] Hinschius, *KR* II 277ff, 436ff; Werminghoff, *op.cit.* 148f, 151, 167f.

[9] *Summa* on D.60 pr. v. *ecce ex parte*, ed. Singer 152 (continuing the text of n.5): ". . . Dignitas vero amministrandi in ipsa electione plene traditur: cum enim archidiaconus eligitur, plene instituitur et instituendo eligitur. Sic de decano et archipresbitero exaudiendum et de ceteris huiusmodi. Et ideo quia in ipso electionis articulo omnis quam habiturus est potestas confertur archidiacono—quam quidem habere non posset, nisi in ordine magno—in eo gradu eligitur, in quo plenitudo dignitatis perseveratura cognoscitur. Cum autem quis in episcopum eligitur, non continuo plenam

To measure the magnitude of Rufinus's achievement in the realm of constitutional theory, it is necessary merely to compare his concepts with those of most earlier writers. For example, the conception of the Church as a symmetrical or, so to speak, pyramidal hierarchy was a common element in medieval thought prior to the *Decretum*,[10] and this idea appeared prominently among Gratian's doctrines.[11] Indeed, the hierarchical order of heaven provided the paradigm for the graded offices in the Church.[12] And within the Church's hierarchy, "the higher the grade," as Gratian remarked, "so much the greater authority is found."[13] But even with Gratian's subsequent explanation that the superior has the "power to rule and command" and the inferiors have the "duty of obedience," such assertions were far from providing a clear and systematic elucidation of the effective authority enjoyed by the prelates on the different levels of the hierarchy. It was not enough simply to say, with Gratian, that "the lesser are to be judged by the greater,"[14] or that a bishop might appeal from a judicial sentence by his metropolitan to the latter's superior, the primate.[15] Although Gratian recognized the necessity of formulating a doctrine which would explain the jurisdiction inherent in the major offices of the Church and which would distinguish the differences in the powers belonging to the various offices, his attempts lack sharpness, consistency,

---

potestatem adipiscitur, sed usque in consecrationem differtur: et ideo tunc satis est, si etiam ex subdiaconatu eligatur. . . ."

[10] D.21 c.1 (from Isidore's *Etymologiae*); D.25 c.1 (cf. Heintschel, *Mediaeval Concept* 26-32).

[11] It was, in fact, an unquestioned assumption within Gratian's thought; cf. D.23 pr.: ". . . a summo [ecclesiastico officio] incipientes, et usque ad ultimum gradum descendentes. . . ."

[12] Eugene III to archbishop Henry of York (1151), ed. W. Holtzmann, *PU England* II (Abh.Göttingen 15: Berlin 1936) 231 no.66: "Ad instar . . . celestis ordinis catholica ecclesia est constituta in terris; sicut enim celestium spirituum alii sunt superiores absque elatione et propensius secreta diuina rimantur, alii inferiores sine inuidia et mandatis superiorum letantur et humiliter obsecuntur, ita in ecclesia catholica alii patriarche siue primates, alii archiepiscopi siue metropolitani, alii episcopi statuuntur."

[13] D.21 dict.p.c.3.   [14] D.21 rubr.c.4.

[15] For example, D.99 pr.

and general applicability.[16] Gratian's contemporary, the great
Bernard of Clairvaux, was surely aware of the difficulties and
possibilities of this problem, as he tried to point out the various ways in which the Roman bishop is distinguished from all
others. Addressing his disciple, pope Eugene III, St Bernard
stated:

> In primacy, you are Abel; in governing, Noah; in patri-
> archate, Abraham; in order, Melchisedech; in dignity,
> Aaron; in authority, Moses; in judgeship, Samuel; in power,
> Peter; in anointment, Christ.[17]

In this list Bernard detailed nine different modes of preeminence by which one official can stand above another
(*primatus, gubernatus, patriarchatus, ordo, dignitas, auctoritas, iudicatus, potestas, unctio*), and he asserted that in each
of these respects, with a figure from the Old or the New Testament as model, the Roman pontiff holds the foremost place.
But in spite of—or, one might better say, because of—the
rhetorical virtuosity of this passage, it is a eulogy, rather than
a juridically useful definition. In other words, the lawyers and
constitutional theorists still needed a broad-reaching but precise conception of jurisdiction and of jurisdictional preeminence, a conception which could be applied, more or less
appropriately, to every office and rank within the Church.
Master Rufinus filled this need.

A Pseudo-Isidorian letter in the *Decretum* states that St
Peter "first received the power of binding and loosing from
the Lord . . . , but the other apostles received honor and
power with him in equal partnership."[18] Tradition dictated
that St Peter was succeeded by the bishops of Rome, just as
the other apostles were the predecessors of the other bishops,

---

[16] See C.9 q.3 pr. and C.9 q.3 dict.p.c.21; also, above, Ch.IIB.

[17] *De consideratione* 2.8.15, *PL* 182 751: "Quis es? Sacerdos magnus,
summus pontifex. Tu princeps episcoporum, tu haeres apostolorum, tu
primatu Abel, gubernatu Noe, patriarchatu Abraham, ordine Melchisedech,
dignitate Aaron, auctoritate Moyses, iudicatu Samuel, potestate Petrus,
unctione Christus."

[18] D.21 c.2.

while the seventy-two disciples of Christ prefigured the hierarchical role of the priests.[19] The suggestion of an "equal
partnership" (*par consortium*) among all the apostles could
therefore scarcely be reconciled with the vigorous claims of
an ascendent papacy, nor could the strongly curialist senti-
ments of canonists like Rufinus easily accept the implication
that St Peter (= Roman pontiff) enjoyed no special power
over the other apostles (= other bishops). To meet this
challenge without completely discarding the statement in the
Decretum, Rufinus created a schema on the different forms
of hierarchical preeminence.[20] There are, he explained, three
ways in which a cleric can achieve superiority to other clerics:
by his *consecratio*, by his *ordo*, and by his *dispensatio* or
administratio. As consecration is the act which bestows full
authority on the bishop, the dignity of *consecratio* is the
familiar *auctoritas* shared by all bishops. By virtue of their
auctoritas, all bishops are equal, but any bishop is superior
to all priests lacking the episcopal consecration. In Rufinus's
view, every priest—of whatever rank—has the same *ordo* as
any other priest. Hence, a bishop differs from lesser priests
not in his orders, but in his office and rank, for the episcopate

---

[19] Again, D.21 c.2; Gratian restated this traditional idea (D.21 pr. §3).
[20] *Summa* on D.21 c.2 v. *pari consort. hon. et pot.*, ed. Singer 45: "Ab
hoc dissentit illud, quod est in dist.lxxx., cap.ii.; ibi enim dicitur quod inter
ipsos apostolos non par fuit institutio, sed unus prefuit omnibus, scil. Petrus.
Sed prelatura in clericis provenit aliquando ex dignitate consecrationis,
aliquando ex dignitate ordinis, aliquando ex dignitate dispensationis vel
amministrationis; hec autem amministratio aliquando est spiritualium aliquando secularium rerum. Et quidem ex dignitate consecrationis prelatura
illa est, qua episcopus ceteris sacerdotibus preminet; ex dignitate ordinis
prefertur subdiacono diaconus; ex dignitate amministrationis rerum secularium prestat archidiaconus non tantum aliis, sed etiam ipsi archipresbitero. . . . Amministrationis rerum secularium ideo diximus, quia in
spiritualium rerum amministratione non archidiaconus archipresbitero,
potius e contrario archipresbiter archidiacono preficitur. Petrus igitur ex
prerogativa consecrationis apostolorum primorum neminem excellebat, quia
omnes in pontificatus apicem consecrati sunt. Itidem propter dignitatem
minoris ordinis non submittebantur ei; omnes enim sacerdotes erant, extra
quem ordinem nullus superior reperitur: episcopatus enim et huiusmodi
non proprie sunt ordines, sed dignitates. Ex dispensationis autem dignitate
apostolos ceteros anteibat, quia ipse aliis predicandi officium et alia huiusce-
modi dispensabat: in duobus itaque prioribus ceteri apostoli cum eo pari
consortio honorem et potestatem acceperunt, sed in hoc ultimo ei impares
fuerunt."

is a *dignitas*, deriving from consecration, rather than an *ordo*. Similarly, although Rufinus placed the subdiaconate among the "holy orders," it is the dignity of his *ordo* which sets the deacon over the subdeacon. Once again, Rufinus drew the distinction between the *administratio spiritualium* and *secularium*. Through his administration of the *spiritualia*, the dean has precedence over the archdeacon and the lesser grades, but correspondingly, in his administration of the *secularia*, the archdeacon is superior to the dean as well as to the minor officials. For the purposes of Rufinus's gloss on the Pseudo-Isidorian text, *administratio* was the crucial concept. With respect to the episcopal *auctoritas*, and also through the priestly *ordo*, St Peter was equal to the other apostles. But by virtue of his *administratio*, Peter was truly Prince of the apostles, for with this power he was above the other apostles and could give them orders.

The meaning of master Rufinus's analyses cannot be missed: As coined by Rufinus, the *administratio* summarized the entire sphere of Church government and ecclesiastical jurisdiction, clearly distinct from the sacramental competencies of bishop and priest. In more limited and specific terms, one could properly speak of an episcopal *administratio*, and even of an *administratio* inhering in the offices of lesser prelates. But there was also, in Rufinus's constitutional system, a special "administration" which belonged to the successors and vicars of St Peter. This papal *administratio* was the supreme ecclesiastical jurisdiction which distinguished the Roman pontiff from all other prelates.

3. The Imperial Office

Master Rufinus composed his *Summa* between 1157 and 1159, during the pontificate of the militantly anti-imperial Hadrian IV. Indeed, Rufinus was writing in the aftermath of the famous clash between Frederick Barbarossa and the papal legates at Besançon,[1] and his political thought belongs to the

[1] Rahewin, *Gesta Friderici* 3.8-10, 3rd ed. G. Waitz and B. von Simson

climate of opinion in papal circles at that time. Like his ecclesiastico-constitutional theories, Rufinus's conception of the relations between papacy and empire was both original and influential. In fact, his political doctrine and his constitutional thought were closely interwoven, for the formula *auctoritas-administratio* had a political dimension.[2]

In a long commentary on an eleventh-century text in the *Decretum*, Rufinus developed the central idea in a bold new conception of empire and papacy. Within the *Decretum*, this chapter is ascribed to Nicholas II; in actuality, however, it was written by Peter Damian in 1059. The passage which served as a springboard for Rufinus and for so many later canonists was the evocative statement that

> [Christ] entrusted the rights of the earthly and also of the heavenly empire to [St Peter,] the bearer of the keys of eternal life (*beato eternae vitae clavigero terreni simul et celestis imperii iura commisit*).[3]

(Hanover 1912) 174ff. See also H. Schrörs, *Untersuchungen zu dem Streite Kaiser Friedrichs I. mit Papst Hadrian IV. 1157-58* (Freiburg im Breisgau 1916), but cf. W. Ullmann, "Cardinal Roland and Besançon," *Sacerdozio e Regno da Gregorio VII a Bonifacio VIII* (Miscellanea Historiae Pontificiae 18: Rome 1954) 107-25.

[2] The following pages are intended only as a brief sketch of the relation between Rufinus's political and constitutional ideas. Obviously, in this context, I cannot present an extended account of Rufinus's notion of empire, and I have made no attempt here to trace his massive influence on the later tradition of canonistic political thought: these tasks must be reserved for a separate study.

The importance of Rufinus's political doctrine has been estimated by Alfons Stickler, "Sacerdozio e Regno . . . nei Decretisti e Decretalisti fino alle Decretali di Gregorio IX," *Sacerdozio e Regno* 20-22, and by Friedrich Kempf, *Papsttum und Kaisertum bei Innocenz III.* (Miscellanea Historiae Pontificiae 19: Rome 1954) 208f. For a more detailed analysis, see Sergio Mochi Onory, *Fonti canonistiche dell'idea moderna dello Stato* (Milan 1951) 84-94, 110-17 (evaluations by E. M. Meijers, *Tijdschrift voor Rechtsgeschiedenis* 20 [1952] 113-25, and by Brian Tierney, "Some Recent Works on the Political Theories of the Medieval Canonists," *Traditio* 10 [1954] esp. 600f); also, Marcel Pacaut, *Alexandre III* (Paris 1956) 340-60. On Rufinus's later influence, see, in addition, the study by Stickler, "Imperator vicarius Papae: Die Lehren der französisch-deutschen Dekretistenschule . . . über die Beziehungen zwischen Papst und Kaiser," *MIÖG* 62 (1954) esp. 201ff.

[3] D.22 c.1: ". . . Illam [scil. Romanam ecclesiam] uero solus ipse funda-

The original meaning of the text was politically harmless. Peter Damian was tersely reformulating the much-quoted Biblical verses in which Christ gives the "keys of the kingdom of Heaven" to St Peter and tells him that whatever he shall bind on earth (that is, in the *terrenum imperium*) shall also be bound in Heaven (that is, in the *celeste imperium*).[4] The power of the keys meant primarily the priestly power to absolve from sin, and Peter Damian certainly intended that the *iura terreni et celestis imperii* should be interpreted in that sense. Damian's statement is embedded in a long discussion, singling out the Roman See and passionately defending its unique preeminence. St Peter as key-bearer and the "rights of the earthly and heavenly empire" were mentioned casually, merely in passing, so to speak, for Damian's main concern was the assertion of papal supremacy—but only with regard to other bishops, metropolitans, and patriarchs. Far from wishing to subject the emperor to the papacy, Peter Damian revered the lofty dignity of the emperor, for "no one superior to him could be found in the human race."[5]

In his canonical collection, bishop Anselm of Lucca interpreted Damian's statement of 1059 as evidence "that the Roman Church instituted other ecclesiastical offices," and that the Roman Church was founded by Christ alone.[6] Nor did Gratian and the earliest decretists regard Damian's remarks as more than a substantiation of papal primacy *within* the organization of the Church, and in fact, the "rights

---

uit, et super petram fidei mox nascentis erexit, qui beato eternae uitae clauigero terreni simul et celestis imperii iura commisit. Non ergo quelibet terrena sententia, sed illud uerbum, quo constructum est celum et terra . . . Romanam fundauit ecclesiam. . . ." Cf. *Matt.* 16.17-19; Damian's original text (excerpted in D.22 c.1) is printed as *Opusculum* 5, *PL* 145 91f. On the sources and history of this text, see J. Joseph Ryan, *Saint Peter Damiani and His Canonical Sources* (Toronto 1956) 59f.

[4] Jean Rivière, *Le problème de l'Église et de l'État au temps de Philippe le Bel* (Louvain 1926) 387-93 and esp. 389-91. Also, Ryan, *op.cit.* 60.

[5] *Opuscula* 56.4, *PL* 145 812: "Eo [scil. imperatori] superior quisquam in humano genere reperiri non potuit"; Rivière, *op.cit.* 387f, 392.

[6] *Collectio canonum* 1.63 rubr., ed. Thaner 31; Damian's text also appears in Deusdedit, *Collectio canonum* 1.167, ed. Wolf von Glanvell 106f.

of the earthly and heavenly empire" remained a nonpolitical concept until Rufinus.[7]

Although Rufinus fully understood the original implications of the "rights" of the two "empires," he decisively rejected the interpretation based on this original meaning.[8] His own *re*interpretation was simple, daring, and obvious: The "heavenly empire" consists of the clergy, the "earthly empire" is composed of "secular men and secular things." Therefore, since St Peter had the rights of both empires, the pope, "who is the vicar of St Peter," seems to hold the same authority over the secular world and over the "community of clerics."[9] In this manner, Rufinus enlarged and transformed Peter Damian's purely ecclesiastical conception of papal power until that power included the entire world of politics and affairs. To put the matter differently, the power of the keys had become a political form of power, and primacy was

---

[7] D.22 pr., and esp. D.22 rubr.c.1: "Romana ecclesia ceterarum primatum obtinuit"; also, Kempf, *Papsttum* 206. In their commentaries on D.22, the *iura utriusque imperii* are mentioned neither by Paucapalea, *Summa*, ed. J. F. von Schulte (Giessen 1890) 21, nor by Roland, *Summa*, ed. Thaner 6, nor by the *Summa Parisiensis*, ed. McLaughlin 22.

[8] *Summa* on D.22 c.1 v. *terr. s. et cel. imper. iura comm.*, ed. Singer 48: ". . . Alii sic exaudiunt: 'terreni simul et celestis imperii iura commisit,' i.e. ei dedit, ut quecunque ligaret vel solveret super terram, essent soluta vel ligata in celo." This passage appears at the end of the long gloss given in the following note. In the usual decretistic fashion, Rufinus offered this explanation as an alternative interpretation of the *Decretum*'s text—but as one which he himself did not believe.

[9] *Ibid.* 47f: "Celeste imperium celestium militum i.e. clericorum universitatem cum his, que ad eos pertinent, dicit; terrenum vero regnum vel imperium seculares homines secularesque res appellat: per hoc ergo videtur quod summus pontifex, qui beati Petri est vicarius, habet iura terreni regni. Sed animadvertendum est quod ius aliud est auctoritatis, aliud amministrationis. Et quidem ius auctoritatis quemadmodum in episcopo, ad cuius ius omnes res ecclesiastice spectare videntur, quia eius auctoritate omnia disponuntur; ius autem amministrationis sicut in yconomo, iste enim habet ius amministrandi, sed auctoritate caret imperandi: quicquid aliis precipit, non sua, sed episcopi auctoritate indicit. Summus itaque patriarcha quoad auctoritatem ius habet terreni imperii, eo scil. modo quia primum sua auctoritate imperatorem in terreno regno consecrando confirmat et post tam ipsum quam reliquos seculares istis secularibus abutentes sola sua auctoritate pene addicit et ipsos eosdem post penitentes absolvit. Ipse vero princeps post ipsum auctoritatem habet seculares regendi et preter ipsum officium amministrandi; etenim nec apostolicum secularia nec principem ecclesiastica procurare oportet, ut infra d. xcvi. Cum ad verum ventum est. . . .'"

74

transformed into suzerainty. By thus changing the definition of *terrenum imperium*, master Rufinus prepared the way for his attack upon the empire.

The simple statement that the pope possesses supreme quasi-political rights over laymen as well as over clerics could never have sufficed in a law-centered age. To command respect, the notion required a firm legal basis, and precisely this foundation had been lacking before Rufinus. No one would have denied that the emperor as a *person* was subject to the Church. But before the 1150's the theory that the emperor's *office* was subordinate to the papacy had found neither an adequate legal justification nor adequate historical precedents.

To face this problem, Rufinus resorted to one of the main principles in his doctrine of ecclesiastical office: "There is one right of authority, another of administration" (*ius aliud est auctoritatis, aliud administrationis*). Applying this principle —as usual—to the structure of the Church, he continued:

> Indeed, there is a right of authority, as in the bishop, to whose rights all ecclesiastical matters seem to refer, since all things are regulated by his authority. There is, on the other hand, a right of administration, as in the *oeconomus*, for he properly has the right to administer but lacks the authority to govern. Whatever he commands others to do, he orders not by his own authority but by that of the bishop.

Here, the supreme power and the final decision remain in the hands of the bishop, who controls all of the affairs of his diocese. His delegate, the *oeconomus*, has no independent "authority to govern" but can "command others" insofar as he is entitled to use the bishop's authority.[10]

---

[10] Terminologically, the episcopal *auctoritas imperandi* derived from the Early Middle Ages via the *Decretum*: Pope Symmachus contrasted the ecclesiastical *auctoritas imperandi* with the layman's *necessitas subsequendi*, and this formula, already well known during the Age of Reform, appeared twice in the *Decretum* (D.96 c.1; C.16 q.7 c.23). Cf. also the duality *libertas inperandi* and *necessitas obediendi* (D.63 dict.p.c.8; above, Ch.IIA

By discussing the relations between the *oeconomus* and the bishop, Rufinus added little to a constitutional theory which he explored more fully in other parts of his *Summa*, for the *oeconomus* and his *ius administrandi* are clearly comparable to the archdeacon and his *administratio secularium*.[11] But with regard to the roles of bishop and *oeconomus*, Rufinus's conception of the administrative structure of a diocese is nonetheless significant and instructive, since he considered it a model for politics, a political microcosm exemplifying a structural uniformity of the ecclesiastical and political realms. For, as Rufinus explained, the relations between pope and emperor are arranged "accordingly" (*itaque*):

Accordingly, with respect to authority, the pope has the right of the earthly empire . . . , since . . . with his own authority he confirms the emperor in the earthly kingdom by consecrating him, and further, solely by his own authority of punishment, the pope judges the emperor as well as other laymen when they misuse worldly things, and afterwards he absolves them when they repent. Indeed, second to the pope, the prince himself has the authority to rule laymen, and independent of the pope, he has the office of administering. In fact, it is proper neither for the pope to administer secular affairs, nor for the prince to administer ecclesiastical affairs.[12]

The imperial coronation at Rome provided Rufinus with one of the two arguments on which he based the papal sovereignty in the "earthly empire": By crowning and anointing him, the pope "confirms the emperor in the earthly kingdom" (*imperatorem in terreno regno . . . confirmat*). Having no precise or technical legal significance, this "confirmation" meant simply

---

n.30), as well as the formula *regendi et iubendi potestas* vs *obsequendi necessitas* (D.21 dict.p.c.3), and the papal *auctoritas regendi et disponendi* in the election decrees of 1059 and 1060 (D.23 c.1; D.79 c.9).

[11] *Summa* on D.60 pr. v. *ecce ex parte* etc., ed. Singer 151f (above, Ch.IIIB n.5).

[12] Above, n.9.

a general "strengthening" in office. It is perhaps remarkable that Rufinus did not assert the constitutive character of the imperial coronation. That is, he did not describe the emperor's powers as the object of a grant or delegation by the pope at the time of the coronation in Rome.[13] Within his commentary on Peter Damian's formula, Rufinus ignored the source of the emperor's power and treated only the relation between pope and emperor.[14]

The papal "right of the earthly empire" authorizes the Roman pontiff to judge and to govern the entire lay world of "secular men and secular things." Whenever they abuse this power, the emperor and all lesser laymen are subject to papal judgment, which can actually bypass the emperor to correct those who are subject to imperial power. In other words, not only the emperor and his office are within the papal jurisdiction, but also those *under* the emperor are subject to the pope.[15] As described by Rufinus, this papal omnicompetence is an effluence of the priestly power to impose penance and to absolve from sin. At first glance, Rufinus seems to justify merely a papal right to intervene in secular affairs "by reason of sin" (*ratione peccati*). Yet his doctrine ascribes more to the papacy than the power to remit sins and the Church's

13 Two decades later, as an extension of Rufinus's ideas, this doctrine was unambiguously stated by the *Summa Inperatorie maiestati* on D.22 c.1 v. *terreni* (Stickler, *MIöG* 62 [1954] 201 n.69 on 202). If Rufinus had wanted to push to its logical conclusion the parallel between bishop-elect and emperor, he might have suggested that the emperor receives the *officium administrandi* from election, and his *auctoritas* from the imperial coronation (above, n.9). Of course, such an assertion would have drastically altered the main point of his argument.

14 But cf. the *Summa* on D.4 (= D.3 dict.p.c.3) v. *officium vero*, and on D.8 c.1 v. *quo iura* etc., ed. Singer 13, 21f; also, his *De bono pacis* 2.9, *PL* 150 1617.

15 With this assertion, Rufinus foreshadowed the later canonistic claim that the pope is the *iudex ordinarius omnium*, but in this respect Rufinus's concept of the universal papal judgeship resembles the extremist vision of Alanus Anglicus (direct papal jurisdiction over all laymen), rather than the more moderate view of Huguccio (papal *plenitudo potestatis* over all clerics). Most recently, John A. Watt, *The Theory of Papal Monarchy in the Thirteenth Century* (New York 1965) esp. 46-51, 81-85, 93f; also, for Gratian's contribution to this theory, see my article, "*Plenitudo potestatis*: Evolution of a Formula from Gregory IV to Gratian," *SGrat* 13 (1968) nn.70-85.

coercive power, for in Rufinus's view, the Roman pontiff holds far-reaching governmental powers. Rufinus admitted that the emperor possesses a secondary *auctoritas*, since immediately under the "supreme patriarch" the monarch has the "authority to rule secular men." Note well: The emperor holds this authority immediately "after" the Roman pontiff (*post ipsum*), who therefore shares and supervises it.[16] Unlike the pope's governmental *auctoritas*, which extends both to the clergy and to the laity, this imperial *auctoritas* is restricted to the emperor's rule over laymen and remains subject to the Roman pontiff. As Rufinus asserted, it is not proper for the pope to have direct charge of secular affairs without an intermediary, and hence, the emperor has a special "office of administering" (*officium administrandi*)—a form of power which the pope does not share. It is not difficult to guess the rationale and scope of the emperor's "office of administering," for canonists generally agreed that some governmental acts—such as waging war, or judging a capital crime—are inconsistent with clerical status.[17] On papal-imperial relations, the drift of Rufinus's thought is clear: he is suggesting that the emperor's *auctoritas* and *officium administrandi* are directly derivative from the superior papal *auctoritas*, and that the emperor is simply the Roman pontiff's agent in secular affairs.

[16] *Summa* on D.22 c.1 (above, n.9). Throughout this long commentary, one should note Rufinus's careful diction: Subtly manipulating his terminology and thereby highlighting the difference in rank between the ecclesiastical and the secular, Rufinus played off the pope's *terrenum imperium* against the emperor's *terrenum regnum*, and the ecclesiastical *auctoritas imperandi* against the imperial *auctoritas regendi*.

In general, on the idea of an imperial *auctoritas*, see Mochi Onory, *Fonti* 87-94; Robert Folz, *L'idée d'Empire en Occident du Ve au XIVe siècle* (Paris 1953) 123; R. Holtzmann, "Der Weltherrschaftsgedanke des mittelalterlichen Kaisertums und die Souveränität der europäischen Staaten," *HZ* 159 (1939) 251-64; *id.*, "Dominium mundi und Merum imperium," *ZKG* 61 (1942) 191-200. For criticism of R. Holtzmann's theory, see Fritz Rörig, "Heinrich IV. und der Weltherrschaftsanspruch des mittelalterlichen Kaisertums," *DA* 7 (1944) 200-03; also, W. Holtzmann, *Das mittelalterliche Imperium und die werdenden Nationen* (Cologne 1953) 18f.

[17] For example, Rufinus, *Summa* on C.23 q.5 c.8 v. *De occidendis* etc., ed. Singer 409; in general, see below, Ch.IXB.

Within Rufinus's scheme, the quasi-delegated character of the imperial office is particularly evident through his analogy between the emperor and the *oeconomus*. From the Early Middle Ages, at least from the fifth century, the *oeconomus* or *vicedominus* was a "manager of the church's property" (*ecclesiae facultatum dispensator*).[18] His function was to administer the material resources of an episcopal church—indeed, his duties were much like those of an archdeacon. In the twelfth century, as legal practice became more complex, the role of the *oeconomus* became better defined. He had to represent the bishop in worldly matters, especially in business affairs but also in cases at law. Unlike the *procurator*, the *oeconomus* often held a more or less permanent office, which outlasted the individual cases and transactions initially assigned to him.[19] Although the *oeconomus* was generally expected to be a cleric, his office was not related to any rank in the regular Church hierarchy, since it could be held by anyone under the rank of bishop. He was, in fact, deputy to a bishop (or to an ecclesiastical corporation, such as an episcopal church or a monastery). And his delegated powers, his commission, enabled him to act as representative in the court and the market. With this analogy, then, Rufinus was implying that the emperor is a subordinate officer whose powers are limited and delegated.

To sum up: In his commentary on Peter Damian's phrase, master Rufinus created a new political logic. Indeed, his theory produced a revolution in medieval political thought, and throughout the next half-century the duality *auctoritas-administratio* dominated the canonists' theories on the relations between papacy and empire.

18 Ducange, *Glossarium* VI (1886) 31 s.v. "oeconomus"; also, Theodor Hirschfeld, "Das Gerichtswesen der Stadt Rom vom 8. bis 12. Jahrhundert wesentlich nach stadtrömischen Urkunden," *AUF* 4 (1912) 522ff.

19 Within the *Decretum*, the *oeconomus* is repeatedly mentioned; for example, Gratian included a decree of the Council of Chalcedon (D.89 c.4, C.16 q.7 c.21), prescribing that every episcopal church should have an *oeconomus*, who should be chosen from the clergy of that church and should administer the church's resources.

4. Rufinus's Thought: Sources and Significance

For the purposes of law and government, the resources of twelfth-century Latin were imposing. Among the many synonyms for governing power were: *auctoritas, potestas, administratio, regimen, gubernatio, imperium, ius, iurisdictio,* and *cura.* By 1157 these terms had been applied and reapplied in a bewildering variety of contexts, and usually with little effort to narrow their meaning. Most of the available expressions were characterized more by vagueness and ambiguity than by the sharpness and clarity needed for the creation of a systematic constitutional theory.[1] As a prerequisite for the construction of his system, then, master Rufinus first faced the task of selecting and defining terms appropriate to a technical vocabulary. Indeed, Rufinus's achievement was especially remarkable in the sphere of juridical and constitutional semantics, for he endowed his terms with a precision which cannot be found in earlier canonistic writings. In his discussions of office and jurisdiction, the main expressions have the air of well-established technical terms, as though they stood at the end of a long tradition.

Rufinus's political ideas have received far more attention than his constitutional doctrines, and it is commonly assumed that he gave the highest prominence to his political theory. At first glance, one might well conclude that Rufinus first developed his concept of papal *auctoritas* and imperial *administratio,* and then applied these terms in his discussions of ecclesiastical office. At least on the level of terminology, Rufinus could have taken his initial inspiration from the Gelasian duality of pontifical *auctoritas* and imperial *potestas.*[2] Moreover, it would not have been difficult for Rufinus

---

[1] See above, Ch.IIв.

[2] Gelasius's famous formula was, of course, available within the *Decretum* (D.96 c.10), as quoted by Gregory VII (*Reg.*8.21, ed. Caspar 553-55); cf. also D.96 c.6 and D.10 c.8. In general, see Caspar, *Geschichte des Papsttums* II 64ff, 756, and for a more recent interpretation, cf. W. Ullmann, *The Growth of Papal Government in the Middle Ages* (London 1955) 19-28.

to settle on the word *administratio* as an equivalent for the imperial office. In the twelfth century the monarch or lay official was often designated an *administrator*, just as his governing power was often termed an *administratio*. Applied to secular government within the *Decretum*, these terms could suggest that the power of rule was a public trust, and they could find a place in statements on the moral responsibility of government for the protection of churches, widows, and orphans.[3] On the other hand, *administratio* and its cognates were rooted in the terminology of Roman law, where they referred simply to the exercise of a public office by a magistrate.[4] Hence, in the twelfth century *administratio* could appear as an entirely neutral synonym for government, *administrator* as a straightforward synonym for ruler or official.[5] Nonetheless, it is improbable that Rufinus devised his political doctrine before his ecclesiology, and equally unlikely that the Gelasian formula seriously influenced the development of his ideas. Like other canonists before and after him, master Rufinus was primarily a canon lawyer and only secondarily a political theorist. The technicalities of Church law were his daily concern, and marriage law was surely more important for him than public law. As a matter of course, he was more often occupied with the organizational problems of a diocese than of the empire, more often conscious of the constitutional character of the episcopal than of the imperial office. Consequently, even if Rufinus had not drawn the instructive analogy between emperor and *oeconomus*, one would have to assume that he simply applied to papal-imperial relations the conceptual scaffolding which he

---

3 C.23 q.5 dict.p.c.25, c.26; D.96 c.11; Pacaut, *Alexandre III* 327.

4 *Dig.* 50.8; *Cod.* 1.49, 11.31. Also, Roman private law commonly discussed the *libera administratio* of property by a son, slave, or proctor.

5 The *regni administratio* is mentioned by Rahewin, *Gesta Friderici* 3.25, 3rd ed. Waitz and Simson 198, and by Hadrian IV (W. Holtzmann, *PU England* II 270 no.90). See also George H. Williams, *The Norman Anonymous of 1100 AD* (Cambridge, Mass. 1951) 223 ("administratio publicarum rerum"); Gerhoh of Reichersberg, *Comm. in ps.LXIV*, in *MGH LdL* III 451 ("reipublicae amministratores"); Suger, *Ep.*14, *PL* 186 1353.

had constructed for his description of ecclesiastical office. In short, the origins of Rufinus's thought and terminology do not lie in the realm of politics.

Of course, *administratio* was a common term for various forms of ecclesiastical power,[6] and Rufinus was undoubtedly familiar with it in this context. He probably did not know Gerhoh of Reichersberg's reference to the episcopal *regalia* as an *administratio*, with the implication that the monarch delegates these secular powers to the bishop.[7] And in all likelihood, Rufinus had never read Bernard of Clairvaux's assertion that the bishop should serve others and not himself, since the episcopal office is a "ministry" (*ministerium*) rather than a "lordship" (*dominium*).[8] Yet Rufinus must have known the canonistic uses of the expressions *administrator* and *administratio*. Referring to the "ecclesiastical judge" as the "administrator of ecclesiastical laws," Gratian used the word *administrator* to signify an official who is duly empowered as the competent judicial authority.[9] Within the *Decretum*, the term *administratio* could designate, in a general way, the governing power of a bishop,[10] or it could indicate the right to use sacramental power, as distinct from the power itself.[11]

Though certainly aware of the diction within the *Decretum*, Rufinus did not have to draw directly upon this terminology in the elaboration of his constitutional doctrine. It is, however, possible to trace several of Rufinus's key terms to their common source, and thus to reveal one of the influences on his thought. Distinguishing between a bishop's powers of

---

[6] In 1076, for example, the German bishops mentioned the papal *rerum ecclesiasticarum administratio; MGH Const* I 107 no.58.

[7] *De edificio Dei* c.23, *MGH LdL* III 153: "regales et militares administrationes." Cf. Heinrich Mitteis, *Lehnrecht und Staatsgewalt* (Weimar 1933) 424f: "Als Lehnsobjekt . . . die Regalien . . . sind in erster Linie die . . . vom König an die Kirchen zum Zweck der Ausübung im staatlichen Interesse vergabten Hoheitsrechte. Die Regalienleihe ist also eine Rechtsleihe."

[8] *De moribus et officio episcoporum tractatus* c.1, *PL* 182 812; *ministerium* and *administratio* were sometimes used interchangeably.

[9] C.11 q.1 dict.p.c.30.   [10] C.7 q.1 cc.4, 31, dict.p.c.11.

[11] C.24 q.1 dict.p.c.37: ". . . amministratio interdicitur, potestas non aufertur . . ." (above, Ch.IIB n.30); in this context, *administratio* is equivalent to *executio*.

jurisdiction and his sacramental powers, Rufinus designated the former as "full power with respect to administration" (*plena potestas quoad administrationem*) and the latter as "full power with respect to the office of authority" (*plena potestas quoad auctoritatis dignitatem*).[12] Here the phrase *plena potestas* seems equally useful in a formula for sacramental powers and in one for jurisdictional powers. There was, however, an ambiguity in Rufinus's terminology, since in other contexts *plena potestas* could refer to episcopal jurisdiction,[13] or to the jurisdictional *and* sacramental powers of a consecrated bishop.[14] Within his own diocese, even a bishop-elect may suspend lesser clerics from the exercise of those jurisdictional powers and duties which Rufinus entitled the *administratio procurationum*.[15] From these three terms— *plena potestas*, *administratio*, and *procuratio*—an important source of Rufinus's constitutional terminology becomes evident: the expression *plena potestas* derived from Roman law, for in the Justinian *Code*, that phrase signified the full powers by which an agent or "proctor" (*procurator*) acts with binding consequences for his principal.[16] In the *Digests*, the expression *libera administratio* had the same sense.[17] Without specifically mentioning *plena potestas*, the twelfth-century civil lawyers were familiar with the idea of proctorship.[18] The

---

12 *Summa* on D.23 c.1, ed. Singer 52 (above, Ch.IIIA n.4).

13 *Id.* on C.10 pr. v. *quidam laicus*, ed. Singer 300: "episcopus in sua parrochia plenam disponendi habeat potestatem."

14 *Id.* on D.60 pr., ed. Singer 152 (above, Ch.IIIB n.9); *plena auctoritas* and *plenitudo auctoritatis* could also denote the sacramental plus the jurisdictional competence. Elsewhere, however, Rufinus emphasized the purely jurisdictional element in the phrase *plena auctoritas*; *id.* on D.11 c.2 v. *plena auctor.*, ed. Singer 27: "Plena auctoritas illa dicitur, que in se continet preceptum et generalitatem."

15 *Id.* on D.23 c.1, ed. Singer 52.

16 *Cod.* 2.12.10: "Si procurator . . . plenam potestatem agendi habuit, rem iudicatam rescindi non oportet. . . ." In general, see Gaines Post, "*Plena potestas* and Consent in Medieval Assemblies," *Traditio* 1 (1943) 356-64 (= *Studies* 92-102).

17 *Dig.* 3.3.58: "Procurator, cui generaliter libera administratio rerum commissa est, potest exigere, novare, aliud pro alio permutare."

18 Rogerius (mid-12th century) and Azo (ca.1150-ca.1230) used the formula *generalis et libera administratio* for the full powers of a proctorial

lawyers of the Church also appropriated it, for in the early 1180's a canonist commented on the *plenaria potestas* of proctors.[19] Although earlier evidence is missing, the idea surely came to their attention even before the 1180's, and during the thirteenth century this Romano-canonical *plena potestas* was a common concept. Master Rufinus was well acquainted with the medieval literature of Roman law,[20] and in constructing his theory of office, he quarried some of the foundation stones from those writings. In particular, he extracted several essential terms from the Romanistic definitions of a proctorial mandate.[21] It is obvious that in some sense he considered these terms applicable to ecclesiastical office, though the mere use of this terminology cannot prove that he conceived the jurisdictional powers of office as proctorial in character, that is, as derivative or delegated.[22] St Augustine had remarked that the prelate holds ecclesiastical property as a proctor representing the poor, and he thereby emphasized the prelate's solemn responsibility in the administration of his church's properties.[23] Gratian quoted Augustine's statement, and a decretal of Alexander III stressed the limits to the bishop's freedom of administrative action, "since the bishop . . . is the proctor, not the owner, of the ecclesiastical properties."[24] Of course, Rufinus was aware that the idea (and presumably also the terminology) of proctorship implied

---

mandate. The 13th-century legists, however, used this expression as well as *plena potestas*, commonly equating the two phrases. Again, Post, *op.cit.* 357f.

[19] *Ordo iudiciarius Bambergensis* (ca.1182-85): "Procurator super his, quae ad ipsam procurationem spectare noscuntur, plenariam recipit potestatem" (J. F. von Schulte, *SB Wien* 70 [1872] 300, quoted by Post, *op.cit.* 357). At the end of the 11th century, Bonizo of Sutri considered the term *plenaria potestas* interchangeable with *plenitudo potestatis*; Benson, *SGrat* 13 (1968) n.62.

[20] Singer, *Summa des Rufinus* Einleitung pp. cx-cxi, cxviii-cxx.

[21] Tierney, *Foundations* 120.

[22] *Ibid.*

[23] C.23 q.7 c.3: "non sunt illa nostra, sed pauperum, quorum procurationem gerimus."

[24] X 3.24.2: ". . . cum episcopus et quilibet praelatus . . . ecclesiasticarum rerum sit procurator, non dominus, conditionem ecclesiae meliorare potest, facere vero deteriorem non debet."

limitations on the bishop's power. But did Rufinus regard the cathedral chapter as the "principal" whom the bishop represented? And did he consider the bishop's jurisdictional powers derivative from the chapter? Rufinus never explicitly asserted such a relation between bishop and chapter, although he believed that the bishop should exercise his jurisdictional powers "with the presence of his chapter" and that the chapter itself could exercise these powers *sede vacante*.[25] On one occasion, however, Rufinus did maintain the derivative character of episcopal jurisdiction. In his address to Alexander III and to the prelates assembled at the Third Lateran Council, he explained:

> Through the Roman Church, the power of the keys and the tribunals are granted to all bishoprics.[26]

Here the bishop's judicial prerogatives derive from and are sanctioned by the papacy. Still, Rufinus made this assertion two decades after the completion of his *Summa*, and this extreme view cannot be found within the *Summa*.[27]

As a model and precedent for the crucial terms *auctoritas* and *administratio*, Rufinus could have found a cognate duality in theological discussions of the power to administer sacraments. Justifying the dogma that an evil man can perform a baptism, St Augustine distinguished between the "power" to baptize (*potestas*), which belongs to God alone, and the "ministry" of baptism (*ministerium*), which is carried out by men. Augustine's statement reappeared in the *Decretum*,[28] and twelfth-century theologians regularly contrasted divine *potestas* and human *ministerium*.[29] A few years before Rufinus

25 *Summa* on D.23 c.1, ed. Singer 52 (above, Ch.IIIA n.4).
26 *Sermo*, ed. Morin, *Atti della Pontif. accad. rom. di archeologia* 3rd ser., *Memorie* 2 (1928) 119: ". . . per [Romanam ecclesiam] omnibus sedibus claues et tribunalia dispensantur. . . ."
27 See, for example, the brief discussion of papal *plenitudo potestatis* in the *Summa* on C.25 pr. v. *Sancta Romana ecclesia*, ed. Singer 421f.
28 De cons. D.1 c.26.
29 Peter Lombard, *Sententiae* 4.5.2, *PL* 192 851; Petrus Comestor and Radulphus Ardens used the same formulation (Anciaux, *Théologie* 496 n.4, 511 n.1).

completed his *Summa*, however, Peter Lombard explained that in the remission of sins, God exercises his power as "originator" or "author" (*auctor*), while the priest is merely the "agent" or *minister* of this act.[30] The duality *auctor* and *minister*, which certainly antedated Peter Lombard's discussion,[31] was influential in the later twelfth century,[32] and its similarity to the Rufinian formula *auctoritas-administratio* is obvious.

Yet Rufinus's theory of *auctoritas* and *administratio* required more than merely a subtly elaborated terminology, and in the last analysis, his reliance upon the traditions of theology and of Roman law brings us no closer to the major source for his doctrine of *auctoritas-administratio*. In all probability, the primary impetus for the formulation of this theory came from the challenge of describing the Church's hierarchy in precise juridical terms. How do the various offices of the Church differ in rank and power? To answer this question, Rufinus seems to have appropriated and refined the concept of hierarchy which Hugh of St Victor had developed in his treatise *On the Sacraments of the Christian Faith*.[33] "Spiritual power in the clergy," Hugh stated, "is arranged with different grades (*gradus*) and orders of dignities (*ordines dignitatum*)."[34] As Hugh explained, the hierarchy contains seven "grades" of cleric, from porter upward to priest.[35] In "grade" and in

---

[30] *Sententiae* 4.5.3, *PL* 192 852; one cannot be certain that Rufinus made use of Peter's *Sentences* (Singer, *Summa des Rufinus* Einleitung p.cxxi).

[31] Letter of Pseudo-Clement I (Hinschius, *Decr. Ps.-Isid.* 62): "Auctores quidem vite nostrae parentes non sunt, sed ministri." Following Pseudo-Isidore, the Anglo-Norman Anonymous described God as *auctor* and the bishop as *minister* of the grace bestowed in royal consecrations (*MGH LdL* III 679).

[32] *Summa Omnis qui iuste iudicat* on C.1 q.1 dict.p.c.42: "Per auctoritatem, solus Spiritus sanctus peccata remittit; per ministerium, . . . sacerdotes . . ." (Anciaux, *op.cit.* 552). For similar statements by Radulphus Ardens and Peter of Roissy, see Anciaux, *op.cit.* 511 n.1, 585.

[33] Singer, *Summa des Rufinus* Einleitung p.cxx, has noted Rufinus's use of the *De sacramentis Christianae fidei* in the *Summa* from C.27 on. The *De sacramentis* was written around 1134.

[34] *De sacramentis* 2.3.1, *PL* 176 421.

[35] *Id.* 2.3.5, *PL* 176 423: ". . . Sequuntur deinde septem graduum promotiones. . . . Hic gradus [scil. sacerdotum] dispares in eodem ordine habet

Master Rufinus

"order," a priest is superior to a deacon. On the other hand, a deacon and an archdeacon belong to the same "grade" with respect to their "sacrament" (*sacramentum*), but the archdeacon has greater "power" (*potestas* or *potestas in ministerio*), for "he has the care of churches and he tries ecclesiastical cases." Similarly, within the "order" of priesthood all priests have the same "sacrament," but some have more "power."[36] In other words, among priests there are "unequal dignities within the same order," for the "princes of priests"—that is, the bishops—are above all others.[37] The "power" of the bishops includes their unique sacramental prerogatives, which are not shared by lesser priests.[38] Throughout, there is a strict hierarchical arrangement.[39] On

---

dignitates. Nam post sacerdotes altiores sunt principes sacerdotum, id est episcopi. Supra quos iterum sunt archiepiscopi; et supra illos qui dicuntur primates, supra quos quidam patriarchas constituere volunt; alii eosdem primates et patriarchas dicunt. . . . Post hos omnes sequitur summus pontifex. . . . Cui vice Petri principis apostolorum praesidenti, omnis ecclesiasticus ordo obtemperare debet, qui solus praerogativa dignitatis claves habet ligandi omnia et solvendi super terram. . . ."

[36] *Id.* 2.2.5, *PL* 176 418f: "Omnis ecclesiastica administratio in tribus constat: in ordinibus, in sacramentis, in praeceptis. Ordines consideramus in personis praelatorum, sacramenta in ministerio eorum, praecepta in conversatione subiectorum. . . . De ordinibus hoc primum attendendum est, quod alii sunt secundum gradum differentem, sicut sic diaconus et sacerdos, alii in eodem gradu secundum potestatem excellentem, sicut diaconus et archidiaconus. Unus gradus est in sacramento, non tamen una potestas in ministerio. Diaconus enim sacerdoti ministrat in sacramento corporis et sanguinis Christi. Archidiaconus autem hoc plus habet, quod praeter ministerium altaris sub episcopo et vice episcopi curam habet ecclesiarum et causas ecclesiasticas examinat et ministeria dispensat. Similiter sacerdos et pontifex sive summus sacerdos unus gradus est in sacramento, diversa tamen potestas in ministerio, quia cum utrisque corporis et sanguinis Christi consecrandi, baptizandi, catechizandi, praedicandi, ligandi, solvendi, una quodammodo sit dignitas, pontificibus tamen ecclesias dedicandi, ordines faciendi, manus imponendi, sacri chrismatis consecrandi, communem super populum benedictionem faciendi, singularis data est potestas. Sic itaque alia est differentia graduum in sacris ordinibus, alia est in eodem gradu differentia dignitatum."

[37] *Id.* 2.3.5, *PL* 176 423 (above, n.35).

[38] *Id.* 2.2.5, *PL* 176 419 (above, n.36).

[39] *Id.* 2.2.4, *PL* 176 418: "In utraque potestate [scil. terrena et spirituali] diversi sunt gradus et ordines potestatum, sub uno tamen utrinque capite distributi, et quasi ab uno principio deducti, et ad unum relati. . . . Spiritualis potestas [caput] habet summum pontificem. . . . Ad potestatem summi pontificis pertinent quae spiritualia sunt. . . ."

87

an ascending scale, Hugh distinguished simple bishops from archbishops, and archbishops from primates or patriarchs. Finally, though he was uncertain whether patriarchs are higher than or identical with primates, he was sure that the pope stands above them all.

> Every ecclesiastical order must obey him who presides in place of Peter, the prince of the apostles, and who alone, by the prerogative of his dignity, has the keys of binding and loosing all things on earth.[40]

Hugh nicely summed up the point that he was trying to make:

> There is one difference of grades among the holy orders; there is another difference of dignities within the same grade.[41]

It is evident that Hugh perceived the need for distinguishing between a hierarchy of sacramental powers and a hierarchy of jurisdiction. Nonetheless, in contrast with Rufinus's constitutional doctrine, Hugh's theory suffers from crucial weaknesses. For a theoretically precise justification of the pope's supremacy over other bishops and other priests, the traditional reference to the keys of St Peter was insufficient. Correspondingly, allusions to "superior power" and to a "difference of dignities" did not adequately explain the jurisdictional preeminence of one prelate over another. Moreover, when Hugh singled out several expressions to designate jurisdictional functions (*potestas, potestas in ministerio, dignitas*), he used the same terms for sacramental powers. The result is far from satisfactory, for it fails to draw a sharp line between the jurisdictional and the sacramental capacities. Thus, though he was fully aware of the problem, and though he ventured a solution, Hugh did not clarify the meaning of his terms, nor did he apply them with rigor and consistency to the different powers of all levels and offices within the Church. The degree of Rufinus's indebtedness to each of his various sources can-

[40] *Id.* 2.3.5, *PL* 176 423 (above, n.35).
[41] *Id.* 2.2.5, *PL* 176 419 (above, n.36).

not be firmly established, but it is likely that for his concept of office and hierarchy, he borrowed most heavily from Hugh of St Victor. Still, since Rufinus's doctrine was lucid, precise, and thoroughly systematic, it went far beyond Hugh's, which furnished, at the most, a starting point and a foundation.[42]

With Rufinus's theory of *auctoritas* and *administratio*, the Christian Church had at hand, for the first time in its history, a carefully elaborated idea of jurisdiction, as well as a doctrine which distinguished incisively between the sacramental and the jurisdictional spheres of action.[43] The constitutional theory of *auctoritas* (or *consecratio*), *ordo*, and *administratio* was applicable to every office in the Church. It could portray the sacramental hierarchy which culminates in the bishop's office and, with equal clarity, the jurisdictional hierarchy culminating in the Roman pontiff. Unlike the various conceptions of the episcopal *regalia*, the Rufinian doctrine of office was purely ecclesiastical in character, implying no involvement with feudal political institutions and no obligation to any secular prince. Moreover, Rufinus used his technical terms to explain, in a new way, the juridical significance of ecclesiastical election, and they served as the basis for a radical new theory of the relations between pope and emperor. Within all of these areas, Rufinus's innovations determined, in large measure, the substance and the direction of later canonistic thought.[44]

[42] In his explanation of office, Rufinus did not appropriate verbatim even a single phrase from Hugh, but by a comparison of Hugh's text (above, n.36) with Rufinus's major statements (cf. esp. *Summa* on D.21 c.2, ed. Singer 45; above, Ch.IIIB n.20), one can see the theologian's influence upon the canonist. Some terms appeared in both explanations (*administratio, potestas, dignitas, ordo*), but these terms were in the general domain. More significantly, Hugh's contrasting of *sacramentum* and *potestas in ministerio* foreshadowed Rufinus's thought and terminology. Above all, the two men shared a common approach to a problem which had not been frequently discussed.

[43] For Gratian and the earlier period, cf. above, Ch.IIB.

[44] His influence upon the doctrines of office and election will be treated in the following chapters, though his role in the development of political thought lies outside the scope of this study. Certain later decretists incorporated the *ius patronatus* into their discussions of *auctoritas* and *administratio*; see Appendix 2.

CHAPTER IV

ELECTORAL CONFIRMATION
AND THE BISHOP-ELECT

1. Decretistic Definitions

Rufinus's theories of office and election remained the foundation of decretistic and early decretalistic thought on these subjects. Writing in the 60's of the twelfth century, not long after Rufinus, master Stephen of Tournai took over the Rufinian doctrine of election.[1] To this familiar material, however, he added a new element.

Just as in Rufinus's system, Stephen's theory of election presupposed a congruent theory of office. With very few changes, Stephen appropriated Rufinus's conceptions of ecclesiastical office. For example, he took over the distinction between *consecratio, ordo*, and *administratio*.[2] Similarly, with only slight deviations from Rufinus's theory, the French canonist explained the riddle of a subdeacon's eligibility for the episcopate and ineligibility for the archidiaconate. The terminology of office was still fluid, and in this discussion Stephen differentiated between an "office of ministry" (*dignitas ministerii*), like the archidiaconate, and an office which was both a "ministry" and a "sacrament" (*ministerium* and *sacramentum*), like the episcopate. Though Stephen bor-

---

[1] For Stephen of Tournai, J. F. von Schulte's edition, *Die Summa des Stephanus Tornacensis über das Decretum Gratiani* (Giessen 1891), is incomplete; on Stephen, see Stephan Kuttner, "Les débuts de l'école canoniste française," *Studia et documenta historiae et iuris* 4 (1938) 194ff.

[2] *Summa* on D.21 c.2 v. *pari consortio*, ed. Schulte 31.

rowed the expressions *ministerium* and *sacramentum* from Hugh of St Victor, who also influenced his political doctrine, it is easy to see that Stephen's term *ministerium* was identical with Rufinus's *administratio*, and correspondingly, that the term *sacramentum* was merely a variant of the Rufinian *auctoritas* or *consecratio*. However, Stephen also offered an alternative explanation for this inconsistency in the hierarchical system: formerly, "the subdiaconate was not considered among the holy orders." But the subdeacon's status had changed, and in his own time, as Stephen remarked, the subdeacon was believed to have holy orders. Hence, Stephen asserted that a subdeacon can, in fact, become an archdeacon or dean.[3]

Like Rufinus, Stephen used the papal election decree of 1059 as a pretext for some general observations on episcopal election and on the powers granted by election:

From their election alone [bishops] are approved; from the confirmation of their election, they obtain power. For when the election has been confirmed, they can forbid the divine office and, for a just cause, they can suspend clerics from their benefices. . . . However, they cannot remove orders from someone, since one cannot give that which one has only from his consecration. For an elected official has the power of administration, not the authority of dignity. . . .[4]

---

[3] After his paraphrase of Rufinus's doctrine, Stephen continued (*id.* on D.60 pr., ed. Schulte 86f): ". . . Vel ita dicamus: Auctoritates, quae prohibere videntur subdiaconos in archidiaconum vel praepositum aut decanum eligi, loquuntur secundum eum statum, quando subdiaconatus inter sacros ordines non computabatur, modo autem, quia pro sacro ordine habetur, non solum in istos, sed etiam in episcopos subdiaconi possunt eligi." For Hugh's terminology, cf. his *De sacramentis* 2.2.5, PL 176 419 (above, Ch.IIID n.36).

[4] *Id.* on D.23 c.1 v. *sicut vere eis papa*, ed. Schulte 35: "i.e. sicut iam consecratus esset. Hinc habes, quod electus papa ante consecrationem habet potestatem regendi romanam ecclesiam, et omnes facultates disponendi. Nec est contrarium, quod alibi habetur scil. quod episcopi se magis existiment ex electione approbatos. Et revera ex sola electione approbantur, ex confirmatione electionis etiam praemissam potestatem consequuntur. Confirmata enim electione possunt etiam divinum officium interdicere et a

Here at last the effects of confirmation have been defined: The jurisdictional power of office, the "power of administration" (*potestas administrationis*), is no longer derived from election or consecration—it is acquired solely through electoral confirmation. In this respect, Stephen was the first to define the consequences of this confirmation, and his definition still remains essentially valid within the *Codex iuris canonici*. In other respects, his theory is identical with that formulated by Rufinus, from whom he borrowed it. It should be noted that Stephen, even more clearly than Rufinus, referred the metropolitan's confirmation exclusively to the election rather than to the consecration, whereas the older view, still visible in the election decree, related the metropolitan's consent primarily to the consecration of the new bishop.

Because the "power of administration" is won by a bishop only when his election has been confirmed, one may well ask: Within Stephen's theory, what is the meaning of election? The act of election brings a sort of approval, an *approbatio*, for "from their election alone, bishops are approved." Since it confers no power, one may speculate that there remains only one possible effect for this *approbatio*: in some way, the electors' "approval" guaranteed that the *electus* had a claim upon confirmation and upon the full powers of his office. In any case, Stephen seems uneasy in his insistence upon confirmation, seems reluctant to deprive the election of its effectiveness. Or one might say that for Stephen, the "approval" and the confirmation were two parts of a single juridical act,

---

beneficio clericos ex iusta causa suspendere, non tamen sine capituli sui auctoritate, ordines autem auferre alicui non potest, quia nec dare valet, quod tantum ex consecratione sua habet. Habet enim electus potestatem administrationis, non auctoritatem dignitatis. . . ." During the past century, the ecclesiastical regulations governing the right to administer an office have received surprisingly little attention from the legal and constitutional historians of the Church. However, see the careful, useful, and—unfortunately—seldom-cited work by Carl Gross, *Das Recht an der Pfründe* (Graz 1887); also, Gillmann, *AKKR* 113 (1933) 463-85.

separated in time, and culminating in the effective bestowal of power.

Evidently, then, Stephen of Tournai was the first to formulate precisely the effects of electoral confirmation, and his concept of election is thereby substantially different from Rufinus's. However, writing only thirty years after Rufinus's *Summa*, master Huguccio stated that Rufinus was among those canonists who would make the jurisdictional powers dependent upon electoral confirmation.[5] Any such assertion by Huguccio must command respect, for he had an unexcelled knowledge of decretistic literature, and quite possibly he even knew Rufinus personally. It is curious, therefore, that a careful reading of Rufinus's *Summa* does not justify Huguccio's remark. Huguccio may simply have been wrong. Indeed, this is not the only instance where Huguccio ascribed to Rufinus an opinion which cannot be found in the latter's *Summa*.[6] Moreover, on the idea of office, Huguccio considered Rufinus's theories either irrelevant or incomprehensible— because in this context Rufinus ignored the effects of electoral confirmation.[7] At all events, *after* writing his *Summa*, Rufinus probably accepted the new meaning of electoral confirmation, and Huguccio may have known this revised view from a gloss or lecture.[8]

[5] *Summa* on D.63 c.10, v. *subscripta relatio* (See Appendix 3, lines 12-19): ". . . Rufinus, Jo(hannes) et Simon . . . in hoc quidem conueniunt, quod ex nuda electione, idest nondum superioris auctoritate confirmata, nil iuris acquiritur electo, nec efficitur prelatus illius ecclesie ante confirmationem . . ."

[6] See below, n.30, and Appendix 3, lines 8-15; also, Singer, *Summa des Rufinus* Einleitung pp. lvii-lviii.

[7] Huguccio, *Summa* on D.60 c.2 v. *nullus* etc. *nisi presbiter vel diaconus*: ". . . Cur ergo ex inferioribus gradibus potest eligi episcopus—quia ex subdiaconatu—quam archidiaconus vel diaconus et huiusmodi? Rufinus suam voluit assignare rationem, scil. quia dignitas istorum consistit tantum in administratione, et talis dignitas plene confertur in electione; cum enim tales eliguntur, instituuntur, et cum instituuntur, eliguntur, quod non est in episcopo. Sed hoc falsum est, quia ante eliguntur et postea confirmantur et ab aliis eliguntur et ab aliis confirmantur. Nulla est ergo talis solutio aut, si est aliqua, a nullo intelligitur . . ." (Singer, *op.cit.* Einleitung p.lvii).

[8] Singer, *op.cit.* Einleitung p.lviii.

The Bishop-Elect

When one wishes to trace the history of a specific disagreement between Rufinus's ideas and Stephen's, one should turn to the influential *Summa* prepared by master John of Faenza soon after 1171. Because John admittedly compiled his *Summa* largely by excerpting the works of Rufinus and Stephen, John's judgments are especially useful, for they sometimes show whether Rufinus or Stephen was primarily responsible for determining the direction of canonistic thought on a particular problem. In his discussion of the papal election decree of 1059, John began by quoting almost verbatim from Rufinus.[9] One sees familiar Rufinian expressions which were not used in this context by Stephen, such as the episcopal "full power with respect to administration" (*plena potestas quoad administrationem*) and "with respect to authority" (*quoad auctoritatem*). But then, in midstream, John changed horses: that is to say, in the middle of his explication he abandoned the Rufinian text and took up Stephen's thought and wording, almost verbatim. From Stephen he borrowed the statement that an elected bishop receives the power of administration through his confirmation.[10] By thus ratifying Stephen's innovation, John demonstrates the firm establishment of the new direction in the decretistic tradition.

Heavily dependent on Rufinus, the *Summa Inperatorie maiestati*, an anonymous product of the French School, was

[9] Johannes Faventinus, *Summa* on D.23 (Gross, *Recht an der Pfründe* 99). On electoral theory in general, Johannes borrowed heavily from Rufinus; cf. also his *Summa* on D.60 (Gross, *op.cit.* 100).

[10] Johannes, *Summa* on D.23: "episcopi se magis ex electione existiment approbatos, quia tamen ex sola electione dumtaxat approbantur, ex confirmatione tamen electionis etiam premissam potestatem consecuntur" (Gross, *op.cit.* 99). Both before and after this passage, Johannes has derived his text from Rufinus's *Summa* ad loc., ed. Singer 52; cf. Stephen's remarks, above, n.4. Stephen's influence is also visible in the *Summa Elegantius in iure diuino* 3.58: "Sicut autem consecratio sic electi in episcopum confirmatio ad metropolitanum spectat, que antequam electioni accedat nullam habet electus episcopalium rerum dispositionem. Ex electione enim . . . episcopi se tantum nouerint approbatos. Ex confirmatione uero patrimonium et facultates ecclesie disponendi potestas conceditur, adeo ut possit electus clerico beneficio suspendere, si ad hoc capituli fauore iuuetur. Ordinem uero quem non potest dare non potest auferre, quia hoc consecrationis priuilegium est . . ." (from page-proofs of edition by G. Fransen and S. Kuttner).

written in Carinthia between 1175 and 1178.[11] The unknown decretist paid homage to master Rufinus in the most direct way, by quoting long passages from Rufinus's *Summa* practically verbatim. With scarcely a change in wording, for example, he presented Rufinus's formulation of the hierarchical paradox concerning a subdeacon's eligibility for the episcopal office, and to explain this paradox, without any alteration he quoted Rufinus's distinction between an office of *auctoritas* and one of *administratio* as well as the subdistinction of the *administratio spiritualium* and *secularium*.[12] However, the anonymous author did not appropriate Rufinus's brilliant discussion of *auctoritas* and *administratio* in the context of electoral theory; instead, he took over the key terms with which Hugh of St Victor had described the various levels and functions of the ecclesiastical hierarchy.[13] According to the *Summa Inperatorie maiestati*, each basically different ecclesiastical rank consists either of an "order" (*ordo*) such as the priesthood or diaconate, or of a "dignity" (*dignitas*):

> Some dignities are minor, some are major. . . . The major dignities, such as the episcopate, are conferred by election, by confirmation of the election, and by consecration. Election belongs to the clergy, consent belongs to the people, confirmation belongs to the metropolitan.[14]

[11] Formerly known as the *Summa Monacensis*.

[12] *Summa Inperatorie maiestati* on D.60 pr. v. *ecce ex parte* etc. (Clm 16084 fol.9ra). Also, cf. *id.* on D.60: "§ Possumus dicere quod hanc dignitatem, scilicet archidiaconatum, non precedit illa electio, ut statim in electione qui merito digni sint illa dignitate [eam acquirant], set secus est in episcopali dignitate, quam non solum precedit electio set et consecratio" (Clm 16084 fol.9ra-b).

[13] That is, one might have expected the anonymous decretist to take over Rufinus's commentary on D.23 c.1, which markedly influenced later decretists. For Hugh, see above, Ch.IIID n.36.

[14] *Summa Inperatorie maiestati* on D.23 pr. v. *breuiter*: "Distinctio graduum consistit in ordinibus et dignitatibus. Ordinum alii sunt maiores, alii minores. Minores dantur sola uocatione et benedictione et uestimentorum et uasorum distributione, ut [*scr.* et] diaconatus et infra. Maiores uero dantur et uocatione et benedictione et consecratione, ut presbiteratus. Dignitatum alie sunt minores, alie maiores. Minores dantur sola uocatione et sedium impositione, ut archidiaconatus, decanatus. Maiores autem, episcopatus, dantur ex electione, ex electionis confirmatione, et consecratione. Cleri est eligere, plebis consentire, metropolitani confirmare. Electio

The Bishop-Elect

The anonymous summist was undoubtedly aware of the complexities within this problem, as well as the terminological ambiguities in earlier electoral doctrines, for he distinguished clearly between the election by the clergy, "which is properly called election," and popular consent or the metropolitan's approval, which were sometimes also—"incorrectly"—called election.[15] Though the anonymous decretist's ideas lack the polish and originality of Rufinus's discussion, they nevertheless provide a new element of clarity. For Gratian and for Rufinus, election and consecration were the two essential stages in the acquisition of the episcopal office, but in the *Summa Inperatorie maiestati*, a third step has become explicitly necessary. Together with election and consecration, electoral confirmation fulfilled an indispensable function in the bestowal of office upon a bishop.[16] Master Rufinus's constitu-

---

autem quandoque est concors et non canonica, quandoque canonica et non concors. Quando concors et non canonica, non ualet; quando uero canonica et non concors, ualet. Canonicam autem tria faciunt: eligendi potestas, electi ydoneitas, electionis sollempnitas. Sollempnitas in tribus consistit: in denominatione, in decreti subscriptione, et in obedientie exhibitione. Hec omnia non attenduntur in apostolico, quia in eo tantum sufficit electio et consecratio, quia ibi quorum est eligere eorum est consecrare et confirmare. Docet autem Nicholaus in hoc capitulo *In nomine* quis debeat eligi in apostolicum et a quibus et qualiter et ubi et quando" (Clm 16084 fol.4va). A somewhat shorter version of this passage can be found in the same *Summa*, on D.79 pr. v. *apostolicus* (Clm 16084 fol.12ra).

15 *Summa Inperatorie maiestati* on D.62 pr. v. *breuiter monstratum*: "Electio tripliciter dicitur: aut est nominantis, ut cleri, aut consentientis, ut populi, aut approbantis, ut metropolitani et concilii. Primo modo quidem proprie dicitur electio, aliis duobus improprie, et secundum hanc distinctionem diuersa oportet intelligi capitula, nec clero, nec populo, nec metropolitano et concilio attribuendam electionem" (Clm 16084 fol.9rb). See also Peter of Blois, *Speculum iuris canonici* 49, ed. T. A. Reimarus (Berlin 1837) 91: ". . . electio dicitur triplex, scilicet aut nominantis, aut consentientis, aut approbantis. Prima clerici, IIda populi, IIIa metropolitani, sed prima proprie dicenda [*ed.* danda] est electio, reliquie improprie." Peter wrote these *distinctiones* about 1180, under the influence of the *Summa Inperatorie maiestati*.

16 Because of their esteem for Gratian's authority, the decretists continued to quote the older theory transmitted to them in the *Decretum*. For example, *Summa Inperatorie maiestati* on D.64 pr. v. *hinc considerandum*: "Due sunt que faciunt episcopum: electio et consecratio . . ." (Clm 16084 fol.10vb); here, the anonymous author was quoting Rufinus's remark (*Summa* on D.64 pr. v. *hinc considerandum est* etc., ed. Singer 158). Further examples among later decretists could easily be listed, but it will soon

tional thought had absorbed much from the Church's customary law, which since the beginning of the Middle Ages had guaranteed to almost everyone the right of giving consent in an episcopal election, and Rufinus had therefore asserted that the comprovincial bishops as well as the metropolitan should give postelectoral approval to a new bishop. The *Summa Inperatorie maiestati*, however, distinguished between the consent of the people and the confirmation by the metropolitan. The confirmation of the election is an essential act, explicitly restricted to the competent ecclesiastical superior, that is, to the metropolitan.[17]

Writing shortly before 1179, Simon of Bisignano took a more radical view of electoral confirmation than earlier decretists had done, for he did not in any way qualify his insistence upon confirmation as the key to the duties and rights of office.[18] Speaking of bishops, Simon stated, "Before confirmation, their election is without effect." During the decade following Simon's *Summa*, this extreme opinion on electoral confirmation continued to make headway among decretists. For the anonymous *Summa Tractaturus magister* (1175-91) of the French school, the elected Roman pontiff is "true pope" (*verus papa*) possessing "the management of

---

be evident that this older conception was no longer an accurate description of contemporary theory or practice. Above, Ch.IIA n.3.

[17] Note, however, that unlike Stephen and John of Faenza, the anonymous summist does not discuss the powers acquired through electoral confirmation.

[18] *Summa* on D.23 c.1 v. *electus tamen sicut verus papa auctoritatem obtinet regendi ecclesiam*: "Hinc collige, quod summus pontifex statim cum eligitur, potest res ecclesie amministrare, clericos suspendere et prebendas dare. Deponere vero et consecrare non potest, quia hoc ex consecratione provenit. Et hoc ideo, quia ab eisdem eligitur et confirmatur. Secus in episcopis, quia eorum electio ante confirmationem est irrita" (Josef Juncker, "Die Summa des Simon von Bisignano und seine Glossen," *ZRG KA* 15 [1926] 403). *Id.* on D.79 c.9 v. *concessa electo auctoritate* etc.: "Hinc collige electum posse prebendas dare, alienationem rerum ecclesiasticarum facere, et omnia que ad dispositionem temporalium pertinent facere; suspendere etiam clericos potest. Ea uero que ex consecratione proueniunt ante consecrationem non potest facere, et hoc in summo pontifice est uerum, nam statim cum eligitur confirmatur, ab eisdem enim eligitur a quibus et confirmatur . . . , in aliis uero hoc non obtinet antequam eorum electio confirmetur . . ." (BN 3934A fol.61va; Rouen 710 fol.72ra).

The Bishop-Elect

temporal affairs," but no other *electus* has any administrative rights before his confirmation.[19] The judgment of the French *Summa Et est sciendum* (1181-85) was similar,[20] and following this work closely, the Anglo-Norman *Summa Omnis qui iuste iudicat* (around 1186) gave immediate full powers to the elected pope but "no rights" (*nihil iuris*) to any other clerical *electus*.[21]

[19] *Summa Tractaturus magister* on D.23 c.1 v. *sicut uerus papa*: "quantum ad dispositionem temporalium, quod tamen secus est in aliis, quia ante confirmationem electionis non habent ius disponendi aliquid de rebus ecclesie. Dominus autem papa ex ipsa electione consequitur confirmationem . . ." (BN 15994 fol.7va). *Id.* on D.60 c.1 v. *nullus episcopus nisi sit dia. archi.* etc.: "infra e. c.ult. contra. Set aliud est in dignitate amministrationis temporalis, ubi ex ipsa electione consequitur plenitudinem potestatis, ut hic, aliud in dignitate cure spiritualis, ubi non ex electione set ex consecratione. Vnde et ibi oportet eligi talem qualis futurus est in ipsa amministratione, hic autem non eligi set consecrari, uel potius eligi potest quis ad istas etiam dignitates in subdiachonatu set non institui nisi prius ordinetur in superioribus ordinibus, . . . ut habet generalis consuetudo" (BN 15994 fol.19va).

[20] *Summa Et est sciendum* on D.23 c.1 v. *disponendi facultates*: "Nota, quod papa, statim cum eligitur, potest omnia dispensare ut papa, quia statim est eius confirmata electio. Cardinales enim eligunt et eligendo confirmant. . . . Ceteri vero clerici electi nil ex electione possunt facere, antequam sit confirmata electio. . . . Sed nunquid potest omnia electus, que potest postea? Dico, quod si episcopus in papam eligitur, statim omnia potest. Nil enim ordinis uel unctionis ei postea confertur excepto pallio. Si vero electus esset presbiter, tum posset quidem suspendere, beneficia dare, non autem degradare. Set nunquid posset episcopis precipere, ut eius auctoritate episcopum degradarent? Quere, lector . . ." (Gillmann, "Die Dekretglossen des Cod. Stuttgart. hist. f. 419," *AKKR* 107 [1927] 214). *Id.* on D.61 c.11 v. *episcopus cum fuerit*: ". . . Nihil iuris acquiritur postulato per sinplicem postulationem, quia nec electo per sinplicem electionem . . ." (Gillmann, *op.cit.* 221f). The *Summa Et est sciendum* was formerly cited as the *Glossae Stuttgardienses*.

[21] *Summa Omnis qui iuste iudicat* (= *Summa Lipsiensis*) on D.23 c.1 v. *disponendi*: "Nota quod papa statim cum eligitur potestatem habet disponendi res ecclesie, quia statim est eius confirmata electio; cardinales eligunt et eligendo confirmatur. . . . Ceteri clerici electi nichil iuris habent ante confirmationem quoad res ecclesie. . . . Set numquit omnia potest papa electus que postea potest? Dici potest quod si episcopus in papam eligitur statim omnia potest, nichil enim ordinis uel unctionis ei postea confertur excepto pallio. Si uero electus esset presbiter, suspendere tantum posset et dare beneficia, non autem degradare, quia hoc prouenit ex consecratione. Quidam tamen dicunt quod nec suspendere potest antequam consecretur. Item possetne episcopis precipere ut auctoritate eius episcopum degradarent? Item queri potest, si presbiter electus esset in papam, an possit accusari de simonia cum deberet in episcopum ordinari, et uidetur quod non, quia cum sit papa non potest accusari nisi de heresi. . . . Hodie tamen non posset reuocari in dubium electio, cum non sit electus nisi a duabus partibus eli-

Electoral Confirmation

In the period just before the Third Lateran Council, Bernard Balbi of Pavia wrote a treatise on elections—indeed, the first canonistic treatise on that subject.[22] The concluding chapter of this work discusses the acquisition of administrative and sacramental powers by a newly elected officer of the Church. After drawing the Rufinian distinction between an office of *consecratio* and one of *administratio*, he laid down the general principle that before his confirmation in the "dignity" to which he has been elected, an *electus* cannot exercise the powers of that office, for the election does not really take effect before the confirmation:

> After the confirmation, if it is a dignity of administration, he will be able to fulfill the duties of his dignity, provided that he has those priestly orders which are required by his dignity; for instance, to fulfill the duties of his dignity, an archdeacon must be a deacon, and an archpriest must be a priest.[23]

---

gatur" (Rouen 743 fol.9ra). *Id.* on D.79 c.9 v. *concessa electio* [sic] *auctoritate disponendi* [sic]: "quod est speciale in papa, qui eligendo confirmatur et confirmando eligitur. . . . Secus de aliis prelatis, quibus ante confirmationem non licet. . . . Ea uero que ex consecratione proueniunt non potest ante consecrationem facere, ut deponere" (Rouen 743 fol.37va).

[22] On Bernard's *Summa de electione*, see Schulte, *Geschichte der Quellen* I 178f. On his collection of decretals, the *Compilatio prima*, see Kuttner, *Repertorium* 322f; Stickler, *Hist. iur. can.* I 225ff; also the edition by Friedberg, *Quinque compilationes antiquae* (Leipzig 1882). Bernard's glosses were probably the first explication of his own collection. In addition, see Bernard's *Summa decretalium*, ed. E.A.T. Laspeyres (Regensburg 1860), the first *summa titulorum* on a decretal collection; the *Summa de electione* was also edited there by Laspeyres (pp.307-23). With this latter work and his *Summa de matrimonio*, Bernard became one of the pioneers in the monographic genre.

[23] *Summa de electione* 4, ed. Laspeyres, *Summa decretalium* 322f: "Postremo consideratione dignum occurrit, quid electus ex electione consequatur. Ubi notandum, quod dignitas alia est administrationis, alia consecrationis; administrationis, ut archidiaconatus, archipresbyteratus, prioratus et huiusmodi; consecrationis, ut episcopatus, abbatia et similia. Generaliter itaque sciendum, quemlibet electum ante confirmationem dignitatis, ad quam electus est, officio fungi non posse. Licet enim canonice sit electus, quia tamen suspensa et quodammodo infirma est ante confirmationem electio, nondum habet electus potestatem exequendi, sicut si pro me lata est sententia, licet iusta sit, si est per appellationem suspensa, nondum tamen valeo actionem rei iudicatae proponere . . . ; quia enim ex alieno pendet arbitrio, necesse

99

Except for the added necessity of confirmation, this is a neat summary of Rufinus's theory. Bernard continued:

> Clearly, if it is a dignity of consecration, after the confirmation but before the consecration he will have the power to manage the affairs of the church. . . . Nevertheless, he will not be competent to depose, just as he cannot ordain. . . .

Bernard emphasized the necessity of confirmation, and indeed, for the powers of administration, he assigned the constitutive moment principally to the confirmation. Nonetheless, like Stephen of Tournai, Bernard found this formulation too strong. To qualify this position, he remarked that before the confirmation "the election is suspended and, in a certain sense, ineffective" (*suspensa et quodammodo infirma*), and therefore the *electus* does not yet have the right to exercise the duties of his office (*potestas exequendi*). This is, of course, a tacit admission that the election has a degree of effectiveness. For a clarification, he found the analogy of a court case which is still *sub iudice* because of an appeal: even though the court has reached its decision, that verdict cannot be carried out, since "it is suspended by the appeal" (*sententia . . . est per appellationem suspensa*). Bernard might have added that for an election as well as for an appealed verdict, a decision has been made, and the probable execution of that decision is simply a matter of time. For Bernard, the effectiveness of election was limited, but in his theory an unconfirmed *electus* was not entirely without rights and powers:

> Through his election the *electus* seems to have acquired a certain right (*aliquid iuris*)—which is apparent for this

---

est confirmatoris arbitrium expectare. . . . Post confirmationem autem, si est dignitas administrationis, poterit suae dignitatis officium exercere, dum tamen sit eius ordinis, qui a sua dignitate requiritur; necesse est enim ad explendum suae dignitatis officium, archidiaconum esse diaconum, et archipresbyterum esse sacerdotem. . . . Plane si fuerit dignitas consecrationis, post confirmationem ante consecrationem potestatem habebit res ecclesiasticas disponendi. . . . Non tamen deponere, sicut nec ordinare valebit. . . ."

Electoral Confirmation

reason, since he can demand confirmation, and his bishop will have to confirm the election.[24]

Here, evidently, the *electus* automatically has a claim upon confirmation and the right to administer. In this formulation Bernard was hinting at a new conception of ecclesiastical election and pointing out a new direction which was finally, a decade later, followed and explored. Soon after Bernard's electoral treatise, Sicard of Cremona wrote his *Summa* (1179-81).[25] In the Rufinian tradition, Sicard was familiar with the distinction between

a dignity for the administration of spiritual or secular matters, such as the archdeacon's or archpriest's dignity . . . and a dignity of authority and administration, such as the episcopal dignity.[26]

[24] *Id.* 2.1.7, ed. Laspeyres, *ibid.* 313: ". . . ex electione aliquid iuris videtur acquisisse electus, quod inde apparet, quia confirmationem petere potest, et eius episcopus electionem confirmare debebit . . ."; Gillmann, *AKKR* 113 (1933) 467.

[25] For the ascription of Sicard to the French school, see Kuttner, "Réflexions sur les brocards des glossateurs," *Mélanges Joseph de Ghellinck* II (Gembloux 1951) 783ff.

[26] *Summa* on D.60: "Querunt quidam, cum episcopus maior sit archidiacono et archipresbytero, cur ex inferioribus ordinibus assumatur? Sicut de suo queritur, ita de suo soluunt, dicentes quod est dignitas:

—amministrationis spiritualium uel secularium, ut archidiaconi, archipresbyteri. Hec in electione plene confertur, et ideo in eligendis debitus ordo requiritur.

—auctoritatis et amministrationis, ut episcopalis. Hec in quantum est amministrationis in electione plene confertur, in quantum est auctoritatis usque ad consecrationem differtur, et ideo quod minus est in electione poterit conferri in consecratione.

Set michi uidetur, licet non nichil dicere uideantur, quod hec sit superstitiosa solutio, tum propter ecclesie consuetudinem, tum propter nouam constitutionem. Duplex est igitur causa harum prohibitionum: procacitas et dignitas. Nam propter procacitatem quorumdam ad hos ordines promoueri nolentium, statutum est ut qui in his ordinibus non fuerint, diaconatu scilicet et presbyteratu, ad has dignitates nullatenus assumantur, archidiaconatum scilicet et archipresbyteratum. . . . Propter dignitatem statutum est ut nullus eligatur in episcopum nisi in sacris ordinibus constitutus. . . .

Queritur cum sit prepositi amministratio secularis, scilicet in temporalibus, cur tanta districtio requiritur in ordinibus? Resp.: Alicubi prepositi habent amministrationem temporalium tantum et in istis forte non tanta requiritur ordinum districtio. Alicubi habent cum amministratione temporalium etiam amministrationem spiritualium, curam uidelicet animarum, et in istis sine

The Bishop-Elect

Though master Rufinus had used this distinction in order to explain the subdeacon's paradoxical eligibility for the episcopate, Sicard refused to accept Rufinus's explanation, which he dismissed as an "unreasonable solution" (*superstitiosa solutio*). Yet when Sicard posed the question, "How great is the power of an *electus*?" he based his answer on Rufinus's distinction. As Sicard remarked, an *electus* can have the "administration of temporal matters but not the authority of spiritual affairs."[27] This was, of course, a standard conception, but in his explanation of it Sicard's ideas were less orthodox:

> From the fact that someone is elected, he should consider himself not promoted (*prelatus*) but approved (*comprobatus*).

In other words, through his election, an official is endorsed or "approved" (*comprobatus*) but not yet fully "elevated" (*prelatus*) to the higher rank of his new office. With the term *prelatus*, in this context Sicard was undoubtedly referring to the status of an official with sacramental as well as jurisdictional powers, that is, with both *auctoritas* and *administratio* —and of course, since "authority" comes from consecration

---

dubio requirenda est premissa districtio" (Clm 11312 fols.27v-28r). Cf. D.60 dict.p.cc. 3, 4.

[27] *Id.* on D.62: "Queritur quanta sit potestas electi. Videtur quod nulla, nam ex eo quod quis eligitur, non prelatum set se existimet comprobatum. . . . Econtra, quia potestatem habet facultates ecclesie disponendi. . . . Resp.: Duplex est . . . dignitas amministrationis et auctoritatis. Habet igitur electus canonice amministrationem temporalium set non auctoritatem spiritualium, non enim ordines et similia dare uel auferre potest, quia non habet. Aiunt quidam quod ualeat interdicere officium et beneficium, quod non credo, simpliciter et perpetuo, set tantum in sua iurisdictione, sicut episcopus non potest alienum parrochianum simpliciter excommunicare nisi in casu manifeste depredationis, puto tamen eum ab ecclesie sue liminibus sequestrare. Quod ergo dicitur se magis comprobatum, intellige de electione deliberationis uel denuntiationis cum subscriptione uel confirmatione, quod non tenet in apostolico, in cuius electione non requiritur alia confirmatio, quia maiorem non habet, unde quam cito est electus, tam cito habet amministrationem. Vel hoc dicitur ad compescendam electorum elationem, licet enim scientia doctior, uita sanctior ceteris esse debeat, non tamen ex eo quod prefertur ceteris melior intelligitur . . ." (Clm 11312 fol.30v).

rather than from election, a simple *electus* could not be a *prelatus*. In Sicard's idea of "approval," one hears a strong echo of the electoral theory formulated by Stephen of Tournai—indeed, both canonists derived their conceptions from the same passage in the *Decretum*.[28] Still, there is a difference, for Stephen used the notion of "approval" to moderate the force of the confirmation requirement: "approval" accompanies the election, the right to administer comes from the confirmation. For Sicard, however, this "approval" is far more than mere endorsement by the electors: full "approval" presupposes the simple act of election and requires also confirmation by the ecclesiastical superior. When the election has been confirmed in this way, the *electus* is "approved" (*comprobatus*), and he can then administer the temporalities of his church, for he then has full jurisdictional powers.

During the three decades between Rufinus's *Summa* and Huguccio's, the role of electoral confirmation became firmly established within the Church's constitution. There was disagreement over the details—the precise rights which belonged to the power of jurisdiction—but the decretists were unanimous in the judgment that an *electus* cannot administer jurisdictional powers until his election has been confirmed. According to the theory and practice of that period, however, the hierarchical superior's confirmation was not the only factor which served to render the election valid and effective. For master Gratian, an episcopal election had to be ratified

---

[28] For Stephen's conception of an *electus* as *approbatus*, see above, n.4; for Johannes Faventinus's conception, taken over from Stephen, cf. above, n.10. The common source for the idea of "approval" is C.8 q.1 c.20, by St Jerome: ". . . ex eo, quod ipsi electi sunt, se magis existiment conprobatos. . . ." Note that Sicard follows Jerome almost verbatim—far more closely than Stephen. Of course, Jerome was not discussing the powers of an *electus*; rather, he was warning against pride of office among bishops (as Sicard explained: ". . . hoc dicitur ad compescendam electorum elationem . . ."). Cf. Gratian's summary, C.8 q.1 rubr.c.20: "Ex electione non proficiuntur episcopi, sed conprobantur." Cf. also the formulary for an episcopal election decree from the Early Middle Ages, in the *Liber diurnus* no.2, ed. E. de Rozière (Paris 1869) 17: ". . . quaesumus . . . uti . . . virum venerabilem . . . cuius vitam et honestos mores apud nos habemus bene et optime comprobatos, hunc nobis apostolatus vester . . . episcopum consecrare dignetur. . . ."

with an election decree solemnly signed by the clerical electors (*cum solempnitate decreti omnium subscriptionibus roborati*).[29] This solemn "undersigning" (*subscriptio*) of the decree was necessary for the formal announcement and publication of the election. Rufinus and Stephen paid little attention to electoral *subscriptio*, but some of the later decretists asked themselves whether the act of election obligates the electors to abide by their decision, whether they can still change their minds until they have signed the election decree, or whether, as a third possibility, their choice is flexible until the election has been confirmed.[30] As Bernard of Pavia clearly recognized, the answer to this question depended directly upon the concept of election. If an *electus* obtains any rights through simple election, the electors have granted him something—and have bound themselves, even without the solemn "undersigning." In Bernard's opinion, as soon as the result of a canonical election has been announced, whether or not it has been undersigned, the electors are no longer allowed to change their minds.[31] On the other hand, Simon of Bisig-

---

29 D.60 rubr.c.11.

30 Huguccio neatly summed up these three possible interpretations of *subscriptio* (see Appendix 3, lines 1-15). To Rufinus, Johannes Faventinus, and Simon of Bisignano, however, master Huguccio ascribed the view that prior to the *subscriptio*, the electors can alter their choice. Cf. Rufinus's *Summa* on D.61 c. 17 v. *cum decreto*, ed. Singer 154: "id est cum scriptura, ubi eius electio et clericorum subscriptio contineatur." This simple statement certainly does not justify Huguccio's assertion, and no better evidence for such a view can readily be found (Singer, *Summa des Rufinus* Einleitung pp.lvii-lviii). Either Huguccio was simply wrong, or else Rufinus expressed this opinion somewhere outside of his *Summa*—in a gloss, for example, or in a lecture. In support of the view ascribed to Rufinus, Huguccio cited C.27 q.1 c.36 (Appendix 3, line 11), which concerns the binding character of the written *professio* (or *scriptura*) by one entering the monastic life; it is possible that Huguccio here confused Rufinus with master Roland Bandinelli, whose glosses might bear the same initial (R.) and who had discussed this monastic version of "*subscriptio*" (*Summa* ad loc., ed. Thaner 123). In any case, on the question of *subscriptio*, Huguccio was apparently referring primarily to Simon of Bisignano, whose wording was similar to his own (below, n.32).

31 *Summa de electione* 2.1.7, ed. Laspeyres, *Sum. decr.* 313: ". . . Super hoc autem dicunt plerique, referre, an ipsa electio sit subscripta, vel coram episcopo vel in publico pronuntiata, quae pronuntiatio, ut dicunt, valet pro subscriptione . . . et tunc dicunt clericos eam revocare non posse, an ipsa electio nondum sit subscripta, vel coram episcopo vel in publico pronuntiata,

nano found justification in the *Decretum* for a different conclusion:

> If the clergy elects someone but does not sign [the election decree], . . . they are allowed to change the election, if they wish.[32]

For, as Simon explained, this *subscriptio* "belongs, in a certain sense, to the substance of an election, and confirms it." Of course, Simon's view of *subscriptio* was entirely consistent with his idea of election, which he considered "null and void" (*irrita*) before confirmation by the competent superior. In a similar vein, Sicard of Cremona believed that proper "approval" of an election requires *subscriptio* as well as electoral confirmation.[33] Although the question of *subscriptio* often reappeared in later discussions of ecclesiastical election, it was finally settled by Gregory IX, who declared that when an election has been publicly announced, the electors can no longer alter their decision.[34]

---

et tunc fatentur eos posse revocare. . . . Mihi autem sine melioris praeiudicio sententiae dicendum videtur, quod, ex quo canonice facta electio saltem in capitulo fratrum pronuntiata fuerit, sive subscripta est sive non subscripta, dummodo populus non contradicat, cuius est electioni consentire, iam non licebit clericis mutare electionis arbitrium. . . . Hoc autem maxime, quia ex electione aliquid iuris videtur acquisisse electus. . . ." Cf. above, n.24.

[32] *Summa* on D.63 c.10: "*ne quid, quod ad cautelam pertinet, omittamus.* Non refertur hoc ad subscriptionem, que quodam modo de substantia electionis est et eam confirmat. . . . Hinc expresse colligitur, quod si clerici aliquem eligunt, nec subscribunt, nec eum intronizant, licet eis, si voluerint, mutare electionem . . . , post subscriptionem nequaquam . . ." (Juncker, *ZRG KA* 15 [1926] 342f). At this point in the margin of the Bamberg MS of Simon's *Summa*, a further statement appears: "Licet autem ipsi mutare non possint, non tamen ex sola electione aliquod ius electo acquiritur antequam confirmetur, nec posset electus cogere eligentes, ne procederent nec removere[nt]" (Juncker, *loc.cit.*). Elsewhere, Simon drew a similar inference but shifted the emphasis slightly; *id.* on D.28 c.13: ". . . Hinc collige electionem posse mutari maxime antequam sit confirmata a superiore . . ." (Juncker, *op.cit.* 343). Cf. above, n.18.

[33] *Summa* on D.62: ". . . Quod ergo dicitur se magis comprobatum, intellige de electione deliberationis uel denuntiationis cum subscriptione uel confirmatione . . ." (Clm 11312 fol.30v; full text above, n.27).

[34] *X* 1.6.58: "Publicato scrutinio variare nequeunt electores, cum sit facienda collatio, et electio celebranda. Ad quod per superiorem, si oportuerit, compellantur."

So far as the simple bishop-elect was concerned, the decretists doubted neither the indispensability of confirmation, nor the metropolitan's competence to grant (or, with cause, to withhold) the confirmation. In fact, their only serious argument about the source of the bishop-elect's confirmation can be seen in the divergent answers to a question posed by the *Summa Et est sciendum*: "But if the metropolitan church is vacant, by whom will the election of a provincial bishop be confirmed . . . ?" The *Summa Et est sciendum* suggested that during such a vacancy, the suffragan's election could be confirmed either by a *visitator*, if one were present, or by the primate, if there were a primatial jurisdiction over the metropolitan church. But the anonymous decretist did not believe that the cathedral chapter had this power.[35] Still, a different doctrine was more usual. As a general principle, master Rufinus had already noted that "when the bishop has died," the cathedral chapter may exercise the episcopal jurisdiction, and one of Lucius III's decretals assigned to the chapter, *sede vacante*, the task of judging heretics.[36] In practice as well as in theory, during a vacancy in a metropolitan see, its chapter might confirm the elections of any new bishops within the province.[37]

Underlying the new requirement of electoral confirmation was a more or less traditional conception of the Church's constitution as a systematically structured hierarchy, pyramidal in form.[38] Although this constitutional concept contained, in its bare outlines, no significant innovation, it was transformed by the decretists. In the succinct formulation by

---

[35] *Summa Et est sciendum* on D.64 c.5 v. *extra conscientiam metropolitani*: "Set quid si vacat metropolis, a quo confirmabitur electio provincialis episcopi vel cuius auctoritate consecrabitur? Forte a visitatore, si ibi est, sin autem, a primate, si habet. Non autem credo capitulum maioris ecclesie hoc posse . . ." (Gillmann, *AKKR* 107 [1927] 242).

[36] Rufinus, *Summa* on D.23 c.1, ed. Singer 52 (above, Ch.IIIA n.4); *X* 5.7.9 (1184). On this problem, see the lucid summary by Tierney, *Foundations* 127-30.

[37] Hinschius, *KR* II 577 n.5.

[38] See, for example, the elegant simile by Eugene III (above, Ch.IIIB n.12).

Electoral Confirmation

Simon of Bisignano, this principle asserted simply that the metropolitan confirms the bishop, the pope confirms the metropolitan.[39] Or, as Ricardus Anglicus stated at greater length,

> The bishop confirms all who are placed below him . . . , the archbishop [confirms] the bishop . . . , and so on, step by step, up to the pope, for election pertains to inferiors . . . , confirmation to superiors. . . .[40]

Of course, decretists were aware that in the diversity of practice explained by "diversity of custom," the constitutional principle inherent in this pyramidal hierarchy was not always followed: inferiors did not always perform the election and superiors did not always bestow confirmation. Nonetheless, the canonist usually disapproved of such deviations from the hierarchical principle.[41] Within the general conception of the Church's constitution as a hierarchy, the important—and new—element had appeared with the demand that electoral confirmation precede the exercise of jurisdictional powers, for this new requirement gave weight and meaning to the relation between the successive levels of the hierarchy.

[39] *Summa* on D.63 c.10 v. *nostrum spectatur arbitrium*: "Hinc collige quod sicut in confirmatione episcopi archiepiscopi est consensus necessarius . . . , sic in confirmatione archiepiscopi summi pontificis desideratur consensus . . ." (Rouen 710 fol.70rb). Simon's view does not take into account the doubts and questions raised by canonists concerning the confirmation of the metropolitan's election; these will be discussed below, Ch.VIB.

[40] *Distinctiones decretorum* on D.63: "Quis debeat confirmare, et quidem episcopus confirmat omnes infra se positos . . . , archiepiscopus episcopum . . . , et sic gradatim usque ad papam, nam electio pertinet ad inferiores . . . , confirmatio ad superiores . . ." (Zwettl 162 fol.107v). For proof that Ricardus was not (as formerly believed) Richard de Lacy, see E. M. Meijers, "Ricardus Anglicus et R. de Lacy," *Tijdschrift voor Rechtsgeschiedenis* 20 (1952) 89f; for the proper name and identity (= Richard de Mores), S. Kuttner and E. Rathbone, "Anglo-Norman Canonists of the Twelfth Century," *Traditio* 7 (1949-51) 329ff. Similar text in Raymond of Peñafort's *Summa iuris* 2.33, ed. Rius Serra 123.

[41] *Glossa Palatina* on D.60 c.1 v. *sit archidiaconum* instituere: ". . . set clerici eligunt archidiaconum, episcopus confirmat. Vel diuersitas est consuetudinis alicubi: alibi utrumque facit episcopus, alibi utrumque clerici, set hoc male fit . . ." (Vat.Pal. 658 fol.16va; Vat.Reg. 977 fol.45ra). See A. M. Stickler, "Il decretista Laurentius Hispanus," *SGrat* 9 (1966) 463-549, who assigns the authorship of the *Glossa Palatina* to Laurentius.

The Bishop-Elect

2. Canonical Theory and Practice

The various decretistic theories on the rights and powers of a bishop-elect were indeed important for the developing concept of the episcopal office, but they constitute only part of the picture. In the second half of the twelfth century and also in the thirteenth, the practical business of ecclesiastical administration gave rise to conflicts and uncertainties about the bishop-elect's right to administer. The papal decretals from that period furnish the best record of these legal questions. Although they are clearly and closely related to the new decretistic doctrines on election and confirmation, prior to 1200 these decretals do not frequently reflect the subtle theorizing of the decretists. To be sure, on occasion Alexander III and later twelfth-century popes quoted readily from the *Decretum*.[1] Moreover, Innocent III showed an exceptional ability to assimilate complex decretistic concepts into his decretals.[2] Still, when compared to the fine distinctions drawn by the decretists and early decretalists in their didactic works, the stuff of the decretals usually seems simple and straightforward. With their intensely matter-of-fact tone and their preoccupation with the immediate and the concrete, these documents were vehicles for canonical practice, embodying papal solutions to the practical administrative and juridical problems which had arisen in different dioceses and which had been referred to the pope.

Even when it did not originate as a statement of general policy, a decretal might soon acquire general validity through its use as model and precedent in the papal chancery and in the law schools. It is therefore important to determine the first appearances of this new requirement, electoral confirmation, within the realm of official Roman policy: In one of his undated decretals, Alexander III sent instructions to the

---

[1] Marcel Pacaut, *Alexandre III* 313ff; Walther Holtzmann, "Die Benutzung Gratians in der päpstlichen Kanzlei im 12. Jahrhundert," *SGrat* 1 (1953) 325-49, esp. 345ff (also repr. in his *Beiträge zur Reichs- und Papstgeschichte des hohen Mittelalters* [Bonn 1957] 177-96, esp. 193ff).
[2] See below, Ch.Vc.

bishop-elect of Hereford concerning the provision of a suitable income for a certain cleric. From Alexander's wording, the capacity to grant a prebend was unmistakably linked to electoral confirmation (*cum fueris confirmatus*), and without being explicitly stated, the legal principle was clearly implied: the power to bestow a benefice derives from the confirmation.[3] Indeed, an early gloss on this decretal explains straightforwardly that "before his confirmation, an *electus* does not have the power of conferring a benefice."[4] For the date of this decretal, one must look to the history of the diocese. Hereford was ruled by a bishop-elect in 1163, when the distinguished theologian Robert of Melun was elected to succeed the former bishop, who had been translated to London. And in 1173 Robert Foliot was elected to the vacant bishopric of Hereford but was not consecrated till October of the following year.[5] Hence, this decretal was originally dispatched in either 1163 or 1173-74—and the latter date is far more probable.[6]

[3] *Comp.I* 1.4.19 (*X*——): "... nos ... ipsum tuae prudentiae duximus commendandum fraternitati tuae ... mandantes, quatinus ei pro reuerentia beati Petri et obtentu fidelitatis suae aliquam de ecclesiis ad tuam diocesim spectantibus si qua uacat, uel cum primo uacauerit, unde possit uitae suae sufficienter et honeste percipere, cum fueris confirmatus, concedas ..." (ed. Friedberg, *Quinque compilationes antiquae* 3). Though this decretal was republished in eleven 12th-century collections, the recipient is properly entitled an *electus* only twice (*Cheltenhamensis*: "Lincoln. electo," and *Tanneriana* [correctly, though added in the margin]: "Hereford. electo"); for this and other information (below, nn.4f), I am extremely grateful to the late Professor Holtzmann.

[4] Anon. gl. on *Francofortana* 22.13 (*Comp.I* 1.4.19) v. *confirmatus*: "Nota ante confirmationem electum non habere potestatem beneficium conferendi, ut supra de electionibus Nosti, C.vii. q.i. Illud" (present in two MSS, BM Egerton 2901 and BN 3922A, as relayed to me through the kindness of Professor Holtzmann). The decretal *Nosti* is *X* 1.6.9; presumably the other citation is a mistake and should refer to C.8 q.1 c.20 (discussed above, Ch.IVₐ n.28).

[5] According to the text of this decretal in *Cheltenhamensis*, the name of the *lator presentium* was Walconinus. Identification of this Walconinus (or perhaps Walkelinus) might firmly establish the decretal's date, but he does not appear in the standard accounts: William W. Capes, *Charters and Records of Hereford Cathedral* (Hereford 1908); Z.N. and C.N.L. Brooke, "Hereford Cathedral Dignitaries in the Twelfth Century," *The Cambridge Historical Journal* 8 (1944) 1-21, 179-85.

[6] In general, few of Alexander's early decretals have been preserved.

In the same vein, writing to the bishop of Worcester around 1174 or 1175, Alexander discussed the postelectoral powers of Geoffrey Fitzroy, who had just acceded to the bishopric of Lincoln:

> As a prudent and wise man, you know that our beloved son Geoffrey, bishop-elect of Lincoln, has no power to grant honors or prebends or otherwise to dispose of the church's property, since his election is not yet confirmed. . . .[7]

Alexander was especially concerned that Geoffrey should not confer the vacant archdeaconry of Northampton. However, if the grant had already been made, the pope prescribed that Geoffrey should speedily revoke it, but that if Geoffrey then failed to comply, the bishop of Worcester should step in and revoke the concession "without right of appeal."

In the middle years of the twelfth century, when a decretal mentioned electoral confirmation, it still referred to the older idea of a nonconstitutive consent, and it still carried no implications about the prelate-elect's right to administer.[8] By the mid-1170's, however, two decretals had discussed electoral confirmation and had accepted the meaning assigned to it by Stephen of Tournai and later decretists. Does this fact imply direct decretistic influence? In other words, can one conclude that this concept of electoral confirmation first appeared in the schools of canon law and later emerged in administrative practice and in Curial policy? Since both

---

[7] *Comp.I* 1.4.18 (*X* 1.6.9): "Nosti sicut vir prudens et sapiens, quomodo dilectus filius G. dictus Lincolniensis electus concedendi honores vel prebendas aut alias disponendi de rebus ecclesie, cum sua nondum sit electio confirmata, non habeat facultatem . . . et si . . . prebendam cuiquam . . . concessit, ei auctoritate nostra precipias, ut concessionem suam . . . studeat revocare . . ." (reedited by W. Holtzmann and E. W. Kemp, *Papal Decretals Relating to the Diocese of Lincoln in the Twelfth Century* [Publications of the Lincoln Record Society 47: Hereford 1954] 18f no.7).

[8] *Collectio Lipsiensis* 31.4 (Eugene III): ". . . electio autem celebrata romano pontifici siue metropolitano proprio cum electorum subscriptionibus presentanda est, ut illius iudicio, cuius interest manum consecrationis imponere, si idonea est, approbetur, si minus canonica reprobetur" (Friedberg, *Quinque compilationes* 197). Also, see above, Ch.IIA n.71.

Electoral Confirmation

decretals discuss the constitutive effects of electoral confirmation as something self-evident, apparently the pope assumed that the English recipients were familiar with the requirement. Consequently, it is likely that by 1175 the requirement was no longer new. Because relatively few of Alexander's early decretals have been preserved, the evidence is perhaps not entirely conclusive. Nonetheless, in all probability these two decretals reflect an innovation by the schools, and the influence of learned jurists on Curial practice. Contemporaries did not miss the central point of these two decretals. By the time of Alexander's death in 1181 or soon thereafter, among English decretalists it was possible to regard this principle explicitly as a general rule of law: "An *electus* cannot administer the church's properties, unless his election has been confirmed."[9] Within two decades after Alexander's death, both of these decretals had entered numerous collections, including the *Compilatio prima* around 1190, and within these collections, the two decretals usually appeared under the title "On election and the power of an *electus*."[10] That is to say, canonists viewed the two decretals primarily as juridical statements on the administrative capacities of a bishop-elect.

Not long after the issuance of these two decretals, one of the constitutions of the Third Lateran Council speaks of a bishop's election, confirmation, and administration of ecclesi-

[9] The decretalist who provided the chapter headings in the Royal Collection extracted this principle as a rubric: "Electus disponere de rebus ecclesie non potest, nisi electione eius confirmata" (BM Royal 15.B.IV fol.115ra); Charles Duggan, *Twelfth-Century Decretal Collections and Their Importance in English History* (London 1963) 81-84. The first official appearance of this canonical requirement in two Alexandrian decretals directed to English recipients should not be interpreted as evidence that (a) the requirement itself originated in England, or (b) the requirement was first imposed on English bishops-elect. As Duggan points out (*op.cit.* esp. 118-24, 132-35, 140-51), apparently a higher proportion of Alexander's decretals addressed to Englishmen was *preserved*, than of his decretals to Continental recipients.

[10] Friedberg, *Quinque compilationes* pp.xii, 197; W. Holtzmann, "Die Dekretalensammlungen des 12. Jahrhunderts (I): Die Sammlung Tanner," *Festschrift zur Feier des zweihundertjährigen Bestehens der Akademie der Wissenschaften in Göttingen* II, philologisch-historische Klasse (Berlin 1951) 120f.

111

The Bishop-Elect

astical property, and it distinctly suggests—or rather, assumes
—that this was a fixed temporal sequence of events in any
accession to the episcopate.[11] The constitution takes a curious
precaution, stipulating that until after the canonical interval
in which the bishop-elect should receive his consecration, the
benefice which he held before his election should not be given
to another cleric. The significance of this provision is somewhat obscure, for in the view of contemporary canonists, the
confirmation of his election should render the bishop-elect's
former benefice vacant. In explanation of this clause, Bernard
of Pavia proposed the possibility that an *electus* might not
obtain his consecration, and in that case he could easily return
to his benefice and "to his prior status."[12] Or perhaps, Bernard added, this precaution should be followed as a matter
of courtesy (*de urbanitate*), rather than as a strict canonical
regulation (*non de necessitate*).

Near the end of the twelfth century a confirmed bishop-
elect attempted to discipline the unruly clerics of his diocese,
who then resisted him by denying his right, as a mere *electus*,
to exercise this form of power. When the question was
referred to Rome, Celestine III upheld the bishop-elect.

---

[11] *Conc. Lat. III* c.2 (*X* 1.6.7 §2): "Cum vero electus fuerit, et confirmationem electionis acceperit, et ecclesiasticorum bonorum administrationem
habuerit, decurso tempore de consecrandis a canonibus diffinito, is, ad quem
spectant beneficia, quae habebat de illis disponendi liberam habeat
facultatem."

[12] Gl. on *Comp.I* 1.4.16 §1 (*X* 1.6.7): ". . . Set quare dicit 'decurso tempore,' nonne statim post electionis confirmationem poterit electi beneficium
aliis assignare? Responderi potest quod intervenerat electo locus penitendi,
vel quod magis placet, dicas, quod sepe contingit, ut ex vicio eleccionis
etiam post confirmacionem electus non possit obtinere consecracionem. . . .
Quia igitur talis casus posset intervenire et tunc oporteret electum ad prio-
rem statum redire, merito interim locus eius ac beneficium debet in
suspenso manere. Vel dicas hoc de urbanitate, non de necessitate" (Gillmann, *AKKR* 113 [1933] 467 n.4).

Alanus seems to have been uncertain about this provision; see his
Apparatus on *Comp.I* 1.4.16 v. *decurso* tempore: "Maxime quoniam si ante
illud tempus perfecte translatus esset, et ante posset beneficia eius alii
conferre ille ad quem pertineant, . . . illa potissimum ratione, quia recipiendo episcopum intelligitur renuntiare aliis beneficiis. . . . Aliud tamen est
in aliis dignitatibus que habentur ex iure consuetudinis cum minoribus beneficiis, hic enim non eo ipso quod dignitatem recipit prestimoniis renuntiare
intelligitur . . ." (Clm 3879 fol.3va).

Electoral Confirmation

Under normal circumstances, Celestine asserted, disciplinary powers can be freely exercised as soon as the *electus* has received his confirmation.[13] For as Laurentius remarked in a gloss on Celestine's decretal, and as the canonists—beginning at least in the later twelfth century—generally agreed, since the right to excommunicate belongs to the *potestas iurisdictionis*, rather than to the *potestas ordinis*, it is conferred by electoral confirmation.[14] And in 1199, when the unconfirmed bishop-elect of Penne prematurely and "irreverently" undertook the administration of his diocese by accepting oaths from laymen and clerics alike, Innocent III declared his election, together with all of his administrative acts, null and void.[15] Indeed, Alanus explained that "to judge, to accept oaths of fealty from vassals, to give investitures and prebends, to confirm prelates-elect"—all these pertain to the sphere of *iurisdictio*.[16] In order to bypass these stringent regulations, unconfirmed prelates-elect sometimes assumed special proctorships or adopted other ingenious expedients enabling them to administer. Hence, at the Second Council of Lyons in 1274, it was necessary to prohibit the uncon-

[13] *Comp.II* 1.3.7 (*X* 1.6.15): ". . . clerici tuae dioecesis . . . nonnulli . . . correctionem ecclesiasticam per contemptum eludunt, dicentes, quod potestatem non habeas eos, nisi tibi specialiter apostolica sedes indulserit corrigendi. Respondemus igitur quod . . . tu eos auctoritate nostra suffultus excommunicationi appellatione cessante subiicias. . . . Etiam haec [scil. excommunicationis sententiam etc.] sine speciali mandato exsequi posses, cum ex quo electionis tuae confirmationem accepisti, de talibus et consimilibus, praeter ea, quae maioris inquisitionis discussionem exigunt, et ministerium consecrationis desiderant, quod iustum est et ecclesiasticae convenit utilitati statuendi habeas liberam facultatem."

[14] Gl. in Tancred's *Gl.ord.* on *Comp.II* 1.3.7 v. *excommunicationi*: "Confirmatus ergo excommunicare potest non solum electus in episcopum set electus in abbatem. . . . Unde patet quod excommunicare iurisdictionis est, non ordinis, unde et uisitator ecclesie excommunicare potest, cum liberam habeat administrationem . . ." (Clm 3879 fol.101va).

[15] *Comp.III* 1.6.2 (*X* 1.6.17): ". . . Verum quoniam electus a vobis ante confirmationem obtentam administrationi episcopatus se irreverenter immiscuit, recipiendo tam a clericis quam a laicis iuramenta . . . electionem de ipso factam exigente iustitia duximus irritandam, quicquid ex ea et ob eam factum est denunciantes penitus non tenere."

[16] Gl. in Tancred's *Gl.ord.* on *Comp.II* 1.3.7 v. *de talibus*: "ad iurisdictionem pertinentibus, puta: iudicare, sacramenta fidelitatis a uasallis accipere, inuestituras et prebendas dare, electos confirmare. . . . Hec enim in confirmatione conferuntur . . ." (Clm 3879 fol.101va).

113

The Bishop-Elect

firmed *electus* from taking any part in the administration of his church, even through a representative, and from administering the Church by having himself appointed as an *oeconomus* or *procurator* during the interim before his consecration.[17]

The electoral treatises by Egidius of Bologna and by William Naso undoubtedly reflected the procedure which had become standard in the episcopal elections of many cities by the mid-thirteenth century. According to this procedure, immediately following an election the *Te Deum* was sung, and thereafter the bishop-elect was enthroned near the altar. At this point, these treatises assert: "The prelate-elect should take care that he does not meddle in the administration before he has been confirmed."[18] From this indication, it is likely

[17] *Conc. Lugd. II* c.4 (*VI* 1.6.5): ". . . sancimus, ut nullus . . . administrationem dignitatis, ad quam electus est, priusquam . . . electio confirmetur, sub oeconomatus vel procurationis nomine, . . . in spiritualibus vel temporalibus, per se vel per alium, pro parte vel in totum, gerere vel recipere, aut illis se immiscere praesumat. . . ."

[18] Egidius, *Tractatus Ad intelligentiam decretalis Quia propter*: ". . . Facta electione mox publicent in communi, idest in capitulo et coram populo, sollempniter cantando alta uoce 'Te Deum laudamus' et ducendo ipsum ante altare et installando ipsum. Caueat tamen ne aliquid administret ante confirmationem nisi sit ualde remotus ultra Ytaliam et electus in concordia, tunc propter necessitatem et utilitatem in temporalibus et spiritualibus administrat, eodem titulo Nichil, in fine . . ." (Bamberg Can. 47 fol.127v); the exceptional status of the *ualde remoti* will be discussed below, Ch.VIc. Egidius's treatise enjoyed considerable popularity in the 13th and early 14th centuries; seven other MSS are known. Though it has been ascribed to Egidius Fuscararius (Miroslav Boháček, "Zur Geschichte der Stationarii von Bologna," *Symbolae Raphaeli Taubenschlag dedicatae* II [Eos: Commentarii Societatis Philologae Polonorum 48 (1956)] 248-51), it cites no decretals later than the 4th Lateran Council, and hence was probably composed before the late 13th century (W. Ullmann, "The Disputed Election of Hugh Balsham, Bishop of Ely," *Cambridge Historical Journal* 9 [1949] 261 n.16). Eventually I hope to include his *Tractatus* in a collective edition of several 13th-century electoral treatises.

Almost identical to Egidius's wording in this passage was a portion of William Naso's long gloss in his *Lectura* on *X* 1.6.42; cf. esp. the statement: ". . . Caueat tamen electus ne prius quam fuerit confirmatus immisceat se amministrationi . . ." (Vienna 2083 fol.49va-b). William's gloss also appeared, virtually verbatim, in Montecassino MS 136 fols.209-210 as a separate work (*Inc.*: "Tres sunt forme que fiunt in electionibus . . ."), which, like Egidius's treatise, explicates *Quia propter* (= *X* 1.6.42); R. Trifone, "Gli scritti di Guglielmo Nasone conservati nella Biblioteca di Montecassino," *Rivista di storia del diritto italiano* 2 (1929) 258. In

114

that an explicit warning—not to undertake the *administratio* prior to confirmation—was often a customary part of electoral procedure.[19] Indeed, when an *electus* was examined before his confirmation, he could be asked "if he has meddled in the administration of his temporalities or spiritualities."[20] Understandably, therefore, in episcopal documents of the thirteenth century, bishops-elect began to use the title *electus et confirmatus*, instead of the older and simpler title *electus*, in order to stress the legitimacy of their administrative acts.[21]

Throughout the last quarter of the twelfth century and the opening years of the thirteenth, the unanimous judgment of popes, councils, and decretalists—in full agreement with contemporary decretists—pronounced upon the prelate-elect's right to exercise his jurisdictional powers: there can be no administrative rights before the election has been confirmed. Similarly, canonical practice and procedure further reinforce the impression that no bishop-elect could break this rule and come away unscathed.

---

general, see S. Kuttner and B. Smalley, "The 'Glossa ordinaria' to the Gregorian Decretals," *EHR* 60 (1945) 103-05.

[19] To be sure, the requirement of confirmation before administration finds no explicit mention in Laurentius de Somercote's *Tractatus de formis electionum episcoporum faciendarum* (ed. A. von Wretschko, *Der Traktat des Laurentius de Somercote, Kanonikus von Chichester, über die Vornahme der Bischofswahlen, entstanden im Jahre 1254* [Weimar 1907]), or in Hostiensis's unedited *Tractatus Almo ac beatissimo patri* (Vienna 2238 fols.1r-9v; Vienna 2209 fols.50r-54r; etc.); on the latter, see Wretschko, "Ein Traktat des Kardinals Hostiensis mit Glossen betreffend die Abfassung von Wahldekreten bei der Bischofswahl," *Deutsche Zeitschrift für KR* 17 (1907) 73-88.

[20] Thomas Walsingham, *Gesta abbatum monasterii sancti Albani,* ed. H. T. Riley, II (Rolls Series: London 1867) 12: ". . . si se immiscuit administrationi [ed. ad ministrationem] temporalium aut spiritualium. . . ."

[21] G. Schmidt, *UB des Hochstifts Halberstadt* II 136-49 nos.868ff (Halberstadt 1253ff); *Westfälisches UB* VII (Münster 1908) 742 no.1623 (Osnabrück 1277); W. Altmann and E. Bernheim, *Ausgewählte Urkunden zur Erläuterung der Verfassungsgeschichte Deutschlands im Mittelalter* (4th ed. Berlin 1909) 346 no.168 (Paderborn 1279); and often.

CHAPTER V

THE DISSENT OF MASTER HUGUCCIO

1. In Defense of the Bishop-Elect

Beginning with Rufinus, the decretists spun the
different and often divergent threads of their electoral
theories. Near the end of the twelfth century, these various
threads were finally woven together by the most brilliant of
the decretists: Huguccio of Pisa.[1] At some time between 1188
and 1192 he stopped work on his massive but still incomplete *Summa decretorum*, which clearly shows his mastery of
preceding decretistic literature. Confronted by the problems
of electoral theory, he borrowed much from the earlier decretists, but with great originality he joined the various strands
into a new, complex, and harmonious pattern.[2]

[1] Numerous studies on Huguccio have appeared in the recent past. In
particular see: Gaetano Catalano, "Contributo alla biografia di Uguccio da
Pisa," *Il diritto ecclesiastico* 65 (1954) 3-67; Corrado Leonardi, "La vita e
l'opera di Uguccione da Pisa decretista," *SGrat* 4 (1956-57) 39-120; and
esp. Alfons M. Stickler, "Uguccio de Pise," *DDC* VII (1963) 1355-62.
Under the auspices of the Institute of Medieval Canon Law, a collaborative
edition of Huguccio's *Summa decretorum* is being directed by Father
Stickler. Two articles by Luigi Prosdocimi deal with the MSS and textual
problems (*SGrat* 3 [1955] 349-74; 7 [1959] 251-72).
For this study, my examination of Huguccio's thought has been based
on two MSS (Clm 10247 and Vat.Arch. C.114); for Appendix 3, an additional MS (Vat. 2280) was collated.
[2] Huguccio knew the works of the Bolognese masters, such as Rufinus,
John of Faenza, and Simon of Bisignano, and he was also familiar with
the production of the other schools: *Summa Inperatorie maiestati, Summa
Et est sciendum, Summa Parisiensis*, and *Summa Omnis qui iuste iudicat*.
Influence from Bernard of Pavia's *Summa de electione* seems to me prob-

The Dissent of Master Huguccio

Many passages in the *Decretum* served Huguccio as pretexts for elaborating his conceptions of office and election; like his predecessors he found Nicholas II's papal election decree of 1059 an excellent springboard from which to discuss the constitutive moment in ecclesiastical elections. Huguccio started by facing a familiar question: Does every *electus*, even before confirmation, have the right to administer the affairs of his church? Although no canonist of Huguccio's generation actually believed that an unconfirmed *electus* may administer freely, it still seemed at least theoretically possible to defend a positive answer to this question and to justify this position with texts from the *Decretum*.[3] Moreover, in their explications of the *Decretum*, the decretists had a marked tendency to generalize from particular cases, to frame widely applicable principles of law on the basis of single events recorded in Gratian's chapters. And sometimes, through its phrasing, a gloss on the 1059 election decree might have seemed to refer indifferently to any *electus*—pope or bishop or any other.[4]

---

able, and the eventual edition of Huguccio's *Summa* will undoubtedly reveal other influences.

[3] Huguccio, *Summa* on C.12 q.1. c. 13 v. *dispensator*: "arg. quod electus potest administrare res ecclesiasticas etiam ante confirmationem, quia ut hic dicitur, ex quo prelatus est, statim efficitur dispensator rerum ecclesiasticarum, set prelatus efficitur ex ipsa electione . . ." (Gross, *Recht an der Pfründe* 102). *Id.* on D.63 c.20 v. *eius*: "scil. electi. . . . Ipsi electo et ordinando administratio ecclesie concedenda est et est argumentum, quod electus eo ipso, quod canonice electus est, consequitur ius administrationis, ante enim quam ab episcopo confirmetur et ordinetur, cura huius ecclesie committitur electo. . . . . . . est ibi alia lectio inutilis . . . *eius*, scil. archidiaconi . . . et ita est argumentum, electum nichil iuris consequi ex electione antequam confirmetur" (Gross, *op.cit.* 117). More than a century later, Huguccio's remarks were still remembered; cf. Guido de Baysio, *Rosarium* on C.8 q.2 c.2: "Dicunt quidam quod hic de confirmato loquitur . . . ex sola enim electione secundum eos non efficitur quis praelatus. Sed secundum Ala(num), Hu(guccionem) et Lau(rentium) si recte capitulum inspiciatur aperte dicitur quod ex electione efficitur quis praelatus et videtur statim habere administrationem rerum ecclesiae"; Tierney, *Foundations* 126 n.1.

[4] *Apparatus Ordinaturus* on D.23 c.1 v. *disponendi*: "Arg. quod quibus ex canonica et iusta electione disponendi et administrandi ius sequitur, ut . . ." (Clm 10244 fol.11vb); dating from the 1180's, this work has been most recently studied by J. Kejř, "La genèse de l'Apparat 'Ordinaturus' au Décret de Gratien," *Proceedings of the Second International Congress of Medieval Canon Law, Boston College 1963*, ed. S. Kuttner and J. J. Ryan (Monumenta iuris canonici, Subsidia 1: Vatican City 1965) 45-53, with

117

The Bishop-Elect

Still, to be sure, master Huguccio was closely following the main decretistic tradition when he distinguished between the constitutive effect of election in the case of a pope and in the case of any other *electus*:

> Some say that this [right of immediate postelectoral administration] is peculiar to the pope, for in being elected he is confirmed and in being confirmed he is elected. In fact, he is elected and confirmed simultaneously and by the same people. And therefore, from the very fact that he is elected, he immediately has the full power of administering, just like other *electi* after confirmation. Other *electi* are elected before they are confirmed, and they are elected by some and confirmed by different people, and for this reason they do not have the power of administering before their confirmation.[5]

---

further studies in *SGrat* 12 (1967) by Kejř (pp.143-64) and by A. M. Stickler (pp. 111-41). Anon. gl. (probably Simon of Bisignano) ad loc.: "§ Hinc collige electum non posse clericos deponere, potest tamen eos suspendere et res ecclesiasticas amministrare . . ." (Juncker, *ZRG* KA 15 [1926] 403).

[5] *Summa* on D.23 c.1 v. *disponendi omnes facultates eius*: "Et est arg. quod quilibet electus etiam ante confirmationem habet ius disponendi et administrandi res ecclesiasticas . . . et dicunt quidam hoc esse speciale in papa, ipse enim eligendo confirmatur et confirmando eligitur, simul enim et ab eisdem eligitur et confirmatur, et ideo statim ex quo est electus habet plenam potestatem administrandi sicut alii post confirmationem, alii enim ante eliguntur quam confirmentur, et ab aliis eliguntur et ab aliis confirmantur, et inde est quod non habent potestatem administrandi ante confirmationem. Set distinguo: ante habent potestatem administrandi, idest ius administrandi, set non habent executionem illius iuris in actu. . . . Set ecce papa est electus et nondum est episcopus, potest deponere uel degradare clericos? Potest suspendere uel excommunicare? Vtique, et ut generalem faciam doctrinam, omnia potest que sunt tantum iurisdictionis set non illa que sunt ordinis. Potest ergo deponere, degradare, excommunicare, suspendere, prebendas dare et auferre et huiusmodi, set non potest clericos ordinare, crisma conficere, altaria uel ecclesias consecrare et huiusmodi. Prima enim potius sunt iurisdictionis quam ordinis, hec autem ex ordine proueniunt, nam insacratus uel inordinatus consecrare uel ordinare non potest . . ." (Clm 10247 fol.22ra). See also his remarks on the election decree of 1060, *id.* on D.79 c.9 v. *anathemate*: ". . . Videtur quod electus in episcopum plenam habeat potestatem administrandi et disponendi de rebus ipsius ecclesie ipso actu, set hoc speciale est in papa . . . ipse enim eligitur confirmando et confirmatur eligendo, a quibus enim eligitur, et confirmatur, et ideo eligendo confirmatur, ergo statim habet plenam

The Dissent of Master Huguccio

It must be emphasized that this was not Huguccio's theory; rather, he was reporting the opinion of others (in this instance, Simon of Bisignano and the *Summa Omnis qui iuste iudicat*).[6] In part, Huguccio himself agreed with this conception, for of course he ascribed full administrative powers to a newly elected pope. And if the pope was not a bishop before his election, still he can immediately perform all duties which are based on his "power of jurisdiction" (*potestas iurisdictionis*); he can, for example, depose and degrade clerics.[7]

It is clear that from Rufinus to Huguccio, the decretistic discussions of ecclesiastical office and election presupposed a more or less precise distinction between an official's jurisdictional powers and his priestly powers (*potestas ordinis*). There was not always agreement over the content of the two powers and the boundary between them—for instance, did the right to depose and degrade a cleric belong to the *iurisdictio* or to the *ordo*?—but the basic distinction was always present, informing the decretist's thought. At first, however, the terminology had a wild and luxuriant variety. In the papal election decree of 1059, the *auctoritas regendi et disponendi* was the quasi-technical term for the papal jurisdictional powers. Rufinus was responsible for the crystalline formulation of the terms *auctoritas* and *administratio*, a ubiquitous and extremely useful duality, based on a clearer sense of this distinction than had been possible in the preceding centuries. For Rufinus, however, the jurisdictional powers could also be designated as *potestas, dispensatio, exercitium, ius diocesanum*, and *regimen*. Even within the Decretum, such further terms as *dispositio* and *executio* had been applied to

---

potestatem, sicut alii electi in episcopos habent post confirmationem . . ." (Gross, *Recht an der Pfründe* 122 n.37).

[6] Cf. above, Ch.IVA nn.18, 21.

[7] Among 12th-century decretists, Huguccio was practically alone in the belief that the right to depose or degrade a cleric belongs to the *potestas iurisdictionis*. However, cf. also the *Apparatus Ordinaturus* on D.23 c.1 v. *auctoritatem*: ". . . alii [electi] cum deinde fuerint confirmati possunt . . . deponere set non con[secrare] . . ." (Clm 10244 fol.11vb).

aspects of jurisdictional competence.[8] Master Huguccio must tentatively be credited with the introduction of *iurisdictio* as a precise technical term and with the further polishing of the basic distinction. In fact, strictly speaking, the duality *iurisdictio* and *ordo* did not exist before Huguccio, although of course, in a broader sense, the framework had already been constructed by Rufinus. At all events, Huguccio's version proved decisive: to the present day, Church law has operated with his sharp terminological distinction between the *potestas iurisdictionis* and the *potestas ordinis*.[9]

Except for his insistence that the power of deposition belongs to the *potestas iurisdictionis*, master Huguccio's notion of papal election and of the consequent administrative rights was thoroughly traditional. Radical, however, was his conception of the more general principle, relating to the preconfirmatory administrative powers of all other *electi*:

Before [confirmation], they have the power of administering, that is, the right of administering, but they do not have the execution of that right in the act [of administration].[10]

Thus, defying the unanimous conviction of all decretists from Stephen of Tournai to the *Summa Omnis qui iuste iudicat*, Huguccio asserted that even before confirmation any

[8] On the development of the varying terminology surrounding the jurisdictional powers, see van de Kerckhove, *Études franciscaines* 49 (1937) 421ff.

[9] Cf. van de Kerckhove, *Études franciscaines* 49 (1937) 423, who noted Huguccio's application of the equation *administratio = iurisdictio*, but who failed to appreciate the precision with which Rufinus had already drawn the line between the jurisdictional and the sacramental powers. Moreover, the first substantive *and* terminological distinction between *ordo* and *iurisdictio*, which van de Kerckhove ascribed to the period 1215-50 (*op.cit.* 453f), was actually drawn in the late 12th century. See Alfons M. Stickler, "Vergessene Bologneser Dekretisten," *Salesianum* 14 (1952) 488f, and the comment in the *Summa Reginensis* on D.96 c.1 v. *anathema*: ". . . hec potestas magis pertinet ad iurisdictionem quam ad ordinem" (Stickler, *op.cit.* 488). This Bolognese work was written about 1190, probably by Peter of Benevento; in general, see Stickler, *op.cit.* 487ff and esp. 502f (for the authorship). The *Summa Reginensis* was heavily dependent upon Huguccio, and in fact, Huguccio has priority for the first formulation of this duality: ". . . prima enim potius sunt iurisdictionis quam ordinis . . ." (above, n.5).

[10] Above, n.5.

The Dissent of Master Huguccio

electus has the power of administering. In this discussion of
Nicholas II's election decree, with deceptively simple terminology and with great originality Huguccio briefly summarized his theory of the stages on the way to full powers of
office, but in a commentary on electoral *subscriptio* he elaborated these ideas in more detail.[11] Because this distinction
between different forms of administrative power is extraordinarily complex and has, at the same time, fundamental importance, it will require an extended analysis.

MATRIMONIUM SPIRITUALE

Mysticism seldom flourishes in the dry world of constitutional law. Especially in the twelfth and early thirteenth centuries, when the constitutional theorists were seeking sharper
distinctions on such problems as office and jurisdiction, mysti-
cal concepts might have seemed a hindrance, rather than a
help, to this endless search. Yet in his analysis of the bishop-
elect's powers, master Huguccio successfully invoked a mystic
concept to introduce new precision, clarity, and balance into
the tradition of decretistic thought.

Huguccio was thoroughly aware of the conflicting decretistic notions of electoral *subscriptio* and *confirmatio*, and his
fully developed theory of election was an answer to these
disagreements. The first step in his conception of election is
"active nomination" (*nominatio activa*), which meant the
simple act of election by the electors.[12] From this, no rights
are acquired. The second stage is the "passive nomination"
(*nominatio passiva*), that is, the consent of the *electus*, and
from this alone, nothing is acquired. Huguccio was undoubt-

---

[11] *Summa* on D.63 c.10 v. *subscripta relatio*; because of its central significance, the full text of this gloss has been edited in Appendix 3.

[12] Appendix 3, lines 24ff: ". . . electio dicitur nominatio tam actiua
quam passiua, scilicet nominatio eligentium et nominatio eius qui eligitur.
Ex hac electione sic simpliciter intellecta nullum ius acquiritur alicui electo
nec ob hoc efficitur prelatus. Item electio dicitur uinculum quod ex mutuo
consensu, scilicet eligentium et electi, contrahitur inter eos, cum enim isti
consentiunt in illum et ille uersa uice in istos, contrahitur inter eos matrimonium spirituale, ut ille iam dicatur sponsus istius ecclesie uel istorum
clericorum et hec ecclesia sponsa ipsius. . . ."

edly familiar with the Roman law principle—and with its canonistic derivative—prescribing that "not sexual intercourse, but consent makes a marriage."[13] Applying this Romano-canonical rule to the ancient formula that a bishop is married to his church, he remarked that election is thus a bond between electors and *electus*—through the "mutual consent" (*mutuus consensus*) of electors and *electus*, a "spiritual marriage" (*matrimonium spirituale*) is contracted between them.[14] This moment, in which the newly elected official becomes the spouse of his church, is the true promotion to the new office: at that instant, the *electus* becomes the "prelate of that church" (*prelatus illius ecclesie*).[15]

In itself, Huguccio's use of marriage as a metaphor was far from original. For centuries the ritual surrounding the bishop's consecration had included a ceremonial act of marriage between the bishop and his church. According to Roman

---

[13] *Dig.* 50.17.30: "Nuptias non concubitus, sed consensus facit." *Dig.* 35.1.15: "Cui fuerit sub hac condicione legatum 'si in familia nupsisset,' videtur impleta condicio statim atque ducta est uxor, quamvis nondum in cubiculum mariti venerit, nuptias enim non concubitus, sed consensus facit." This formula was taken into the *Decretum.* Cf. C.27 q.2 pr.: "consensus . . . est efficiens causa matrimonii, iuxta illud Ysidori: 'Consensus facit matrimonium' "; and cf. also C.27 q.2 cc.1-6, 9, and dict.p.c.2. Also deriving from Roman law, the canonistic notion of "affection" was sometimes considered equivalent to "consent"—and might therefore be decisive in creating a marriage; *Caesaraugustana* 10.4: "Nuptias non concubitus, sed affectus facit" (Fournier and LeBras, *Histoire des collections canoniques* II 280). In general, see John T. Noonan, "Marital Affection in the Canonists," *SGrat* 12 (1967) 479-509, who also discusses the concept of *consensus.*

[14] The idea of a marriage between bishop and church was based—like the nuptial mass itself—upon the marriage between Christ and the Church, a concept deriving from St Paul (*Ephes.* 5.22ff). The important article by Josef Trummer, "Mystisches im alten Kirchenrecht: Die geistige Ehe zwischen Bischof und Diözese," *Österreichisches Archiv für KR* 2 (1951) 62-75, traces this idea but does not discuss Huguccio's role in transforming it; see also Ernst H. Kantorowicz, "Mysteries of State," *Harvard Theological Review* 48 (1955) 79 n.49 (= *Selected Studies* [Locust Valley, N.Y. 1965] 390).

[15] Appendix 3, lines 51ff: "ex secunda [electione], scilicet cum altrinsecus consensus accedit, aliquod ius ei acquiritur, scilicet efficitur prelatus illius ecclesie. . . ." *Ibid.*, lines 116f: ". . . ex mutuo consensu contrahitur [scil. uinculum matrimonii spiritualis] et ex quo electus efficitur prelatus. . . ." The status of a "prelate," as conceived by Huguccio, is very different from that of Sicard's *prelatus*; cf. above, Ch. IVA n.27.

usage since the tenth century, during the consecration, as the metropolitan placed the ring on the bishop's finger, he said:

> Receive the ring, the sign of faith, so that, adorned with pure faith, you may preserve without harm your bride, namely, the holy church of God.[16]

In the eleventh century, even when the emperor handed over ring and crosier to the prelate-elect, the ring was nonetheless regarded as a wedding ring,[17] and it continued to be a commonplace of theology that the ring represents, in Hugh of St Victor's words, "the sacrament of faith, by which the Church, whose guardians and preceptors are the bishops and prelates, is espoused as the bride of Christ."[18] Indeed, the Gregorian reformers' indignation over lay investiture—the prince's bestowal of ring and crosier—focused mainly on the ring.[19] Because of the ring's inherently sacramental character, the lay monarch seemed to arrogate to himself the administration of a sacrament. As Placidus of Nonantula explained, the ring is a "sign of eternal mystery," designating "the mystery of the most sacred conjunction, namely of Christ and his Church." In the episcopal consecration, when he accepts the ring from the metropolitan, the new bishop reenacts Christ's role, for thereby "in the place of Christ he is joined to

---

[16] *Ordo* 35B.35, ed. M. Andrieu, *Les Ordines romani du haut moyen-âge* (5 vols. Louvain 1931-61) IV 108: "Ad anulum digito imponendum: 'Accipe anulum, fidei scilicet signaculum, quatinus sponsam, Dei sanctam videlicet ecclesiam, intemerata fide ornatus, illibate custodias.'" For an episcopal consecration, the same text appears in the *Pontificale Romanum saec.XII* 10.28, ed. M. Andrieu, *Le Pontifical romain au moyen-âge* (4 vols. Vatican City 1938-41) I 149. At his consecration the pope receives the ring with the same words, except for the significant addition of the word *universalis* (". . . Dei videlicet sanctam universalem ecclesiam . . ."); *Pontificale Romanae Curiae* 13B.18, ed. Andrieu, *Pontifical romain* II 374.

[17] Theodericus, *Vita et passio Conradi archiepiscopi* c.2, *MGH SS* VIII 215: "[Electus Treverensis] suscepit a manu regia pontificatus insignia, scilicet pastoralem baculum et sponsalem ecclesiae anulum, interim dum sacri crismatis unctione ordinaretur sponsus ecclesiae."

[18] *De sacramentis christianae fidei* 2.4.15, *PL* 176 438: "Annulus sacramentum fidei significat, quo sponsa Christi ecclesia subarrata est, cuius custodes et paedagogi episcopi sunt et praelati. . . ."

[19] Below, Ch.VII; in general, see the three volumes of the *MGH LdL* Index s.v. "anulus."

the Holy Church."[20] Thus the earlier tradition concentrated its attention on the sacramental and allegorical features of the bishop's marriage to his church, noting constantly its typification of Christ's marriage to the entire Church. Huguccio, however, broke with this tradition when he applied the new juridical—specifically, Romano-canonical—concept of marriage to the marriage between bishop and church. With this innovation, it was natural for Huguccio to shift the moment of marriage from a sacramental rite—the consecration—to a merely administrative act—the prelate-elect's consent to his election.[21]

The signing of the election decree adds nothing to the constitutional significance of the electoral act, for the electors' *subscriptio* is only "a solemnity and a precaution" (*sollemnitas et cautela*). By itself, the "active nomination" by the electors, which is the first step in the electoral procedure, is binding upon them, and afterward they cannot change their decision and elect another person.[22]

[20] *Liber de honore ecclesiae* c.55, *MGH LdL* II 590: ". . . Episcopus etiam, cum benedicitur, baculum de manu archiepiscopi accipit, simul et anulum . . . ut signum aeterni misterii se percepisse cognoscat. . . . In anulo vero misterium sacratissimae coniunctionis, Christi videlicet et eius aecclesiae, designari certissimum est. Quae ideo in episcopo celebrantur, quia vice Christi aecclesiae sanctae coniungitur. . . ."

[21] The canonistic tradition accepted Huguccio's juridical concept of *mutuus consensus* as the bishop-elect's *matrimonium spirituale* (to be discussed below, in Sections 2 and 3 of this chapter), but the *ordines* conservatively adhered to the older notion of the episcopal consecration as the marriage ceremony. In fact, long before Huguccio, decretists drew parallels between the marriage of bride and groom, and the marriage of Christ with the Church; see Rufinus's extended discussion of marriage (*Summa* on C.27 q.2 pr., ed. Singer 440-49). It was, perhaps, therefore inevitable when—also before Huguccio—a decretist asserted that the "spiritual marriage" between the bishop and his church "is begun in election"; *Summa Elegantius in iure diuino* 3.52: "spirituale matrimonium quod est inter spiritualem sponsum et sponsam, pontificem uidelicet et ecclesiam, electione initiatur, consecratione consummatur" (from page-proofs of edition by G. Fransen and S. Kuttner). The terminology describing different steps or stages within marriage (*initiatum, ratum, consummatum, perfectum*) was already present in the *Decretum* (e.g. C.27 q.2 dict.p.c.34, dict.p.c.35, rubr.cc.35-37, dict.p.c.39), which in turn was following earlier models.

[22] Appendix 3, lines 4ff: ". . . propter subscriptionem nec plus nec minus quam ante [potest irritari electio], subscriptio enim non fit nisi ad sol-

The Dissent of Master Huguccio

The main question—to define the precise rights and powers of a *prelatus*—is still not answered by these preliminary distinctions. Moreover, as Huguccio himself tells us, canonical practice furnished no clue, for it varied from place to place:

In some places, according to custom an *electus* administers before his confirmation, but the general custom of the Church is opposed to this.[23]

Thus the earlier tradition of preconfirmatory administration, which was still visible in the *Decretum*, remained a real fact of canonical practice "in some places." The "general custom of the Church" (*generalis ecclesie consuetudo*) was against the *prelatus*'s right to administer before confirmation—one may be sure that this "general custom" was the Church's newly emerging Common Law, which was applied under the canonists' direction and which insisted upon confirmation before administration, as all of the decretists from Stephen of Tournai to Huguccio testify. Neither in theory nor in practice was there complete and universal agreement about the new requirement of electoral confirmation in all of its aspects, and against the background of this split, master Huguccio seems to have been trying to create a middle way, or indeed, trying to reconcile opposites.

Unwilling to take the extreme position of Simon of Bisi-

---

lempnitatem et cautelam. . . ." *Ibid.*, lines 75ff: ". . . clerici post primam electionem concorditer et legitime factam sua auctoritate nulla alia causa interueniente nisi quia uelint, sine peccato non possunt mutare uoluntatem suam in alium. . . ." See also his *Summa* on D.63 c.10 v. *relatio*: "dicit ergo 'relatio,' id est electio nobis relata, et no(ta) secundum quosdam hic duplicem assignari causam, quare electio possit cassari, scilicet quia non fuit subscripta et quia quidam illorum, ad quos spectat eligere uel consentire, aberant, et secundum illos facta fuit illa notula Io(hannis Faventini). Nam post subscriptionem non est locus penitentie. Quam notulam credo falsam, quia innuit, non loquitur de electione. Ego ex ui ipsius littere dico, quod hic tantum una assignatur causa, scilicet absentia illorum. Non enim assignatur causa, ut minus uel magis possit cassari electio, set propter quorundam absentiam, ut iste sit sensus . . ." (Gillmann, *AKKR* 113 [1933] 485).

23 Appendix 3, lines 60ff: ". . . in quibusdam locis electus ante confirmationem de consuetudine administrat, set generalis ecclesie consuetudo tenet in contrarium. . . ."

gnano, of the *Summa Omnis qui iuste iudicat,* and of other decretists, Huguccio refused to deny all administrative powers to an unconfirmed ecclesiastical official, and he found a compromise formula—the distinction between the "power" or "right of administering" (*potestas* or *ius administrandi*) and the "act of administering" or the "execution of the right in the act" (*actus administrandi = executio iuris in actu*). By playing off *potestas* against *actus* here, Huguccio evoked the technical language of philosophy and implied that the prelate-elect's powers exist in potentiality or "potency" (*potentia*), rather than in the act.[24] Through "mutual consent" the *electus* receives the "right of administering," but the limitations upon his power are clear, for it is a right to administer "not immediately but afterward" (*non statim sed postea*). Time, then, is the important factor; the *electus* has the power through his election, but only in the future will he be able to use that power directly. Until the ecclesiastical superior confirms the bond of "spiritual marriage," the *electus* cannot use his administrative rights, for until the confirmation, the "mutual consent" is "suspended" and must be considered temporarily ineffective.[25] Nonetheless, even before confirmation, the *electus*'s rights are not to be disregarded. Interpreting *confirmatio* etymologically, master Huguccio (who was a lexicographer as well as a canonist) explained that it means "to

[24] *Summa* on D.23 c.1 v. *disponendi* etc.: "ante habent [electi] potestatem administrandi, idest ius administrandi, set non habent executionem illius iuris in actu . . ." (above, n.5). Appendix 3, lines 65ff: ". . . consequitur inde [electus] administrationem quoad ius, idest ius administrandi non statim set postea, set non consequitur actum administrandi, scilicet ut in ipso actu posset administrare statim quasi: non habet executionem. . . ."

[25] Appendix 3, lines 28ff: ". . . uinculum . . . ex mutuo consensu . . . eligentium et electi contrahitur inter eos, cum enim isti consentiunt in illum et ille uersa uice in istos, contrahitur inter eos matrimonium spirituale . . . nisi ille clericus subsit alii prelato, tunc enim tales consensus tanquam inualidi suspenduntur quousque ille prelatus consentiat . . . si consentit, statim facti ualidi generant et faciunt matrimonium inter illos. . . ." Cf. also *ibid.,* lines 111ff: ". . . Quid ergo confirmat metropolitanus? Non potest dici quod confirmet primam electionem, idest nominationem, actionem uel passionem, que fuit in eligentibus uel electo, quia illa iam non est de necessitate. Compellimur dicere quod confirmat uinculum illud quod ex mutuo consensu contrahitur. . . ."

strengthen what is weak and to make it stronger" (*infirmum firmare et firmius reddere*).[26] Clearly, a right cannot be confirmed (that is, made stronger) if it does not exist! At his confirmation, the power which the *electus* has already gained through his election is finally transformed into a fully effective and usable power.

To explain in greater detail his complex conception of election, Huguccio returned to his lively analogy with marriage: the "mutual consent" of electors and *electus*, that is, the "spiritual marriage" between them, corresponds to the act of marriage between a man and woman, which both in canon and in Roman law was based on verbal consent. Carrying his analogy further, Huguccio, remarked vividly:

After his confirmation, the *electus* undertakes sexual intercourse, that is, he undertakes the governing of his church.[27]

Huguccio appropriated this striking metaphor—the equation of ecclesiastical administration and sexual intercourse—from a Pseudo-Isidorian text within the *Decretum*,[28] but he trans-

[26] Appendix 3, lines 109ff: ". . . Quod autem dicunt ante confirmationem nil iuris conferri electo stare non potest, quia quid est confirmare nisi quod est quasi infirmum firmare et firmius reddere. . . ."

[27] Appendix 3, lines 36ff: ". . . si [superior electioni] consentit, statim facti ualidi [consensu] generant et faciunt matrimonium inter illos, quod tandem quasi carnali commixtione perficitur. Ex quo electus post confirmationem ad concubitum, idest ordinationem illius ecclesie, accedit. . . . Sicut enim in matrimonio carnali precedit matrimonium in desponsatione per uerba de presenti et postea sequitur carnalis commixtio, sic et hic in mutuo consensu precedit matrimonium spirituale et postea sequitur quasi carnalis commixtio, cum iam ecclesiam disponit et ordinat. . . ." *Ibid.*, lines 70f: ". . . Idem est in marito et uxore tempore menstrui uel partus uel dierum quadragesimalium. . . ." The term *desponsatio de presenti* means simply the act of marriage. In general, see A. Esmein, *Le mariage en droit canonique*, 2nd ed. rev. R. Génestal (2 vols. Paris 1929-35); Piero Rasi, *Consensus facit nuptias* (Milan 1946); for recent bibliography, Feine, *RG* I 381f.

[28] C.7 q.1 c.39: "Sicut alterius uxor nec adulterari ab aliquo . . . permittitur, sic nec uxor episcopi, que eius ecclesia . . . indubitanter intelligitur, eo uiuente absque consilio eius et uoluntate alteri iudicare, uel disponere, aut eius concubitu, id est ordinatione, frui, non conceditur . . ." (Hinschius, *Decr. Ps.-Isid.* 139). On the other hand, it is not likely that Huguccio was familiar with the even stronger metaphor by Humbert of Silva Candida, who denounced a layman's administration of a church as the "violation" of the bishop's wife (*Adversus simoniacos* 3.11, *MGH LdL* I 211f):

formed its meaning. The "act of administering" is comparable to the consummation of the "spiritual marriage" and the *electus*'s inability to exercise his powers prior to confirmation (so Huguccio continues) resembles a husband's sexual abstinence at the time of his wife's menstruation or childbirth. Behind his colorful language, Huguccio's meaning is clear: Even when their "conjugal" rights are not used—or cannot be used—the rights themselves remain undiminished, and the legal status of the *electus* (or, let it also be said, the status of the husband) is unimpaired.

In Huguccio's theory, there are perhaps echoes from Stephen of Tournai's equation *electio = approbatio*, which seemed to imply a claim on confirmation and the conferring of a real power.[29] Far stronger, however, was the influence from Bernard of Pavia's electoral treatise. At least a decade before Huguccio's *Summa*, Bernard wrote that an unconfirmed election is "suspended" and "weak" (*suspensa et quodammodo infirma*), and that before his confirmation an *electus* does not have the "power of execution" (*potestas exequendi*).[30] Moreover, Bernard had even explored the analogy between electoral consent and marital consent:

> There are certain things which are contracted by consent alone, such as . . . marriage, certain things, such as election, in which consent is insufficient unless other ceremonies are added. . . .[31]

Because Bernard was here considering the "consent of the people," rather than the "mutual consent of electors and *electus*," he found the analogy inapplicable. Still, in general,

---

"sacerdotis uxor ab aliis violatur, quandocumque ecclesia a laicis, quibus non pertinet, administratur vel ordinatur."

[29] Above, Ch.IVA nn.4, 28.
[30] Above, nn.24f, and Ch.IVA n.23.
[31] *Summa de electione* 2.1.7, ed. Laspeyres, *Sum. decr.* 314: ". . . notandum quod quaedam sunt, quae solo consensu contrahuntur, ut votum et matrimonium . . . , quaedam, in quibus consensus non sufficit, nisi aliae sollemnitates addantur, ut electio. . . ."

The Dissent of Master Huguccio

Bernard's views strikingly anticipate several of Huguccio's key points. Indeed, on the level of terminology as well as of idea, the similarities between Huguccio's and Bernard's conceptions of election are too great for mere coincidence. The fundamental distinction between a power and the right to execute that power, however, can be traced back even beyond Bernard of Pavia. Indeed, within Huguccio's *Summa* it was already a general mode of thought, applicable to other problems than electoral theory. For example, Huguccio used this basic distinction to define the papal power of the material sword (*potestas gladii materialis*), the Church's right to armed coercion. According to this conception, the pope held the power of the material sword but had to delegate the exercise of this power (*actus exequendi*).[32] Huguccio himself furnishes the indispensable clue to the origins of this important distinction, for with reference to his electoral theory, he remarked:

> It is the same thing in the case of a deposed or suspended priest or bishop, who has holy orders (*ordo*) but not the execution (*executio*) of these orders.[33]

Similar was Huguccio's explanation of a vassal's obligation of fealty to an excommunicated lord: the excommunication suspends the effectiveness of the vassal's duty (*executio obligationis*), but the full force of the fealty is restored as soon as the lord has made his reconcilation with the Church. Again Huguccio found an analogue "in a suspended or deposed cleric," and another counterpart—once more from marriage law—in the suspension of conjugal rights following an adultery.[34] So far as Huguccio and the other decretists are

[32] Stickler, "Der Schwerterbegriff bei Huguccio," *Ephemerides iuris canonici* 3 (1947) 201-42.
[33] Appendix 3, lines 68ff: ". . . Idem est in presbitero uel episcopo deposito uel suspenso, qui habet ordinem set non executionem eius. . . ."
[34] *Summa* on C.15 q.6 c.4 v. *absoluimus*: ". . . in hoc casu [scil. excommunicatione domini] remanet obligatio fidelitatis, set interdicitur eius executio interim, dum dominus est in excommunicatione, non enim interim tenentur uassalli exequi fidelitatem et participare domino, set facta recon-

concerned, this distinction between *potestas* and *executio* originated within the *Decretum* itself. Discussing the priestly powers of monks, Gratian explained that monks with priestly ordination have all priestly powers—nonetheless, the monk does not have a right to the "execution of his power" (*executio suae potestatis*) until he has been elected to a specific office and installed by the bishop with the abbot's consent.[35]

Paucapalea followed Gratian in this regard, and in the same vein, master Roland distinguished between "holy orders and the permission to execute holy orders" (*ordo et licentia ordinis exequendi*), since both are necessary "for the administration of the priestly office" (*ad sacerdotalis dignitatis administrationem*). Moreover, in order to use the priestly powers, one must be entrusted with a parish or congregation.[36] Treating a similar problem with his characteristic precision, Rufinus played off the "reality of the sacrament" (*veritas sacramenti*) against the "execution of the office" (*executio officii*); also for Rufinus, although a priest's sacramental powers may be thoroughly valid, he may nonetheless be unable to use them.[37] From Stephen of Tournai to Huguccio, the later decretists drew the same distinction.[38] Thus, for their

ciliatione ita tenentur seruire domino sicut et ante. . . . Idem est in clerico suspenso uel deposito, quia retinet ordinem, set impeditur in eo executio ordinis quousque absoluatur uel restituatur. Idem est inter uirum et uxorem adulteram uel inter uxorem et uirum adulterum, remanet quidem inter eos uinculum coniugale, set eius executio quo ad exigendum impeditur quousque adulter uel adultera agat penitentiam" (Vat.Arch. C.114 fol.229va).

[35] C.16 q.1 dict.p.cc. 19, 25 (for both texts, see above, Ch.IIB n.36); C.24 q.1 dict.p.c.37 (above, Ch.IIB n.30).

[36] Paucapalea, *Summa* on C.16 q.1, ed. Schulte 86f; Roland, *Summa* on C.16 q.1, ed. Thaner 37f (above, Ch.IIB n.39).

[37] Rufinus, *Summa* on D.70 pr. v. *ab episcopis alterius civitatis*, ed. Singer 161f; *id.* on C.9 q.1 pr. v. *quod ordinatio*, ed. Singer 298 (for both texts, Ch.IIB n.32).

[38] For example, *Summa Parisiensis* on C.2 q.7 dict.p.c.27 §2 v. *sola administratione*, ed. McLaughlin 113: "uterque enim unctus sed solus administrabat Saul." Stephen of Tournai, *Summa* on C.16 q.1 dict.p.c. 19 v. *dedicatione*, ed. Schulte 222 (above, Ch.IIB n.39); *id.* on D.70 pr., ed. Schulte 95f: ". . . Tribus namque modis irrita dicitur ordinatio sacerdotis, scil. quoad sacramenti veritatem, quoad executionem, quoad beneficium. . . . Nec dicimus executionem, quae publice populo a suo sacerdote debetur, sed quae circa confectionem ipsius sacramenti respicitur. Nam re vera

formulations of electoral theory, Bernard of Pavia and master Huguccio merely had to transplant a common conception from the sphere of sacramental powers to the area of those jurisdictional powers which are conferred by election. Indeed, within the realm of secular jurisdictional powers, Stephen of Tournai had already used a similar distinction to suggest that the emperor could make a grant of jurisdiction without any accompanying assignment of a province; thereby the official would have the "title" or "name" but not the necessary *administratio*.[39]

Through their insistence upon electoral confirmation before administration, the canonists and popes of the period between Rufinus and Huguccio diminished the significance of election, for they transformed it into a ceremony through which a prelate could be chosen but by which no power could be transferred to him. In other words, they deprived the electors of effective power, for if the *electus* acquires no rights through the electors' choice, the election itself could almost be omitted. A decade after Huguccio's *Summa*, Alanus expressed offhand the ultimate and logical conclusion of this new tendency within the Church's constitution, when he asserted that "every bishop has his bishopric from the pope." Obviously Alanus could not entirely ignore the electors, and he therefore softened this astonishing remark by his further explanation: "Yet nonetheless the pope does not bestow [the bishopric], but canonical election by clerics does."[40] Master

---

qui ecclesiae attitulatus non est, exequi divina ministeria populo publice non potest. . . ." Huguccio, *Summa* on C.16 q.1 dict.p.c.19: ". . . tamen non habent executionem quoad actum exteriorem, quasi [quia?] non debent actum exequendum exercere, tamen habent executionem quoad ius" (van de Kerckhove, *Études franciscaines* 49 [1937] 423). Bernard of Pavia, *Summa decretalium* 1.7, ed. Laspeyres 10: ". . . notandum, quod resignatio non abstulit episcopo potestatem, sed executionem."

39 Stephen, *Summa* on C.16 q.1 dict.p.c.19 v. *dedicatione*, ed. Schulte 222 (continuation of text given above, Ch.IIB n.39): ". . . quemadmodum et si dominus imperator concedat alicui iurisdictionem vel iudicandi potestatem et non assignet ei provinciam seu populum, quem iudicet, habet quidem titulum, i.e. nomen, sed non administrationem. . . ."

40 *Apparatus Ius naturale* on D.96 c.6 v. *cursu*: ". . . quilibet episcopus

Huguccio clearly understood the significance of the historical development summed up by Alanus, and he opposed it. Refusing to render the electoral act meaningless, he vigorously attacked this position and affirmed the electoral rights of the lower clergy:

> Who would be so foolish as to say that it does not belong to the clergy to create a pastor and prelate for itself, but that it belongs to a superior? Doesn't the clergy create the prelate for itself, just as the princes create the emperor, even though he is afterwards confirmed by the pope?[41]

If the clergy really "creates" its prelates, the electoral act must have some constitutive effect, even though the effect may be neither complete nor temporally immediate. These remarks are of course consistent with Huguccio's main conception: the *electus* has the full rights of his office at the moment of election, but the rights can be used only after the confirmation.

In order to summarize Huguccio's contribution, one can perhaps best use a terminology which first emerged soon after

---

habet episcopatum a papa, set tamen papa non tribuit set canonica clericorum electio . . ." (A. M. Stickler, "Alanus Anglicus als Verteidiger des monarchischen Papsttums," *Salesianum* 21 [1959] 362). To be sure, one should remember that Alanus's remark is special pleading: his main point is to state his position on the controversial question of "two swords," as the context shows clearly.

Alanus's authorship of the *App. Ius nat.* was demonstrated by Professor Kuttner. For this ascription, and for a list of Alanus's other works, see Kuttner, "Bernardus Compostellanus Antiquus," *Traditio* 1 (1943) 289 n.52; *id.*, "Johannes Teutonicus, das vierte Laterankonzil und die Compilatio quarta," *Miscellanea Giovanni Mercati* V (Studi e testi 125: Vatican City 1946) 619f and nn.11f. See also, in general, Stickler, *Salesianum* 21 (1959) 346-406. Two recensions of the *App. Ius nat.* have been preserved: a shorter one completed ca. 1192, and a longer one dating ca. 1202. In this study, the longer version is cited (based on two MSS: BN 15393 and Paris Maz. 1318).

41 Appendix 3, lines 117ff: ". . . Preterea quis esset adeo stultus, qui diceret non esse clericorum sibi facere prelatum et pastorem, set maioris? Numquid clerici non faciunt sibi prelatum, sicut principes imperatorem, licet postea confirmetur a papa?" Huguccio's analogy between episcopal and imperial elections played an important role in later political thought; the subsequent debate on this question cannot, however, be traced here.

The Dissent of Master Huguccio

the great Pisan wrote his *Summa*. The *ius ad rem petendam* is a right which asserts a claim upon something, while the *ius in re* designates a fully exercisable right.[42] From the beginning of the thirteenth century, this duality played a large role in legal thought, and although Huguccio did not coin these terms, his electoral theory first created the full substance of this distinction. Reluctant to deprive the lower clergy of electoral power by denying the constitutive effect of election, and unable to oppose the Curial and canonistic tendency of his age, which ascribed constantly greater importance to the act of confirmation, master Huguccio succeeded in splitting the right of administration into two parts: a *ius ad rem*, deriving from election, and a *ius in re*, deriving from confirmation.[43]

2. The Triumph of Huguccio's Compromise

Master Huguccio's electoral theory achieved widespread acceptance almost immediately. This is not to say that perfect unanimity followed the publication of Huguccio's *Summa* around 1190. As the canonists well knew, even at the beginning of Innocent III's pontificate, there was still disagreement over the rights of an *electus*.[1] And after the diffusion of the Huguccian doctrine, an occasional statement seems to insist strongly upon preadministrative confirmation. For example, one of the *notabilia* on the *Compilatio prima* asserted flatly:

[42] In general, see the works cited below, Ch.VB n.18.
[43] Cf., however, the remarks by Friedrich Kempf in his important study on *Papsttum und Kaisertum bei Innocenz III.* (Rome 1954) 113, interpreting Huguccio's doctrine as a statement that both the *ius ad rem* and the *ius in re* derive from election.

---

[1] Vincentius Hispanus, *Apparatus* on *Comp.III* 1.6.5 v. *seu nominatione*: ". . . etiam usque ad tempora inno(centii III) dissensio fuit inter magistros, an per electionem ius acquiratur . . ." (Gillmann, *AKKR* 113 [1933] 475 n.3). Johannes Galensis, gl. on *Comp.III* ad loc.: ". . . Verumtamen dicunt quidam, cum unus tantum nominatur, tunc ei ius acquiritur, cum plures autem secus. Set hoc non probant, cum etiam usque ad tempus domini innocentii fuerunt opiniones, an electione ius acquiratur . . ." (Gillmann, *loc.cit.*). Both passages were written between 1210 and 1215.

Note that the right to administer is acquired through confirmation.[2]

It is of course characteristic of genres like the *notabilia* or *generalia* that they called attention to particular legal statements or formulated general principles of law—even to the point of exaggeration or oversimplification. Hence, after 1190, such bald statements on the powers of an *electus* no longer reflect accurately the views of most contemporaries.

In part, the remaining disagreements over this problem resulted from the nature of canonistic scholarship, for the canonist was, at least to some degree, the prisoner of his text: his first responsibility was to explain the meaning of a specific passage, and only secondarily did he point out the relation to other texts or give his own opinion. In other words, the self-contradictions of the canonist reflect equivalent inconsistencies among the decretals or within the *Decretum*. However, most of these self-contradictions vanish as soon as one can determine the canonist's own judgment in the matter. Although Johannes Teutonicus wholeheartedly agreed with Huguccio's electoral theory, in his commentary on the *Compilatio tertia* Johannes admitted that one of Innocent III's decretals seems to be an argument against the preconfirmatory rights of an *electus*, and similarly, despite some apparent contradictions in his theory, Laurentius Hispanus was anxious to defend the *electus*'s rights.[3]

---

[2] *Notabilia Nota per exteriora deprehendi* on *Comp.I* 1.4.18: "Nota per confirmationem ius administrandi acquisitum" (BN 14320 fol.127ra).

[3] Johannes Teutonicus, *Summula* on *Comp.III* 5.1.3 v. *et deicit etiam ab obtento*: "§ Ergo videtur quod per solam electionem nullum ius acquiritur . . ." (Gillmann, *AKKR* 113 [1933] 480 n.2). Laurentius Hispanus, *Apparatus* on D.63 c.15: ". . . nos dicimus quod postea [electio] mutari non potest, acquiritur igitur electo ius aliquod ex sola electione . . ." (BN 15393 fol.49rb). Id., *Apparatus* on *Comp.III* 5.1.3 v. *set non deicit*: "§ Arg. nullum ius habere in re ante confirmatione, habet tam[en ius] petendi confirmati[onem] honeste . . ." (Gillmann, *op.cit.* 474 n.2). *Id.* on *Comp.III* 1.4.5 v. *nullum ius*: "§ Et ita per postulationem nullum ius acquiritur. . . ." Immo videtur nec etiam per electionem. . . . Nam licet non possint resilire, ei tamen propter hoc non est ius acquisitum. . . . Set satis potest dici, quod ius aliquod, per quod possit aliquid in ecclesia disponere, non est ei adquisitum ante confirmationem, nec per electionem nec per postulationem" (Gillmann, *op.cit.* 473 nn.1ff).

The Dissent of Master Huguccio

Another example: In one of the manuscripts of Ricardus Anglicus's *Generalia*, composed between 1191 and 1198, the English canonist seems to have formulated a simple postulate of law, without any modification: "Before his confirmation, an *electus* has no rights."[4] Because it is unqualified, this curt principle seems extraordinarily strong, even harsh; moreover, its position in a long series of legal generalities adds to its forcefulness.

However, this statement did not adequately represent the complexity of Richard's conception—in the more complete manuscripts of his *Generalia* and also in his *Apparatus* on the *Compilatio prima*, written between 1193 and 1198, Richard took a far less extreme stand.[5] Although he believed that an *electus* cannot administer before confirmation, he did not agree with the general proposition that an *electus* has "no rights" (*nullum ius*) before his confirmation, for there is surely a difference between an official who has no right to administer and one who has absolutely no rights at all. That is to say, Richard was concerned with certain other preconfirmatory rights of an *electus*, outside the realm of administration. For example, he regarded the completed elec-

4 *Generalia* on *Comp.I* 1.4.19: "Rubrica. Electum ante confirmationem nullum ius habere . . ." (Nuremberg Cent. V.95 fol.1rb); Kuttner, *Mélanges de Ghellinck* 779f.

5 *Apparatus* on *Comp.I* 1.4.19 v. *confirmatus*: "Arg. electum ante confirmationem nullum ius habere. . . ." Solutio: Ante confirmationem secundum quosdam nil iuris habet electus, post confirmationem habet ea que sunt iurisdictionis, non que sunt ordinis . . . , et secundum eos mutari potest electio quam illi concedunt quia hic non tantum electi et eligentium consensus expectatur set etiam confirmatoris. Ego dico quod [*scr.* qui] postquam eligentes [*scr.* eligentis] consentiunt in electum et ipse in eos, neutra pars penitere potest altera inuita . . . nec confirmator sine iusta causa negare potest confirmationem . . . , ante confirmationem tamen administrationem non habet . . ." (Clm 6352 fol.3va-b). A similar text can be found in a more complete version of Richard's *Generalia* (Bamberg Can. 45 fol.40rd). Cf. also his *Distinctiones decretorum* on D.63: "Electio an mutari possit, et quidem initiatur electio in deliberatione, perficitur in pronuntiatione, consumatur in confirmatione. In primo casu tamen mutari potest . . . , aliter autem nequaquam nisi accusatione proposita et ordine iudiciario habito . . ." (Zwettl 162 fol.107v). Also, *id.* on D.63: "Quid potestatis consequatur electus, et quidem cum electionem de se factam approbat ecclesie sponsus efficitur per mutuum consensum, et electoribus cessantibus ipse confirmationem petere potest . . . , nondum autem confirmatus non habet temporalium uel spiritualium amministrationem . . ." (Zwettl 162 fol.107v).

135

tion, which presupposed the mutual consent of electors and *electus*, as binding on both parties. Moreover, by emphasizing that "without just cause" the confirmation cannot be withheld from the *electus*, Richard limited the hierarchical superior's competence of judgment and freedom of action— an important safeguard for the *electus*. In this way he protected the *electus* against arbitary decisions by the electors or by the ecclesiastical superior, and under normal circumstances his *electus* should automatically receive the confirmation and, with it, the right to administer.

Bernard of Pavia finished his electoral treatise before 1179, more than a decade before master Huguccio stopped work on his *Summa*, and as we have seen, in some respects Bernard's conception of election foreshadowed Huguccio's. But shortly after the Pisan canonist laid down his pen, Bernard wrote a *Summa* on his own collection of decretals, the *Compilatio prima*—which affords us a perfect opportunity to measure the diffusion of Huguccio's theory. Even in his electoral treatise, that is to say, even without the imposing authority of Huguccio's *Summa*, Bernard had taken a moderate position, in which he defended the rights of an *electus*. It is not surprising, therefore, that in his *Summa decretalium* Bernard appropriated the new notion of ecclesiastical elections: through "mutual consent" the *electus* is married to his church, and he can immediately demand the confirmation of his election.[6]

The *electus*'s rights were emphasized also by Richard's

[6] *Summa decretalium* 1.4.5, ed. Laspeyres 8: "Hanc autem potestatem habet electus, quia, dum approbat de se factam electionem, ecclesiae sponsus efficitur propter mutuum consensum, unde electoribus cessantibus ipse potest petere confirmationem, . . . nondum vero confirmatus non habet temporalium vel spiritualium administrationem . . . , sed post confirmationem habet utramque. . . ." Around 1215, this statement was appropriated by Damasus, *Summa titulorum* on *Comp.I-III*, De electione et electi potestate (BN 14320 fol.152). See also Bernard, *op.cit.* 1.4.4, ed. Laspeyres 7f: "Nunc videamus, an electio facta mutari possit, ad quod dicendum, quod electio initiatur in deliberatione, perficitur in pronunciatione, consummatur in confirmatione. Initiata mutari potest, perfecta non potest . . . nisi sit non canonica . . . , consummata nec mutari nec cassari potest, nisi accusatione proposita et ordine iudiciario habito. . . ."

The Dissent of Master Huguccio

compatriot, the distinguished canonist Alanus Anglicus, who later became regent master at Bologna.[7] In his *Apparatus* on the *Compilatio prima*, composed between 1201 and 1210, Alanus followed Richard's theory and, ultimately, the electoral treatise by Bernard of Pavia: solely through his election, an *electus* does obtain a certain right, for

> From that right he can demand confirmation and thus, in consequence, the episcopate and the power of administering. . . . Once received, therefore, the confirmation bestows on him, so to speak, the possession of the ecclesiastical property. . . . On the other hand, from his election he cannot demand the church's separate pieces of property, since it is not yet certain that he is the prelate of the church. . . .[8]

Alanus was fully familiar with Huguccio's electoral doctrine, for in both versions of his *Apparatus* on the *Decretum*, he summarized the Pisan canonist's theory with crystalline clarity.[9] Around 1202, when he revised and enlarged this

[7] On Alanus, see above, Ch.Va n.40.

[8] Alanus, *Apparatus* on *Comp.I* 1.4.18 v. *non habeat facultatem*: "§ Per electionem tamen ius est sibi acquisitum in ipso episcopatu. . . . Et ex illo iure potest petere confirmationem et ita per consequens episcopatum et administrandi potestatem. . . . Confirmatio igitur habita tribuit ei quasi possessionem rerum ecclesiasticarum, si ab ecclesia possideantur, vel ius petendi, si non possideantur. Et hec vera sunt, si alius non sit in possessione, qui contendat se canonice institutum, quoniam si alius faciat de institutione controversiam, non debet alius confirmari, . . . et si confirmatus fuerit, quid faciat interim confirmatio, non video, cum prius habuerit ius petendi episcopatum ex electione sicut modo. Singulas autem res ecclesie petere non potest, cum nondum sit certum eum esse prelatum ecclesie . . ." (Gillmann, *AKKR* 113 [1933] 469 n.3).

[9] *Apparatus Ius naturale* on D.63 c.10 v. *subscripta*: "§ Arg. electionem ante subscriptionem non tenere, et clericos alium eligere posse, et electo nullum ius acquisitum esse. . . . Illud certum est, quod electus amministrationem rerum ecclesie habet post confirmationem et non ante. . . . Set et ipsa confirmatio iuris prius competentis uidetur firmatio, et ita ante confirmationem uidetur aliquod ius acquisitum electo, et secundum Vg(uccionem) ex electione et electi consensu legitimo, idest de licentia sui prelati adhibito, si clericus est alterius ecclesie, ius ei est acquisitum, et quia matrimonium inter episcopum et ecclesiam est contractum, cuius iuris executionem in confirmatione consequitur, et sicut principes imperatorem dicuntur facere, et ita clerici prelatum electione. . . . Vnde post talem mutuum consensum uota sua mutare non possunt, ante autem possunt. Alii dicunt quod siue electus consensit siue non, usque ad subscriptionem possunt electionem

Apparatus, Alanus was willing to accept any one of several solutions to the problem of an *electus*'s rights—including Huguccio's compromise. Thus Alanus noted that "confirmation is the strengthening (*firmatio*) of a right previously belonging" to the prelate-elect. Further, he restated Huguccio's view that "after such mutual consent" the votes can no longer be changed, but Alanus then added:

> Some say that whether the prelate-elect has consented or not, [the electors] can revoke the election until the *subscriptio* . . . , others that [it can be revoked] until the confirmation.

With regard to the *electus*'s and the electors' rights, however, Alanus's preference differed strikingly from the theory formulated by Huguccio, who had observed that "in some places" custom guarantees administrative rights to the *electus* even before confirmation. Still, in this respect, master Huguccio had rejected custom as a criterion.[10] But for Alanus, local custom was precisely the touchstone:

> I have recourse first to the custom of a place, and I comply with what is practiced concerning this matter in that place according to custom.

Yet custom might give no guidance, and in this event, Alanus typically recommended referring the matter "to the decision of a judge" (*arbitrio cognoscentis*), who "when he has weighed the circumstances" of the particular case, would choose "among the aforementioned opinions." Or, as a further

---

reuocare ut hic, alii quod usque ad confirmationem. . . . Ego nullam istarum opinionum pro iure recipio, set primo ad loci consuetudinem recurro, et hoc quod circa hanc materiam ex consuetudine obtinet in illo loco obseruo. Si autem consuetudo nichil de hoc habeat, arbitrio de hoc cognoscentis committo, ut inter predictas opiniones quam imitetur ex bono et equo circumstantiis perpensis consideret, uel si placet, scilicet, quod supra dixit Vg(uccio) teneat, eius enim opinionem uidetur Innocentius approbare . . ." (BN 15393 fol.49ra-b). The shorter and earlier version of *App. Ius nat.* ad loc. reproduces Huguccio's views without any of the discursive additions given above (cf. BN 3909 fol.12va). Cf. below, Ch.Vc n.1.

10 Above, Ch.VA n.23.

alternative, Alanus suggested following the pope's preference. Because Alanus primarily favored custom, however, it is tempting to believe that even during the early thirteenth century and even in the law of the Church, his respect for customary law was already characteristically English. Indeed, like Alanus, Ricardus Anglicus allowed a considerable weight to customary law, and he remarked that in England the force of custom is decisive.[11]

Huguccio's two main contributions to electoral theory—the clear distinction between a right and the exercise of the right (*ius* and *executio*), and the metaphor of "mutual consent" as a "spiritual marriage"—remained current throughout the thirteenth century. The anonymous author of the French *Apparatus Ecce uicit leo* (1202-10) asserted that through his election an *electus* has rights—for the electors cannot reverse their decision—but he gains the power to use those rights (*iuris executio*) only through his confirmation.[12] The decretalist Vincentius Hispanus heavily stressed the rights obtained from election: even though the electors merely go through the forms of election without really giving their consent, or even if they should change their minds after

---

[11] Ricardus, *Apparatus* on *Comp.I* 2.17.3 v. *deductis expensis*: ". . . Quod autem de decimis dicitur, plus consuetudine quam ratione apud anglicos obtinet" (Gillmann, *AKKR* 107 [1927] 636). *Id.* on *Comp.I* 3.26.4 v. *diminutione*: ". . . non tamen in anglia, quia longissimo tempore contraria inolevit consuetudo . . ." (Gillmann, *op.cit.* 636f). A study of decretistic and early decretalistic conceptions of *consuetudo* would be welcome. In fact, Innocent III took over a Romanistic notion of "custom" (*X* 1.4.8): ". . . contra consuetudinem . . . quae optima est legum interpres. . . ." Cf. *Dig.* 1.3.37: "optima enim est legum interpres consuetudo." Innocent, however, often denounced existing customs as abuses. Cf. *X* 1.4.7 ("haec non tam consuetudo, quam corruptela merito sit censenda") and *X* 1.8.5 ("talis consuetudo dicenda sit potius corruptela").

[12] *Apparatus Ecce uicit leo* on D.23 c.1 v. *sicut uere papa auctoritatem* etc.: "Istud 'sicut' non est nota similitudinis set expressum ueritatis . . . et est arg. quod ex sola electione adquiritur ius electo, et hoc uerum est . . . de papa et speciale, quia non habet superiorem, . . . qui statim post electionem potest omnia facere, que pertinent ad iurisdictionem: episcopos deponere . . . set non que ad ordinem, unde consecrare non potest, nam [*scr.* num] qui ordinem non habet dare ordinem non potest. . . . In aliis prelatis est recte, quod ex electione ius eis adquiritur et quod non possunt ab eligentibus reprobari, . . . non tamen habent iuris executionem donec post confirmationem . . ." (Laon 371*bis* fol.7vb).

the election, nonetheless the *electus* becomes a *prelatus* and the "spiritual marriage" is valid.[13] In the same vein, Tancred remarked that even against the opposition of those who have elected him, an *electus* has the right to demand confirmation.[14] In his *Glossa ordinaria* on the *Decretum* (1215-17), Johannes Teutonicus took over both elements of the Huguccian doctrine. After briefly mentioning the rights which derive from "consent," Johannes explained:

> If you ask, "What rights are acquired by an *electus* through his election?", I say that he acquires the right of prelature and the right of administering but not the exercise of prelature or of administration. For no new rights are acquired through confirmation, but only the exercise of those rights . . . , for election creates the emperor. . . .[15]

[13] Vincentius, *Apparatus* on *Comp.III* 1.4.4 v. *diffidere:* ". . . Ubi autem ius est acquisitum alicui ut in electione, sive eligatur in concordia sive non, non possunt eligentes variare, etiam si diffidant de iure suo . . ." (Gillmann, *AKKR* 113 [1933] 478 n.1). *Id.* on *Comp.III* 1.6.6 v. *nequiverint:* ". . . Set aliud in postulatione, per quam non acquiritur ius postulato, aliud in electo" (Gillmann, *op.cit.* 476 n.1). *Id.* on *Comp.III* 1.6.6 v. *volente:* "Id est, consentiente. Non enim sufficit sola voluntas, ubi facto opus est. . . . Set pone, quod eo consentiente ipsi dissentiunt. Dixit pe(trus) apulus: Opus est, ut aliquo tempore mutuus consensus concurrat, qui solus facit matrimonium. . . . Unde in eo casu non esset electio confirmanda . . . set superior ex offitio suo potest conpellere eos consentire, ne illuderetur is, cui esset electio presentanda . . . et si alium eligerent pendente coactione, teneret electio et eligentes essent graviter puniendi. Ego credo contrarium. Immo iste est electus, confirmabitur et consecrabitur et conpellentur eligentes istum recipere et erit prelatus, licet eis displiceat. Et aliud est in carnali matrimonio, ubi nunquam erit matrimonium, nisi consensus intervenerit, et si cum alio contraheret, teneret matrimonium carnale, licet putetur. Secus ubi aliqui dicunt: Nos eligimus talem, licet in veritate non consentiant nec velint eum, efficitur prelatus et est ibi matrimonium spirituale" (Gillmann, *op.cit.* 478 n.3).

[14] *Gl.ord.* on *Comp.I* 1.4.18 v. *non habeat facultatem:* "§ Facultatem habet petendi confirmationem contradicentibus electoribus . . ." (Gillmann, *AKKR* 113 [1933] 481 n.5). Id., *Gl.ord.* on *Comp.III* 1.6.5 v. *nominatione:* ". . . Cum enim per nominationem ius non acquiratur nominato, recedi ab ea potest. . . . Et ideo expone: § id est vocatione, quia ex quo electus et vocatus est quis, ius acquisitum est illi" (Gillmann, *op.cit.* 483 n.1). Tancred's *Gl.ord.* on *Comp.I* was written between 1210 and 1215, his *Gl.ord.* on *Comp.III* after 1220.

[15] Johannes Teutonicus, *Gl.ord.* on D.63 c.10 v. *relatio:* "Ex hoc loco quidam dixerunt, quod electio posset variari usque ad subscriptionem, sed post, non. . . . Alii dicunt usque ad confirmationem esse ambulatoriam voluntatem eligentium . . . unde et priora stipendia retinet usque ad con-

The Dissent of Master Huguccio

To be sure, upon occasion Johannes might admit that an unconfirmed *electus* has "an extremely slender right" (*tenuissimum ius*)—but the right existed. And in the same tradition, a few years later Raymond of Peñafort asserted that the *electus*'s consent assures to him the immediate right to demand his confirmation and consecration.[16] Even as late as 1300, Huguccio's system still commanded adherents. Because of the "spiritual marriage" resulting from "mutual consent,"

firmationem . . . nec cogitur inscribere, qui excipit contra electum non confirmatum, quia non deiicitur ab obtento sed ab obtinendo. . . . Item qui ante confirmationem non renuntiat electus episcopatui, cum adhuc nihil iuris sit consecutus. . . . Sed tu dicas, quod per consensum eligentium ius est acquisitum electo, dum tamen ipse consentiat, vel consentire velit. . . . Si quaeras, quale ius acquiritur electo per electionem, dico quod ius praelaturae et ius administrandi sed non exercitium praelaturae vel administrationis, per confirmationem enim nihil iuris novi acquiritur sed tantum exercitium . . . electio enim facit imperatorem. . . . Item subscriptio non est de electione sed de solemnitate. . . ." Id., *Summula* on *Comp.III* 1.6.6 v. *etiam subscriptam*: ". . . Ego dico per solam electionem esse acquisitum ius prelature sive alterius rei, licet non habeat exercitium illius. Nam sola electio facit imperatorem. . . . Unde licet electio non sit publicata, set singuli sua vota expresserint, non possunt revocare consensum tanquam rem non integram. . . . Nam et consensum minus legittimum non possunt revocare . . . quia nemo conscilium [!] potest mutare in alterius iniuriam . . ." (Gillmann, *AKKR* 113 (1933) 480 no.2). Cf. also *id.* on *Comp.III* 1.5.2 v. *et electus confirmatus*: "§ Ergo ante confirmationem potest. Quod verum est, cum adhuc tenuissimum ius habet . . ." (Gillmann, *op.cit.* 481 n.1).

16 Raymond of Peñafort, *Summa iuris* 33, ed. José Rius Serra, *Opera omnia* I (Barcelona 1945) 123ff: ". . . Consequitur electus ex electione hoc quia dum approbat electionem de se factam contrahitur matrimonium spirituale inter ipsum et ecclesiam per mutuum consensum eligentium et electi. . . . Unde electoribus cessantibus ipse potest petere confirmationem et consecrationem. . . . Non tamen habet administrationem spiritualium vel temporalium ante confirmationem . . . nisi sit in partibus valde remotis . . . vel nisi sit electus in papam, qui eligendo confirmatur et confirmando eligitur. . . . Sed post confirmationem consequitur administrationem tam temporalium quam spiritualium . . . adeo quod inter confirmationem et missionem in possessionem non sit gradus, hoc est dicere si post confirmationem appellaretur, non ideo suspenderetur missio in possessionem, licet alias, scilicet, quando post sententiam appellatur, suspendatur executio. . . . Solet queri utrum decretum sit de substantia electionis ita quod non valeat electio sine ipso . . . sed dic cum Johanne quod licet in electione requiratur decretum cum subscriptionibus canonicorum, tamen electio sine ipso pro facta tenet. . . ." This work was probably left unfinished in 1222; on the edition, see Stephan Kuttner, "The Barcelona Edition of St. Raymond's First Treatise on Canon Law," *Seminar* [= Annual Extraordinary Number of *The Jurist*] 8 (1950) 52-67. In part, Huguccio's influence came through Bernard of Pavia, perhaps directly, or perhaps indirectly via a later decretalistic *summa*; cf. above, n.6.

> The confirming official is not bestowing a right but rather is approving a right already acquired. . . . Confirmation does not bestow the right of office or of administering, but the exercise of administration. . . .[17]

One could surely find many more texts to illustrate the spread of Huguccio's electoral doctrine, but it is obvious enough that his ideas exerted an enormous influence, both directly and indirectly.

One of the more important effects of the Huguccian tradition was the attempt to define the specific right, the *ius*, which an *electus* enjoyed, for from this speculation the canonists created a new duality: the *ius ad rem petendam* and the *ius in re*.[18] They can be only roughly translated—the *ius ad rem petendam* is a "claim upon something sought," and the *ius in re* might be rendered as a "right over something." The first is potential and suspended, the second actual and effective. These expressions played a significant role in the legal thought of the Late Middle Ages, and indeed, far more than mere technical terms, they were major concepts for the canonists, Romanists, and feudal lawyers of that period. The *ius ad rem* corresponds approximately to Bernard of Pavia's *aliquid iuris* and to Huguccio's *ius administrandi*, while the *ius in re* is equivalent to Bernard's *potestas exequendi* and to Huguccio's *executio iuris*.[19] In fact, the distinction between the parts of this duality may be traced directly back to the electoral theories developed by Bernard and Huguccio. However, for the first formulation of this new juristic duality, one must turn to the *Summa Animal est substantia*, one of the last productions of the French school, written between

[17] *Responsa doctorum Tholosanorum* q.45 ed. E. M. Meijers (Haarlem 1938) 106.

[18] On this duality, see Hinschius, *KR* II 652f; Gross, *Recht an der Pfründe* passim; Gillmann, *AKKR* 113 (1933) 463-85 (with further literature cited on pp.463-66), and on analogues in 13th-century feudal and Roman law, E. M. Meijers, *Études d'histoire du droit* IV (Leiden 1966) 175-89.

[19] Above, Ch.IVA nn.23-24; Ch.VA n.24.

1206 and 1210.[20] The anonymous author created the new terms as by-products of his theorizing on the rights of an *electus*: through election, the *electus* has the *ius ad rem petendam*, that is, a claim upon confirmation and the right to administer, and from that moment the electors are no longer free to change their minds. Through confirmation, the *electus* receives the *ius in re*, the full right to administer with all jurisdictional powers.[21]

From Bernard of Pavia to Tancred, most of the canonists who discussed electoral theory were conscious of an intimate connection between an *electus*'s rights and the prohibitions against the electors' changing their decision, for as soon as the *electus* has obtained something of his right to administer, the electors can no longer revoke it.[22] According to Bernard

20 The *Summa Animal est substantia* was formerly known as the *Summa Bambergensis*. Gillmann has found the term *ius in re* during the period 1210-15 (*op.cit.* 474 nn.2f; above, n.3). The coining of the term *ius ad rem petendam*, however, was ascribed by Gross to Innocent IV in the mid-13th century (*op.cit.* 166ff, 288ff); according to Gillmann, this term was formulated by Tancred soon after 1220 (*op.cit.* 483f). Hence, by tentatively assigning to the *Summa Animal est substantia* (1206-10) the authorship of this expression, one pushes the origin of the *ius ad rem* more than ten years back.

21 *Summa Animal est substantia* on D.23 c.1 v. *sicut*: "Illud est speciale in summo pontifice, quod ex ipsa electione confirmatur et statim habet potestatem et ius in omnibus illis que sunt iurisdictionis, que autem sunt consecrationis non habet antequam sit consecratus. Vnde antequam sit consecratus non potest ordinem conferre. . . . Alii autem episcopi nullam habent administrationem nec aliquod ius in re donec confirmati fuerint, ex electione enim nullum consequuntur ius in re . . . tamen consequuntur ius ad rem petendam. Vnde illi qui eligerunt eum non possunt ab eius electione resilire nec eum accusare nisi ex noua causa emergente. . . . Ille qui eligit facit testimonium pro electo, set quando confirmatur consequitur ius in re et consequitur ea que sunt iurisdictionis, sicut et papa, unde statim tenetur administrare circa utilitatem ecclesie, sicut est de tutore . . . ; ea autem que sunt ordinis siue consecrationis non adquiruntur ante consecrationem, set tantum per alium potest ea explere. Vnde potest mandare alium episcopum ut faciat ordines in suo episcopatu" (Bamberg Can. 42 fol.106va-b).

22 Typical of the negative position, however, is the *argumentum* extracted by Gilbertus Anglicus, *Apparatus* on *Cum terra* (= *Comp.II* 1.3.6) in his *Collectio decretalium* v. *tamdiu electores*: "Arg. quod voluntas eligentium usque ad confirmationem sit ambulatoria et quod electione ius non acquiritur electo . . ." (Gillmann, *AKKR* 113 [1933] 472 n.1). An even earlier exponent of this view was the author of the *Summa Reginensis* on D.61 c.13 v. *liberum de eo*: ". . . ar. ad questionem, utrum etiam postquam unanimiter elegerint possunt tamen ante confirmationem tam electionem

of Pavia and Alanus Anglicus, however, through electoral confirmation a bishop-elect acquires absolute security in the tenure of office, since after the confirmation he can be removed from office only by the same legal proceedings which would be required to deprive a fully consecrated bishop of his dignity.[23] Equally important was the belief shared by most of these canonists, that from the moment of his election the *electus* has a legitimate claim upon almost automatic confirmation. Indeed, there existed in that period the widespread conviction that an "uncontested and canonical election" (*electio concors et canonica*) should be immediately confirmed.[24] Moreover, if the competent superior (usually the metropolitan) refused to confirm such an election, the cathedral chapter might request the pope to confirm it.[25]

3. Innocent III and Master Huguccio

The major reason for the enormous success of the Huguccian formula was its adoption by Huguccio's greatest student, Lothar of Segni, who in 1198 ascended the throne of Peter as pope Innocent III. Indeed, weighing the different conceptions of an *electus*'s rights, Alanus Anglicus preferred local

---

mutare [quam] voluntatem, et ar. quod sic et ita credo, quia nondum est pastor eorum" (Stickler, *Salesianum* 14 [1952] 498).

[23] Alanus, *Apparatus* on *Comp.I* 1.4.18 v. *confirmata*: "Confirmatio rerum ecclesiasticarum administrationem tribuit . . . et facit quod sine speciali licentia pape ecclesiam non potest dimittere electus . . . facit etiam quod electus ab episcopatu non repellitur nisi sollempni accusatione instituta sicut contra episcopum . . ." (Clm 3879 fol.4ra). On Bernard of Pavia, cf. above, n.6. Innocent III held the same opinion.

[24] Innocent III, *X* 1.6.20 (1200): ". . . preter opinionem omnium qui nichil obstare credebant quin statim concors et canonica deberet electio confirmare . . ." (= C. R. Cheney and W. H. Semple, eds., *Selected Letters of Pope Innocent III concerning England* [London 1953] 16 no.6). The term *electio concors* is commonly—and incorrectly—taken to mean a "unanimous" rather than an "uncontested election." On *electio concors*, see Hinschius, *KR* II 671 n.6; one should note that contemporaries were not always careful in the use of this term. It is perhaps significant that after this decretal had appeared intact in Gilbertus Anglicus's *Collectio* and in *Comp.III*, the recension for the *Liber extra* omitted this passage on the obligation of immediate confirmation.

[25] Cheney and Semple, *op.cit.* 17 no.6; Innocent III, *Reg.* 9.163, *PL* 215 990.

custom as the chief criterion, but he remarked that perhaps Huguccio's doctrine should be accepted, "for Innocent seems to approve of his opinion."[1] Within the first three years of his pontificate, in three different decretals and in an important sermon, the great canonist-pope broadcast Huguccio's electoral theory—ecclesiastical election as a "spiritual marriage" based upon "mutual consent"—to a new and wider public, as well as to the limited classroom audience reached by the learned works of canonistic scholarship. In 1200 Innocent sent instructions to the archbishop of Genoa and to two other bishops concerning a disputed election:

> . . . Since it is established that the election of this provost has been celebrated and also undersigned by the greater and wiser part of the chapter, if the provost has consented to his election, so that by mutual consent of the electors and *electus* a conjugal bond, as it were, has been spiritually contracted, you should confirm his election. . . . Even if the provost has not yet consented to his own election, if he nevertheless wants to consent . . . , you should confirm his election.[2]

From this, one might assume that Innocent followed his teacher in every aspect of electoral theory. Especially when

[1] *Apparatus Ius naturale* on D.63 c.10 v. *subscripta*: ". . . quod . . . dixit Vg(uccio) teneat, eius enim opinionem uidetur Innocentius approbare . . ." (BN 15393 fol.49rb; above, Ch.Vʙ n.9).

[2] *X* 1.6.21: ". . . Discretioni vestrae . . . mandamus, quatenus, cum constet, electionem de praeposito memorato a maiori et saniori parte capituli celebratam etiam et subscriptam, si dictus praepositus eidem electioni consenserit, ut per mutuum consensum eligentium et electi quasi coniugale vinculum spiritualiter sit contractum . . . , vos . . . electionem . . . confirmetis ipsius . . . , etiamsi a partibus in eum fuerit compromissum, cum electores a tali electione sic resilire nequiverint. . . . Etiamsi dictus praepositus nondum electioni de se factae consenserit, eo tamen consentire volente . . . , vos electionem ipsius nihilominus confirmetis." For another example of Innocent's stress on the constitutive character of the bishop-elect's consent, cf. *X* 1.6.33 (1208). In general, Innocent used Huguccio's metaphor as a new language in which to describe election: if "mutual consent" created a *matrimonium spirituale* between electors and *electus*, the election of a fully consecrated bishop (who was, of course, already "married") would logically create between them a *spirituale adulterium*—as Innocent said when the bishop of Worms was elected to the archbishopric of Mainz (*X* 1.6.23).

the pope asserted that the electors may not reverse their decision, he seems concerned to protect the *electus*'s rights as fully as possible.[3] Still, although the main outlines of the original doctrine are present, in a decretal issued on 21 January 1199, Innocent had already introduced some subtle and significant changes into the various elements of Huguccio's theory:

> . . . It should not be doubted that after canonical election and confirmation, there is contracted between the persons of the electors and the *electus* a spiritual marriage, to which the episcopal dignity [that is, the episcopal consecration] actually adds nothing. . . . For this reason, since the bond between a bishop and his church is no greater than that of an *electus*, especially when he has been confirmed, the same law—indeed, absolutely the same, and no different— prevails in both cases. . . .[4]

[3] In general, three modes of election were permissible: *per scrutinium*, *per compromissum*, and *per inspirationem*. See *Conc. Lat. IV* c.24 (*X* 1.6.42) and Despraires, *L'élection des évêques* 23ff. Innocent was referring specifically to the second method, *electio per compromissum*, according to which "the power of electing is entrusted to some suitable men." The *compromissarii* were obliged to elect the one on whom the *maior et sanior pars* was agreed; *X* 1.6.32 (1208) and *VI* 1.6.29. There is no reason to believe that Innocent regarded the other two forms of election as more easily revocable.

[4] *X* 1.7.2: ". . . Sicut enim episcopus consecratus sine licentia Romani pontificis suam non debet ecclesiam derelinquere, sic et electus et confirmatus praeter eius assensum suam deserere nequit ecclesiam, cui est matrimonialiter alligatus, cum non debeat in dubium revocari, quin post electionem et confirmationem canonicam inter personas eligentium et electi coniugium sit spirituale contractum, cui profecto episcopalis dignitas nihil addit. . . . Unde, cum non sit maius vinculum episcopi ad ecclesiam, quam electi, maxime cum fuerit confirmatus, immo idem penitus, et non aliud, idem iuris obtinet in utroque. Sicut ergo episcoporum translatio, vel etiam depositio et cessio, sic et electorum post confirmationem spiritualis ratione coniugii soli est Romano pontifici reservata. Licet usque ad tempora ista quod cautum fuerat de episcopis expressum non fuerat de electis, propter expressam tamen similitudinem, vel identitatem potius, nemini poterat videri dubium subtiliter intuenti, cum de similibus idem iudicium sit habendum." Cf. Innocent IV, *Apparatus* on *X* 1.7.2 v. post electionem et confirmationem canonicam: "post consensum autem suum ante confirmationem posset, cum habeat tenue ius. . . ." The phrase *tenue ius* is taken from Johannes Teutonicus (above, Ch.V B n.15). See also Innocent III, *X* 1.7.4 (1200): ". . . Sicut legitimi matrimonii vinculum, quod est inter virum et uxorem, homo dissolvere nequit . . . sic et spirituale foedus coniugii, quod

Innocent was aware that in the canonical teaching of an earlier period the prescriptions designed for a consecrated bishop did not make adequate provision for the situation of an *electus*. However, "because of the clear similarity, or rather, identity" of the two, he believed that the same principles are applicable to both. In the manner of Huguccio, Innocent could remark that the legal status of bishop and *electus* are equal, that the "bond" of "spiritual marriage" between a bishop and his church is the same as that between a church and an *electus*—but, Innocent hastened to add, "especially when the *electus* has been confirmed."

On the first anniversary of his own consecration as bishop of Rome (that is, on 22 February 1199), Innocent devoted a sermon to the "spiritual marriage" between a bishop and his church. Regarding his consecration as "the day on which this spiritual marriage was consummated," he pointed out the analogy between a "carnal" and a "spiritual marriage":

> A carnal marriage . . . between a man and woman is begun in betrothal, ratified in consent, consummated in sexual intercourse. Thus also a spiritual marriage . . . between a bishop and his church is said to begin in election, to be ratified in confirmation, to be consummated in consecration.[5]

From the decretistic tradition, Innocent has derived the three

---

est inter episcopum et eius ecclesiam, quod in electione initiatum, ratum in confirmatione, et in consecratione intelligitur consummatum, sine illius auctoritate solvi non potest, qui successor est Petri et vicarius Iesu Christi. . . ."

[5] Innocent III, *Sermones de diversis* 3, *PL* 217 663: "Solet dici carnale coniugium, quod est inter virum et feminam, initiatum, ratum, et consummatum. Initiatum in desponsatione, ratum in consensu, consummatum in copula. Sic et spirituale coniugium, quod est inter episcopum et ecclesiam, initiatum dicitur in electione, ratum in confirmatione, consummatum in consecratione. . . ." *PL* 217 665: ". . . solus consensus inter legitimas personas efficit matrimonium. . . ." Cf. Innocent IV, *Apparatus* on *X* 1.7.2: "*contractum*, consummata tamen consecratione . . . *nihil*, quoad veritatem matrimonii," and on *X* 1.7.4: ". . . per consensum enim eligentium et electi et confirmantis, quoad substantiam, plenum est matrimonium . . . nihil enim adiicit consecratio. . . ."

stages in the accession of a bishop, "begun–ratified–consummated" (*initiatum–ratum–consummatum*), but whereas Bernard of Pavia and Huguccio considered the confirmation (or administration) as the "consummation" of the "spiritual marriage,"[6] Innocent has shifted the emphasis from confirmation to consecration as the fulfillment of the "spiritual marriage." In his sermon Innocent then drew the same distinction which he had already used in his decretal a month earlier:

> Because of the mutual consent of the electors and the *electus*, the *electus* becomes their bridegroom—especially when the marriage is confirmed.[7]

Caught between the Huguccian conception, which based the "spiritual marriage" solely on the "mutual consent," and the stricter tradition, which emphasized the role of electoral confirmation, Innocent split the theoretical hair even more finely:

> One can distinguish . . . between a bridegroom (*sponsus*) and a husband (*vir* or *coniunx*). . . . An *electus* is called a bridegroom before the confirmation—namely, before he knows [his bride], that is, before he administers. However, he is called a husband after the confirmation, and especially after the consecration, when at last he administers fully.[8]

Innocent was obviously uneasy and unsure in his attempt to define the dubious position of an unconfirmed *electus*. The result of this uneasiness is an ambiguity in the doctrines of the great canonist-pope, and a marked difference between his theories and his teacher's. It is apparent that Innocent

---

[6] Above, Ch.VB n.6, and Ch.VA n.27. Cf., however, the *Summa Elegantius in iure diuino*, which stated that the spiritual marriage "is consummated in consecration" (above, Ch.VA n.21).

[7] *PL* 217 666: ". . . propter mutuum consensum eligentium et electi, utique sponsus eorum efficitur, praesertim cum electio confirmatur. Sed antequam consecretur, nec nomen pontificis, officium vindicabit. . . ."

[8] *Ibid.*: ". . . Inter sponsum [*ed.* sponsam] autem et virum, et inter sponsum et coniugem distingui potest in spiritualibus: quod sponsus appellatur electus ante confirmationem, videlicet antequam cognoscat, id est antequam administret; vir autem appellatur post confirmationem, et maxime post consecrationem, cum iam plenarie administrat. . . ."

felt compelled to transform the Huguccian doctrine by assigning to electoral confirmation the effects which Huguccio had ascribed to "mutual consent": the "spiritual marriage" is contracted "after canonical election *and* confirmation." Contemporary canonists noticed this tension within Innocent's electoral theory, and some of them did not place him unqualifiedly in the train of Huguccio's followers.[9] In Innocent's terminology, after election an ecclesiastical office is still "something about to be possessed" (*obtinendum*), but from the moment of electoral confirmation it is already "something possessed" (*obtentum*).[10] After the confirmation an *electus* has the same status as a consecrated bishop, for then, like a full bishop, only with the permission of the Roman pontiff can he be transferred, deposed, or allowed to leave his church. Thus, while appropriating the language and the general scheme of his great teacher, Innocent applied Huguccio's concepts with far less concern for the preconfirmatory rights of an *electus*.

[9] Johannes Teutonicus, *Gl.ord.* on D.100 c.1 v. *viduatis*: ". . . post confirmationem electi iam est matrimonium inter eum et ecclesiam, De transla(tione) praela(torum) Inter corporalia. . . ." Also, Johannes Galensis, gl. on *Comp.III* 1.6.6 v. *quasi coniugale vinculum*: "§ Unde isti statim acquiritur ius . . . et no(ta) quod hic dicit 'quasi,' quia ratum matrimonium incipit esse in confirmatione, arg(umentum) . . . Inter corporalia . . ." (Gillmann, *AKKR* 113 [1933] 475 n.3). The decretal *Inter corporalia* (1199) is *X* 1.7.2 (above, n.4). In this regard, Johannes Galensis seems close to the doctrine of Huguccio, who said that the metropolitan confirms the *uinculum* created by the "mutual consent" (above, Ch.VA n.25); however, Huguccio stressed the "mutual consent," whereas the Welsh decretalist emphasized the confirmation.

[10] *X* 5.1.16 (1203): ". . . cum opponitur, ut quis a promotione officii vel beneficii excludatur, si ante confirmationem obiicitur, non cogitur quisquam inscribere, quia crimen, hoc modo probatum, impedit promovendum, sed non deiicit iam promotum. Post confirmationem vero, cum scilicet ordinandus fuerit aliquis aut etiam consecrandus, quia etiam ab obtinendo repellit, et deiicit ab obtento, ad extraordinariam quidem poenam secundum arbitrium iudicis discreti, citra vinculum tamen inscriptionis, est excipiens adstringendus, si defecerit in probando, pro eo, quod, crimine sic probato, perdit quod per electionem et confirmationem ei fuerat acquisitum: sed ob hoc prius habita non amittit. . . ."

CHAPTER VI

THREE EXCEPTIONS:

PAPA, METROPOLITANUS, EXEMPTUS

1. The Roman Pontiff-Elect

the mið-twelfth century was, of course, familiar with Nicholas II's papal election decrees of 1059 and 1060, and their presence in the *Decretum* guaranteed both their accessibility and their wide diffusion. For the generation following Gratian, however, historical events, rather than academic interest, assured the urgent importance of these two documents: in 1159 there was a double election to the papacy. Immediately, the issue was hotly debated. All documents relevant to papal elections were studied assiduously[1]—and of course the decree of 1059 was a prime authority. Indeed, soon after this disputed election, the decree of 1059 was cited extensively in a publicistic work inspired by the controversy.[2] In general, then, the double election of 1159 and the consequent schism furnished the historical context of later theories and legislation about the constitutional status of the Roman pontiff-elect.[3]

[1] As archbishop Theobald of Canterbury wrote to Henry II in 1160; W. J. Millor and H. E. Butler, eds., *The Letters of John of Salisbury* I (London 1955) 216 no.125.

[2] *Dialogus de pontificatu sanctae Romanae ecclesiae*, in *MGH LdL* III 534, 539 (on the *electus*'s right to administer immediately), 544. Perhaps attributable to Rahewin, this work was composed in 1162-63.

[3] In general, Paolo Brezzi, "Lo scisma inter regnum et sacerdotium al tempo di Federico Barbarossa," *Archivio della R. Deputazione romana di storia patria* 63 (1940) 1-98 and esp. 35ff; for a shorter account of the

The election decree of 1059 denounced any uncanonically elected Roman pontiff as the "destroyer of all Christendom," and it pronounced terrible judgments against him. But as the disputed election of 1159 clearly demonstrated, the decree of 1059 had failed to answer a key question: In case of a split among the electing cardinals, which is the true pontiff-elect, and which is the "destroyer"? In 1159 cardinal Roland Bandinelli had received the larger share of the votes, and had taken the name Alexander III. Still, to weigh votes, rather than merely to count them, was characteristic of this age, and one might have to determine the "greater and sounder part" (*maior et sanior pars*) of the electors.[4] Consequently, cardinal Octavian's minority of votes did not necessarily prejudice his position seriously,[5] and his supporters accepted him as pope Victor IV. Since both claimed to have been properly elected and enthroned, by what canonical criteria could one choose between them?

The schism of 1159 reveals the uncertainties in twelfth-century thought on the elevation of a pope. As the two rival parties formulated their official versions of the events, they touched upon some of the obscurities and the tensions within contemporary constitutional doctrine. According to the passionately partisan account given by Alexander himself, these uncertainties became manifest in a dramatic scene which occurred immediately after his election:

> Hereupon, Octavian burst forth in such audacity and insanity that, like a maniac, with his own hands he violently tore from our neck the mantle with which, according to

---

elections, see Pacaut, *Alexandre III* 102-05; I was unable to find a copy of the older work by H. Meyer, *Die Wahl Alexanders III. und Viktors IV.* (Göttingen 1876).

4 G. Barraclough, "The Making of a Bishop in the Middle Ages," *CHR* 19 (1933-34) 277f, and more recently, Leo Moulin, "Sanior et maior pars: Studio sull'evoluzione delle technice elettorale negli ordini religiosi dal VI al XIII secolo," *Studi politici* 6 (1959) 364-93.

5 The *maior et sanior pars* (or *sanior et melior pars*) were claimed for Victor; see Rahewin (?), *Dialogus*, in *MGH LdL* III 533, and Rahewin, *Gesta Friderici* 4.76, 80, 3rd ed. Waitz and Simson 321, 332.

The Bishop-Elect

the custom of the Church, Otto, the prior of the [cardinal-] deacons, had garbed us, . . . and he carried it away amid a tumultuous uproar. However, since some of the senators had watched this crime, one of them . . . snatched the mantle from the madman's hand. But with a roar he immediately turned his flaming eyes toward a certain chaplain of his, who had come instructed and prepared for this, crying out and signaling that he should quickly produce the mantle which he had craftily brought with him. When this had been brought without delay, the self-seeking Octavian . . . assumed the mantle at the hands of that same chaplain and of a certain cleric of his. . . .[6]

Alexander concluded his narrative by ridiculing Octavian for reversing the mantle as he put it on: an indication (in Alexander's view) of Octavian's crookedness. Of course, the events of 1159 did not represent the first appearance of the papal mantle in the ceremonial and symbolism of the Roman court. Already mentioned in the Donation of Constantine, a scarlet or purple mantle had been a prominent part of the papal costume since the mid-eleventh century, when the resurgent papacy began to assert its imperial character.[7] Customarily conferred right after the election, this garment of imperial purple was borne "as a sign of the *imperium*" uniquely inherent in the bishopric of Rome.[8] In the mid-

[6] Alexander related this story in an encyclical letter written soon after his election and preserved in two slightly variant versions. See Rahewin, *Gesta Friderici* 4.61, 3rd ed. 300f (to the bishop of Bologna); my translation is adapted from that by C. C. Mierow (*The Deeds of Frederick Barbarossa* [New York 1953] 291). Cf. *Ep.* 1, *PL* 200 70f (to the archbishop of Genoa). Retelling these events, Alexander's biographer followed the encyclical closely; Boso, *Vita Alexandri III*, ed. L. Duchesne, *Liber pontificalis* (3 vols. Paris 1886-1955) II 397f.

[7] On the mantle (*mantum, cappa, chlamys, pluviale*), see: Wasner, *Apollinaris* 8 (1935) 118-21, 279-81; H.-W. Klewitz, "Die Krönung des Papstes," *ZRG KA* 30 (1941) 120; Kantorowicz, *Laudes regiae* 138; Eduard Eichmann, *Weihe und Krönung des Papstes* (Munich 1951) 34; Ullmann, *Growth of Papal Government* 317f. The use of the mantle as an imperial and royal emblem need not concern us here.

[8] Dictatus of Avranches c.11: "Solus [papa] utitur rubra cappa in signum imperii vel martirii" (S. Löwenfeld, "Der *Dictatus papae* Gregors VII.," *NA* 16 [1891] 200).

twelfth century and perhaps even earlier, the prior of the cardinal-deacons performed the enmantling as an act of investiture, for when he bestowed the mantle upon the pontiff-elect, the prior solemnly announced:

> I invest you with the Roman papacy, so that you may preside over Rome and the world.[9]

The ring and the mitre were conferred immediately after this investiture.

Just as the purple mantle emphasized his imperial prerogatives, the mitre stood for the pope's episcopal status.[10] In the twelfth century, since mantle and mitre were the central symbols of the papal office, a pope could abdicate by laying them aside.[11] Indeed, in twelfth-century thought, the enmantling could completely overshadow the election as the crucial step in the promotion of a Roman pontiff,[12] the donning of the mantle was tantamount to the acceptance and assumption of the office,[13] and possession of the mantle could form part of the pontiff-elect's claim to his office.[14] It is scarcely surprising, therefore, that Victor IV and his supporters vehemently contradicted Alexander's report about the violent seizure of the papal mantle. For the judgment of these two sharply con-

---

[9] Gregory X, *Ordo romanus* 13 c.2, *PL* 78 1105: " 'Investio te de papatu Romano, ut praesis urbi et orbi.' " Also, *Ordo rom.* 14 c.10, *PL* 78 1126. Written in the earlier 14th century, *Ordo* 14 drew on a ceremonial composed around 1200, and preserves its usages with little alteration; see Michel Andrieu, "L'Ordinaire de la Chapelle Papale et le Cardinal Jacques Gaétani Stefaneschi," *Ephemerides liturgicae* 49 (1935) 230-60, and Kantorowicz, *op.cit.* 132. From the reference to the *dignitas papatus* in the anonymous *Dialogus* (below, n.21), it is evident that in the mid-twelfth century, similar wording was already in use.

[10] Kantorowicz, *op.cit.* 137f.

[11] Boso, *Vita Honorii II*, ed. Duchesne, *Lib. pont.* II 379; also, Klewitz, *op.cit.* 120.

[12] Pandulph, *Vita Honorii II*, ed. Duchesne, *Lib. pont.* II 327, where the enmantling of the antipope Celestine II is stressed but his election is not even mentioned.

[13] Id., *Vita Calixti II*, ed. Duchesne, *Lib. pont.* II 322: ". . . vix cappa rubea amiciri sustinuit donec nuncii redientes a Roma . . . electionem ipsam canonice iureque firmarent."

[14] For a description of the antipope Burdinus (Gregory VIII) as "electus et manto coopertus," see J. M. Watterich, *Pontificum Romanorum vitae* (2 vols. Leipzig 1862) II 108; Hinschius, *KR* I 262 n.3.

flicting accounts, it is significant that in the immediate aftermath of the election, Alexander's version was widely accepted, and the alleged dismantling was bitterly resented.[15] Undoubtedly, each party adapted its arguments to capitalize on the advantages of its position. Alexander's adherents could point to their imposing majority of votes.[16] The partisans of Victor IV, however, built their case mainly on his possession of the papal mantle and on their conception of its constitutional meaning. In 1160, convoked by Frederick Barbarossa and attended mainly by his loyal imperial prelates, the Council of Pavia explained the canonicity of Victor's accession to office.

> These are the points which were canonically proven in the Council of Pavia concerning the election of the lord pope Victor: At the request of the people and by the consent and desires of the clergy, the lord Octavian (and no one else) was solemnly enmantled by the cardinals in the church of St Peter at Rome. . . . He was installed on the throne of St Peter, the *Te Deum laudamus* was solemnly chanted for him, and the name Victor was given to him.[17]

Thus, for Victor's supporters, the elements in the elevation of a pope were: election, enmantling, enthronement, the singing of the *Te Deum*, and the adoption of the papal name. Yet the enmantling did not simply fill a place in the sequence of ceremonies which, taken together, effectively promote a

---

[15] Boso, *Vita Alexandri III*, ed. Duchesne, *Lib. pont.* II 398: ". . . commota est universa civitas. Clamabant pueri contra ipsum Ecclesie invasorem, dicentes: 'Maledicte, filius Maledicti, dismantacompagnum! Non eris papa! . . .'" The mob was punning on Octavian's family name, Maledetto; *dismantacompagnum* seems to mean "dismantler of his colleague" (Duchesne, *loc.cit.* nn.3f). Also (as some canons of St Peter's wrote to Barbarossa), when a deacon of the Curia defended Alexander's account, he was rebuked for this "falsehood" by Alexander himself; Rahewin, *Gesta Friderici* 4.76, 3rd ed. 322. Finally, the incident was mentioned in an anonymous verse dialogue written soon after 1159 (vv.31f; *MGH LdL* III 550). Note, moreover, Gerhoh of Reichersberg's effort to view both claims objectively (*De investigatione Antichristi* 1.53f, *MGH LdL* III 362f).

[16] For an analysis of the division, see Pacaut, *Alexandre III* 103-05.

[17] Rahewin, *op.cit.* 4.77, 3rd ed. 324; also *id.* 4.62, 80, 3rd ed. 306, 332.

Roman pontiff-elect to his new dignity. Rather, the enmantling performed a crucial function. According to the acts of the same Council, an inquiry was made on the day after the election:

> Coming to the lord chancellor [Roland] and to the cardinals who were with him, the rectors of the Roman clergy wanted to know if he had been enmantled, as some were saying. They found him neither enmantled nor altered by any sign of office, and . . . they learned from his own mouth . . . that he had never been enmantled, and that this was falsely attributed to him.[18]

Clearly, it was essential for Victor's adherents to deny that Alexander had lawfully assumed the mantle, since they considered the mantle the distinguishing mark of a true pontiff-elect. In this respect, the ceremonial enmantling might seem to have had only declarative significance.[19] It had, however, other dimensions. On the question of priority, for example, Victor's partisans claimed that he had received the mantle before Alexander,[20] and they asserted that he was thereby the first to hold "the office of papacy."[21] Moreover, the Council

[18] *Id.* 4.77, 3rd ed. 324 (adapted from Mierow trans. p.314); also, *id.* 4.76, 77, 3rd ed. 322, 326f.

[19] Such is the view of Wasner and Eichmann, but cf. the interpretations by Klewitz and Kantorowicz, who ascribe greater constitutional importance to this ceremony; see above, n.7.

[20] As Eberhard of Bamberg wrote to Eberhard of Salzburg: "domni Victoris inmantatio prior, illa posterior, quo solo Innocentius Anacleto prevaluit, cum Anacletus plures et maximae scientiae et auctoritatis haberet electores" (Rahewin, *op.cit.* 4.81, 3rd ed. 336). To the adherents of Victor IV in 1159, the double election of 1130 may have seemed an extremely promising precedent, since a minority of the cardinals had indeed voted for pope Innocent II in 1130. There is, however, no warrant for Eberhard of Bamberg's statement that the prior enmantling of pope Innocent was his sole advantage over Anacletus II. On the background, proceedings, and aftermath of the papal elections of 1130, the principal older accounts are: Engelbert Mühlbacher, *Die streitige Papstwahl des Jahres 1130* (Innsbruck 1876); Hans-Walter Klewitz, "Das Ende des Reformpapsttums," *DA* 3 (1939) esp. 371-87; P.F. Palumbo, *Lo scisma del MCXXX* (Rome 1942). These must now be supplemented by Franz-Josef Schmale, *Studien zum Schisma des Jahres 1130* (Cologne 1961).

[21] Rahewin (?), *Dialogus*, in *MGH LdL* III 530: ". . . dignitatem papa-

of Pavia maintained that Alexander had not only admitted his own lack of the mantle, but had given an explicit order to his supporters, "Go and obey him whom you see enmantled."[22] Indeed, when Dante wanted to identify one of the damned as a former Roman pontiff, the condemned soul merely had to say that he had been "vestito del gran manto" (*Inferno* canto 19).

Now to sum up the significance of the mantle in the schism of 1159: Despite their familiarity with the papal election decrees of 1059 and 1060, Victor and his adherents drew no sharp distinction between constitutive and declarative acts. They viewed the entire sequence of acts—election, enmantling, enthronement—as constitutive, but they stressed the enmantling, since the lawful possession of the mantle seemed the touchstone of any genuine pontiff-elect. Precisely because it furnished a visible sign indicating the properly elected pontiff, the enmantling was, for Victor's partisans, the decisive and effective act in the making of a pope.[23] In short, they regarded the enmantling as a uniquely important ceremony, both constitutive and declarative.

*

Though they did not contribute directly to the solution of the crisis which appeared in 1159, the decretists steadily elaborated the theory underlying papal election, and they

---

tus sive iuste sive iniuste prior visus est et animo et corpore possedisse. . . ." This statement appears in the author's introduction, rather than in the dialogue itself, and it therefore certainly expresses his own opinion. Cf. also *ibid.* 536f, 544.

22 Rahewin, *Gesta Friderici* 4.80, 3rd ed. 332: "Probatum est, quod . . . Rolandus . . . expresse confessus est se numquam fuisse inmantatum et expresse dixit: 'Ite et obedite ei, quem inmantatum esse videtis.' " Almost verbatim, *id.* 4.77, 3rd ed. 327.

23 The Council of Pavia gave the following account of the deliberations and actions undertaken by Alexander's supporters: " 'Quoniam modo sumus sine pastore et sine capite, faciamus nobis dominum,' et postea inmantaverunt eum [scil. Rolandum] et cantaverunt ei 'Te Deum laudamus' . . ." (*id.* 4.77, 3rd ed. 327). Alexander's backers were, of course, aware of the opposing party's emphasis on the mantle; see Boso, *Vita Alexandri III,* ed. Duchesne, *Lib. pont.* II 399, and the anonymous verse dialogue mentioned above, n.15 (vv.101f; *MGH LdL* III 551).

occasionally discussed the problem of a disputed election in the bishopric of Rome. As the decretists were aware, a double election within a simple bishopric should be settled by the metropolitan. Moreover, Nicholas II's decree of 1059 explicitly recognized the metropolitan's role in an episcopal election, and for a papal election, the decree asserted:

> Since the Apostolic See is superior to all churches in the whole world and therefore cannot have a metropolitan over itself, the cardinal-bishops certainly fulfill the office of the metropolitan.[24]

It is easy to discern, behind this metaphor, one of the ancient requirements for the accession of any bishop: the metropolitan's consent and, specifically, his participation in or approval of the bishop's consecration.[25] Of course, the metropolitan was the superior of his suffragan bishops, but clearly the cardinal-bishops could not be superior to the Roman pontiff in that way. In what sense, then, did the cardinal-bishops play the part of the metropolitan? To explain this paradox, master Rufinus noted that they are not superior to the pontiff-elect merely because they consecrate him. But perhaps, he rather lamely suggested, since the cardinal-bishops themselves—unlike the pontiff-elect—have received their episcopal consecration, they are "more consecrated" (*sacratiores*) and are therefore superior to him in that one respect, though not *simpliciter*.[26]

The analogy between cardinal-bishops and metropolitan provided no theoretical protection against the dangers of a double election to the papacy. Gratian was aware of this difficulty, but had no solution for it. In the *Decretum* he included

[24] D.23 c.1 §3: ". . . Quia sedes apostolica cunctis in orbe terrarum prefertur ecclesiis atque ideo super se metropolitanum habere non potest, cardinales episcopi proculdubio metropolitani uice funguntur, qui uidelicet electum antistitem ad apostolici culminis apicem prouehant."

[25] Within the election decree, a more apt analogy would have been the role played by the suffragan bishops in "confirming" the election of their metropolitan and in consecrating him. Below, Ch.VI B nn.42, 46.

[26] *Summa* on D.23 c.1 v. *Quia vero* etc. *metrop. vice fung.*, ed. Singer 49f.

a decree of the emperor Honorius, prescribing that when there are two claimants to the papal office, neither candidate is acceptable.[27] Rejecting this doctrine, however, Gratian denied its applicability if one of the two candidates has been canonically elected and enthroned.[28] Even more, since Gratian believed that no judge is competent to decide a contested papal election,[29] he left the question open, and the early decretists found no better answer. As Gratian clearly saw, the recognition of any competent judge would threaten the supremacy of the Roman pontiff within the Church's constitutional theory. For example, the *Summa Inperatorie maiestati* thought that a council may approve and confirm an ecclesiastical election,[30] and the early decretists could have applied this doctrine to disputed papal elections. In fact, during the schism between Alexander III and the antipope Victor IV, Victor's supporters regarded the judgment and the favorable decision by the Council of Pavia as the appropriate confirmation of his election.[31] This protoconciliar theory was, however, unlikely to gain many followers among the early decretists, most of whom believed that a pope can be judged only for heresy—if, indeed, he can be judged at all.[32] Nonetheless, some early students of the *Decretum*

[27] D.79 c.8.
[28] D.79 dict.p.c.8: "Hoc autem capitulum non de eo intelligendum est, qui uno per apostasiam ordinato a cardinalibus et religiosis clericis apostolicae sedi intronizatur, etiamsi ille apostaticus ita cathedram B.Petri violenter tenuerit, ut canonica electio intra urbem fieri non ualeat." Also, D.96 pr.: "Illud autem Honorii Augusti . . . nullius momenti esse probatur. . . ."
[29] C.3 q.1 dict.p.c.6: ". . . Sed hoc [cf. D.79 c.9] in eo tantum casu intelligitur, quo apostolica sedes per uiolentiam occupatur, quo casu iudex non inuenitur, cuius offitio ille apostaticus possit excludi. . . ."
[30] On D.62 pr. v. *breuiter monstratum* (above, Ch.IVA n.15).
[31] Rahewin, *Gesta Friderici* 4.80, 3rd ed. 333: "placuit reverendo concilio, ut electio domni Victoris . . . approbaretur et confirmaretur et electio Rolandi penitus cassaretur." See also the statement by Barbarossa in 1160 (*MGH Const* I 264 no.189): "aecclesia Dei . . . domnum Victorem papam in patrem spiritalem et universalem pontificem confirmavit. . . ."
[32] Tierney, *Foundations of the Conciliar Theory* 57-67 and passim. See, for example, the opinion of Rufinus (*Summa* on D.79 pr., ed. Singer 169): "Si vero duo per contentionem ordinati fuerint, tunc ambobus reprobatis tertius eligatur; si autem unus perverse, alter iuste est electus, tunc illo deiecto iste cathedram optinebit. Qui deinceps a quoquam nisi pro heresi damnari non poterit. . . ."

158

observed, with obvious reference to the election decree of 1059, that in the event of a papal schism the cardinals act as metropolitan and therefore can judge a pope. Stephen of Tournai opposed this view (and, incidentally, defended Gratian) by explaining that the cardinals take "the place of the metropolitan in the confirmation of the election, not in the power of judgment."[33] In other words, the cardinals confirm the pope's election, but they are not superior to him, nor can they judge him in any way. Stephen's statement was not unprecedented, for in the earlier twelfth century one could encounter the notion that the cardinals simultaneously elect and confirm the Roman pontiff.[34]

In this form, the idea of simultaneous election and confirmation had little juridical meaning. After Stephen of Tournai, however, later decretists appropriated and developed it as a part of their electoral theory. Distinguishing between the election of a bishop of Rome and the election of any other bishop, the *Summa Inperatorie maiestati* pointed out:

Not all of these things [that is: election, confirmation, and consecration] are observed with regard to the pope, since for him alone election and consecration are sufficient, for in this case those who elect also consecrate and confirm.[35]

Taking a similar position on the election of a pope, Simon of Bisignano remarked:

When he is elected, he is immediately confirmed, for

[33] *Summa* on C.3 q.1, ed. Schulte 190: "Quo casu dicunt quidam male distinguere hic Gratianum, et aiunt cardinales eum locum obtinere in electione summi pontificis quem metropolitanus obtinet in electione cuiuslibet episcopi, et ideo quod iudices esse posse ipsius. Ad quod respondetur quia tenent locum metropolitani in confirmatione electionis, non in potestate iudicii."
[34] Pandulph, *Vita Paschalis II*, ed. Duchesne, *Lib. pont.* II 296: "'. . . te ad summi pontificatus apicem et eligimus et confirmamus.'" Similarly, the acclamatory election of the antipope Gregory VIII in 1118: "Et nos laudamus et confirmamus dominum Gregorium" (Watterich, *Pontificum Romanorum vitae* II 108).
[35] On D.23 pr. v. *breuiter* (above, Ch.IVA n.14).

he is elected by the same people by whom he is also confirmed.

The newly elected bishop of Rome, therefore, automatically has "everything which pertains to the management of temporal affairs."[36] There is thus no true confirmation of a papal election, for if the same persons elect and confirm, they are merely ratifying their own action. Along the same lines, Sicard of Cremona thought that in a papal election,

No other confirmation is needed, since he has no superior. Hence, as soon as he is elected, he immediately has the right to administer.[37]

As the *Summa Tractaturus magister* expressed it, the Roman pontiff-elect is immediately the true pope "with respect to the management of temporal affairs," since "from the election itself he receives the confirmation."[38] Markedly similar was the doctrine set forth by the *Summa Et est sciendum.*[39] Of course, not all canonists gave unqualified agreement to the notion that a Roman pontiff-elect actually needs or receives electoral confirmation.[40] Still, many accepted this idea, and in the 1180's the *Summa Omnis qui iuste iudicat* cast it in a terse formulation which was repeated by later canonists from Huguccio to Hostiensis, "By being elected, he is confirmed, and in being confirmed, he is elected."[41] Through his election,

---

36 *Summa* on D.79 c.9 v. *concessa electo auctoritate* (above, Ch.IVA n.18).

37 *Summa* on D.62 (above, Ch.IVA n.27).

38 On D.23 c.1 v. *sicut uerus papa* (above, Ch.IVA n.19). See also the *Summa Reuerentia sacrorum canonum* on D.23 c.1 v. *electus tamen*: "ipsa electione confirmatus, quod in eo speciale est, et est argumentum, ea que per electionem facta sunt non rescindi" (Erfurt Ampl. qu. 117 fol.119vb).

39 On D.23 c.1 v. *disponendi facultates* (above, Ch.IVA n.20).

40 Alanus, *Apparatus Ius naturale* on D.23 c.1 v. *uice*: ". . . quantum ad confirmationem et consecrationem, ipsi [scil. cardinales episcopi] eligunt, confirmant et consecrant, immo in tantum rata est electio, quod non sit necessaria confirmatio" (BN 15393 fol.18ra). Johannes Andreas, *Gl.ord.* on *VI* 1.7.1 v. *videbantur*: "Inferiores praelati a suis praelatis confirmantur et instituuntur . . . , sed papa a nemine confirmatur, unde . . . sine superiore instituitur. . . ."

41 On D.79 c.9 v. *concessa electio auctoritate disponendi* [sic]: "quod

therefore, the Roman pontiff-elect instantly acquires full jurisdictional powers and the exercise of those powers, both *potestas* and *executio*.[42] Of course, the decretists never imagined that mere election can confer sacramental power. As the *Summa Et est sciendum* and the *Summa Omnis qui iuste iudicat* carefully explained, everything depends on the prior status of the newly elected pope. If he was only a priest before his elevation, he gains only jurisdictional authority by virtue of the election, but if he was already a bishop at the time of his election, he can immediately use both his jurisdictional and his sacramental powers.[43]

In the papal election decrees of 1059 and 1060 the enthronement was, for normal circumstances, the constitutive ceremony, whereas the right of immediate postelectoral administration was a special stipulation for extraordinary and unsettled conditions. To Gratian, the solemn enthronement still seemed a key ceremony in the elevation of a Roman pontiff,[44] and during the schism of 1159 the supporters of Victor IV were careful to include proper enthronement among his claims.[45] A mere two decades after the *Decretum*, however, beginning with Stephen of Tournai, the decretists unanimously assumed that the right to administer the jurisdictional powers was automatically conferred by the election itself, without any other ceremonies or sanctions. That is, appar-

---

est speciale in papa, qui eligendo confirmatur et confirmando eligitur . . ." (Rouen 743 fol.37va). Cf. *id.* on D.23 c.1 v. *disponendi* (above, Ch.IVᴀ n.21). The Anglo-Norman canonist's formula derives from the *Summa Et est sciendum* (above, Ch.IVᴀ n.20) and ultimately from Rufinus (above, Ch.IIIʙ n.9). For its later influence, see: Huguccio, *Summa* on D.23 c.1 v. *disponendi* (above, Ch.Vᴀ n.5), and Hostiensis, *Summa aurea* 1.6 no.18. In his sermon on the first anniversary of his consecration, Innocent III not only paraphrased this formula, but also quoted Nicholas II's decree of 1059 to support it; *Sermones de diversis* 3, *PL* 217 663.

[42] *Apparatus Ecce uicit leo* on D.79 c.2: ". . . statim post electionem habet papa plenariam potestatem, executionem, administrationem, et est speciale in eo quia non habent alii prelati nisi post confirmationem" (Tierney, *Foundations* 144 n.2).

[43] Above, Ch.IVᴀ nn.20f.

[44] D.79 pr.; also, D.79 dict.p.c.8 (above, n.28).

[45] Above, n.17.

ently not long before the 1160's the exception had become the rule.

In order to solve once and for all the problem which had made the protracted schism possible, the Third Lateran Council devoted the first of its twenty-seven constitutions to the question of papal elections.[46] Alexander III explicitly intended this constitution to amend and to supplement, rather than to replace, existing legislation, and he therefore considered the major provisions of Nicholas II's decrees still in force. The constitution prescribed that in case of a split election, even though a minority may elect a candidate of their own, two-thirds of the cardinals can make a binding choice. On the other hand, even a majority of the cardinals, if less than two-thirds, cannot validly elect a pope.[47] Unlike Nicholas II's decree of 1059, the Council's first constitution does not discuss in any form the papal enthronement or the consecration, and omits all word of lawful influence or consent by the *clerus et populus* or by the emperor.[48] Similarly, there is no mention of the enmantling, the acclamations, or the coronation. All of these acts—enmantling, enthronement, consent, and so forth—have been officially relegated to the status of incidental ceremonies. In 1159 Alexander himself (and also, of course, his rival Victor IV) had been elevated by a protracted process which included a series of inseparable acts. After 1179, however, by ecclesiastical law, election alone

[46] *X* 1.6.6.

[47] The origins of this two-thirds requirement deserve further study. Shortly before the Third Lateran Council, for example, Simon of Bisignano asserted that a two-thirds majority is equivalent to unanimity in an ecclesiastical election (*Summa* on D.85 c.1 v. *ab omnibus fuerat electus* [sic]): "idest duabus partibus, nam omnes dicuntur facere quod due partes faciunt . . ." (Rouen 710 fol.72rb). Gilbert Foliot seems to have made the earliest suggestion of a two-thirds requirement in papal elections; A. Morey and C.N.L. Brooke, eds., *The Letters and Charters of Gilbert Foliot* (Cambridge 1967) 176 no.133 (1160), and for Gilbert's sources (esp. *Cod.* 10.32.45), *ibid.* n.4.

[48] Of course, Victor IV's party had invoked the emperor's consent in support of Victor's claims. Rahewin, *Gesta Friderici* 4.80, 3rd ed. 333: "christianissimus imperator . . . electionem domni Victoris recepit et approbavit." Rahewin (?), *Dialogus*, in *MGH LdL* III 532: "electio mea [scil. Victoris IV] . . . consensu imperatoris . . . confirmata est et roborata."

sufficed for the promotion of a pope to the full rights of his office, except for the sacramental powers deriving from episcopal consecration. And after 1179 neither the enmantling nor the enthronement was ever again considered constitutive. Of course, these ceremonies continued to be performed at each papal accession, but with purely declarative significance. In short, the Third Lateran Council's constitution defined the minimal and decisive act in the creation of a pope: whoever is elected by at least two-thirds of the cardinals "should be regarded by the entire Church, without any exception, as the Roman pontiff."[49] Obviously, whoever was thus "regarded as the Roman pontiff" was immediately expected to exercise full jurisdictional powers in administering the papacy and the Church. As Alexander pointed out, after a disputed election in a lesser church, the competent superior may determine which is the "greater and sounder part" of the electors, and the superior can then confirm their act. But Alexander justified a special procedure in papal elections by explaining the uniqueness of the Roman See, from which "there can be no recourse to a superior." With this statement, Alexander placed himself in the tradition of the decretistic commentaries on the decree of 1059, and he gave the full force of law to the decretists' thought. For like the decretists, he maintained that election alone is decisive, and he believed that beyond and after a proper election by the cardinals, there is no competent authority which can judge and further validate or annul the election of a Roman pontiff. As an ancient

49 *X* 1.6.6: ". . . Statuimus ergo, ut, si forte . . . inter cardinales de substituendo summo pontifice non poterit esse plena concordia, et duabus partibus concordantibus pars tertia concordare noluerit aut sibi alium praesumpserit nominare, ille absque ulla exceptione ab universali ecclesia Romanus pontifex habeatur, qui a duabus partibus concordantibus electus fuerit et receptus. . . . Praeterea si a paucioribus quam a duabus partibus aliquis electus fuerit ad apostolatus officium, nisi maior concordia intercesserit, nullatenus assumatur. . . . Ex hoc tamen nullum canonicis constitutionibus et aliis ecclesiis praeiudicium generetur, in quibus debet maioris et sanioris partis sententia praevalere, quia quod in eis dubium venerit superioris poterit iudicio diffiniri. In Romana vero ecclesia speciale aliquid constituitur, quia non poterit ad superiorem recursus haberi."

maxim of the Church asserted, "The pope is to be judged by no one."[50] According to the Third Lateran Council, a Roman pontiff-elect is in precisely the same position. Of course, Alexander had denied the Council of Pavia's right to sit in judgment over him, and had insisted that "although he should judge all, he himself was willing to be judged by no one."[51] Indeed, in the opinion of Alanus Anglicus, Alexander's statement that "there can be no recourse to a superior" clearly excluded even a general council of the Church from the judgment of a papal election.[52]

By the end of the twelfth century, the most widely held theory of episcopal election stressed the bishop-elect's consent as the act which effectively promotes him and joins him to his church. For a surprisingly long time this concept found no place in the theory of papal election. Finally, however, Hostiensis asserted that the papal jurisdiction derives not from the election itself, but from the pontiff-elect's consent to his own election. With this remark, Hostiensis assimilated Huguccio's idea of consent and applied it for the first time to papal elections. In fact, Hostiensis viewed the pontiff-elect's consent as an integral part of the election itself, for prior to this consent, as he explained, one should speak of a "pontiff-designate" (*nominatus*), rather than of a "pontiff-elect" (*electus*).[53] Probably from the beginning of the thirteenth century, the official ceremonial explicitly required the Roman pontiff-elect's consent after the election and before the enmantling.[54] Clarifying the juridical meaning of this consent

50 D.40 c.6; Tierney, *Foundations* 57 esp. n.3.

51 Rahewin, *Gesta Friderici* 4.79, 80, 3rd ed. 330, 333.

52 *Apparatus* on *Comp.I* 1.4.15 (= X 1.6.6) v. *superiorem*: "Ergo concilium generale non est maius collegio cardinalium, quod potest concedi . . ." (Clm 3879 fol.3va).

53 *Lectura* on X 1.6.6 v. *et receptus*: "Illud quod ibi dicit, 'electus tamen sicut verus papa etc.,' intelligi debet de illo, qui iam consensit electioni sive nominationi de se factae, cui ad potestatis plenitudinem consecratio nihil addit. . . . Ante consensum vero suum non potest dici quod illam habeat potestatem, et proprie loquendo non potest dici electus, sed potius nominatus . . ."; Ronald J. Cox, *A Study of the Juridic Status of Laymen in the Writing of the Medieval Canonists* (Washington, D.C. 1959) 79.

54 *Ordo rom.* 13 c.2, 14 c.10, PL 78 1105, 1126.

and carrying Hostiensis's argument one step further, John of
Paris and Augustinus Triumphus suggested that the pontiff-
elect's consent actually constitutes the confirmation of his
election. Their identification of consent and confirmation successfully explained Hostiensis's ascription of constitutive
power to this consent, since electoral confirmation sanctioned
the administrative and jurisdictional rights of all lesser
bishops-elect.[55]

There were, in fact, a few minor restrictions on Roman
pontiffs-elect. According to the ceremonial authorized by
Gregory X, if a newly elected pope has not yet been consecrated as a bishop, in his letters he must confine himself to
the title "pontiff-elect, servant of the servants of God"
(*electus servus servorum Dei*). Moreover, the bull appended
to his letters should show, on one side, the heads of the
apostles, but the other side, which would normally bear his
name, should be left blank. At the end of each letter, he was
expected to explain this sphragistic irregularity with a special
formula provided for the purpose.[56] Yet these were restrictions on the form, rather than on the substance, of a pontiff-
elect's power, for most contemporaries recognized the validity
of any administrative enactment in a letter from a pontiff-
elect. For example, an archdeaconship was bestowed in a
letter from pope Hadrian V, who reigned for less than six
weeks (11 July to 18 August 1276) and died before receiving
the episcopal consecration or even priestly ordination.
Repeatedly copied into manuscripts containing treatises and
documents relevant to ecclesiastical election, Hadrian's letter
appeared under the rubric, "Thus writes an unconsecrated
pope" (*Papa non consecratus sic scribit*), and the letter

---

[55] John of Paris, *Tractatus de potestate regia et papali* 25, ed. Jean
Leclercq, *Jean de Paris et l'ecclésiologie du XIIIe siècle* (Paris 1942) 260:
"assensus pape sine superiore confirmatio est." Augustinus Triumphus,
Summa de potestate ecclesiastica 4.5: ". . . consentire electioni de se facte
est eius confirmatio, quia statim habet omnem papalem iurisdictionem . . ."
(quoted by Cox, *op.cit.* 78f n.25).

[56] *Ordo rom.* 13 c.4, *PL* 78 1106.

apparently found its way into formulary books.[57] Despite widespread agreement on the rights and powers of a pontiff-elect, however, occasional dissenting voices could be heard. Before his election as pope Clement V, Bertrand de Got was archbishop of Bordeaux and hence did not need episcopal consecration. In such cases, thirteenth- and early fourteenth-century procedure omitted the ordination and consecration, but included the ceremonial acts which would otherwise have directly followed the consecration: the bestowal of the *pallium*, and the coronation with the papal tiara.[58] In fact, there was a delay of more than five months between Clement's election and his coronation, and since coronation was considered the constitutional equivalent of consecration in such cases, he was attacked for having unlawfully administered his office before being crowned. According to his opponents,

> Before the honor of his coronation, the Supreme Pontiff must not intrude upon the granting of provisions, reservations, dispensations, and other favors; must not sign himself simply "bishop" in letters, but "bishop-elect"; and also must not use the bull on which his name is represented.[59]

Here the papal coronation not only plays the role of the

[57] In conferring the archdeaconry, Hadrian entitled himself *electus episcopus servus servorum Dei*, correctly used only the *bulla dimidia*, and explained his use of this bull; A. Chroust, "Ein Brief Hadrians IV.," *NA* 20 (1895) 233f. Also: Wilhelm Diekamp, "Zum päpstlichen Urkundenwesen des XI., XII., und der ersten Hälfte des XIII. Jahrhunderts," *MIÖG* 3 (1882) 613; A. von Wretschko, *Traktat des Laurentius de Somercote* 4 esp. n.1; cf. Fritz Schillmann, ed., *Die Formularsammlung des Marinus von Eboli* (Rome 1929) 217f no.1398. On the *bulla dimidia*: Harry Bresslau, *Handbuch der Urkundenlehre für Deutschland und Italien* (2 vols. repr. Berlin 1958) II 570.

[58] *Ordo rom.* 13 cc.6-8, *PL* 78 1108-10; and esp. *Ordo rom.* 14 cc.12-19, *PL* 78 1127-31. On *Ordo* 14, see above, n.9.

[59] *Extrav. com.* 5.10.4: ". . . nonnulli, prout accepimus, . . . asserere non verentur, quod summus pontifex ante suae coronationis insignia se non debet intromittere de provisionibus, reservationibus, dispensationibus et aliis gratiis faciendis, nec se in literis episcopum simpliciter, sed electum episcopum scribere, nec etiam uti bulla, in qua nomen exprimatur ipsius. . . ." Clement was elected on 5 June 1305 and crowned on 14 November 1305. In 1904 Clement's condemnation of this doctrine was partially repeated in Pius X's *Vacante Sede Apostolica* §88 (*CIC* Documenta no.1).

episcopal consecration, sanctioning the full title of "bishop" and the use of the papal name, but also fulfills the function of an accepted election, since the administrative enactments of an uncrowned pope are invalid. With this curious doctrine, Clement's critics may have been influenced by a contemporary concept of the imperial coronation, which some regarded as jurisdictionally constitutive.[60] In any case, their doctrine had no success, and the Church's entire tradition of constitutional thought supported Clement in his condemnation of it.

To conclude: From 1059 to the thirteenth century, both in law and in theory, the development of papal election consistently served to emphasize the uniqueness of the papacy among the bishoprics of Latin Christendom. In the decrees of 1059 and 1179, as well as in the doctrines of the canonists, the election of the Roman pontiff was explicitly contrasted to the election of any lesser prelate, "since the Apostolic See is superior to all churches in the whole world." And throughout this period, the extraordinary character of papal election matched the unique quality of the papal jurisdiction conferred by election or, in later theory, by the acceptance of the election. Once accepted, election brings the Roman pontiff immediately "to the fullness of power," *in plenitudinem potestatis.*[61]

2. The Powers of the Metropolitan-Elect

The canonistic prescriptions on the right to administer were largely concerned with the most typical case of an *electus*: a bishop-elect in an ordinary diocese. But from the remarks of the canonists and from the decretals, it is clear that special regulations governed the administrative rights of the various bishops directly under the Roman pontiff. Indeed, for a typology of ecclesiastical office, one must fling the net wider, since the metropolitan's status was unique in several respects.

---

[60] See the classic essay by Fritz Kern, "Die Reichsgewalt des deutschen Königs nach dem Interregnum: Zeitgenössische Theorien," *HZ* 106 (1911) 39-95 and esp. 42-50.

[61] Innocent III, *Sermones de diversis* 3, *PL* 217 663, 665; Hostiensis, *Commentaria* on *X* 1.6.6 v. *et receptus* (above, n.53).

The Bishop-Elect

Latin Christianity was familiar with such high-sounding designations as "primate" and "patriarch." Because the rights of a *primas* were discussed by Gratian and by a few of the *Decretum*'s chapters, decretists sometimes assigned to the "primate" a jurisdictional superiority over the metropolitan. More commonly, however, like the term "archbishop," *primas* and *patriarcha* were essentially honorific titles, which enhanced the holder's dignity and rank but which brought no jurisdictional increment above and beyond his episcopal powers. The metropolitan always had the rank and title of—at least—an archbishop, and in fact, he was often simply called *archiepiscopus* in contemporary writings. But within the main medieval tradition, as head of an ecclesiastical province the metropolitan held the only distinct jurisdiction midway between the bishops and the pope.[1] In terms of his sacramental powers and his jurisdictional powers, the metropolitan was, in every sense, a bishop, and by the thirteenth century, he normally passed through the usual stages on the way to the full powers of office: election, confirmation, consecration. Moreover, there was no significant difference between his consecration and that of any other bishop.

But because the metropolitan was *more* than a bishop, there were particular powers—the *ius metropoliticum*—pertaining exclusively to his office. His competence included the right to confirm the elections of the suffragan bishops in his province and to consecrate them, the right to call provincial synods and to preside over them, and also general supervision and discipline within the province. Since the earlier Middle Ages, the metropolitan's right to exercise these supra-

[1] On the metropolitan's position within the Church's constitution, see Hinschius, *KR* II 1ff; Feine, *RG* I 207ff, 321ff; and the works cited below. The following pages are not an attempt at a full treatment of this complex topic. Rather, the intent here is merely to point out that the metropolitan-elect was considered subject to the rules which bound most prelates-elect, and that it was not always easy to reconcile the older regulations for a metropolitan-elect and the newer ones for a simple bishop-elect. Incidentally, a thorough reexamination of the *ius metropoliticum* in the light of 12th- and 13th-century canonistic materials would be instructive.

episcopal powers was dependent upon his possession of the *pallium,* a narrow cloth band worn around the neck, shoulders, and chest as the insignia of the archiepiscopal dignity. A twelfth-century archbishop of Trier, for example, did not have the *pallium* and therefore considered himself incapable of maintaining order within his province; his unruly enemies, he complained, did not fear him and feel compelled to obey him, since his disciplinary powers were ineffective without the *pallium.*[2] Bestowal of the *pallium* was, in general, a papal prerogative. Although the garment was originally a mere decoration and distinction, Gregory the Great connected it firmly with the metropolitan's special powers. At least since Paschal II's pontificate, the newly elected metropolitan took an oath of obedience to the pope, and the effective *ius metropoliticum* dated from the taking of this oath as well as from the receipt of the *pallium.*[3]

Appropriating from Urban II a new term for the *pallium,* Paschal II defined the significance of its bestowal:

With the *pallium,* the fullness of the episcopal office is granted, since according to the custom of the Apostolic See and of all Europe, before he has received the *pallium*

---

[2] See the monograph by Johanne Heydenreich, *Die Metropolitangewalt der Erzbischöfe von Trier bis auf Baldewin* (Marburger Studien zur älteren deutschen Geschichte II 5: Marburg 1938) 26, 156; similar studies of other metropolitan sees should be undertaken.

[3] Hinschius, *KR* II 23ff and esp. 31ff; Feine, *RG* I 108ff, 207ff, 321ff; and in general, Curt-Bogislav von Hacke, *Die Palliumverleihungen bis 1143* (Göttingen 1898). See, for example, D.100 pr.: "Episcopos autem ordinare ante pallium acceptum nec archiepiscopo, nec primati, nec patriarchae licet. . . ." Johannes Teutonicus, *Gl.ord.* on D.100 pr. v. *episcopos:* ". . . eorum dignitas [scil. archiepiscoporum] videtur esse imperfecta sine pallio . . . nisi habeant pallium, non possunt episcopalia exercere officia. . . ." On the *ius pallii,* see D.100 and X 1.8 (*De usu et auctoritate pallii*) and their glosses. The right to crown and anoint the German kings could also depend upon possession of the *pallium;* Ulrich Stutz, *Der Erzbischof von Mainz und die deutsche Königswahl* (Weimar 1910) 17 n.1, 23f. Yet such a right could derive from confirmation: in 1260 Alexander IV ordered the bishops of Prague and Olmütz—in the place of the unconfirmed archbishop-elect of Mainz—to crown and anoint the king of Bohemia (*MGH Ep.saec.XIII* III 470 no.508).

a metropolitan is not allowed to consecrate bishops or to hold a synod.[4]

Almost two centuries later this conception of the *pallium* was enshrined in William Durandus's *Pontifical*, where he quoted the customary Roman formula for the handing over of the *pallium*: ". . . With this *pallium*, accept the fullness of your office, and the power to hold councils and to consecrate bishops." In Durandus's *Pontifical*, on the other hand, the papal *pallium* was bestowed without mention of any specific powers, since the Roman pontiff's full jurisdiction derives from election alone.[5] Indeed, aware of the possible conflict between the theory of papal election and the theory of the *ius metropoliticum*, an Anglo-Norman canonist proposed an ingenious solution:

> But before receiving the *pallium*, can [the Roman pontiff-elect] hold councils and consecrate a bishop, since the *pallium* is necessary in these matters . . . ? By all means, the *pallium* must be immediately conferred in the election.[6]

4 *X* 1.64. For Urban's phrase, see JL 5464.

5 William Durandus, *Pontificale* 1.14.66, ed. Andrieu, *Pontifical romain* III 393: ". . . cum apud sedem apostolicam palleum alicui traditur, archipresbiter ecclesie romane illud sumens de altari sibi dicit hoc modo: 'Accipe palleum sumtum de corpore beati Petri et in hoc palleo accipe plenitudinem officii tui et potestatem celebrandi concilia et consecrandi episcopos.' " This work was completed between 1293 and 1295. Cf. the formula whereby the pope received the *pallium*, in *Pontificale romanae Curiae* 13B.20, ed. Andrieu, *op.cit.* II 374: "Accipe pallium, plenitudinem scilicet pontificalis officii, ad honorem . . . Dei et . . . Marie . . . et beatorum apostolorum Petri et Pauli et sancte romane ecclesie"; the papal formula dates from the beginning of the 13th century. For a thorough summary of the rights included within the *ius metropoliticum*, see Durandus, *Pontificale* 3.30, ed. Andrieu, *op.cit.* III 661f.

6 Honorius, *Summa quaestionum*: ". . . Set numquid [papa electus] ante acceptum pallium potest concilia celebrare uel episcopum consecrare, cum ibi necessarium sit pallium . . . ? Immo statim in illa electione conferri debet pallium . . ." (Zwettl 162 fol.197ra). Also, Boncompagno of Florence (*Rhetorica antiqua* 2.1.2) published a formulary letter purportedly written by Honorius III to announce his election, at which two cardinal-bishops, as *compromissarii*, "nostris humeris pallium apostolicum imposuerunt" (Vat.Arch. H.13 fol.46vb). In common practice, however, the *pallium* was conferred during the pope's consecration; above, n.5, and *Ordo* 36.46, 40A.7, 40B.7, ed. Andrieu, *Ordines romani* IV 203, 297, 308.

Papa, Metropolitanus, Exemptus

In general, then, the metropolitan's "fullness of the episcopal office" (*plenitudo officii pontificalis*) represented the totality of those powers based upon possession of the *pallium*. A century after Urban II and Paschal II, Innocent III asserted that also the title *archiepiscopus*, as well as the *plenitudo officii*, is dependent upon the *pallium*; before receiving the *pallium*, even if he is already a consecrated archbishop, a metropolitan-elect has no right to an archbishop's title and name.[7] Urban's expression, the *plenitudo officii pontificalis*, was immediately and widely adopted as a technical term for the increment of priestly and jurisdictional power which accompanied the *pallium*. The emphasis in the expression is upon the word *pontificalis*, for the wearing of the *pallium* was a privilege to which the metropolitan was entitled only within the churches of his own ecclesiastical province and only during the solemn celebration of certain festivals and ceremonies.[8] In other

[7] In the *Vita Arnoldi archiepiscopi Moguntini*, written soon after 1160, ed. Jaffé, *Bibl.* III 612, Arnold's consecration is described: "Et demum—duobus viris apostolice sedis legatis hinc inde suffultus—per impositionem manus ministeriumque episcoporum suorum plenitudinem officii sui sollempnissime est adeptus et nomen." If this account is accurate, even in the later 12th century the *plenitudo officii* and the archiepiscopal title could still depend simply upon the episcopal consecration. Immediately after this consecration, Arnold did in fact begin to use the title *archiepiscopus*; Hermann Krabbo, *Die Besetzung der deutschen Bistümer unter der Regierung Kaiser Friedrichs II. 1212-1250* (Berlin 1901) 131 n.2. Before the first appearance of the expression *plenitudo officii pontificalis* in 1092 (JL 5464), some 11th-century terms for the *pallium* were: *dignitatis insigne, supplementum totius sacerdotalis ordinis, plenitudo omnis sacerdotalis dignitatis, pontificatus plenitudo* (Hinschius, *KR* II 33f; Hacke, *Pallium-verleihungen* 116-18). Innocent III was apparently the first to prohibit explicitly the use of the title *archiepiscopus* before receipt of the *pallium* (*X* 1.8.3 [1200]); but cf. Hacke (*op.cit.* 115f), who maintains that this doctrine appeared in the 11th century or even earlier. Like *archiepiscopus*, the titles *primas* and *patriarcha* were dependent on possession of the *pallium* (Hinschius, *KR* II 31).

[8] Albert Hauck, *Kirchengeschichte Deutschlands* (3rd and 4th ed. 5 vols. Leipzig 1911-29) IV 21 n.2: in the 12th-century documents accompanying the bestowal of the *pallium*, the term *plenitudo officii* was a precise and unambiguous formula. See also the letter by Innocent III (1207), *Reg.* 10.134, *PL* 215 1230: "Cum sine pallio metropolitanus non possit plenitudinem pontificalis officii exercere, gravis quidem . . . ecclesiae . . . immineret iactura, si circa eius antistitem donatio pallii nimium differretur. . . ."

D.100 c.6 (Gregory I): "Pallium tibi transmisimus, quo fraternitas tua

words, it was a liturgical garment, and it stressed the priestly character rather more than the jurisdictional powers of the metropolitan's office.

The pope, however, could wear the *pallium* "always and everywhere" (*semper et ubique*), since as head of the Roman province, he is, so to speak, a universal metropolitan.[9] As Innocent III formulated this claim to universality, the papal *pallium* signifies the papal "fullness of ecclesiastical power" (*plenitudo ecclesiasticae potestatis*), whereas the other metropolitans are called merely "to a share in the solicitude—but not to the fullness of power" (*in partem sollicitudinis, non in plenitudinem potestatis*).[10] Although *plenitudo officii* remained, in general, the technical term for the metropolitan's powers, Innocent surely found it natural on this occasion to substitute the term *plenitudo potestatis*, which was a favorite

---

intra ecclesiam ad sola missarum solempnia utatur." Cf. D.100 dict.p.c.3. The rule against using the *pallium* anywhere except *infra ecclesiam* was interpreted by Celestine III (1193) to mean *infra quamlibet ecclesiam provinciae* (*X* 1.8.1). Cf. also two decretals by Innocent III, *X* 1.8.5, 6.

9 The claim to universality had been vigorously asserted at least since the Reform Papacy. For example, Gregory VII, *Dictatus pape* 2, *Reg.* 2.55a, ed. Caspar 202: "Quod solus Romanus pontifex iure dicatur universalis." See also the parallel texts cited by Caspar (*loc.cit.*), and especially his Index s.v. "universalis." Note the striking term *universalis papa* in the oaths of fealty taken by the Norman princes to Alexander II and Gregory VII; Deusdedit, *Collectio canonum* 3.288, ed. Wolf von Glanvell I 395, and Gregory's *Reg.* 1.21a, 8.1a, ed. Caspar 34, 514. In 1062 Damian described the pope as *universalis pontifex* (*Disceptatio synodalis*, in *MGH LdL* I 78), and in 1064 stated that "papa vero . . . solus est omnium ecclesiarum universalis episcopus" (*Opusculum* 23 c.1, *PL* 145 474); see the excellent discussion by Ryan, *St Peter Damiani* 85, 103-05. Correspondingly, around 1076 Bernold of Constance stressed the ubiquity of the pope's *universalis et principalis potestas* (*Apologeticus* c.23, *MGH LdL* II 88); Benson, *SGrat* 13 (1968) nn.67f. On the other hand, Gratian repeated Gregory the Great's prohibition against the use of the title *universalis* (D.99 dict.p.c.3, cc.4-5); the topic needs further study.

10 *X* 1.8.4 (1204): ". . . Sane solus Romanus pontifex in missarum solenniis pallio semper utitur et ubique, quoniam assumptus est in plenitudinem ecclesiasticae potestatis, quae per pallium significatur; alii autem eo nec semper, nec ubique, sed in ecclesia sua, in qua iurisdictionem ecclesiasticam acceperunt, certis debent uti diebus, quoniam vocati sunt in partem sollicitudinis, non in plenitudinem potestatis." Innocent's idea was anticipated by Bonizo of Sutri (*Liber de vita christiana* 3.108, ed. Perels 108), who identified the metropolitan's *pallium* with the *pars sollicitudinis* entrusted to him by the Roman pontiff; see my article in *SGrat* 13 (1968) n.60.

expression in his vocabulary. But since *plenitudo potestatis* referred primarily to the pope's jurisdictional rather than sacramental powers, Innocent thereby shifted the meaning of the *pallium* and gave added weight to its jurisdictional character. In this sense, the uniqueness of the papal *pallium* stresses the overwhelming superiority of papal jurisdiction. Master Huguccio had already equated the pope's *plenitudo potestatis* with the ubiquitous papal jurisdiction, characterized by "universality" (*generalitas*)—everywhere in Christendom, the pope has the same jurisdiction which a bishop has within his own diocese.[11] While distinguishing between the pope's *pallium* and the metropolitan's *pallium*, Raymond of Peñafort used the term "fullness of ecclesiastical power" (*plenitudo ecclesiasticae potestatis*) to explain both. Of course, Raymond did not intend to place pope and metropolitan on the same jurisdictional level, but was following a tradition which can be traced back to Gratian, who discussed the *plenitudo potestatis* of the metropolitan and the *pars sollicitudinis* of the suffragan bishops. For Gratian, the metropolitan's relation to his suffragan bishops might be regarded as identical with the pope's relation to the metropolitans according to the conceptual scheme of Huguccio and Innocent III. In this respect, Raymond was implicitly ascribing to the metropolitan a certain quasi-universality of jurisdiction within the various dioceses of his province.[12]

CONFIRMATION, CONSECRATION, *Ius pallii*

During the second half of the twelfth century, the requirement of electoral confirmation assumed new meaning. This development was as applicable to the metropolitans as to

---

[11] *Summa* on D.11 c.2 (Tierney, *Foundations* 146).

[12] Raymond of Peñafort, *Summa iuris* 2.34, ed. Rius Serra, *Opera* I 129: "Significat autem pallium in papa plenitudinem ecclesiastice potestatis. . . . In metropolitano significat metropoliticam plenitudinem ecclesiastice potestatis. . . ." Gratian apparently defended the metropolitan's *plenitudo potestatis* (C.9 q.3 pr.) but later soundly rejected this view (C.9 q.3 dict.p.c.21), allowing the metropolitan to interfere within a suffragan's diocese only when the suffragan is corrupt or negligent. On Gratian's ideas: Benson, *op.cit.* nn.70-85.

other bishops: like that of any other bishop, the election of a metropolitan had to be confirmed. Thus there were two systems which could be used to define and limit the metropolitan's right to administer. The key question is: Considering the complexity of the new pattern formed by election, confirmation, and consecration, could the older rights of the *pallium* be integrated into the new system? Where did one draw the line between the metropolitan's simple episcopal powers and his special prerogatives as metropolitan, or, differently expressed, between the *episcopalia* and the *archiepiscopalia*? Conflict and contradiction were unavoidable, and no single satisfactory answer emerged.

Let us illustrate the problem: In 1198 Innocent III wrote the patriarch of Antioch to charge him with the illegal transfer of an archbishop-elect to an episcopal see. Of course Innocent regarded any bishop-elect or archbishop-elect—"especially if he has been confirmed"—as wedded to his see. Hence Innocent's careful definition of the archbishop-elect's constitutional status:

> Although L. had not yet been consecrated as archbishop, nevertheless he had received the gift of confirmation, and insofar as it was lawful for him, he had administered his archiepiscopal rights.[13]

So far as he properly could (*quantum ei licuit*), the archbishop-elect had executed the duties of his office (*archiepiscopalia*), but a part of these duties—whether deriving from the consecration or from the *pallium*, Innocent did not specify—were not yet within his powers. A generation earlier, Alexander III had defined some of the powers acquired by a metropolitan-elect through confirmation. Solely on the basis of his own confirmation, a metropolitan-elect without the *pallium* could confirm the election of one of his suffragan

---

[13] *X* 1.7.1: "Licet enim dictus L. nondum fuisset in archiepiscopum consecratus, confirmationis tamen munus receperat, et archiepiscopalia, quantum ei licuit, ministrarat. . . ."

bishops and he could also order one of the fully consecrated suffragans to consecrate an *electus*.[14] However, even if a metropolitan has been properly elected, confirmed, and consecrated, until he has received the *pallium* he is not personally entitled to exercise his metropolitical rights. Without the *pallium*, for instance, solely on the basis of his powers as a consecrated bishop, the metropolitan cannot consecrate a bishop-elect even in his own province. As Innocent III explained, such acts are forbidden to a consecrated metropolitan who lacks the *pallium*, "since he seems to do that not as a simple bishop but as an archbishop."[15]

There were of course misunderstandings, and there was some resistance to the complex regulations which restricted a newly elected metropolitan. For example, in 1261 complaints were lodged against Henry of Vistingen, the archbishop-elect of Trier, and the resultant proceedings dragged out for eleven years.[16] Henry was accused of having confirmed the election of a suffragan bishop, Philip of Metz, and of having ordered Philip to be consecrated—all this while his own election had not yet been confirmed. In the course of the long proceedings, it was further charged that Henry had usurped the archiepiscopal title, had held a synod, and had taken part in the consecration of an altar—all this without having received the *pallium*. In answer to the assertion that he had

[14] *X* 1.6.11: "Suffraganeis alicuius metropolitani, ad mandatum ipsius metropolitani, post confirmationem electionis suae, etiamsi pallium non receperit, licitum est aliquem electum, qui ad eius iurisdictionem pertinet, consecrare. . . ." Johannes Teutonicus, *Gl.ord.* on D.100 c.1 v. *episcoporum*: ". . . si ipse [scil. metropolitanus electus] non habeat pallium, tamen aliis mandare posset consecrationem. . . . Sed ipse electus licet sit consecratus, iura episcopalia non potest exercere ante receptum pallium: nec virgines consecrare, nec ordinare clericos, nec synodum celebrare. . . . Sed numquid electus in archiepiscopum et confirmatus potest confirmare eos, qui sunt electi in episcopos? Dico quod sic. . . ."

[15] *X* 1.6.28 §1 (1202): ". . . cum non liceat archiepiscopo sine pallio convocare concilium, conficere chrisma, dedicare basilicas, ordinare clericos, et episcopos consecrare, multum profecto praesumit, qui, antequam impetret pallium, clericos ordinare festinat, cum id non tanquam simplex episcopus, sed tanquam archiepiscopus facere videatur."

[16] Heydenreich, *Metropolitangewalt* 28ff, 162f; Krabbo, *Besetzung* 150ff; *Gesta Henrici archiepiscopi et Theoderici abbatis* 4ff, 51ff, *MGH SS* XXIV 414ff, 444ff.

misused the title *archiepiscopus*, Henry made the familiar plea of "custom," that it was usual and customary in Germany for a confirmed archbishop-elect, even without the *pallium*, to bear this title.[17] As a defense against the charge of having participated in a consecration although he did not have the *pallium*, he affirmed his belief that even lacking the *pallium*, his own episcopal consecration entitled him to consecrate, "since he did that not as archbishop but as bishop" (*quia istud non tamquam archiepiscopus, sed tamquam episcopus faciebat*).[18]

The restriction upon the use of the title *archiepiscopus* derived from a deep-rooted medieval conviction that the bearer of an office or rank had to fulfill all of the prerequisite forms and ceremonies before he had a right to the title. One can perhaps express this even more strongly: To a very large degree, in the Middle Ages the title *was* the office, and the powers of the office were inherent in the title itself. The validity of a seal—and thereby, of a document—depended not only upon the issuer's right to the title inscribed on the seal, but also upon the absolute agreement of the title on the seal with the title given at the beginning of the document. Before his consecration, a bishop-elect would use the title ELECTVS on his seal.[19] Similarly, on the coins of a bishop-elect, his name was followed by the legend ELECTVS, and after his consecration his coins show the full title EPISCOPVS.[20]

---

[17] Gerard of Bremen (elected 1219) and Siegfried of Mainz (elected 1230) similarly used the archiepiscopal title before receiving the *pallium*; Krabbo, *op.cit.* 136f, 147f.

[18] Archbishop Henry apparently appropriated—and inverted—the wording of Innocent III's decretal (*X* 1.6.28; above, n.15).

[19] Harry Bresslau, *Handbuch der Urkundenlehre für Deutschland und Italien* II 615. Also, on the medieval conception of *nomen*, see the interesting discussion by Heinrich Mitteis, *Die deutsche Königswahl und ihre Rechtsgrundlagen bis zur Goldenen Bulle* (2nd ed. Brünn 1944) 160ff. Yet one should not exaggerate this tendency in medieval thought, for canonists were skillful at distinguishing—in Stephen of Tournai's words—between an official's *nomen* or *titulus* and his *administratio* (above, Ch.VA n.39).

[20] Arthur Engel and Raymond Serrure, *Traité de numismatique du moyen âge* II (Paris 1894) 577f. The same could also hold true for the coins issued by officials with higher rank. Archbishop Adolph of Cologne (1193-

The constitutional situation of a metropolitan-elect was, however, somewhat more complex. After his election and confirmation, he could use the title *electus*. After receiving the *pallium* he could use the title *archiepiscopus*. But midway between these two levels there was an intermediate stage, which followed his own episcopal consecration and in some cases lasted for years. After this consecration the metropolitan-elect was in an ironic and ambiguous position, for although he was already a fully consecrated bishop, he was forbidden to use that title. What other titles could he adopt?

He might have called himself *archielectus*, a term which would readily suggest that he was something more than a mere *episcopus electus*—indeed, this fantastic word was actually coined and applied to some twelfth- and thirteenth-century archbishops-elect of Trier and Cologne.[21]

In fact, the thirteenth century witnessed an attempt to create a new archiepiscopal title for the interim between consecration and the receipt of the *pallium*, and the origins of the new title are sufficiently clear: even before the mid-twelfth century, a bishop might occasionally entitle himself

---

1205) first issued coins with the title ELECTVS, later with the title ARCHIEPIS-COPVS (*ibid.* 605). Gregory of Montelongo, patriarch of Aquileia (1251-69), struck coins with the legend GREGORI(us)-ELECTVS, and later with the legend GREGORIV(s)-PA(triarcha); *ibid.* 797.

21 In these actual usages, the term meant simply *archiepiscopus electus*, and did not imply that the prelate-elect had received his episcopal consecration. For Trier (1169), see Heinrich Beyer et al., *UB zur Geschichte der . . . mittelrheinischen Territorien* II (Coblenz 1865) 35; for Cologne (1193), Joseph Heinrich, "Kaiser Heinrich VI. und die Besetzung der deutschen Bistümer," *RQSchr* 51 (1956) 214; and for another instance at Cologne (1228), *MGH SS* XXIV 347. The prefix *archi-* was of course readily applied in the High Middle Ages, and especially frequently to designate an archbishop or pope; for example, *archipater* (*MGH Const* II 318 no.233), *archipontifex* (*ibid.* II 361 no.262), *archipraesul* and *archisacerdos* (J. F. Niermeyer, *Mediae latinitatis lexicon minus* [Leiden 1954ff] 56ff).

In order to avoid the modest title *electus*, another possibility—less imaginative but more precise—was explored by Christian II of Mainz between his consecration (before 5 August 1249) and his receipt of the *pallium* (after 1 November 1249). Successively, he adopted first the title "electus confirmatus et consecratus," then "electus et consecratus in archiepiscopum Moguntinum," and finally "consecratus in archiepiscopum Moguntinum"; Krabbo, *Besetzung* 148ff.

humilis minister.[22] Between the mid-twelfth century and 1220, the archbishops of Trier and of Canterbury sometimes used the title *humilis minister*, sometimes the title *archiepiscopus*. There was no real distinction between these two terms, and they had no special constitutional significance in Trier.[23] If an archbishop called himself a "humble minister," the epithet was, of course, purely formulary, revealing nothing about the prelate's character and little about his conception of his own office; the popes bore the proud title *servus servorum Dei*, and *humilis minister* could well have similar shadings of meaning.[24] At all events, by the early thirteenth century, the term *humilis minister* was firmly established as a possible equivalent for the title *archiepiscopus*.

In February of 1216 Engelbert of Altena was elected to the archbishopric of Cologne, his election was confirmed in May of the same year, and he was consecrated in September of 1217.[25] Between February 1216 and September 1217, Engelbert referred to himself as an *electus*. Moreover, his seals display this title, and they show Engelbert without any of the usual episcopal ornaments. In April of 1218 the *pallium* was sent to Engelbert, and after that date he bears the title *archiepiscopus* in his documents and on his seals, where Engelbert is properly depicted in full archiepiscopal costume, with mitre, staff, and *pallium*. But what about the period between the consecration in September 1217 and the bestowal of the *pallium* in April 1218? Some documents issued by Engelbert in 1218 ascribe to him the title *minister*. Similarly, some of Engelbert's coins were stamped with the

[22] For example, Ivo of Chartres ("Ivo humilis ecclesiae Carnotensis minister"), ed. Jean Leclercq, *Correspondance* (Paris 1949) nos. 36, 41-43 and often. Also, *MGH Const* I 388 no.281 (Strasbourg 1181-86).

[23] Heydenreich, *Metropolitangewalt* 26ff. Thomas Becket's use of *minister humilis*: Morey and Brooke, eds., *Letters . . . of Gilbert Foliot* 189 no.144 (April 1163).

[24] Indeed, Hillin of Trier (1152-69), the first metropolitan to adopt the title *minister* in this fashion, used it in combination with the title *servus* (*humilis minister et servus*); Heydenreich, *op.cit.* 26f. On the origin of the title *servus servorum Dei* in the documents of Gregory the Great, see Caspar, *Geschichte des Papsttums* II 457f.

[25] Krabbo, *Besetzung* 132ff.

legend MINISTER.[26] Above all, the seals on documents during that interim bear the title "Engelbert, by the grace of God, minister of the holy church of Cologne" (+ ENGILBERTVS DI. GRA. SANCTE COLONIENSIS ECCLESIE MINISTER), and the accompanying image shows Engelbert with his episcopal insignia, that is, with mitre and staff—but without the *pallium*. In precisely the same fashion, Gerard of Bremen used the title *minister humilis* between his consecration (1219) and his winning of the *pallium* (1223).[27] The title *minister* similarly served archbishop Conrad of Cologne from 1239 to 1244, and correspondingly, he was described as MINISTER on his coins.[28] These German archbishops failed in their attempt to create an intermediate level between the status of an *electus* and the status of an *archiepiscopus*. On the whole, the Curia continued to designate a consecrated metropolitan as an *electus* until he had received the *pallium*, and the popes never recognized the title *minister* as a special rank for a metropolitan-elect during the interim between consecration and *pallium*. One can speculate that in this attempt, the German archbishops were aware of the connections between the title *minister* and the new technical term *administratio*, for through this new title they wished to imply that even without the *pallium* a consecrated metropolitan-elect has a higher *administratio spiritualium et temporalium* than a mere *electus*.

The spheres of the sacramental and the jurisdictional, of the bishop's *spiritualia* and of his *temporalia*, were first distinguished clearly in the second half of the twelfth century. But before the decretists sharpened the boundary between the *potestas ordinis* and the *potestas iurisdictionis*, the rights which accompany the *pallium* had already been listed and defined. In the predecretistic era, no distinctions were drawn between different kinds of power bestowed by the

---

26 Engel and Serrure, *Traité* II 605.
27 Krabbo, *op.cit.* 136ff.
28 On Conrad's titulature, see Krabbo, *op.cit.* 140ff; on his coinage, Engel and Serrure, *op.cit.* II 605.

pallium, but it is not at all surprising that the decretists undertook to classify the powers of the *pallium*: If one paid attention primarily to the metropolitan's right to consecrate his suffragan bishops, the *pallium* seemed essentially a matter of "holy orders or anointment" (*ordo vel unctio*), as an anonymous decretist of the French school described it.[29] Another French canonist, however, pointed out that

> Before he has received the *pallium* a metropolitan is prohibited from doing many things which belong to his jurisdiction, such as the convocation of a council.[30]

Obviously the decretists were here applying their own characteristically precise new mode of thought—the division of all ecclesiastical power into *ordo* or *iurisdictio*—to the older pattern of the metropolitan's rights. The *ius pallii* was thus split into the same two elements which are inherent in any episcopal office, and in this way the new conceptual framework, created by Rufinus and used so flexibly and effectively by the decretists, was adapted to the *pallium*: as Raymond of Peñafort remarked, the metropolitan needs the *pallium* in order to have "the full right to administer" (*plena administratio*).[31]

After the middle of the twelfth century, electoral confirma-

---

[29] *Summa Et est sciendum* on D.23 c.1 v. *disponendi facultates*: ". . . Nil enim ordinis vel unctionis ei [scil. episcopo qui in papam eligitur] postea confertur excepto pallio . . ." (Gillmann, *AKKR* 107 [1927] 214). *Id.* on D.100 c.1 v. *ac per hoc episcoporum consecratio*: "Hinc canon videtur innuere ante pallium archiepiscopum non posse episcopum consecrare . . ." (Gillmann, *op.cit.* 203).

[30] *Summa Animal est substantia* on D.23 c.1 v. *sicut*: ". . . De metropolitano dicit Hug(uccio) quod ex perceptione pallii confirmatur, set nonne uidemus quod metropolitanus administrat antequam perceperit pallium? Vnde dicunt alii quod ex electione confirmatur, sicut papa, et hoc uerum est, et hoc de illo qui non habet primatem. Quod tamen dicitur, quod metropolitanus multa prohibetur facere que sunt iurisdictionis ante pallii perceptionem, ut conuocare concilium, istud est ex causa, quia metropolitani erant negligentes in petendo pallio . . ." (Bamberg Can.42 fol.106va-b).

[31] *Summa iuris* 2.34, ed. Rius Serra, *Opera* I 129: ". . . electi [scil. metropolitani] post confirmationem et consecrationem indigent pallio, ut plenam habeant administrationem. . . ." In this context, *plena administratio* is obviously a technical term, borrowed not from the old *ius pallii* but from the newer canonistic administrative law.

tion became the constitutive moment in the acquisition of episcopal jurisdiction. Like any other bishop, through the confirmation of his election, a metropolitan had the simple "power to administer" (*potestas administrandi*). To what extent this power was immediately effective only within his own archdiocese, and to what extent it operated in all of the dioceses within his province, one cannot say with certainty.[32] Moreover, from the moment of confirmation, he could even exercise some of his special powers as metropolitan.[33] Still, a part of the metropolitan's jurisdictional and sacramental competence derived not from electoral confirmation but from the *pallium*. Since the pope's grant of the *pallium* sanctioned the metropolitan's "full administration," it is clear that the indispensability of the *ius pallii* rendered the metropolitan-elect dependent on the Roman pontiff. But did the requirement of electoral confirmation have the same effect? To phrase the question differently, did the pope have the jurisdictional right to confirm the election of any metropolitan?

One must remember that in its fully developed form, electoral confirmation was, during the second half of the twelfth century, still a new requirement. Consequently, there was still considerable uncertainty about the meaning and application of the rule. In 1177, for example, Alexander III charged the new archbishop of Salzburg with the offense of receiving his consecration before the arrival of the papal letter confirming his election. Against this accusation, the archbishop defended himself with the plea of custom and cited as examples the archbishops of Trier and Cologne:

---

[32] On the metropolitan's exercise of his *potestas administrandi* following his confirmation, see the statement at the end of Innocent IV's commentary on *X* 1.6.34 (below, n.54), and Hinschius, *KR* II 31f. It is not clear whether a confirmed metropolitan-elect had the *potestas administrandi* in his capacity as bishop or as archbishop. In this respect, Innocent III's distinction between an action performed by a metropolitan-elect *tanquam simplex episcopus* and one performed *tanquam archiepiscopus* (above, n.15) is illuminating, for it might suggest—but cannot prove conclusively—that a metropolitan-elect could have the administrative rights of a "simple bishop" merely within his archdiocese.

[33] Above, n.14.

Even though we were not confirmed by you before our consecration, it should not harm us much, since in our land such things have customarily been done.[34]

There is no reason to doubt the truth behind the archbishop of Salzburg's plea. Indeed, in the late twelfth century and early thirteenth, canonists still observed—with strong disapproval—the continuity of older custom, for in some places bishops-elect and especially metropolitans-elect continued the practice of undertaking their administrative responsibilities even before their confirmation.[35]

As we have seen, among the decretists and early decretalists there was a marked tendency to rationalize the Church's constitution, that is, to make it systematic and consistent by viewing it as a pyramidal hierarchy.[36] On the one hand, this notion might lead a canonist to distinguish only three main levels in the hierarchy—bishop, metropolitan, pope—and therefore to require papal confirmation of any metropolitan's election.[37] Equally, however, a decretist might ascribe to the "primate" an intermediate jurisdiction between metropolitan and pope. Within the *Decretum*, if a *primas* had jurisdiction over a province, his consent was, like the metropolitan's approval, necessary for the consecration of a bishop.[38] In fact, Gratian stated:

[34] *Chronicon Magni presbyteri Reicherspergensis* anno 1177, *MGH SS* XVII 504: "Dicimus etiam quod etsi ante consecrationem a vobis non essemus confirmati, non multum nobis noceret, tum quia in terra nostra talia consueverunt fieri, sicuti in multis exemplum habere poteritis, ut in Treverensi, in Coloniensi, et in multis aliis"; Albert Diegel, *Der päpstliche Einfluss auf die Bischofswahlen in Deutschland während des 13. Jahrhunderts* (Berlin 1932) 17f.

[35] Huguccio, *Summa* on D.63 c.10 (above, Ch.VA n.23). Also, *Apparatus Ecce uicit leo* on D.23 c.1 v. *obtineat*: ". . . in omnibus electionibus . . . electus non habet liberam administrationem nec potestatem exequendi gladium nisi fuerit confirmatus, ut extra de electione Nosti, set archiepiscopi hodie non confirmati administrant, set male faciunt . . ." (BN n.a. 1576 fol.45vb).

[36] See the end of Ch.IVA (esp. Ch.IVA n.40).

[37] Simon of Bisignano, *Summa* on D.63 c.10 (above, Ch.IVA n.39).

[38] D.65 dict.p.c.3; D.65 cc.4, 5, and esp. rubr.c.4. In its original context, D.65 c.4 referred to the powers of a papal vicar, rather than of a *primas*.

Primates and patriarchs have different names, but the same office. As often as may be necessary, bishops appeal from archbishops to primates. . . . Also, archbishops owe obedience to primates in all things which have been justly commanded . . . by them.[39]

Indeed, in order to distinguish the primate from the metropolitan, a decretist might describe the *primas* as the competent superior within a kingdom, just as the metropolitan was in charge of an ecclesiastical province.[40] Of course, whenever a metropolitan was considered subject to a primate, a canonist might require the metropolitan's election to be confirmed by the primate. For example, a French decretist explained,

Some say that from election alone, [the metropolitan] is confirmed, just like the pope. And this is true . . . with regard to the one who does not have a primate [over him].[41]

Here the French decretist's analogy between the elections of pope and metropolitan indicates clearly that a metropolitan—unless he is under a primate—could administer immediately after his election; in any case, the Roman pontiff cannot confirm his election. Of course, master Huguccio did not share the French decretist's antipapal outlook on this question, but Huguccio did recognize that some metropolitans, either by custom or because they are subject to a primate, are not confirmed by the pope. Moreover, Huguccio envisioned even the possibility that the pope might allow a primate to bestow

---

[39] D.99 pr.: ". . . Primates et patriarchae diuersorum sunt nominum, sed eiusdem offitii. Ab archiepiscopis, quoties necesse fuerit, episcopi ad primates appellant. . . . Debent quoque obedientiam primatibus archiepiscopi in omnibus, que sibi ab eis fuerint iuste inperata." Also, D.99 cc.1-2, D.80 cc.1-2; in general, on the conception of the *primas* from Pseudo-Isidore to the early 12th century, see the valuable account by Horst Fuhrmann, "Studien zur Geschichte mittelalterlicher Patriarchate," *ZRG* KA 39 (1953) 112-76; 40 (1954) 1-84; 41 (1955) 95-183 (esp. 115f, 178).

[40] Sicard of Cremona, *Summa* on D.80 (Rouen 710 fol.13rb).

[41] *Summa Animal est substantia* on D.23 c.1 v. *sicut:* ". . . Vnde dicunt alii quod [metropolitanus] ex electione confirmatur, sicut papa, et hoc uerum est, et hoc de illo qui non habet primatem . . ." (Bamberg Can.42 fol.106va-b).

the *pallium* on a metropolitan under his jurisdiction.[42] Johannes Teutonicus similarly believed that normal procedure requires either the pope or the primate to confirm a metropolitan's election.[43]

Yet these discussions on the primate's jurisdiction belong to the realm of mere constitutional theory, with little foundation in constitutional practice. A different theory was, however, far closer to the realities of procedure: according to custom, most twelfth-century metropolitans were consecrated by their own suffragan bishops. Moreover, the *Decretum* stressed the suffragans' right to consecrate their metropolitan.[44] At least since the mid-twelfth century, a canonical principle had asserted that whoever consecrates should also confirm.[45] It was therefore not entirely illogical when some canonists maintained that a metropolitan's suffragans may confer his confirmation as well as his consecration. Bernard of Pavia, however, opposed this doctrine. Although he admitted that the consecrator is normally also competent to confirm

[42] *Summa* on D.63 c.9 v. *consentimus*: "tuam confirmando electionem, et est arg. quod electio metropolitani a papa confirmatur. . . . Quid ergo? Dici potest quod hoc non obseruatur odie nisi in illis qui nullo medio subsunt apostolico . . . , nisi forte dicatur quod quilibet archiepiscopus hoc ipso intelligitur confirmari a papa, quia quilibet ab eo recipit pallium. . . . Immo et in quibusdam locis non obseruatur hoc etiam in illis qui subsunt pape nullo medio, set confirmantur et consecrantur a suis suffraganeis. Est enim regulare quod quilibet archiepiscopus accipit pallium a papa, nisi papa uolens deferre primati eius primati mittat pallium et ab eo accipiat archiepiscopus. Item archiepiscopus qui habet primatem preter papam ab illo debet confirmari et a suffraganeis consecrari. Ille qui subest pape nullo medio a papa debet confirmari, nisi de consuetudine et consensu pape tacito uel expresso. In aliquo loco fit aliter, scilicet quod confirmetur et consecretur a suis episcopis etiam inconsulto papa" (Clm 10247 fol.69ra).

[43] *Gl.ord.* on D.63 c.9: "confirmando electionem tuam. Et ita papa confirmat omnes metropolitanos. . . . Quod verum est cum non habent primatem, sed ei nullo medio subsunt . . . nisi velis dicere quod eo ipso quod quis recipit pallium a papa, intelligitur confirmari ab ipso. Imo et plerique archiepiscopi non confirmantur nec consecrantur nisi a suis subditis, nec petitur confirmatio a papa sed tantum pallium. . . ." Cf., however, *id.* on D.51 c.5 v. *convenientibus*: "Hic habes quod metropolitanus consecrandus a suffraganeis. . . . Arg. contra [C.24 q.1 c.33], ubi dicitur quod a papa sit consecrandus, sed primum est de iure, papa tamen iam praescripsit contra ius illud."

[44] D.66 pr.; D.66 c.1.

[45] *Coll. Lips.* 31.4 (above, Ch.IVb n.8), and see below, n.46.

the election, he argued that suffragans do not even have the right of consecration "from strict law . . . but [only] from privilege." Rather, "confirmation should always be referred to the superior," and consequently, Bernard declared, the confirmation of any metropolitan's election "pertains to the Roman pontiff."[46] Along somewhat different lines, master Huguccio explained the practice of confirmation by the suffragans as a consequence of diversity in local custom: a metropolitan directly under the Roman pontiff "may be confirmed and consecrated by his own bishops, even without the pope's having been consulted," although Huguccio believed that confirmation by the suffragans was proper only "by custom and with the tacit or express approval of the pope."[47] As a further variation on this theme, the cathedral chapter of the metropolitan church occasionally confirmed the election of their new prelate.[48] But such variations in theory and practice should not obscure the fact that by the end of Innocent III's reign, papal confirmation of a metropolitan's election had become more or less standard procedure. Because of the theoretical link between confirmation and consecration, it is not surprising that, increasingly, the Roman pontiff also consecrated the metropolitans.[49] Finally, in 1257 Alexander IV decreed that "the prelates-elect of churches which pertain, with no intermediary, to the Roman Church" must receive their consecration in Rome—a rule which presumably included metropolitans-elect.[50]

---

[46] *Summa de electione* 3.1, ed. Laspeyres, *Sum. decr.* 320: ". . . confirmatio semper ad maiorem est referenda. . . . . . . ab eo enim quis est confirmandus, a quo et consecrandus. . . . Quodsi archiepiscopus eligitur, eius confirmatio ad Romanum pontificem spectat . . . nec obiicias ad comprovinciales episcopos confirmationem archiepiscopi pertinere debere, sicut et consecrationem, cum nec ipsa quoque consecratio eis ex stricto iure conveniat, sed ex privilegio competat. . . ."

[47] Above, n.42.

[48] Hinschius, *KR* II 577 n.5 (Magdeburg 1283, Mainz 1288).

[49] *X* 1.6.44 §2 (discussed below, Ch. VIc n.12); Hinschius, *KR* II 577, 590, 600; Barraclough, *CHR* 19 (1933-34) 285-87.

[50] The decree itself has been lost and is known primarily through a letter from Alexander to the patriarch of Aquileia, *MGH Ep.saec.XIII* III 451 no.487 (1259): ". . . nobis humiliter supplicantes, ut cum eadem

The Bishop-Elect

In their efforts to create a uniform Common Law for the Church, the decretists and early decretalists had to take account of this confusion and to harmonize these various conflicts which arose from the rapid changes within canon law. Discussing the question whether metropolitans' elections should be confirmed by the pope, master Huguccio tried to resolve some of these contradictions. Although he did not fully succeed in solving these problems, he added a new element to the tradition:

> It may perhaps be said that since every archbishop receives the *pallium* from the pope, through this very act he is confirmed by the pope.[51]

In other words, Huguccio was willing to identify the bestowal of the *pallium* with the confirmation of the election, thus assimilating the newer administrative law to the old *ius pallii*. A decretal of Innocent III on a disputed election to the archbishopric of Armagh shows the logical consequence of this identification, for here Innocent implied that metropolitans

---

ecclesia [scil. Bambergensis] . . . tanta prematur sarcina debitorum, ut idem electus [scil. Bertholdus] propter hoc nequeat absque ipsius ecclesie gravi dispendio personaliter sedem apostolorum adire pro confirmationis et consecrationis munere obtinendo, confirmari electionem huiusmodi et impendi eidem electo consecrationis munus—non obstante constitutione a nobis edita, ut electi ecclesiarum, que ad Romanam ecclesiam nullo medio pertinent, ad eandem sedem pro consecratione sua personaliter teneantur accedere—in illis partibus faceremus. . . ." See also Johannes de Oxenedes, *Chronica* anno 1257, ed. Henry Ellis (Rolls Series: London 1859) 210, where the decree is mentioned—but with reference only to *quilibet exemptus in abbatem electus*. Also, see the *Continuatio chronici Florentii Wigorniensis* II (English Historical Society: London 1849) 186, for the misfortunes of the abbot-elect of Bury St Edmunds, who was forced by this decree to go to Rome in person for his confirmation and benediction; William E. Lunt, *Papal Revenues in the Middle Ages* (New York 1934) II 219. From another papal decree issued in 1257, it is evident that Alexander urgently wished to tighten the regulations for all prelates *immediate sub papa* and to bind them more closely to the Roman See; cf. his *Reg.* 3.615, ed. Charles Bourel de la Roncière et al., *Les Reg. d'Alexandre IV* (Paris 1902ff) 677 no.2206: ". . . nonnulli . . . prelati obtinuerunt sibi . . . concedi, ut non teneantur Sedem eandem [scil. Apostolicam] usque ad certa tempora visitare, contra formam prestiti iuramenti. . . . Nos igitur . . . indulgentias et concessiones huiusmodi patriarchis, archiepiscopis, episcopis, abbatibus et aliis . . . prelatis concessas, auctoritate presentium revocamus. . . ."

51 Above, n.42.

186

should seek the "confirmation with the *pallium*" from the Roman See. On the basis of this decretal, Johannes Teutonicus asserted that the linking of *pallium* and electoral confirmation was part of Innocent's policy.[52] Clearly, if electoral confirmation and the *pallium* were granted simultaneously (together with the episcopal consecration, of course), the metropolitan-elect would obtain his episcopal jurisdiction and his full archiepiscopal prerogatives at the same moment—thus the constitutional problem would disappear.[53]

There were, however, even further ambiguities. A metropolitan was said to receive the "fullness of office" (*plenitudo officii*) with the *pallium*. In a slightly different sense, an archbishop might obtain the *plenitudo officii* through his consecration, and as Innocent IV pointed out, an abbot-elect gained

[52] *X* 1.6.28 (1202): ". . . quousque posset electus [scil. metropolitanus] confirmationem cum pallio a sede apostolica obtinere . . ."; this decretal will be discussed below, Ch.VIc. Johannes Teutonicus, *Gl.ord.* on D.100 c.9 v. *ordinatum*: ". . . hoc est regulare, ut a suis suffraganeis consecretur archiepiscopus, . . . et potest perpendi . . . quod metropolitanus etiam sine licentia summi pontificis potest consecrari, et ad papam non spectat, ut videtur, nisi datio pallii. Alii dicunt istud obtinere, ubi metropolitanus habet primatem, vel cum hoc habet ex consuetudine. Hodie tamen vult papa, quod petatur ab eo confirmatio cum pallio, ut extra De electio(ne) cap. Quod sicut (*X* 1.6.28)." Even in the later 12th century, the Curia may already have seen a close connection between the *pallium* and the *confirmatio*, as the pope's *confirmatio* was required with increasing regularity. In the 1170's and 1180's, for example, two successive archbishops of Braga received in Rome "litteras domni pape ad suffraganeos ipsius ecclesie et ad capitulum, in quibus continebatur, quod recognoscerent eum tamquam proprium archiepiscopum habentem pallium et confirmationem a Romana ecclesia"; ed. Carl Erdmann, *PU Portugal* (Abh.Göttingen 20, 3: Berlin 1927) 384. Yet this policy never became fixed, for frequently throughout the 13th century the *pallium* and the confirmation were acquired at different moments. To cite a single example, the archbishop-elect of Salzburg was confirmed in March 1285 and was granted the *pallium* in May 1285; F. Kaltenbrunner, *Actenstücke zur Geschichte des deutschen Reiches unter den Königen Rudolf I. und Albrecht I.* (Mittheilungen aus dem Vaticanischen Archive 1: Vienna 1889) 302ff, 308f nos.268, 273f. Naturally, the episcopal consecration was carried out between the confirmation and the grant of the *pallium*; for the sequence in this instance, see Kaltenbrunner, *op.cit.* 305.

[53] The metropolitan-elect was normally expected to go to Rome for his *pallium*, but of course this arduous trip might be delayed for many reasons. If the confirmation *and* the *pallium* were to be simultaneously acquired in Rome, it was urgently necessary for the unconfirmed metropolitan-elect to have interim powers; this difficulty will be discussed in the next section.

The Bishop-Elect

the *plenitudo officii* through his "benediction" (*benedictio*), which was equivalent to episcopal consecration.[54] Thus, this technical term could also refer to the sacramental powers of an abbot as well as the special prerogatives of a metropolitan. The word *officium* itself added still another note of confusion, for *officium* could mean simply "office"—but in the first half of the thirteenth century, it could equally well denote specifically either the *potestas ordinis* or the *potestas iurisdictionis*.[55] On the other hand, an abbatial benediction could be considered a substitute for electoral confirmation, and the abbot's administrative powers—his general right to govern his monastery—could be derived from the benediction, rather than from confirmation. By this interpretation, an abbot's *plenitudo officii* would include not only his sacramental competence but also his jurisdictional powers.[56] It is apparent that the canonists

[54] Innocent IV, *Apparatus* on *X* 1.6.34 v. *coronamus*: ". . . In pallii autem datione, non credimus necessario examinationem faciendam, nec propter exceptionem differendam, quia consequitur ad priora, et quia ibi fit manus impositio. In benedictione autem abbatum credimus necessariam examinationem, cum fiat manus impositio, et ibi ordinandi potestatem accipiat. . . . Sed licet abbates in benedictione plenitudinem officii recipiant, non tamen per eam intelligitur dari confirmatio, vel administratio in temporalibus, quod ex eo apparet, quia ante habet hoc, sicut in archiepiscopo videmus, qui ex confirmatione potestatem recipit administrandi, tamen dicitur postea in susceptione pallii recipere plenitudinem pontificalis officii, quod apparet tantum intelligendum esse de spiritualibus. Melius dicitur, quod plenitudo officii quandoque sumitur pro confirmatione, infra eo(dem) Nihil § fi., sed aliquando aliter, sicut apparet in archiepiscopis, qui in pallii datione recipiunt plenitudinem officii, et tamen ante sunt confirmati et administrant."

[55] *Glossa Palatina* on C.24 q.1 c.4 v. *quia excommunicatus* (identical text in Johannes Teutonicus's *Gl.ord.* ad loc.): ". . . si ab officio tantum [sit suspensus] ea non poterit que officii sunt, puta celebrare et similia; set ea poterit que iurisdictionis sunt, ut dare prebendas et excommunicare, quia hoc iurisdictionis . . ." (van de Kerckhove, *Études franciscaines* 49 [1937] 452; for the correction of a false ascription here, see also Kuttner, *Repertorium* 81ff). The opposite interpretation of *officium* is given by Innocent IV, *Apparatus* on *X* 1.10.1 v. *et alia*: ". . . cum conferre lectoratum non sit officii tantum, sed ordinis . . . non poterit [abbas] ordinem conferre, nisi sit benedictus. . . ."

[56] Alexander III, *X* 1.10.1 (1169): "Statuimus . . . ut, si episcopus . . . substitutos abbates . . . benedicere . . . renuerit, eisdem abbatibus liceat proprios monachos benedicere, et alia, quae ad officium huiusmodi pertinent, exercere. . . ." Bernard of Parma, *Gl.ord.* on *X* 1.10.1 v. *substitutos*: "Et confirmatos, quia ante nihil facere vel disponere possunt." Cf., however, Innocent IV, *Apparatus* ad loc.: ". . . Per hanc benedictionem intelligitur

did indeed ring the changes in their use of the term *plenitudo officii*, but even these diverse interpretations did not exhaust the possibilities of that flexible expression: according to a decree of the Fourth Lateran Council, the various officials directly under the pope—a group which included some bishops and abbots as well as all metropolitans—were said to receive the *plenitudo officii* through electoral confirmation.[57] In this sense, the *plenitudo officii* embraced the sum of those jurisdictional and administrative powers which an *electus* normally acquired at the moment of confirmation.

3. *Immediate sub papa*

The exceptional status of a newly elected pope, possessing full jurisdictional powers, should not be surprising, since the absence of any hierarchical superior renders the papacy a truly exceptional office within the Church. Prior to 1200 and in many instances long after 1200, the papal decretals were uncompromising in their insistence upon the precedence of confirmation before a bishop-elect's administration. Even master Huguccio's defense of the bishop-elect was essentially theoretical, for it did not augment in practice the administrative and jurisdictional powers of an unconfirmed *electus*. All the more startling, therefore, is a decretal issued by Innocent III in 1202 and afterward endowed with the full authority of

---

data cura monasterii, quia succedit in locum confirmationis, nec est facienda aliqua examinatio, vel inquisitio in hac benedictione. . . ." With these remarks, Innocent has apparently contradicted himself; cf. above, n.54. Further, note the formula used in the abbatial benediction, as given by William Durandus, *Pontificale* 1.20.25, ed. Andrieu, *Pontifical romain* III 407: "Accipe plenam et liberam potestatem regendi hoc monasterium et congregationem eius et omnia quae ad illud interius et exterius spiritualiter et temporaliter pertinere noscuntur."

[57] *X* 1.6.44 §2 (below, Ch.VIc n.12). The term *plenitudo officii* sometimes also referred specifically to the powers acquired through episcopal consecration; Hostiensis, *Commentaria* on *X* 1.6.34, 1.6.5, 1.23.4. In the 12th century, moreover, the term could be used in a nontechnical sense, to mean the "full powers of office" (or even "good standing") of a bishop; see Paul Kehr, *PU Spanien* I (Abh.Göttingen 18, 2: Berlin 1926) 333 no.61 (1153).

binding law, when it was taken into the *Compilatio tertia*.[1] John of Salerno, cardinal-legate for Scotland and Ireland, had written from the latter province in order to ask Innocent's advice in settling a complicated dispute over a double election to the vacant archbishopric of Armagh,[2] and this decretal is Innocent's answer. The church of Armagh had a special prominence in this period, for since the early twelfth century the archbishop of Armagh had acted as metropolitan of all Ireland.[3] As a legal controversy, the electoral dispute was extraordinarily complex, and most of the issues are not of immediate importance. Indeed, besides other disagreements, the parties were even divided along national lines in a way that rings familiar to modern ears. The English were absolutely unwilling to have an Irishman as archbishop, and the Irish asserted that if an Englishman presided over the cathedral of Armagh, "that church and the peace of the entire land would not be suitably provided for"; Innocent himself mentioned the *simplicitas et ruditas* of the Irish. An election was held to fill the vacancy, but the circumstances were extremely irregular, even uncanonical, and an appeal was sent to the Holy See. Despite the first election and the appeal, a few days later a second election was held, and the abbot of Bangor was elected—but some of the proper electors were absent from this election. On the following Sunday, without waiting either for electoral confirmation or for the *pallium*, the abbot received his episcopal consecration, and he immediately proceeded to ordain an acolyte and to exercise his administrative rights. Thereupon the papal legate suspended the abbot, and he gave the administration of the church to the archdeacon of Armagh. The archdeacon, however, abused

---

[1] X 1.6.28 (= *Comp.III* 1.6.13).

[2] On John of Salerno, cardinal-priest of St Stephen's, see Helene Tillmann, *Die päpstlichen Legaten in England bis zur Beendigung der Legation Gualas (1218)* (Bonn 1926) 90; also, P. J. Dunning, "The Letters of Innocent III to Ireland," *Traditio* 18 (1962) 234 and Calendar no.22.

[3] Austin Lane Poole, *From Domesday Book to Magna Carta 1087-1216* (Oxford History of England 3: Oxford 1951) 304.

his *administratio* by selling a silver *tabula* belonging to his church for twenty-five marks.

As one of the arguments against the abbot of Bangor's claim, Innocent remarked that "the abbot, having been thus elected, presumed to administer before receiving his confirmation."[4] Nonetheless, this transgression did not decisively prejudice the abbot's claim. In fact, Innocent expressly instructed his envoy to wink at the violation of this canonical precept:

> Though the election was held before you had arrived in Ireland, and though the archbishop-elect immediately began to administer, you can ignore this fact. For as you know, considering the needs of the churches, the Roman Church permits this in the case of the metropolitans of England, France, Germany and other remote places, when their elections have been uncontested. For if the archbishop-elect did not receive the temporalities (*regalia*) before he can obtain his confirmation with the *pallium* from the Apostolic See, his church, meanwhile lacking an administrator, would suffer great damage. . . .[5]

Innocent's reason for this stipulation—"the needs of the churches"—was undoubtedly sound: there were real dangers for an ecclesiastical province which was distant from Rome and which might be left untended during the necessarily long interval before the confirmation of the metropolitan's election. To be sure, even at the very beginning of the Middle Ages,

---

[4] *X* 1.6.28: ". . . Quartum, quia praefatus abbas sic electus ante confirmationem obtentam administrare praesumpsit. Quintum, quia in die consecrationis suae ordines celebravit, cum nondum pallium obtineret. . . ."

[5] *X* 1.6.28: ". . . Ceterum, cum, antequam tu ad partes Hibernicas pervenisses, illa fuerit electio celebrata, et electus ipse statim coeperit ministrare, tu satis id potes sub dissimulatione transire, cum id, sicut nosti, de metropolitanis Angliae, Franciae, Alemaniae et aliarum partium remotarum, qui concorditer sunt electi, Romana ecclesia patiatur, ecclesiarum utilitate pensata, quia, si tanto tempore, quousque posset electus confirmationem cum pallio a sede apostolica obtinere, regalia non reciperet, ecclesia, quae interim administratore careret, non modicum incurreret detrimentum. . . ." The Armagh election is certainly not a good example of an *electio concors*.

it had been recognized that because of the slowness and difficulty of a long journey, it might be impractical to insist upon the consent and participation of all suffragan bishops at the elevation of a new bishop. Special canonical measures provided for such circumstances, and some of these provisions reappeared in the *Decretum*, where Innocent had certainly read them and approved of the idea behind them.[6]

For Innocent, the metropolitans in regions distant from Rome clearly enjoyed an exceptional status, which entitled them to administer immediately after their elections without waiting for papal confirmation. Further, Innocent presupposed that the cardinal-legate was already fully acquainted with his special right of the metropolitans in "remote places." Indeed, this state of affairs was, in all likelihood, quite well known. Ten or fifteen years earlier, Innocent's teacher, master Huguccio, had noted that some prelates-elect do, in fact, administer even before confirmation,[7] and in similar vein the French *Apparatus Ecce uicit leo* had observed that "today, unconfirmed archbishops administer"—to which he caustically added, "but [in this respect] they act badly."[8] Various canonists had pointed out that some metropolitans, although directly under the pope, are confirmed by their own suffragan bishops.[9] Of course, where the metropolitan is elected by his own suffragans, as in the church of Armagh, confirmation of the election could thereby be automatic and immediate. Automatic confirmation, simply by virtue of election, might even be considered distinctive and appropriate for the metropolitan. As the *Summa Animal est substantia* explained, "A metropolitan [who does not have a primate] is confirmed through election, just like the pope."[10] Obviously, then, the metropolitan, like the pope, can administer immediately after

---

[6] D.64 cc.1, 7; for another Innocentian decretal using the same argument, cf. *X* 1.8.6: "Cum sis in partibus remotissimis. . . ."

[7] *Summa* on D.63 c.10 v. *subscripta relatio* (above, Ch.VA n.23).

[8] On D.23 c.1 v. *obtineat* (above, Ch.VIB n.35).

[9] Bernard of Pavia (Ch.VIB n.46); Huguccio (Ch.VIB n.42); Johannes Teutonicus (Ch.VIB n.43).

[10] On D.23 c.1 v. *sicut* (Ch.VIB n.41).

his election. Now to return to the Armagh controversy: The
abbot of Bangor's testimony corroborates the general tenor
of these assertions about the metropolitan's postelectoral
administrative rights. As a plea to defend himself against the
charge of preconfirmatory administration, the abbot, supported by others from that region, stated that custom had
always allowed this right.[11] One need not take Innocent's
words too seriously, therefore, when he speaks of a tradition
of papal *permission* for the metropolitans' practice of administering directly after their elections. Huguccio and the other
decretists, in agreement with the abbot of Bangor, were discussing a usage of long standing, a customary usage which
had never depended on papal permission. Indeed, it seems
certain that this "right" to administer had always been a
matter of normal practice in the metropolitan sees outside of
Italy—a practice which was never even questioned until the
twelfth-century decretists developed their theories on the
prerequisites to ecclesiastical administration.

In 1215, at the Fourth Lateran Council, the special "right"
of immediate postelectoral administration was extended also
to the "exempt" bishops and abbots in distant lands, that is,
to bishops and abbots who were not subject to a local metropolitan or bishop but were directly under the pope.[12] All

[11] *X* 1.6.28: ". . . abbatem canonicorum regularium de Benger in archiepiscopum elegerunt, et ipsum, sicut consuetudinis esse dicebant, sequenti
die dominica in episcopum consecraverunt; qui post inunctionem suam,
antequam missarum solennia finirentur, quendam in acolythum ordinavit, et
administrare praesumpsit. Cumque ipsum super hoc graviter redargueres,
dicebat ipse, ac confitebantur alii de partibus ipsius, quod talis consuetudo
erat hactenus in Hibernia observata. . . ."
[12] *Conc. Lat. IV* c.26; *Comp.IV* 1.3.11 (*X* 1.6.44 §2): "Ceterum qui ad
Romanum pertinent immediate pontificem, ad percipiendam sui confirmationem officii eius se conspectui, si commode fieri potest, personaliter reprae-
sentent, aut personas transmittant idoneas, per quas diligens inquisitio super
electionibus et electis possit haberi, ut sic demum per ipsius circumspec-
tionem consilii sui plenitudinem officii assequantur, cum eis nihil obstiterit
de canonicis institutis, ita, quod interim valde remoti, videlicet ultra Italiam
constituti, si electi fuerint in concordia, dispensative propter necessitates
ecclesiarum et utilitates in spiritualibus et temporalibus administrent; sic
tamen, ut de rebus ecclesiasticis nihil penitus alienent. Munus vero benedictionis seu consecrationis recipiant, sicut hactenus recipere consueverunt."
Because this decree applied to *all* who were directly subject to the pope, it

those who depend upon the pope for electoral confirmation should come to Rome personally for this approval, or should at least send "suitable persons" who can answer questions about the election and the *electus*. If, however, their province or diocese is located outside of Italy, and if the election was uncontested, they may, "through a dispensation" (*dispensative*) for the needs of the church, administer the *temporalia* and *spiritualia* even before confirmation. Like Innocent's decretal of 1202, this constitution of the Fourth Lateran Council was designed to avoid an administrative interregnum, with all of its consequent dangers. But simple distance was not the only possible source of delay; in matters of electoral confirmation, the Apostolic See maintained especially rigorous standards. Although for other churches the election decree was a sufficient guarantee of canonical election, the "custom of the Roman Church" generally insisted that as a prerequisite to the granting of electoral confirmation, two persons who had taken part in the election should personally give their testimony in Rome.[13]

Quite probably the status of the "exempt" bishops and abbots resembled that of the metropolitans in still another respect: just like the metropolitans before the decretal of 1202, even before the Fourth Lateran Council the *exempti* were probably inclined to regard immediate postelectoral administration as their customary right.[14] To be sure, the

---

thus superseded the passages in the decretal of 1202 (*X* 1.6.28) which are relevant to the administrative rights of a metropolitan-elect; hence, when the decretal of 1202 and this decree were republished in the *Liber extra*, the pertinent passages from the earlier decretal were omitted.

[13] Innocent IV, *Apparatus* on *X* 1.6.44 v. *aut personas*: "de iure enim est quod solum decretum sufficit ad probationem canonicae electionis . . . sed consuetudo Ro(manae) ecclesiae est, quod non confirmat aliquem electum, nisi sint presentes apud sedem apostolicam duo de his qui interfuerint electioni. . . ."

[14] Gl. on *Comp.III* 1.6.13 v. *metropolitanis*: "§ numquid in illis tantum? Credo quod idem est in episcopis uel abbatibus exemptis, in aliis non, supra e.t. c.ii." (Clm 3879 fol.163vb). Gl. on *Comp.III* 1.6.2. v. *irreverenter*: " . . . Solutio: illud in remotis partibus tolleratur [*add. alt. man.*: tam in spiritualibus quam temporalibus, ut infra, e.t. Nichil uel Qualiter], hic autem in aliis se miscuit, uel illud tolleratur in metropolitanis tantum, ut in illo

papacy had been extremely tolerant toward the metropolitan in the exercise of his administrative rights prior to electoral confirmation—but was much less tolerant toward this practice when carried on by an *exemptus*. In 1208 Innocent bitterly attacked the position held by an exempt abbot in Germany, who had asserted that according to the "custom in those parts," an *exemptus* need not seek electoral confirmation from the pope or from a papal legate.[15] In any case, the Council's constitution provided a "general dispensation" for these exempt bishops and abbots, as well as for the metropolitans, to administer before confirmation.[16] Even under these circumstances, however, the canonists believed that the unconfirmed *electus* did not have an absolutely unrestricted right to administer. During the interim between election and confirmation, for example, he could not alienate the property of his church, nor could he accept an oath of obedience from

---

c.Quod sicut" (Clm 3879 fol.158vb). Except for the addition, which was obviously written after the 4th Lateran Council (*Nichil* = *Conc. Lat. IV* c.26), these two glosses are in the same hand and should, in all likelihood, be ascribed to Johannes Galensis and thereby to the period before 1215.

[15] *X* 1.4.7: ". . . [abbas] de monasterio Hermionensi, quod ad Romanam ecclesiam noscitur pertinere nullo mediante . . . se . . . excusans illius terrae allegavit consuetudinem generalem, asserens, quod pro electionis confirmatione vel obtinenda etiam benedictione . . . summus pontifex vel eius legati non erant aliquatenus requirendi, cum in illis partibus consuetudo talis hactenus sit servata. . . . Cum igitur haec non tam consuetudo, quam corruptela merito sit censenda . . . ipsam mandamus . . . non servari."

[16] Because of one of the glosses on *Conc. Lat. IV* c.26, the question arises: What does *dispensative* mean? Vincentius, *Apparatus* on *Conc. Lat. IV* c.26 v. *ultra ytaliam*: "§ Nota provinciales appellare valde remotos et possunt, si electio in concordia est facta, amministrare et hoc dispensative. Set quis dispensabit? Dico, quod papa dispensabit hic, et est ius conmune, quod quilibet electus potest uti iure huius constitutionis et potest conferre prebendas . . ." (Gillmann, *AKKR* 109 [1929] 259 n.5). By using future tense, Vincentius seems to imply that a separate dispensation will have to be granted in each case. However, Vincentius was, in all probability, the first commentator on these constitutions (Kuttner, *Repertorium* 370). The later and more mature opinions of Johannes Teutonicus and Innocent IV agree that the decree itself is a "general dispensation," and hence, automatically effective in advance (below, nn.18f). But did Vincentius really wish to suggest that *quilibet electus* can take advantage of this constitution? Probably not. Cf. another gloss on c.26 by Vincentius, v. *alienent*: ". . . Hic enim agitur de hiis, qui subsunt immediate domino pape . . ." (Gillmann, *op.cit.* 234).

a subject.[17] Moreover, when there was a papal legate present in the province, the "general dispensation" for these officials in "remote places" was invalid; before administering his office, the *electus* must first be confirmed by the legate.[18] In the view of Innocent IV, the very jurisdiction exercised by these unconfirmed metropolitans and *exempti* was extraordinary, since it had been directly sanctioned by the pope. The

[17] *X* 1.6.44 §2: ". . . ut de rebus ecclesiasticis nihil penitus alienent . . ." (above, n.12). Also, Johannes Teutonicus, *Gl.ord.* on *Comp.IV* 1.3.11 v. *administrent*, ed. Antonius Augustinus, *Opera omnia* IV: *Antiquae collectiones decretalium* (Lucca 1769) 620: "In tribus reperio, quod ex sola electione habetur ius administrandi. In exemptis, qui sunt ultra Italiam, ut hic; et in archiepiscopis transmontanis . . . et in Romano pontifice. . . . Sed pone, quod ille qui sic administrat, postea tempore confirmationis, cum non reperitur idoneus, cassatur eius electio, numquid ea, quae medio tempore fecit, cassanda sunt? . . . Dico, quod quidquid fecit circa spiritualia, illud ratum habebitur. Similiter quidquid in temporalibus fecit recipiendo, non autem dando. . . ." For an opposing interpretation, which probably should not be taken too seriously, cf. Vincentius, *Apparatus* on *Conc. Lat. IV* c.26 v. *ultra ytaliam*: ". . . potest [electus valde remotus] conferre prebendas, et licet postea non confirmetur per papam, tamen valebunt ea, que contulit . . ." (Gillmann, *AKKR* 109 [1929] 259 n.5). Perhaps for Vincentius, the bestowal of a prebend was an act of simple administration rather than an alienation. Also, Innocent IV, *Apparatus* on *X* 1.6.44 v. *administrent*: ". . . sed obedientiam a subditis recipere non debet." For any *electus*, confirmation was a prerequisite to the acceptance of an oath.

[18] Innocent IV, *Apparatus* on *X* 1.4.7 v. *consuetudinem*: "quae erat, ut tales abbates sine licentia papae transirent, et sine confirmatione ministrarent, quorum neutrum facere poterat. . . . Hodie autem, licet non sit mutatum in Italia in administratione, tamen hodie ex generali dispensatione pape ultra Italiam constituti et concorditer electi possunt in temporalibus et spiritualibus ministrare, infra De elect(ione) Quod sicut et c.Nihil, sed hic cum in prouincia essent legati, a quibus poterant confirmationem habere, non prodest consuetudo." Also, William of Mandagout, Commentary on his own treatise *De iure electionis novorum praelatorum* c.56 v. *confirmatione* (Cologne 1602) fol.104r-v: "Nota, quod ante confirmationem non debet electus in spiritualibus vel temporalibus per se, vel per alium . . . administrare tanquam electus, vel tanquam procurator aut oeconomus, vel alias qualitercumque . . . nisi sit ultra Italiam constitutus, ac immediate ecclesiae Romanae subiectus, et in concordia electus, si enim haec tria in eo concurrant, bene potest administrare . . . sic tamen, quod de rebus ecclesiasticis nihil penitus alienet. . . . Quod est verum, nisi sit legatus in provincia, a quo confirmatio possit peti, tunc enim non debet administrare. . . ." William composed his electoral treatise and his own commentary on it shortly before 1285; Schulte, *Geschichte der Quellen* II 183ff. See also the decretal by Boniface VIII, *VI* 1.6.36 §1: "Huiusmodo vero legatus [scil. de latere], qui maius post Romanum pontificem in provincia sibi decreta imperium censetur habere, archiepiscoporum, episcoporum et exemptorum electiones potest ex officio confirmare. Alii autem legati hoc nequeunt. . . ."

implications were similar when other jurists compared these unconfirmed prelates to specially appointed "proctors."[19]

In their discussions of the metropolitans and *exempti* in the lands remote from Italy, the decretalists noted that the same arguments—distance, delay, and the needs of the church —could also be applied to any *electus*, even to one who was not immediately subject to the pope. As Johannes Teutonicus remarked:

Isn't the same reasoning valid for other *electi* who are distant from their metropolitan? It seems that is the case . . . and it can be said that if [such an *electus*] administer those things for which a delay would be dangerous and which would be destroyed in the course of time, it does not seem that by this he has meddled in the administration. . . .[20]

[19] Innocent IV, *Apparatus* on *X* 1.6.44 v. *administrent*: "Isti ex sola electione administrationem habent a papa . . . et sic administrare possunt, ac si prelati essent confirmati. Alii dicunt quia sunt ut visitatores vel procuratores. . . ."

[20] *Summula* on *Comp.III* 1.6.13 v. *metropolitanis*: "§ transmontani metropolitani ex sola electione habent ius amministrandi, similiter illi qui subsunt pape tantum. . . . Set numquid eadem est ratio in aliis electis qui sunt remoti a suo metropolitano? Satis uidetur quod sic . . . et potest dici quod si amministrat ea quorum mora est periculosa et que tractu temporis essent peritura, per hoc non uidetur se immiscuisse amministrationi . . ." (Clm 3879 fol.163vb). Johannes took the opposite position in his *Gl.ord.* on *D.*23 c.1 v. *et disponendi*: ". . . Qui transmontani [archiepiscopi vel exempti] sunt, statim possunt administrare. . . . Sed certe videtur, quod in omnibus, idem iuris est, ut si electus non posset intrare possessionem rei, ad quam est electus, nihilominus pro possessore est habendus. . . ." The last clause in this passage is characteristic of Johannes's adherence to the Huguccian tradition. Johannes presented both sides of the question in his *Apparatus* on *Comp.IV* 1.3.11 v. *administrent*, ed. Augustinus, *Opera* IV 620: ". . . Sed quid si suffraganeus aliquis valde remotus est a suo metropolitano, numquid eo modo ratione remotionis poterit ministrare? Videtur quod sic, ne si nimia subtilitate circa res ecclesiarum laboremus, res ipsarum in medio depereant . . . et sic ista subtilitas eis in perniciem verteretur. . . . Secus tamen videtur, quia cum istud hic dispensative statuatur, ut hic dicitur, dispensatio non est trahenda ad similia . . . nec excusat hic periculum aliquod. . . ." Also, Vincentius, *Apparatus* on *Conc. Lat. IV* c.26 v. *ultra ytaliam*: ". . . Pone, quod archiepiscopus non vult confirmare electum in concordia et appellat ad papam, nuncquid interim administrabit? Arg. est hic, quod sic. Set non credo. Hic enim agitur de hiis, qui subsunt immediate domino pape . . ." (Gillmann, *AKKR* 109 [1929] 234).

Still, the decretalists were unwilling to accept this argumentation, and even Johannes himself did not consistently defend this position. At least the principle had been established that the administrative rights could be effectively separated from the juridical act which normally conferred them: the *administratio* could, under exceptional circumstances, precede the electoral confirmation. Of course, the Roman pontiff had the power to confirm any election whatsoever,[21] or he could, if he chose, confer the *administratio* without confirming the election. For example, in 1206, because of their fear of Philip of Swabia, the cathedral chapter of Constance did not dare request the archbishop of Mainz to confirm the election of William of Staufen, and they asked Innocent to confirm William's election and accordingly to grant him full administrative rights. In effect, such an action on Innocent's part could have given exempt status to the bishopric of Constance and might thereby have placed it directly under the Roman See. Innocent, however, was generally anxious to protect the rights of the metropolitans, and he usually tried to avoid usurping their prerogatives.[22] Therefore, "considering the needs of the church of Constance," Innocent granted the *administratio spiritualium et temporalium* to the bishop-elect, but he insisted that William should nonetheless receive the electoral confirmation from his own metropolitan, the archbishop of Mainz, "at an opportune time."[23]

[21] As Innocent III distinctly intimated in a letter of 1206 (below, n.23).
[22] Helene Tillmann, *Papst Innocenz III.* (Bonn 1954) 293.
[23] Letter to the provost, dean, and chapter of Constance (1206), *Reg.* 9.163, *PL* 215 990: "... Verum, quia propter metum principis, cuius incursibus est ecclesia Constantiensis exposita, confirmationem electionis eiusdem ausi non estis a ... Maguntino archiepiscopo postulare, ne propter confirmationis dilationem ecclesia vestra in spiritualibus et temporalibus incurrere valeat detrimentum, nobis humiliter supplicatis, ut ... electionem ipsam auctoritate apostolica confirmare, ac dicto electo administrationem tam spiritualium quam temporalium committere dignaremur. Nos igitur, necessitatem Constantiensis ecclesiae attendentes ... administrationem tam spiritualium quam temporalium eidem W. duximus committendam, in qua idem se talem studeat exhibere, quod a metropolitano suo confirmationis gratiam, et consecrationis munus consequi mereatur tempore opportuno"; on this text, see Tillmann (*loc.cit.*). This terminology was also used in rather different circumstances. For example, after a subdeacon and

Either by going to Rome himself or by sending "suitable persons," an exempt bishop or abbot had to obtain his electoral confirmation from the pope, but the *exemptus* was not generally consecrated by the Roman pontiff.[24] By decree of Alexander IV in 1257, however, prelates-elect directly subject to the papacy had to go to Rome for their electoral confirmation and also for consecration.[25] Except for compelling reasons and with explicit permission from Rome, such an *electus* no longer had the option of sending "suitable persons" to give testimony at the Curia. And two decades after Alexander's decree, Nicholas III reiterated this requirement, stipulating further that the *electus* must depart for Rome within one month after consenting to his own election (or receiving notice of it), and must bring all necessary documents with him.[26] Still, these provisions did not affect the non-Italian prelate-elect's right to administer before confirmation.

---

papal chaplain was elected to the archbishopric of Capua, the election was challenged. Upon examining the case, Innocent did not regard the irregularities as serious. Innocent was personally acquainted with the *electus*, and he vouched for the subdeacon's character and education. However, neither he nor anyone else, as it seems, was sure that the *electus* had reached the canonical age of thirty years. The disposition of the case is interesting: Innocent III, *X* 1.6.19 (1200): ". . . Nos ecclesiae pariter et personae providere volentes . . . quia propositum vestrum providum intelleximus, et ideo propter urgentem necessitatem et evidentem utilitatem ecclesiae Capuanae, quam in hac parte potius approbamus, volumus ipsum firmiter perdurare, praefatum subdiaconum nostrum . . . vobis in procuratorem concedimus, liberam administrationem ei tam in temporalibus quam in spiritualibus committentes." Innocent has appointed the *electus* as *procurator* and has granted him the *administratio*—but without really confirming the election.

24 Abbots received a *benedictio* rather than the *consecratio* given to bishops-elect. Correspondingly, an exempt abbot was confirmed by the pope, but he might obtain his benediction elsewhere; *Chronicon abbatiae de Evesham* anno 1214 [properly: 1215 or after], ed. William D. Macray (Rolls Series: London 1863) 259.

25 Above, Ch.VIB n.50.

26 *VI* 1.6.16. Provision is made for exceptions, difficulties, and special circumstances, but—despite the constitution's obscure wording—this basic requirement is discernible. A constitution of the 2nd Council of Lyons (c.5 = *VI* 1.6.6) had already established that every *electus* must consent to his election within one month, and within three months must request his confirmation; even after Nicholas's decree, this constitution continued to have validity for prelates-elect who were subject to a metropolitan rather than to the papacy.

Finally, however, Boniface VIII abandoned Innocent III's tolerant and sensible policy toward the metropolitans and *exempti* outside of Italy. One of Boniface's decretals commanded that any *electus* who is directly subject to the Roman See should not undertake the administration of his church without written confirmation of his election, and that no one should obey such an *electus* until the letter of confirmation has been shown.[27] On this question the Fourth Lateran Council had firmly established the canonical norm for the thirteenth century,[28] and Boniface was clearly trying to reverse the direction of papal policy of the previous hundred years. Understandably, therefore, in the fourteenth century a non-Italian *exemptus* might still seek special permission to administer before his confirmation.[29] Because Boniface's decretal was only an *extravagans*, rather than a part of the *Corpus iuris canonici*, his innovation was not immediately and unquestionably accepted.[30] Innocent III's policy had indeed struck deep roots in administrative thought and practice.

[27] *Extrav. com.* 1.3.1: ". . . sancimus, ut episcopi et alii praelati superiores, necnon abbates . . . qui apud dictam sedem [scil. apostolicam] promoventur, aut confirmationis, consecrationis vel benedictionis munus recipiunt, ad commissas eis ecclesias et monasteria absque dictae sedis literis huiusmodi, eorum promotionem, confirmationem, consecrationem seu bendictionem continentibus, accedere, vel bonorum ecclesiasticorum administrationem accipere non praesumant, nullique eos absque dictarum literarum ostensione recipiant, aut eis pareant vel intendant. . . . Similiter quoque episcopi, praelati, abbates . . . et alii . . . solito fidelitatis et obedientiae iuramento non praestito. Illi etiam pontifices, quos apud praedictam sedem pallium continget recipere, absque literis traditionis ipsius pallii nequaquam ab eadem discedant. . . ."

[28] *X* 1.6.44 (above, n.12).

[29] In 1395 the monastery of St Albans, directly subject to the Roman See, received a perpetual indult entitling the abbot-elect to administer immediately after election; *Calendar of Entries in the Papal Registers Relating to Great Britain and Ireland: Papal Letters* IV, ed. William H. Bliss and J. A. Twemlow (Rolls Series: London 1902) 517f.

[30] Cf. Oldradus de Ponte, *Consilia* no.51.

PART TWO

THE BISHOP-ELECT BETWEEN
CHURCH AND MONARCHY

CHAPTER VII

OFFICE, *REGALIA*,
AND INVESTITURE:
THE AGE OF REFORM

1. The Episcopal Office and the *Regalia*

At no other time in the Church's history has the episcopal office been the object of such intense scrutiny and deep concern as during the eleventh and early twelfth centuries. Indeed, the major ideological conflicts of this period can be largely summed up as a crisis provoked by divergent concepts of office.[1] Simony was widespread, and from the end of the tenth century, reformers were demanding its abolition. In the late 1050's, the reformers extended their attack to include lay investiture, and the papacy incorporated this program in legislation. Yet simony was still the main target of the reformers until Gregory VII issued a new series of decrees against lay investiture between 1075 and 1080. Then followed the Investiture Struggle: almost fifty years of conflict between popes and emperors, with the control of the imperial episcopate as the chief prize at stake. In the course of the struggles over simony and lay investiture, as the contestants were forced to defend and define their positions, they formulated new theories of the episcopal office, which in turn

---

[1] The crisis in the evolving conceptions of the papal, imperial, and royal offices cannot be discussed within the framework of this study. Moreover, some crucial issues in the history of the episcopal office—such as the validity of the sacramental powers of a simoniac or heretical bishop—will be given only cursory attention here.

The Bishop-Elect

reflected their positions and aggravated the differences between them. Reformers and simoniacs, imperial supporters and papal partisans, contended long and bitterly over these ideas of office. By the early twelfth century, some had lucidly analyzed the various functions and appurtenances of the bishop: sacramental competence, jurisdictional powers, fiscal rights, and different forms of property.[2] The acceptance of such concepts made possible the eventual settlement of the Investiture Struggle.

During the eleventh and early twelfth centuries, in the ceremonial act of investiture, the monarch granted to a new prelate the symbols of his office: the ring and the crosier. Investiture was the sign and symbol of the king's power over the episcopate and of his right to control episcopal appointments. Sometimes an election preceded the investiture, sometimes an election followed it as a formality expressing consent to the king's choice, often the election was dispensed with altogether. In any case, the investiture was the decisive step in the elevation of the bishop.[3]

Episcopalis dignitas continet res

According to the customary investitive formula used in the

[2] On these developments, the studies by Carl Mirbt, *Die Publizistik im Zeitalter Gregors VII.* (Leipzig 1894), and Anton Scharnagl, *Der Begriff der Investitur in den Quellen und der Literatur des Investiturstreites* (Kirchenrechtliche Abh. 56: Stuttgart 1908), are essential, and the even older work by Julius Ficker, "Ueber das Eigenthum des Reichs am Reichskirchengute," *SB Wien* 72 (1872) 55-146, 381-450, can still be read with profit. For a lucid survey, see Z. N. Brooke, "Lay Investiture and Its Relation to the Conflict of Empire and Papacy," *PBA* 25 (1939) 217-47. Arnold Pöschl, *Die Regalien der mittelalterlichen Kirchen* (Festschrift der Grazer Universität für 1927: Graz 1928), is useful, though sometimes confused and misleading; critical review by A. Degener, *ZRG KA* 19 (1930) 719-29. Further, two important articles must be consulted: Irene Ott, "Der Regalienbegriff im 12. Jahrhundert," *ZRG KA* 35 (1948) 234-304; Hartmut Hoffmann, "Ivo von Chartres und die Lösung des Investiturproblems," *DA* 15 (1959) 393-440. See also Jean Gaudemet, "Régale (Droit de)," *DDC* VII (1959-60) 493-532, who assesses without exaggeration the historian's difficulty in treating the *regalia* (p.494): "Obscurité des origines, imprécision des concepts, diversités régionales, variations historiques."

[3] In addition to the works cited in the previous note, see Carlyle, *Mediaeval Political Theory* IV 25-39, 49-60; Hauck, *KG* III 52-56.

mid-eleventh century, as the monarch handed over the symbols to the future bishop, he said simply, "Receive the church."[4] Since the reign of Otto the Great, emperors had richly endowed their bishoprics with lands, rights, and jurisdictional powers. However vague, the formula of investiture was rooted in the monarch's continuing proprietary claims to these ecclesiastical possessions, and it undoubtedly embraced the church's lands as well as the church building itself.[5] Indeed, the formula even suggested that the ruler was conferring the bishop's office, and in fact, eleventh-century Germany commonly described the investiture in the most general terms as the bestowal of the episcopal office, without any attempt to distinguish between the temporal and the spiritual elements attached to that office. When it was said that the prince had granted the *regimen pastorale* or *cura pastoralis* or *episcopatus* to a newly invested bishop, it must have seemed as though the grant included the bishop's purely ecclesiastical functions.[6]

Until the reformers began to attack the custom of investiture with ring and staff, there was little reason to examine it critically and to explain its meaning. Prior to the late 1050's, therefore, most contemporaries did not grasp the full implications of the terminology applied to investiture. Indeed, it is

4 Peter Damian, *Ep.*1.13, *PL* 144 221: "Sane cum baculum ille tuis manibus tradidit, dixitne: 'Accipe terras atque divitias illius ecclesiae,' an potius, quod certum est: 'Accipe ecclesiam'?"

5 Ficker, *SB Wien* 72 (1872) 107-09, 420f; Ulrich Stutz, "The Proprietary Church as an Element of Mediaeval Germanic Ecclesiastical Law," *Mediaeval Germany 911-1250*, ed. G. Barraclough (2 vols. Oxford 1938) II 35-70.

6 Some other 11th-century expressions for the object conferred by investiture were: *episcopium, pontificium, praesulatus, munus pontificatus*. For different opinions on the meaning of investiture in the earlier 11th century, see Ficker, *loc.cit.*; Hinschius, *KR* II 536f; Scharnagl, *op.cit.* 6f; Hauck, *KG* III 53-56. More or less typical is the view of Scharnagl: "So haben auch die Zeitgenossen diese Investitur . . . als Uebertragung des bischöflichen Amtes, der cura pastoralis [verstanden, ohne zwischen Spiritualien und Temporalien zu unterscheiden]. Das war keineswegs eine durch den Gebrauch von Ring und Stab geweckte, irrtümliche Anschauung, sondern entsprach völlig den Tatsachen. Der König schien nicht nur das Amt zu vergeben, sondern vergab es wirklich und, wie seine Worte zeigen, bewussterweise. Der Investierte besass das volle ius in re, alle geistlichen und weltlichen Rechte."

probable that very few even reflected on this question. Yet in an age which did not consider investiture a controversial act, perhaps the fluid terminology of the chroniclers and of the ceremonial formula did not accurately represent the views of thoughtful men. For one thing, it is clear that investiture was not regarded as the conferment of sacramental powers and of all spiritual prerogatives. After his investiture, a new bishop held only the title of an "elect," and he still needed the episcopal consecration. Far from asserting that investiture was sufficient warrant for the exercise of sacramental powers, in 1046 the emperor Henry III was ready to try and to condemn the duly invested archbishop-elect of Ravenna for wearing the episcopal costume during the celebration of mass—an unauthorized act, since that prelate had not been consecrated.[7] Even the most passionately royalist of later writers, founding their theories of kingship on the king's anointed and hence priestly character, denied that the monarch can bestow sacramental powers.[8] Of course, so long as an invested but unconsecrated prelate did not lay claim to any purely sacramental prerogatives, no one questioned his right to administer his office without further restrictions, in some cases even for a substantial period of time.[9] But in exercising his purely ecclesiastical jurisdiction, the invested bishop-elect was acting with the sanction of unexamined custom: there is no reason

[7] Anselm, *Gesta episcoporum Leodiensium* c.58, *MGH SS* VII 224: ". . . Wigerus . . . archiepiscopatum Ravennatem ab ipso imperatore Heinrico acceperat, isque antequam episcopus ordinaretur, biennio presbiter tantum cum dalmatica et sandaliis missarum sollempnia celebraverat. Unde pro . . . hac maxime quasi temeritate accusatus, ad palatium evocatur. . . ." Anselm's account of this incident (see also below, n.12) is contemporary, well informed, and highly reliable; Wilhelm Wattenbach & Robert Holtzmann, *Deutschlands Geschichtsquellen im Mittelalter: Deutsche Kaiserzeit* I (2nd ed. Tübingen 1948) 146-48.

[8] See, especially, the Anglo-Norman Anonymous of 1100 (below, Ch. VIIB n.44), *Tractatus* 4, *MGH LdL* III 667. Cf. also Wido of Osnabrück (*MGH LdL* I 466f), who argued that royal anointment made the monarch a *sacerdotalis ministerii particeps*, but he claimed for the king nothing more than an unspecified *facultas de ecclesiasticis disponendi*.

[9] Rudolf Bonin, *Die Besetzung der deutschen Bistümer in den letzten 30 Jahren Heinrichs IV. 1077 bis 1105* (Jena 1889) 48f, 113ff.

to assume that this procedure harmonized fully with the canonical norms of the early eleventh century. For the clarification of these norms, there is one invaluable clue: the trial of the archbishop-elect of Ravenna in 1046.[10] Among the bishops present at this trial was Wazo of Liège. When the emperor asked for his opinion, Wazo's reformist principles conflicted with his proven loyalty to Henry. Speaking as a German bishop, Wazo at first tactfully disclaimed any right to judge an Italian prelate, but when the emperor reminded him of his duty to obey, Wazo expressed his real views. Implicitly rejecting the obligation of obedience to Henry, he explained—undoubtedly using *obedientia* and *fidelitas* as technical terms—that every imperial bishop owes "obedience" to the Roman pontiff, but "fealty" to the emperor.[11] With a further distinction between "secular things" and the "divine office," Wazo pointed out that each bishop is responsible to the emperor for his *secularia*, to the pope for whatever concerns his *divinum officium*. Whatever offense

10 Above, n.7. Also, Ernst Steindorff, *Jahrbücher des Deutschen Reichs unter Heinrich III.* (2 vols. Leipzig 1874-81) I 254, 295-97; Hauck, *KG* III 578f.

11 That *obedientia* could be considered a technical term within the Church may be seen from the oaths taken by 11th- and 12th-century bishops promising "obedience" to their metropolitans. See the texts of the oaths sworn by bishops and other prelates subject to the archbishops of Besançon and Sens, as published by Georg Waitz, "Obedienzerklärungen burgundischer und französischer Bischöfe," *NA* 3 (1878) 195-202; though there is considerable variation, most commonly the bishops promised "subiectionem et reverentiam et obedientiam."

By denying the obligation of "obedience," Wazo perhaps drew on an even older tradition. In his relation to the emperor, Hincmar of Reims had recognized the vassal's duties of *auxilium et consilium*. Though willing to swear that he would be *fidelis*, Hincmar objected to an oath requiring him to be *fidelis et obediens et adiutor*, since he considered this obligation superhuman and potentially in conflict with his episcopal office. Wazo could have appropriated this idea directly, for Hincmar's statement appeared in a MS preserved at Liège; see *PL* 125 1125f. On Hincmar's reluctance to swear "obedience in all things" as demanded by Charles the Bald at Ponthion (876), see Mitteis, *Lehnrecht und Staatsgewalt* 63f, and cf. Charles E. Odegaard, "The Concept of Royal Power in Carolingian Oaths of Fealty," *Speculum* 20 (1945) 284-87. Along similar lines, Benzo of Alba contrasted the prelate's obligation of *militia* to the king, and his duty of *obedientia* to the metropolitan (*Ad Heinricum IV imperatorem* lib.iv Prologus, *MGH SS* XI 634). The duality *fidelitas-obedientia* reappeared in Gerhoh of Reichersberg's writings (below, Ch.VIIIc n.65).

The Bishop-Elect

the archbishop-elect has committed "against the ecclesiastical order," its judgment pertains only to the pope. However, Wazo continued,

> If he has managed something negligently or disloyally in the *secular things which have been entrusted to him by you*, it is undoubtedly your business to demand an accounting.[12]

With this remark on the bestowal of the *secularia*, Wazo can only have meant the emperor's investiture of the archbishop-elect.[13] Wazo himself had been invested by Henry, and in criticizing the emperor, he neither attacked nor defended the practice of investiture, which he simply took for granted. What matters here is Wazo's oblique reference to investiture as the act conferring the "secular things" which the bishop holds by vassalage. In Wazo's thought, then, the *secularia* apparently included everything imperial in origin: lands, rights, secular jurisdiction.[14] On the other hand, the term "divine office" undoubtedly embraced the bishop's sacramental prerogatives, but perhaps—though one cannot be sure of this —Wazo would also have considered ecclesiastical jurisdiction

---

[12] Anselm, *op.cit.* c.58, *MGH SS* VII 224: "super his iudicium episcoporum exquiritur. Respondentibus quibusdam ad voluntatem imperatoris, quibusdam vero hesitantibus, venitur ad Wazonem episcopum; illo multum excusante, Italicum episcopum nequaquam a se cisalpino debere iudicari, imperator iterum, ut ammonitus per oboedientiam super hoc facto iudicii sententiam edicat, vehementer insistit. Ita coactus, tandem quod super his sentiret aperuit: 'Summo,' inquiens, 'pontifici oboedientiam, vobis autem debemus fidelitatem. Vobis de secularibus, illi rationem reddere debemus de his quae ad divinum officium attinere videntur, ideoque mea sententia quicquit iste contra ecclesiasticum ordinem admiserit, id discutere pronuntio apostolici tantummodo interesse. Si quid autem in secularibus, quae a vobis illi credita sunt, negligenter sive infideliter gessit, procul dubio ad vestra refert exigere.' Consentientibus huic sententiae caeteris episcopis, nullius iudicio eo die episcopatum perdidisset, nisi ipse ultro imperatori redderet baculum cum anulo."

[13] The term *investitura*, it should be noted, was rare before the mid-11th century; Hinschius, *KR* II 536 esp. n.6.

[14] A similar duality, *episcopale officium* and *secularia*, reappeared 40 years later in the treatise by Guido of Ferrara; see below, n.71. The significance of Wazo's distinction (*secularia* vs *officium*) has received little attention; cf. Gerd Tellenbach, *Church, State, and Christian Society* 104, who notes that "it foreshadows the division between temporalities and spiritualities."

and even some forms of property pertinent to the "ecclesiastical order" and to the "divine office."[15] One can at least be certain that he did not regard the *divinum officium* as the object of an imperial investiture. And even though the assembled bishops thereby had to oppose the emperor, they accorded unanimous agreement to Wazo's opinion: obviously the distinction between *secularia* and *divinum officium* did not strike them as a shocking innovation. Wazo presented this distinction almost as though it were self-evident, and of course, the distinction itself was incidental to his main argument, whose sole purpose was to prove the trial an unlawful encroachment upon the autonomous sphere of ecclesiastical authority. Indeed, it is not too rash to conclude that his concept of office and investiture was widely held among the imperial bishops of the earlier eleventh century.

Wazo of Liège was a reformer. Yet long before his dispute with Henry III, the distinction between the secular and the spiritual elements of office had been serving a less lofty purpose. As the struggle for the reform of the Church opened, simoniacs ingeniously used this distinction as an expedient to check the mounting criticism of simony.[16] Even before 1000, simoniacs denied that they were buying sacraments and sacramental powers (*benedictio qua percipitur gratia Spiritus sancti*) but admitted the purchase of their ecclesias-

---

[15] *Divinum officium* was, of course, a technical term for the mass and other rites. Yet in 11th-century usage, the word *officium* sometimes clearly included episcopal jurisdiction or referred to positions (e.g. the archidiaconate) primarily and explicitly requiring the exercise of jurisdictional rather than sacramental powers. See Gregory VII, *Reg.* 5.18, 6.5b (c.12), 6.35, ed. Caspar 381, 406, 450; also, Bernold of Constance, *De damnatione schismaticorum* c.21, and his *Apologeticus* c.6, *MGH LdL* II 55, 66.

[16] The simoniacs' views are known mainly from the reformers' polemics. There must once have been a small body of works defending the simonists, but with one exception, all have disappeared. Written after 1072 (Hoffmann, *DA* 15 [1959] 396 n.14), the one surviving treatise has been edited by S. Hellmann, "Anecdota aus Codex Cusanus C 14 nunc 37," *NA* 30 (1905) 24-33 (see esp. pp.27f). In general, one should not assume that the debate on simony was ever a serious two-sided argument: the simoniac's position was never popular; Mirbt, *Publizistik* 80f, 367-69. Even more often than my footnotes will indicate, for many points in this chapter I am indebted to H. Hoffmann's excellent article on Ivo of Chartres (above, n.2).

The Bishop-Elect

tical and episcopal properties (*res ecclesiarum vel posses-siones episcopi*).[17] Thereafter, simoniacs and reformers disagreed fundamentally in their conceptions of the episcopal office. Around 1031, in a letter to the archbishop of Milan, Guido of Arezzo vigorously opposed the view that one could sell the properties of a church without selling the consecration itself.[18] Through the influence of Guido's letter, the simoniacs' argument and his counterargument became well known. Echoing Guido's remarks, cardinal Humbert of Silva Candida leveled an attack "against those who say that they have bought, not the consecration, but the properties of the church."[19] In the 1060's, reiterating the familiar argument, two chaplains of duke Godfrey the Bearded asserted that it is lawful to purchase a bishopric (*episcopatus*), "so long as one receives the consecration gratis." Horrified by their opinion, Peter Damian composed a detailed refutation of it, and reporting their doctrine to pope Alexander II, he lamented, "Alas! a new heresy has arisen in our time."[20] In Germany during

---

[17] Reported by Abbo of Fleury, *Apologeticus*, in *PL* 139 465f; see also the statement quoted by Aimoin, *Vita sancti Abbonis* c.10, *PL* 139 398.

[18] *Epistola ad archiepiscopum Mediolanensem*, in *MGH LdL* I 6: "Si quis autem obiecerit non consecrationes, sed res ipsas, quae ex consecratione proveniunt, vendi, videtur quidem aliquid dicere, nichil autem penitus sapere. Nam cum corporalis ecclesiae aut episcopus vel abbas aut tale aliquid sine rebus corporalibus et exterioribus in nullo proficiat, sicut nec anima sine corpore temporaliter subsistit, quisquis eorum alterum vendit, sine quo alterum habere non provenit, neutrum invenditum derelinquit." Despite the detailed study by Michel, "Die antisimonistischen Reordinationen und eine neue Humbertschrift," *RQSchr* 46 (1938) 25-41, ascribing this letter to Humbert of Silva Candida, the case against Guido's authorship is inadequate; see Hoffmann, *op.cit.* 395.

[19] *Adversus simoniacos* 3.1 (rubr.), *MGH LdL* I 198: "Contra eos, qui dicunt se non consecrationem, sed res ecclesiae comparasse"; also, *id.* 3.2, 4, *ibid.* 199-202. Fundamental for the interpretation of Humbert's thought are the numerous works by Anton Michel; see his article on "Die folgenschweren Ideen des Kardinals Humbert und ihr Einfluss auf Gregor VII.," *SGreg* 1 (1947) 65-92, with bibliography (p.65 n.1).

[20] To Alexander, Damian wrote (*Ep.*1.13, *PL* 144 219): "Nova, proh dolor! nostro tempore haeresis orta est. . . . Nonnulli . . . clericorum . . . hoc pertinaciter dogmatizant: Non ad simoniacam haeresim pertinere, si quis episcopatus a rege . . . per interventum coemptionis acquirat, si tantummodo consecrationem gratis accipiat. Unde cum nuper in excellentissimi ducis Gothfredi versaremur alloquio, duo quidam ex capellanis eius . . .

the later 1070's, one could readily hear similar presentations of the simoniacs' case.[21] Throughout the last quarter of the century, when reformers denounced the simonists' traditional defense, they usually cited Guido's letter to support their attack. At the same time, as a weapon in the reformers' hands, Guido's letter gained added authority from the fact that it was generally ascribed to a pope "Paschalis" or "Paschasius."[22] In their canonical collections, leading canonists—Anselm of Lucca, Deusdedit, and Ivo of Chartres—incorporated the entire letter or at least the passage disputing the simoniacs' position.[23] Nonetheless, toward the end of the century, there was still uncertainty over the limits and the meaning of simony. Maintaining the old defense, bishop Otbert of Liège could still argue that he had never sold "the grace of God," but had simply "exacted his price for the ecclesiastical possessions."[24] In the same decade Urban II received an inquiry, "Whether it is simoniacal to sell ecclesiastical property?" Referring to the view held by his "blessed predecessor Paschal," Urban explained that since the Church's property is, like the Holy Spirit, the "gift of God," the purchase or sale of ecclesiastical property is simoniacal.[25]

At the foundations of their thought, many reformers shared a body of common assumptions. As Abbo of Fleury ex-

---

hanc non cessabant disseminare doctrinam. . . ." For his letter to the chaplains, see *Ep.*5.13, *PL* 144 358-67 esp. 364f; both letters should be dated 1061-68.

[21] Bernard of Constance, quoted by Bernold, *De damnatione schismaticorum* Ep.2 c.32, *MGH LdL* II 42; *Gesta Treverorum* Continuatio c.11, *MGH SS* VIII 184 (see below, n.68).

[22] Mirbt, *Publizistik* 6; Hoffmann, *DA* 15 (1959) 395f. Cf. Placidus of Nonantula, *De honore ecclesiae* c.101, *MGH LdL* II 618; the letter reappeared twice in Gerhoh of Reichersberg's works (*MGH LdL* III 249f, 424f).

[23] Friedberg, apparatus ad C.1 q.3, c.7 (n.48); Thaner, in *MGH LdL* I 4.

[24] *Chronicon sancti Huberti Andaginensis* c.78, *MGH SS* VIII 612: "contestatus non se in benedictionibus suis gratiam Dei vendidisse, sed potius eas gratis contulisse; non autem sibi videri iniustum, si de possessionibus ecclesiasticis suum exigeret commodum, quas non habentibus distribuebat ad habendum."

[25] *Ep.*273, *PL* 151 529-33 esp. 529f (JL 5743). Placidus of Nonantula quoted Urban's letter extensively (*op.cit.* cc.52, 78, 101, *MGH LdL* II 589, 602, 618), and Gratian republished a long passage (C.1 q.3 c.8).

plained, the episcopal office together with all appurtenances is an indivisible unit. Christ is the ultimate proprietor of every church, and each church with all of its property must be subject to the power of its bishop.[26] Though developed with greater complexity and subtlety, the same doctrine reappeared in cardinal Humbert's writings. Maintaining that visible matter and its invisible adjuncts cannot be sold apart from one another, he argued that whoever buys a tree is primarily buying its abstract form and only secondarily buying the matter of which it is composed.[27] Even theologically, Humbert was preoccupied with the idea of unity: God loves unity, he asserted.[28] In his constitutional thought, the idea of unity expressed itself as the unity and inseparability of office and property, for without the possessions, the office ceases to exist and the bishop cannot fulfill his duties. Moreover, he remarked,

> The episcopal dignity contains the possessions consecrated to God, and is contained by them, or rather in them, as a thing which is itself consecrated by God.[29]

From Abbo in the late tenth century to Placidus of Nonantula in the early twelfth, reformers justified their antisimonist stand by recourse to the metaphor of the human body and soul, which cannot be separated without destroying the temporal

---

[26] *Ep*.14, *PL* 139 441: "eius est pars, cuius est totum." See also his *Apologeticus* (*PL* 139 466) and the letter quoted by Aimoin, *Vita S. Abbonis* c.10, *PL* 139 398: "Cuius vero possessio est ecclesia, nisi solius Dei?"

[27] *Adversus simoniacos* 3.2, *MGH LdL* I 200; Humbert used similar argumentation in his attack on the Eucharistic doctrine of Berengar of Tours. In general, see the lucid account by Gerhart Ladner, *Theologie und Politik vor dem Investiturstreit* (Baden near Vienna 1936) 17, 57f, 137f.

[28] *Adv. simoniacos* 3.24, 25, *MGH LdL* I 229f; Ladner, *op.cit.* 34, 57f, 138.

[29] *Adv. simoniacos* 3.2, *MGH LdL* I 200: "Sic episcopalis dignitas potius possessionem, quam possessio episcopalem dignitatem vindicat. Et tamen tale est episcopale officium, ut sine his, quibus debet impendi vel adhiberi, non sit officium, velut si quis dicatur habere licentiam agrum colendi, et ei ager, quem colat, desit. . . . Quicquid inseparabiliter quodlibet continet aut inseparabiliter continetur a quolibet, neutrum eorum sine altero vendi aut comparari valet. Continet autem episcopalis dignitas res Deo sacratas, continetur quoque ab eis, immo in eis, utputa et ipsa a Deo consecrata. . . ."

life of the individual.[30] Even stronger was a theological analogy in which the simoniacs' defense was compared with the heretical separation of Christ's human and divine natures.[31] Thus the distinction between office and property was tainted by its association with simony, and as a weapon against this abuse, the unitary concept of office and property found a firm foothold in the growing movement for reform. With cardinal Humbert's slashing attack upon lay investiture in his *Three Books Against the Simoniacs* (1057-58), the campaign against investiture made its first appearance as a part of the much older struggle against simony. The two offenses were closely connected in Humbert's thought: the secular princes practice simony "under the false name of investiture."[32] Since antiquity, churchmen had inveighed against the "simoniac heresy," but they did not regard this expression as a mere figure of speech, for as Humbert explained, it is heretical to believe that the Holy Spirit can be purchased.[33] Following a similar chain of ideas, Humbert also denounced lay investiture as a heresy.[34] In fact, other reformist doctrines on simony were equally applicable to the long-standing custom of investiture with ring and staff. Discussing simony, Humbert had argued that the simonist inevitably purchases the consecration as well as the ecclesiastical properties, and that office and property are inseparably joined. In his critique of lay investiture, he invoked the traditional concept of the episcopal office as an indivisible unit. His idea of investiture thus developed along familiar lines: the ring and crosier represent the bishop's office in the broadest sense

---

[30] Abbo, *Apologeticus*, in *PL* 139 466; id., *Ep*.14, *PL* 139 441; Guido of Arezzo (above, n.18); Peter Damian, *Ep*.1.13, *PL* 144 219f; Placidus, *De honore ecclesiae* c.82, *MGH LdL* II 605. For a different application of this metaphor, see Humbert, *op.cit.* 3.21, *MGH LdL* I 225.

[31] Abbo, *Ep*.14, *PL* 139 441; Damian, *Ep*.5.13, *PL* 144 365.

[32] *Adv. simoniacos* 3.6, *MGH LdL* I 206: "Nonne saeculi principes prius vendiderunt et vendunt ecclesiastica sub falso nomine investitionis . . . ?"

[33] Jean Leclercq, "'Simoniaca heresis,'" *SGreg* 1 (1947) 523-30; Humbert, *op.cit.* 1.3, 20, *MGH LdL* I 106, 134.

[34] *Id.* 3.29, *ibid.* I 235f; this view was restated by Bruno of Segni, *Ep*.4, *ibid.* II 565, and Geoffrey of Vendôme, *Libellus* 4, *ibid.* II 690.

(*cura pastoralis*), and for the exercise of his episcopal functions, they are even more indispensable than the consecration
itself. Lay hands may not even touch the bishop's ring, much
less confer it.[35] Nonetheless, in the investiture, lay princes
administer "ecclesiastical sacraments," and this sacramental
act is just as valid as a baptism performed by a layman. By
bestowing spiritual symbols, the monarch arrogates to himself
the "entire pastoral authority," for he unlawfully grants to the
new bishop the "entire episcopal office" (*omne episcopale
officium*). Yet at the time of the episcopal consecration, the
metropolitan reinvests the bishop with the ring and staff: an
absurdity, in Humbert's view, since the "sacrament" of investiture, like a baptism administered by a layman, cannot be
repeated. With the original investiture, the prince consigns
the office, the powers, and the appurtenances to the bishop,
once and for all.[36]

Just as the attack upon lay investiture is reminiscent of the
campaign against simony, similarly the simoniacs' defense
could be used to vindicate lay investiture. Sometime between
1061 and 1068, in their apology for the simonists, the chaplains of duke Godfrey the Bearded argued that through the
king's investiture, a prelate receives only the property and

---

[35] *Adv. simoniacos* 3.6, 12, 15, *MGH LdL* I 205, 213, 217.

[36] *Id.* 3.6, *ibid.* 205: "Quid enim ad laicas pertinet personas sacramenta
ecclesiastica et pontificalem seu pastoralem gratiam distribuere, camyros
scilicet baculos et anulos, quibus praecipue perficitur . . . tota episcopalis
consecratio? Equidem in camyris baculis . . . designatur, quae in eis committitur, cura pastoralis. . . . Quicumque ergo his duobus aliquem initiant,
procul dubio omnem pastoralem auctoritatem hoc praesumendo sibi vendi-
cant. . . . Sic [enceniatus baculo et anulo] metropolitanum aggreditur, non
. . . requirit aut recipit eius iudicium, sed solum exigit . . . servitium, quod
ei solum in oratione et unctione est relictum. Quid enim sibi iam pertinet
aut prodest baculum et anulum, quos portat, reddere? Nunquid quia a
laica persona dati sunt? Sed etiam a laico baptisma datum non est iteran-
dum, sed oratione et unctione a sacerdote, si supervivitur, supplendum. . . .
Unde palam est omne episcopale officium in baculo et anulo eis datum, sine
quorum initiatione et auctoritate episcopari nequeunt, cum sine unctione
visibili constet sanctis apostolis hoc attributum in sola perceptione curae
pastoralis, quae baculo et anulo visibiliter monstratur et datur. Rogo ergo,
cur redditur quod habetur . . . ?"

land of his church, but does not acquire any sacrament.[37] Thus simony and lay investiture are comparable, since neither aims at the bestowal of any spiritual powers, and both refer solely to the transfer of the Church's property. The chaplains' defense was logical and, indeed, inevitable: the investor delivers what the simonist has purchased. Their justification established a crucial precedent: for the first time, investiture was explicitly treated as an act of conveyance with purely temporal (or more specifically, proprietary) implications.

Peter Damian had the task of answering the two chaplains.[38] He was relentlessly opposed to simony, and insofar as their defense of lay investiture was linked to their defense of simony, it was obvious that he would deal severely with both. Nonetheless, though he considered lay investiture unjust,[39] he was generally willing to recognize the royal prerogative in episcopal promotions and to tolerate lay investiture, at least so long as princes exercised their power responsibly.[40] Since his attack upon the chaplains' concept of investiture was uncharacteristic as well as vehement, one may well ask why he showed such uncompromising hostility to lay investiture in this specific context. Against their argument, he pointedly recalled that an investing prince says to a new bishop, "Receive the church," but does not use the narrower formula, "Receive the lands and wealth of that church."[41] Objecting to the use of ecclesiastical symbols in the ceremony of investiture, Damian implied that if a different symbol—a "simple

[37] Peter Damian, *Ep.*5.13, *PL* 144 364: "E contra contenditis, quoniam investituram ille suscipit ecclesiasticae facultatis, non munus [*ed.* minus] percipit gratiae spiritualis. Acquirit ecclesiae praedium, non ecclesiastici charismatis sacramentum." The emendation was suggested to me by Professor K. M. Woody.

[38] In general, see: Scharnagl, *Begriff der Investitur* 22-25; Owen J. Blum, *St. Peter Damian* (Washington, D.C. 1947) 22-24; Fridolin Dressler, *Petrus Damiani* (Studia Anselmiana 34: Rome 1954) 138-42.

[39] *Ep.*1.13, *PL* 144 222: "cavenda sit haeresis illa [simoniaca] . . . saecularibus . . . principibus, qui licet iniuste, aliquo modo tamen ecclesias futuris rectoribus tradunt"; also, *Disceptatio synodalis,* in *MGH LdL* I 78.

[40] *Ep.*5.10, 7.2, *PL* 144 353, 436; *Opusculum* 22, *PL* 145 468.

[41] Above, n.4.

staff," instead of a crosier—were granted by the prince, such an investiture would neither concern the Church nor affect ecclesiastical property: it would confer merely "the stewardship of a proctor" administering purely secular properties.[42] Of course, the introduction of a secular symbol and a narrower formula into the ceremony would not have satisfied Damian. His disagreement with the chaplains was unbridgeable, since he could not accept their fundamental doctrine on the separability of an office or church from its properties. Indeed, he undoubtedly considered the idea of such a separation a mere pretext, for as he explained, whoever is invested with the "earthly properties of a church" expects to be consecrated, and in practice, investiture confers a solid claim upon the consecration.[43] To disjoin properties from a church, he charged, is the work of a schismatic.[44] Clearly, though Peter Damian was politically and theologically far more moderate than the fiery Humbert, he followed his late colleague's rigorous views on the inseparability of the episcopal office and its appurtenances: "the episcopal dignity contains the possessions."[45]

[42] *Ep*.1.13, *PL* 144 220: "dum te dicis a principe terrena duntaxat ecclesiae commoda percepisse, asseris te quodammodo villicum, non ut sacerdotali fungaris officio, constitutum. Dic, inquam, cuius erat figurae, quam sane habebat speciem investitura haec, quam in manibus tuis princeps ille deposuit? Porro si surculus, si simplex baculus, merito tibi laetus applaude; quia, sicut asseris, non ad sacerdotis officium, sed ad procuratoris initiatus es villicatum. . . . At si saecularis ille princeps, accepta vel promissa pecunia, pastoralem tibi tradidit baculum, qua fronte poteris episcopalis ordinis excusare commercium?"

[43] *Ibid*.: "nisi per hanc investituram ille [scil. princeps] secuturi sacerdotii tibi prius imprimeret titulum, futurus ordinator nequaquam per manus impositionem sacerdotii tibi traderet sacramentum."

[44] *Ibid*. 221: "Quod si bona ecclesiae sine ecclesia suscepisti, schismaticus es atque sacrilegus, qui bona ecclesiae ab ecclesia dividis. . . . Quod si ecclesiam suscepisti, quod omnino negare non potes, procul dubio factus es simoniacus. . . . Tunc enim consecrationem evidentissime coemisti, cum id, propter quod ad consecrationem promovendus eras, venaliter accepisti. Sic enim unum pendet [*ed.* pende] ex altero, ut qui terrena ecclesiae bona suscipit, ad gratiam consecrationis aspiret; et qui consecratione perficitur, bona ecclesiae in usus egentium et caetera pietatis opera dispensanda conservet. . . ." Also, *Ep*.5.13, *PL* 144 364f.

[45] See the discussions above (nn.20, 30f, 37, 39f, 42-44), and notice that Damian identified the consecration as the moment in which the prelate receives the administration "of the church's properties" (*Ep*.1.13, *PL* 144

Office, *Regalia*, and Investiture

Now, a brief glance backward: In the second quarter of the eleventh century, the distinction between office and property was equally useful to a strict Gelasian like Wazo of Liège, trying to protect the Church from imperial domination, and to the simonists, denying the purchase of sacramental powers. Preoccupied with the struggle against simony, however, Humbert's thought was guided by the antisimoniac doctrine of earlier reformers on the unity of office and property. Consequently, in attacking the simonists' argument, he also had to reject the position of Wazo and other imperial bishops, who assumed that lay investiture confers only the *secularia*. Since the idea of a purely secular investiture thus antedated Humbert's attack, an appropriate defense of investiture was already at hand. But the distinction between office and property was discredited by repeated use in defense of simony, and in the 1060's or 1070's, a defender of lay investiture was likely to defend simony as well. It is not surprising, therefore, that Humbert's concept of office and investiture prevailed among the reformers. Nonetheless, the distinction between office and property was making new headway. In 1073 an Angevin charter lucidly prescribed the count's investiture with the "temporal possessions" as the normal prerequisite to the ecclesiastical investiture with the "care of souls."[46] Such was the situation when Gregory VII took up the problem of lay investiture.

---

221): "licet ecclesiasticae facultatis mentio in ipsa manus impositione non fiat, is tamen qui consecratur, bonorum ecclesiae dispensator efficitur."

[46] *Gall. Chr.* XIV Instr.150 no.9: "Facta est autem electio ista annuente comite Fulcone, . . . a quo etiam dono rerum temporalium ad idem monasterium pertinentium suscepta; praesentata est deinde Eusebio, . . . Andecavensis urbis episcopo, ad [ed. ab] benedictionis suscipiendum mysterium; ut cui comes exterius tradiderat auctoritate sua dominium, episcopus quoque debita benedictione consecrans ex more ecclesiastico curam committeret animarum." Though the other evidence is not entirely above suspicion, similar distinctions seem to have been drawn elsewhere in France during this period, perhaps as early as 1066; Hoffmann, *DA* 15 (1959) 400f.

N.B. The Angevin charter deals with the investiture of an abbess. At various points in the present study, materials concerned with abbots or abbesses are used to illustrate the evolution of the episcopal office. Where such sources are cited without special qualification, it should be assumed that the conclusions are also valid for the episcopate.

The Bishop-Elect

Regalia AND *Spiritualia*

During the first two years of his pontificate, Gregory VII countenanced the practice of lay investiture, so long as "the gift of the bishopric" (*donum episcopatus*) was conferred gratis.[47] At the Lenten Synod of 1075, however, he forbade the royal right of appointment to bishoprics and condemned lay investiture, but he did not publicize this decree.[48] In 1077, giving instructions for a synod, he ordered his legate, bishop Hugh of Die, to enjoin the French episcopate from consecrating anyone who received "the gift of a bishopric" from a layman.[49] Finally, in 1078, again at the Lenten Synod, Gregory issued a general prohibition against all lay investiture with bishoprics, and he threatened offenders with anathema. Moreover, he explicitly forbade the "ancient usurpation" practiced by laymen in the enfeoffment of clerics with things which have previously been given to God and which therefore belong to the Church as unencumbered property.[50] Obviously directed against the monarch's proprietary claims to the Church's wealth, this unambiguous provision had its roots in the tradition created by earlier reformers, who viewed the "possessions consecrated to God" as inseparable and indistinguishable from the episcopal office. Nonetheless, since the authentic texts of these decrees have been lost, and since Gregory was never lavish in explanation of these prohibitions,

[47] *Reg.* 1.21, 1.35, ed. Caspar 35, 56f; Scharnagl, *op.cit.* 27-29.

[48] *Ibid.* 30f; Arnulf, *Gesta archiepiscoporum Mediolanensium* 4.7, *MGH SS* VIII 27; cf. Hugh of Flavigny, *Chronicon* anno 1074 (!), *MGH SS* VIII 412.

[49] *Reg.* 4.22, ed. Caspar 333; the synod's decree has been lost.

[50] The decree is summarized by Berthold, *Annales* anno 1078, *MGH SS* V 308f: "In laicos quoque cuiuscumque dignitatis data est sententia anathematis, sive clericos, nec non in omnes personas, quicumque contra sacrorum canonum decreta episcopatus, abbatias, praeposituras, qualescumque aecclesias, decimas, vel quascumque aecclesiasticas dignitates, cuilibet clerico seu cuicumque personae iuxta usurpationem suam antiquam in beneficium dare, et quod domino Deo prius canonica et legitima traditione in proprietatem et servitium legaliter delegatum est, hoc quasi proprium quiddam et hereditarium laica et non consecrata Deo manu, consecratis Deo altaris et aecclesiasticae dispensationis ministris procurandum et ordinandum contradere seu praestare omnino praesumpserint."

perhaps their significance requires comment. Did he intend to draw a distinction between the episcopal office and its purely temporal possessions, and thereby to leave open the possibility of a lawful investiture with these temporalities?[51] In fact, Gregory did once distinguish between the temporal and spiritual elements of the episcopal dignity. Following a double election in Le Puy, one of the candidates went to Rome and laid his case before the pope, who entrusted to this bishop-elect the governmental and administrative responsibility for the bishopric (*regimen totius episcopatus*) but forbade him to exercise the sacramental powers (*episcopale officium*). Gregory then ordered the "clergy and people" to show the bishop-elect due reverence and to furnish him with aid in the defense of their church.[52] Since Gregory's grant implied full jurisdictional powers over the people of Le Puy as well as the necessary means of defense, the bishop-elect's competence evidently included those temporal appurtenances which belonged, at least in the standard view held by twelfth-century France, to the royal prerogative.[53] More significant

51 Against the consensus of earlier scholars, Scharnagl (*op.cit.* 27-41) and more recently Brooke (*PBA* 25 [1939] 228-33) have tried to demonstrate the presence of this distinction in Gregory's policy. If their view is correct, Gregory himself could scarcely be considered a Gregorian, and he might well have accepted the terms finally agreed upon in 1122; see Scharnagl, *op.cit.* 69, and G. Barraclough, *The Origins of Modern Germany* (2nd ed. Oxford 1947) 129. However, Scharnagl's interpretation has been contested by various scholars, including Augustin Fliche, *La réforme grégorienne* (3 vols. Louvain 1924-37) II 181 n.1, and Hoffmann, *op.cit.* 397-400.

52 *Reg.* 1.80 (13 April 1074), ed. Caspar 114: "regimen totius episcopatus vestri sibi commisimus eo tenore, ut . . . de pontificali officio se non intromittat, sed quemcumque voluerit episcoporum religiosorum patrie vestre ea, que ad episcopale officium pertinent, facere commoneat. Vos [scil. clerum et populum] itaque apostolica auctoritate ammonemus, ut sibi debitam in omnibus reverentiam exhibeatis et ad defensionem ecclesie vestre adiutorium vestrum fideliter impendatis." Le Puy was a royal bishopric and was also directly subject to the pope. In general, see Alfons Becker, *Studien zum Investiturproblem in Frankreich* (Saarbrücken 1955) 56-58, 194f, who has, however, confused the two candidates (both called Stephanus); cf. Caspar, *op.cit.* 114 n.2.

53 Phrases like *regimen ecclesiae* commonly indicated the administration of temporal property; for an example, Damian, *Ep.*5.13, *PL* 144 364. See also his *Ep.*5.10, *PL* 144 353, where he plays off the administrative *cura ac sollicitudo totius episcopatus* against the sacramental *episcopalia officia*; I owe this reference to the kindness of Professor Woody.

than Gregory's distinction between *regimen* and *officium*, therefore, was his assumption that the right to bestow this *regimen* pertained to the Church and to the Roman pontiff.

The events of 1078 in Germany might well suggest that Gregory regarded his decrees as a partial prohibition, which did not affect the king's right to bestow temporalities. After an election in the see of Augsburg, the archbishop of Mainz consecrated and enthroned the *electus*, and at the same time invested him with ring and staff. The anti-king Rudolph of Rheinfelden then granted to the new bishop "whatever belonged to royal authority" in the sphere of "ecclesiastical property" (*quicquid regii iuris fuerit in procurandis bonis ecclesiasticis*).[54] Thus Rudolph and his supporters distinguished between the spiritualities, which only the Church can confer, and the "ecclesiastical property" which pertains to the royal prerogative. Moreover, since Rudolph did not claim to bestow churches, tithes, or offices, he believed that he was obeying the recent synodal decrees, and some German Gregorians were willing to regard his actions in that light.[55] Coming at the very end of the proceedings, Rudolph's "investiture" did not interfere with canonical election, and unlike most investitures performed by Henry IV, it could not be construed as the direct royal appointment of a bishop. Indeed, at his own election in 1077, Rudolph had promised to observe

[54] For the text, see the following note; the reference to *bona ecclesiastica* makes it clear that the episcopal properties deriving from royal grant were the central part (though not necessarily all) of the *regium ius*. Cf. Georg Waitz, *Deutsche Verfassungsgeschichte* (8 vols. repr. Graz 1955) VIII 457 n.1, interpreting *regium ius* as "Hoheitsrechte," and Scharnagl, *op.cit.* 37, asserting the impossibility of a reliable interpretation.

[55] Berthold, *Annales* anno 1078, *MGH SS* V 309f: "Wigoldus . . . in episcopum consecratus et ordinatus est. Cui rex post peracta legittime omnia quae ad ordinationem ipsius pertinebant, videlicet anulo, virga pastorali et cathedra episcopali ab archiepiscopo Mogontino susceptis, ex sua parte quicquid regii iuris fuerit in procurandis bonis aecclesiasticis diligenter commendavit. Cavebat namque, ut oboedientissimus erat in omnibus, quod in Romana synodo nuper canonice diffinitum . . . et prohibitum est, ne quis laicorum aecclesias et aecclesiasticas decimas et dignitates personis aliquibus quasi proprium suum praestiterit, sive contra canones sibi usurpare praesumpserit."

the Gregorian rules on the freedom of episcopal elections.[56] Still, there is no evidence that Gregory approved of this investiture or of the principle underlying it. And though the pope apparently never reproached Rudolph for this act, it is scarcely surprising that he was content to leave the anti-king in undisturbed possession of this limited prerogative, at least for the moment.

To the partisans of Henry IV, Rudolph's role at Augsburg did not seem markedly different from the rights exercised by Henry himself in the elevation of bishops. Since German Gregorians participated in the events at Augsburg, Wenrich of Trier objected to the double standard by which Rudolph's and Henry's acts were judged. Gregory's policy, as Wenrich explained, was a personal attack on Henry, and was animated "not from zeal for religion, but from hatred of the prince." Nonetheless, apart from its motives and its violence, the scholasticus of Trier acknowledged a measure of justice in the Gregorian program, which he summarized as an attempt to free forever the Church's lands from all secular control, and to end royal appointment and investiture of bishops.[57] The Gregorian reply to these statements came from Manegold of Lautenbach, who vehemently denied that Gregory sought to remove the Church's property entirely from lay hands. Significantly, however, Manegold did not deny that Gregory

[56] Bruno, *Saxonicum bellum* c.91, ed. H. E. Lohmann (MGH Deutsches Mittelalter 2: Leipzig 1937) 85: "Tamen quaedam sunt ibi causae . . . , quas . . . deberet emendare, scilicet ut episcopatus non pro pretio nec pro amicitia daret, sed unicuique ecclesiae de suis electionem, sicut iubent canones, permitteret." In general, see W. Berges, "Gregor VII. und das deutsche Designationsrecht," *SGreg* 2 (1947) 202-04.

[57] Wenrich, *Epistola* c.8, *MGH LdL* I 297: "Illud sane, quod de aecclesiasticis ventilatur beneficiis ab omni secularium iure perpetua emunitate asserendis, de episcopis quoque manu principis in episcopatum minime introducendis, etsi pro rei novitate primo sui aspectu offensionem generat, aliquam tamen speciem rationis exhibet, si non res vel tali tempore mota vel tali impetu properata vel tali foret contentione agitata. Quis enim non videat, non ex religionis zelo, sed ex principis odio haec actitari, cum personis per sacram Rodulfi dexteram non introductis, sed subintroductis, benedictiones non negentur, pallia domum transmittantur, . . . nostris autem episcopis, archiepiscopis legitime electis, communi assensu receptis, laica etiam communio interdicatur."

aimed to liberate the Church's lands entirely from the king's control. As Manegold noted, at the November Synod of 1078 Gregory forbade laymen to hold tithes but "nowhere made mention of lands (*beneficia*)."[58] In other words, laymen may not hold tithes from bishops, but may hold "benefices" from them. Thus Manegold's discussion deals with the relation between bishops and their vassals, rather than the relation between bishops and the king.[59] Manegold's assertion is doubly strange, since Wenrich himself never alluded to Gregory's decree against lay possession of tithes. Obviously, in his remark on Gregory's attempt to free the Church's "benefices," Wenrich was concerned with the relation between monarch and bishops, and with the monarch's proprietary claim to all or part of the Church's lands. In this respect, Manegold's attack was irrelevant to Wenrich's original statement. Unable to meet Wenrich's statement head-on, Manegold interpreted it with absolute literalness and thereby ignored its real meaning; the trick is familiar to every debater. Hence Manegold could correctly point out that Gregory did allow laymen—as vassals—to hold "ecclesiastical [that is, lay] benefices" from bishops. From Manegold's quibbling argument, one can only conclude that he tacitly admitted the essential accuracy in Wenrich's concept of the Gregorian program.[60] Although the distinction between temporalities

---

[58] Manegold, *Ad Gebehardum liber* c.50, *MGH LdL* I 399: "Unde et illud, de ecclesiasticis beneficiis quod dicunt ab omni secularium iure perpetua immunitate auferendis, penitus falsum repperit, quemcumque eius decreta perlegere non piguerit. Nam nusquam beneficiorum mentionem fecit, sed decimas tantum, quas tam sub lege quam sub gratia ad usus tantum pietatis concessas divina testatur auctoritas, a laicis possideri prohibuit. . . . Statutum vero eius de episcopis per manum principis in episcopatum non introducendis quam sit catholicum, quam ecclesiastice dispensationi congruum et necessarium, liquido possent cognoscere, si decreta apostolica . . . vellent legere."

[59] Already explained by W. von Giesebrecht, "Die Gesetzgebung der römischen Kirche zur Zeit Gregors VII.," *Münchner historisches Jahrbuch* (1866) 138 esp. n.42. For the decree of the November Synod to which Manegold alludes, see Gregory's *Reg.* 6.5b (c.7), ed. Caspar 404: "Decimas, quas in usum pietatis concessas esse canonica auctoritas demonstrat, a laicis possideri apostolica auctoritate prohibemus."

[60] Any intelligible interpretation of Manegold's argument presupposes— and the assumption is perhaps too generous—that he understood Wenrich's position.

and spiritualities would have enabled him to refute Wenrich effectively, Manegold neither drew this distinction in theory nor defended Rudolph's application of it in practice.[61] Moreover, he was not the only German Gregorian who insisted that all ecclesiastical properties belong unequivocally to the Church: in 1078 bishop Altman of Passau forcefully expressed the same view.[62] In short, outside of the immediate circle of Rudolph's supporters, German Gregorians refused to accept any distinction between ecclesiastical office and ecclesiastical property.

On Gregory's conception of office and property, the synod of Poitiers in January of 1078 offers striking evidence. Under the leadership of his legate, Hugh of Die, the first canon of this council decreed that no cleric should receive from a layman "the gift of a bishopric or abbey or church *or any ecclesiastical properties.*"[63] The last phrase is unambiguous: the legate explicitly prohibited even an investiture confined to the temporalities. Does this uncompromising decree reflect Gregory's position? In fact, the pope neither disavowed nor ratified this canon. Still, it is clear that after the synod of Poitiers, the legate retained his full confidence.[64] Moreover, though Gregory occasionally found it necessary to check Hugh's reformist zeal, these restraints upon the legate should be regarded as mere tactical directives, not as differences of objective. After reviewing and, in some cases, lightening Hugh's sentences against six French bishops, Gregory expressly justified a cautious policy:

Since the custom of the Holy Roman Church . . . is to

61 Cf. Brooke, *PBA* 25 (1939) 230, and Hoffmann, *DA* 15 (1959) 400, for a different view of Manegold.

62 *Gesta Treverorum* Continuatio c.11, *MGH SS* VIII 184.

63 Mansi XX 498: "Decrevit sancta synodus, ut nullus episcopus, abbas, presbyter vel quaelibet persona de clero accipiat de manu regis vel comitis vel cuiuslibet laicae personae donum episcopatus vel abbatiae vel ecclesiae vel aliquarum ecclesiasticarum rerum." Later synods of Gregory's reign were, however, less explicit. The November Synod of 1078 forbade any *investitura episcopatus vel abbatie vel ecclesie,* and the Lenten Synod of 1080 similarly failed to clarify the status of the ecclesiastical properties; *Reg.* 6.5b (c.3), 7.14a (cc.1, 2), ed. Caspar 403, 480f.

64 *Reg.* 5.17, 20, 22, 23, 6.2, 3, ed. Caspar 378-80, 383f, 386-88, 393-96.

The Bishop-Elect

tolerate some things, even to ignore some things, [we have followed] the moderation of prudence rather than the rigor of the canons.[65]

Here Gregory surely intended no criticism of Hugh's principles, which represented the correct meaning of the Church's laws as Gregory himself conceived them. Indeed, common sense indicated that the reformers' program could not be imposed at a single stroke, for as Gregory once explained to Hugh, "Lofty buildings are built gradually."[66]

Thus, if not beyond all doubt, it is nonetheless practically certain that Gregory's own views are to be seen in the unmistakable wording of the decree promulgated by Hugh of Die, and in the stance taken by such German supporters as Manegold of Lautenbach and Altman of Passau.

If the concept of an investiture limited to the temporalities alone had been restricted to Rudolph of Rheinfelden and his circle, this idea might have died with him. In 1078, however, the idea made its first appearance among the supporters of Henry IV, when it was advocated by Egilbert, provost and scholasticus of Passau.[67] After the Lenten Synod of that year, in obedience to the pope's command, the staunch Gregorian bishop Altman of Passau read aloud in his church the synod's prohibition against lay investiture. Thereupon the provost publicly defied his bishop, attacked Gregory's decree, and announced his own adherence to the "Henricians." In defense of Henry, Egilbert asserted the king's right to grant the temporalities—but not the spiritualities—"to anyone he wanted, free or for a price."[68] With this statement, Egilbert affirmed

65 *Reg.* 5.17 (9 March 1078), ed. Caspar 378: "Quia consuetudo sancte Romane ecclesie . . . [est] quedam tolerare quedam etiam dissimulare, discretionis temperantiam potius quam rigorem canonum [secuti sumus]. . . ."

66 *Reg.* 2.43 (5 January 1075), ed. Caspar 180.

67 The scholarly consensus assigns this priority to Guido of Ferrara (1086). Cf. Scharnagl, *Begriff der Investitur* 49; Ott, *ZRG* KA 35 (1948) 238; Hoffmann, *op.cit.* 404.

68 *Gesta Treverorum* Continuatio c.11, *MGH SS* VIII 184: "Dicebat [Egilbertus] autem, imperatori licere, nec idcirco ecclesiae consorcium amittere, si non spiritualia sed regalia sua gratis preciove cui voluerit inpendat. Quae utique non sua, sed iuxta Romanam consuetudinem regalia beati Petri vel

the royal right of direct appointment to bishoprics, and accepted the traditional simoniac doctrine on the lawfulness of selling the temporalities of a church. Unlike the earlier defenders of simony, however, his primary concern was the king's right of investiture. After much argument, bishop Altman excommunicated the provost as a partisan of the "simoniac faction." Nevertheless, Egilbert's subsequent career did not suffer, for Henry sent him as envoy to Gregory's November Synod of 1078, and in January of 1079, considering Egilbert the only acceptable candidate for the vacant archbishopric of Trier, Henry forced him upon the reluctant electors assembled there.[69] The prominence of the new archbishop undoubtedly lent added weight to his views.

At the instigation of other imperial partisans and of the antipope Clement III, in 1086 bishop Guido of Ferrara wrote *On the Schism of Hildebrand.*[70] Near the end of this treatise, the essential elements in Egilbert's concept of investiture reappeared with new sharpness and clarity. Every bishop, Guido asserted, has "two rights," one spiritual, the other secular. Separating the "episcopal office" from all secular affairs, Guido identified this *officium* exclusively with "spiritual" or "divine things," which do not concern the monarch and are not subject to him. On the other hand, the bishop's secular appurtenances belong permanently to the emperors, and if these *secularia* are not regranted by each newly suc-

---

ecclesiae pociori iure possunt appellari. Sed utinam qui ad ecclesiasticae dignitatis culmen venire desiderant, non . . . artificiosi colore commenti symoniacae hereseos sibi machinamenta confingant, asserentes se non spiritualia sed terrena terrenis acquirere, cum . . . non [tam] appetant curam pastoralem quam honorem temporalem." There is some confusion of chronology here (cf. *id.* c.10, *ibid.* 183), and the chronicler is heavily biased in Gregory's favor, but as Meyer von Knonau points out (*Jahrbücher* III 188), the account is "wohl als glaubhaft anzunehmen." However, the use of the word *regalia* in this context most probably reflects the standard terminology of the 12th century, and cannot be ascribed with certainty to Egilbert.

[69] *Gesta Trev. Cont.* c.11, *MGH SS* VIII 184f; Meyer von Knonau, *loc.cit.*

[70] *MGH LdL* I 532, 567. In general, see Mirbt, *Publizistik* 40f, 504-07, 510-12; Scharnagl, *op.cit.* 48-54; Ott, *op.cit.* 238f.

ceeding emperor, they revert to him.[71] Earlier discussions of
the bishop's *secularia* had emphasized only the lands and
properties deriving from royal grant, but Guido contributed
a concrete enumeration of distinct prerogatives: manors and
landed properties (*curtes, praedia*), secular judicial power
(*iudicia* or *placita secularia*), fiscal rights (*vectigalia, tributa*), and undefined public rights or powers (*publica iura*).[72]
Without the royal grant, a bishop does not even have power
over the peasants, stewards, and servants subject to his
church.[73] Moreover, these *secularia* include all types of
ecclesiastical property, excepting only the altars and church
buildings themselves. That is, Guido did not even explicitly
exempt the tithes and offerings from the imperial authority
to which all *secularia* are subject.[74] Guido's distinction
between the episcopal office and its secular appurtenances
enjoyed a marked advantage over the similar doctrine pro-
pounded by Egilbert and by the chaplains of duke Godfrey
the Bearded, for Guido's theory was not discredited by any
attempt to defend the indefensible "simoniac heresy." Above
all, however, Guido's treatise introduced the new idea of a
purely temporal investiture into the swelling stream of polemical writings.

71 *De scismate Hildebrandi* 2, MGH LdL I 564: "Duo siquidem iura
conceduntur episcopis omnibus, spirituale vel divinum unum, aliud seculare;
et aliud quidem caeli, aliud vero fori. Nam omnia quae sunt episcopalis
officii spiritualia sunt, divina sunt, quia, licet per ministerium episcopi,
tamen a sancto Spiritu conceduntur. At vero iudicia secularia et omnia,
quae a mundi principibus et secularibus hominibus aecclesiis conceduntur,
sicut sunt curtes et praedia omniaque regalia, licet in ius divinum transeant,
dicuntur tamen secularia, quasi a secularibus concessa. Itaque divina illa a
sancto Spiritu tradita imperatoriae potestati constat non esse subiecta. Quae
vero sunt ab imperatoribus tradita, quia non sunt aecclesiis perpetuo iure
manentia, nisi succedentium imperatorum et regum fuerint iteratione concessa, dicuntur profecto quodammodo regibus et imperatoribus subdita, quia
nisi per succedentes imperatores et reges fuerint aecclesiis confirmata,
revertuntur ad imperialia iura."
72 *Ibid.* 565f: "omnia placita secularia et iuditia et regalia et publica
iura et vectigalia scilicet et tributa regum sunt et imperatorum, vel ab illis
aliis tradita."
73 *Ibid.* 566.
74 *Ibid.* 565: "Unde . . . est . . . imperatoribus concessum, ut aecclesiarum
investituras habeant, non dico parietum sacrorum et altarium, quae non
sunt eorum, sed aecclesiasticarum rerum."

Office, *Regalia*, and Investiture

Though Guido also used other expressions to indicate the bishop's secular appurtenances, by dubbing them the *regalia* he created a standard technical term for all time. To be sure, in Guido's discussion, the word *regalia* was not free from ambiguity, and he did not distinguish this term sharply from the various expressions to which he gave the same meaning.[75] As a term for the secular—and royal—business of the episcopate, the word *regalia* was not unknown at the beginning of the eleventh century.[76] A generation before Guido, the papal chancery had coined a new expression, "the *regalia* of Saint Peter," to designate the secular power and jurisdiction of the papacy in Central Italy, the pope's sovereign prerogative as secular ruler.[77] Moreover, in the charters of Henry IV, the term *regalia* had appeared, referring in a general way to royal authority[78] or more specifically to the mass of rights and

[75] See above, nn.71f, 74, and the following: "imperialia iura et regalia" (*ibid.* 565 line 3); "omnia regalia et omnia publica iura" (*ibid.* line 40); "seculare ius" (*ibid.* 566 line 6). In Guido's phrase "curtes et praedia omniaque regalia" (above, n.71), the *regalia* may stand in contrast with the *curtes* and *praedia*, or could equally well include them (cf. Ott, *op.cit.* 238f).

[76] Thangmar, *Vita Bernwardi episcopi* c.7, *MGH SS* IV 761: "divina ac regalia benignissime amministrabat."

[77] In 1059 and after, the Norman princes swore to preserve, defend, and recover the *regalia sancti Petri*; similarly the patriarch of Aquileia in 1079. See Deusdedit, *Collectio canonum* 3.285, 288, ed. Wolf von Glanvell 394, 396; Gregory VII, *Reg.* 1.21a, 6.17a, 8.1a, ed. Caspar 36, 429, 515. In general, see Ernst H. Kantorowicz, *The King's Two Bodies* (Princeton 1957) 185 n.293.
  The sovereignty implicit in the concept of the papal *regalia* was undermined by the *Tractatus de investitura episcoporum* (1109), a semiofficial statement of the imperial position. As the anonymous author pointed out, the emperor has the right to invest all bishops-elect, "exceptis quos papa Romanus investire et consecrare debet ex antiquo dono regum et imperatorum cum aliis que vocantur regalia, id est a regibus et imperatoribus pontificibus Romanis data in fundis et reditibus" (*MGH LdL* II 498). From this view, the papal and the episcopal *regalia* are on almost the same level, for they are markedly similar: both derive from royal grant and take their name from this fact. On this point, the author of the *Tractatus* drew his wording mainly from a forged privilege of Leo VIII (below, Ch.VIIʙ n.18 and Ch.VIIIc n.24).

[78] *MGH DD Heinrici IV* 123 no.94 (1062 for the abbey of Kempten): "pristinam libertatem et ad sola regalia respectionem regali nostro iure ac potestate concedimus et confirmamus, . . . ut nullus . . . predictam abbatiam a nostro iure, scilicet a regalibus abalienare presumat."

powers pertaining to the royal prerogative.[79] Most probably, Guido appropriated the word *regalia* from the usage of the imperial chancery.[80] With this term, he implied that these rights, powers, and possessions remained attached to the royal prerogative, were still subject to royal proprietary claims, and were simply delegated to the bishop. Indeed, one might well say that the papal *regalia* signified the pope's regality, whereas in Guido's thought, the bishop's *regalia* formed the basis of his subjection to the regality of the emperor.[81]

2. Investiture and the Concordat of Worms

In September of 1122, after a half century of struggle between empire and papacy, the emperor Henry V and the legates of pope Calixtus II came to an agreement at Worms. Each side issued a charter embodying its concessions and assurances to the other party.[1] In many ways, this Concordat of Worms was an unusual treaty, but in no way was it more extraordinary than in the number of details which it did *not*

[79] *Ibid.* 385 no.293 (1077 for Aquileia): "comitatum Fori Iulii et villam . . . omneque beneficium, quod Ludouicus comes habebat in eodem comitatu situm, cum omnibus ad regalia et ad ducatum pertinentibus, hoc est placitis collectis fodro districtionibus universis omnique utilitate . . . tradidimus." Cf. also *MGH DD Conradi II* 282 no.207 (1034 for Bamberg): "in comitatu . . . et in omnibus appendiciis eius districtum mercatum theloneum . . . piscationes venationes, et quicquid ad nostrum ius ducisque pertinet, . . . in proprium ius donamus."

[80] Cf. Ott, *op.cit.* 236, who suggests the papal expression *regalia sancti Petri* as the origin of Guido's term; however, see below, following note.

[81] Consequently, Guido's conception of the episcopal *regalia* is much closer to the meaning of *regalia* in the imperial charters than to the idea embodied in the *regalia sancti Petri*. Guido surely had no wish to suggest that the bishop holds his *regalia* without obligation. In general, the two uses of the term were antipathetic; see above, n.68.

[1] For Henry's charter, see *MGH Const* I 159f no.107; for Calixtus's, *ibid.* 160f no.108. The meaning of the Concordat is best elucidated in the masterly analysis by Adolf Hofmeister, "Das Wormser Konkordat: Zum Streit und seine Bedeutung," *Forschungen und Versuche zur Geschichte des Mittelalters und der Neuzeit: Festschrift Dietrich Schäfer* (Jena 1915) 64-148, with voluminous citation of sources and a thorough evaluation of the scholarly controversies; his views have been compactly restated by Geoffrey Barraclough, *Mediaeval Germany* I 98-101. Of the earlier literature, see especially the important monograph by Schäfer, *Zur Beurteilung des Wormser Konkordats* (Abh.Berlin 1905 no.1: Berlin 1905), and the numerous works of Ernst Bernheim.

settle. During the conferences leading to the Concordat, both sides studied the documents from earlier papal-imperial diplomacy, especially the detailed documents from the dramatic negotiations of 1111.[2] Since both parties in 1122 were aware of the crucial precedents, the simple brevity of the Concordat's two charters was deliberate. In general, the Concordat had both the virtues and the defects of an armistice, for like any truce, its main purpose was to halt the fighting, and it provided no fundamental remedy for the causes of the conflict. Intended as a practical compromise, the Concordat attempted neither a doctrinaire separation of Church and monarchy—the fiasco of February 1111 was sufficient warning—nor the complete fulfillment of either party's objectives.[3]

In the imperial charter, Henry V renounced "investiture with ring and crosier," and he promised "canonical election and free consecration" for the bishops and abbots of his empire. With the guarantee of "canonical election," Henry abandoned the long-standing imperial practice of directly appointing bishops. The emperor made these concessions explicitly to the Roman Church, which never dies, and consequently the concessions were permanently binding on his successors. Since Henry's renunciation of the traditional right of investiture was a revolutionary act, a formal grant in perpetuity was legally indispensable.[4]

Through its personal style of address, however, Calixtus II's privilege had formal validity for Henry V, but not for his successors on the imperial throne.[5] This stylistic usage did

---

[2] Bernheim, *Das Wormser Konkordat und seine Vorurkunden* (Breslau 1906) 6.

[3] Hofmeister, *op.cit.* 95f.

[4] Schäfer, *op.cit.* 3f. By a comparative study of 11th- and 12th-century documents, Hofmeister (*op.cit.* 72-85) has demonstrated the clear distinction between the forms used in a charter which was valid only for the recipient's lifetime, and the forms designed for a permanent grant. As Hofmeister points out (*op.cit.* 77), Paschal II's concession of February 1111, which proposed to restore all of the *regalia* to Henry V, also implied the radical overthrow of an existing legal situation—and therefore had to employ the permanent form; see *MGH Const* I 141 no.90.

[5] *MGH Const* I 161 no.108: "Ego Calixtus . . . tibi dilecto filio Heinrico Dei gratia Romanorum imperatori augusto concedo, electiones episcoporum

not necessarily imply that the various rights conceded by Calixtus would disappear with Henry V's death. Rather, Henry and the German princes undoubtedly considered these concessions an already well-grounded part of imperial custom. From this standpoint, the Calixtinum was more a recognition (or, one might almost say, a confirmation) of certain existing rights than a grant of new ones. Indeed, a personal charter valid during Henry's lifetime may have seemed the appropriate form, since it would discourage the inference that traditional imperial rights were based upon papal generosity.[6] Certainly, however, the papal Curia was anxious to assert the personal character of the Calixtinum,[7] and most probably, Henry and the princes would have preferred the obvious future advantages of a perpetual grant, but were unable to win this concession in the hard bargaining at Worms.[8]

Specifically, the Calixtinum's provisions were: German episcopal and abbatial elections should take place at the

---

et abbatum Teutonici regni, qui ad regnum pertinent, in praesentia tua fieri, absque simonia et aliqua violentia; ut si qua inter partes discordia emerserit, metropolitani et conprovincialium consilio vel iudicio, saniori parti assensum et auxilium praebeas. Electus autem regalia per sceptrum a te recipiat et quae ex his iure tibi debet faciat. Ex aliis vero partibus imperii consecratus infra sex menses regalia per sceptrum a te recipiat. . . ."

[6] Against earlier authorities and subsequent criticism, Schäfer has successfully defended his interpretation of the Calixtinum as a personal concession to Henry V alone (*op.cit.* 3-7, 84-94); this view was further developed by Hofmeister (*op.cit.* 72-85, 116f and passim).

[7] Otto of Freising, *Chronica sive historia de duobus civitatibus* 7.16, 2nd ed. Hofmeister (MGH SS.rer.Germ. Hanover 1912) 331: "Hoc [privilegium, scil. Calixtinum] pro bono pacis sibi soli et non successoribus datum dicunt Romani."

[8] The Pravilegium of 12 April 1111 (*MGH Const* I 144f no.96) was written while Paschal was entirely in Henry's power, and it was therefore largely tailored to the emperor's specifications. Nonetheless, as Hofmeister has shown (*op.cit.* 77f), it was a personal grant for Henry alone, and Hofmeister is at least half convinced that Henry himself chose the personal form. Yet there were serious limits to the pressures which Henry could exert upon Paschal, and it is no more reasonable to suppose that Henry dictated this form, than to infer that Paschal refused to yield on this one point; see Hofmeister, *op.cit.* 95, and Hoffmann, *DA* 15 (1959) 424 n.136. Moreover, the papal report on the events of April 1111 emphasized the personal nature of the grant to Henry; *Relatio Paschalis*, in *MGH Const* I 149 no.99: "Restabat illa exactionis et extorsionis portio, ut de investiture permissione privilegium regi personaliter scriberetur"; Hofmeister, *op.cit.* 79 n.2.

imperial court.[9] After a contested election in Germany, the emperor should support the "sounder part" (*sanior pars*) of the electors and the more suitable candidate; however, the emperor's right to decide the dispute was further qualified by the provision that he should settle the conflict only after hearing the counsel and verdict of the metropolitan and the comprovincial bishops (*metropolitani et conprovincialium consilio vel iudicio*).[10] And with his scepter, the emperor should grant the *regalia* to German prelates-elect before their consecration.[11] In Burgundy and Northern Italy, however, the *electus* should receive the *regalia* within the six months following his consecration; regalian investiture was thus relegated to a minor position in the non-German parts of the empire.

From a strict Gregorian viewpoint, election and consecration were the only two indispensable elements in the making of a bishop. As Geoffrey of Vendôme explained, the clergy are the vicars of Christ in the election of a bishop, the metropolitan and the other officiating bishops are the vicars of Christ in the consecration.[12] This Gregorian emphasis on election and consecration implied, of course, the superfluousness of the monarch's investiture. Yet the Calixtinum assured

[9] Such is Hofmeister's sound interpretation of the phrase "in praesentia tua" (*op.cit.* 87-94). The English kings found the *electio in capella regis* an effective device for controlling episcopal elections; Constitutions of Clarendon c.12, ed. William Stubbs, *Select Charters*, 9th ed. rev. H.W.C. Davis (Oxford 1913) 166.

[10] Hermann Krause, "Consilio et iudicio: Bedeutungsbreite und Sinngehalt," *Speculum historiale*, ed. Clemens Bauer (Munich 1965) 416-38.

[11] Here the scepter symbolized royal power and the act of concession, but did not represent the thing transferred; on this kind of investiture, see H. Mitteis, *Lehnrecht und Staatsgewalt* 508-11, and F. L. Ganshof, *Feudalism*, trans. P. Grierson (London 1952) 111f. Originally suggested as a compromise by the *Disputatio vel defensio Paschalis papae* in 1112 (*MGH LdL* II 665), the investiture *per sceptrum* was less offensive to the reformers than investiture with ring and staff, since the scepter was not actually given to the prelate and therefore could not so readily represent the bestowal of an ecclesiastical office; Mitteis, *op.cit.* 510.

[12] *Libelli* 2, *MGH LdL* II 684: "Tota itaque ordinatio episcopi in sola electione consistit et consecratione, si tamen illam electio recta praecesserit. . . . Sunt autem vicarii Christi clerici in electione, episcopi in consecratione." Cf. also above, Ch.IIA n.3.

Henry of a far-reaching authority over both election and consecration in Germany. The elections at the imperial court would inevitably be influenced by the emperor's wishes, and he had a decisive voice in any disputed election. Moreover, the emperor's investiture was to precede the consecration. With these concessions, therefore, Calixtus surrendered key points of the Gregorian program, and at least in Germany, the Concordat of Worms represents a limited victory for the emperor. Yet with its narrow provisions, the Concordat left many problems unsolved, and left much room for the free play of power. Even more clearly after Henry V's death in 1125, the relative power of the monarch was always a central factor determining his control over the promotions to the German episcopate. Strong rulers, like Frederick Barbarossa and Henry VI, exerted a broad and not easily definable influence over German ecclesiastical elections. They went far beyond the rights explicitly conceded by the Calixtinum, and their sanctions derived from the custom and usage recognized by the imperial princes, rather than from a papal grant.[13] On the other hand, the German monarchs of the thirteenth century were forced to abandon much of this imperial prerogative in episcopal elections.[14]

Seen under the rubric of constitutional law rather than of politics, the Concordat left much room for a more detailed juridical definition of regalian investiture. Indeed, within the Concordat, the key term *regalia* was neither defined nor explained, but was simply left to the reader's understanding.[15] Informed contemporaries undoubtedly interpreted the term

---

[13] Below, Ch.VIIIc.   [14] Below, Ch.X.

[15] In fact, within the Concordat, the term *regalia* had two broad but commonly recognized meanings, one primarily episcopal and the other literally regalian, that is, referring to royal prerogative rights; in general, see Ott, *ZRG KA* 35 (1948) esp. 272-97, and Kantorowicz, *King's Two Bodies* 185 n.293. As mentioned in the Calixtinum, the *regalia* were simply the German bishops' temporalities; in Germany, the term's context was feudal. In Henry's charter for Calixtus, however, the emperor promised to restore and preserve the *regalia sancti Petri;* on these *regalia*, see above, Ch.VIIA n.77. In Italy during the reign of Barbarossa, the word *regalia* referred primarily to fiscal prerogative.

by reference to the more explicit documents of 1111.[16] Nonetheless, the requirement of investiture before consecration constituted a kind of definition, for with the *regalia* the German *electus* won the right to receive his consecration. This requirement was, however, no radical innovation. Before 1122, the Concordat's prescribed sequence of investiture and consecration had been the normal practice in the empire, with the status of well-established custom—even though Paschal II had condemned it as "a custom intolerable to the Church."[17] Moreover, a full generation before the Concordat, this prescribed sequence was already an articulate program, keynoted by imperialist forgers in the 1080's.[18] Around 1100, Hugh of Fleury advocated the precedence of investiture before consecration,[19] and imperialist pamphleteers of the early twelfth century echo the same refrain.[20] In April 1111, when pope Paschal granted the "Pravilegium" to Henry V and recognized thereby the emperor's prerogative in the elevation of bishops, the precedence of investiture appeared prominently among the pope's concessions.[21] In this respect, then, the Concordat sanctioned and crystallized the existing policy and customary law of the empire, but did not create new law. Long after Henry V's death in 1125, this regulation was still considered binding in Germany.[22] However, even in imperial circles, the Calixtinum was not regarded as the juridical basis for this

---

[16] Especially *MGH Const* I 141 no.90; Ott, *op.cit.* 257.

[17] *MGH Const* I 141 no.90 (12 February 1111): ". . . mos inolevit ecclesiae intollerabilis, ut episcopi electi nullomodo consecrationem acciperent, nisi prius per manum regiam investirentur. . . ."

[18] See the spurious decree of Hadrian I (*MGH Const* I 660 no.446; excerpted in D.63 c.22), and the two spurious privileges of Leo VIII: the *Privilegium minus* (*ibid.* 667 no.448; excerpted in D.63 c.23), and the *Privilegium maius* (*ibid.* 673 no.449). The imperialist forgeries of the 1080's are discussed in two articles by Karl Kordan, "Der Kaisergedanke in Ravenna zur Zeit Heinrichs IV., *DA* 2 (1938) 85-128, and "Ravennater Fälschungen aus den Anfängen des Investiturstreites," *AUF* 15 (1938) 426-48; also, Ullmann, *Growth of Papal Government* 352-58.

[19] *Tractatus de regia potestate* 1.5, *MGH LdL* II 472.

[20] *Tractatus de investitura episcoporum*, in *MGH LdL* II 501; also, Gregory of Catino, *Orthodoxa defensio imperialis* 3, *MGH LdL* II 537.

[21] *MGH Const* I 145 no.96, and *ibid.*142 no.91.

[22] In the early 1220's, Eike von Repgow asserted its continuing validity (below, Ch.VIIIc n.31).

requirement. Indeed, after Henry V's death, the Calixtinum was explicitly cited only once in support of imperial rights. Even in that one instance, Otto of Freising implies that the accepted custom of the imperial court was decisive for the precedence of investiture before consecration.[23] For as the German bishops explained to the pope in the late twelfth century, immemorial tradition and the "approved usage" (*usus approbatus*) of Germany dictated the sequence of investiture and consecration. Any violation of this official sequence constituted, in their opinion, the "dismemberment" of the empire and the "utmost diminution of its rights."[24]

In the early and mid-twelfth century, contemporaries disagreed on the evaluation of this customary sequence, and on its significance for the royal prerogative. If the king disapproved of a bishop-elect, could he withhold the investiture at will? If the king delayed or refused the investiture, could the Church proceed with the consecration of the *electus*?[25]

[23] *Gesta Friderici* 2.6, 3rd ed. Waitz and Simson 106f: "Tradit enim curia et ab ecclesia eo tempore, quo sub Heinrico V de investitura episcoporum decisa fuit inter regnum et sacerdotium controversia, sibi concessum autumat, quod, obeuntibus episcopis, si forte in eligendo partes fiant, principis arbitrii esse, episcopum quem voluerit ex primatum suorum consilio ponere, nec aliquem electum ante consecrandum, quam ab ipsius manu regalia per sceptrum suscipiat." The key phrase here is "Tradit enim curia . . ."; it should be noted that the subsequent clause ("et ab ecclesia . . . autumat") merely furnishes a secondary justification (or explanation) of the official imperial position on episcopal promotions. Cf. also Otto's *Chronica* 7.16, 2nd ed. Hofmeister 331; and Paul Kopfermann, *Das Wormser Konkordat im deutschen Staatsrecht* (Berlin 1908) 9f.

[24] Wichman of Magdeburg and his suffragans to Urban III (December 1186), *MGH Const* I 445 no.315; Adalbert of Salzburg and his suffragans to the cardinals, *ibid.* 447 no.316. The bishops were expressing their objections to Urban's consecration of the uninvested Folmar of Trier. With more loyalty than accuracy, the bishops asserted that the pope's procedure was unprecedented; in fact, Innocent II consecrated an uninvested archbishop of Trier in 1131.

[25] On these questions, the uncertainty of 12th-century thought is reflected in the differing interpretations of modern scholars; a clear and consistent picture of the relevant 12th-century legal norms is unlikely to emerge from the scanty surviving evidence. For a survey of scholarly views, see Schäfer, *Zur Beurteilung* 21, and Hermann Rudorff, *Zur Erklärung des Wormser Konkordats* (Weimar 1906) 20-23. Two basic positions can be discerned: Some assert the reality of a lawful and far-reaching royal veto power (e.g., Hinschius, *KR* II 561 n.1); others deny the king's legal right to withhold investiture from anyone chosen by a canonical election, though they admit

On the one hand, the right to withhold the investiture would carry with it the right to raise serious obstacles for—or even to veto—an undesirable candidate. If strictly maintained, this right would render the ruler's consent indispensable to a bishop-elect. On the other hand, many churchmen understandably regarded consecration as a purely ecclesiastical act, which did not concern the monarchy. And after 1122, the customary sequence of investiture and consecration was occasionally reversed; such instances would place heavy pressure on the monarchy to accept the *fait accompli* and to invest the consecrated bishop. The Concordat of Worms simply stipulated the sequence, but it did not explain the consequences if the prescribed sequence should be reversed, nor did it settle the question of the emperor's right to withhold the investiture. Yet it is clear that in imperial thought prior to the Concordat, the right of investiture implied a right of veto. This claim is already distinct in the program formulated by imperialist forgers in the 1080's:

> Unless [a bishop-elect] is approved and invested by the king, he may be consecrated by no one.[26]

Here, instead of a mere statement prescribing the sequence of investiture and consecration, the consecration of an uninvested bishop-elect is expressly and unmistakably forbidden. It goes without saying that the Gregorian program could never be reconciled with such a royal "right" of veto. Moreover, Paschal II was fully aware of—and solidly opposed to—the veto power implicit in imperial custom and policy.[27] A right of veto was still claimed under Barbarossa, and as late as the

the *de facto* exercise of such a right (e.g., Scharnagl, *Begriff der Investitur* 131f). Dealing with this topic, however, scholars often assume that the same legal norms were accepted equally by the German monarchy and by the Roman Church. In fact, at least two separate claims existed and were always potentially in conflict.

[26] *MGH Const* I 660 no.446: "nisi a rege laudetur et investiatur, a nemine consecretur"; similarly *ibid.* 667 no.448, 673 no.449 (above, n.18). See Bernheim, *ZKG* 7 (1885) 310f.

[27] *MGH Const* I 141 no.90 (above, n.17); Paschal was familiar with the imperialist forgeries cited above (nn.18, 26).

1150's, Gerhoh of Reichersberg denounced this royal practice. Indeed, Gerhoh considered the customary precedence of
investiture a threat to canonical procedure, since the king
could easily force an invested prelate-elect upon a church.
As Gerhoh pointed out, the suitability of an invested *electus*
could not always be examined by the ecclesiastical superior,
for the investiture might serve as a guarantee of the consecration.[28] In twelfth-century practice, the papacy and a few of
the German ecclesiastical princes did not recognize a binding
obligation to observe the official sequence,[29] for they were
prepared equally to ignore the prescribed sequence when an
opportunity presented itself, and to observe the sequence
when it was expedient or inevitable.

On the imperial side, the problem of power could be
equally decisive. For example, in 1131 an uninvested archbishop-elect of Trier received his consecration from the pope.
Because of this violation, Lothar III at first withheld the
regalia from the archbishop, but since he knew that the
powerful archbishop could readily become a dangerous
opponent, Lothar accepted the archbishop's excuse and reluctantly invested him.[30] Nonetheless, twelfth-century emperors
and prelates placed value on the official sequence, and their
emphasis would be inexplicable if they had not regarded the
investiture as a truly indispensable prerequisite to the consecration. Their attitude derived from their concept of German
customary law, and it implied, as a possible sanction, the
threat of refusing the investiture to violators. Hence, in 1131,

[28] Gerhoh, *Commentarius in psalmum LXIV*, in *MGH LdL* III 451f; id.,
Liber de novitatibus huius temporis c.12, *ibid.* 297: "sicut iam alicubi
factum scimus personis quibusdam inordinate purpuratis, antequam veste
alba prout oportuit induerentur, dum, necdum spiritaliter post electionem
examinati aut consecrati, sunt regalibus amplificati et ita nimis confortati,
ut postmodum non potuerunt examinari, sed oporteret eos ad placitum
regis et militum consecrari." See below, Ch.IXA.

[29] Above, n.24; also, below, Ch.VIIIA and B.

[30] Baldericus, *Gesta Alberonis* cc.12f, *MGH SS* VIII 250f. Though this
incident concerns a consecrated archbishop and therefore cannot directly
illustrate the king's right to refuse investiture to a bishop-elect, one is
entitled to infer that *a fortiori*, with a good reason the king could withhold
the investiture from an *electus*.

Lothar considered himself justified in punishing a breach of this imperial custom by withholding the *regalia*, although political realism prevented the full assertion of his rights in this case.[31] In imperial thought, the prescribed sequence undoubtedly seemed to guarantee that the emperor's consent would remain a necessity for bishops-elect. And in many elections, the electors felt strong pressure to designate only a candidate who would prove acceptable to the emperor.[32] Indeed, as conceived by twelfth-century Germany, the official sequence was an essential part of the royal prerogative, which might—by the strictest possible interpretation—even include the right to veto an undesirable candidate.

Throughout the twelfth century, the precedence of investiture remained a fundamental element of German customary law. Still, occasionally in the twelfth century and commonly in the thirteenth, a violation of this rule might provoke no reaction from the emperor.[33] One may speculate that the chief cause of this indifference lay in the regulation itself, which related the investiture primarily to the prelate's consecration and hence to his sacramental powers. The main weakness of this rule—and the probable reason for its steadily lessening importance—was its failure to answer a central question: What powers does the investiture confer upon an *electus*?

The Calixtinum answered this question straightforwardly: Calixtus's charter assured Henry that in Germany, each "*electus* should receive the *regalia* from you by way of the scepter."[34] Indeed, this declaration clearly implied that the investiture conveys to the *electus* all of the powers

---

[31] Cf., however, the view of Schäfer, *Zur Beurteilung* 23: "Er . . . weicht . . . vor dem Papst zurück. Von einem Recht kann also nicht die Rede sein."

[32] At Trier in 1131 the canons were convinced that only imperial support could persuade the laity to accept their candidate. Hence, in electing a new archbishop, they stipulated that their choice was conditional upon king Lothar's willingness to invest the *electus*, as well as upon papal consent; see the canons' letter to Innocent II, as quoted by Baldericus, *op.cit.* c.10, *MGH SS* VIII 249. Numerous examples of pressure from the emperor himself can be found in the reign of Barbarossa.

[33] Note, for example, the case of bishop Hartwig of Regensburg in 1155 (below, Ch.VIIIc n.18).

[34] Above, n.5.

and possessions summed up in the *regalia*. Yet Calixtus used precisely the same expression for the Burgundian and Italian bishops, who were to receive the investiture within six months of their consecration. It is hardly credible that these non-German bishops were expected to await a long deferred investiture before exercising their secular jurisdiction and administering their properties.[35] Apparently, then, Calixtus's statement cannot be interpreted as a generally applicable stipulation that everywhere in the empire, the investiture effectively confers the *regalia*, and that before the investiture an *electus* may not administer his *regalia* in any way. In fact, it would not be easy to find among the eleventh-century sources an explicit and detailed assertion of such jurisdictional consequences for the act of investiture. Moreover, during the later eleventh and early twelfth centuries, it was possible to imagine an act of investiture without any juridically constitutive significance, that is, without any important effects. Cardinal Humbert had asserted—with indignation—that the prince's investiture conveys even the sacramental and purely ecclesiastical facets of the bishop's office, so that in the subsequent ecclesiastical investiture during the consecration, the metropolitan is performing a hollow ceremony.[36] From a somewhat different point of view, when a later Gregorian claimed the Church's absolute rights over all properties ever conferred upon it, he concluded that any act of lay investiture therefore conveys nothing and is hence "superfluous and vain."[37] Though both of these Gregorian doctrines denied the central juridical meaning in the act, one was referring solely to ecclesiastical investiture, the other solely to lay investiture.

Nonetheless, for practical men, investiture meant the effective conveyance of properties and rights through a symbolic

---

[35] C. Volkmar, "Das Verhältnis Lothars III. zur Investiturfrage," *FDG* 26 (1886) 486. This question needs further investigation.

[36] *Adversus simoniacos* 3.6, *MGH LdL* I 205 (above, Ch.VIIa n.36).

[37] Geoffrey of Vendôme, *Libellus* 4, *MGH LdL* II 691 (below, n.42).

act of concession.[38] And in eleventh-century imperial practice, the king's investiture was constitutive, for it formally inaugurated the new prelate into full possession of his jurisdictional and administrative powers.[39] Moreover, eleventh-century usage was clearly reflected in the formula of investiture, as the king said to the future bishop, "Receive the church" (*Accipe ecclesiam*).[40] Here the word *ecclesia* stands for the entire bishopric taken as a whole, without any distinction between office and property, between spiritual and temporal aspects. As eleventh-century Germany viewed the investiture, the entire office with all of its appurtenances—the *regimen pastorale* or *cura pastoralis*—was transferred when the crosier was handed over to the new prelate.[41] Episcopal consecration was, of course, considered a necessity, but it added nothing to those governmental powers conferred on the bishop-elect at the moment of his investiture.

By 1100 the monarchists and the moderates of both camps were attempting to define, with a clarity and precision which had not previously been needed, the legal and constitutional significance of royal investiture. With their denial that this investiture confers any sacramental or spiritual prerogative, these theorists were forced to spell out the meaning of investiture, and to assert that the king's investiture is constitutive for the bishop-elect's power over his secular properties and jurisdiction.[42] As Ivo of Chartres explained, the investiture

[38] Julius Ficker, *Vom Heerschilde* (Innsbruck 1862) 34; Mitteis, *Lehnrecht und Staatsgewalt* 500-11; Ganshof, *Feudalism* 110-12.

[39] Carlyle, *Mediaeval Political Theory* IV 25-39, for a convenient summary; also, Hauck, *KG* III 53ff, and Hinschius, *KR* II 535ff.

[40] Peter Damian, *Ep.*1.13, *PL* 144 221 (above, Ch. VIIᴀ n.4).

[41] Thietmar of Merseburg, *Chronicon* 2.21, ed. R. Holtzmann 62f (= *MGH SS* III 749f): ". . . inperator . . . curam . . . ei baculo committens pastoralem . . ."; cf. *id.* 2.21, *ibid.* 63. See also Hinschius, *KR* II 536 n.7, and Scharnagl, *Begriff der Investitur* 6f (above, Ch.VIIᴀ n.6).

[42] Around 1119 Geoffrey of Vendôme was reluctantly ready to allow investiture "in order to avoid scandal and schism," so long as the investiture was carried out with some other symbol than ring and staff. Though a Gregorian, Geoffrey admitted the royal origin of the Church's properties, and continuing royal jurisdiction over them, and even admitted the constitutive

The Bishop-Elect

bestows the ecclesiastical lands and other properties (*villae ecclesiasticae et alia bona exteriora*).[43] Around 1100 the Anglo-Norman Anonymous admitted that the king can confer no ecclesiastical *ordo*, but maintained that through the king's investiture the bishop-elect receives the rights of property (*possessio temporalium rerum*) and jurisdiction over his diocese (*potestas regendi populum* or *dominatio in populum*).[44]

---

character of the king's investiture (*Libelli* 4, *MGH LdL* II 691f): "Subtrahe ius humanum, possessiones [episcopus] amittit, quibus ipse corporaliter sustentatur. Non enim possessiones haberet ecclesia, nisi sibi a regibus donarentur et ab ipsis non quidem divinis sacramentis, sed possessionibus terrenis investiretur. . . . Ex iure autem humano tantum illis debemus, quantum possessiones diligimus, quibus ab ipsis vel a parentibus suis aecclesia ditata et investita dinoscitur. . . ." Then Geoffrey supports this position with a well-known quotation from St Augustine, basing all property rights on human and imperial law (*Tractatus in evangelium Iohannis* 6.26, *PL* 35 1437). Immediately thereafter, however, Geoffrey qualifies his surprising concession and reduces its significance (*MGH LdL* II 692): "Possunt itaque sine offensione reges post electionem canonicam et consecrationem per investituram regalem in aecclesiasticis possessionibus concessionem, auxilium et defensionem episcopo dare, quod quolibet signo factum extiterit, regi vel pontifici seu catholicae fidei non nocebit." In the same discussion, Geoffrey contends that, once given to the Church, ecclesiastical possessions are permanently the Church's property. When Geoffrey further asserts that in the investiture the king gives to the Church something which the Church already owns, he concludes that such an investiture "superfluum est et vanum, non tamen videtur criminosum" (*ibid.* 691). Thereby, Geoffrey has clearly contradicted himself, and has denied that the royal investiture effectively confers rights upon a bishop; at the most, such an investiture could merely confirm preexistent rights. In short, Geoffrey's apparent concession represents neither the abandonment nor even the serious modification of his generally uncompromising stand. Because of his inconsistency, there is no fully satisfactory account of Geoffrey's doctrines. See Mirbt, *Publizistik* 529f; Scharnagl, *op.cit.* 112-19; Carlyle, *op.cit.* IV 149-52; Hoffmann, *DA* 15 (1959) 416f; and for the best analysis, Becker, *Studien zum Investiturproblem* 153-57.

43 *Ep.*60, ed. Leclercq I 246f; in general, Hoffmann, *op.cit.* 405-16.

44 *Tractatus* 4 ("De consecratione pontificum et regum"), *MGH LdL* III 667; also, *Tractatus* 5 ("De Romano pontifice"), *ibid.* 685. The Anonymous's doctrine on investiture was, of course, ancillary to his more central idea of the anointed king's prerogatives within the Church; see Williams, *Norman Anonymous* 188f. In fact, the Anonymous usually avoided the verb *investire*, preferring the more neutral term *instituere*, which could equally refer to the ceremonial elevation of bishop or king (Williams, *op.cit.* 185 n.625). As explained by the Anonymous, the bishop receives from the king jurisdictional powers which are more than merely secular and regalian, for they seem to encroach upon and to include part of the *forum externum*, a much later term for a purely ecclesiastical form of jurisdiction.

The author of these tractates is generally designated either as the Anony-

Office, *Regalia*, and Investiture

Similarly, the archimperialist Gregory of Catino stressed the confirmation of secular property rights as the main effect of investiture.[45] Equally explicit was the doctrine set forth by Hugh of Fleury between 1102 and the end of 1104. Hugh visualized two ways in which a bishop could be selected: royal appointment, or election "by clergy and people."[46] After an election, if the bishop-elect is deemed worthy, the king must consent; if the *electus* is unworthy, king and people must withhold their consent. And following the election, the king invests the bishop-elect with "secular properties" (*res seculares*) and "worldly powers" (*terrenae potestates*). Finally, the bishop-elect receives his "spiritual powers," his *cura animarum*, from the archbishop, who bestows the ring and staff. However, though he accepted the principle of election, Hugh passionately defended the royal right of appointment. To be sure, in making an appointment, the king should act only "with the counsel and consent of the metropolitan."[47] When the king appoints a bishop, he confers upon him "the

mous of York or as the Norman Anonymous. Authorship and provenance (Rouen or York) have been much debated and are still *sub judice*; the problem and the scholarly literature are discussed at great length by Williams (*op.cit.* 1-127), whose conclusions have recently been criticized by Norman F. Cantor, *Church, Kingship, and Lay Investiture in England 1089-1135* (Princeton 1958) 174-97, 238-47. Since the question of authorship does not directly concern the present study, the author is cited here simply as the Anglo-Norman Anonymous.

45 *Orthodoxa defensio imperialis* 5, *MGH LdL* II 538: "secularium rerum seu temporalium atque corporalium possessionum omniumque ecclesiae eiusdem bonorum iuris confirmationem."

46 *De regia potestate* 1.5, *MGH LdL* II 472: "Igitur rex instinctu Spiritus sancti potest, sicut existimo, praesulatus honorem religioso clerico tribuere. Animarum vero curam archiepiscopus debet ei committere. . . . Ubi vero eligitur episcopus a clero vel populo secundum morem ecclesiasticum, nullam vim ac perturbationem eligentibus rationabiliter rex per tyrannidem debet inferre, sed ordinationi legitime suum adhibere consensum. At si reprehensibilis ille qui eligitur fuerit inventus, non solum rex, sed nec plebs provintiae debet electioni ipsius suum assensum favoremque tribuere. . . . Post electionem autem, non annulum aut baculum a manu regia, sed investituram rerum secularium electus antistes debet suscipere, et in suis ordinibus per annulum aut baculum animarum curam ab archiepiscopo suo, ut . . . terrenis et spiritalibus potestatibus suae auctoritatis privilegium conservetur."

47 *Id.* 2.3, *ibid.* 489: ". . . speramus, ut si rex aut quislibet pius princeps praesulatus honorem viro sancto ordinabiliter tribuere vult, ne hoc suo solo faciat arbitrio, sed consilio et consensu metropolitani episcopi."

dignity of prelacy" (*honor praesulatus*).[48] Within his theory, Hugh's concept of the *honor praesulatus* is of key importance.[49] Since Hugh did not mention a requirement of investiture following a royal appointment, presumably the royal appointment itself either included an investiture or produced the same juridical effects as investiture.[50] Of course, the *honor praesulatus* did not include any spiritual or sacramental prerogatives,[51] but the appointee had a strong claim upon the episcopal consecration. Thus a royal appointee, holding the *honor praesulatus*, and a duly invested bishop-elect enjoyed the same rights and powers. Though Hugh's theory was less clear and systematic than ambitious, it attempted to formulate the constitutional status of a prelate-elect to whom the king has granted secular powers and properties, and it was the most imaginative of the early attempts at such a definition.

With only partial success, these theorists were trying to articulate the principle that investiture marks the effective beginning of the bishop-elect's regalian rights. An obvious corollary implied that prior to his investiture, a bishop-elect may not enter upon the powers and income from his *regalia*. Of course, imperial custom sanctioned these two principles, but as long as the lawfulness of investiture itself was in dispute, this aspect of custom could scarcely achieve the status of universally recognized law. In his negotiations with the papacy, therefore, Henry V sought formal and explicit recognition of investiture as a constitutive act. In May 1107 Henry sent the archbishop of Trier and other envoys to confer with

48 *Id.* 1.5, 2.3, *ibid.* 472, 488f.

49 However, Heinrich Böhmer, *Kirche und Staat* 165f, regards the idea of the *honor praesulatus* as the "Achilles' heel" of Hugh's theory; see also Scharnagl, *Begriff der Investitur* 90-93, and Becker, *Studien zum Investiturproblem* 152. Benzo of Alba had already coined the expression *honor praesulatus* to indicate the dignity which the prelate receives from the king (*Ad Heinricum IV imperatorem* lib.iv Prologus, *MGH SS* XI 634).

50 Scharnagl, *op.cit.* 92.

51 Cf. Böhmer, *op.cit.* 166, and the correction by Scharnagl, *op.cit.* 93 n.1; also, Becker, *loc.cit.*

Office, *Regalia*, and Investiture

Paschal II at Châlons. Suger of St Denis was present at Châlons, and has left a detailed résumé of the issues discussed there. According to Suger, the archbishop explained to Paschal the customary "right of the empire" in episcopal elections, stipulating that investiture with ring and staff was an indispensable prerequisite to the prelate's jurisdictional and administrative powers,

> For otherwise [the bishop] must in no way occupy the cities and castles, margraviates, tolls, and whatever things belong to the imperial dignity.[52]

Though abbot Suger's account is open to serious question in some respects, there is no reason to doubt his accuracy on this point.[53] At Châlons, presumably for the first time,

[52] *Vita Ludovici grossi regis* c.10, ed. H. Waquet (Paris 1929) 56-58: "Talis est domini nostri imperatoris pro qua mittimur causa. Temporibus antecessorum nostrorum, sanctorum et apostolicorum virorum magni Gregorii et aliorum, hoc ad jus imperii pertinere dinoscitur, ut in omni electione hic ordo servetur: antequam electio in palam proferatur, ad aures domini imperatoris perferrea, et si personamb deceat, assensum ab eo ante factam electionem assumere; deinde in conventu, secundum canones, peticione populi, electione cleri, assensu honoratorisc proferre, consecratumd libere nec simoniace ad dominum imperatorem pro regalibus, ut anulo et virga investiatur, redire, fidelitatem et hominium facere. Nec mirum; civitates enim et castella, marchias, thelonea et queque imperatorie dignitatis nullo modo aliter debere occupare. . . ."

[53] Suger's presentation and the other sources have been analyzed by Bernard Monod, "La question des investitures à l'entrevue de Châlons (1107)," *Revue historique* 101 (1909) 80-87. The unreliability of Suger's report has been stressed by Hinschius (*KR* II 540 n.5), Johannes Bauermann ("Die Frage der Bischofswahlen auf dem Würzburger Reichstag von 1133," *Kritische Beiträge: Festschrift R. Holtzmann* [Berlin 1933] 121f), and Ott (*ZRG KA* 35 [1948] 251f). Monod (*op.cit.* 82, 85f) and Becker (*op.cit.* 222 nn.101f), however, have only minor reservations about this account, while Hauck (*KG* III 894f) and Hoffmann (*DA* 15 [1959] 422) have no reservations whatsoever.

The question of credibility reflects serious textual difficulties (cf. the superscript letters in n.52): (a) Since "perferre" lacks a direct object, Ott (*op.cit.* 252 n.73) proposes "electionem" as object, and Waquet (*op.cit.* 59) supplies "le nom du candidat" there. (b) Obviously, "persona" is the correct form; Ott, *op.cit.* 252 n.74. (c) If not emended, "honoratoris" would be the genitive singular of *honorator* (no other examples are known); it would then mean "bestower of an office or fief" and would refer to the emperor (thus Meyer von Knonau, *Jahrbücher* VI 46; Waquet, *op.cit.* 58 n.1). Hence, Monod emended "honoratoris" into "imperatoris." As Bauer-

imperial spokesmen tried to build an important regulation into the public law accepted equally by papacy and empire: the requirement of investiture before administration of the regalities. The negotiations at Châlons broke down, but apparently the pope objected mainly to the imperial embassy's demand of homage from the bishops, and to its insistence upon investiture with ring and staff.[54] That is, the imperial claim to the *regalia* and the requirement of an imperial bestowal before occupancy of the *regalia* seem not to have been the major stumbling blocks at Châlons.

Four years later, in February 1111, Henry and Paschal agreed to a radical solution incorporating the same requirement in a different fashion.[55] Henry promised to renounce

---

mann has shown, however, "honoratoris" should read "honoratorum" (*loc.cit.*); on the role of the *honorati* in elections, see Ch.VIIIв esp. nn.4-17. (d) Because one cannot reconcile "consecratum" with the imperial program requiring investiture before consecration, Monod—probably correctly— emended "consecratum" into "electum" (*op.cit.* 81-86). Although Monod considered the phrase "consecratum libere nec simoniace" meaningless, the papal and imperial chanceries did *not* find phrases like *libera consecratio* meaningless; cf. *MGH Const* I 142 no.91 (1111), 159 no.107 (1122).

54 Cf. Ott's argument that Henry probably did not actually demand homage in 1107 (*op.cit.* 252). Though generally well informed, Suger was not necessarily familiar with German custom. Moreover, the *Vita* was written about 1144, thirty-seven years after the event; at sixty-three, a man may well confuse the details of an incident occurring when he was twenty-six. His résumé of the imperial position on elections could easily have been influenced by French usage, which prescribed royal consent as prerequisite to an election; see Hinschius, *KR* II 540 no.5, and Ott, *loc.cit.*, but cf. Monod, *op.cit.* 82ff. Further, as described by Suger, the sequence of investiture and consecration is directly opposed to the consistently defended views of imperial spokesmen. Again Suger was probably influenced by his conception of French usage, for in France after the 1140's consecration generally preceded investiture, although in 1107 the investiture was normally prior; on the changing sequence in France, see Becker, *op.cit.* 167f, 244 n.206 (quoting a letter from Suger in 1149). On the other hand, this difficulty disappears if one accepts the emendation conjectured by Monod and others, replacing *consecratum* with *electum*. In any case, the various reasons for doubting Suger's report do not seem to affect his statement on the imperial requirement of investiture before "occupation" of the *regalia*.

55 *MGH Const* I 134-42 nos.83-90; Meyer von Knonau, *Jahrbücher* VI 141-65. Karl Pivec has ascribed to David, a royal chaplain, the composition of the documents relevant to these negotiations: "Studien und Forschungen zur Ausgabe des Codex Udalrici," *MIÖG* 46 (1932) 258-89, and "Die

Office, *Regalia,* and Investiture

the practice of investiture with ring and staff. Paschal recognized the royal origin of the various *regalia*—"the cities, dukeships, margraviates, mints, manors, and the other things pertaining to the service of the kingdom"—and he complained that because of the *regalia,* "the ministers of the altar have become ministers of the court."[56] In return for Henry's concession, therefore, Paschal ordered the imperial bishops to renounce their *regalia,* which would then revert to Henry and his successors in perpetuity. To be sure, Paschal left a large loophole open to Henry and to the ecclesiastical princes of Germany: the agreement would not have deprived all imperial prelates of the regalities, for in certain instances Henry could grant the *regalia* to individual prelates, but the regalian rights and properties would no longer be customarily appurtenant to the episcopal and abbatial offices. In the words of Paschal's charter:

> We forbid and under pain of anathema we prohibit any bishop or abbot, present or future, to usurp the *regalia* . . . and hereafter, except by grace of the king, to intrude himself upon the *regalia.*[57]

By "usurpation" of the regalities, the charter means simply the seizure, occupancy, or administration of the *regalia* without royal permission. In other words, according to the papal

---

Bedeutung des ersten Romzuges Heinrichs V.," *MIöG* 52 (1938) 222-25. Pivec's view has been effectively contested by Friedrich Hausmann, *Reichskanzlei und Hofkapelle unter Heinrich V. und Konrad III.* (MGH Schriften 14: Stuttgart 1956) 83-86, 310-19, who proposes the chancellor, Adalbert of Mainz, as the most probable author of these documents.

[56] *MGH Const* I 141 no.90 (12 February 1111).

[57] *Ibid.*: "Interdicimus etiam et sub districtione anathematis prohibemus, ne quis episcoporum seu abbatum, presentium vel futurorum, eadem regalia invadant . . . nec se deinceps nisi per gratiam regis de ipsis regalibus intromittant." Cf. Paschal's earlier promise (*ibid.* 138f no.85), made by his representative in the course of the negotiations leading to this agreement, and note that it included the former provision but omitted the latter ("nec se . . . intromittant"). Thus the "loophole" was added to the agreement at the last moment, after February 4th and before the promulgation on February 12th.

document, imperial bishops and abbots would no longer have a normal expectation of carrying out the necessary formalities and then receiving the *regalia*. Some prelates might still hold *regalia*, but only "by grace of the king," and not simply by virtue of office; obviously they could enjoy the *regalia* only so long as they retained the king's favor. By twelfth-century standards, royal confiscation of a bishop's *regalia* was an exceptional penalty,[58] but by the terms of Paschal's charter, royal bestowal of the *regalia* would have become the constitutionally exceptional act. The documents of February 1111 did not specify the forms by which the *regalia* should henceforth be conferred. Nonetheless, it is clear that these exceptional grants of the *regalia* by royal "grace" would take place only on Henry's terms, for it is inconceivable that Henry

---

[58] As we shall note in other contexts, the *regalia* were regarded as belonging primarily to the episcopal church, rather than to the individual bishop. The king could not confiscate the *regalia* without cause, and confiscated *regalia* eventually had to be returned to the bishop's successor. See *MGH Const* I 209 no.149 (*Libri feudorum* 2.40): ". . . si clericus, veluti episcopus vel abbas, beneficium habens a rege datum non solummodo personae sed aecclesiae, ipsum propter suam culpam perdat, eo vivente et ecclesiasticum honorem habente, ad regem pertineat, post mortem vero eius ad successorem revertatur." Also, Otto of Freising, *Gesta Friderici* 2.12, 3rd ed. Waitz and Simson 114: ". . . Hartwici Bremensis et Ulrici Halberstadensis, regalia personis tantum, quia nec personis, sed aecclesiis perpetualiter a principibus tradita sunt, abiudicata fuere." Barbarossa was quick to threaten confiscation as the penalty for failure to fulfill feudal obligations (such as homage); Rahewin, *Gesta Friderici* 4.35, *ed.cit.* 275 (= *MGH Const* I 250 no.179): "Episcoporum Italiae ego quidem non affecto hominium, si tamen et eos de nostris regalibus nichil delectat habere. Qui si gratanter audierint a Romano presule: 'quid tibi et regi,' consequenter quoque eos ab imperatore non pigeat audire: 'quid tibi et possessioni.' Nuncios nostros non esse recipiendos in palatiis episcoporum asserit. Concedo, si forte aliquis episcoporum habet in suo proprio solo et non in nostro palatium. Si autem in nostro solo et allodio sunt palatia episcoporum, cum profecto omne quod inedificatur solo cedat, nostra sunt et palatia"; for the sources of Barbarossa's thought, see D.8 c.1 (St Augustine) and *Dig.* 41.1.7.10. Note Barbarossa's use of this threat as a weapon during the papal schism; Rahewin, *id.* Appendix anno 1165, *ed.cit.* 348: "Albertus Frisingensis . . . coactus iuravit obedire Paschali . . . quamdiu regalia habere vellet." In 1227 Frederick II threatened to confiscate the *temporalia bona* (that is, the regalian properties) of prelates who refused to celebrate mass during the interdict; J.L.A. Huillard-Bréholles, *Historia diplomatica Friderici secundi* (7 vols. Paris 1852-61) III 51.

would have conferred the *regalia* without the safeguard of a close bond between himself and the favored prelate.[59] In short, those prelates holding *regalia* would have continued to be "ministers of the court," and "the service of the kingdom" would still have been strictly required. Whatever form they might have assumed, these exceptional grants of the *regalia* would have been explicitly constitutive, effectively conveying the regalian rights and properties to the favored prelates. Of course, the revolutionary agreement of February 1111 was never put into execution, for when Paschal's charter was solemnly read aloud in St Peter's before the German ecclesiastical and lay princes, the foreseeable storm of opposition broke out. In the tumult, as it became evident that the pope could not enforce his decree on the German episcopate, Henry announced that the agreement with Paschal was void.[60]

To clarify the meaning of investiture was important. Yet the full value of a sharpened definition can be seen only against the background of contemporary Gregorian doctrine. Placidus of Nonantula must serve as the prime example, since he alone systematically elaborated the implications of the high Gregorian position on the problem of the *regalia*. Writing near the end of 1111, Placidus's thought reveals the extent to which the Church's property had become, for all parties, the key issue.[61] As Placidus explained, the practice of investi-

[59] One may assume that the bestowal would have been signalized by an investiture, though under some other symbol than the ring and staff. One can only conjecture, however, about the form of the oath (and of any other obligation) which Henry would have exacted from a bishop before conferring the *regalia* on him; see Ott, *op.cit.* 252-58.

[60] Henry had promised conditionally to give up investiture with ring and staff, for he had stipulated that his promise depended on the Church's and the princes' consent to the entire agreement; Ekkehard of Aura, *Chronicon* anno 1111, *MGH SS* VI 244. It is scarcely surprising that the hardheaded monarch expected the princes' reaction to the papal charter; even Paschal may have anticipated opposition, since he threatened anathema against resisting prelates. However, Henry's reservations about the practicability of the agreement do not affect the interpretation of his concept of investiture.

[61] Mirbt, *Publizistik* 524-28; Scharnagl, *Begriff der Investitur* 103-10; Carlyle, *Mediaeval Political Theory* IV 132-40; Ott, *op.cit.* 246-50.

ture implies that the emperor has a proprietary right to the Church's possessions,[62] and that a bishop cannot hold castles and lands unless he has received them "from the emperor's hand."[63] Along similar lines, Placidus lucidly summarized the imperial claim that investiture is a constitutive act: "Without investiture, no one can have an ecclesiastical office and the worldly properties of his church."[64] With equally acute perception, Placidus attacked the foundations of the imperial position. Since he believed that the emperor was categorically forbidden to invest churchmen, Placidus was obviously unwilling to admit that the emperor's investiture could be, in any respect, constitutive. Moreover, pointedly avoiding even the word *regalia*, Placidus refused to recognize a distinction between the *regalia* and any other properties or privileges pertaining to the Church.[65] "Just as one who separates the body from the soul destroys the man," he stated, "he who separates the *corporalia* from the *spiritualia* of a church destroys the church."[66] Not only tithes and offerings, but also cities, castles, lands, even "dukeships and margraviates" and other secular offices belong to the Church as incontestable property.[67] For "whatever has once been given to the Church belongs to Christ in perpetuity, nor can it in any way be alienated from the Church's possession."[68] According to Placidus's system, when a bishop is consecrated, the metropolitan must invest the new bishop with the crosier, as a sign that the bishop has then received the lordship over the "worldly properties" (*terrenarum rerum dominium*) which his church possesses, and these "worldly properties" include everything which the emperor claimed as *regalia*. It is evident

---

[62] *De honore ecclesiae* cc.68, 82, 118f, *MGH LdL* II 596, 605, 625f.
[63] *Id.* c.43, *ibid.* 587.
[64] *Id.* c.85, *ibid.* 610: ". . . nemo sine investitura praesulatum ecclesiasticum et terrenas res aecclesiae habere praevaleat."
[65] Ott, *op.cit.* 247-49.
[66] *De honore ecclesiae* c.41, *MGH LdL* II 586.
[67] *Id.* Prologus, cc.43, 91, 151, *ibid.* 568, 587, 614, 634f.
[68] *Id.* cc.7, 43, 56, *ibid.* 577, 587, 591.

that in place of the constitutive investiture claimed by imperial custom and policy, Placidus has substituted a purely ecclesiastical investiture by the metropolitan. Yet for the new bishop, the metropolitan's investiture was constitutive only in a special and limited sense, since the bestowal of the crosier signified a divine bestowal of "worldly properties"; in Placidus's view, then, the new bishop actually received dominion over his temporal possessions "from the hand of the Lord."[69] Indeed, within the ceremonial of an episcopal investiture and consecration, the metropolitan acts "in the place of Christ."[70] Thus Placidus regarded the ecclesiastical investiture as primarily symbolic and declarative, but considered the divine conferment truly constitutive. There seems to be a contradiction, however, when Placidus observes in another passage that a bishop-elect must administer the properties of his church.[71] With this remark, Placidus was apparently asserting that election, rather than ecclesiastical investiture or divine bestowal, was the constitutive moment. Yet Placidus's inconsistency does not affect the main point of his argument against the imperial conception of investiture. By either of Placidus's

[69] *Id.* c.55, *ibid.* 590: "Episcopus etiam, cum benedicitur, baculum de manu archiepiscopi accipit, simul et anulum. Baculum quidem, ut bene populum regat . . . se percepisse cognoscat. . . . Unde et nos intellegere decet ideo institutum episcopos vel abbates baculum de manu episcopi, cum consecrantur, accipere, ut noverint se terrenarum rerum, quae aecclesia possidet, de manu Domini veraciter tunc accepisse dominium. . . ." There was, of course, nothing unusual in this stress on the importance of the metropolitan's investiture with ring and staff; for contemporary examples among the Gregorians, see the *Disputatio vel defensio Paschalis papae*, in *MGH LdL* II 665f, and Geoffrey of Vendôme, *Libelli* 4, *MGH LdL* II 691. The striking element in Placidus's doctrine is the assertion that this investiture—or rather, its divine counterpart—is constitutive and confers full property rights over *all* of the church's *corporalia*.

[70] After stating that consecration and investiture are inseparably linked ("Is enim sacratur qui investitur . . ."), Placidus asserts (*De honore ecclesiae* c.82, *MGH LdL* II 605): ". . . electus . . . ab archiepiscopo, qui vice Christi eum benedicit, investiri et consecrari debet."

[71] *Id.* c.56, *ibid.* 591: "Electus autem res aecclesiae gubernare et ad utilitatem tam animarum quam corporum dispensare debet." For further evidence of this uncertainty in Placidus's thought, cf. his Prologus, *ibid.* 568: ". . . qui consecratus est tam parvas quam magnas possessiones, quae Deo sanctificatae sunt, in potestate habeat. . . ."

interpretations, the sanction for the administration of property lies with the Church, whether God and the metropolitan confer them in the investiture, or the clergy in the election. And in either case, there is no room for an imperial investiture.[72]

---

[72] It has often been noted that Placidus made concessions to time-honored usage and to the imperial prerogative; *id.* cc.37, 56, 82, 86, 118, *ibid.* 585, 591, 605, 612, 625, but cf. *id.* c.153, *ibid.* 635. See, especially, *id.* c.93, *ibid.* 615: ". . . cum pastor aecclesiae canonice electus, investitus et consecratus fuerit, tunc per se vel per suos fideles imperatorem adeat et de rebus aecclesiae sibi commissis imperiale praeceptum expetat. Quod ei piissimus imperator . . . libentissime concedens firmare dignetur, quod sui praedecessores illi aecclesiae concessisse manifestum est, promittens . . . suam . . . defensionem in omnibus." The *imperiale praeceptum* embodies a promise of protection and a confirmation of the bishop's property rights, though it certainly does not indicate an imperial investiture; cf. Mirbt, *Publizistik* 528, and the preferable account in Scharnagl, *Begriff der Investitur* 108f. Properly seen against the background of Placidus's deepest convictions, these various concessions do not seem to modify seriously the strictness of his high Gregorian position.

CHAPTER VIII

THE *REGALIA* AND
THE BISHOP-ELECT:
IMPERIAL VIEWS

1. The Roman Concordat of 1133

for compelling reasons, neither the supporters of the emperor nor the partisans of the papacy were truly satisfied with the Concordat of Worms. Shortly before the compromise of 1122, as Henry clung tenaciously to his time-honored right of investiture with ring and crosier, with unusual solidarity the secular princes of Germany had vigorously backed the emperor's claim, and had denounced their opponents as "wreckers."[1] Nor did the agreement of 1122 really bring the Investiture Struggle to a decisive conclusion. Since investiture remained a live issue for more than a decade after 1122, in a literal sense the Investiture Struggle still continued.[2] Indeed, even Lothar III, far more compliant

[1] As archbishop Adalbert of Mainz complained to Calixtus II late in 1122 or early in 1123; Jaffé, *Bibl.* V 518ff: "Sed quia tam inperium quam inperator tamquam hereditario quodam iure baculum et anulum possidere volebant—pro quibus universa laicorum multitudo inperii nos destructores inclamabat—nullo modo potuimus his inperatorem exuere. . . ."

[2] The date 1122 is, of course, firmly embedded in 20th-century historical thought, and even distinguished historians are sometimes tempted to forget that the problem of investiture did not suddenly vanish in September of that year. For an example of this tendency, see Z. N. Brooke, "Lay Investiture and Its Relation to the Conflict of Empire and Papacy," *PBA* 25 (1939) 217: "[The] history . . . of Lay Investiture . . . is confined within the space of fifty years, from . . . 1075 to the settlement at Worms in 1122. . . . There was no epilogue after 1122." In reality, the developments discussed in the following pages can properly be regarded as an epilogue to the Investiture Struggle.

than the three Henrys who preceded him, eventually proved reluctant to forget the valuable rights which Henry V had relinquished in the compromise of Worms.[3] The newly elected Innocent II, driven from Rome by the supporters of the anti-pope Anacletus, met Lothar at Liège in March 1131, offered him the imperial coronation, and requested his help in expelling the "tyrant" from the Apostolic See.[4] Lothar accepted this responsibility, and set in motion the machinery for an expedition to Italy, but he knew that his aid was indispensable —and he placed a high price upon it. For as Lothar explained to Innocent, his deep concern was "the extent to which the kingdom had been weakened by its love for the churches, and with how great a loss to itself it had surrendered their investiture."[5] Since his own election in August 1125, there were undoubtedly incidents which convinced Lothar that the royal prerogative had been crippled by Henry V's concessions to the Church. For one thing, Lothar may have been unable to prevent the election of hostile prelates in Germany. Equally dangerous were the possible violations directed against his royal right of investiture: either consecration before investiture, or seizure of the *regalia* before investiture. In fact, however, there is no positive evidence that any such incidents occurred between August 1125 and March 1131.[6] Whatever the specific symptoms were at Liège King Lothar proposed a strong remedy:

[3] On Lothar, the work by Wilhelm Bernhardi, *Lothar von Supplinburg* (Jahrbücher der deutschen Geschichte: Leipzig 1879), is still fundamental. For Lothar's relations with the Church, see also the old but still useful study by C. Volkmar, "Das Verhältnis Lothars III. zur Investiturfrage," *FDG* 26 (1886) 437-99. For more recent accounts, see Schäfer, *Zur Beurteilung* 8-37; Hauck, *KG* IV 118ff; and in opposition to some of Hauck's views, Karl Hampe, "Kritische Bemerkungen zur Kirchenpolitik der Stauferzeit," *HZ* 93 (1904) 393-407. The important article by Johannes Bauermann, "Die Frage der Bischofswahlen auf dem Würzburger Reichstag von 1133," *Kritische Beiträge zur Geschichte des Mittelalters: Festschrift für Robert Holtzmann* (Berlin 1933) 103-34, has become a standard authority.

[4] On the double election of 1130 and its aftermath, see the studies cited above, Ch.VIA n.20.

[5] Otto of Freising, *Chronica* 7.18, 2nd ed. Hofmeister 335.

[6] The likeliest violator was, of course, archbishop Conrad of Salzburg, and the election of 1126 at Regensburg (the only one held in his province during those years) would have been the most probable occasion for an

> Thinking that he had an opportune time, the king stubbornly insisted that the investiture of bishops, which the Roman Church had taken away from his predecessor . . . with the greatest efforts and many dangers, should be restored to himself.[7]

In effect, Lothar was demanding the restoration of the pre-1122 form of investiture: that is, the reestablishment of investiture with ring and staff.[8] Badly frightened, Innocent and his retinue were saved from Lothar's importunity only by the eloquent intervention of St Bernard.

In the two years following the meeting at Liège, Lothar had ample chance to reflect that his relations with the German episcopate were deteriorating further. During that period an archbishop of Trier and a bishop of Regensburg—and perhaps other German prelates as well—received the episcopal consecration before the regalian investiture. On both occasions the new prelates had also administered the *regalia* prior to the investiture.[9] It was clear that the pope and a part of the German episcopate were prepared simply to ignore the customary law of the empire. Moreover, it was obvious that if these violations became common in Germany, they would soon transform the investiture into a meaningless formality there, just as in Italy. Lothar was in a serious predicament,

---

incident; unfortunately, about this election the sources are almost silent. In eight episcopal elections between August 1125 and March 1131, it is certain or highly probable that investiture preceded consecration. For twelve other elections during that period, nothing pertinent is known about the elevation of the new bishop. Moreover, in no one of these twenty elections can one be certain that the bishop-elect seized the *regalia* before his investiture. On these elections, see Volkmar, *op.cit.* 464-76, and Schäfer, *op.cit.* 8-32, with supplementary data provided by Hauck, *KG* IV 950-73 and passim. The unpublished dissertation by S. Lietzmann, "Königtum und Reichsepiskopat vom Wormser Konkordat bis Barbarossa" (Berlin 1944), was not accessible to me.

7 Ernald, *Vita Bernhardi* 1.5, *PL* 185 271f; the sources on the meeting at Liège have been conveniently assembled by Bernhardi, *Lothar* 358-60 nn.19f.

8 Lothar's demand has been variously interpreted; see below, n.16.

9 Schäfer, *op.cit.* 21-23; the two cases will be discussed in detail.

for he was personally "devoted to the rights of the Church,"[10] and he owed his royal election in large part to German ecclesiastical princes. Consequently, he was neither temperamentally inclined nor politically able to conduct an all-out struggle against the papacy and the recusant prelates. In addition, by the time of his imperial coronation on 4 June 1133, Lothar was closely tied to Innocent by a group of far-reaching agreements which a contemporary accurately described as a "treaty" (*foedus*).[11] Lothar had already promised his help against Innocent's rival, and in his imperial coronation oath he solemnized his obligation to Innocent and the Roman Church.[12] For his own part, Innocent conferred the imperial crown on Lothar. Of mutual advantage was Innocent's investiture of Lothar with the Tuscan patrimony of the countess Matilda.[13] However, when Innocent granted to Magdeburg and to Hamburg-Bremen full recognition of their old claims to jurisdiction over neighboring non-German dioceses, his measures primarily rewarded Norbert of Magdeburg and Adalbero of Hamburg-Bremen for their loyalty, rather than Lothar for his services.[14] In general, these various concessions

---

[10] Anselm of Gembloux, *Continuatio Sigeberti* anno 1125, *MGH SS* VI 380; many similar texts in Bernhardi, *Lothar* 794ff.

[11] Below, n.15.

[12] Even before the meeting at Liège, Lothar had recognized Innocent as lawful pope—and had thereby thrown away the bargaining power which a more calculating prince would have exploited to great advantage. For Lothar's encyclical letter condemning the antipope, see *MGH Const* I 167 no.114, and for his coronation oath, *ibid.* 168 no.115.

[13] *Ibid.* I 169f no.117 (8 June 1133); in general, Bernhardi, *Lothar* 481-85. To be sure, the papacy derived the only advantage from the way in which Lothar received the Matildine lands; the papal court viewed this investiture, even without an act of homage, as evidence that the emperor was a papal vassal.

[14] Gnesen and its Polish suffragans were thereby declared subject to Norbert, while the Danish and Swedish bishoprics were subject to Adalbero, rather than to the archbishop of Lund. For the grant to Norbert, see JL 7629 (4 June 1133); Innocent's main motive is explicitly stressed. For the grant to Adalbero, JL 7622-26 (27 May 1133). It is obvious that both grants were at least potentially and indirectly useful to Lothar's foreign policy, though in fact, Gnesen and Lund remained independent of German jurisdiction; Bernhardi, *Lothar* 485-89.

and agreements may well have seemed to Lothar one-sided, and they certainly did not materially help his position in relation to the ecclesiastical princes of Germany. Immediately after his imperial coronation, therefore, Lothar repeated the stipulation made two years earlier at Liège:

> Crowned . . . in confirmation of the treaty which he had concluded with the pope, the emperor rashly demanded that the investiture of bishoprics—in other words, the liberty of the churches—should be relinquished to him by the lord pope.[15]

Once again, Lothar was demanding the restoration of investiture with ring and staff; for the second time, he sought to nullify the central provision in Henry V's concession of 1122.[16] Lothar had rightly assessed the weaknesses of Innocent's character and of his political position. Precariously holding only a part of Rome, the hard-pressed pontiff still needed his "treaty" with Lothar, and he was on the point of

[15] *Vita Norberti* c.21, *MGH SS* XII 702: "Coronatus autem imperator ad honorem imperii et ad firmamentum foederis, quod cum papa pepigerat, investituras episcopatuum, libertatem videlicet ecclesiarum, sibi a domino papa concedi minus consulte postulavit." It is unlikely that *foedus* refers to any written treaty. Rather, it should be interpreted as a body of mutual obligations, inherent in the papal and imperial offices, and arising from Lothar's and Innocent's particular circumstances. The term is too narrowly explained by Roger Wilmans (*MGH SS* XII 702 n.89), who identifies it as Lothar's coronation oath. For Bernhardi, *Lothar* 478 n.40, the *foedus* was "das Gesammtverhältnis, insbesondere die Kaiserkrönung." Most perceptively, Mühlbacher, *Streitige Papstwahl* 199f, sees it as the "Gegenseitigkeit der Verpflichtungen."

[16] According to Bernhardi, at Liège and Rome Lothar was merely asking for "eine Verbriefung des Wormser Concordats" (*Lothar* 478 n.40). Along similar lines, Hauck regards as "unmöglich" a demand to restore investiture with ring and staff, and asserts that Lothar was simply demanding a change for the better (*KG* IV 148f). There is no evidence for (or against) Volkmar's statement that at Liège, Lothar also sought a change in his position with relation to the Italian episcopate (*FDG* 26 [1886] 476-78 and cf. 484); in other respects, Volkmar's interpretation is sound. After correctly assessing the demand of 1131 (*Zur Beurteilung* 32ff), Schäfer is curiously uncertain whether the demand of 1133 refers to investiture *baculo et anulo* or to investiture *per sceptrum*; in fact, it is clear that Lothar was consistently exercising his right of investiture *per sceptrum*. The prevailing verdict is summed up by Hofmeister, *Forschungen und Versuche: Festschrift D. Schäfer* 110, and by Bauermann, *Kritische Beiträge: Festschrift R. Holtzmann* 111f and esp. nn.34f.

The Bishop-Elect

granting Lothar's demand. Nonetheless, Lothar's policy reveals a certain political naïveté, for even if Innocent had yielded, his decree could scarcely have been enforced against the inevitable opposition of German prelates like Adalbert of Mainz and Conrad of Salzburg. It was fortunate for everyone, therefore, when once again an influential churchman intervened to rescue the hesitant pope—this time, archbishop Norbert of Magdeburg, who stiffened the pope's resistance and dissuaded the emperor from his stand.[17] In principle, however, archbishop Norbert was not opposed to imperial influence in the elevation of bishops,[18] and he may well have negotiated the ensuing compromise between Lothar and Innocent: Four days after the imperial coronation, the pope granted Lothar a charter dealing with the question of regalian investiture,[19] and thereby Innocent made a major addition to the "treaty" between the emperor and himself. After this concordat of June 1133, the issue of investiture with ring and crosier never reappeared in the relations between papacy and empire.[20]

[17] The similar course of events at Liège in 1131 and at Rome in 1133—first, the imperial demand, then weakness on the pope's part, and finally, successful opposition from an important churchman—has seemed more than merely accidental; most recently, Bauermann admits to "gewisse Bedenken gegen den Bericht" (*op.cit.* 112 n.35). Since there are several, mutually independent sources for the events at Liège, their accuracy cannot seriously be questioned. However, the *Vita Norberti* is the only source for the imperial demand at Rome. Could the *Vita Norberti* have appropriated an account of the meeting at Liège, changed the time and place, and substituted St Norbert's name for St Bernard's? Though the *Vita Norberti* is not an irreproachable source, it is undoubtedly reliable in this account. As Bernhardi has pointed out (*Lothar* 478 n.40), the charter of 8 June 1133 is far more than "eine gewisse Bestätigung" (in Bauermann's words) of the historical reality of Lothar's demand at Rome, for this charter shows beyond any doubt that the problem of investiture had just previously been renegotiated. On the value of the *Vita Norberti* c.21, see Richard Rosenmund, *Die ältesten Biographien des heiligen Norbert* (Berlin 1874) 82-95, and esp. Mühlbacher, *Streitige Papstwahl* 180-211.

[18] See below, Ch.VIIIв nn.10f, 16.

[19] *MGH Const* I 168f no.116 (8 June 1133); the charter is preserved in fragmentary condition.

[20] Most of the evidence for investitures with ring and staff after 1133 is questionable. On the alleged investiture of the bishop of Prague with *baculus et anulus* in 1136, see Bernhardi, *Lothar* 560 n.1; on the supposed cases at Utrecht in 1196 and 1249, see Robert Boerger, *Die Belehnungen*

Regalia and the Bishop-Elect

In this papal privilege of 1133, the wording is as careful and cautious as in Calixtus II's charter for Henry V, for like the Calixtinum, Innocent II's grant was personal in form, valid for Lothar's lifetime but not intended for his successors.[21] Though Innocent's assurances to Lothar were clothed in ambiguity, at first glance they seem perfectly fashioned as vague expressions of benign intent toward the emperor. Praising Lothar for his devotion to the Church and for his opposition to the antipope, Innocent announced that in the coronation he was conceding to Lothar "the fullness of the imperial office":

> Wishing, therefore, not to diminish but to increase the majesty of the *imperium*, we grant you the fullness of the imperial office, and by these presents, we confirm the required and canonical customs.[22]

At the very least, Innocent was here emphasizing the value of the imperial coronation, and the importance of his own role as bestower of the imperial title. Within these resounding phrases, however, there was grave danger for the theoretical position of the emperor. Innocent's language was strikingly different from Paschal II's restrained statement in 1111, when he asserted that "through the ministry of our priesthood, the Divine Majesty" had elevated Henry V to the imperial dignity.[23] By claiming that he himself was granting "the fullness of the imperial office," Innocent almost maintained that the imperial coronation was a constitutive act, in which the

---

der deutschen geistlichen Fürsten (Leipzig 1902) 21-24. On Matilda's threatened reinstatement of investiture with ring and staff in England (1141), R.H.C. Davis, *King Stephen* (Berkeley 1967) 61; for Scandinavia, Feine, *RG* 224 n.9.

[21] Ernst Bernheim, *Zur Geschichte des Wormser Concordates* (Göttingen 1878) 50.

[22] *MGH Const* I 168 no.116: "Nos igitur, maiestatem imperii nolentes minuere sed augere, imperatorie dignitati[s plenitu]dinem tibi concedimus et debitas et canonicas consuetudines presentis scripti pagina confirmamus."

[23] In the Pravilegium of 12 April 1111, *MGH Const* I 145 no.96: "Ad cuius . . . coronae et imperii dignitatem tuam . . . personam . . . per nostri sacerdotii ministerium maiestas divina provexit." The document reflects Henry's pressure on Paschal.

257

Roman pontiff conferred an office together with all of its powers. Moreover, some may have sensed the resemblance between Innocent's term, the *imperatoriae dignitatis plenitudo*, and the contemporary expression *plenitudo officii pontificalis*, which summarized the powers granted to an archbishop-elect with the bestowal of the *pallium*.[24] In Innocent's charter, however, the claim is partly veiled, the language is far from explicit, and the threat is latent.[25] Yet it is significant that Innocent's term reappeared twenty-four years later, in the famous incident at Besançon, when Hadrian IV enraged the imperial princes with his statement that in Barbarossa's imperial coronation, the Roman See had conferred the *plenitudo dignitatis* on him.[26]

Even more indefinite was Innocent's confirmation of "the required and canonical customs." Here, Innocent was surely referring to the emperor's relations with the German church,

---

[24] As Bauermann has remarked (*op.cit.* 113 n.37); on this expression, see above, Ch.VIB esp. nn.3-8. Equally suggestive would have been the phrase *plenitudo potestatis*; on its pre-1133 meanings, see Benson, *SGrat* 13 (1968) esp. n.67.

[25] Hauck goes too far in his statement that Innocent viewed the coronation as "eine Übertragung des Reichs" (*KG* IV 154). With equal exaggeration, Hofmeister describes Innocent's assertion as "eine förmliche Investitur mit dem Kaisertum, mit denselben Ausdrücken, die der Lehensherr seinem Mann gegenüber gebraucht!" (*Forschungen und Versuche: Festschrift D. Schäfer* 109 n.3); in fact, Hofmeister regards the Innocentianum as more significant for the relations between pope and emperor than for the constitutional development of the empire.

Cf. Innocent's earlier letters to Lothar (JL 7411) and to the German princes (JL 7413), referring to the coronation as the acceptance of the *imperialis dignitatis plenitudo*; also, the description of the Liège meeting in the *Annales sancti Disibodi* anno 1131, *MGH SS* XVII 24: "Dominus papa regem ad comprimendam tirannidem Petri Leonis . . . Romam invitabat, plenitudinem imperii in eadem Romana civitate, sicut decebat, offerens." The topic deserves a separate discussion.

[26] Rahewin, *Gesta Friderici* 3.9 and esp. 3.10, 3rd ed. Waitz and Simson 176: "Precipue tamen universos accenderat, quod in premissis litteris . . . dictum fuisse acceperant, dignitatis et honoris plenitudinem sibi a Romano pontifice collatam. . . ." Yet one may suspect that if Hadrian had avoided the inflammatory and ambiguous term *beneficium*, a simple claim to bestow the *plenitudo dignitatis* would not have provoked so prolonged a controversy. For an attempt to explain away the term *beneficium* and to assert that Hadrian acted in good faith, see W. Ullmann's article on this incident (above, Ch.IIIc n.1). Cf. the comparable phrase *plenitudo corone* in the Treaty of Constance (1153); *MGH Const* I 201, 203 nos.144f, and P. Rassow, *Honor imperii* (2nd ed. Darmstadt 1961) 118.

but by simply guaranteeing these "customs" without explanation of their nature, he carefully avoided making a specific commitment to Lothar. Indeed, with this expression, the pontiff did not even expressly renew the provisions of the Calixtinum,[27] much less turn back the clock to the constitutional practices of an earlier age. Rather, Innocent merely promised just treatment, suitable to the properly precedented rights of the imperial office in its relation to the German church. Innocent himself may well have held a strict and antimonarchical conception of these "canonical customs."[28] Nonetheless, it is clear that in the opinion of Lothar and most German bishops, a papal confirmation of "the required and canonical customs" would imply the ratification of one of the usages formerly prescribed by the Calixtinum, since customary practice in Germany still required investiture as the normal prerequisite to consecration.

But in its final sentence, Innocent's charter went far beyond the Calixtinum, for it brought a valuable new concession: a stipulation that no one who is elevated to the episcopal or abbatial office in Germany "should dare to usurp or to seize the *regalia*" before having requested them from Lothar.[29] Here Innocent's diction is no less obscure than in his assurances on "the fullness of the imperial office" and on "the required and canonical customs."[30] Though the Calixtinum

27 On this point, see Bernhardi, *Lothar* 480 n.48; Schäfer, *Zur Beurteilung* 36; Hofmeister, *op.cit.* 111 n.3. There is no evidence for the contrary view, defended by Volkmar, *FDG* 26 (1886) 485f, and by Hampe, *HZ* 93 (1904) 405f.

28 Of course, Innocent himself was not bound, in any respect, by the provisions of his own charter. For example, he could continue to believe that consecration might "canonically" precede investiture. In consecrating the uninvested archbishop of Trier (March 1132), he had already shown that he did not consider investiture a necessary prerequisite to consecration.

29 *MGH Const* I 169 no.116: "Interdicimus autem, ne quisquam eorum, quos in Teut[onico] regno ad pontificatus honorem vel abbatie regimen evocari contigerit, regalia usurpare vel invadere audeat, nisi eadem prius a tua [potes]tate deposcat, quod ex his, quae iure debet tibi, tue magnificentie faciat."

30 As Hampe has noted, this lack of clarity has contributed to the broad spectrum of divergent scholarly opinion on the Innocentianum. Volkmar, *op.cit.* 483-88, presents the Innocentianum as an extremely significant gain

had specifically referred to the investiture of an *electus*, the Innocentianum used a clumsy circumlocution in order to avoid this expression; thereby, Innocent left the sequence of investiture and consecration unclear. Equally obscure is Innocent's statement that the new prelate must "request" (*deposcere*) the *regalia*. Did Innocent mean to imply that a mere request by a prelate is sufficient warrant for seizure and administration of the *regalia*? In fact, the document ignores the question of the emperor's right to refuse the prelate's request for the *regalia*, and it by-passes the corollary question of the prelate's rights in the event of such a refusal. Yet the ambiguities in the Innocentianum were a matter of policy. Indeed, a comparison of Innocent's charter with earlier papal documents on investiture shows unmistakably that the papal chancery composed this grant with earlier usage in mind.[31]

---

for Lothar. Somewhat more reserved are Hampe, *op.cit.* 405f ("ein wenn auch bescheidener Erfolg Lothars"); Hofmeister, *op.cit.* 109f ("eine ausdrückliche, wenn auch abgeschwächte Anerkennung seines Rechts"); and Bauermann, *op.cit.* 114. On the other hand, Bernhardi, *Lothar* 479, sees therein the danger of an "Abschwächung der durch das Wormser Concordat dem Kaiser zugestandenen Gerechtsame." Even more negative is Hauck, *KG* IV 155, who thinks that the stipulation on investiture had "geringe Bedeutung" for Lothar and that the confirmation of the *consuetudines* implied "eine Erschütterung des Rechtsstandes [des Reichs]."

[31] As most commentators have noticed. The following table indicates the main borrowings; for the models, see *MGH Const* I nos.96, 90, 108:

Innocentianum	*Models*
Nos igitur . . . imperatorie dignitatis plenitudinem tibi concedimus et debitas et canonicas consuetudines presentis scripti pagina confirmamus.	*Pravilegium (no.96)*: Illam igitur dignitatis prerogativam . . . nos . . . dilectioni tuae concedimus et presentis privilegii pagina confirmamus.
Interdicimus autem, ne quisquis eorum, quos . . . ad pontificatus honorem vel abbatiae regimen evocari contigerit, regalia . . . invadere audeat, nisi eadem prius a tua potestate deposcat,	*Renuntiatio regalium (no.90)*: Interdicimus etiam . . . ne quis episcoporum seu abbatum . . . eadem regalia invadant . . . nec se deinceps nisi per gratiam regis de ipsis regalibus intromittant.
quod ex his, quae iure debet tibi, tuae magnificentiae faciat.	*Calixtinum (no.108)*: quae ex his iure tibi debet, faciat.

Though it may not be surprising that the Calixtinum's wording was followed in part, it is ironic that Paschal II's renunciation of the *regalia* and the notorious Pravilegium influenced the Innocentianum even more extensively. From these borrowings, one can conclude nothing more significant than the

It is, of course, obvious that the Innocentianum was the product of hard negotiation. Presumably, therefore, in this charter Innocent had made his maximum concessions, and Lothar's minimum conditions had been met.

In general, then, the charter's murky diction reveals the papacy's determination not to revalidate the Calixtinum,[32] and to yield as little as possible in the crucial question of investiture. Through such deliberate obscurities, the papacy had guarded itself, for a strict Curialist interpretation of Innocent's charter could vastly reduce its value to Lothar.[33] Still, despite the careful ambiguities of the papal chancery, it is clear that in the practical thinking of the imperial court, the Innocentianum would be interpreted as a simple and straightforward prohibition, categorically forbidding any German bishop-elect to administer his temporalities prior to his investiture.[34] The tangible consequences of this restriction were serious, for without his investiture, a German prelate-elect could neither exercise his secular jurisdiction, nor command his vassals, nor enjoy the income from the regalian properties attached to his office and his church. Lothar gained more from this requirement than he would have won from papal recognition of investiture as a necessary prerequisite to consecration.[35] Far more clearly than the Calixtinum, the Inno-

---

fact that Innocent's charter was composed with the greatest possible care, and that every word was deliberate; cf., however, Bauermann, *op.cit.* 113 n.37, 114 n.39.

[32] With the expectation of an affirmative answer, Bauermann has asked (*op.cit.* 115 n.42): "Setzt die teilweise Korrektur in der Regalienbestimmung, bei Übergehung der anderen Punkte, nicht auch voraus, dass man päpstlicherseits das Calixtinum im übrigen noch als Norm betrachtete?" In fact, the papacy manifestly did *not* wish to recognize the Calixtinum's provisions as a norm.

[33] For an example, see Conrad of Salzburg's interpretation (below, Ch.VIIIв n.35). In general, one may agree with Bernheim, *Lothar III. und das Wormser Konkordat* (Strasbourg 1874) 42, that the Innocentianum was "a masterpiece of papal diplomacy"; cf. Bernhardi, *Lothar* 479.

[34] At the Würzburg meeting of the imperial court in September 1133, Lothar did not concern himself with such semantic subtleties; the meeting is discussed below.

[35] Of course, if Innocent had explicitly granted a complete or partial renewal of the Calixtinum *in addition to* the final sentence of the Innocentianum, the overall concession would have been even more valuable to Lothar.

centianum explicitly recognized and protected a crucial element of the royal prerogative: the monarch's proprietary claim to the *regalia*. Although Lothar's original demand at Rome was refused, Innocent's grant was a substitute which could serve as a powerful safeguard against any future violations like the recent ones at Trier and Regensburg.

In defining the juridical content of investiture, the Roman concordat of 1133 was explicitly valid only for the kingdom of Germany. This fact implied a further widening of the growing gulf between the constitutional position of the German episcopate and that of the episcopate in the other two kingdoms of the empire. Of course, the differences between conditions in Germany and in the rest of the empire had long existed, and had been formalized in the Concordat of Worms.[36] Moreover, as we have seen, the concordat of 1133 did not alter the customary sequence of investiture and consecration, either in the German bishoprics or elsewhere. Indeed, it was silent on that question. Rather, within Germany, the Roman concordat ratified a *second* function of investiture as a prerequisite to the administration of the *regalia* as well as to the episcopal consecration.

Even though the Innocentianum defined the constitutive effects of regalian investiture, it did not truly give new juridical significance to that act, nor impose a new requirement upon the German bishops.[37] Rather, this regulation had deep roots in the German past, for long before the concordats of 1122 and 1133, it was a standard part of imperial practice. Indeed, this rule was an object of negotiation in 1111, and it had been assumed in more than one publicistic treatise.[38] Because the regulation already belonged to imperial public law, it did not depend upon the Innocentianum. Strictly speaking, therefore, Lothar had small reason to regret that the

---

[36] On the constitutional significance of the *regalia* as a key to the status of the episcopate, and on the divergence in Germany, Burgundy, and Italy, see Ott, *ZRG* KA 35 (1948) 272ff.

[37] Schäfer, *Zur Beurteilung* 36.

[38] Above, Ch.VIIв.

Regalia and the Bishop-Elect

Innocentianum was granted to himself personally and not to his successors, for he could be confident that this crucial requirement would outlast the Innocentianum. Still, by providing a papal guarantee of a traditional regulation, the Innocentianum strengthened its legal foundations at a moment when they were visibly crumbling. Since the ecclesiastical princes of Germany were subject to the Roman See as well as to imperial law, the authority of the papacy was now added to the force of imperial custom. After 1133, Church and papacy had to recognize that this regulation was, so to speak, one of "the required and canonical customs."

2. Lothar III vs Conrad of Salzburg

Armed with his new imperial title and with the Innocentianum, Lothar returned from Italy, and on 8 September 1133 he presided over a meeting of the imperial court in Würzburg. The major business on the agenda concerned the familiar and pressing problem which had occupied Lothar at Liège and Rome: the investiture of bishops as an expression of royal prerogative. Against a background of heated debate on questions of episcopal election and investiture, Lothar faced urgent decisions there. The emperor's policies and the issues debated at Würzburg moved archbishop Conrad of Salzburg to compose a publicistic treatise soon after the meeting.[1]

[1] On the Würzburg meeting, the basic source is the very brief but reliable account in the Annalista Saxo, and Conrad's treatise is an invaluable supplement. All earlier scholarly comments on this Reichstag have been superseded by Johannes Bauermann's important article, published in 1933 in *Kritische Beiträge: Festschrift R. Holtzmann* 103-34, where he has edited the fragmentary remains of Conrad's treatise (pp.132-34). It was probably written immediately after the meeting—that is, in the autumn of 1133—and certainly no later than the spring of 1134. One cannot even determine the original length of the treatise, which is now poorly preserved on both sides of a badly mutilated piece of parchment, and which may once have been much longer. Gerhoh of Reichersberg knew the treatise, for he cites it in the 1150's (*Commentarius in psalmum LXIV*, in *MGH LdL* III 451). Though Gerhoh asserts that one of the topics in the letter was "copiose tractatum," a reliable estimate cannot be squeezed from this indefinite phrase.

Because my interpretation of the treatise diverges markedly from Bauermann's at several points, a detailed analysis will be necessary.

The Bishop-Elect

Though written as a letter to archbishop Norbert of Magdeburg, it is an open letter, designed for publication.[2] Indeed, it is the last in the long tradition of polemical treatises directly and primarily inspired by the problem of election and investiture.[3] In the realm of theory, the court argued over the proper role of the leading laymen, the *honorati*, in the elevation of a bishop.[4] The term *honorati* derived ultimately from Leo the Great, who considered the wishes of these "eminent men" (*arbitrium* or *testimonium honoratorum*) an important factor in the creation of a bishop.[5] Between the later eleventh century and the second quarter of the twelfth, Leo's doctrine, with minor variations in its wording, was appropriated in several canonical collections.[6] As the twelfth century realized clearly, the canonical collections transmitted and publicized this doctrine.[7] By 1133 the formula was familiar, and after

[2] Careful workmanship, conceptual subtlety, and lucid argumentation clearly suggest the intention of publication. Moreover, within the surviving portions of Conrad's letter, everything concerns the Würzburg meeting either directly or indirectly, and these statements could scarcely have been news to Norbert, who had taken an active part in this Reichstag. Gerhoh's acquaintance with the letter does not necessarily indicate widespread publication, since he had close relations with Conrad; see Peter Classen, *Gerhoch von Reichersberg* (Wiesbaden 1960) 66f and passim.

[3] Written in 1128-29 and slightly revised in 1138, Gerhoh's earliest work, the *Opusculum de aedificio Dei* (*MGH LdL* III 136-202), might almost fit the same description; Classen, *op.cit.* 40ff.

[4] On the *honorati*, see Bauermann, *op.cit.* 108f, 117-24.

[5] Leo I, *Ep.*10, cc.4, 6, *PL* 54 632, 634 (quoted above, Ch.IIA n.8). Cf. also *Ep.*40, 167, *PL* 54 814, 1200.

[6] Between 1083 and 1087, it appeared in Deusdedit's *Collectio canonum* 1.119, ed. Wolf von Glanvell 86; as Deusdedit's source, Wolf von Glanvell cites Anselm, *Collectio canonum* 6.13, but I am unable to find the text in Thaner's edition of Anselm's collection. Between 1110 and 1120, Leo's statement reappeared in the first recension of the *Caesaraugustana*; see Friedberg's apparatus ad D.63 c.27 (n.274). In general, Leo I's remarks on election were frequently republished in the late 11th- and early 12th-century collections, but by omitting this particular letter, compilers were perhaps showing their distaste for the prominent role assigned there to the lay *honorati*.

[7] Gerhoh of Reichersberg mentions the opinion of certain "reges mali et symoniaci," who believed that "secundum canones consensus honoratorum requirendus . . . est in electionibus episcoporum" (*Comm. in ps.LXIV*, in *MGH LdL* III 451). Also, Suger, *Vita Ludovici* c.10, ed.

Regalia and the Bishop-Elect

1140, when Gratian republished it in his *Decretum*, it was a commonplace.[8] To the twelfth-century mind, the term *honorati* referred primarily to the nobles,[9] yet its meaning could be extended to include a monarch.[10] Though Conrad of Salzburg and Norbert of Magdeburg did not share a common definition of the *honorati* in their debate,[11] neither of them was mainly concerned with defining the limits and membership of the category of *honorati*.[12] In fact, at Würzburg the dispute hinged upon a particular kind of *honorati*: the lay "advocates" of

Waquet 58: "secundum canones, electione cleri, assensu honoratorum, peticione populi"; the necessity of emending *honoratoris* (which appears in all MSS and was accepted by Waquet) into *honoratorum* is ably shown by Bauermann, *op.cit.* 121f. The notion of the *petitio plebis* (or *populi*) was well known, also deriving from Leo I; see D.62 c.1 and Friedberg's apparatus (nn.1f).

Because Bauermann overlooked the canonistic transmission of Leo's doctrine on the *honorati*, he encountered difficulties in explaining the introduction of this term into 12th-century usage. As tentative explanations, he suggested archbishop Norbert's antiquarianism (*op.cit.* 119), or possible influence from Henry V's demands at Châlons in 1107 (as described by Suger, *loc.cit.*), or influence from French customary practice (*op.cit.* 122f, 125 n.79). These explanations are, of course, unnecessary.

[8] D.63 c.27.

[9] The more distinguished among the lay participants in 12th-century episcopal elections were variously designated as *principes, nobiles, comites, ministeriales, optimates, priores, capita populi, proceres, cives, divites,* and so forth; Franklin Geselbracht, *Das Verfahren bei den deutschen Bischofswahlen in der zweiten Hälfte des 12. Jahrhunderts* (Weida 1905) 101f, 106, 121-23 and passim. There was apparently little precision in the application of most of these terms. When the *honorati* were mentioned as electors together with the *clerus et populus*, the term *honorati* seems to be equally general; for some examples from 1150-51, see Jaffé, *Bibl.* I 453, 470, 472 nos.324, 340f. Also, Heinz Zatschek, "Wibald von Stablo," *MIÖG* Ergänzungsband 10 (1928) 406, 409ff, and Bauermann, *op.cit.* 123 n.75.

[10] According to Gerhoh (below, n.16), Norbert thought that kings should be included within the category of *honorati*. Since Gerhoh had read Conrad's letter in its original form, his testimony must be accepted. Also, see the following note.

[11] Conrad's letter to Norbert (Bauermann, *op.cit.* 133): "Talibus questionibus [scil. imperatoris] ad respondendum coartatus, verba vestra potui quidem auribus corporis audire, sed non potui cor adponere ad respondendum vobis [nec] ad inquirendum a vobis denomen honoratorum, quod cum sit generale omnium, qui in sublimitate sunt, sive regis quasi precellentis sive ducum advocatorum ad vindictam malefactorum, laudem vero [bonorum] sive etiam aliarum in populo di[gnitatum . . .]." Cf. 1 *Tim.* 2.2, and esp. 1 *Petr.* 2.13f: "sive regi quasi praecellenti sive ducibus tamquam ab eo missis ad vindictam malefactorum, laudem vero bonorum."

[12] Cf., however, the view of Bauermann, *op.cit.* 108f.

The Bishop-Elect

episcopal churches.[13] Archbishop Conrad was indignant over
a scandal which afflicted the Church:

> This scandal is the new presumption of the advocates, who
> ascribe to themselves unheard-of rights in the election of
> bishops, as though a bishop could not be elected unless
> they consent.[14]

In opposition to Conrad's view, archbishop Norbert accepted
Leo the Great's doctrine and defended the general principle
that "the consent of the *honorati* is necessary in the election
of bishops"; from this theorem, one could conclude that the
advocati rightfully had an influential role in episcopal elections.[15] Scarcely less controversial was Norbert's vindication
of royal consent. In his judgment, the consent of the king as
well as of the *honorati* was truly indispensable in the making
of a bishop, for without this twofold consent, the election
was ineffective.[16] Conrad of Salzburg, on the other hand, was

---

13 Conrad's letter to Norbert (Bauermann, *op.cit.* 134): "officium iudicandi populum . . . nunc sub Christi sacerdotio debent habere [nostr]i
honorati, quo nomine solos advocatos [. . .] significari." Also, *ibid.*:
"inquam, an ad illos tales honoratos pertinuerit al[iquid] de spiritualium
rerum dispositione et deo in rebus [divi]nis ministrantium electione?"

14 *Ibid.* 132: "Scandalum hoc est advocatorum nova presumptio, qui sibi
nescio quid iuris [adiu]dicant in eligendis episcopis, quasi non possit eligi
episcopus [nisi consenti]a[n]t."

15 Where the top of the parchment was cut away, a line of Conrad's text
was lost, and his discussion resumes in the middle of a sentence (*ibid.*):
"quod advocati episcoporum electionibus debeant interesse propter hoc,
scilicet, quod vos in curia Werzburg habita dixistis honoratorum consensum
in episcoporum election[ibus] esse debere."

16 On this point, Norbert's opinion cannot be extracted from the remaining portions of Conrad's letter. However, cf. Gerhoh, *Comm. in ps.LXIV*,
in *MGH LdL* III 451: "Voluerat enim ille [scil. Norbertus] inter honoratos
cuiusque civitatis etiam potestativos principes vel reges reipublicae amministratores esse comprehensos: quod sacrorum canonum censura omnino
contradicit." Then Gerhoh quotes several canons at length, and soon thereafter continues his discussion (*ibid.* 452): "Nam spiritales et religiosi viri
habent consulere, canonici eligere, populus petere, honorati assentire. Qui
tamen si consilio religiosorum patrum et electione clericorum ac peticione
populi concurrente in unum noluerint prebere assensum, non propter hoc
erit irrita [electio], si alias est canonica. Quia neque regibus neque honoratis
eam cassandi est ulla potestas, sed, ut Symachus papa dicit, subsequendi
necessitas." Though the two quoted passages are widely separated in
Gerhoh's text, the second passage is comprehensible only as a continuation

Regalia and the Bishop-Elect

simply and flatly opposed to the influence of *all* laymen, kings and lesser dignitaries alike, in episcopal elections. From his lifelong policy as well as from his letter to Norbert, it is clear that Conrad was no more inclined to recognize the necessity of royal consent than was archbishop Adalbert of Mainz, who was horrified when Lothar played a dominant role in the deposition of a newly elected bishop of Basel and in the selection of a successor.[17] The argument between Conrad and Norbert could not be finished at Würzburg, for Conrad came into sharp conflict with the emperor, and thereafter he could no longer put his heart into the discussion.[18]

The debate of the two archbishops was closely connected to recent events in Germany. Indeed, the question of the *honorati* and the other issues discussed at Würzburg afford a rare insight into the relation between theory and practice in the early twelfth century: Three episcopal elections had taken place since May 1132, as Lothar was preparing to depart for Italy. At Würzburg, Lothar confirmed the bishop-elect of Augsburg, but with papal approval he quashed the election held at Basel.[19] The third case, bishop Henry of Regensburg, posed special problems for the emperor.

---

of his diatribe against Norbert's views; hence the opinion which Gerhoh attacked in the second passage must be ascribed to Norbert. Gerhoh's mention of the *honorati cuiusque civitatis* refers simply to any prominent laymen with close ties to an episcopal *civitas*; the term applies nicely to the *advocatus* of an episcopal church.

[17] On the Basel election, see below, n.19. The remark appears in a letter from Adalbert to Otto of Bamberg, written early in 1134; *Codex Udalrici* no.264, ed. Jaffé, *Bibl.* V 451: "destructionem ecclesiasticae libertatis ingemiscimus. . . . Quid nunc restat ad cumulum doloris nostri? Cum videamus canonicas episcoporum electiones ad nutum principis cassari, et pro beneplacito suo ipse substituat, quos libuerit. Hoc in Basiliensi ecclesia factum est." One can scarcely doubt that Conrad of Salzburg shared Adalbert's view of this case. There is, however, no reason to conclude that Norbert of Magdeburg was also opposed to Lothar's intervention in the Basel elections.

[18] Above, n.11.

[19] Annalista Saxo, anno 1133, *MGH SS* VI 768: "Ibi confirmantur electiones episcoporum Heinrici Ratisponensis et Walteri Augustensis. Et quia Heinricus Basiliensis episcopus a papa omnino degradatus fuit, Adalbero Nienburgensis abbas . . . eidem canonica electione cleri et populi per consilium inperatoris successit"; also, *Gesta archiepiscoporum Magdeburgensium* anno 1133, *MGH SS* XVI 184, almost verbatim (but without the phrase "a papa"). Undoubtedly the pope supported Lothar's decision, but

The Bishop-Elect

When Henry of Regensburg was elected sometime between May and July of 1132, Lothar was about to leave for Italy and his imperial coronation. The election was engineered by an *advocatus* of Regensburg, Frederick of Bogen, with support from other enemies of duke Henry the Proud of Bavaria.[20] In all probability, by 1132 Frederick of Bogen had lost the position of advocate, for at least since 1129 duke Henry had been the chief advocate of the Regensburg church.[21] In danger of losing his influence over the most important Bavarian bishopric, the powerful duke asked Lothar to withhold the investiture from the bishop-elect, and "charging that the election was not canonical," he requested the pope to forbid his consecration. Innocent was ready to comply with the duke's wishes, and he dispatched an experienced legate to Germany. The nuncio arrived too late, however, for in the meantime the uninvested bishop-elect had gone to his metropolitan, archbishop Conrad of Salzburg,

---

apparently Lothar himself was primarily responsible for this deposition; on this point, the Annalista Saxo's account must be supplemented by the well-known letter from Adalbert of Mainz (above, n.17). Though Bernhardi asserts that the deposition of the bishop of Basel must have taken place during the emperor's visit to Basel in November 1133 (*Lothar* 509f), Bauermann rightly defends the unambiguous testimony of the Annalista Saxo, placing the event in Würzburg (*op.cit.* 104, 125f). The reason for Lothar's opposition to Henry of Basel is not known.

[20] *Historia Welforum* c.19, ed. E. König (Stuttgart 1938) 32 (= *MGH SS* XXI 464): "Ratisponenses . . . Heinricum . . . , machinante advocato cum aliis aemulis ducis, eligunt." For an account of the election and the ensuing struggle, see Bernhardi, *Lothar* 498ff, and Sigmund Riezler, *Geschichte Baierns* I (Gotha 1878) 612ff.

[21] An episcopal church might have two (or even more) *advocati*, but one of them usually gained predominancy over the others; G. Waitz, *Deutsche Verfassungsgeschichte* VII 330-34, 337, 371. On duke Henry as *advocatus*, see Thomas Ried, *Codex diplomatico-chronologicus episcopatus Ratisponensis* (2 vols. Regensburg 1816) I 188 (1129); *Monumenta Boica* I 141 (1130), with the title *archiadvocatus*, indicating the duke's claim to a paramount position over all other advocates, if any; also, a questionable document in *Monumenta Boica* XIII 149 (1129?). Henry the Proud's position was not uncommon, for as duke of Saxony, Lothar himself had been advocate of Verden; Herbert W. Vogt, *Das Herzogtum Lothars von Süpplingenburg* (Quellen und Darstellungen zur Geschichte Niedersachsens 57: Hildesheim 1959) 115.

who had consecrated him without delay.[22] Henry the Proud armed for war, and after initial reverses, he overawed the formidable Bavarian coalition behind Frederick of Bogen and bishop Henry of Regensburg. Abandoned by his relatives and allies, bishop Henry made terms. As a sign of reconciliation and perhaps also as an indemnity, bishop Henry invested the duke with a substantial countship belonging to the church of Regensburg and located on the river Inn.[23]

It is unlikely that a zealous reformer like archbishop Conrad of Salzburg would have consecrated a suffragan bishop if he had seen any serious irregularities in the election.[24] From a purely ecclesiastical point of view, therefore, one can assume that bishop Henry's election was canonical. As advocate of the Regensburg church, Henry the Proud could be considered one of the *honorati* of Regensburg, and according to Leo the Great's formula, his consent was required. Apparently, duke Henry did claim that his consent to the election at Regensburg was indispensable, and from his standpoint, it is probable that the election seemed uncanonical precisely

[22] *Historia Welforum* c.19, ed. König 32-34 (= *MGH SS* XXI 464): "Quod dux in iniuriam sui factum [scil. electionem] compensans, ad depositionem eius [scil. electi Ratisponensis] omnimodis laborabat et apud imperatorem, ut investituram ei negaret, et apud apostolicum, ut consecrationem eius interdiceret, calumpnians electionem eius non esse canonicam satagebat. Ille vero inter huiusmodi discrimina metropolitanum suum festinanter adiit et consecrationem ab eo suscipiens, nuntium apostolici prevenit." See Bernhardi, *Lothar* 499f; on the legate, Azzo of Acqui, see Johannes Bachmann, *Die päpstlichen Legaten in Deutschland und Skandinavien 1125-1159* (Historische Studien 115: Berlin 1913) 32f.

[23] *Historia Welforum* c.22, ed. König 42 (= *MGH SS* XXI 466): "Non multo post compositio quoque inter ipsum [ducem] et episcopum [Ratisponensem] fit, et comitatus ille, quem ecclesia Ratisponensis circa Enum fluvium habet, ab episcopo ei in beneficio conceditur." On these events, Bernhardi, *Lothar* 500-04. The date of this enfeoffment cannot be firmly established, and the indefinite phrase "non multo post" is not very instructive. Still, the bishop was in no position to postpone his reconciliation with the duke. In any case, the enfeoffment had apparently taken place before the coronation at Rome in June—and hence, long before the assembly at Würzburg.

[24] Conrad's achievements as reformer are discussed by Albert Brackmann, *Die Kurie und die Salzburger Kirchenprovinz* (Berlin 1912) 33-41; also, Classen, *Gerhoch* 58-67. The dissertation by C. Meyer, *Erzbischof Konrad I. von Salzburg* (Jena 1868), was not accessible to me; a new biography of Conrad would be desirable.

because of the failure to secure this consent.[25] But when arch-bishop Conrad attacked "the new presumption of the advocates," was Henry the Proud the chief object of his condemnation? Of course, duke Henry's opposition to the bishop-elect of Regensburg was not the only conspicuous recent instance of an advocate attempting to influence an episcopal election. At Trier in 1131 the count-palatine, who was also advocate of the cathedral, played a dominant role in the tumultuous elections.[26] By the time of the Würzburg meeting, however, the settlement of the conflict at Trier was more than a year old, and the influence of the advocate had been successfully excluded. Moreover, the election of a suffragan undoubtedly concerned Conrad more intimately than an election outside of his province. Indeed, throughout his letter to Norbert, the problem of Regensburg still rankled.[27] All things considered, there is little doubt that Conrad's anger was directed against Henry the Proud, who, as advocate of the cathedral, had dared to usurp a decisive voice in the Regensburg election and had invoked both papal and imperial sanctions to this end.[28] In Conrad's view, papal backing did not extenuate the duke's offense. In this respect, Conrad's strictness is not surprising, for despite papal cooperation with

25 In 1205 a bishop of Regensburg implicitly recognized the Bavarian duke's claim to a role in the episcopal elections, for he granted the duke the right to participate in the electoral deliberations "just like one of the canons or *ministeriales*"; Ried, *op.cit.* I 290 no.307. On the other hand, apparently duke Henry the Lion did not take over the position of advocate of Regensburg.

26 Baldericus, *Gesta Alberonis* c.10, *MGH SS* VIII 248, quoting a letter from the canons of Trier to Innocent II. On another form of intervention by advocates, cf. a decree of Innocent II in 1137 (JL 7851), directing that no *rex vel imperator seu advocatus* could exercise the *ius spolii* in Trier.

27 Conrad recurs to the question of Regensburg once again in the largely illegible portion of the letter; see Bauermann, *op.cit.* 134.

28 Above, n.22. In the surviving portions of Conrad's letter, Henry the Proud is never explicitly mentioned, and Bauermann was reluctant to identify duke Henry as one of the presumptuous advocates whom Conrad was attacking (cf. *op.cit.* 118 n.50). Note that within his letter, Conrad wanted Norbert to indicate the specific *honorati* whom he had in mind (above, n.11), for as Conrad explained with the help of a scriptural citation, the word *honorati* is common to all in high places—to kings, dukes (!), and lesser officials.

the emperor, archbishop Adalbert of Mainz denounced Lothar's intervention at Basel as "the destruction of ecclesiastical liberty."[29]

By receiving his consecration before his investiture, bishop Henry of Regensburg had placed himself in a vulnerable position. Nonetheless, at the Würzburg meeting Lothar confirmed the bishop in his office and invested him with the *regalia*.[30] Although the emperor had been far from pleased with the irregular proceedings during his absence from Germany, he apparently reserved his anger for archbishop Conrad, whom he severely reproached for having consecrated Henry.[31] Behind this reproof stands the customary German insistence upon investiture as prerequisite to consecration, a sequence which Lothar regarded as standard. Indeed, Lothar had already shown that he might demand satisfaction for a violation of this customary sequence—as he did when the archbishop of Trier, not yet invested with the *regalia*, had been consecrated by the pope in March 1132. Also, prior to his investiture, the new archbishop had used armed force to overawe the hostile laity of Trier, and had thereby usurped a regalian right.[32] Because the archbishop had been consecrated before his investiture, Lothar at first refused to grant him the *regalia*. However, the archbishop cleared himself by offering to swear that he had been forced by the pope to accept his consecration, and that he had not intended any detriment to Lothar's honor.[33] It does not seem coincidental that both at Trier and at Regensburg the offense was twofold: reversal of the proper sequence of investiture and consecration, followed

---

[29] Above, n.17.
[30] Above, n.19.
[31] Conrad's letter to Norbert (Bauermann, *op.cit.* 132): "imperator me redarguit et per grav[ia verba mihi] imputavit quod dominum Ratisponensem consec[ravissem]."
[32] Baldericus, *Gesta Alberonis* c.12, *MGH SS* VIII 250; nonetheless, there is no record that Lothar explicitly objected to Albero's seizure of the *regalia*. In general, see Richard Martini, *Die Trierer Bischofswahlen vom Beginn des zehnten bis zum Ausgang des zwölften Jahrhunderts* (Historische Studien 72: Berlin 1909) 52-63.
[33] Baldericus, *op.cit.* c.13, *ibid.* 250f.

by unlawful seizure of the *regalia*. By the strictest ecclesiastical standards of the early 1130's, the consecration undoubtedly seemed sufficient warrant for any administrative act.

On principle, archbishop Conrad repudiated the prescribed sequence of investiture and consecration, and he had acted on this conviction as early as 1125, at the assembly which gathered to elect a new king after Henry V's death. On the first day of this Reichstag, Conrad consecrated a suffragan bishop-elect who had not received his investiture. At that moment there was, of course, no king to perform the investiture, but if Conrad had chosen to honor the customary sequence, he need only have waited a few days for the election of a king.[34] To be sure, in his letter to Norbert, Conrad reluctantly conceded the lawfulness of the emperor's right to invest a bishop-elect with the *regalia*, though he characteristically explained it as a right based on the consent of the Church.[35]

[34] Bishop Reimbert of Brixen, as told in the *Narratio de electione Lotharii* c.1, *MGH SS* XII 510; also, *Vita Chuonradi* c.21, *MGH SS* XI 76. See Bernhardi, *Lothar* 28f; Hampe, *HZ* 93 (1904) 400; Schäfer, *Zur Beurteilung* 8f.

[35] In Conrad's own words (Bauermann, *op.cit.* 132f): "Non autem graviter ferre [potuissem] ab illo al[iquam] servitutem erigi de regalibus pertinentiis, [que, sicu]t nostis, consensit ecclesia esse a sceptro imperiali suscipienda." Despite the rough similarity in the Calixtinum's wording (above, Ch.VII$_B$ n.5), one may question whether this statement really is, in Bauermann's phrase (*op.cit.* 116), a "deutlicher Hinweis auf das Calixtinum"; Conrad knew how to be explicit when he chose to be. Note that in describing the right of investiture as based on the consent of the Church, Conrad asserted nothing more than Paschal II had claimed in the Pravilegium of 12 April 1111 (*MGH Const* I 145 no.96): "Illam igitur dignitatis prerogativam, quam predecessores nostri vestris predecessoribus catholicis imperatoribus concesserunt . . . , nos quoque dilectioni tuae concedimus et . . . confirmamus, ut regni tui episcopis . . . electis investituram virgae et anuli conferas."

Moreover, Bauermann concluded that Conrad recognized the continuing validity of the Calixtinum (*op.cit.* 116 n.44): "Konrad war also der Auffassung, dass der Papst [Calixtus II] namens der Kirche handelte, sein Zugeständnis mithin nicht nur für die Dauer seiner Regierung galt." This assertion contains two misconceptions: First, the real question was not whether Calixtus made his grant "in the name of the Church" and hence for more than "the duration of his reign." It goes without saying that Calixtus acted in the name of the Church. Rather, the serious question concerns the fact that the Calixtinum and the Innocentianum were grants to the individual emperor and *not* to the emperor's successors, with the clear implication that each of these two grants was valid only for the life-

Moreover, since Conrad repeatedly and explicitly mentioned the investiture of an *electus episcopus*, he obviously recognized the fact that German prelates were customarily invested before their consecration.[36] Yet there is a considerable difference between a simple awareness of an existing custom and an acceptance of that custom as a binding principle of law. In fact, Conrad did not admit that regalian investiture was necessarily prerequisite to the episcopal consecration, for in his view, an archbishop had an unqualified right to consecrate a suffragan bishop, whether or not the suffragan had been invested. Consequently, when the emperor rebuked Conrad for having consecrated the bishop of Regensburg, Conrad considered this reproach an attack upon "the dignity of all archbishops."[37]

To all participants in the meeting at Würzburg, the elevation of the bishop of Regensburg must have seemed a test case, involving fundamental principles generally applicable to the German episcopate. Indeed, the case of Regensburg was a trial which would establish the value of the Innocentianum for Lothar and for the royal prerogative. At Würzburg, therefore, the central issue under debate was not limited to the sequence of investiture and consecration. As a statement of principle, Lothar proclaimed that "the entire bishopric of Regensburg was his" (*totum Ratisponensem episcopatum suum esse*).[38] The remark is neither immediately clear nor

time of the reigning emperor. Second, Conrad could not have recognized the continuing validity of the Calixtinum, since he believed that investiture need not precede consecration.

36 Below, n.38. There is, however, no warrant for assuming that in Conrad's judgment the Innocentianum specified the precedence of investiture before consecration.

37 Conrad's position is clearly implied at two points in his letter; see the following note, at the beginning and again at the end of the quotation.

38 Conrad's letter to Norbert (Bauermann, *op.cit.* 132f): "imperator me redarguit et per grav[ia verba mihi] imputavit, quod dominum Ratisponensem consec[ravissem], quo dicto cunctorum archiepiscoporum [imminuit] dignitatem. [Dixit] autem Ratisponensem episcopatum esse suum, quo dicto usus [est in] proprietatem [suam] convertere vota fidelium, pretia peccatorum, patrimonia pauperum, redemptiones animarum, qui in [alios] usus iuste transferri non possunt nisi in quos [date] sunt. Non autem graviter ferre [potuissem] ab illo al[iquam] servitutem erigi de regalibus pertinentiis,

self-explanatory.[39] At first glance, it seems to assert proprietary rights over the church of Regensburg and all of its property.[40] To be sure, there was nothing intrinsically improbable in such extreme pretensions, for in 1131 the burgrave of Trier claimed to hold the archiepiscopal palace and revenues in fief, "to rule the land and to administer all things in the bishopric," leaving to the archbishop only the purely sacramental functions.[41] Still, for the interpretation of Lothar's claim to "the entire bishopric of Regensburg," everything depends upon the word *episcopatus*. Most simply, this term could refer to the episcopal office as a purely ecclesiastical function, but it is obvious that Lothar was not claiming the *episcopatus* in this sense. In the eleventh century, *episcopatus* had another meaning, for it sometimes indicated the episcopal office together with all the rights and properties per-

---

[que, sicu]t nostis, consensit ecclesia esse a sceptro imperiali suscipienda, de quo nec dari nec suscipi debent ali[que] ecclesiastica; unde laudamus discrecionem domini et patris nostri Innocencii pape, qui electos episcopos tam diu a regalium intromissione vel administratione significavit extraneos esse debere, quoadusque talia exposcant a domino imperatore; ab administratione vero rerum ecclesiasticarum non prohibet electum episcopum, etiam antequam ei porrigantur ipsa regalia per sceptrum, que si cui electorum dominus imperator nollet omnino prestare vel si electus ipse negligeret hec expostulare, nichilominus tamen electus et promotus episcopus deberet ecclesiam sibi commissam regere et omnes ecclesiasticas facultates eius dispensare. Que, ut prudentia vestra novit, cum ita se habeant, non immerito gra[vi]a mihi erant verba domini mei imperatoris absque distinctione regalium et ecclesiasticarum rerum totum Ratisponensem episcopatum suum esse dicentis et eundem electo regulariter episcopo et a nobis consecrato interdicentis." Where Bauermann made no attempt to fill a lacuna, I have offered conjectures ("imminuit," "est in," "suam," "alios"); the other restorations are his. For the source of the statement "quo dicto usus . . . sunt," see a letter of Urban I, in Hinschius, *Decr. Ps.-Isid.* 144 (JK 87).

[39] One must be extremely cautious in any interpretation of Lothar's policies at Würzburg, since they are known only through Conrad's letter to Norbert. Conrad was scarcely an unprejudiced witness, for in such an apologia he surely did not intend to present Lothar's views and actions in the most favorable possible light. It is inconceivable that Conrad would misrepresent matters of fact in a letter to a well-informed man who had just attended the meeting under discussion, but he undoubtedly emphasized only those facts which suited his purpose and which could be interpreted to advantage. In short, even if we had the full text of Conrad's letter, by itself his account could not furnish a fully reliable picture of the issues at Würzburg.

[40] Such is Bauermann's interpretation (*op.cit.* 110-15).

[41] Baldericus, *Gesta Alberonis* c.12, *MGH SS* VIII 250.

taining to it.[42] If Lothar was claiming the Regensburg *episcopatus* in this eleventh-century sense, his statement would recall his repeated demand for the restoration of investiture with ring and staff, that is, for the restoration of investiture in its pre-1122 form. Further, it might seem plausible that on the basis of his proprietary claims, the emperor was affirming his unlimited right to the bishopric of Regensburg and to the appointment of its bishop.[43] One might even conclude that Lothar was claiming the cathedral itself as his own, calling it "my church," and asserting that all of its appurtenances belonged to him, in precisely the fashion which the strictest Gregorians had considered characteristic of their royal adversaries.[44]

But the term *episcopatus* was protean, for it had still another meaning. At the trial of the bishop of Durham in 1088, though archbishop Lanfranc sharply distinguished the *episcopatus* from the *regalia*, the confused reply of the bishop presupposed that *episcopatus* and *regalia* were identical.[45] In fact, eleventh-century clerics ingeniously denied the charge of simony by asserting that it is lawful to purchase the *episcopatus* (that is, the episcopal properties), so long as the episcopal consecration is obtained free of charge.[46] Ivo of Chartres

[42] In this 11th-century sense, the *episcopatus* was the object of royal investiture; see Ficker, *SB Wien* 72 (1872) 92f, 106f, and the review by Georg Waitz, *Göttingische gelehrte Anzeigen* 21 (1873) 627 (= *Gesammelte Abh.* I 580). And in this sense, the *investitura episcopatus* or *donum episcopatus* was forbidden by the Reform Papacy. For a few examples, see Gregory VII, *Reg.* 4.22, 5.11, 6.5b, 7.14a, ed. Caspar 330ff, 364, 403, 480; Mansi XX 498 (1078), XXI 74 (1112).

[43] As Bauermann has concluded (*op.cit.* 110-15).

[44] Placidus of Nonantula, *De honore ecclesiae* c.118, *MGH LdL* II 625: "Ergo qui dicit: 'Meae sunt ecclesiae, et ego feci eas,—de regno enim meo factae sunt et mihi servire debent, et non possunt habere rectores, nisi ego dedero'—nonne quod Dei est in ius proprium vendicat?" Note that Lothar apparently spoke of *episcopatus noster*, rather than *ecclesia mea* (or *nostra*); the terminology is significant.

[45] Simeon of Durham, *Libellus de iniusta vexatione Willelmi episcopi* c.10, ed. T. Arnold (Rolls Series: London 1882-85) I 179. Also, *id.* c.13, *ibid.* I 184, where *episcopium* is contrasted with *feudum*; and S. Loewenfeld, *Epistolae pontificum Romanorum ineditae* (Leipzig 1885) 63 no.129 (JL 5397), for a letter of Urban II using the term *episcopatus* in the sense of *regalia*. In general, see Hoffmann, *DA* 15 (1959) 402f.

[46] Petrus Damiani, *Ep*.1.13, 5.13, *PL* 144 219, 364f (above, Ch.VIIA n.20).

regarded investiture as the king's concession of a purely temporal *episcopatus*.[47] Under Frederick Barbarossa, one finds the *episcopatus* tightly linked to *regalia*, so that the two terms together summed up the landed properties of a bishopric, the bishop's secular jurisdiction, and his lordship over his vassals.[48] In contrast to such purely ecclesiastical terms as *diocesis* or *parochia*, the terms *episcopatus* and *episcopium* commonly referred to the area in which the bishop held lands and other temporal possessions, and over which he held secular jurisdiction.[49] Indeed, it was natural to clarify the concept of the *episcopatus* by explaining it as a "dukeship" (*ducatus*).[50] Moreover, in Barbarossa's charters, where the *episcopatus* appears as the object of investiture, it is clearly identical with the *regalia*.[51] Similarly in twelfth-century France, documents declare that the *episcopatus* remains in the king's hands during the vacancy of a royal bishopric.[52] In the dispute at Würzburg, Lothar's statements were based upon this common equation, *episcopatus* = *regalia*. Thereby, the emperor was

---

[47] *Ep*.60, *PL* 162 73.

[48] For example, *Chronicon Magni presbyteri Reicherspergensis* anno 1169, *MGH SS* XVII 490: "Archiepiscopus [Salzburgensis] . . . resignavit ipsum episcopatum et omnia regalia in gratiam [inperatoris] . . . , sicque inperator toto episcopio Salzburgensi pro velle suo potitus est." Also, *id.* anno 1174, *ibid.* 498: ". . . toto episcopatu cum omnibus regalibus per sceptrum ei [scil. electo Salzburgensi] concessis . . ."; immediately thereafter, the archbishop-elect conferred fiefs on various secular princes. Correspondingly, the expression *ius episcopatus* referred to the feudal lordship of a prince-bishop. When a piece of land belonged to the *ius episcopatus*, it was simply held in fief from the bishop; F. Huter, *Tiroler UB* 1st Abt. I (Innsbruck 1937) 269 no.481 (1194).

[49] Adam of Bremen, *Gesta Hammaburgensis ecclesiae pontificum* 3.46, 3rd ed. B. Schmeidler (MGH SS.rer.Germ.: Hanover 1917) 188; in general, Theodor Mayer, *Fürsten und Staat* (Studien zur Verfassungsgeschichte des deutschen Mittelalters: Weimar 1950) 280ff, 290ff; also Karl Bosl, "Würzburg als Reichsbistum," *Aus Verfassungs- und Landesgeschichte: Festschrift . . . Theodor Mayer* I (Constance 1954) 173, 178f.

[50] Karl Zeumer, *Quellensammlung zur Geschichte der deutschen Reichsverfassung* (2nd ed. Tübingen 1913) 18f no.15: Barbarossa's grant for the *episcopatus* and *ducatus* of Würzburg (1168).

[51] *MGH Const* I 207 no.147; other instances cited by Ficker, *SB Wien* 72 (1872) 106f.

[52] For example, Louis VII, referring to the bishopric of Paris in 1161, claimed the "episcopatus et regale"; Edmond Michellet, *Du droit de régale* (Ligugé 1900) 23. Similar terminology appears as early as the 9th century (*ibid.* 21).

simply asserting his right to "the entire *regalia* of Regensburg," and his pretensions scarcely seem radical.[53] Lothar's claim only becomes fully comprehensible against the background of recent events. Not long before the meeting at Würzburg, bishop Henry of Regensburg had invested duke Henry the Proud with an extensive countship along the Inn.[54] Strictly speaking, however, this enfeoffment was illegal, for at the time, bishop Henry himself had not yet been invested. Lothar knew of this incident,[55] but needless to say, he would not have wished to revoke the enfeoffment and to dispossess his son-in-law of valuable lands. It is not surprising, therefore, that at Würzburg, Lothar refrained from drastic action against bishop Henry, and confined himself to a rebuke. In this context, then, the emperor declared that "the entire bishopric of Regensburg was his." The statement is neither obscure nor extreme, for Lothar was simply claiming that the *regalia* of Regensburg must remain in the emperor's hands till the

[53] If Lothar had claimed the Regensburg *episcopatus* in its 11th-century sense, he would surely have encountered staunch opposition from Norbert and from other prelates at Würzburg. Yet within Conrad's letter to Norbert, there is not the slightest indication that Lothar faced opposition from anyone except Conrad himself. Indeed, Conrad's letter is consistently cordial and polite toward Norbert, but it seems to arise from basic disagreements between the two archbishops.

Bauermann, on the other hand, recognizes the difference between Norbert's and Conrad's views on the rights of the *honorati*, but he believes that the two prelates agreed on fundamentals and were united in their opposition to the emperor's policy at Würzburg (*op.cit.* 117f). As evidence for such agreement, Bauermann cites Norbert's firm resistance to Lothar's demand at Rome in June 1133. Against Bauermann's argument, one can only assert the considerable distinction between a demand for the restoration of investiture with ring and staff and a claim to proprietary rights over the regalian lands of a bishopric. One should also note the opening statement in Conrad's letter, immediately after the salutation (Bauermann, *op.cit.* 132): "Apostolo monente, ut id ipsum dicamus omnes et non sint [in nobis] scismata, nostri precipue debet esse studii, qui dicimur [past]ores in populo, ut concordemus et consonemus exemplo et verbo." Cf. 1 *Cor.* 1.10 ("ut idipsum dicatis omnes, et non sint in uobis schismata"). In short, at the very beginning of his letter, Conrad exhorts Norbert to join him in striving for harmony and agreement between themselves. Conrad's statement does not suggest perfect unanimity.

[54] Above, n.23; this incident was overlooked by Bauermann.

[55] In all probability, it had been discussed in Rome between 4 June and 8 June 1133; in any case, Lothar would have been informed by his son-in-law, duke Henry.

investiture of the new incumbent. If the terminology of the thirteenth century had been available to him, Lothar could have asserted that with regard to the regalian properties, the election confers a mere *ius ad rem*, whereas the investiture confers a *ius in re* (or, as one might say, a *ius in regalibus*).

The assembly at Würzburg provided a perfect opportunity for publicizing the Innocentianum to the ecclesiastical princes, and Lothar certainly familiarized the court with the contents of the charter.[56] Moreover, there is little doubt that even before the discussions at Würzburg, both Conrad and Norbert were fully aware that bishop Henry of Regensburg had just bestowed a fief on the duke of Bavaria.[57] Nevertheless, in his letter to Norbert, Conrad made no excuses for his suffragan, nor did he even mention the act of enfeoffment.[58] Since Conrad recognized the absolute authority of Innocent's charter, and since he defended bishop Henry, it is clear that he did not regard the bishop's act as an offense against the major provision of the Innocentianum.[59] Indeed, one can only conclude that Conrad considered his suffragan's behavior entirely lawful. In defense of bishop Henry, Conrad applied the twofold conception of ecclesiastical property—a distinction which was, by 1133, a commonplace. Asserting that "nothing ecclesiastical may be given or received" in an investiture, Conrad explicitly endorsed the Innocentianum's prohibition against administration of the *regalia* before the bishop-elect has requested his investiture. However, Conrad went on to say, Innocent II had *not* forbidden the uninvested bishop-elect to undertake "the administration of ecclesiastical affairs"

---

[56] Though he had not accompanied the Roman expedition, archbishop Conrad was well acquainted with the document's text; note his use of the unusual word "exposcat," adapted from "deposcat" in the Innocentianum (above, n.38, and Ch.VIIIA n.29).

[57] One may assume that Conrad was well informed about major developments in his own province; Norbert must have known about bishop Henry's action at least since the negotiations at Rome in June.

[58] Such, at least, is the case in the surviving portions of the letter.

[59] In his letter Conrad apparently did not raise the question of the charter's validity *ex post facto*.

Regalia and the Bishop-Elect

(*administratio rerum ecclesiasticarum*).[60] In Conrad's view, these "ecclesiastical affairs" included the bishop-elect's ecclesiastical jurisdiction and his ecclesiastical properties.[61] For as Conrad argued, even if the bishop-elect fails to request the *regalia*, or if the emperor refuses to grant them, nevertheless the prelate must "rule the church entrusted to him and administer all of its ecclesiastical properties." Thus Conrad's conception of *episcopatus* included or implied four elements: the *regalia* deriving from investiture, the bishop-elect's jurisdiction over his church and its clergy (*ecclesiam sibi commissam regere*), the bishop-elect's supervision of his purely ecclesiastical properties (*ecclesiasticas facultates dispensare*), and of course the sacramental prerogatives deriving from episcopal consecration. Since Conrad did not regard the investiture as an indispensable prerequisite to the *regimen ecclesiae*, to the administration of the *facultates ecclesiasticae*, or to the consecration, he evidently considered it possible for a bishop to omit the investiture altogether and to leave the *regalia* in the emperor's hands indefinitely.[62] In general, Conrad feared that when the *regalia* were not kept separate and distinct from the Church's "ecclesiastical properties," the Church was thereby subjected to an intolerable "slavery."[63] And in the specific case of Regensburg, Conrad contended that Lothar was imposing such a slavery, for by neglecting the distinction between the *regalia* and the *res ecclesiasticae*,

---

[60] Bauermann wrongly interprets the *res ecclesiastice* as the "geistliche Funktionen" (*op.cit.* 116); Hoffmann, *DA* 15 (1959) 432 and esp. n.165. Clearly, Conrad was not seeking what Bauermann calls "eine Trennung von Regalien und Kirchenamt" (*op.cit.* 116 n.43); in fact, such a separation was presupposed equally by the Calixtinum and the Innocentianum. Moreover, both charters implicitly separated the *regalia* from the episcopal office *and* from the nonregalian properties. Hence, it is misleading to speak of a simple distinction between "Kirchengut und Kirchenamt" or between "regalia und ecclesiastica" (cf. Bauermann, *op.cit.* 113f).

[61] The phrase does not indicate solely the nonregalian properties; cf., however, Hoffmann, *loc.cit.*

[62] Hoffmann, *op.cit.* 432f.

[63] As usual, Conrad's wording is careful, and he avoids calling the imperial right of regalian investiture a *servitus*; cf., however, Bauermann's remark (*op.cit.* 116): "er sieht darin eine *servitus*."

the emperor was appropriating the purely ecclesiastical properties of the bishopric.[64] Thus archbishop Conrad's indignant charge against Lothar reduces itself to a marked difference in their conceptions of the *regalia*.

Suspicious of the obligations arising from the feudal bond between the ruler and the German episcopate, archbishop Conrad was bitterly opposed to the customary demand for homage and fealty from bishops, and he refused to do homage and fealty either to Lothar or later to Conrad III.[65] Yet of course archbishop Conrad was never one of those who, like Arnold of Brescia, were entirely opposed to the bishops' possession of the *regalia*. Since he considered tenure of the *regalia* a lawful practice, the next question concerned the boundary between the *regalia* and the *res ecclesiasticae*. It was not merely an academic question, for contemporaries could maintain that in several respects, different regulations governed those lands classified as *regalia* and those classed as *res ecclesiasticae*.[66] With regard to the boundary between the *regalia* and the *res ecclesiasticae*, Conrad's thought was in sharp contrast to Lothar's. Understandably, the emperor believed that Henry the Proud's countship on the Inn pertained to the *regalia* of Regensburg. Indeed, it is probably not too much to assume that in claiming "the entire bishopric of Regensburg" with "harsh words" (as Conrad called them), Lothar asserted his rights over *all* of the bishopric's lands

---

[64] The nature of these ecclesiastical properties is unmistakably explained in Conrad's letter (above, n.38): "vota fidelium, pretia peccatorum, patrimonia pauperum, redemptiones animarum." These various properties might be summed up as *oblationes*, and of course, Church lands could also be reckoned as *oblationes*; Gerhoh of Reichersberg, *De aedificio Dei* c.25, *MGH LdL* III 154.

[65] *Vita Chuonradi archiepiscopi Salisburgensis* c.5, *MGH SS* XI 66.

[66] As Gerhoh of Reichersberg explained in a letter to the Bamberg chapter (1165), *UB des Landes ob der Enns* I (1852) 312 no.69: "Quod enim in commutationibus rerum ecclesiasticarum secundum canones requirenda est collaudatio et subscriptio clericorum, non pertinuisse dinoscitur ad nostram actionem, qua de regalibus potius quam ecclesiasticis rebus agebatur, ac proinde magis eam decuit roborari collaudatione principum regni coram ipso principe principum Friderico Augusto"; in general, see Classen, "Der Prozess um Münsteuer (1154-76) und die Regalienlehre Gerhochs von Reichersberg," *ZRG GA* 77 (1960) 324-45, esp. 335.

during an episcopal interregnum, and refused to recognize any of these lands as belonging unconditionally to the Church (*absque distinctione regalium et ecclesiasticarum rerum*).

Against Lothar's view, Conrad apparently thought that duke Henry's new fief belonged among the "ecclesiastical properties" of Regensburg, rather than among the bishopric's *regalia*. Here Conrad's concept of the *regalia* recalls the theorizing during the Investiture Struggle.[67] The distinction between regalian lands and other forms of regalian property was, of course, an old one.[68] Moreover, in the negotiations between pope and emperor early in 1111, some ecclesiastical lands were clearly reckoned as part of the *regalia*,[69] and apparently other lands were considered the "hereditary possessions" of the churches.[70]

Far more instructive, however, is the similarity between Conrad's idea of the *regalia* and the earliest doctrines of his protégé, Gerhoh of Reichersberg.[71] It is, of course, likely that Conrad's career as reformer impressed Gerhoh deeply.[72] The practical-minded Conrad had no experience as a publicist, and in preparation for a polemic, it would have been natural for him to arm himself with the theorists' arguments. At least since 1126 Conrad had known and trusted Gerhoh, and by 1133 Gerhoh had already written three works. Indeed, it is highly probable—and would not be at all surprising—that before composing his letter to Norbert, Conrad studied the earliest of Gerhoh's writings, the *Opusculum de aedificio*

---

[67] On the evolution of the idea of the *regalia* from the late 11th century to 1125, see Ott, *ZRG KA* 35 (1948) 235-58.

[68] *De investitura episcoporum*, in *MGH LdL* II 500-02; the *fundi* are set off against *mobilia*, *res ecclesiastice*, and specified *iura civitatum*.

[69] *MGH Const* I 138f, 141 nos.85, 90; also, Placidus of Nonantula, *De honore ecclesiae* c.151, *MGH LdL* II 634.

[70] *MGH Const* I 141 no.90. Henry V did not consistently categorize Church lands (*praedia*) as a part of the *regalia*, though he claimed both (*ibid.* 150 no.100).

[71] Since Gerhoh's early conceptions of the *regalia* will be discussed in detail below, they need only a brief summary here; for the main scholarly literature, see esp. Ch.IXA n.16.

[72] Classen, *Gerhoch von Reichersberg* 66f.

Dei.[73] In this treatise Gerhoh distinguished three kinds of ecclesiastical holdings: tithes and offerings, lands, and "public offices" (*publicae functiones*).[74] Gerhoh maintained that all tithes and offerings unquestionably belong to the Church; also, although he admitted the royal origin of some ecclesiastical lands, he insisted upon their inalienability and their freedom from any obligation to the monarchy. On the other hand, Gerhoh believed that the Church should renounce the *regalia* in a narrower sense—that is, dukeships, countships, and other "public offices." Obviously, archbishop Conrad did not accept everything in Gerhoh's program, since Conrad vigorously exercised the powers of his own "public offices." Indeed, in February 1111, during the hot dispute following Paschal II's order that the imperial bishops should return their *regalia* to the king, Conrad asserted that he would rather have his head cut off than give his consent to the pope's decree![75] Moreover, it is possible (though it cannot be proven) that Conrad disagreed with another of the doctrines in Gerhoh's *De aedificio Dei*, for Conrad may have recognized that *some* Church lands are truly royal property

[73] Classen has found no evidence that Gerhoh influenced Conrad (*loc.cit.*). However, distinguishing between *regalia* and *res ecclesiastice* (above, n.38), Conrad used precisely the same expression which Gerhoh had used in drawing his fundamental distinction between the three forms of ecclesiastical property (*De aed. Dei* c.25, *MGH LdL* III 154):

Epistola Conradi	*De aedificio Dei*
Que, ut prudentia vestra novit, *cum ita se habeant,* non immerito gravia mihi erant verba domini mei imperatoris absque distinctione regalium et ecclesiasticarum rerum. . . .	*Que cum ita se habeant,* patet ecclesiarum facultates trifariam esse distinctas: in decimarum vid. oblationes, et agrorum possessiones, nec non regales ac publicas functiones.

The general similarity of wording and of topic is obvious. Note further that the italicized expression appears both times in the same context. Although the expression itself was not uncommon, it was also not essential to either argument, and therefore this verbatim recurrence seems scarcely accidental.

[74] Below, Ch.IXA nn.23f.

[75] Gerhoh of Reichersberg, *De investigatione Antichristi* 1.25, *MGH LdL* III 333f; cf. also Otto of Freising, *Chronica* 7.14, 2nd ed. Hofmeister 327, and the *Vita Chuonradi archiepiscopi Salisburgensis* c.9, *MGH SS* XI 68. Since Conrad was actually threatened with violence on that occasion, it was not solely a sense of the melodramatic which prompted this defiant statement.

and therefore subject to the obligations imposed by other *regalia*. Still, at Würzburg, when he defended an uninvested bishop's right to confer a fief, Conrad apparently shared, at least in part, Gerhoh's tendency to regard ecclesiastical lands as the unconditional property of the Church. Though more conventional in terminology, Conrad's twofold distinction between *regalia* and *res ecclesiasticae* corresponds closely—but, to be sure, not perfectly—to Gerhoh's tripartite distinction: tithes and offerings, lands, and "public offices." In all probability, Conrad viewed tithes, offerings, and *most* ecclesiastical lands as part of the *res ecclesiasticae*; hence he needed only two categories, instead of the three used by Gerhoh. Thus, by diminishing the mass of rights and properties which the Church should acknowledge as royal, both Gerhoh and Conrad sought to limit the Church's obligations toward the monarchy. In particular, archbishop Conrad's narrowed conception of the *regalia* threatened to erode the meaning of investiture and the value of the Innocentianum.

3. Investiture as a Constitutive Act

During his troubled reign, king Conrad III lacked the power to enforce effectively the requirement that, for the ecclesiastical princes of Germany, investiture must precede consecration. It is, moreover, equally unlikely that Conrad was able to enforce consistently, in practice, the crucial principle which had been recognized at Rome and reaffirmed at Würzburg in 1133: the constitutive character of investiture.[1]

[1] Based on the wording of the *Vita Eberhardi* 4, *MGH SS* XI 99, the prevailing view has maintained that Eberhard I of Salzburg was consecrated before his investiture. Pointing out that the *Vita Eberhardi* is not always reliable in dating events, Adolf Hofmeister has expressed strong doubts about this view ("Zur Erhebung Eberhards I. auf den Salzburger Erzstuhl 1147," *ZKG* 29 [1908] 71-78), and has supported his reservations by citing a charter in which Eberhard, on the day after his consecration, granted a manor which formed part of his *regalia* (W. Hauthaler and F. Martin, eds., *Salzburger UB* II [Salzburg 1916] 360-62 no.251). However, because almost nothing is known about the proceedings in the 46 German episcopal promotions under Conrad, one is perhaps equally justified in accepting the authority of the *Vita Eberhardi*, which would warrant the conclusion

The Bishop-Elect

Yet the principle survived, and even under Conrad's uncertain leadership, undoubtedly some prince-prelates were reluctant to violate this principle.[2] The survival of the principle must be credited to the strength which it gained from the firm stand taken by Conrad's predecessor, Lothar III. Indeed, not least among Lothar's achievements was his successful struggle to preserve the royal prerogative in promotions to the episcopate. Against such powerful opponents as Conrad I of Salzburg, he had not only maintained but enhanced the value and meaning of regalian investiture, precisely at a moment when this vital part of the prerogative faced the threat of virtual extinction. Under Barbarossa, once again the fundamental law of the empire effectively prohibited prelates-elect from administering the *regalia* before their investiture.[3]

FREDERICK BARBAROSSA

Assigning high importance to the loyal support of the German church, Frederick I was, on the whole, successful in his efforts to exercise effective control over accessions to the episcopate.[4] His prerogative included the right to confirm an

that the prescribed sequence of investiture and consecration was reversed on 11 May 1147, *and* that the principle forbidding the administration of *regalia* by an uninvested prelate was violated on 12 May 1147. Even Barbarossa did not succeed in enforcing these two principles consistently.

Though a full reevaluation of Lothar's and Conrad's ecclesiastical policies would be desirable, it does not belong in the present study.

[2] See Conrad's order to Wibald, abbot-elect of Corvey, in *MGH Const* I 178 no.123 (1146): Because of his absence, Wibald's church has suffered *tam in temporalibus quam in spiritualibus*, and to remedy this *grave damnum*, Wibald should receive his investiture and thereby become a *pater spiritualis et prudens dispensator* of his church.

[3] Long ago summarized by Georges Blondel as a principle belonging to the "droit général de l'empire" (*Étude sur la politique de l'empereur Frédéric en Allemagne* [Paris 1892] 238), the juridically constitutive character of regalian investiture has received surprisingly little attention in scholarly studies. It has been briefly noted by: Georg Phillips, *Der Ursprung des Regalienrechts in Frankreich* (Halle 1870) 33; Ficker, *SB Wien* 72 (1872) 134; Boerger, *Die Belehnungen der deutschen geistlichen Fürsten* 61f, 121f; Albert Werminghoff, *Verfassungsgeschichte der deutschen Kirche im Mittelalter* (2nd ed. Leipzig 1913) 58. For more detailed remarks, see Hofmeister, *Forschungen und Versuche: Festschrift D. Schäfer* 111-15; and Friedrich Baethgen, "Der Anspruch des Papsttums auf das Reichsvikariat," *ZRG KA* 10 (1920) 184ff.

[4] In addition to the standard histories of the empire, the German church,

election—a right which, as in earlier reigns, might be associated with the act of investiture.[5] "By the imperial authority," he could "make good" any deficiency in an election—here, his language is reminiscent of the thirteenth-century papacy's claim, by virtue of the papal "plenitude of power," to "make good" any "defect" in an election.[6] Thoroughly traditional, of course, was his assertion of the right to decide a disputed election.[7] Yet he went far beyond this (and, thereby, far beyond anything conceded in the Calixtinum) in maintaining that in the event of a double election, he himself could settle the issue by selecting and appointing a third person.[8] Even without the occasion of a split election, however, Frederick unequivocally insisted upon an imperial right of direct

---

and the papacy, see: Georg Wolfram, *Friedrich I. und das Wormser Konkordat* (Marburg 1883); P. Scheffer-Boichorst, *Kaiser Friedrichs I. letzter Streit mit der Kurie* (Berlin 1866); Rudolf Jordan, *Die Stellung des deutschen Episkopats im Kampf um die Universalmacht unter Friedrich I. bis zum Frieden von Venedig* (Würzburg 1939).

[5] *Annales Ottenburani (minores)* anno 1180, *MGH SS* XVII 316: "cognita abbatis electione, quia canonice facta est, ab ipso tandem principe confirmatur, et per regalia sublimatur." This conception of an electoral confirmation linked to the act of investiture was easily transferred to the relations between the emperor and a vassal-king; Rahewin, *Gesta Friderici* 3.25, 3rd ed. Waitz and Simson 197f: ". . . nuncii regis Datiae N., nuper electi, principis adeunt presentiam, postulantes, quatinus investituram de regno suo regi mittere ac electionem de ipso factam ratihabitione confirmare dignaretur. . . ." In exchange for the oath of fealty, the vassal-king was to receive the "regni administrationem de manu principis" (*ed.cit.* 198).

[6] *MGH Const* I 328 no.233 (1167): ". . . si quid in electione ipso presente defuerit, ipse [scil. A. Aquensis ecclesie prepositus] imperiali auctoritate suppleat. Quamvis enim sine electione, dictante iusticia, in quamlibet personam hunc honorem [scil. Cameracensem episcopatum] conferre possemus, ecclesie tamen vestre deferimus et dilectum nostrum P(etrum) et non alium per sollempnitatem electionis maluimus sublimare, quam de imperiali iusticia in huius dignitatis apicem collocare. . . ." For the papal diction, cf. *X* 1.6.39 (Innocent III); and often later.

[7] Otto of Freising, *Gesta Friderici* 2.56, *ed.cit.* 161: archbishopric of Cologne (1156).

[8] Implicit in Otto of Freising's remark on the tradition of the imperial court (*op.cit.* 2.6, *ed.cit.* 106; text: above, Ch.VIIB n.23). The claim to this "right" was expressed even more clearly under Henry VI; *Vita Alberti episcopi Leodiensis* 5, *MGH SS* XXV 143, and Gilbert of Mons, *Chronicon hanoniense* anno 1191, *MGH SS* XXI 578. On the *ius devolutionis* in general, see Godehard J. Ebers, *Das Devolutionsrecht* (Kirchenrechtliche Abh. 37-38: Stuttgart 1906) 163-69.

appointment, though in practice he did not often use this "right."[9] Moreover, in open opposition to the canonical norms generally accepted during the previous hundred years, Frederick included within his prerogative the right to transfer a bishop from one see to another.[10]

Equally important to Barbarossa was control over the *regalia*. Appealing to a familiar principle of Roman law, he claimed full proprietary rights over the *regalia*, in Italy as well as Germany—they are, he stated, "our *regalia*."[11] In return for the *regalia*, he expected both homage and fealty, since possession of *regalia* was, in his view, a form of feudal tenure: "Those things which are held from the empire, are held by feudal law."[12] Frederick could refuse to invest a prelate-elect with the *regalia*, and, further strengthening the emperor's veto power, the imperial court vigorously defended the traditional sequence of investiture and consecration.[13] Moreover, for due cause, Frederick could confiscate the *regalia* of an invested and consecrated bishop.[14] In the strained circumstances of the papal schism, imperial bishops could expect the confiscation of their *regalia* if they adhered to Alexander III.[15] Though actually administered by individual prelates, *regalia* were perpetually assigned to particular churches, and under feudal law, if a prelate kept his ecclesiastical office after confiscation, the *regalia* remained in the

[9] *MGH Const* I 327 no.231 (1167): ". . . nos de superabundanti iure imperii personam . . . elegerimus . . ."; also,, above, n.6.

[10] Otto of Freising, *op.cit.* Epistola Friderici, *ed.cit.* 2: "Cicensem episcopum Wichmannum ad archiepiscopatum Magdeburgensem transtulimus"; also, *Gesta Frid.* 2.6, 2.8, *ed.cit.* 106, 109.

[11] Rahewin, *Gesta Frid.* 4.35, *ed.cit.* 275 (= *MGH Const* I 250 no.179; text: above, Ch.VIIB n.58). See also Frederick's reference to *temporalia nostra* (below, n.17), and his conviction "quod res episcopales decedente episcopo ad eamdem manum . . . redierunt de cuius munere constat eas descendisse . . ." (*MGH Const* I 327 no.231 [1167]).

[12] *MGH Const* I 236 no.169 (1157): ". . . ea, que ab imperio tenentur, iure feodali possidentur . . ."; Mitteis, *Lehnrecht* 425f. Gerhoh of Reichersberg was, during this period, generally opposed to the requirement of homage; similarly Hadrian IV, specifically for the Italian bishops (Classen, *Gerhoch von Reichersberg* 178f).

[13] *MGH Const* I 445, 447 nos.315f (1186); see above, Ch.VIIB n.24.

[14] Otto, *Gesta Frid.* 2.12, *ed.cit.* 114 (above, Ch.VIIB n.58).

[15] Rahewin, *Gesta Frid.* Appendix anno 1165, *ed.cit.* 348 (above, Ch.VIIB n.58).

emperor's hands until the prelate's death allowed the installation of a successor.[16]

Within this sphere, a central feature of Barbarossa's concern to preserve his prerogative was his reassertion of the principle forbidding administration of the *regalia* prior to investiture. Beyond any doubt, this principle belonged to the standard "ideas of the court" (*rationes curiae*) during his long reign. With evocative phrasing, he maintained that regalian investiture confers on the prelate-elect the "fullness of honor in temporal things," just as the subsequent consecration brings the "fullness of office in spiritual matters."[17] In 1155, however, bishop Hartwig of Regensburg was tried for granting fiefs before having received the *regalia* from the emperor.[18] That is to say, bishop Hartwig was charged with administering the temporalities of his church prior to his own investiture. To be sure, the circumstances of the bishop's transgression might seem extenuating: he had already been consecrated, the emperor was away in Italy at the time, and, curiously, the bishop was apparently unaware of this imperial regulation.[19] Nonetheless, Frederick fined bishop Hartwig

---

[16] *MGH Const* I 209 no.149 (above, Ch.VIIB n.58).

[17] *MGH Const* I 321 no.226 (1165): ". . . Volumus enim absque omni dubio, ut sicut in temporalibus nostris plenitudinem honoris a nobis accepit, ita et plenitudinem officii in spiritualibus consequatur et habeat." This phrase, *plenitudo honoris*, was not confined solely to ecclesiastical princes; in 1174 Barbarossa granted *investitura in omni plenitudine honoris* and *regalia cum omni plenitudine honoris et utilitatis* to a lay count (*MGH Const* I 337f no.241). On the extended meanings of *honor* in the feudal and monarchical context, see Schäfer, "Honor, citra, cis im mittelalterlichen Latein," *SB Berlin* (1921) 372-78, and in general, Peter Rassow, *Honor imperii: Die neue Politik Friedrich Barbarossas 1152-1159* (2nd ed. Darmstadt 1961) esp. 58-61.

[18] Otto of Freising, *Gesta Frid.* 2.44, *ed.cit.* 152: "Impetitur . . . Hardewicus, qui noviter per electionem cleri et populi et metropolitani sui consecrationem pontificatum eiusdem civitatis acceperat. Regalia siquidem, quae iuxta rationes curiae nulli episcoporum militi, antequam de manu principis suscipiantur, tradere licet, ipse huius rei nescius impremeditate, morante adhuc in Italia principe, tradiderat. Ob ea in causam positus, dum et factum inficiari qualitatemve facti defendere nequit, compositionis incurrit noxam. Caeteri quoque, qui ab eo susceperant, quique iuxta suam conditionem et sortem in plusve minusve consimili pena dampnatur. . . ."

[19] By being consecrated before his investiture, bishop Hartwig had reversed the sequence prescribed by the Calixtinum; nonetheless, apparently this irregularity was not the offense with which he was charged.

one hundred marks, and all those who had accepted fiefs from the bishop were subjected to fines which varied according to their rank.

In Regensburg the lesson was well learned, for when another episcopal election was held there in 1167, representatives of the electors went to Barbarossa and pleaded the poverty of their church. As an exceptional favor, the emperor granted their request, "although it seems opposed to the custom of our court," and with Frederick's permission the bishop-elect could then take immediate possession of the "palaces and all the revenues and fiefs and offices and castles and courts of the bishopric" and could administer them freely even before receiving the emperor's investiture.[20] In 1162 the uninvested bishop-elect of Hildesheim also took the precaution of consulting Barbarossa, who was in Italy, and of securing the emperor's permission to accept oaths of fealty from the vassals of his church, as well as to organize the church's resources "with free power." In this case Barbarossa had every reason to give this special privilege to the new bishop-elect, who could thereby bring his contingent of knights to Frederick in Italy, where the emperor finally bestowed the investiture.[21] When the canons of Lübeck cathedral elected the provost of Segeberg and Keven to the vacant bishopric in 1186, the new bishop-elect showed due caution. Frederick was in Italy at the time of this election, and for almost a year the bishop-elect remained at Keven as provost, "lest he should seem to undertake anything rashly," until the emperor's return finally allowed him to receive his investiture.[22] Indeed,

[20] *MGH Const* I 329 no.234; Wolfram, *Friedrich I.* 97.
[21] *Chronicon Hildesheimense* c.22, *MGH SS* VII 856: "Hermannus . . . ab omnibus electus, a fidelibus aecclesiae, consulto tamen prius imperatore, qui eo tempore in Ytalia morabatur, sacramentum fidelitatis suscepit, cunctisque negociis suis et comodis circa redditus episcopales libera potestate dispositis, cum milicia domnum imperatorem in Ytaliam secutus, regalium investituram . . . adeptus est."
[22] Arnold of Lübeck, *Chronica Slavorum* 3.14, ed. J. M. Lappenberg (MGH SS.rer.Germ. Hanover 1868) 100f: ". . . ne temere aliquid aggredi videretur, mansit in prepositura sua Kevena toto anno illo, donec circa hiemem revertente imperatore de Italia occurreret ei cum archiepiscopo in

Regalia and the Bishop-Elect

when a twelfth-century bishop-elect conferred a charter of investiture, at the beginning of the charter he might clarify his status—and justify his action—with the explanation that "he had already received the *regalia* from the hand of his lord, the emperor Frederick."[23] Under Barbarossa, the German church was clearly learning to respect the prohibition against "usurping or seizing the *regalia*" before investiture. Yet the principle needed occasional restatement, undoubtedly because it was still sometimes violated. At Augsburg in 1179 the archbishop of Salzburg referred to the imperial court a question concerning one of his suffragans, the bishop of Gurk. The exceptional relation of Gurk to Salzburg formed the historical background of the archbishop's question, for an earlier archbishop of Salzburg had founded the bishopric of Gurk, and the archbishop was therefore the bishop's temporal lord as well as his ecclesiastical superior. Consequently the archbishop, instead of the emperor, customarily invested the bishop-elect.[24] In Augsburg the archbishop's query was:

Gellinhusen. Ubi accepta pontificali investitura de manu ipsius, reversus est cum archiepiscopo Bremam, sicque . . . consecratus est. . . . Inde . . . venit Lubeke." Prior to investiture, an attempt by the bishop-elect to undertake any part of his episcopal prerogative—either the *regalia* or the *potestas ordinis*—would surely have been *temeritas*. However, Hermann Heineken, "Die älteste Münzprägung der Bischöfe von Lübeck," *Forschungen und Versuche: Festschrift D. Schäfer* 206f, explains the bishop-elect's long delay in Keven as a manifestation of his reluctance to receive the investiture from duke Bernard of Saxony and of his desire to be directly under the emperor. This interpretation does not take account of the reason explicitly given by Arnold.

[23] F. Huter, *Tiroler UB* 1st Abt. I 241 no.448 (Trent 1189): "Dominus Conradus in Tridentina sede episcopus electus, qui de manu domini Federici imperatoris iam regalia susceperat, investivit . . . de wardia et custodia castri de Lichtenstaine. . . .' "

[24] Normally the archbishop also elected, confirmed, and consecrated the *electus*; in general, see Wilhelmine Seidenschnur, "Die Salzburger Eigenbistümer in ihrer reichs-, kirchen- und landesrechtlichen Stellung," *ZRG KA* 9 (1919) 177-287; Jakob Obersteiner, "Das Bistum Gurk in seiner Entwicklung und in seiner reichs- und kirchenrechtlichen Stellung," *Österreichisches Archiv für KR* 8 (1957) 185-208.
In the early 1080's the spurious *Privilegium minus* of Leo VIII (*MGH Const* I 667 no.448; D.63 c.23) asserted that archbishops and bishops "ab eo [scil. rege] investituram accipiant et consecrationem unde debent, exceptis his quos imperator pontifici et archiepiscopis concessit"; see above, Ch.VIIв n.18. And indeed, such were the archbishop of Salzburg's

The Bishop-Elect

Whether . . . the bishop-elect of Gurk may lawfully grant to anyone any kind of fief from among the properties of the church of Gurk, before the bishop-elect is invested by the archbishop of Salzburg with the administration and possession of that bishopric.[25]

Following the judgment pronounced by the bishop of Bamberg, the imperial court decreed:

Neither the bishop-elect of Gurk *nor any other* [*bishop-elect*] can or should transfer any fief to anyone, before he himself is invested by his own lord.[26]

Here it is worth noting that imperial prelates approved and even—under unusual circumstances—appealed to this imperial principle.

During the papal schism, however, through its devotion to Alexander III, Salzburg itself became an island of resistance to Frederick's ecclesiastical policy, and the harsh struggles between emperor and archbishops highlight the importance which Barbarossa attached to his control over the *regalia*. In fact, archbishops Conrad II and Adalbert III were the chief violators of the imperial regulations on the *regalia*.[27] Though archbishop Conrad II requested the *regalia* three times, Barbarossa consistently refused him. When Conrad seized the castles and other *regalia* in 1165, his act was tantamount to a declaration of war. Because Conrad had received

---

exceptional rights over Gurk, granted by Henry IV on 4 February 1070 (Obersteiner, *op.cit.* 187). Also, *Glossa Palatina* on D.63 c.23 v. *exceptis*: "quia ipse imperator quibusdam archiepiscopis quorumdam inuestituram concesserat" (Vat.Pal. 658 fol.17rb; Vat.Reg. 977 fol.48rb).

25 *MGH Const* I 383f no.278.

26 *Ibid.* 384 no.278: ". . . nec Gurcensis electus nec quisquam alius possit aut debeat aliquid feodum in quemquam transferre, antequam ipse a suo auctore sit investitus."

27 In general, see the works cited above, n.4, and the long article, now more than a century old, by Wilhelm Schmidt, "Die Stellung der Erzbischöfe und des Erzstiftes von Salzburg zu Kirche und Reich unter Kaiser Friedrich I. bis zum Frieden von Venedig (1177)," *Archiv für österreichische Geschichte* 34 (1865) 3-144; a fresh study of this topic would be welcome.

neither the *regalia* from the emperor nor the *spiritualia* from the imperial antipope, Frederick viewed Conrad's seizure as robbery, confiscated Salzburg's *regalia*, and granted them to vassals.[28] Events moved similarly under Conrad's successor, archbishop Adalbert III. Having received his consecration without preliminary regalian investiture, Adalbert administered his church's properties, accepted oaths of fealty, and bestowed fiefs. Frederick refused to recognize the new archbishop, and Adalbert could not gain the emperor's favor even by handing over to him the temporal possessions of Salzburg, which Frederick then simply distributed to laymen.[29] As the Salzburg clergy explained to Alexander III in 1170,

> Our church . . . has been almost annihilated by many calamities, principally for this reason, that after his promotion, our lord [Adalbert] . . . neglected to request the *regalia* from the emperor according to the custom of the German princes.[30]

This complaint assumes general recognition of the constitutional rule and of its political implications: under a strong emperor, an uninvested prelate could not administer the *regalia* without the gravest risk.

THE THIRTEENTH CENTURY AND AFTER

The verdict of the German jurists was unanimous on this requirement. In the early 1220's the distinguished magistrate,

[28] *Annales Reicherspergenses* anno 1166, *MGH SS* XVII 472f; Henry of Salzburg, *Historia calamitatum ecclesiae Salzburgensis* c.2, ed. B. Pez, *Thesaurus anecdotorum novissimus* (6 vols. Augsburg 1721-29) II,iii 202f; W. Schmidt, *op.cit.* 59-80.

[29] *Chronicon Magni presbiteri Reicherspergensis* anno 1169, *MGH SS* XVII 489f; R. Jordan, *Stellung des deutschen Episkopats* 131-38.

[30] H. Sudendorf, ed., *Registrum oder merkwürdige Urkunden für die deutsche Geschichte* I (Jena 1849) 70 no.27 (= A. von Jaksch, *Monumenta historica ducatus Carinthiae* [Klagenfurt 1896-98] I 204 no.268): "ecclesia nostra . . . paupercula et multis calamitatibus pene annullata maxime pro eo, quod dominus noster post introitum suum . . . regalia secundum consuetudinem principum Teutonicorum ab imperatore requirere neglexit"; Wolfram, *Friedrich I.* 89.

The Bishop-Elect

Eike von Repgow, crystallized this imperial principle in his *Sachsenspiegel*:

> When one elects bishops or abbots or abbesses . . . they should receive the investiture first and the consecration afterward. If they have received the investiture, they may use their feudal rights then and not sooner.[31]

Although these assertions seem to summarize key clauses in the Calixtinum and the Innocentianum, one should not infer that Eike's statements derived their legal force from these two documents, nor even that Eike was personally familiar with either of the two. Once again, the sanction came from custom. Just as the "approved usage" in twelfth-century Germany dictated the temporal precedence of regalian investiture before consecration, custom similarly required investiture as a prerequisite to the administrative acts of a prelate-elect, and Eike restated both of these doctrines as segments of the customary law, the *usus approbatus*, valid in northeastern Germany. Later German law books—specifically: the *Deutschenspiegel* and the *Schwabenspiegel*—reaffirmed the imperial principle of investiture as antecedent to administration.[32] The testimony of these two customaries bears witness to the general acceptance of this imperial doctrine in south Germany during the mid-1270's. In the *Schwabenspiegel*, however, there is a noteworthy omission: although the compiler of the *Schwaben-*

---

[31] *Sachsenspiegel* Landrecht 3.59 §1 (152), ed. Karl A. Eckhardt (MGH Fontes iuris Germanici antiqui n.s.1: Hanover 1933) 142: "Swen men kûset bischopphe oder ebde oder ebdischen, die den herschilt habit, daz lên sollen se vore untfân unde die bîsorge nâ. Swenne se daz lên untfangen habent, sô mogen se lênrecht thûn unde nicht îr." In general, see Fritz Salomon, "Der Sachsenspiegel und das Wormser Konkordat," *ZRG GA* 31 (1910) 137-45, and, for some corrections, Hofmeister, *Forschungen und Versuche: Festschrift D. Schäfer* 111-15.

[32] *Schwabenspiegel* Landrecht 110 §3, ed. Heinrich G. Gengler (2nd ed. Erlangen 1875) 99: "So man kiuset bischove oder aepte oder aeptissinne, die gefürst sint, die enmugen dehein lehen gelihen, ê daz si ir reht enphahen von dem künige." Also, Julius Ficker, ed., *Der Spiegel deutscher Leute* Landrecht 306 (Innsbruck 1859) 139: "Swenne man chieset Byscholf oder aebte oder abtessinne. die den herschilt habent. daz lehen sullen si vor enphahen. swenne si daz lehen vor enphangen habent so mugen si lehen reht tûn vnd niht e."

spiegel closely followed Eike von Repgow's prohibition of administration before investiture, he did not bother to discuss the sequence of investiture and consecration. One may, perhaps, conclude that in the world mirrored by the *Schwabenspiegel*, the jurisdictionally constitutive character of regalian investiture was still a crucial aspect of customary law, but the sequence of investiture and consecration, no longer of central significance, could be ignored.[33]

During the thirteenth century and even beyond, the German monarchs continued to press the same point. Thirteenth-century imperial documents repeatedly charted the episcopal "interregnum" as a period extending from the death of one incumbent to the investiture of his successor. For example, the German rulers frequently stated that certain secular offices subject to a bishopric automatically become vacant when the new bishop-elect receives his *regalia*, so that the bishop-elect can then make appointments to those offices at his own pleasure.[34] During the thirteenth and early fourteenth centuries, the diction and the formulas of the imperial chancery unambiguously presented the investiture as a constitutive act, conclusively ending the episcopal "interregnum." Sometimes a charter of investiture enumerated the specific powers, rights, and properties thereby transferred to a bishop-elect.[35] An imperial document might specify that through investiture the prelate-elect acquired "full and free power of judging in civil and criminal cases," or "free authority to rule . . . and to exercise temporal jurisdiction over vassals and subjects."[36] But after the mid-thirteenth century, chancery usage most

[33] In contrast to Eike, the *Schwabenspiegel* reveals a strongly pro-Curial bias, which would furnish an alternative—but, I believe, less satisfactory—explanation for this omission.

[34] *MGH Const* II 443 no.332 (1240): ". . . quia de manu nostra regalium receperat investituram, legitime vacare debeant universa officia ecclesie Hersveldensis, exceptis quatuor principalibus, que post se consequentiam suam trahunt. . . ." Similar, *ibid.* II 443 no.333 (1240), 465 no.358 (1250).

[35] Eduard Winkelmann, *Acta imperii inedita* I (Innsbruck 1880) 5f no.7 (1205); *MGH Const* IV 178 no.206 (1306); and in many other charters.

[36] H. Böhmer, *Acta imperii sel.* 312 no.385 (1268); *MGH Const* III 190 no.205 (1278).

commonly summed up the *regalia* simply as "the administration of the temporalities" (*administratio temporalium*), an expression which suggested the conferment of full secular jurisdiction over men, prerogatives, and property.[37] Often in highly concrete terms, imperial documents stressed the constitutive nature of investiture by denying to the uninvested *electus* the exercise of these various jurisdictional powers and, above all, by denying him the right to grant fiefs and properties. As Frederick II defined it, the vacancy of a see comes to an end only with the investiture of the new *electus*, since the temporalities—such as tolls, customs, mints, minor magistracies, and the secular courts—remain in the emperor's hands "until the *electus* receives the *regalia* from him."[38] In 1223, with an impressive list of German bishops present, Frederick II's court decided that a prelate "who has not received his insignia from the imperial hand" may not subinfeudate any of his church's holdings.[39] In the same year Frederick's son asserted that if an *electus* grants a fief to anyone, or alienates or mortgages any property prior to his own investiture, the act is invalid and must be revoked.[40] Also, if an uninvested *electus* gave rights of citizenship to a new inhabitant of his city, the king could nullify these rights and

[37] H. Hoogeweg, *Westfälisches UB* VI (Münster 1898) 167 no.583 (1253); *MGH Const* III 637 nos.647f (1274); *ibid.* III 421 no.434 (1290); R. Wilmans, *Westfälisches UB* III (Münster 1871) 497f no.966 (1275); Fritz Kern, *Acta imperii, Angliae et Franciae ab a.1267 ad a.1313* (Tübingen 1911) 42 no.64 (1290); and often elsewhere. The meaning of the term *administratio* and its application to the *regalia* has already been discussed (above, Ch.IIID n.7).

[38] *MGH Const* II 285 no.212 (1238): ". . . quilibet imperator . . . percipere debet integraliter et vacantibus ecclesiis omnia [scil. theloneum, moneta, officium sculteti, et iudicium seculare necnon et consimilia] usque ad concordem electionem habere, donec electus ab eo regalia recipiat. . . ."

[39] *MGH Const* II 117f no.94: ". . . nulli ecclesiarum prelato, qui insignia sua de manu imperiali non receperit seu qui non teneat clippeum, qui vulgariter dicitur herschilt, liceat possessiones ecclesie cui preest alicui infeudare, ita quod ipsum feudum perpetuo sit apud feudatarium permansurum."

[40] Henry (VII), *MGH Const* II 397 no.282: ". . . Donationes mansorum, concessiones feudorum, obligationes pignorum ante regalium receptionem facte sint in irritum revocande. . . ."

restore the unfortunate burgher to serfdom.[41] In other words, enactments requiring secular jurisdiction were null and void if performed by a prelate-elect without the *regalia*.

Familiar with the official conception of regalian investiture, for obvious reasons the vassals of imperial bishops were reluctant to render fealty to an ecclesiastical prince who had not yet been invested, and on occasion they even refused allegiance to a bishop-elect who lacked the *regalia*.[42] In documents granting or announcing the investiture of a prelate-elect, the German king sometimes concluded by commanding the vassals and subjects to obey their new ecclesiastical lord.[43] Such commands were, of course, formulary, but the formulas were not entirely empty, since they neatly expressed the jurisdictional meaning of a prelate-elect's investiture as understood by his vassals. Indeed, local custom at Verdun dictated special precautions to ascertain the jurisdictional competence of every new bishop-elect, for in the usage of Verdun, as a commission of inquiry reported to Rudolph of Hapsburg,

Neither the temporal justice nor the fealty of the bishopric of Verdun nor the keys of the city have been delivered over to the bishops . . . until they have shown to the chapter of Verdun and to the city the letter from the German king concerning the *regalia*.[44]

[41] Rudolph of Hapsburg, royal edict (1289), ed. H. Wartmann, *UB der Abtei Sanct Gallen* III (St Gall 1882) 255 no.1064: "Cum . . . quidam sub iurisdictione abbatum sancti Galli constituti a quibusdam abbatibus, qui nondum a nobis erant investiti de regalibus, ius civium receperint, . . . nos, volentes recepta huiusmodi iniuste et illicite iura civium reprobare, . . . mandamus, quatenus tales, qui iura premissa receperunt enormiter, pro servis habeatis, ut prius ante receptionem extiterant, ac ipsos a legitimis civium iuribus prorsus iudicetis expertes. . . ."

[42] As at Liège in 1245 (*MGH Ep.saec.XIII* II 64 no.90). Also, after each of two successive promotions to the see of Verdun, once in 1246 and again in 1253, it was necessary for the pope to command the vassals of the bishopric, under the grim threat of punishment as rebels, to take the oath of fealty to the uninvested bishop (*ibid.* II 117 no.155, and III 208 no.242); see below, Ch.XB.

[43] Hoogeweg, *Westfälisches UB* VI 167 no.583 (1253); Böhmer, *Acta imperii sel.* 312 no.385 (1268); Wilmans, *Westfälisches UB* III 497f no.966 (1275); Kern, *Acta imperii* 42 no.64 (1290); and often.

[44] Report to Rudolph of Hapsburg on an inquest concerning the imperial

It is not unlikely that elsewhere, too, before demanding fealty from his vassals or taking over the secular court, a new bishop-elect was required to present evidence of his investiture.

Before the mid-thirteenth century imperial custom strictly insisted that a bishop-elect appear in person to receive his investiture from the monarch. But thereafter, beginning with William of Holland and Richard of Cornwall, the German rulers more and more frequently waived this requirement in individual cases, either granting the *regalia* to the prelate-elect by letter or ordering him to receive the investiture from a designated imperial vicegerent.[45] However, despite this relaxation of the requirements for investiture, and despite the waning of German monarchical power, the insistence upon investiture before administration did not disappear, and concern over lawful possession of the *regalia* is still visible in the early fourteenth century. For example, unable to go in person to king Henry VII for his investiture, the bishop of Cambrai requested and received from Henry special permission to administer the temporalities of his church provisionally, until he could make the trip; and twice the bishop requested and received from Henry postponements of the deadline for his investiture.[46] Two such grants were made also to the next bishop of Cambrai, who was thereby allowed, as a special privilege, to administer his temporalities before his investiture.[47] In the same fashion, the uninvested bishop of Münster received extraordinary permission to administer his temporalities and his fiefs for a year.[48] Similar exemptions were still

---

frontier (1288), *MGH Const* III 398 no.410: ". . . la justice temporelz ne li fiei de l'aveschiei de Verdun ne les clers [i.e. clefs] de la dite citey ne ont estei delivrei as evesques, . . . c'est a dire a trois evesques trespasseis, tant qu'il horent moustrei au chapistre de Verdun et a la citei les lettres dou roy d'Alemengne de lors regales. . . ."

[45] Boerger, *Belehnungen der deutschen geistlichen Fürsten* 115ff.

[46] *MGH Const* IV 235f nos.267-69 (1309).

[47] *Ibid.* IV 290ff nos.337, 340 (1309-10); for the eventual investiture, see Winkelmann, *Acta imperii inedita* II (Innsbruck 1885) 243 no.382.

[48] *Westfälisches UB* VIII: *Die Urkunden des Bistums Münster von 1301-1325*, ed. R. Krumbholtz (Münster 1913) 196 no.556 (1310).

granted during the reign of Louis the Bavarian.[49] Thus, although the fourteenth century still honored the ancient imperial requirement of investiture before administration, often the requirement was literally honored in the breach. Apparently, imperial prelates found it at least expedient, and perhaps necessary, to get special dispensations in order to administer lawfully before receiving the investiture. By this prudence, however, the ecclesiastical prince of the fourteenth century was undoubtedly showing far more concern for the obedience of his subjects and the fealty of his vassals than for imperial sanctions or for an imperial principle apart from its possible consequences. Indeed, even the clergy of his own cathedral chapter might require his investiture as a condition of their obedience.[50]

Regale sacerdotium

Temporal possessions and secular jurisdiction brought to the bishop a special status. As tenants-in-chief of the king, the English archbishops and bishops formed part of the baronage.[51] Constitutionally, the German bishops were on at least equal terms with the lay nobles, for they were "not only bishops but also princes and lords."[52] In addition to the princely rank held by almost all German bishops, a few prelates—the archbishop of Cologne and the bishop of Würzburg —enjoyed a special ducal status; to symbolize and signalize their dukedom, these prelates issued coins showing the banner with which lay dukes and counts were invested.[53] Indeed, as

[49] Boerger, *Belehnungen* 122.

[50] *De antiqua consuetudine Alamanie,* and evidently also by the laws and customs of her own church, the abbess of Essen could not subinfeudate her vassals prior to her own investiture; see Sigmund Riezler, *Vatikanische Akten zur deutschen Geschichte in der Zeit Kaiser Ludwigs des Bayern* (Innsbruck 1891) 700 no.1933 (1338), and Baethgen, *ZRG* KA 10 (1920) 185, 189f (= *Mediaevalia* 122, 125f). Apparently from the customs of Cambrai, even the dean and the cathedral chapter seem to have been unwilling to obey an uninvested bishop-elect; Riezler, *op.cit.* 195 no.412 (1324). Also, above, n.44.

[51] Constitutions of Clarendon c.11, ed. Stubbs, *Select Charters* 166.
[52] *MGH SS* XXIII 928f; Hauck, *KG* V 66.
[53] Boerger, *Belehnungen* 28-35.

the imperial court observed in a decree of 1240, the German prince-bishop held both the "spiritual" and the "temporal" swords."[54] In imperial thought, the investiture with the *regalia* was the specific act which elevated the bishop-elect to the level of an imperial prince.[55]

To style the bishop a prince was commonplace. Yet in twelfth- and thirteenth-century constitutional thought, there were moments of extravagance, verging almost on playfulness, for in their attempts to portray the dignity and power of the ecclesiastical prince, contemporaries went far beyond the designation of the bishop as a mere temporal lord. The tenth century heard the first statement of the theme. Writing to his brother, archbishop Bruno of Cologne, Otto the Great rejoiced that a "royal priesthood" (*regale sacerdotium*) had come to his empire. Indeed, Bruno united in himself the offices of archbishop and "archduke," and combined the virtues of "both priestly religion and royal strength."[56] Especially since the Age of Reform, the papacy had increasingly reflected the attributes of a royal—or even imperial—office.[57] Following the papal example, the episcopal office with its princely status and its *regalia* began to acquire overtones of regality.

Of course, medieval men were familiar with Isidore of

[54] *MGH Const* II 444 no.333 (1240): ". . . sententiatum exstitit ad instantiam principis memorati [scil. electi Brixinensis], quod ratione gladiorum, spiritualis videlicet et materialis, quibus sua episcopalis dignitas est fulcita. . . ." The most recent addition to the extensive literature on the two swords is the interesting and controversial study by H. Hoffmann, "Die beiden Schwerter im hohen Mittelalter," *DA* 20 (1964) 78-114.

[55] For a charter of investiture by Conrad III (1150), see K. F. Stumpf, *Die Reichskanzler vornehmlich des X., XI. und XII. Jahrhunderts* (Innsbruck 1865-83) no.3569: "In consortium principum nostrorum suscepimus. . . ." Also, Hoogeweg, *Westfälisches UB* VI 167 no.583 (1253); *MGH Const* IV 1134 no.1133 (Salzburg 1313); Winkelmann, *Acta imperii inedita* II 231 no.356 (1309), 243 no.382 (1310); and often.

[56] Ruotger, *Vita Brunonis* c.20, ed. I. Ott (MGH SS.rer.Germ. n.s.10: Weimar 1951) 19. It should be stressed that the ducal power was *personally* held by Bruno in addition to the archiepiscopal office, and that the dukeship was *not* attached to his office or his church.

[57] On the "regalization" or "imperialization" of the papacy, see P. E. Schramm, "Sacerdotium und Regnum im Austausch ihrer Vorrechte," *SGreg* 2 (1947) 403-57, and Ullmann, *Growth of Papal Government* esp. ch.10.

Regalia and the Bishop-Elect

Seville's etymological explanation that rulers are called kings by virtue of exercising the kingly function (*reges a regendo vocati*).[58] In this sense, anyone who ruled might be called "king." At least as significant for the notion of the *regale sacerdotium*, however, was its scriptural foundation in the First Epistle of Peter—"You are a chosen people, a royal priesthood"—a classic statement which could be readily applied to the entire clergy.[59] On this authority, Hugh of St Victor interpreted the cleric's tonsure (that is, his *corona*) as a sign "that he is raised to royal power in Christ," and in similar fashion, a contemporary viewed the clergy as "kings" who "have their kingship in God."[60] Both for Hugh and for the unknown contemporary, this concept is eschatological, and, since it presupposes the cleric's "rejection of all temporal things," has little to do with the powers exercised by prelates on this earth.

In the generation of publicists around 1100, however, a far more concrete and terrestrial notion appeared, a notion which exalted the bishop and, because of his jurisdiction or even more particularly because of his *regalia*, regarded him as a monarch: according to the fervently royalist Anglo-Norman Anonymous of 1100, the bishop is a quasi-ruler endowed with administrative and jurisdictional powers, or, so to speak, a deputy with something of the king's royalty. And when the bishop succeeds to these powers through the royal investiture,

---

[58] *Etymologiae sive origines*, ed. W. M. Lindsay (2 vols. Oxford 1911) 9.3.4, 7.12.17; id., *De ecclesiasticis officiis* 2.4.4, PL 83 780.

[59] 1 *Petr*. 2.9: "Vos estis genus electum, regale sacerdotium."

[60] Hugh of St Victor, *De sacramentis christianae fidei* 2.3.1, PL 176 421: "coma capitis clerico in modum coronae tondetur . . . , ut per hoc detur intelligi, quod ad regiam in Christo potestatem assumitur." Cf. also C.12 q.1 c.7 (ascribed by Gratian to St Jerome, but apparently composed in the late 11th or, even more probably, early 12th century): ". . . [clerici] sunt reges, id est se et alios regentes in virtutibus, et ita in Deo regnum habent. Et hoc designat corona in capite. Hanc coronam habent ab institutione Romanae ecclesiae in signo regni, quod in Christo expectatur. Rasio uero capitis est temporalium omnium despositio. . . ." In general, see the valuable article by Luigi Prosdocimi, "Chierici e laici nella società occidentale del secolo XII," *Proceedings of the Second International Congress of Medieval Canon Law*, ed. S. Kuttner and J. J. Ryan (Vatican City 1965) 105-22.

he becomes thereby a *rex*, a lesser "king" subject to a greater king. Indeed, the pope "is a supreme pontiff insofar as he is a king."[61] Politically far more moderate than the Anglo-Norman Anonymous, Hugh of Fleury remarked of the bishop:

> He is called . . . a king because of the leadership which he must show to the people. . . . For the bishop seems . . . to have also the royal dignity.[62]

Even a Gregorian like Geoffrey of Vendôme could draw the same inference. Through the ecclesiastical investiture with ring and staff, as Geoffrey explained, the metropolitan grants to the new bishop a jurisdictional *cura pastoralis*, and thereby the metropolitan transforms him into a "duke of the Church" (*dux ecclesiae*), or even into a "king of the Church" (*rex ecclesiae*).[63] Still more, through his consecration the bishop has become the "vicar of Christ" and the "lord and emperor of Christians" (*dominus et imperator christianorum*).[64] Here, by asserting that the grant of a purely ecclesiastical jurisdiction confers royal or even imperial character on a bishop, Geoffrey has implicitly denied that regalian investiture can bestow such status. For Gerhoh of Reichersberg, however, the very term *regalia* suggested that the regalian prelate was a *rex*. As Gerhoh imagined it, churchmen with *regalia* might well have boasted:

---

[61] *Tractatus* 4, *MGH LdL* III 667: "Quod si quis dicat quod etiam sacerdos rex sit—omnis enim, qui regit rex iure potest appellari—hic pro eis melius facere videtur, ut rex instituatur per regem, minor per maiorem." Cf. also *ibid.* III 665, 672, 675, 685. For the statement that the *sacerdotium* is also *regale* ("quod est a rege dirivatum"), see *ibid.* III 668. On the pope's regality (*ibid.* III 679): "Nec offendatur domnus papa in his, que de rege dicta sunt, quoniam et ipse summus pontifex est, in quantum rex est." In general, (Kantorowicz, *King's Two Bodies* 56 n.30.

[62] *De regia potestate et sacerdotali dignitate* 1.10, *MGH LdL* II 477: "Hic [episcopus] . . . vocatur . . . rex propter ducatum, quem praebere populo debet. . . . Nam et regalem dignitatem habere . . . videtur episcopus"; Kantorowicz, *op.cit.* 56 n.30.

[63] Geoffrey of Vendôme, *Libelli* 2, 3, 7, *MGH LdL* II 685, 689, 697.

[64] Id., *Libelli* 3, 7, *ibid.* II 687, 695.

Regalia and the Bishop-Elect

Possessing not only the *sacerdotalia* in tithes and offerings but also many *regalia* from the donation of kings, we are, in a certain sense, both kings and priests of the Lord.[65]

In another of his works Gerhoh pointed out that Christ was clad both in white and in purple garments, signifying His priestly and imperial rule, and with Christ as model, the bishop partakes of the same twofold character. For by investing the bishop with his *regalia*, the monarch confers upon him the purple garment of imperial rule.[66] In the thirteenth century, from the fact that the archbishop of Canterbury has various governmental and judicial duties in the service of the king, Francis Accursius could derive the conclusion that "the title of king is properly applied to the archbishop."[67] Addressing himself to the same point, an anonymous French pamphleteer asserted that

Any bishop is temporal and spiritual lord in his own city, and thus he is a monarch holding both forms of principality there.[68]

[65] *De investigatione Antichristi* 1.69, *MGH LdL* III 388: " 'At,' inquiunt, 'nos qui non solum sacerdotalia in decimis et oblationibus, set et regalia multa ex regum donatione tenemus, quodammodo et reges et sacerdotes Domini sumus, ideoque a populo non solum obedientiam in ecclesiasticis, sed et fidelitatem nobis iurari exigimus ad defensionem videlicet regalium simul et pontificalium beati Petri.' " Gerhoh's hypothetical spokesmen here were apparently the pope and the higher Roman clergy, but these remarks (with the possible exception of the last phrase) would be equally applicable to the German bishops. See Kantorowicz, *op.cit.* 185 n.294.

[66] Gerhoh, *Liber de novitatibus huius temporis* c.12, *MGH LdL* III 296f; cf. *Luc.* 23.11, and *Ioh.* 19.2.

[67] Francis Accursius, *Arenga coram domino papa* (1278) §§ 26f: "Cum enim rex a regendo dicatur et cum . . . sententiis regat rex, . . . et sic potest etiam vilissimo iudici ecclesiastico hoc vocabulum adaptari, cum subditos habeat regere. . . . At tum proprie Cantuariensi archiepiscopo regis vocabulum adaptatur, cum facta secularia regni habeat gubernare, . . . quia ad parlamenta regis sicut baro alius consuevit vocari et in secularibus negociis regi suum prebere consilium et assensum." See George L. Haskins and E. H. Kantorowicz, "A Diplomatic Mission of Francis Accursius and His Oration before Pope Nicholas III," *EHR* 58 (1943) 436, 446; the full text of the "harangue" is edited on pp.440-47.

[68] *Quaestio in utramque partem*, ed. M. Goldast, *Monarchia* II (Frankfurt 1614) 1067: "Sicut dicimus quod aliquis episcopus est dominus tempo-

Indeed, it is not surprising that precisely because of their princely status directly under the ruler, thirteenth-century German bishops could draw upon the same tradition of thought and could regard themselves with pride as truly a *regale sacerdotium.*[69]

---

ralis et spiritualis in sua civitate et sic est ibi monarcha utrumque obtinens principatum, sic ergo concedimus quod papa habet monarchiam utriusque potestatis in urbe, non tamen in orbe"; Wilks, *Journal of Theological Studies* n.s.8 (1957) 71. In this passage the anonymous author is close to the assertion that the bishop (or pope) is *rex in civitate sua* and has the attributes of sovereignty.

[69] This concept is implicit in the complaint of several German bishops over their subjection to the duke of Saxony (*MGH Const* II 633 no.460 [1252]): ". . . sub eo non posset dici regale sacerdotium sed ducale. . . ." For the episcopate, the desire to hold directly of the king or emperor was a recurrently stated theme; cf. also the bishop of Lausanne's attempt to avoid subordination to duke Berthold of Zähringen (*MGH Const* I 388 no.281 [1181-86]), and the efforts by the bishop of Prague to remain independent of the duke of Bohemia (Gerlach of Mühlhausen, *Continuatio Vincentii Pragensis* anno 1182, *MGH SS* XVII 693).

CHAPTER IX

THE CHURCH
AND THE *REGALIA*

1. The Legacy of 1122

chere is a famous conversation in Sir Arthur Conan Doyle's *Silver Blaze*, often retold, for it is a favorite exemplum among historians. Discussing the case with an inspector from Scotland Yard, Sherlock Holmes commented on the curious incident of the dog in the nighttime. With magnificent lack of imagination, the inspector remarked, "The dog did nothing in the nighttime." "That," replied Holmes, "was the curious incident."

Our case is comparable: After shaking and transforming the political and ecclesiastical institutions of Europe through almost two generations, the first great struggle between empire and papacy—a conflict in which the question of lay investiture was a central concern—ended with an uneasy compromise at Worms in 1122.[1] The Concordat of Worms was well publicized, and copies of the two documents composing the Concordat were deliberately and widely disseminated throughout Europe.[2] Obviously, contemporaries recognized the importance of this armistice between empire and papacy, and among the chroniclers recording the event there was a tendency to emphasize Henry V's concessions to the Church

---

[1] This paragraph and the next one follow closely the discussion by A. Hofmeister, *Forschungen und Versuche: Festschrift D. Schäfer* 100-09, 121f.

[2] *Ibid.* 99f, esp.100 n.1.

The Bishop-Elect

more than Calixtus II's concessions to Henry.[3] The official biography of Calixtus in the *Liber pontificalis* and the papal records in the *Liber censuum* reveal the full text of Henry's charter, but bypass the Calixtinum.[4] Above all, though the Concordat was concluded scarcely two decades before the publication of the *Decretum*, and though Gratian's massive compilation embraces most of the twelfth century's major ideas and concerns, it contains neither of the two documents, nor even a passing mention of them![5] The dog did indeed behave strangely.

Curialists and reformers were profoundly dissatisfied with the settlement at Worms, and almost immediately there was opposition to the legal arrangements which the Concordat sanctioned. Hence the "conspiracy of silence" about the embarrassing papal concessions to Henry V.[6] On Calixtus II's accession in 1119, a well-wisher had congratulated him with the hope that in the struggle for the Church's liberty, the new pontiff would be the "emperor of a victorious triumph."[7] In fact, Calixtus chose to put a bold face on the treaty of 1122 and to publicize it as a victory for the papacy. At his orders, a new fresco in the Lateran Palace proclaimed this triumph, evidently depicting Henry V in the act of making his grant to the Church and apparently reproducing the text of the emperor's charter. In this painting, however, the Calixtinum seems to have been ignored, for only by this silence could one consider the Concordat a victory.[8] But despite Calixtus's

[3] *Ibid.* 97-99.
[4] Boso, *Vita Calixti II*, ed. Duchesne, *Lib. pont.* II 378; similarly, Cencius, *Liber censuum*, ed. P. Fabre and L. Duchesne (3 vols. Paris 1905-52) I 368, II 93.
[5] Sägmüller, *Bischofswahl* 18; Hofmeister, *op.cit.* 102 n.1.
[6] Hoffmann, *DA* 15 (1959) 434.
[7] J. Ramackers, *PU Frankreich* VI (Abh. Göttingen 3rd ser. 41: Göttingen 1958) 87f no.30.
[8] Mentioned by Pandulph, *Vita Calixti II*, ed. Duchesne, *Lib. pont.* II 322, III 168, the picture was copied in the later 16th century by Onophrius Panvinius. In general, see Duchesne, *op.cit.* II 325f, 378f, and P. Lauer, *Le palais de Latran* (Paris 1911) 162ff, 478; corrections by Hofmeister, *op.cit.* 121f, by Hoffmann, *op.cit.* 433, and, above all, by Gerhart Ladner, "I mosaici e gli affreschi ecclesiastico-politici nell'antico Palazzo Latera-

public attitude, most papal partisans were far from pleased with the Concordat, which they regarded as provisional, as an interim agreement made on unfavorable terms. Though he had been instrumental in the negotiation of the treaty, archbishop Adalbert of Mainz was soon complaining that the elections in the emperor's presence simply legalized the intimidation of the electors:

> Through the opportunity of [the emperor's] presence, the Church of God must undergo the same slavery as before, or an even more oppressive one.[9]

In 1123, when the two documents of the Concordat were read aloud to the prelates gathered at the First Lateran Council, for understandable reasons Henry V's charter was ratified. But when the assembled churchmen heard the Calixtinum, a great clamor arose as the indignant audience shouted its opposition to these concessions: *"Non placet, non placet!"* The tumult was eventually quieted—not without difficulty—by the explanation that, "To reestablish peace, such things should not be approved, but tolerated."[10] In 1125 the death of Henry V furnished the perfect occasion for an attack upon the imperial prerogatives which Calixtus had recognized in 1122. Since the Curialists and reformers did not forget the limited validity of the papal concessions, they could feel reassured that the charter given to Henry had expired with his death, for as they declared at Rome, the Calixtinum "was granted to him alone and not to his successors."[11] Indeed, when the German princes met to elect Henry's successor, the entire issue was reopened. At this gathering the reformers apparently enunciated a program which opposed all imperial

nense," *Rivista di archeologia cristiana* 12 (1935) 269-80, esp. 272f, fig.5; id., *Die Papstbildnisse des Altertums und des Mittelalters* I (Vatican City 1941) 199ff.

[9] Jaffé, *Bibl.* V 519; see also E. Bernheim, "Die Praesentia regis im Wormser Konkordat," *Historische Vierteljahrschrift* 10 (1907) 197f.

[10] Gerhoh of Reichersberg, *Libellus de ordine donorum S. Spiritus*, in *MGH LdL* III 280.

[11] Above, Ch.VIIв n.7.

influence upon episcopal elections, as well as the practice of election in the emperor's presence, and the precedence of investiture before consecration.[12]

After 1122 there was, within the imperial realms, a broad spectrum of opinion on the episcopal *regalia*. To be sure, most German prelates not only accepted the *regalia* but also freely recognized the attendant obligations to the emperor. Still, even after the Concordat of Worms, critics continued to denounce the role of the *regalia* in the life of the Church. The criticism came from two directions: so to speak, from the Left and from the Right. The radical critics of the *regalia* were opposed to all ownership of property by the Church. Concerned over the secularization of the Church as a consequence of wealth, they feared the nexus of feudal relations because it involved the Church in worldly matters and in problems of property, that is, because it deflected the Church from that poverty which would best serve its other-worldly mission. As the extreme example of this position, Arnold of Brescia preached that bishops holding *regalia* are inescapably damned, and that all clerics should live solely from first-fruits, offerings, and tithes.[13] Fear of the Church's growing wealth could drive an Arnold of Brescia into heresy, but a pale reflection of Arnold's views can be seen even in some of the most rigidly orthodox of twelfth-century churchmen. St Bernard of Clairvaux, for instance, suspected the Church's wealth as a potential source of spiritual weakness and corruption, and though he defended the papal *plenitudo potestatis*, he insisted that the pope should rule "in matters of crime, not in matters of property" (*in criminibus, non in possessionibus*).[14] Except for the renunciation briefly offered by Paschal II, however,

12 *Narratio de electione Lotharii* c.6, *MGH SS* XII 511; K. Hampe, *Deutsche Kaisergeschichte*, 10th ed. rev. F. Baethgen (Heidelberg 1949) 109-11.

13 Otto of Freising, *Gesta Friderici* 2.28, 3rd ed. Waitz and Simson 133: "Dicebat enim [Arnaldus] nec clericos proprietatem nec episcopos regalia nec monachos possessiones habentes aliqua ratione salvari posse"; see also Carlyle, *Mediaeval Political Theory* IV 343-46.

14 *De consideratione* 1.6, *PL* 182 736.

those in positions of power and authority seldom seemed to share this suspicion of the Church's worldly wealth. Although most were reluctant to relinquish any part of the properties and rights administered by the Church, some of them retained their concern over the *regalia* because, through the *regalia*, the emperor could exercise a continuing control over ecclesiastical elections and over ecclesiastical property. For this reason, as a chronicler explained near the end of the twelfth century,

> The lord pope was strongly opposed to the power and esteem which the lord emperor had in the episcopal churches and greater abbeys.[15]

Here the Gregorian tradition survived in the continuing struggle to limit imperial influence on the episcopate and to assure the Church's freedom from lay domination.

As a specific example of these two tendencies in criticism, Gerhoh of Reichersberg managed to adopt both positions: on the one hand, fearful over the danger that the Church's power and wealth had brought corrupting influences; on the other hand, concerned to keep the Church's property, and anxious over the danger that the *regalia* would serve as a lever for lay control over the Church.[16] Throughout a literary career which stretched from the late 1120's to the late 1160's, he regarded the prelates' possession of *regalia* as a crucial problem for the Church, and as the central issue in the rela-

---

[15] Gilbert of Mons, *Chronicon hanoniense* anno 1192, *MGH SS* XXI 580: "Dominus papa potestati et dignitati, quam dominus imperator in ecclesiis episcopalibus et abbatiis maioribus habebat, valde erat contrarius."

[16] Important recent studies of Gerhoh have largely replaced earlier works. In general, see Damien Van den Eynde, *L'oeuvre littéraire de Géroch de Reichersberg* (Rome 1957), and especially the authoritative biography by P. Classen, *Gerhoch von Reichersberg* (Wiesbaden 1960). Through the excellent edition by D. and O. Van den Eynde and P. Rijmersdael, *Opera inedita* (2 vols. Rome 1955-56), the incomplete edition by E. Sackur (*MGH LdL* III 131-525) is partially superseded. For Gerhoh's views on the *regalia*, see: Carlyle, *op.cit.* IV 347-60; Ott, *ZRG KA* 35 (1948) 258-72; Erich Meuthen, *Kirche und Heilsgeschichte bei Gerhoh von Reichersberg* (Leiden 1959) 60-86; and above all, Classen, *op.cit.* esp. 41-44, 100-02, 146f, 177-79, 236f, 296f, 317.

tions between *regnum* and *sacerdotium*. In 1142 he even urged the summoning of a general council to solve the problem.[17] Though his specific doctrines on the *regalia* were not typical of any school or group, there were undoubtedly many who shared his grave concern over the state of the Church and over the unhappy legacy of the Investiture Struggle. In his first work, a treatise *On God's Edifice*, written only six years after the Concordat, his attitudes reflect the savage violence of the conflict which had just ended, as well as the uneasiness of the peace established at Worms. Indeed, his essay may well be viewed as a commentary on the Concordat or, more precisely, on the unhappy condition of the Church following the compromise of 1122.[18] In his opinion, however, the monarchs did not bear the chief responsibility for the failure of the Church's spiritual mission. Rather, the main object of his attack was the dual status of the imperial bishop, half cleric and half warrior, who owes homage and fealty in return for his *regalia*, who must parcel out his church's lands to his vassals, and who must serve the monarch by leading his contingent of knights into war. Thus Gerhoh believed that the root of the problem lay in the feudal bonds linking the prelate to the king above and to his vassals below. As the worst example of the secularized prince-prelate, Gerhoh singled out archbishop Adalbert I of Mainz, whose "sumptuous banquets" were daily attended by "many princes and knights."[19] Gerhoh's attack on Adalbert highlights one of the crucial changes which had emerged in the immediate aftermath of the Concordat: Before the Concordat, of course, Adalbert had led the German Gregorians in the struggle for the Church's freedom,[20] but since 1122 the reform movement

---

[17] *De ordine donorum sancti Spiritus*, in *MGH LdL* III 280 (= ed. Van den Eynde, *Op. ined.* I 85); Classen, *op.cit.* 102, 198.

[18] Classen, *op.cit.* 41. The 1st recension of the *Opusculum de aedificio Dei* was prepared in 1128-29, the 2nd (only slightly revised) in 1138.

[19] *De aed. Dei* cc.23f, 72, *MGH LdL* III 153f, 177. Sackur (p.153 n.1) wrongly ascribed these references to Adalbert II; cf. Classen, *op.cit.* 47 n.54.

[20] To be sure, long after 1122 Adalbert still showed deep concern for the Church's *libertas*; see above, n.9 and Ch.VIIIв n.17.

had concentrated its attention on a new program. Like most German prelates, Adalbert enjoyed his princely status and administered his *regalia* with enthusiasm. In contrast to such former Gregorians, however, men like Gerhoh, working for the reform of the clergy and especially of the cathedral chapters, were now the leaders of the reform movement in Germany.[21]

The Church's primary difficulty, Gerhoh maintained, stems from the possession of *regalia*, which blur the proper boundary between the secular and ecclesiastical spheres. In his own words:

> Truly, the *regalia* and the *ecclesiastica* are so much mingled that a bishop would now seem to rob the monarchy if he wanted to refuse the Church's properties to knights.[22]

To unravel this confusion and to counter the secularization of the episcopate, Gerhoh distinguished three categories of ecclesiastical property: tithes and offerings, landed estates, and royal offices.[23] First, the tithes and offerings of the faithful (*decimae, primitiae, oblationes*) belong inalienably to the Church, and no layman may hold them without sacrilege. Second, the Church's lands (*agri, villae*) are "for the use of the poor" and must remain forever in the Church's possession. As his third category, Gerhoh pointed out the secular offices held by prince-prelates (*regales ac publicae functiones* or *regales et militares administrationes*). These "dukeships, countships, tolls, and mints pertain to the secular world," and the Church can easily afford to give them up, for "they cannot be administered by bishops without a certain apostasy from their order."[24] From his threefold distinction, it is evi-

21 Classen, *op.cit.* 46f, 317.
22 *De aed. Dei* c.14, *MGH LdL* III 145: "Sic etenim confusa sunt regalia et aecclesiastica, ut iam videretur episcopus regnum spoliare, si aecclesiae facultates militibus vellet denegare."
23 *Id.* c. 25, *ibid.* 154; in general, on the *regalia* and other forms of property or jurisdiction, see also *id.* cc.8, 16f, 21, 23, 34, *ibid.* 140, 147-49, 152-54, 159.
24 *Id.* cc.22, 23, *ibid.* 153. Gerhoh qualified this argument by admitting

dent that Gerhoh could never have agreed with Arnold of Brescia, who believed that "neither clerics owning property, nor bishops holding *regalia*, nor monks having possessions could, on any account, be saved."[25] Indeed, almost twenty years after writing the treatise *On God's Edifice*, Gerhoh opposed one of Arnold's followers in a disputation at Rome on the question of the *regalia*.[26] The threefold distinction makes it equally apparent that Gerhoh did not endorse Paschal II's renunciation of the *regalia*.[27] In 1111 Paschal had recognized the regalian character of much of the Church's land and had included these lands in his renunciation. In contrast, Gerhoh admitted the royal (literally: regalian) origin of some ecclesiastical lands but refused to relinquish them.[28] To support his argument, Gerhoh devised a further distinction between a ruler's private or dynastic wealth (*res privata*), which he can freely give to the Church, and the property held by the ruler in his public capacity (*res publica* or *regni facultas*), which he can alienate only with the consent

---

the principle that anything given to the Church is thereafter inalienable, and by refusing to explain how the Church could lawfully alienate these *regales et militares administrationes* ("Quibus ego ad presens non respondeo, sed illud simpliciter affirmo").

[25] Above, n.13. For a comparison of the ideas and careers of Gerhoh and Arnold, see the valuable remarks by Classen, *op.cit.* 105-07, 130f, 225, who perhaps overstresses the similarity of their thought (cf. esp. pp.106, 183).

[26] Mentioned in *Comm. in ps.LXIV* and in *Liber de novitatibus huius temporis* c.11, *MGH LdL* III 447, 296; though deposited in the papal archives, Gerhoh's transcript of the disputation is lost. In general, see Classen, *op.cit.* 130f, 418f. Primarily concerned with the *regalia* of St Peter, the debate undoubtedly also dealt with the problem of the episcopal *regalia*.

[27] Cf. Carlyle, *Mediaeval Political Theory* IV 350, and Ott, *ZRG KA* 35 (1948) 266f; for the preferable interpretation, Classen, *op.cit.* 43f.

[28] Classen, *op.cit.* 42 n.14. It is, of course, significant that although Gerhoh's list of specific *regalia* derived from the documents produced by the negotiations of 1111 (*MGH Const* I 138f, 141 nos.85, 90), his list of *regalia* (unlike the enumeration of 1111, which cites *curtes* as *regalia*) omits all mention of ecclesiastical lands. See *De aed. Dei* cc.23, 25, and *De investigatione Antichristi* c.24, *MGH LdL* III 153f, 333; also, cf. Ott, *op.cit.* 263f, 271.

of his magnates.[29] By minimizing the extent of the ecclesiastical lands originally granted from the king's public property (*villae regalis pertinentiae*), Gerhoh implied that the monarchs had enriched the churches almost exclusively from their private holdings.[30] Like the offerings of any private person, a king's private grants were, in Gerhoh's view, unencumbered and inalienable property of the Church. Since the bishops' obligation to the king could not be based on his private gifts to the churches, but only on gifts made from public property, and since Gerhoh maintained that little ecclesiastical land derived from this latter source, he could feel that he had practically refuted the royal claims to service by bishops in return for their churches' lands. In any case, as he explained, the bestowal of *regalia* does not necessarily secularize the Church, for Constantine the Great conferred *regalia* (that is, public property) on the churches without demanding military service. Rhetorically, Gerhoh asked:

> Who granted to the bishop the power of summoning knights to arms and of administering the other duties of a duke— a power which neither the blessed Sylvester nor any other bishop had . . . under Constantine?[31]

For his own age, however, Gerhoh believed that if the *regalia* in the narrower sense—that is, the bishops' secular offices— were returned to the monarch, there would no longer be any reason for the dangerous feudal bond between bishop and king or vassal. Few, if any, German prelates would have supported Gerhoh's wish to relinquish the regalian offices, but it seems probable that some of his contemporaries (for example, archbishop Conrad of Salzburg) shared, at least in part,

---

[29] *De aed. Dei* c.21, *MGH LdL* III 152. Ott (*op.cit.* 261-63) interprets this passage as evidence for the influence of Romano-canonical thought and as evidence for a concept of State distinct from the person of the king; against her view, however, cf. the reservations expressed by Kantorowicz, *King's Two Bodies* 172 n.250, and Classen, *op.cit.* 43 esp. n.21.

[30] *De aed. Dei* cc.17, 21, *MGH LdL* III 149, 152.

[31] *Id.* c.21, *ibid.* 152.

his determination to see the Church hold her lands freely, without any obligation to the king.[32]

In the 1120's and 1130's, with his radical solution to the problem of the *regalia*, Gerhoh had hoped to clear the way for ecclesiastical reform, but without either impoverishing the Church or undermining the empire. Though this reformist objective remained, in general, a lifelong concern, the years between 1138 and 1142 mark a watershed in the development of his views on the *regalia*. It is unnecessary to trace in detail the transformations of these later views—indeed, the task would be imposing, since Gerhoh's doctrine on the *regalia* altered in each new work[33]—but a few crucial elements must be noted: With his *Book on the Order of the Gifts of the Holy Spirit* in 1142, Gerhoh abandoned his utopian proposal to relinquish the regalian offices. Despite much uneasiness, he was resigned to the Church's possession of these *regalia*, but he stipulated that monarchs should demand neither service nor tribute in return for the Church's lands and that the regalian offices should be administered by secular judges. Moreover, he asserted that the Concordat of Worms had introduced homage by bishops into German usage, and he never gave up his opposition to the custom by which bishops did homage to kings.[34] In fact, only late in his life did he explicitly admit that bishops might lawfully swear fealty to kings.[35] The privileges granted by Calixtus II in the Concordat were, he believed, an "extorted concession,"[36] and he vigorously attacked the various provisions of the Calixtinum.[37] By 1142

[32] Above, Ch.VIIIB.
[33] Classen, *op.cit.* 8f; it is therefore misleading to divide the evolution of his thought neatly into an early, middle, and late phase (cf. Ott, *op.cit.* 259).
[34] *De ordine donorum S. Spiritus*, ed. Van den Eynde, *Op. ined.* I 110, 83f (cf. 75); *De investigatione Antichristi* 1.72, *MGH LdL* III 392f.
[35] *Liber de novitatibus huius temporis* c.12, *MGH LdL* III 297; *De inv. Antichristi* 1.72, *ibid.* 392f.
[36] *De ordine donorum S. Spiritus*, in *MGH LdL* III 280.
[37] There is, of course, no evidence that Gerhoh regarded the Calixtinum as still valid; his explicit attacks were directed against the Calixtinum as a historical document, his implicit attacks were against existing custom (which could, in part, be traced back to the Calixtinum and beyond).

The Church and the *Regalia*

Gerhoh was jubilant over the fact that episcopal elections were no longer held in the king's presence,[38] and it goes without saying that he denied to the emperor any right to settle a disputed election.[39] In opposition to prevailing imperial custom, Gerhoh consistently urged the precedence of consecration before investiture. As he explained, Christ donned first the white garment given by Herod and signifying priestly office, and only later the purple robe of royalty mockingly bestowed by Pilate's soldiers. In Gerhoh's view, the bishop should follow Christ's exemplary procedure by receiving first his episcopal consecration and then his *regalia*.[40]

Gerhoh's views clearly reflect the violence of the conflicts between *imperium* and *sacerdotium*. In France, on the other hand, since lay investiture was never the occasion for an all-out protracted war between monarchy and papacy, one can speak more accurately of an "investiture problem" than of an Investiture Struggle.[41] There is consequently no contemporary French counterpart to Gerhoh. With relative ease, French thinkers were reconciled to the Church's bond with the secular monarchs, a bond which recognized not only the ruler's proprietary rights over the possessions which he and his predecessors had bestowed upon the churches, but also the obligations of prelates toward their princely benefactors. St Bernard of Clairvaux, for example, did not contest the bishop's duty to his monarch. In a treatise on the episcopal office, he took it for granted that the prelate is bound to participate in the king's "courts, councils, affairs, and military expeditions."[42] Writing about 1134, Hugh of St Victor tranquilly accepted a similar position:

[38] Above, n.36. Already in *De aed. Dei* c.8, *MGH LdL* III 142, Gerhoh did not consider election *in presentia regis* a normal procedure: "episcopi . . . facta electione ad palatium ire compelluntur, quatenus a rege . . . regalia suscipiant."

[39] *Comm. in ps.LXIV*, in *MGH LdL* III 452.

[40] *Liber de novitatibus huius temporis* c.12, *MGH LdL* III 296f (cf. *Luc.* 23.11, *Ioh.* 19.2); also, *Comm. in ps.LXIV*, in *MGH LdL* III 452.

[41] Pointed out by Becker, *Studien zum Investiturproblem* 7.

[42] *De moribus et officio episcoporum* 8.31, *PL* 182 829; W. Williams, *Saint Bernard of Clairvaux* (Manchester 1935) 252.

313

With regard to earthly possessions, earthly princes . . .
sometimes concede only utility to a church, sometimes both
utility and power.[43]

By "utility," Hugh meant simply the usufruct of the property,
but by "power," he indicated a grant of secular jurisdiction
over the subjects inhabiting the lands conferred upon a
church. To be sure, a prelate holding full regalian rights, both
utilitas and *potestas*, must exercise his secular jurisdiction
indirectly, through a lay adjutant. Under all circumstances,
the prince's prerogatives are unimpaired: An endowed church
must acknowledge that its secular power remains royal in
character, and that the royal claim upon its possessions is
inalienable. In return for the possessions, "if reason and
necessity should demand," the prelate owes obedience
(*obsequium*) to the prince.

Thus, despite the distress of certain reformers, most
twelfth-century churchmen accepted the *regalia* and the
attendant royal rights in a matter-of-fact way. Still, although
many prelates, within the empire and elsewhere, were reconciled—often quite happily—to the possession of *regalia*, the
papacy remained uneasy over this continuing custom.[44] During successive negotiations with three German kings, Innocent
III tried to limit the monarchical rights arising from the
tenure of *regalia* by imperial bishoprics and abbeys. As a
result, in 1209 Otto of Brunswick renounced his claims to
the income from "properties . . . of vacant churches," and in
1213 Frederick II made the same concession, repeating it in
1216 with the added renunciation of any claim to the rever-
sion of regalian jurisdictional rights during an episcopal

---

[43] *De sacramentis* 2.2.7, *PL* 176 419f.
[44] Except for the unsatisfactory book by Pöschl (above, Ch.VIIᴀ n.2),
specialized studies of the *regalia* have generally concentrated on the
12th century. Scattered remarks on the 13th-century *regalia* can be found
in various works, but it would be useful to have a systematic study which
also treated the Church's legislation on these rights. For the first half of
the 13th century, see the brief discussion by Erich Klingelhöfer, *Die
Reichsgesetze von 1220, 1231-32 und 1235* (Weimar 1955) 11-20, 130-37.

vacancy.[45] Nonetheless, Innocent's attempts were not markedly successful, for thereafter Frederick II enjoyed the income from the *regalia* of vacant bishoprics.[46] Later in the thirteenth century the papacy made similar efforts in its relations with the kingdom of Sicily.[47] And as Gerhoh of Reichersberg had once hoped, eventually the question of the *regalia* even found its way onto the agenda of a general council: In 1274 the Second Council of Lyons recognized *old* claims to the *regalia*, based upon a founder's privilege "or from ancient custom," but it flatly prohibited any *new* claims to regalian rights in church or monastery.[48]

2. Canonistic Verdicts on the *Regalia*[1]

It is, perhaps, not surprising that master Gratian omitted from the *Decretum* all of the crucial documents on the agreements and near-agreements negotiated between empire and papacy during the first third of the twelfth century.[2] Yet with the vast range of the *Decretum*'s contents, he could not completely avoid such issues as lay investiture and the *regalia* of bishops.[3] Earlier canonical collections afforded Gratian many

[45] Philip of Swabia (1203), *MGH Const* II 9ff nos.8f; Otto of Brunswick (1209), *ibid.* 37 no.31 (= Kempf, *RNI* 401 no.189); Frederick II (1213, 1216), *MGH Const* II 58, 68, nos.47, 56.

[46] *MGH Const* II 285 no.212 (above, Ch.VIIIc n.38).

[47] For example, *MGH Ep.saec.XIII* III 516 no.539 §§19, 23 (1263).

[48] *Conc. Lugd. II* c.12 (*VI* 1.6.13).

[1] Most of this section has appeared in my article on "The Obligations of Bishops with 'Regalia,'" *Proceedings 2nd Int. Cong. of Med. Can. Law*, ed. Kuttner and Ryan, 123-37. I should like to thank the Institute of Medieval Canon Law for permission to reprint this material here.

[2] Moreover, these early 12th-century documents found virtually no echo in the decretists' works. As a striking but isolated example of indirect influence, the word *privilegium* (*MGH Const* I 572 no.399) reappeared about 1169 in the *Summa Elegantius in iure diuino* 1.104 (kindly pointed out to me by Professor Kuttner in the page proofs of the forthcoming edition). The word was presumably transmitted by Gerhoh of Reichersberg, *De aed. Dei* gl. ad c. 154, and *De investigatione Antichristi* c.25, *MGH LdL* III 190, 335.

[3] For Gratian's views on the *regalia*, see A. Stickler, "Magistri Gratiani sententia de potestate Ecclesiae in Statum," *Apollinaris* 21 (1948) 55f, 62f; Francesco Marchesi, "De rationibus quae intercedunt inter Ecclesiam et res publicas in Gratiani Decreto," *SGrat* 3 (1955) 187f; and above all, the analysis by Hoffmann, *DA* 15 (1959) 434-37.

texts relevant to these problems, and these collections also offered him a variety of conflicting positions about them. Characteristically, Gratian presented material on both sides of the question. Included in his *distinctio* on ecclesiastical election, two imperialist documents forged during the struggles of the late eleventh century insist that the emperor's consent and investiture are prerequisite to any episcopal consecration. Still, for Gratian's dialectic of opposing positions, the value of these two texts was their testimony favoring imperial influence in papal elections—needless to say, Gratian himself did not actually accept the validity of this imperial "right"—and Gratian's rubrics indicate no concern here with the issue of investiture.[4] In a *quaestio* largely devoted to problems of ecclesiastical property, however, several *capitula* demonstrate that a cleric should never accept a church from the hands of a layman.[5] For as Gratian asserted, "churches as well as ecclesiastical property" are exclusively at the bishop's disposal, and apparently, in Gratian's view these *res ecclesiarum* were the "tithes" and "offerings" of the faithful.[6] Even more sharply to the point, Gratian also included here two synodal decrees by Gregory VII and one by Paschal II, all of them forbidding to laymen "the investiture of bishoprics or of any ecclesiastical office."[7] It is clear that Gregory, Paschal, and Gratian agreed on this prohibition against investiture in this broad sense, as the investiture of a bishop with his church and his episcopal dignity, yet their remarks seem

---

[4] D.63 cc.22, 23; see above, Ch.VIIв n.18.

[5] C.16 q.7 cc.14, 16, 17, 20. Cf. also the denunciations of lay domination of or interference with Church property, in C.16 q.7 cc.18, 25.

[6] C.16 q.7 pr.: "Quod autem ecclesias de manu laicorum nec abbati nec alicui liceat accipere omnium canonum testatur auctoritas. Generaliter enim tam ecclesiae quam res ecclesiarum in episcoporum potestate consistunt. Laici autem nec sua, nec episcoporum auctoritate decimas uel ecclesias possidere possunt." For further evidence that in this context Gratian was referring to tithes and offerings, cf. C.16 q.7 cc.1, 3-8 and dict.p.cc.6, 9, 28.

[7] C.16 q.7 cc.12, 13, 17. It is, by the way, noteworthy that an extraordinary number of *capitula* in C.16 q.7 date from the period 1059-1123: cc.1-2, 11-13, 16-20, 25, 39.

equally to leave open the possibility that an investiture specifically confined to the *regalia* would be lawful.

Since Gratian was familiar with the radical Gregorian doctrine expounded by Placidus of Nonantula, it is not surprising that—like Placidus—he avoided the term *regalia*. Nonetheless, Gratian's position was thoroughly moderate, for at least in the case of those bishops who have been granted regalian lands (*predia*), he was readily willing to recognize their dependence upon and obligation to the emperor.[8] Discussing the right of clerics to bear arms and to perform military service, Gratian's remarks echoed Placidus's language, but the canonist's thought differed markedly from the views of Placidus, who had refused to sanction any division between the *corporalia* and the *spiritualia* of a church. Gratian distinguished two kinds of bishop: There are, he wrote, bishops who are content with tithes and offerings, and since they do not hold the *temporalia*, "in every kingdom they are free from all worldly exactions," for they have "nothing in common with the princes of the world."

However, there are others who—not content with tithes and first-fruits—possess lands, towns, castles, and cities. In return for these things, they owe tribute to Caesar, unless by imperial generosity they have gained immunity from this.[9]

[8] C.11 q.1 dict.p.c.26: "Clerici ex offitio sunt subpositi episcopo, ex possessionibus prediorum inperatori sunt obnoxii. Ab episcopo unctionem, decimationes et primitias accipiunt; ab inperatore uero prediorum possessiones nanciscuntur. . . ." Concerned with a legal process between clerics, and *de prediis*, this *quaestio* examines (and denies) the lawfulness of clerics' appearing before a secular judge.

[9] C.23 q.8 dict.p.c.20: ". . . Sed notandum est, quosdam episcopos Leuitica tantum portione esse contentos. . . . His nichil commune est cum principibus seculi, quia temporalia penitus abiciunt, ne eorum occasione legibus inperatorum obnoxii teneantur. Talibus nulla occasio relinquitur occupationis secularis miliciae, quia, cum de decimis et primiciis uiuunt . . . in omni regno a terrenis exactionibus liberi sunt. . . . Porro alii sunt, qui non contenti decimis et primiciis, predia, uillas, et castella, et ciuitates possident, ex quibus Cesari debent tributa, nisi inperiali benignitate immunitatem promeruerint ab huiusmodi. . . ." Cf. Placidus, *De honore ecclesiae* Prologus, *MGH LdL* II 568: "Si vero solummodo decimis et primitiis et

These "lands, towns, castles, and cities" are, of course, Gratian's matter-of-fact summary of the episcopal *regalia*, and though he clearly prefers the bishop to live on tithes, he refuses to condemn the possessor of *regalia*. Nor does his position seem fundamentally altered by his selection, for dialectical purposes within this *quaestio*, of other texts opposed to any obligation of churchmen toward the emperor.[10] And indeed, just as he divided bishops into two classes, in a nearby *dictum* he correspondingly distinguished two kinds of ecclesiastical property: on the one hand, those things which are free of all liability, and on the other, those things for which a bishop "owes the customary obedience to princes, so that he should pay annual tribute to them, and should set off with them to military service when the army is summoned."[11] At the conclusion of this *dictum*, however, Gratian laid down a single restriction on the accountability of bishops holding the *regalia*, namely, that this military service "must not be performed without the consent of the Roman pontiff."[12] What-

---

oblationibus . . . [episcopi] contenti esse voluerint, eorum in voluntate pendeat"; Placidus puts these words into the mouth of an imagined opponent. See also D.63 dict.p.c.28, which Gratian appropriated almost verbatim from Placidus (*op.cit.* c.69, *ibid.* II 597); Sägmüller, *Bischofswahl* 17f.

[10] C.23 q.8 cc.21, 24 (note also their rubrics) and dict.p.c.22.

[11] C.23 q.8 dict.p.c.25: "Hinc datur intelligi, quod de his, que inperiali beneficio, uel a quibuslibet pro beneficio sepulturae ecclesia possidet, nullius iuri, nisi episcopi, teneatur asstricta. De his uero, que a quibuslibet emerit uel uiuorum donationibus acceperit, principibus consueta debet obsequia, ut et annua eis persoluat tributa, et conuocato exercitu cum eis proficiscatur ad castra. Quod tamen hoc ipsum non sine consensu Romani Pontificis fieri debet." Gratian has introduced a confusion by asserting that properties gained *inperiali beneficio* are exempt from obligations. Yet apparently he does not mean to indicate thereby the *regalia*, which he clumsily describes as *donationes uiuorum*. See Hoffmann's ingenious explanation of the phrase "inperiali beneficio" as a reference to the *inperialis benignitas* (above, n.9) which grants immunity from obligations (*DA* 15 [1959] 436).

[12] Cf. Hoffmann, *op.cit.* 436f (and n.183), where he interprets—with misgivings—the phrase "hoc ipsum" (above, n.11) as an inclusive reference to the payment of tribute as well as to the rendering of military service. For Gratian (C.23 pr.), however, the topic of this *quaestio* was "an episcopis . . . liceat . . . arma mouere?"; cf. also C.23 q.8 pr., and note the comments of Bazianus and the *Glossa Palatina* on this point (below, n.28). Gratian's immediately following references to the episcopal *comitatus*

ever may be the form in which Gratian envisioned such consent, he believed that papal disapproval would override even this central obligation required of a bishop in return for his *regalia*.

Although Gratian's concern with investiture and with the *regalia* is certainly genuine, yet it indicates the degree to which, in the view of most churchmen after 1140, the importance of these questions had diminished: these issues had withdrawn from the center of the stage into the wings. For example, in the second half of the twelfth century, the imperial court still required the precedence of investiture before consecration, and in his later writings Gerhoh of Reichersberg still indignantly denounced this sequence as an intolerable abuse. Nonetheless, this question was losing its significance, for though the sequence of investiture and consecration was stressed by the two imperialist forgeries in Gratian's *distinctio* on ecclesiastical election, the decretists were indifferent to this regulation, and they glossed these two documents without even noticing it.[13] In general, following Gratian's lead in the *Decretum*, the Church's later legal thinkers devoted much more attention to their conceptions of ecclesiastical office, election, and jurisdiction than to investiture or to the meaning of the *regalia*. On the *regalia*, the *Decretum* contains no treatise comparable to the long *Distinctio* 63 on ecclesiastical election, and though the *Compilatio tertia* and *Liber extra* have a short *titulus* "On Fiefs" (*De feudis*), containing only two decretals, there is no title *De regalibus* within the early compilations or the *Decretales*.[14] Thus the decretists and early decretalists found only a scatter-

---

(C.23 q.8 rubr.cc.26, 28) do not vitiate this impression, since Gratian was considering primarily the military service arising from the *comitatus* (C.23 q.8 dict.p.c.27). If Gratian had actually required papal consent for the payment of tribute, he would have surpassed in strictness the legislation of Alexander III on the taxation of clerics (*X* 3.49.4), and thereby, he would indeed have foreshadowed, as Hoffmann suggests (*op.cit.* 437), the legislation of Innocent III and Boniface VIII (*X* 3.49.7; *VI* 3.23.3).

[13] See their commentaries on D.63 cc.22, 23.
[14] *Comp.III* 3.16 (= *X* 3.20); both decretals are by Innocent III.

ing of isolated texts, which did not require them to formulate an elaborate and systematic theory on the *regalia*. Still, the *regalia* had neither vanished nor fully lost their significance in the second half of the twelfth century, and consequently the canonists could not regard them as outside the perimeter of their interests.

In their occasional discussions of investiture and of the *regalia*, most decretists found it easy to agree on those general principles sanctioned by the solid authority of Gratian, but the ambiguities and omissions in the *Decretum* encouraged them to disagree on the details and the corollaries. Specifically on the act of investiture, decretists took their cue from Gratian. They found little difficulty in explaining away the two *capitula* in the *Decretum* which seemed to allow a layman the right of investing a prelate with a church or an ecclesiastical dignity. For as Rufinus and Huguccio pointed out, this earlier practice was "antiquated" or "abrogated" by other and more recent legislation.[15] Master Huguccio, however, excepted and justified investiture with the *regalia* as a lawful act. Anticipating the possible objection that a layman could thereby have power over the Church's property, he added that "the *regalia* belong to the Church with regard not to property but to use, for they are given to the Church in fief."[16]

In general, canonistic conceptions of the *regalia* were more

---

[15] Rufinus, *Summa* on D.63 c.22 v. *Adrianus* etc., ed. Singer 157: "Et hoc hodie abrogatum est ex decreto Gregorii septimi [C.16 q.7 c.13] . . . similiter etiam sequenti capitulo derogatur." Also, *id.* on C.16 q.7 pr. v. *quod autem* etc., ed. Singer 368. Huguccio, *Summa* on C.16 q.7 pr. v. *ecclesias de manu laicorum*: ". . . illa [D.63 cc.22, 23] et omnia capitula que uidentur innuere quod laici possint concedere ecclesias uel earum inuestituras antiquata et abrogata sunt autoritate sequentium canonum . . ." (Vat.Arch. C.114 fol.240vb). *Id.* on D.63 c.23 v. *ultimis suppliciis*: ". . . Item quia per sequentia decreta sunt eliminata et abrogata . . ." (Clm 10247 fol.71ra).

[16] Huguccio, *Summa* on D.63 c.7 v. *ecclesias*: "idest ecclesiarum inuestituram, quam nullus debet recipere a laico nisi forte de regalibus" (Vat.Arch. C.114 fol.81ra). *Id.* on C.16 q.7 c.12 v. *interdicimus*: ". . . Item nota quod inuestitura regalium non prohibetur recipi ab imperatoribus uel regibus uel aliis principibus. Set numquid laicus habebit potestatem in rebus ecclesie? Non, regalia enim non sunt ecclesie quo ad proprietatem set quo ad usum, in feudum enim sunt data ecclesie . . ." (Vat.Arch. C.114 fol.241vb).

The Church and the *Regalia*

concrete and thoroughgoing than Gratian's, and contemporary theologians were sometimes similarly concerned to elucidate the practical problems arising from the Church's possession of *regalia*.[17] Sicard of Cremona, writing about 1180, exemplifies this canonistic awareness of the broad range of issues and implications inherent in the episcopal *regalia*.[18] By virtue of the *regalia*, as Sicard explained, a bishop is responsible to Caesar for the payment of tribute, for obedience in those things which concern princes, and for service as a secular judge. Also, as count or duke, the bishop will owe fealty to the emperor. And in a just war, the bishop must aid the prince with his presence on campaign, with his powers of exhortation, and (above all, one might say) with his contingent of knights. Finally, Sicard concluded his account with a curiously restrained recommendation: "It would be more advisable, however, if they did not do these things without an order from the pope." A lucid summary, indeed, highlighting the aspects of particular interest to the Church. At this point it may be worthwhile to examine the views of individual canonists on these various obligations arising from the *regalia*.[19]

The possession of secular jurisdiction and the requirement of service as a secular judge seemed to place the regalian bishop simultaneously and ambiguously in two judicial systems or hierarchies. Indeed, if one of his vassals wished to appeal the bishop's sentence, should the vassal appeal to the king (as the bishop's overlord) or to the pope (as his ulti-

---

[17] The theologians' views on the *regalia* require a separate analysis; for an excerpt from a discussion on this topic by Robert of Courson (*Summa* 26.9), see my article, *Proc. of the 2nd Int. Cong.* 127 n.19.

[18] Sicard, *Summa*: ". . . Clerici quidam regalia possident, de quibus reverentiam cesari recognoscant et in fidelitate, si sunt comites vel duces et in tributis et in mandatis, ad principes non tamen ad Deum pertinentibus, et in iudiciis. Unde et in iusto bello principibus parere tenentur in milites dando, adhortando, ad castra proficiscendo, non tamen arma arripiendo. Consultius tamen esset, si nec ista facerent sine mandato apostolici" (A. Stickler, "Imperator vicarius Papae," *MIÖG* 62 [1954] 186 n.45).

[19] Although many valuable texts have been assembled by Father Stickler in his articles, particularly in "Imperator vicarius Papae," *MIÖG* 62 (1954) esp. 183-86, his remarks are brief, and other scholars have not yet seriously studied the canonistic opinions on the *regalia*.

mate ecclesiastical superior)? There was no simple solution, and canonists argued the question without agreement.[20] Moreover, the bishop's judicial obligations created a danger for the bishop himself and posed a problem for the canonists in their commentaries.[21] As the *Summa Animal est substantia* observed, it might seem unlawful for a bishop to administer secular justice, but "by reason of office," the bishop who is also a count (that is, the bishop with *regalia*) can judge in secular actions—so long as the case does not involve a capital crime.[22] Most decretists were quick to place similar restrictions on the judicial function of bishops.[23] Indeed, for the canonists, that was the crux: clerics may not shed blood. Sometimes, however, even decretists who had sternly forbidden episcopal judgment in *causae sanguinis* took a different position elsewhere in their commentaries, and allowed the bishop to judge in these cases. Typical of such permission was the statement that the pope with his "dukedom" over the States of the Church and the bishop with *regalia* equally

[20] Alanus, *Apparatus* on *Comp.I* 2.20.7 §1 v. *qui nostre sunt*: "Si episcopus habet regalia et uassallus sub episcopo litigans appellare uoluerit, utrum appellabit ad regem uel ad papam. Resp.: Diuersi diuersa sentiunt" (Clm 3879 fol.31va).

[21] Nonetheless, *iurisdictio ciuilis* in episcopal hands did not necessarily seem incongruous to Gratian; cf. C.23 pr.

[22] On C.23 q.8 c.29 v. *committunt*: "quia sepe principes sacerdotibus committunt causas. . . . Dico quod in eo, quod sacerdos, non debet tractare set ratione officii potest, ut si sit comes, dum tamen non sit causa sanguinis" (Stickler, *MIöG* 62 [1954] 186 n.45).

[23] In general, see the texts assembled by Stickler, *MIöG* 62 (1954) 183-86 nn.44f, from which the following examples are taken: *Summa Elegantius in iure diuino*: ". . . licentiam habeant iudicandi excepto criminali quod ad effusionem sanguinis vel corporalis supplicii ponitur, quia . . . mansuetudini sacerdotali non convenit. . . ." *Id.*: ". . . Effusionem vero sanguinis nulli episcoporum sua vel imperatorum auctoritate imperare licet." *Summa Inperatorie maiestati* on C.3 q.6: ". . . clericus enim ad effusionem sanguinis nihil debet machinari." Sicard of Cremona, *Summa*: ". . . dicere possumus, canones penas non iniungere, cum non liceat clericis sanguinem effundere." *Id.*: ". . . apostolico et episcopis . . . non licet . . . sanguinem fundere vel effusionem sanguinis imperare vel iudicium sanguinis agitare." Evrard of Ypres, *Summula decretalium quaestionum*: "Queritur utrum ecclesiastica persona debeat penas corporales exigere vel ad exigendum tradere? R. In sanguinis effusione non; in verberum cohertione sic." *Id.*: ". . . Nec tamen his [regalia possidentibus] nec illis [regalia non possidentibus] licet sanguinem effundere vel iudicium agitare sanguinis. . . ."

The Church and the *Regalia*

have jurisdiction over capital cases (*ius gladii materialis*) but not the right to hear capital cases or to carry out the judgment (*executio iuris*), for they must delegate this power to a layman.[24] Further, a canonist might specifically insist that the bishop refrain from appearing personally as judge for capital offenses, and that he appoint a lay *administrator* to hear the case and to pass judgment in his stead.[25]

Like the bishop's secular judgeship, the bishop's military duties raised the question of his personal right to bear arms. Here, too, the prohibition against the actual shedding of blood was absolute, and the canonists agreed that even on campaign, the bishops themselves were not allowed to fight: "They can do this through others, not in person."[26] In realistic fashion,

[24] *Apparatus Ecce uicit leo* on D.63 c.30 v. *concedo*: ". . . papa habet ducatum et ita ius gladii set non executionem iuris, similiter et episcopi, qui habent regalia" (Stickler, *op.cit.* 180 n.41 on 181). *Summa Et est sciendum* on D.45 c.1 v. *non percussores*: ". . . et apostolicus et quilibet episcopus, qui est comes, potest laico dare potestatem gladii, licet per se eam non valeat exercere" (Gillmann, *AKKR* 107 [1927] 235). *Summa Et est sciendum* on D.22 c.1 v. *terreni simul*: ". . . Sed quid dicemus de hiis iudicibus, qui ab ipso papa temporalem iurisdictionem accipiunt, vel ab episcopis, qui et comites sunt, a quo tales gladii potestatem accipiunt? Forte potest dici, quod ab episcopis potestatem accipiunt et ex potestatis auctoritate executionem vel ab episcopis totum. Quedam enim aliis concedere possumus, que tamen per nos exercere non possumus . . ." (Gillmann, *AKKR* 107 [1927] 214). *Summa Animal est substantia* on D.63 c.30 v. *cum ducatu*: "ergo et papa habet utrumque gladium, materialem et spiritualem, set usum materialis per se non habet . . ." (Stickler, *op.cit.* 183 n.44 on 185). *Summa Inperatorie maiestati* on C.2 q.4: ". . . quilibet episcopus habet executionem aut meram aut mixtam. Si meram, non licet ei interesse curie cruoris. Si mixtam ratione secularis officii potest interesse curie cruoris" (Stickler, *op.cit.* 186 n.45).

[25] *Summa Elegantius in iure diuino*: "Set sunt alii, quibus de imperiali munificentia ducatus, comicie, tributa concessa sunt; hi . . . ius gladii habent, quod tamen non per se set per suffectam personam exercere debent . . ." (Stickler, *op.cit.* 186 n.45). *Id.*: "Patet ergo episcopos, qui super civitates civilem potestatem acceperunt, per se iuditia sanguinis agitare non posse" (Stickler, *loc.cit.*). *Summa Parisiensis* on C.23 q.5, ed. McLaughlin 218: "Quid tamen, si prelatus ecclesie utrumque habeat gladium? Per interpositam personam, per administratores videlicet suos causas, in quibus iudicium sanguinis vertitur, diffinire debet, non autem <per> personam propriam" (Stickler, *loc.cit.*, reads "ante personam propriam").

[26] *Summa Et est sciendum* on D.36 c.3 v. *si quis* [usque] *ad bella non vadit*: ". . . si [prelatus] haberet a principe regalia, potest secum proficisci ad castra" (Rouen 710 fol.126ra; Stickler, *op.cit.* 180 n.41 on 181). *Summa Tractaturus magister* on C.23 q.8 pr.: ". . . Melius est, ut dicatur omnibus [scil. episcopis] esse illicitum [scil. arma mouere] . . . exceptis his, qui possi-

the decretists generally recognized that the bishop with *regalia* was firmly required to accompany his monarch on military expeditions. When the decretists ignored Gratian's ban on military service "without the consent of the Roman pontiff," they tacitly gave additional recognition to the binding character of the bishop's obligation.[27] As an exception, however, Bazianus followed Gratian strictly, for he insisted that a special dispensation (*specialis licentia*) from the pope was necessary for a bishop summoned to go on campaign.[28] Against Bazianus, and taking a far less literal view of Gratian's rule, the *Glossa Palatina* argued that if the war is just, all bishops—"whether or not they have the *regalia*"— may serve, unless specifically prohibited by the pope. In this context, the *Glossa Palatina* distinguished the possessors of *regalia* from the bishops lacking them, and he explained that the regalian bishops *must* serve, whereas the others *may* serve if they wish.[29] Indeed, it is evident that most decretists followed Gratian in assuming the importance of the juridical status conferred upon a bishop by possession of the *regalia*, and therefore in distinguishing between bishops with *regalia*

---

dent regalia, qui possunt hoc agere per alios non per se . . ." (Stickler, *op.cit.* 187 n.46). Alanus, *Apparatus Ius naturale* on C.23 q.8 c.10 v. *precibus adriani*: ". . . Bello tamen personaliter clericus interesse non debet, . . . secundum quosdam nisi habeat regalia a principe, quo casu in propria persona tenetur ad expeditionem ire" (Stickler, *Salesianum* 21 [1959] 369). *Summa Animal est substantia* on C.23 q.8 pr.: ". . . Quid dicemus de illis episcopis, qui ratione regalium cum rege tenentur ire ad prelium? . . . Si autem contra prohibitionem armis usi fuerint nec admoniti deficiant, debent privari omni ecclesiastico beneficio" (Stickler, *MIÖG* 62 [1954] 186 n.45).

[27] C.23 q.8 dict.p.c.25 (above, n.11).

[28] *Glossa Palatina* on C.23 q.8 c.19 v. *uenire*: "bar. dicit, quod episcopi non possunt ire in exercitum, nisi de speciali licentia domini pape, set tamen nec auctoritate pape pugnare. Set tu dic quod ire possunt siue habeant regalia siue non, si iustum est bellum, nisi prohibeantur a papa. Set ea est differentia inter habentes regalia et non habentes, quia habentes tenentur ire, alii non nisi voluerint" (Stickler, *Salesianum* 15 [1953] 591). The initials "bar." are usual for Bazianus.

[29] *Glossa Palatina* on D.18 c.13 v. *preceptione* regia: "infra, xxiii. q.ult. Si uobis et Si quis episcopus [C.23 q.8 cc.28, 27], contra, set hic de hiis qui habent feudum, ibi non. Immo quilibet deberet uenire si uocaretur propter negotium regni" (Vat.Reg. 977 fol.9vb). In this final sentence, the anonymous author seems to obliterate the distinction between bishops with *regalia* and those without, requiring all to obey a summons *propter negotium regni*.

and those without *regalia*. Dwelling upon this distinction between two kinds of bishop, the canonist might draw inferences that touched upon other questions: In a discussion of the emperor's right to give consent to an episcopal election, for example, a French decretist specifically regarded this right as strengthened by the tenure of *regalia* within that bishopric.[30]

Among a group of texts on ecclesiastical councils, Gratian included a decree from a sixth-century synod, asserting that when a metropolitan has summoned a bishop to a council, the bishop must attend unless hindered "by grave infirmity of body" or "by a royal command" (*preceptione regia*).[31] Perhaps the most striking glosses on the concept of the *regalia* were devoted to this *capitulum*, which of course did not discuss the *regalia* in any form. Yet this *capitulum* posed for the decretists the paradox of a bishop owing primary obedience to his monarch rather than his metropolitan. For when one of the early decretists used such a *capitulum* as the springboard for a leap into a discussion of a problem like the *regalia*, he was often followed by later decretists and eventually by the decretalists, who then had to come to terms with the same question. Indeed, it was characteristic of the decretists to build up long-lived traditions of thought on particular themes—though sometimes with scarcely any foundation in the original text provided by Gratian.

Commenting on this *capitulum*, some early students of the *Decretum* explained that if the emperor should summon a bishop holding a "countship" and thereafter the pope should send for the same prelate, the bishop must go first to the emperor and then to the pope. To this doctrine, master

---

[30] *Summa Parisiensis* on D.63 c.16 v. *Reatina*, ed. McLaughlin 55: ". . . Assensus enim imperatoris desideratur, et maxime in eis ecclesiis in quibus habet regalia. . . ." Though the gloss speaks here of the "emperor's assent," one should remember that this doctrine (for which Gratian offered no explicit support) corresponded to the French king's prerogative in the royal bishoprics (that is, the *ecclesie in quibus habet regalia*); see Pacaut, *Louis VII* esp. 63-82. On the other hand, the German situation differed sharply from that in France, for in Germany virtually all bishoprics were "imperial."

[31] D.18 c.13.

The Bishop-Elect

Rufinus objected by distinguishing between an order from a metropolitan and one from the pope. For as he pointed out, a metropolitan may well be subject to the emperor in secular matters, the pope never—hence a papal summons has priority over an imperial command, though the summons of a metropolitan does not.[32] Closely following Rufinus's view in this hypothetical case, Stephen of Tournai firmly asserted that the bishop "must always go first to the pope, even if he has already started off to the king,"—then Stephen added the surprising qualification, "unless perhaps the bishop had taken an oath."[33] All of the decretists were, of course, familiar with the famous letter from bishop Fulbert of Chartres to duke William of Aquitaine, with its classic analysis of a vassal's obligations to his lord, since Gratian had included that eleventh-century letter in the *Decretum*.[34] Needless to say, the decretists were equally familiar with the requirement of an oath of fealty. Indeed, Stephen of Tournai regarded as ordinary and normal the oath of fealty which "bishops and other ecclesiastical persons" swore to "emperors and kings."[35]

[32] Rufinus, *Summa* on D.18 c.13 v. *si episcopus* et post *a. precept. reg.*, ed. Singer 41: "Ex hoc quidam habere volunt quia, si imperator vocaverit aliquem clericum et postea vocaverit eum apostolicus, primo adire imperatorem debet, postmodum apostolicum. Sed longe alia ratio est in apostolico, alia in metropolitano; metropolitanus quippe pro secularibus principi subiacet, summus vero pontifex in nullo ei subest. Nec de alio episcopo hoc est intelligendum, nisi de eo, quem ab imperatore comitatum habere constiterit."

[33] *Summa* on D.18 c.13 v. *praeceptione regia*, ed. Schulte 28: "si prius facta fuit episcopo a rege quam a metropolitano; ad apostolicum vero semper prius debet ire etiam si iam coepisset ire ad regem, nisi forte iurasset. . . . . . . prohibentur ire ad imperatorem causa iudicii suscipiendi, hic permittitur causa negotii regni." The decretists were frequently willing to accept Rufinus's and Stephen's formulations with little change. See, for example, John of Faenza, *Summa* ad loc., and the *Summa De iure naturali* ad loc. (Knut W. Nörr, "Die Summen 'De iure naturali' und 'De multiplici iuris diuisione,'" *ZRG KA* 48 [1962] 138-63 at 154); also, Sicard of Cremona, *Summa* on D.18 (Rouen 710 fol.3rb).

[34] C.22 q.5 c.18; virtually all of C.22 is concerned with the law of oaths. On Fulbert's ideas apart from this letter (*Ep.*58, *PL* 141 229f), see Frederick Behrends, "Kingship and Feudalism according to Fulbert of Chartres," *Mediaeval Studies* 25 (1963) 93-99, and in general, see also Emilio Nasalli-Rocca, " 'Fidelitas' e giuramento di fedeltà nell'opera di Graziano," *SGrat* 2 (1954) 411-23. Fulbert's letter also appeared in *Libri feudorum* 2.6.

[35] *Summa* on C.22 q.5 c.22 v. *nullus*, ed. Schulte 230: ". . . Alii dicunt de sacramento fidelitatis hoc dictum; quod etiam nihil valet, cum videamus episcopos et alios ecclesiasticas personas imperatori et regibus fidelitatem facere."

The Church and the *Regalia*

To solve the potential conflict of duty in the event of summonses from both pope and monarch, the *Summa Et est sciendum* explained that this paradox may refer only to the earlier period in the Church's history, or, he explained, the primacy of the prince's summons might be simply an obligation arising from possession of the *regalia*. Apparently, however, some of the anonymous decretist's contemporaries argued straightforwardly that the bishop should obey the first summons, whether from pope or monarch.[36] While admitting that a king's command may have precedence over that of a metropolitan, decretalists like Ricardus Anglicus and Tancred insisted that the bishop with *regalia* must always give priority to a papal summons, even if he is therefore forced to give up

---

[36] *Summa Et est sciendum* on D.18 c.13 v. *a. preceptione regia*: "Per hoc videtur quod vocatus a papa et principe plus principi deberet quam pape deferre. Quod vel ad tempora nascentis ecclesie refertur vel de his intelligas, qui a principe habent regalia, qui debent que sunt cesaris cesari et que dei deo. Quidam tamen distinguunt, quis eorum vocaverit eum prius, et ei obediet, qui prius vocavit" (Gillmann, *AKKR* 107 [1927] 235). Similar argumentation can be found in the *Distinctiones Monacenses* on D.18 c.13: "Si quis episcopus metropolitanus episcopos prouinciales uocauerit et ipsi non uenerunt postpositis omnibus, excepta graui infirmitate ac preceptione regia, usque ad proximam synodum a fratrum karitate et ecclesie communione priuentur [*scr.* priuetur]. Contra, C.xxiii. q.viii. c.Si quis episcopus [C.23 q.8 c.27] uel omnis constitutus sub ecclesiastica regula, preter consilium uel litteras episcoporum et maxime metropolitani, ad imperatorem perrexerit [*scr.* perrexerunt], et communione et propria dignitate carebit. Resp. Hoc Antiocenum concilium preiudicat Agathensi: uel ad tempus referendum est antiquum, in quo magis regibus cogebantur obedire episcopi quam metropolitanis: uel illud ad episcopos qui regalia habent scilicet teloneum, monetam et huiusmodi, hoc ad eos qui non habent regalia referatur"; I owe this text to the kindness of Father Daniel Shanahan of London.

When a decretist invoked the doctrine of "historical relativism," asserting that what was permissible (or at least tolerable) in an earlier age was no longer proper, he was following Gratian's practice. For Gratian, historical relativism explained the power exercised by earlier monarchs over ecclesiastical elections (D.63 dict.p.c.28), and similarly explained the fact that early medieval clergy had been married (D.28 dict.p.c.13; C.N.L. Brooke, "Gregorian Reform in Action: Clerical Marriage in England 1050-1200," *The Cambridge Historical Journal* 12 [1956] 5). Still, the doctrine of historical relativism was not the only historically based argument by which a decretist might explain and resolve the differing claims of contradictory canons: it was usually simpler to point out that a particular canon had been superseded by more recent legislation (cf. the statements by Rufinus and Huguccio, above, n.15) or was outranked and thus nullified by a canon of greater authority (note the remark above in the *Distinctiones Monacenses*: "Hoc Antiocenum concilium preiudicat Agathensi").

all his *regalia*.[37] In essential agreement with this position, Alanus observed that a papal legate's order has the same force as a summons from the pope himself.[38]

It was, however, master Huguccio who had the surest grasp of the fundamental issue in the bishop's dilemma of the conflicting summonses.[39] For Huguccio defined the question clearly in terms of the superiority of the *sacerdotium* over the *regnum*. Or as his decretalist colleagues might have expressed it with slightly different emphasis, it was a problem *de maioritate et obedientia*. If the priesthood is greater than the royal power, and if the greater should be obeyed by the lesser, how can the king's bidding outrank an ecclesiastical command? Though Huguccio's solution is more lucid and

---

[37] Richard, *Apparatus* on *Comp.I* 2.20.9 v. *in legatione regis*: "arg. quod regia auctoritas excusat. . . . Solutio: Si mandatum regis preueniat mandatum cuiuslibet prelati preter papam, dico regi obediendum maxime si ab eo regalia habuerit, ut xxiii. q.ult. § Ecce quod [C.23 q.8 dict.p.c.20]. Si autem papa uocauerit, exemplo Petri relictis retibus etiam si opus est et omnibus regalibus [*scr.* regularibus] sequantur dominum papam" (Clm 6352 fol.28ra; cf. Gillmann, *AKKR* 107 [1927] 607f). This gloss was repeated almost verbatim by Tancred, *Gl.ord.* on *Comp.I* ad loc. (Gillmann, *loc.cit.*).

[38] Alanus, *Apparatus* on *Comp.I* ad loc.: "hec excusatio sufficeret uocato ab episcopo uel ab archiepiscopo, . . . non uocato a legato [*scr.* allegato] pape, quia non a papa uocato" (Clm 3879 fol.34ra).

[39] Huguccio, *Summa* on D.18 c.13 v. *preceptione regia*: "utrumque enim per se sufficit ad excusationem. . . . Set nonne ordo sacerdotalis excellentior est et altior regali potestate? Sic, . . . et maior potestas preponenda est minori in obedientia. . . . Queritur ergo hic: regia preceptio preponitur uocationi sacerdotali? Set parcitur uerecundie principis in quo scandalum timetur. . . . Alii dicunt quod loquitur in eo casu, cum princeps est legatus Romane curie, sicut nunc multi sunt, et ideo ratione legationis est maior metropolitano. Et intelligitur quod hic dicitur, cum episcopus regalia habet a principe et in regalibus subest ei, et princeps primo precipit ei aliquid quod impedit eum, ne possit uenire, puta precipit ei ut uadat secum in expeditione, ad quod tenetur ratione regalium, et si tali causa abfuerit episcopus, non punietur. Ad uocationem uero pape semper tenetur ire primo, etiam si ante sit citatus a principe, infra xxiii. q.viii. Si quis episcopus, contra, set illud in alio casu intelligitur, scilicet cum episcopus relicto ecclesiastico iudicio pergit ad imperiale, petens cognitionem iudiciorum publicorum, quod nullus clericus debet facere, . . . ergo prohibetur . . . episcopus, ne uadat ad imperatorem causa iudicii, hic permittitur ire causa negotii regni, ad quod tenetur, uel si illud capitulum intelligitur in eodem casu cum isto, quod ego non credo. Dic quod ibi dicitur de illo episcopo qui nil habet ab imperatore, nec subest ei in aliquo, hic dicitur de illo qui subest ei in regalibus" (Clm 10247 fol.16ra).

detailed, it largely follows those of Rufinus, Stephen, Richard, and Tancred in insisting on the absolute preponderance of a papal command in conflict with an imperial order to a bishop possessing *regalia*. Yet before giving his own solution to the paradox, Huguccio cited an alternative explanation offered by unnamed contemporaries:

> When the prince is a legate of the Roman Curia, as many now are, . . . by reason of his legatine office he is greater than the metropolitan.

Hence a bishop would owe prior obedience to such a prince, rather than to the metropolitan. And as a concrete example, Huguccio undoubtedly had in mind primarily the Norman king of Sicily, who claimed the role of papal legate.[40] Indeed, Huguccio could also have thought of Hungary and England as monarchies where this claim was made in the twelfth century. According to the famous report by John of Salisbury, king Henry II boasted that he was, like his grandfather, "apostolic legate" in his own realm, as well as "king . . . , patriarch, emperor, and everything he wanted."[41] Though the disadvantages of Huguccio's alternative explanation were surely obvious, it proposed for certain princes a special authority delegated by the Roman See and thereby justified

[40] Huguccio considered the Sicilian king an outstanding example of a monarch with an unfortunately privileged role in the installation of bishops in his realm. *Summa* on D.63 c.23 v. *inuestiatur*: ". . . Hoc [scil. inuestitura ecclesie] autem fuit speciale priuilegium in persona eius et quorumdam aliorum, sicut hodie est in persona regis Apuli, et male" (Clm 10247 fol.71ra). *Id.* on C.16 q.7 c.12 v. *interdicimus*: ". . . prohibetur recipi inuestituram ecclesie . . . a laico . . . , nisi laicus habeat priuilegium a papa, ut talem inuestituram possit dare, ut Apulus" (Vat.Arch. C.114 fol.241vb). It was no novelty to cite Sicily as an example of remarkable politics, for long before Huguccio wrote his *Summa*, the audacious, ruthless, and effective statecraft of Roger II had created a profound—and usually bad—impression among European thinkers; see Helene Wieruszowski, "Roger II of Sicily: *Rex-Tyrannus* in Twelfth-Century Political Thought," *Speculum* 38 (1963) 46-78.

[41] John of Salisbury, *Ep*.239, *Opera omnia*, ed. J. A. Giles (Oxford 1848) II 114; in general, Josef Deér, "Der Anspruch der Herrscher des 12. Jahrhunderts auf die apostolische Legation," *Archivum historiae pontificiae* 2 (1964) 117-86.

their overriding authority in relation to the bishops of their realms. Or, as one might say, this explanation integrated the ruler into the hierarchy of the Church—above the metropolitan, but below the pope—and thus removed the major objection to the dominance of royal authority.

These arguments might seem purely theoretical—an arid dispute over mere diplomatic protocol. Yet in these discussions one can discern a general characteristic of government during this age: the medieval ruler's need to assert effective control over his subjects in order to preserve an undiminished jurisdiction over them. The *de facto* exercise of power was an integral part of the *de iure* claim. Within the empire, failure to heed a summons was a serious offense: in 1154, Frederick Barbarossa deprived two bishops of their *regalia* for their failure to accompany him on his expedition to Italy.[42] Moreover, in order to ensure that a bishop could appear with his full contingent of vassals, Barbarossa ordered that an imperial bishop's vassal failing to respond to the bishop's summons should be penalized by the loss of his fief.[43]

Correspondingly, this question had more than academic interest to the Church. Since the later eleventh century, the papacy had demonstrated the stress which it placed on the readiness of its ecclesiastical subjects to respond to a summons, for it began to require archbishops to take an oath which included, among its provisions, the promise to appear when called to a council, unless hindered by a "canonical impediment."[44] By the early twelfth century, archbishops-

---

[42] Above, Ch.VIIв n.58.

[43] *MGH Const* I 208 no.148 §3 (1154), 248 no.177 §5 (1158).

[44] T. Gottlob, *Der kirchliche Amtseid der Bischöfe* (Kanonistische Studien und Texte 9: Bonn 1936) 42ff, 176f (text): "Vocatus ad synodum venire non differam nisi prepeditus canonica excusatione uel prepeditione." Almost verbatim, this clause appeared in the highly similar oath which was twice published among the collections of decretals (*Comp.I* 1.4.20 = X 2.24.4). The question remained: What sort of excuse was acceptable as a *canonica prepeditio*? Bernard of Parma (*Gl.ord.* on X 2.24.4) answered this question simply by citing D.18 c.13—in other words, the *regia preceptio* was (at least for Bernard) a valid hindrance. For convenient accounts of the oath's history, see Kantorowicz, *King's Two Bodies* 348ff; *id.*, "Inalienability," *Speculum* 29 (1954) 488-502.

elect normally took this pledge, and by the early thirteenth, exempt bishops-elect followed the same practice.[45] Indeed, Gerhoh of Reichersberg already regarded as superfluous the sworn promise of archbishops and papal suffragans to appear at a synod when summoned, since "according to the canons" this obligation was, he thought, binding even without an oath.[46] Finally, during the thirteenth century, metropolitans required of their suffragan bishops-elect an oath with this provision.[47]

In general, then, the canonists forcefully expressed the Church's grave concern over the various burdens assumed by the prelate at the moment of his fealty and investiture. Needless to say, even canonists who recognized the regalian bishop's obligation to serve his king refused to countenance the practice of elevating a cleric to the episcopate because of his service in the king's *familia*.[48] Moreover, some canonists feared that bishops might prefer to serve in the king's army, rather than to live according to their clerical state.[49] For the canonists were deeply anxious to protect the bishop from all duties inconsistent with his ecclesiastical office, character, and responsibilities. Above all, most canonists sought to

---

[45] Gottlob, *op.cit.* 52ff.

[46] *De investigatione Antichristi* 1.69, *MGH LdL* III 388: "Nam venire vocatum ad synodum debita quidem obedientia est, quae non exhibita . . . etiam non iurata, punire potest secundum canones. . . ."

[47] Although the evidence given by Gottlob (*op.cit.* 160ff, 183f) is dated after the middle of the 13th century, it seems clear that this development began even earlier, as one may judge from a decretal of Gregory IX (*X* 1.33.13), ordering the patriarch of Grado to use only the customary and canonical form (presumably as in *X* 2.24.4) for oaths taken by his suffragans.

[48] Alanus, *Apparatus Ius naturale* on D.63 c.4 v. *fauentem*: ". . . Set nonne regalium ratione debent episcopi regibus et fauere et seruire? Debent quidem postquam electi sunt, set hoc intuitu non debent eligi quia sunt familiares regis" (BN 3909 fol.12va).

[49] *Distinctiones Monacenses* on D.18 c.7: ". . . Resp. Si episcopus animositate principis prohibitus non uenerit ad synodum, excommunicabitur. Si uero pro necessitate regni aliquem secum habuit princeps, et miserit excusationem ad synodum, ei abesse licet"; in the Munich MS there is a marginal gloss, v. *Resp.*: "Vel quia mauult sequi castra quam ecclesiastice discipline doctrinam." Again, I should like to thank Father Daniel Shanahan for providing this text.

preserve intact the bishop's obligation to the Roman pontiff —even if an occasional bishop had to risk the forfeiture of his *regalia* as a result of adhering to this higher obedience. In a final sense, the very presence of these prince-bishops in the alien hierarchy of the secular world disturbed the canon lawyers, as it disturbed others outside of the canonists' lecture halls. That is, it seemed improper that a bishop—possessed with the fullness of the *sacerdotium*—should be subjected to any secular person. Indeed, a canonist might be distressed over the impropriety of a bishop's obligation to kneel before his secular lord.[50] Understandably, even with the admission that a regalian bishop may be under the authority of a monarch, a canonist might specify that this subjection was limited to the sphere of the bishop's temporalities.[51]

Nothing signified the subjection of bishop to monarch quite so clearly as the oath of fealty taken by these prelates. Indeed, some twelfth-century decretists indicated the fundamental disharmony between the claims of customary law and of Church law, between the bishop's role as imperial vassal and the bishop's position under canon law. In Rufinus's words:

> If one objects to the oath of fealty, which today bishops take to the emperor, it should be answered that the canons do not allow everything which custom accepts.[52]

[50] *Summa Et est sciendum* on D.96 c.10 §2 v. *colla principum* etc.: "Quomodo ergo feudum est de principibus, si turbato ordine reuerentie prelatos ecclesie ante sua patiantur genua incurvari?" (Gillmann, *AKKR* 107 [1927] 236).

[51] Alanus, *Apparatus Ius naturale* on D.96 c.7 v. *ligari*: ". . . Licet enim imperator sit maior papa in temporalibus, tamen ei non subest in ecclesiasticis temporalibus . . . et nec aliquis clericus, nisi feudum habeat ab eo" (Stickler, *Salesianum* 21 [1959] 364f). Also Innocent III, in a letter to the emperor Alexius (1201), X 1.33.6 (= *Comp.III* 1.21.2): ". . . non negamus, quin praecellat imperator in temporalibus illos duntaxat, qui ab eo suscipiunt temporalia. . . ."

[52] *Summa* on C.22 q.5 c.22 v. *nullus ex ecclesiastico*, ed. Singer 403: "Si opponatur de iuramento fidelitatis, quod hodie episcopi faciunt imperatori, respondeatur non omnia, que consuetudo habet, canones permittere. Vel dicatur imperatorem non omnino laicum esse, quem per sacram unctionem constat consecratum esse." And under Rufinus's influence, the *Summa Elegantius in iure diuino*: "Si opponitur de iuramento fidelitatis,

Yet Rufinus could find a possible rationale for the bishop's oath of fealty:

> Or it may be said that the emperor, who is known to be consecrated by holy anointment, is not entirely a layman.

In other words, if the emperor really belonged to the *sacerdotium*, the main objection to the oath of fealty would thereby disappear—and this justification of the oath sharply illuminates the chief reason for the canonists' opposition to that practice.[53] In most of their remarks about this network of episcopal obligations, however, canonists were realistic and faithful to the facts of their society, for they recognized that fealty and the *regalia* were deeply rooted in custom. Indeed, for John of Faenza, custom itself—"the best interpreter of the laws" (in the classical phrase which John appropriated from the *Digest*)—sanctioned the bishop's obligation of obedience in return for his *regalia*.[54] With regard to the particular custom of fealty, master Huguccio was less enthusiastic about the value of custom than John of Faenza. Nonetheless, Huguccio clearly discerned the consequences if the Church refused fealty to the princes:

> Such a custom is approved by the Church chiefly on this account, since the churches would be much harmed if they had to lose all the *regalia* by reason of the bishops' unwillingness to take an oath of fealty in return for them.[55]

quod ab episcopis imperatori prestatur, responderi potest, non omnem moderni temporis consuetudinem canonibus concordare, vel quod potius est: imperatorem propter sacram unctionem in numero laicorum non haberi" (Stickler, *MIÖG* 62 [1954] 191 n.51).

[53] For a few more texts on the clerical status of the emperor, see Kempf, *Papsttum und Kaisertum* 127f n.52; the question cannot be pursued further here.

[54] John of Faenza, gl. on C.23 q.8 c.26 v. *nullum omnino*: "Hoc de illis tantum episcopis intelligitur, qui levitica tantum sunt portione contenti, ceteri namque de regalibus et aliis possessionibus suis senioribus servire tenentur. . . . Hoc quoque consuetudo approbat, quae est optima legum interpres" (J. F. von Schulte, *Denkschriften der kaiserlichen Akademie der Wissenschaften* 21, 2 [Vienna 1872] 16); *Dig.* 1.3.37.

[55] Huguccio, *Summa* on C.22 q.5 c.22 v. *nullus* usque *laico*: ". . . Quid ergo dicemus de imperatore cui episcopi faciunt iuramentum fidelitatis?

The Bishop-Elect

This price was too high. Neither the oath of fealty nor any of the bishop's other obligations was an issue which could inspire canonists to follow Paschal II and Arnold of Brescia in advocating the renunciation of the *regalia*.

Talis consuetudo approbatur ab ecclesia presertim ea ratione, quia multum lederentur ecclesie si omnia regalia deberent amittere, ex quo episcopi pro eis iuramentum fidelitatis nollent exhibere . . ." (Josef Juncker, "Summen und Glossen: Beiträge zur Literaturgeschichte des kanonischen Rechts im zwölften Jahrhundert," *ZRG KA* 14 [1925] 453 n.2).

CHAPTER X

THE ECLIPSE OF THE *REGALIA*

1. Confirmation vs Investiture

in their relations with their ecclesiastical feudatories, the emperors ascribed to the regalian investiture substantially the same effects which the Church claimed for electoral confirmation. That is, according to the imperial conception, an *electus* could not administer the temporalities of his church before he had been invested with the *regalia*; according to canonical theory, an *electus* could not administer the temporalities of his church until his election had been confirmed by the competent ecclesiastical superior. Clearly, there is a contradiction here, and indeed, the secular requirement and the ecclesiastical were in danger of serious conflict.[1]

To illustrate the practical consequences of this potential conflict, let us turn to a document which emerged from the circle of French royal legists around 1300. First, the historical background: Claiming the title "Chief See of Gaul" (*prima sedes Galliarum*) and the primacy of the French Church, the archbishopric of Lyons stood as a metropolitan see over an ecclesiastical province of French dioceses. The archdiocese itself, however, stood on imperial soil, and although the archbishop was an imperial prince, successive archbishops enjoyed an almost unbroken record of *de facto* independence from imperial control. The bishop of Autun was one of the archbishop's French suffragans, but the bond between them was

---

[1] Baethgen, *ZRG* KA 10 (1920) 186f (= *Mediaevalia* 123f).

actually even closer, for according to a long-standing reciprocal arrangement, during a vacancy in either see, the other should administer the temporalities until a new incumbent was chosen. There was a similar arrangement between the church of Lyons and the abbey of Savigny, which was subject to Lyons but was on French soil.[2] Hence the archbishop of Lyons was obliged to do fealty to the king of France for the *regalia* of these two possessions. The French attempt to intervene seriously in Lyonnaise affairs—indeed, to annex Lyons—began during the long vacancy of the archiepiscopal throne from 1267 to 1272.[3] Finally, in 1272 Gregory X appointed an important ecclesiastic, Peter of Tarantaise (later pope Innocent V), to the vacant see. At his accession, Peter announced his willingness to take the usual oath of fealty to king Philip III in return for the *regalia* of Autun and Savigny. To this came the reply that he was doing fealty for that part of the archbishopric which lay on the right bank of the Saône (that is, which lay in France, rather than in the empire). The question was left open, and Peter took the oath without specification of his precise feudal holdings.[4] Such was the historical reality behind a juristic memorandum written sometime before 1297 to justify and publicize France's claims to Lyons.[5] On the whole, the assertions of this memorandum represent the fine art of historical falsification for political purposes. Still, the document is useful here, since among its numerous arguments there is a discussion of the legal problems in archbishop Peter's accession: fresh from his "confirmation" at the Roman Curia, archbishop Peter arrived in Lyons and immediately began to administer the temporal possessions and affairs of his archdiocese—without having first rendered homage and fealty to the king of France. The anonymous author expressly denied that the archbishop's fealty was limited to any specific

[2] Fritz Kern, *Die Anfänge der französischen Ausdehnungspolitik bis zum Jahr 1308* (Tübingen 1910) 60f, 96.
[3] *Ibid.* ch.7.
[4] *Ibid.* 102f.
[5] The memorandum has been edited by Kern, *Acta imperii* 201-06 no.274; for a brief discussion, see his *Anfänge* 233.

tenancies; on the contrary, according to the memorandum, the primate of Lyons takes the oath in return "for all the temporalities of his archbishopric" (*de tota temporalitate ipsius archiepiscopatus*).[6] Hence, as the anonymous jurist explained, king Philip deprived the new archbishop of his administrative authority, and when Peter protested, he was told that

> It was generally the custom in the kingdom of France, that no prelate who was obliged to do fealty to the lord king could undertake or administer the temporalities until he had sworn fealty. . . .[7]

Then, according to the memorandum, an objection was raised on the archbishop's side:

> His predecessors, when they had received their confirmation, had always been accustomed to take in hand and administer the temporalities before they swore fealty.

For the royalist author of the memorandum, this was the main point: that the archbishop did not deny his ultimate obligation of fealty to the king of France. For the purposes of our inquiry, the doubtful historicity of the unreliable jurist's tale is a secondary concern. One cannot criticize his discussion of the conflict between the monarchical conception of regalian investiture and the ecclesiastical conception of electoral confirmation, for it is an accurate reflection of thirteenth-century constitutional thought.

Indeed, the potential conflict between electoral confirmation and regalian investiture is already visible by the end of

6 Kern, *Acta imperii* 202 no.274 §5.
7 *Ibid.* 203 no.274 §7: ". . . Responsum fuit sibi [scil. archiepiscopo], quod consuetudo generaliter erat in regno Francie, quod nullus prelatus, qui domino regi facere fidelitatem teneretur, poterat tangere vel administrare temporalia, quousque fidelitatem prestitisset, et quod dominus rex erat et sui predecessores fuerant in possessione vel quasi sic manutenendi regnum suum. Ex parte autem illius archiepiscopi fuit dictum, quod predecessores sui semper confirmatione optenta consueverant tangere et administrare temporalia, antequam fidelitatem prestarent. . . ."

the twelfth century. The Innocentianum of 1133 forbade the uninvested bishop-elect to "seize the *regalia*," which included the right to subinfeudate, and from the beginning of his reign Barbarossa severely punished the bishop-elect who dared, without special permission, to grant fiefs prior to his own investiture. This imperial requirement was still significant as late as the early fourteenth century. And needless to say, the enfeoffment of vassals was an essential duty inherent in the position of the ecclesiastical prince.[8] On the Church's side, in 1199 Innocent III quashed the election of an unconfirmed bishop-elect who had accepted oaths—presumably oaths of fealty—from laymen.[9] Just as Innocent later disclaimed any right to pass judgment on matters of feudal law (*de feudo*), which are the concern of the secular ruler,[10] so also might the pope have asserted here that he was judging the unfortunate prelate by reason of ecclesiastical office, rather than *de feudo*. For according to Alanus, the right "to accept oaths of fealty from vassals" and the right "to grant investitures" were powers which belonged to the *potestas iurisdictionis*, and "these things are conferred in the confirmation" of an episcopal election.[11] In general, the Church was gravely concerned over the maintenance of its property in any form, for it insisted that no bishop could subinfeudate or otherwise alienate properties without the consent of his cathedral chapter,[12] and imperial decrees reinforced this restriction, sometimes adding

---

[8] Ecclesiastical recognition of this obligation is evident in the complaint by Gerhoh of Reichersberg, *De edificio dei* c.14, *MGH LdL* III 145 (above, Ch.IXa n.22).

[9] *X* 1.6.17 (above, Ch.IVb n.15).

[10] In his famous decretal *Novit*, *X* 2.1.13 (ed. Cheney and Semple, *Selected Letters* 64 no.21).

[11] Gl. in Tancred's *Gl.ord.* on *Comp.II* 1.3.7 v. *de talibus*: "ad iurisdictionem pertinentibus, puta: . . . sacramenta fidelitatis a uasallis accipere, inuestituras . . . dare. . . . Hec enim in confirmatione conferuntur . . ." (Clm 3879 fol.101va).

[12] Without such consent, the bishop was specifically forbidden to alienate any properties belonging to the *mensa episcopalis*; Feine, *RG* I 332. Most of the decretals in the *titulus* "De his quae fiunt a praelato sine consensu capituli" (*X* 3.10) expressly prohibit a bishop from alienating property or granting prebends without the chapter's consent.

as a further requirement the emperor's consent.[13] Indeed, after 1215 most churchmen agreed that even the two specially privileged classes—distant archbishops-elect and exempt bishops-elect—could not lawfully alienate properties in any way prior to electoral confirmation.[14] It is not difficult to see that Innocent III, Alanus, and others were laying down principles for the bishop's powers acquired under feudal law, that is, acquired by virtue of the bishop's position within the feudal hierarchy. In other words, even when the bishop was acting in his capacity as feudal lord by accepting oaths and investing vassals, the Church considered these secular prerogatives a part of—or, at least, dependent upon—the bishop's purely ecclesiastical jurisdiction.

The basic problem was, of course, that in their concern for the *regalia*, the emperors regarded the German bishops essentially as imperial princes taking an active part in the administration of the empire, whereas the popes and canonists, armed with precise new concepts of jurisdiction, were determined to stress the primarily ecclesiastical character of the episcopal office. A clear demarcation of the boundary between the realms of ecclesiastical *iurisdictio* and of the ruler's *regalia* would have relieved the tension between these two views of the episcopal office. In 1209, when king Philip Augustus confiscated the *regalia* of two French bishoprics, he took "only those *temporalia* which they held from him feudally, peacefully leaving to them the tithes and other *spiritualia*."[15] That is, Philip Augustus carefully distinguished

13 For a decree of the imperial court requiring the consent of the chapter, see *MGH Const* II 397 no.282 (1223); decrees requiring the consent of chapter and monarch, *ibid.* I 425 no.300 (1184), II 81 no.68 (1219), II 404f no.289 (1225). In 1222, the bishop of Passau asked the imperial court about alienations without consent of chapter and *ministeriales*; see *ibid.* II 391 no.277. These decrees reflect a broad and general concern over alienation of ecclesiastical properties; cf. *ibid.* I 459f no.321 (1188), I 466f no.328 (1190), I 479 no.336 (1191), II 80 no.67 (1219). The consent of those concerned was also expected in transactions affecting a nonecclesiastical *principatus*; see *ibid.* II 70f no.57.

14 Above, Ch.VIc n.17.

15 Guillelmus Armoricus, *De gestis Philippi Augusti* anno 1209, ed. M. Bouquet, *Recueil des historiens des Gaules et de la France*, 2nd ed. rev.

between the *regalia* and the nonregalian appurtenances of the bishoprics, and he asserted his control exclusively over the former.

Still, it is far from certain that the monarchs were always equally scrupulous in adhering to this narrow conception of the *regalia* as the ecclesiastical princes' clearly secular properties and prerogatives, originally deriving from royal grants.[16] And of course on the Church's side, since canonical definition considered the right to administer the *regalia* an element of the episcopal *potestas iurisdictionis*, prominent churchmen sometimes manifestly ignored—and overstepped —the boundary between *iurisdictio* and the *regalia*.

Simply on the level of terminology, there were serious obstacles hindering any attempt to keep distinct the spheres of the *regalia* and of *iurisdictio*. To be sure, in 1133 archbishop Conrad of Salzburg had subtly drawn a line between the *regalia* and the nonregalian spheres of governance and administration, and even in his own time, Conrad's distinction was rare only by virtue of its lucidity. Two generations later the finest canonistic minds—men like Huguccio and Innocent III—could handle the main terms with great precision, sharply distinguishing the monarchical *regalia* from the purely ecclesiastical *temporalia* and *spiritualia*.[17] But elsewhere, even

---

L. Delisle (Paris 1899ff) XVII 82: "Rex eorum regalia confiscavit, scilicet ea tantum temporalia quae ab eo feodaliter tenebant, decimas et alia spiritualia eis in pace dimittens."

[16] As one may judge from the complaints of Conrad of Salzburg and Gerhoh of Reichersberg; above, Ch.VIIIв, Ch.IXв.

[17] Huguccio, *Summa* on C.16 q.7 c.12 v. *interdicimus*: ". . . inuestitura regalium non prohibetur recipi ab imperatoribus uel regibus uel aliis principibus . . . et inde est, quod episcopus licite de illis suscipit inuestituram a laica persona, nec te decipiat similitudo uel scriptura aliqua, ut credas quod patronus laicus possit clericum inuestire de ecclesia uel de rebus ecclesie collatis uel quantum ad spiritualia uel quantum ad temporalia, nullam enim potestatem habet in ecclesia uel in rebus ecclesie collatis . . ." (Vat.Arch. C.114 fol.241vb). Cf. *X* 1.6.32 (1208): ". . . Metropolitanus . . . electionem factam de ipso . . . confirmavit. Qui postea, regalibus receptis a rege ad petitionem . . . capituli a . . . Atrebatensi episcopo de mandato metropolitani . . . fuit in presbyterum ordinatus, et aliquamdiu nullo contradicente liberam et pacificam tam in spiritualibus quam in temporalibus administrationem obtinuit in ecclesia Morinensi. . . ." Innocent's reference to the *regalia* was included in *Comp.III* 1.6.17 but omitted from the *Liber extra*; the *ecclesia Morinensis* was the French royal bishopric of Thérouanne.

in important papal documents, the terms *regalia* and *temporalia* were sometimes regarded as identical.[18] Indeed, it was possible for an early thirteenth-century decretalist to interpret the term *regalia* as the "ecclesiastical property" or "affairs" (*res ecclesiasticae*) which were normally administered by an *electus* only after his confirmation—in short, to interpret the *regalia* unambiguously as the prelate's jurisdiction and as the *temporalia* of his church, rather than as a collection of royal rights and prerogatives which a bishop-elect received from king or emperor at the moment of investiture.[19]

Equally formidable was the terminological ambiguity within imperial parlance. Investing an imperial bishop with the *regalia*, Philip of Swabia described his own grant as the bestowal of "ordinary jurisdiction" on the bishop.[20] In contemporary juristic and administrative usage, *iurisdictio ordinaria* was a technical term for the jurisdictional—and especially judicial—powers inherent in the higher offices.[21] But

[18] *MGH Ep.saec.XIII* III 516 no.539 §19 (1263): ". . . Ab illis autem prelatis et ecclesiis, qui regalia sive temporalia bona tenent . . . a domino regni et aliis dominis temporalibus. . . ." *Ibid.* III 651 no.646 §18 (1265).

[19] Damasus, *Summa titulorum* on *Comp.I-III*, De electione et electi potestate: ". . . facultatem tamen administrandi res ecclesiasticas non consequitur electus nisi confirmetur. . . . Speciale est tantum in archiepiscopis Alamannie et aliarum partium remotarum . . . quia illi ante confirmationem administrant regalia, ut in extra De elec(tione) Quod sicut . . ." (BN 14320 fol.152). Here, Damasus was thoughtlessly following Innocent III's diction in *Quod sicut* (*Comp.III* 1.6.13 [*X* 1.6.28]; above, Ch.VIc n.5), where Innocent mentioned the administration of *regalia* by an unconfirmed *electus*. Yet Innocent—perhaps answering a question referred to him about this particular case—may have intended to indicate the *regalia* in a specifically technical sense. Or Innocent may have used the term carelessly.

[20] Philip of Swabia, investiture of bishop Herman of Valence (1205), ed. Winkelmann, *Acta imperii inedita* I 6 no.7: ". . . In supradictis vero omnibus [possessionibus] et in toto episcopatu ordinariam prefato episcopo concedimus iurisdictionem. . . ."

[21] The expression *iudex ordinarius* derived from Roman law (*Cod.* 1.3.32, 1.37.2, 12.19.2). In the 12th and early 13th centuries it was commonly applied to both the secular and the ecclesiastical hierarchies, which were thereby conceived as parallel in structure. In this mode of thought, jurists were imitating Gratian (C.2 q.6 dict.p.c.33): ". . . Iudicum enim alii sunt arbitrarii, alii ordinarii. Ordinarii uero sunt, qui ab apostolico, ut ecclesiastici, uel ab inperatore, utpote seculares, legitimam potestatem accipiunt . . ." More elaborately, Tancred, *Ordo iudiciarius* 1.1, ed. F. Bergmann, *Pillii, Tancredi, Gratiae libri de iudiciorum ordine* (Göttingen 1842) 91: "ordi-

iurisdictio ordinaria never became a common designation for the regalian powers. In the early thirteenth century a preferable term had already made its appearance as a synonym for the *regalia*: the even more familiar expression *administratio temporalium.*[22] In a letter of 1274 Rudolph of Hapsburg mentions that he has granted the *regalia* and the *administratio temporalium* to a certain abbess, and in that same year he describes a certain abbot as having been "invested with the *administratio temporalium* by the king of the Romans."[23] By a letter of 1290 Rudolph granted the *regalia* to the bishop-elect of Verdun, and to the formula of investiture Rudolph added an evocative phrase: "committing to you . . . the administration of temporal affairs and the plenary jurisdiction of preeminence in the church of Verdun."[24] In another letter of 1290 Rudolph clarified the significance of this imperial diction, for he expressly indicated that the *regalia* were identical with the *administratio temporalium.*[25] Even without rein-

narius iudex est, qui in ecclesiasticis ab apostolico, sicut primates, archiepiscopi, episcopi, in saecularibus ab imperatore, ut duces, marchiones, comites, totalem provinciae vel loci accipit iurisdictionem."

[22] Burchard of Ursberg, *Chronicon,* ed. Oswald Holder-Egger and B. von Simson (MGH SS.rer.Germ. Hanover 1916) 86: ". . . nec iste nec prefatus S[ifridus] Maguntinus potuerunt acquirere temporalium administrationem usque ad mortem Philippi."

[23] *MGH Const* III 637 no.647: ". . . feoda sua regalia et amministrationem temporalium principatus monasterii sui sibi concessimus. . . ." *Ibid.* III 637 no.648: ". . . idem [scil. abbas] imperiali ceptro a Romanorum rege de amministracione temporalium investitus. . . . Mandantes universis predicte abbatie . . . subiectis, quatinus eidem tamquam suo principi in omnibus ad amministracionem temporalium pertinentibus devote ac fideliter pareant et intendant."

[24] Kern, *Acta imperii* 42 no.64: ". . . regalia, feoda et iura principatus pontificalis . . . tibi . . . concedimus, et te . . . investimus . . . de eisdem, administrationem temporalium et iurisdictionem plenariam principatus ecclesie Virdunensis . . . tibi . . . committentes. Quocirca universis . . . ecclesie tue dedimus in mandatis, quatinus tibi tanquam principi nostro et eorum domino intendant in omnibus humiliter ac pareant reverenter." This letter served as a model for the investiture of later bishops of Verdun by king Adolph (1297) and king Albert (1305); *ibid.* 80 no.117 and 107 no.161. The command of obedience at the end of this letter (cf. also above, preceding note) seems to be taken over from papal practice; cf. *MGH Ep.saec.XIII* III 14 no.18 (Innocent IV).

[25] *MGH Const* III 421 no.434: ". . . cum abbatissa Romaricensis post novam suam creationem sua regalia, id est administrationem temporalium, a nobis petere et recipere . . . teneatur. . . ."

forcement from further examples, it is evident that in the later thirteenth century, to express with precision their concept of the *regalia* as the embodiment of secular jurisdictional and administrative rights, the German rulers appropriated the canonists' sharply defined terminology of office.

By the mid-twelfth century, the ancient quarrel over the monarchical investiture of prelates could never flare up again —clearly, there would not be another Investiture Struggle. By the last quarter of the twelfth century, however, the Church had created a new concept of jurisdiction which overlapped with the imperial concept of the *regalia*. Did Church and monarchy clash in a "Regalian Struggle" over the contradiction of the ecclesiastical and the imperial requirements? What solution could be found for the conflict between the requirements of electoral confirmation and regalian investiture? We must turn now to these questions.

2. The Assimilation of the *Regalia*

The tension between these two requirements, investiture and confirmation, is difficult to trace and analyze, for the conflict is visible only in routine administrative acts and in various minor collisions between the Church and the secular princes. It was never the object of a major contest between the two powers, and it never provoked the political or ecclesiological theorists to the creation of a systematic doctrine on this subject. Indeed, contemporary theorists scarcely seem aware of the problem, and not at all surprisingly, neither Church nor monarchy managed to formulate and adhere to a single consistent policy toward it. In a final sense, like the larger conflicts of Church and monarchy in the Middle Ages, the tension between these two requirements was never truly solved.[1] Yet despite the many ambiguities and obscurities,

[1] H. E. Feine, *Die Besetzung der Reichsbistümer vom Westfälischen Frieden bis zur Säkularisation 1648-1803* (Stuttgart 1921) 181ff, 347ff, points out that the relation between the two requirements was still discussed by jurists as late as the 17th and 18th centuries.

from scattered evidence one can discern the rough outlines of the policies and the customary usage adopted by the papacy, the empire, and the French monarchy.

In day-by-day routine or pressed by immediate realities, the papacy often implicitly recognized the importance of the *regalia* for the bishop-elect. Since the monarch commonly received the income from the episcopal *regalia* during a vacancy in the bishopric, this usage sometimes encouraged the protraction of vacancies. A pope might consistently intervene, therefore, as a matter of policy, to shorten the vacancies.[2] Moreover, the thirteenth-century papacy despatched innumerable requests to monarchs, asking them to grant the *regalia* to a newly confirmed bishop-elect.[3] A typical request might be:

> Hoping that . . . this church may profit by growth with regard to both *spiritualia* and *temporalia*, . . . we ask . . . that granting the *regalia* to this bishop-elect, you pour forth on him the grace of your benevolence in such a way that he, supported by the help of your favor, can assiduously . . . prosper in the execution of the pastoral duty. . . .[4]

Although these requests were occasionally expressed in the most urgent terms, from the viewpoint of the Church's constitutional law the papacy had no interest in regalian investi-

---

[2] For example, Innocent IV, *Reg.* nos.316, 1057, 1152, 1301, 3640.

[3] *MGH Ep.saec.XIII* III 275 no.309 (Halberstadt 1254); Alexander IV, *Reg.* no.1115 (Würzburg 1256); Kaltenbrunner, *Actenstücke* (cited above, Ch.VIB n.52) 354 no.335 (Trier 1286), 356 no.336 (Mainz 1289), 432 no.429 (Utrecht 1291); below, n.4 (Verdun); and often.

[4] Gregory X, letter to Rudolph of Hapsburg (1275), ed. O. Redlich, *Eine Wiener Briefsammlung zur Geschichte des deutschen Reiches* (Mittheilungen aus dem Vaticanischen Archive 2: Vienna 1894) 57 no.50: ". . . G(erardum) de G(randisono) electum Virdunensem . . . ipsi ecclesie de fratrum eorundem consilio et apostolice plenitudine potestatis in episcopum prefecimus et pastorem, sperantes, quod . . . eadem ecclesia tam circa spiritualia quam temporalia . . . proficiat incrementis. Quocirca serenitatem regiam rogamus . . . , quatenus regalia electo concedens eidem circa ipsum ita tue graciam benignitatis effundas, ut ipse fultus tui favoris auxilio in executione pastoralis officii possit assidue deo propicio prosperari. . . ."

The Eclipse of the *Regalia*

ture, and only once did the papacy explicitly admit that possession of the *regalia* could alter the jurisdictional competence of a prelate.[5]

In papal thought as early as Innocent III, the secular dignity of an ecclesiastical prince could only be an annex to an essentially spiritual and ecclesiastical office.[6] Thus Innocent included the administration of the *regalia* among the rights and powers derived from electoral confirmation.[7] Indeed, thirteenth-century history furnishes many examples of the Roman pontiffs' refusal to recognize any decisive binding force in the act of investiture, and Innocent himself was already consistently pursuing this policy at the very beginning of the century. For instance, after having been invested by Philip of Swabia, in 1200 the bishop of Würzburg was forced by Innocent to lay down his office.[8] Another case illustrating Innocent's policy: Though already invested with the *regalia*, the bishop-elect of Naumburg had to abandon his claims, to travel to Philip's court and to return the *regalia* to him.[9] In the same vein, when Gregory IX quashed the election of the bishop-elect of Regensburg in 1227, although the bishop-elect had been invested with the *regalia*, Gregory decreed that the bishop-elect's infeudations were invalid and that any alienated fiefs should be restored to the bishopric.[10] Even more revealing is the dispute over Mainz in 1200: immediately after an

[5] This single exception (Alexander IV) will be discussed below, nn.41f.
[6] A paraphrase of the perceptive remark by Tillmann, *Papst Innocenz III.* 73. In general, however, for the topic treated in the next few pages, the fundamental conception owes much to the brief but excellent analysis in the study by F. Baethgen, "Der Anspruch des Papsttums auf das Reichsvikariat," *ZRG KA* 10 (1920) 184-90 (reprinted in his *Mediaevalia* [MGH Schriften 17: 2 vols. Stuttgart 1960] 122-26).
[7] In addition to *X* 1.6.17 (above, Ch.IVʙ n.15), see also *X* 1.6.28 (above, Ch.VIᴄ n.5).
[8] Otto Kuhle, *Die Neubesetzung der deutschen Bistümer unter Papst Innozenz III.* (Berlin 1935) 12-15.
[9] *Chronica S. Petri Erfordensis* anno 1206, *Monumenta Erphesfurtensia saec.XII, XIII, XIV*, ed. O. Holder-Egger (MGH SS.rer.Germ. Hanover 1899) 203f; Tillmann, *Innocenz III.* 73 n.55.
[10] T. Ried, ed., *Codex diplomatico-chronologicus episcopatus Ratisponensis* I 349-51 nos. 367-69; *MGH Ep.saec.XIII* I 277 no. 363; and in general, Krabbo, *Besetzung der deutschen Bistümer* 112-17.

election to the archbishopric, king Philip invested the chosen prelate with the *regalia*. The election was contested, however, and the other candidate appealed to Rome.[11] Innocent instructed a legate to examine the case and particularly to determine whether Philip's candidate had already taken over the administration of Mainz—if so, his claim was lost without hope of appeal.[12] Here the key point is, of course, that under imperial law a duly invested candidate was entitled to administer immediately, whereas Innocent specifically regarded any act of administration by either candidate as a major offense unless sanctioned by electoral confirmation. Moreover, both Innocent III and Gregory IX regarded a bishop-elect's enfeoffment of his own vassals as dependent upon ecclesiastical sanctions, and as revocable at the Church's command. To say the least, papal confirmation of an ecclesiastical *electus* was certainly not facilitated by prior investiture. And obviously, the thirteenth-century papacy was unwilling to accept in any way the twelfth-century conception of regalian investiture as a confirmation of an episcopal election.[13]

THE BISHOP-ELECT AND HIS VASSALS

By 1200 canonical doctrine firmly asserted that an *electus* cannot accept an oath of fealty until his election has been confirmed—and, as an obvious corollary, that a confirmed bishop-elect may accept such oaths. The papacy was entirely

[11] Kuhle, *op.cit.* 28-32; and cf. Philip's own account of the investiture (*RNI* 321 no.136 [= *MGH Const* II 12 no.10]).

[12] *Reg.* 5.14, *PL* 214 964f.

[13] To be sure, the 13th-century papacy occasionally recognized the importance of the prince's assent. In 1200, for instance, after the archbishop of Canterbury had referred an election to Rome because of *defectus natalium*, Innocent III listed the factors to be considered: "concors capituli . . . electio, petitio populi, assensus principis, votum tuum [scil. archiepiscopi Cantuariensis], suffraganeorum suffragia" (*X* 1.6.20). Although the 13th-century papacy did not regard the *assensus principis* as the canonical confirmation of the election, the decretists were sometimes terminologically less careful (e.g. Simon of Bisignano; above, Ch.IIIA n.17). Far more unusual, however, was the identification of investiture and confirmation in the *Glossa Palatina* on D.63 c.22 v. *eligendi:* "idest confirmandi, ut patet per litteram sequentem, 'ab eo inuestituram' ex capitulo sequenti" (Vat.Pal. 658 fol.17rb).

The Eclipse of the *Regalia*

logical, therefore, when it refused to endorse the imperial principle which required investiture as a necessary and sufficient prerequisite to the acceptance of oaths. At this point, a few case histories may remove any remaining obscurity in the Church's constitutional doctrine on regalian investiture, and may illuminate the key principles within papal policy:

CASE NO. 1 (LIÈGE 1238): In the tangled negotiations following the double election at Liège in 1238, when some of the electors appealed to Rome, Gregory IX instructed the archbishop of Reims and the bishop of Cambrai to investigate the case.[14] Of the two candidates, Gregory favored William of Savoy rather than Otto, provost of Aachen. Indeed, Gregory accused Otto of having a bad reputation, a deficiency of learning, and a plurality of benefices; moreover, Otto was a *de facto* excommunicate.[15] Further, Gregory charged,

> Having received the *regalia*, although he was not uncontestedly elected and although his election was not confirmed, . . . he irreverently meddled and is still meddling in the administration of his bishopric.[16]

From Gregory's statement one can readily infer that before the confirmation of his election, Otto had no more right to receive the *regalia* than to administer them. A few weeks later, although the archbishop-elect of Cologne had just confirmed Otto's election, Gregory forbade the dean, chapter, nobles, and *ministeriales* of Liège to render obedience to either candidate till the papacy had confirmed one of the two elections, and also forbade them to give the "castles and fortresses" to

---

14 This conflict has been summarized by J. P. Kirsch, "Das Lütticher Schisma vom Jahre 1238," *RQSchr* 3 (1889) 177-87, with a collection of the main documents (pp.187-203).

15 Gregory IX, *Reg.* no.4587, ed. L. Auvray II 1165 (= Kirsch, *op.cit.* 187ff no.1).

16 *Ibid.*: ". . . dictus tamen prepositus . . . temere . . . est electus, et, receptis regalibus, quamquam in concordia non fuisset electus nec eius electio confirmata, . . . amministrationi episcopatus se irreverenter immiscuit et immiscet. . . ." Also, *Reg.* no.4863, ed. Auvray III 47f (= Kirsch, *op.cit.* 192f no. 4): ". . . [Otto] recepit regalia, confirmationis beneficio non obtento, et . . . amministrationi spiritualium et temporalium ecclesie . . . se impudenter ingessit."

either *electus* before a papal decision had settled the appeal.[17] In January of 1239 Gregory annulled all oaths taken to Otto, revoked all benefices granted by him, quashed his disciplinary acts, and ordered him stripped of all property belonging to the church of Liège.[18] Then in May the pontiff decided the dispute by appointing William of Savoy to the vacant see.[19] Naturally, all debts contracted by Otto were declared not binding on William.[20] And finally, Gregory ordered one of the bishopric's vassals to take the oath of fealty to the new bishop-elect, even though William had not been invested.[21]

CASE NO. 2 (CHÂLONS-SUR-MARNE 1241): In 1241 Gregory IX put an end to the protracted appeal against the episcopal election at Châlons-sur-Marne—a case which had dragged on for three years. As metropolitan, the archbishop of Reims had already confirmed the election of Joffrid, and Gregory decided in favor of the confirmed bishop-elect. Following this decision, the pontiff instructed king Louis IX to grant the *regalia* to Joffrid and to give him "the income received since the time of the confirmation."[22] There is no need to belabor the point: for Gregory IX, royal possession of the *regalia* implied no limitation on the administrative rights of a prelate-elect. Indeed, according to this papal principle, electoral confirmation was the sole touchstone, for even though the king might hold the *regalia* long after the confirmation, at the moment of confirmation and thereafter any profits from the *regalia* were automatically owed to the prelate-elect.

CASE NO. 3 (HALBERSTADT 1253): Ludolf of Schladen was

---

[17] *Reg.* no.4642, ed. Auvray II 1184f (= Kirsch, *op.cit.* 189f no.2).
[18] *Reg.* nos.4710, 4868, ed. Auvray II 1208f, III 50f (= Kirsch, *op.cit.* 190f, 197 nos.3, 9).
[19] *Reg.* no.4863, ed. Auvray III 47f (= Kirsch, *op.cit.* 192f no.4).
[20] Kirsch, *op.cit.* 195 no.7.
[21] Kirsch, *op.cit.* 194 no.5.
[22] Gregory IX, letter to Louis IX (1241), *Reg.* no.5983, ed. Auvray III 474: ". . . regalia ipsius ecclesie ac perceptos a tempore confirmationis fructus, eidem electo facias liberaliter assignari. . . ." Cf. also *Reg.* no.5974, *ibid.* 465-70. On this dispute, which lasted from 1237 to 1244, see Gerard J. Campbell, "Temporal and Spiritual Regalia during the Reigns of St Louis and Philip III," *Traditio* 20 (1964) 360f.

The Eclipse of the *Regalia*

a canon of Halberstadt cathedral, an unscrupulously ambitious man. He spread a false report that the bishop of Halberstadt had lawfully resigned his office. The subsequent events cannot be described more succinctly than in Innocent IV's indignant words:

> Ludolf . . . arranged for himself to be elected as pastor—or rather, pirate—of that church. And while the truth was kept secret, having received the *regalia* from . . . king William, he intruded upon the administration of the bishopric of Halberstadt and seized its castles and other properties. Finally, in reversed order . . . , he received the confirmation of this election from our venerable brother, archbishop Gerard of Mainz, the metropolitan of that place. Neither to the archbishop nor to the king did he make any mention of such misshapen proceedings. . . .[23]

Clearly, Innocent regarded electoral confirmation as prerequisite not only to the administration of the diocese, but also to the acceptance of the *regalia*. Nor could the investiture legitimately confer the administrative rights upon an unconfirmed bishop-elect. One should perhaps add that although Ludolf was confirmed, invested, and eventually even consecrated, the papacy succeeded in overriding his claims and in installing an acceptable candidate.

CASE NO. 4 (REIMS 1299): When Robert of Courtenai was elected to the archbishopric of Reims, he gave his consent to

[23] Innocent IV, letter to bishop Herman of Würzburg (1253), *MGH Ep.saec.XIII* III 206 no.240: ". . . prefatus Ludolfus . . . se de facto in pastorem ipsius ecclesie vel raptorem potius eligi procuravit, et receptis a . . . W. rege Romanorum illustri tacita veritate regalibus, et amministrationi episcopatus Halberstadensis se temere ingerens ac occupans castra et alia bona ipsius, demum ordine prepostero et ex malicia commutato a venerabili fratre nostro G. Maguntino archiepiscopo loci metropolitano huiusmodi electionis confirmationem obtinuit, nullam ipsi vel dicto regi de tam informi processu faciens mentionem. . . ." Ludolf's later vicissitudes can be traced *ibid.* 274f, 363-66, 436f, nos.309, 405, 472; also on Ludolf, G. Schmidt, ed., *UB des Hochstifts Halberstadt* II 136-230 nos. 868-999. In general, see Franz Tenckhoff, *Papst Alexander IV.* (Paderborn 1907) 173f, and P. Aldinger, *Die Neubesetzung der deutschen Bistümer unter Papst Innocenz IV. 1243-1254* (Leipzig 1900) 161-64.

the election and requested the cathedral chapter to give him the properties and prerogatives which they had held since the death of the previous archbishop.[24] After going to Rome, Robert presented the election decree to Boniface VIII and asked for the electoral confirmation. To examine the election and the *electus*, the pontiff named a commission, which apparently discovered an irregularity, for the archbishop-elect resigned his claim upon the church of Reims. Then, on 10 April 1299, Boniface used his papal *plenitudo potestatis* to appoint Robert to the vacant archbishopric, and Boniface immediately announced this appointment (*provisio*) to the cathedral chapter of Reims, to the people and clergy of the archdiocese, to the suffragan bishops of the Reims province, to the vassals of the archbishopric, and to king Philip IV of France.[25] (Direct papal appointment of a prelate—*provisio*—had, of course, the same juridical effects as the confirmation of a canonical election, for the new prelate was entitled *electus* and could fully exercise his jurisdictional powers).[26] The first hint of trouble came two weeks later, on April 25th, when Boniface found it necessary to write the provost, dean, and chapter of Reims: They should, he commanded, restore to the *electus* the castles and the ecclesiastical jurisdiction which they had legitimately held during the vacancy of the archiepiscopal throne.[27] Moreover, they must restore to the archbishop-elect all income received after the moment at which Robert had consented to his election and had thereupon requested from them the *administratio in spiritualibus et*

[24] Boniface VIII, *Reg.* nos.3022, 3024-32, 3045, ed. G. Digard et al. (Paris 1907ff) II 389-401; August Baumhauer, *Philipp der Schöne und Bonifaz VIII. in ihrer Stellung zur französischen Kirche* (Freiburg im Breisgau 1920) 76-80.

[25] *Reg.* no.3022, ed. Digard II 389f.

[26] On papal provisions in general, see works cited, by Feine, *RG* I 304f, and esp. G. Barraclough, *Papal Provisions* (Oxford 1935). Occasionally *confirmatio* and *provisio* were linked as key papal prerogatives in the formulae of 13th-century documents; e.g., *MGH Ep.saec.XIII* III 516 no.539 (1263): "... salva ... tam in faciendis provisionibus et electionibus confirmandis quam in omnibus quibuscumque aliis Romani pontificis ... iurisdictione ac auctoritate plenaria et libera potestate."

[27] *Reg.* no.3045, ed. Digard II 400f.

The Eclipse of the *Regalia*

temporalibus. Almost a century earlier the Fourth Lateran Council had pronounced that a non-Italian metropolitan-elect (like Robert) could administer immediately after election, and, in that tradition, Boniface was defining the *electus*'s request of the temporalities as the jurisdictional termination of the archiepiscopal vacancy.[28] A series of papal letters, dated April 26th and 27th, then made the necessary arrangements for Robert of Courtenai to receive priestly orders, episcopal consecration, and the archiepiscopal *pallium*.[29] On April 27th, Boniface despatched another letter to king Philip the Fair, this time about the *regalia*: He reminded the king that Robert was now lawfully entitled to the *administratio in spiritualibus et temporalibus*, and that Philip should surrender the *temporalia* to the new archbishop-elect, as already requested. Moreover, Boniface continued,

> By whatever name it may be called, the guardianship or custody of ecclesiastical properties during vacancies in the churches was introduced and tolerated by the Church for the benefit of the churches themselves. It must cease as soon as the vacant church has a legitimate person to whom the administration of ecclesiastical properties has been canonically granted, so that no layman—whatever his eminence or status—can [then] administer these properties under pretense of the *regalia* or custody or guardianship, nor can he receive their income. . . .[30]

---

28 Cf. above, Ch.VIc.
29 *Reg.* nos.3026-30, ed. Digard II 392f.
30 *Reg.* no.3031, ed. Digard II 394f: ". . . attendens quod bonorum ecclesiasticorum custodia sive guardia, quocumque nomine nuncupetur, vacationum ecclesiasticarum tempore, pro utilitate ipsarum ecclesiarum extitit introducta et per Ecclesiam tolerata, debetque cessare postquam vacans ecclesia habet personam legitimam cui bonorum ecclesiasticorum administratio canonice est permissa, ita quod, nec pretextu regalium vel custodie sive guardie, persona laica, cuiuscumque foret eminentie sive status, administrare potest in illis proventusque percipere seu temporalia bona tenere; . . . de proventibus seu fructibus, per officiales tuos perceptis a tempore quo dictus in concordia petiit temporalia sibi reddi et hanc custodiam seu guardiam amoveri usque ad tempus quo idem electus in nostra presentia constitutus omne ius . . . pure ac libere in nostris manibus resignavit, plenam satisfactionem impendi facias electo predicto. . . ."

351

In other words, the ruler cannot delay in granting the tempo-ralities to a "legitimate person," that is, to a confirmed bishop-elect, or, even without electoral confirmation, to a non-Italian archbishop-elect. On April 28th, Boniface sent abbreviated versions of this letter to the bishop of Dol, to a certain count Guido, and to the royal counselor Pierre Flote, in the hope that they would attempt to influence the king on behalf of the archbishop-elect and of his rights.[31] In another letter ad-dressed to these three men on the same day and for the same general purpose, Boniface mentioned his own request to Philip, to bestow "the *temporalia*, which are commonly called the *regalia*," upon Robert of Courtenai as a special favor (*de gratia speciali*), even though the archbishop-elect may be unable to visit king Philip at an early date and to take the required oaths and due homage in the king's presence.[32]

From these case histories, three points emerge clearly: First, the papacy was—at the very least—indifferent to the imperial conception of regalian investiture, for the popes refused to recognize the major constitutive effect claimed for the act of investiture. Second, the canonical regulations were far from indifferent to the bishop-elect's enfeoffment of his own vassals and to any other exercise of his feudal juris-diction, which normally presupposed, under Church law, electoral confirmation as a prerequisite. Third, the papacy maintained a lively interest in the feudal rights of prelates and in the relations between these ecclesiastical princes and their vassals. As an early instance of this latter concern, when certain vassals of an English prelate refused to swear fealty to him, Alexander III authorized the prelate to suspend them

[31] *Reg.* no.3032, ed. Digard II 395f.
[32] *Reg.* no.3024, ed. Digard II 391: ". . . regem [Phylippum] . . . horta-mur . . . ut . . . presentialem prestationem sibi faciendam per eum ipsi electo usque ad reditum eius proroget, si forsan ad presentiam regiam non sic festinus accesserit sicut vellet, ac nichilominus ei vel nuntiis suis ad hoc specialiter destinatis temporalia que vulgariter regalia nuncupantur . . . reddat et reddi faciat de gratia speciali, huiusmodi dilatione presentialis pre-stationis homagii non obstante. . . ." Also, *Reg.* no.3025, *ibid.* 391f.

The Eclipse of the *Regalia*

from the tenure of their fiefs till they had taken the customary oath.[33] Indeed, all three of these tendencies are evident in countless papal letters to the vassals of prelates-elect: In 1225, for example, Honorius III wrote to the nobles and *ministeriales* of Paderborn, ordering them to fulfill all their obligations and to swear fealty to their newly confirmed bishop-elect, who, in fact, had not yet received the *regalia*.[34] In ordering vassals to obey, such papal documents commonly ignored the fact that a prelate-elect might not yet have received his investiture, and they directed terrible threats against rebellious vassals who refused obedience to a duly confirmed prelate-elect.[35]

Among the glosses of his great *Apparatus*, Innocent IV once presented a view which was perfectly consistent with the traditional imperial concept of regalian investiture. On the one hand, he asserted, a prelate has a "certain spiritual right" which includes all of the powers acquired through confirmation and consecration, and on the other hand, through investiture a prelate can accept the homage, fealty, and service of his vassals. Thus, according to Innocent's gloss, investiture effectively confers the various *temporalia*.[36] Yet Innocent's apparent accommodation to imperial doctrine could not easily be translated into policy, since the sentences

[33] Letter to the abbot of St Augustine's, Canterbury (1179-81), ed. W. Holtzmann, *PU England* I (Abh.Göttingen 25: Berlin 1930) 469f no.200.
[34] R. Wilmans, ed., *Westfälisches UB* IV 96 no.141: ". . . per apostolica vobis scripta mandamus, quatinus eidem electo . . . plene ac humiliter intendatis, ei sicut tenemini exhibentes iuramenta fidelitatis et in ecclesie sue negotiis assistentes, plene insuper eidem de iuribus ipsi ecclesie a vobis debitis responsuri"; Baethgen, *ZRG KA* 10 (1920) 187 n.2 (= *Mediaevalia* 124 n.45), and for the subsequent investiture, *Reg.imp.* V no. 1571a.
[35] Ried, *Codex* I 349f no.367 (Regensburg 1227; above, n.10); Boniface VIII, *Reg.* no.1743, ed. Digard I 659f (Verdun 1297). Other examples of such papal orders to vassals, with the accompanying threat of sanctions, will appear later in this discussion.
[36] Innocent IV, *Apparatus* on X 1.6.28 v. *nominatio*: ". . . dicemus quod ex inuestitura regum . . . non habebant instituti ab eis aliquod ius spirituale, puta quod possent conferre ecclesias uel canonicatus uel ordinare clericos uel huiusmodi. Potestatem autem horum recipiebant a confirmatore uel consecratore uel quocumque alio ministro spirituali et ecclesiastico. Per inuestituram autem laicorum potest recipere uassalagia et alia temporalia."

of excommunication and deposition against Frederick II created a painful problem for newly elected German bishops under Gregory IX and under Innocent himself. After Frederick's deposition was proclaimed in July 1245, the imperial throne was officially vacant, and even during the previous half-dozen years, a bishop-elect could not lawfully have had any contact with the excommunicated monarch. At least in the realm of legal theory, the harsh dilemma imposed by this circumstance was still unsolved a century later, when a distinguished canonist asked,

> Whether the prelates of the churches, before they receive their fiefs from the king or emperor, can enfeoff their own vassals, if the ruler happens to be excommunicated.[37]

Though strongly pro-papal in outlook, the cautious canonist was unwilling "to declare hastily either pro or con," and nearby in the margin of his manuscript, a scribe commented, "Note these questions, since some seem to need clarification."[38] Despite the complexity of the theoretical problem, however, and despite his own gloss explaining the effect of investiture, Innocent IV acted decisively and realistically in the realm of practice, for he followed the precedents provided by Honorius III and Gregory IX. In January 1245, the bishop of Liège complained that to the great detriment of his church, his vassals refused to do homage and to obey him, since he had never received the *regalia*—and could not receive them from an excommunicated emperor. Innocent simply sent orders to the feudatories, demanding that they render "due homage and other customary services" to their lord.[39] Un-

---

[37] Herman of Schildesche (1327-31), *Contra hereticos* 14, ed. Richard Scholz, *Unbekannte politische Streitschriften aus der Zeit Ludwigs des Bayern 1327-1354* II (Rome 1914) 137: "an prelati ecclesiarum infeodare possint suos vassallos, antequam recipiant feodum a rege vel imperatore, si eum contingat excommunicari: non est meum precipitanter asserere pro vel contra"; Baethgen, *ZRG KA* 10 (1920) 185 n.1 (= *Mediaevalia* 122 n.38).
[38] Scholtz, *op.cit.* 136 note a.
[39] *MGH Ep.saec.XIII* II 64 no.90.

doubtedly provoked by a similar situation, in 1246 Innocent wrote to the vassals of the bishop of Verdun:

> We command that without any delay, you must do homage and take the oaths of fealty owed to our venerable brother, the bishop of Verdun, since in Germany at present he has no emperor or king from whom he could receive the *regalia* of the Verdun church.[40]

Firmly established by midcentury, this policy obviously reflects the intense concern of the papacy and of the bishops-elect themselves over the problematical loyalty of vassals and over the possible loss of property and revenue.

Once in thirteenth-century practice, however, the papacy openly recognized the imperial conception of investiture as a constitutive act: In 1255, Alexander IV asked king William of Holland to invest the bishop-elect of Verdun with the *regalia*, or rather, to invest the bishop-elect's proctor, since the *electus* himself was detained by business at the papal court. Moreover, pope Alexander expressed this wish with great urgency, adding specifically his hope that the investiture could be performed as soon as possible (*qualibet mora vel dilatione postpositis*). As the final part of his request, the pontiff explained his desire that

> This church should not, because of the *regalia*, incur any loss or damage in temporalities and spiritualities.[41]

William died before fulfilling the pope's request, so Alexander took matters into his own hands. Acting "in the place of a king" (*vice regia*), he invested the bishop-elect with the *regalia* of his church.[42] In this bestowal of the *regalia*, Alex-

---

[40] *Ibid.* II 117 no.155: ". . . mandamus, quatinus . . . episcopo Virdunensi homagium et fidelitatis debite iuramenta sine dilatione qualibet, cum nullum ad presens in Theotonia imperatorem [ille] habeat sive regem, a quo [regalia] Virdunensis ecclesie recipere valeat, exhibere curetis"; Baethgen, *op.cit.* 189 (= *Mediaevalia* 125).

[41] *MGH Ep.saec.XIII* III 375 no.417.

[42] *Ibid.* III 390 no.431 (1256): ". . . Nos itaque . . . regalia huiusmodi, cum imperium vacet ad presens, vice regia auctoritate presentium tibi duximus concedenda, ita tamen quod pro ipsis futuro regi Romanorum, cum per sedem apostolicam sua fuerit electio confirmata [fidelitatis debite iura-

ander added that in return for the *regalia*, the bishop-elect should take the customary oath "to the future king of the Romans, when his election has been confirmed by the Apostolic See." (It is striking that Alexander regarded the "future king of the Romans" as a quasi-ecclesiastical official and applied canonical criteria to him: like any bishop, before the confirmation of his election the king of the Romans will have no right to accept an oath of fealty from a vassal.[43]) The regalian investiture of an imperial bishop by the pope was indeed an innovation. But for a pope to stress the importance of regalian investiture and then to take over this imperial function was to admit, by implication, that it had significant —or even indispensable—constitutive effects upon the powers of a bishop or bishop-elect. Understandably, after Alexander's unique venture in the bestowal of *regalia*, the papacy returned to its earlier position.[44]

In all probability, some imperial bishoprics quickly accepted the papal definition of electoral confirmation, rather than regalian investiture, as the effective beginning of the bishop-elect's feudal prerogatives. In other bishoprics, however, apparently clerics and vassals alike adhered more steadfastly to the imperial conception of investiture. Verdun was a prime example of such conservatism, and to this situation

---

menta] exhibeas . . ."; Baethgen, *ZRG* KA 10 (1920) 185f (= *Mediaevalia* 122f).

There were, of course, innumerable papal grants of *administratio temporalium* during the 13th century, but this kind of conferment should not be confused with a papal bestowal of the *regalia*, for in this context, the *administratio temporalium* was conceived as an essentially ecclesiastical form of jurisdiction. A few examples of papal grants of *administratio temporalium*: *PL* 215 990 (Constance 1206); *UB Salzburg* IV nos.2, 28, 49, 79 (Salzburg 1247, Passau 1249, Salzburg 1265, 1270); Innocent IV, *Reg.* no.3136 (Lübeck 1247); *MGH Ep.saec.XIII* III 233 no.267 (Lübeck 1254); Alexander IV, *Reg.* nos.842, 2217 (Verdun 1255, Salzburg 1256); Martin IV, *Reg.* no.177 (Metz 1282).

[43] In a separate study, I hope to trace the canonistic origins and the evolution of this important conception of the imperial office; in general, see Fritz Kern, "Die Reichsgewalt des deutschen Königs nach dem Interregnum," *HZ* 106 (1911) 39-69.

[44] Baethgen, *ZRG* KA (1920) 185f, 189 (= *Mediaevalia* 122f, 125).

the papacy reacted forcefully. In 1246 Innocent IV ordered the vassals of Verdun to obey their uninvested bishop,[45] and soon thereafter, when the see fell vacant, he commanded the dean and chapter not to elect a successor before the arrival of the papal legate then on his way to Verdun.[46] Announcing his appointment of a new bishop-elect in 1253, Innocent wrote separate letters to the chapter, the clergy, and the vassals of Verdun, enjoining obedience on all of them and specifically ordering the vassals to swear fealty to their new lord. Each of the three letters ended with a formula threatening the recipients with spiritual and temporal punishment as "rebels" if they refused to obey.[47] And when Alexander IV briefly assumed an imperial vicarship in 1255, he adopted this unique expedient in order to confer the *regalia* on the bishop-elect of Verdun.[48] Still, as late as 1288, Verdun customarily withheld recognition and obedience from each new bishop-elect till he had shown a letter certifying his investiture with the *regalia*, and in 1297 Boniface VIII threatened severe sanctions against any vassal disobedient to the confirmed bishop-elect of Verdun.[49]

As one of the steps in the accession of a newly elected prelate, the Church prescribed a purely ecclesiastical investiture with ring and staff, the symbols of high ecclesiastical office. Since the Concordat of Worms, this kind of investiture had remained exclusively a prerogative of the Church. It is, of course, evident that the Church firmly denied any significant jurisdictional consequences in the act of regalian investiture. Indeed, the twelfth-century Church could easily have found reasons for identifying the *ecclesiastical* investiture with the new prelate's acquisition of jurisdictional powers, since even before the twelfth century the crosier had been consid-

45 Above, n.40.
46 *MGH Ep.saec.XIII* II 234 no.307 (1247).
47 *Ibid.* III 207f no.242.
48 Above, n.42.
49 *MGH Const* III 398 no.410 (above, Ch.VIIIc n.44); for Boniface VIII, above, n.35.

ered specifically a symbol of jurisdiction and rule.[50] Moreover, as early as the 1170's, the distinction between ecclesiastical investiture and electoral confirmation was perhaps blurred by the fact that the ring and the staff were commonly bestowed upon the *electus* by the hierarchical superior who had just confirmed the election. At the same time, this ecclesiastical investiture was sometimes regarded as identical with the act in which the new prelate ceremoniously took possession of his church (*missio in possessionem*), an act which amounted to a solemn inauguration, following the confirmation and carried out in the presence either of the confirming superior or of the latter's *nuntius*.[51] Also, in the late

[50] The theme was stated as early as Isidore of Seville (*De ecclesiasticis officiis* 2.5.12, *PL* 83 783f): "Huic autem dum consecratur, datur baculus, ut eius iudicio subditam plebem vel regat vel corriget. . . ." In the *ordines* for episcopal consecrations, the same idea reappears; M. Andrieu, "Le sacre épiscopal d'après Hincmar de Reims," *Revue d'histoire ecclésiastique* 48 (1953) 54-62. For a 10th-century example, *Ordo* 35B.37, ed. Andrieu, *Ordines romani* IV 108: "Cum datur baculus, dicit: 'Accipe baculum, sacri regiminis signum, ut . . . pravos corrigas, rectos dirigas in viam salutis eterne, habeasque potestatem erigendi dignos et corrigendi indignos . . .' "; similarly, *Pontificale Romanum saec.XII* 10.27, ed. Andrieu, *Pontifical romain* I 149; and often.

Such liturgical statements had juristic and theological counterparts. Investiture with the *virga pastoralis iudicii* was mentioned by Bonizo of Sutri (*Liber de vita christiana* 2.27, ed. Perels 46). According to Hugh of St Victor, "Baculus . . . iustitiam significat praelatorum, qua subiectos regere debent . . ." (*De sacramentis* 2.4.15, *PL* 176 438). Of course, during the Investiture Struggle the publicists argued constantly over ring and staff; a few examples will suffice: The Anglo-Norman Anonymous considered the *virga pastoralis* a *signum regiminis*, like the *virga regia* (*Tractatus* 4, *MGH LdL* III 674). For Placidus of Nonantula, investiture with the crosier indicated the conveyance of episcopal jurisdiction over property and people (above, Ch.VIIB n.69). The *Disputatio vel defensio Paschalis pape* referred to the "virga qua [ecclesia] regitur" (*MGH LdL* II 666).

[51] Bernard of Pavia, *Summa de electione* 3.3-4, ed. Laspeyres, *Sum. decr.* 321: "§3 . . . Sunt enim nonnulli, qui differentiam [inter institutionem et investituram] in hoc facientes fieri investituram dicunt, cum post confirmationem electionis ille, qui confirmavit, in manu electi annulum vel baculum . . . tribuit, his verbis . . . utendo: 'Investio te de hac dignitate . . .'; institutionem autem fieri dicunt, cum quis in possessionem mittitur, v.g. cum a confirmatore vel eius nuntio in ecclesiam ducitur, in sede locatur . . . et claves eius manibus immittuntur. . . . . invenitur tamen, investituram et institutionem pro eodem accipi. . . . Id autem tene firmissime, institutionem vel investituram alicuius spiritualis a laico fieri non posse. . . . §4. Notandum autem institutionem aliam esse temporalium, aliam spiritualium; utraque autem ad episcopum de ecclesiis suae dioecesis videtur generali iure pertinere. . . ." The ceremonial enthronement following the confirmation could also be regarded as the effective *institutio* of the newly elected prelate; *ibid.* 2.3.4, *ed.cit.* 319f.

twelfth century, the effects of ecclesiastical investiture could be considered remarkably similar to those of electoral confirmation, for this investiture was described then as conferring the exercise of the full powers and rights of office (*dignitas vel beneficium*) and as the point at which the prelate can be deprived of office only by judicial process.[52] According to Raymond of Peñafort, the act of taking possession is not substantially different from the act of confirmation, and there can be no delay or postponement between the confirmation and the installation of the *electus* in his church.[53] In his *Apparatus*, however, Innocent IV gave a concise and even classical presentation to the idea that confirmation alone is sufficient, even without investiture:

> As soon as he has been confirmed, without any other act of taking possession or investiture or installation, an *electus* can immediately administer the affairs of his church, in temporal and in spiritual matters. . . .[54]

Within this passage, Innocent was referring to the purely ecclesiastical installation and investiture.[55] Still, his remark seems to apply equally well to the regalian investiture, for of

[52] Bernard, *Summa decretalium* 3.7.3-4, ed. Laspeyres 72: "§3. Est [institutio] autem facienda post electionis confirmationem; praecedit enim electio, sequitur confirmatio, deinde institutio sive investitura. §4. Effectus institutionis est, ut abinde libere sua dignitate vel beneficio uti possit nec destitui valeat sine rationabili et cognita causa. . . ."

[53] Raymond of Peñafort, *Summa iuris* 33, ed. Rius Serra, *Opera* I 124: ". . . post confirmationem consequitur [electus] administrationem tam temporalium quam spiritualium, preter illa que . . . plus ex ordine quam ex iurisdictione pendent . . . adeo quod inter confirmationem et missionem in possessionem non sit gradus, hoc est dicere si post confirmationem appellaretur, non ideo suspenderetur missio in possessionem. . . ."

[54] Innocent IV, *Apparatus* on X 1.6.15 v. *confirmationem*: "Nota, quod electus quam cito est confirmatus sine alia possessione uel inuestitura uel stallatione statim potest adminstrare res ecclesie sue in temporalibus et spiritualibus tam in colligendis fructibus quam in actionibus intentandis nomine ecclesie sue"; Baethgen, *ZRG KA* 10 (1920) 186 n.1 (= *Mediaevalia* 123).

[55] Note that in the same context with *investitura*, Innocent uses the specifically ecclesiastical terms *possessio* (= *missio in possessionem*) and *stallatio*. Also, the decretal on which Innocent's gloss was based (X 1.6.15) discusses a case involving ecclesiastical discipline for unruly clerics (above, Ch.IVB n.13); it is inconceivable that in the Church's view, regalian investiture should have any effect upon a prelate's ecclesiastical disciplinary powers.

course, in practice, Innocent was quick to insist that regalian investiture was not necessary to the feudal powers and position of an imperial bishop.

But were there any compelling canonical reasons for the Church's insistence that the vassals even of an uninvested bishop-elect owe full fealty to their lord? At least by analogy, decretistic doctrine on the oath of fealty will illuminate the Church's position on the relation between the bishop-elect and his vassals. Of course, the nullification of an oath of fealty—or indeed, of any oath—was an ecclesiastical prerogative.[56] From Gregory VII's famous letter to Herman of Metz in 1081, Gratian excerpted an historical justification of the papal right to absolve subjects from oaths of fealty taken to kings or bishops.[57] Commenting on this passage, Rufinus explained that such oaths are taken "sometimes with regard to persons, at other times with regard to offices." An oath of fealty by one layman to another is personal, and can be terminated only by the lord's excommunication. An oath of fealty to a prelate, however, is sworn because of the secular office which the prelate has received from a lay prince, and such an oath is binding precisely so long as the prelate holds this office.[58] Later decretists did not unanimously accept Rufinus's views on this problem, though they usually accepted

[56] For one example, the *Summa Tractaturus magister* on C.15 q.6 c.3 v. *a regno deposuit*: ". . . Set hic nihil aliud fuit deponere, nisi subditos a iuramento fidelitatis absolvere, quod ius spirituale est sicut et ligare" (Stickler, *MIÖG* 62 [1954] 198 n.63).

[57] C.15 q.6 c.3 (incorrectly ascribed by Gratian to Gelasius I).

[58] Rufinus, *Summa* on C.15 q.6 c.3 v. *Alius item Romanus*, ed. Singer 350: "Hic sciendum est quod iuramenta fidelitatis fiunt aliquando intuitu personarum, aliquando intuitu dignitatum. Et quidem intuitu personarum, sicut illa, que laicis laici faciunt; contemplatione dignitatum, ut ea, que prelatis ecclesiarum a laicis offeruntur, non utique propter ipsas prelatorum personas, sed propter eas quas ipse persone suscipiunt dignitates. Si quis itaque intuitu persone iuraverit alicui fidelitatem, semper iuramento obligatus ei tenebitur, nisi suus dominus ab ecclesia fuerit anathematizatus: interea enim, scil. dum in excommunicatione dominus fuerit, fidelis etiam non debet servire ei. . . . Si autem intuitu dignitatis quis alteri fidelitatem iuraverit, postquam dominus dignitatem illam canonice perdiderit vel legitime, iuratorum ei deinceps obligatus nequaquam erit. . . . Isti enim regi Francorum iuraverant Franci intuitu regie potestatis; postquam ergo rex legitime regnum perdidit, iuramenti vinculum absolutum fuit."

his general approach, as well as his distinction between "office" and "person."[59] In fact, among the decretists it was a commonplace to note, in the words of Alanus Anglicus, "that those who have a fief from a church must do fealty not only to the church but to the prelate."[60] That is, the prelate's vassals owe their fealty equally to his church, episcopate, or office, and to him personally. Indeed, this principle was also accepted by the imperial court under Barbarossa, for when two imperial bishops were deprived of their *regalia*, "the *regalia* were confiscated only from the persons, since *regalia* are granted not to persons but perpetually to churches."[61] As an imperial law explained, the bishop's *beneficium* is "given not only to the person but to the church," and if he loses it through judicial sentence but manages to retain his ecclesiastical office, the *beneficium* reverts to the king till the bishop's death and replacement by a suitable successor.[62]

On the feudal oath to "office" or "person," the consequences of Rufinus's doctrine were most clearly perceived and elaborated by master Huguccio:

> Therefore, when a king or bishop is deposed, all of his vassals by virtue of kingship or episcopate (*episcopium*) . . . are immediately released with regard to him, but not

[59] A dissenting view was held by Sicard of Cremona, *Summa*: ". . . Intuitu dignitatis: et hic dignitate durante permanet obligatus, nisi dominus . . . fuerit excommunicatus. Dignitate vero rationabiliter amissa aiunt quidam, quod evanescit obligatio, set satius est, si apostolica requiritur absolutio" (Stickler, *MIÖG* 62 [1954] 197f n.62). Cf. also the *Summa Parisiensis* on C.15 q.6 dict.p.c.2 v. *A fidelitatis*, ed. McLaughlin 176: ". . . Ea [scil. iuramenta fidelitatis] ergo que fiunt causa dignitatis papa poterit dissolvere si aliquem a dignitate potest deponere. Ea vero que sunt respectu persone, nec papa nec alius poterit absolvere."

[60] *Apparatus Ius naturale* on D.63 c.33 v. *Iohanni*: "arg. quod qui feudum habent ab ecclesia non solum ecclesie set prelato debent fidelitatem facere . . ." (Stickler, *Salesianum* 21 [1959] 360).

[61] Above, Ch.VIIB n.58.

[62] Above, Ch.VIIB n.58. On the other hand, if Paschal II's renunciation of the *regalia* had been carried out in February 1111, thereafter the *regalia* would presumably have been attached solely to the *person* of a bishop, rather than to his office and his church, nor could his successor have asserted any claim to succeed him in possession of the *regalia*. Of course, under these circumstances, the emperor would not have conferred *regalia* on all bishops, but only on those whom he deemed trustworthy.

with regard to the kingship or the episcopate or the successor. For they are always bound to the kingship and the episcopate, and as soon as the successor is installed, they are immediately bound to him with the original obligation.[63]

For the special case of an excommunicated feudal lord, Huguccio had a characteristic doctrine: the vassals of an excommunicated lord still have the "obligation of fealty," but they are not obligated to the "execution" of fealty until the lord is reconciled to the Church.[64] In Huguccio's thought, however, the case of a deposed bishop is a more instructive one, since the same principle seems equally valid for the vacancy left by the death of a bishop and for that left by his deposition. Still, Huguccio did not clarify a further question: At what moment could one say that "the successor is installed" (*successor substituitur*)?[65] Huguccio might have asserted that "the successor is installed" when *electus* and electors give their "mutual consent."[66] But if one regarded electoral confirmation, even without the regalian investiture, as a sufficient installation in office, obviously the vassals of a confirmed bishop-elect were then "immediately bound to him with the original obligation." And such was precisely the view of the thirteenth-century papacy, which regarded elec-

---

[63] *Summa* on C.15 q.6 c.3 v. cum milites *absoluit*: ". . . set distingue: cum quis iurat alicui fidelitatem, aut iurat ei intuitu dignitatis aut intuitu persone. Si intuitu dignitatis, quam cito ille remouetur a dignitate illa, statim et ille desinit ei teneri. Si intuitu persone, puta propter patrimonium eius uel ob aliud, licet ille remoueatur a dignitate illa, non tamen iste absoluitur. Cum ergo rex uel episcopus deponitur, statim omnes uasalli eius intuitu regni uel episcopii ipso iure absoluuntur quo ad illum, set non quo ad regnum uel episcopium uel successorem. Regno et episcopio semper tenentur, et quam cito successor substituitur, statim ei tenentur pristina obligatione. Exigitur tamen et fit noua obligatio ab illis, et hoc ad cautelam, quia solet plus timeri, . . . ne longinquitate temporis obscuretur conditio obligationis . . ." (Vat.Arch. C.114 fol.229va; cf. Mochi Onory, *Fonti* 156).

[64] *Summa* on C.15 q.6 c.4 v. *absoluimus* (above, Ch.VA n.34).

[65] Similar diction was used—with a radically different meaning—in the imperial chancery: a document of 1166 states that the emperor will hold the *regalia* of Cologne "usque ad substitutionem alterius episcopi"; Lacomblet, *Niederrheinisches UB* I 289 no.417.

[66] Above, Ch.VA.

The Eclipse of the *Regalia*

toral confirmation as full warrant for the use of jurisdictional and feudal prerogatives, that is, for the exercise of powers over vassals as well as over ecclesiastical subordinates.

3. The Primacy of Electoral Confirmation

Thus, as a juridical act, electoral confirmation overrode regalian investiture, for the Church chose to ignore or even to assimilate the jurisdictional content ascribed to the *regalia* in imperial doctrine. This potential conflict between investiture and confirmation might have been reconciled in an imaginative but essentially impractical compromise, by simultaneously confirming the election and bestowing the *regalia*. One can, in fact, easily find instances of this, for bishop Otto II of Freising (1184-85), and archbishops Engelbert I of Cologne (1216) and Christian II of Mainz (1249) were confirmed and invested on the same day.[1] Necessarily, however, this procedure was unusual, and at least till the end of the twelfth century the *regalia* were often conferred soon after the election, without any regard for electoral confirmation, which might follow much later.[2] But since investiture and confirmation were rarely simultaneous, there existed the possibility of conflict between the overlapping claims of these two acts. At the very least, the sequence of the two acts could become a question of some significance, just as the sequence of investiture and consecration had once been.[3]

The problem of sequence had already been anticipated in the mid-twelfth century, when Gerhoh of Reichersberg asserted that all *spiritualia* should first be conferred upon the bishop-elect, who is thus a fully "elected and constituted bishop" when he finally receives "the assent of laymen and the grant of the *regalia*." For the special case of a contested

[1] Wolfram, *Friedrich I.* 148; Krabbo, *Besetzung* 133, 148. Other examples could undoubtedly be found.

[2] In 1180, for example, the *electus* of Halberstadt was invested only four days after his election; *Gesta episcoporum Halberstadensium*, in *MGH SS* XXIII 109. In general, Boerger, *Belehnungen* 62.

[3] Above, Ch.VIIв.

election, however, Gerhoh insisted that the ecclesiastical authorities must confirm the election of the successful candidate before the ruler bestows the *regalia* upon him.[4] Here Gerhoh was most probably attacking the imperial prerogative, originally sanctioned by the Calixtinum, of deciding a disputed election.[5] In that respect, his statement looks backward toward 1122, yet it also suggests the position which the Church was to adopt in the thirteenth century. Indeed, by 1200 the Church was ready to insist on the confirmation of *any* election as a prerequisite to the investiture by the monarch.

There were, however, bishoprics which received their *regalia* from other bishops. In these exceptional cases, the procedure is especially instructive, since the interested prelates were free to act without immediate regard for the customs of secular monarchs. That is to say, in these cases the regalian investiture was a purely intra-ecclesiastical matter: Because the archbishop of Salzburg was simultaneously the ecclesiastical superior and the temporal lord of the bishop of Gurk, the archbishop had to confirm his suffragan and grant him the *regalia*. At Gurk, bestowal of the *regalia* followed the confirmation.[6] The other exceptional instance concerns the archbishopric of Lyons and the bishopric of Autun. Between the archbishopric and the bishopric there was a reciprocal arrangement: whenever one was vacant, the other held its *regalia*. The archbishop-elect of Lyons received his temporalities only after his election had been canonically confirmed.[7]

---

[4] *Comm. in ps.LXIV*, in *MGH LdL* III 452.

[5] Gerhoh was, of course, strongly opposed to the Calixtinum's provision prescribing that the emperor should be present at episcopal elections; above, Ch.IXₐ nn.38f.

[6] A. von Jaksch, *Monumenta historica ducatus Carinthiae* I 418 no.538: ". . . Quicumque autem sic ab archiepiscopo nominatus et a capitulo Gurcensi electus fuerit, postquam ab archiepiscopo Salzpurgensi confirmationem petierit et . . . acceperit, teneatur iurare archiepiscopo . . ."; Seidenschnur, *ZRG* KA 9 (1919) 237, and above, Ch.VIIIc nn.24-26.

[7] This requirement was stipulated in 1301; Jean Gaudemet, "Les origines de la régale réciproque entre Lyon et Autun," *Mémoires de la Société pour l'histoire du droit et des institutions des anciens pays bourguignons, comtois et romands* 5 (1938) 21-48 at 31 and esp. n.2.

The Eclipse of the *Regalia*

On the problem of sequence, the Church's position is clear. How, then, did the monarchies respond to this question? Since a resolution of this problem is perhaps more readily visible in some of the French royal bishoprics than in Germany, let us turn to an examination of French usage.[8] At first glance, one might conclude that the French monarchy was satisfied merely to repeat the familiar imperial ban on the exercise of administrative and jurisdictional rights before acceptance of the *regalia*. In the reign of Philip III, for example, a French legist insisted that the bishop of Chartres may administer his *regalia*, "that is, all of his temporalities," only after he takes the oath of fealty to the king.[9] Similarly, from Louis VII to Philip IV, the monarchy normally required the oath of fealty as a prerequisite to the possession and administration of those properties which were held by the king during the episcopal interregnum.[10]

In their relations with the royal bishoprics, the French monarchs enjoyed a right which the contemporary German rulers did not have. Since at least the later twelfth century, the French monarchy claimed and exercised the right to confer the unoccupied prebends or benefices of a vacant bishopric —a valuable privilege, which enhanced the king's ability to reward loyal service and reinforced the clergy's loyalty to the monarchy.[11] In order to defend this important royal

[8] On the *regalia* in 12th-century France, see the analysis by Alfons Becker, *Studien zum Investiturproblem* esp. 160-71, 239-45; for the 13th century, consult Campbell, *Traditio* 20 (1964) 351-83, and Baumhauer, *Philipp der Schöne und Bonifaz VIII.* 55-83. In general, Jean Gaudemet, "Les institutions ecclésiastiques en France du milieu du XIIe au début du XIVe siècle," in: F. Lot and R. Fawtier, eds., *Histoire des institutions françaises au moyen-âge* III: *Institutions ecclésiastiques* (Paris 1962) 171-73, 246-54. Also, above, Ch.VIIA n.2.
[9] Jean Gaudemet, *La collation par le roi de France des bénéfices vacants en régale des origines à la fin du XIVe siècle* (Paris 1935) 36f; also, Campbell, *op.cit.* 355-59, 367.
[10] Exceptions were made; see below, nn.16-21.
[11] The standard work on this royal right of the "spiritual *regalia*" is Gaudemet, *Collation par le roi*; see also the older work by G. Mollat, "L'application du droit de régale spirituelle en France du XIIe au XIVe siècle," *Revue d'histoire ecclésiastique* 25 (1929) 425-46, 645-76, and for a summary, Baumhauer, *op.cit.* 70-83. Despite the assertion by Gaudemet

prerogative, Louis IX formulated a claim which was closely analogous to the imperial doctrine that certain essential episcopal powers are dependent upon the bishop-elect's possession of the *regalia*. The occasion for this assertion was an incident of 1266, when a cardinal, supported by papal authority, granted a prebend in the archdiocese of Reims during a vacancy in the archiepiscopal see. Against this act, Louis protested that his royal right to confer prebends was valid "until the new archbishop receives the *regalia*."[12] That is to say, St Louis defined the bestowal of the *regalia* as the end of the interregnum.

In short, despite a clear similarity to German usage, in some respects French practice was markedly different. The sequence of investiture and consecration provides a further point of comparison. In 1149, acting as regent for the absent Louis VII, Suger confirmed an election at Chartres and asserted that the "ancient custom" of France prescribed a fixed sequence of steps (*redditionis ordo*) in the elevation of a bishop. "In the palace," he explained, the already consecrated bishop "does fealty to king and kingdom and thus at last he receives the *regalia*."[13] It is evident that this procedure was not exceptional. By the mid-twelfth century, then, the precedence of investiture before consecration—still a key

---

(*op.cit.* 43, n.4 on 44), I can find no evidence that contemporary German monarchs made use of this right. On the other hand, the English kings did enjoy the right of patronage in cathedral churches *sede vacante*. In general, see the valuable book by Margaret Howell, *Regalian Right in Medieval England* (London 1962) esp. 171-200, 206-10, which contains numerous English analogues and parallels to the topics treated in Part Two of the present study.

[12] Clement IV to Louis IX (1267), *Gall.Chr.* X Instr.66: no.69: "Quia tu ea ratione videlicet quod vacantes confers in ecclesia ipsa praebendas, a tempore quo tandem ecclesiam pastoris regimine contingit destitui, donec substitutus archiepiscopus regalia recipiat a te, huiusmodi collationem in praeiudicium tuum asseris esse factam"; Gaudemet, *Collation par le roi* 26f.

[13] Suger, *Ep.*10, ed. A. Lecoy de la Marche, *Oeuvres complètes* (Paris 1867) 257: "De regalibus vero, sicut in curia dominorum regum Francorum mos antiquus fuisse dinoscitur, cum episcopus consecratus, et in palatium ex more canonico fuerit introductus, tunc ei reddentur omnia. Hic est redditionis ordo et consuetudo, ut, sicut diximus, in palatio statutus [scil. episcopus] regi et regno fidelitatem faciat, et sic demum regalia recipiat."

The Eclipse of the *Regalia*

point in German constitutional practice—had been quietly abandoned in France. And when Philip II Augustus was about to leave for the Third Crusade in 1190, he standardized the royal procedure in a testament. The regency, he declared, should keep the *regalia* "until the *electus* has been consecrated . . . and then the *regalia*, without objection, should be granted to him."[14]

By emphasizing the consecration as the cue for the royal bestowal of the *regalia*, French practice coordinated the *regalia* with the purely sacramental aspects of ecclesiastical office. In this regard, French usage resembled the practice prescribed by the Concordat of Worms, which established the sequence of investiture and consecration in Germany, Burgundy, and Italy.[15] However, at the beginning of the thirteenth century, a new pattern was emerging in France. As early as 1200, the bishop-elect of Langres received his temporalities soon after his electoral confirmation—and

[14] Philip II (1190), ed. E. J. de Laurière, *Ordonnances des roys de France de la troisième race* I (Paris 1723) 20: "Si forte contigerit sedem episcopalem, vel aliquam abbatiam regalem vacare, volumus ut canonici ecclesiae vel monachi monasterii vacantis veniant ad reginam et archiepiscopum, sicut ante nos venirent, et liberam electionem ab eis petant; et nos volumus quod sine contradictione eis concedant. Nos vero tam canonicos quam monachos monemus, ut talem pastorem eligant, qui Deo placeat, et utilis sit regno. Regina autem et archiepiscopus tamdiu regalia in manu sua teneant, donec electus consecratus sit, vel benedictus, et tunc regalia sine contradictione ei reddantur."

[15] The specific sequence accepted in France (consecration preceding fealty) was, according to the terms of the Calixtinum, applicable only in Italy and Burgundy. English usage in the later 12th century required homage and fealty before the bishop-elect's consecration; Constitutions of Clarendon c.12, ed. Stubbs, *Select Charters* 166, and the work attributed to Glanvill, *De legibus et consuetudinibus regni Angliae* 9.1, ed. Stubbs, *op.cit.* 193.

It is scarcely necessary to add that the precedence of consecration before fealty did not prevent the French king from exercising a decisive influence over episcopal elections. The monarch had adequate safeguards, including the royal "permission to elect" (*licentia eligendi*), the postelectoral royal consent given to the *electus*, and often also permission for the consecration. In short, French royal power over episcopal elections did not have to express itself primarily through the bestowal of the *regalia*. Even so, the king could suspend a bishop and thereby deprive him temporarily of the *regalia*, or could withdraw the *regalia* completely.

before his episcopal consecration.[16] In 1203 for the bishopric of Arras, and again in 1209 for Mâcon, Philip II renounced the royal right to keep (and profit from) the *regalia* during a vacancy, and he granted to the cathedral chapter this right of administering the temporalities. But retaining his right to confer the *regalia* on the new bishop-elect, Philip asserted that the *electus,* "when he has been confirmed," should swear fealty in return for the *regalia.*[17] Note well: "When he has been confirmed," the bishop-elect can receive the temporalities. Clearly, in Langres, Arras, and Mâcon, after 1200 the *regalia* were coordinated with electoral confirmation, that is, with the canonical act which gave full administrative and jurisdictional powers to the *electus.*

This new stress on electoral confirmation was neither a temporary nor an accidental phenomenon in France. At LeMans in 1214, the new bishop-elect refused to swear fealty to Philip II, on the ground that his immediate predecessor had never done fealty to the English kings, who had formerly ruled LeMans. Philip ordered an investigation. If the bishop-elect's predecessor had taken an oath to his Anglo-Norman lord, the new *electus* must thereupon swear fealty to Philip in the same fashion; if not, Philip was willing to forgo the oath of fealty. In either case, however, Philip instructed his agents to hand over the *regalia* as of the very day on which he himself received word of the election's confirmation.[18] A similar arrangement was ratified by Louis VIII in 1223:

[16] In 1200 Hilduin, bishop-elect of Langres, "post meae electionis confirmationem et regalium receptionem," made a grant to the chapter of his cathedral (*Gall.Chr.* IV Instr.196 no.88).

[17] For Philip II's remarks on the case of Arras, see N. Brussel, *Nouvel examen de l'usage général des fiefs en France* (Paris 1750) I 307f: ". . . electum suum confirmatum nobis [canonici] praesentabunt, ut nobis fidelitatem faciat. . . ." Even clearer is Philip's grant to the dean and chapter of Mâcon, *Gall.Chr.* IV Instr.288 no.36: "Electus vero quando confirmatus fuerit ad nos venire debet facta nobis fidelitate ex manu nostra regalia recepturus." This provision did not always accompany the royal abandonment of regalian rights; cf. Philip's grant for Langres in 1203 (*Gall.Chr.* IV Instr.197 no.90).

[18] *Chartularium insignis ecclesiae Cenomanensis quod dicitur Liber albus capituli* (LeMans 1869) 8 nos.14f; Paul Piolin, *Histoire de l'église du Mans* IV (Paris 1858) 260f; Franz X. Barth, *Hildebert von Lavardin (1056-1133) und das kirchliche Stellenbesetzungsrecht* (Stuttgart 1906) 454f.

The Eclipse of the *Regalia*

We acknowledge . . . that when the bishop-elect of LeMans shall be confirmed by his metropolitan . . . , we shall transmit to him his *regalia* by way of the messengers who bring the patent letter of his confirmation. Within forty days after his receiving the *regalia*, the bishop-elect himself will be obliged to come to us in good faith, if we are in the kingdom, and to take an oath of fealty to us. And if he does not come to us within forty days . . . , we shall be able to seize his *regalia* and to hold them until he has taken the oath of fealty to us.[19]

For the bishoprics of Angers and Poitiers, Louis VIII made the same promise.[20] As bishop William LeMaire of Angers testifies, in the early 1290's the same procedure was still customary in his diocese.[21] At least in these six French bishoprics, with the king's concession of the *regalia* closely following the electoral confirmation, there was scarcely a basis for tension between Church and monarchy over the conflicting claims of these two juridical acts. But even when the French monarchy did not enter an explicit agreement linking confirmation of the election and bestowal of the *regalia*, the king was usually content that ecclesiastical regulations should prevail, and that confirmation should precede the request for the *regalia*.[22]

---

[19] *Chartularium* (*Liber albus*) 7f no.13: "Item, recognovimus ei, quod, quando electus Cenomanensis ecclesie erit confirmatus a metropolitano vel ab eo qui potestatem habebit confirmandi, nos reddemus ei regalia sua per nuncios deferentes litteras patentes confirmationis eius. Ipse tamen electus tenebitur bona fide adire nos, si fuerimus in regno, infra quadraginta dies post susceptionem regalium, et nobis iuramentum fidelitatis prestare. Et si infra quadraginta dies ad nos . . . non veniret, nos poterimus saisire regalia sua, et ea tamdiu tenere, quousque nobis fidelitatis fecerit iuramentum . . ."; Piolin, *op.cit.* IV 283ff, and Barth, *op.cit.* 455f.

[20] Charles Petit-Dutaillis, *Étude sur la vie et le règne de Louis VIII* (Paris 1894) 453.

[21] *Liber Guillelmi Maioris*, ed. Célestin Port, *Mélanges historiques* II (Paris 1877) 224-28 and 240-42; the election was confirmed on April 24th, the concession of the *regalia* on April 28th, and the oath of fealty on May 16th.

[22] For example, A. Teulet et al., *Layettes du Trésor des chartes* (5 vols. Paris 1862-1909) II no.3472 (Limoges 1241); Campbell, *Traditio* 20 (1964) 354f. According to a letter of Innocent III, this sequence was apparently usual in Thérouanne (above, Ch.XA n.17).

The Bishop-Elect

Beginning near the end of the twelfth century, a similar tendency is increasingly visible both in the empire and in Sicily: in practice, confirmation normally preceded investiture.[23] One finds, however, no evidence that any particular theory, apart from the Church's constitutional doctrine, contributed to this development. Indeed, pressure from the Church is, by itself, very nearly a sufficient explanation for the monarchs' cooperativeness in accepting this rule. As a concession to Innocent III, for example, Frederick II prescribed that in Sicily, ecclesiastical elections should follow canonical principles and that an unconfirmed *electus* should not administer his bishopric.[24] In the late thirteenth century, imperial charters of investiture sometimes used the formula *electus et confirmatus* immediately after the prelate-elect's name and thereby explicitly emphasized that the prelate-elect had already been confirmed.[25] Even more illustrative is a letter from king Adolph to the archbishop of Trier (1297):

> Since the . . . abbot of the monastery of Epternach . . . cannot come personally . . . to us for the acquisition of the temporalities and rights which he holds from us and from the holy empire, . . . we entrust our duty to you, so that *after he has been canonically confirmed by you,* . . . you should grant the *regalia* to the aforesaid newly created abbot, and receive from him in the usual fashion the oath of fealty owed to us. . . .[26]

23 Needless to say, through the first half of the 13th century, there are still examples of the older usage: investiture without regard to previous confirmation.

24 *MGH Const* II 544 no.413 (1212); to be sure, in this charter Frederick amply protected his own interests by insisting on *assensus regius* as prerequisite to the episcopal enthronement and to the chanting of the episcopal acclamations (Kantorowicz, *Laudes regiae* 119f). Cf. also *MGH Const* II 543 no.412.

25 In a letter addressed "domino Jacobo electo et confirmato ecclesie Virdunensis" (1290), Rudolph of Hapsburg conferred *regalia, administratio temporalium*, etc., on the prelate-elect *in absentia* (Kern, *Acta imperii* 42 no.64). Also, Adolph of Nassau's charter for the bishop of Liège (1294): ". . . Guidonem electum et confirmatum sceptro regio investivimus . . ." (J. C. Lünig, *Teutsches Reichs-Archiv* XVII 512, quoted by Boerger, *Belehnungen* 51).

26 *MGH Const* III 544 no.583: "Cum religiosus abbas monasterii de Epternaco tue dyocesis pro receptione temporalium et iurium, que a nobis

The Eclipse of the *Regalia*

Clearly, by the end of the thirteenth century imperial procedure readily took full account of electoral confirmation as prerequisite to investiture.

The German monarchy's acquiescence to this ecclesiastical requirement could perhaps have been foreseen even under Barbarossa. A revealing episode took place in 1177, during the conclusion of the Peace of Venice between Barbarossa and Alexander III. After the resignation of archbishop Adalbert III of Salzburg, some Salzburg clergy, in the presence of pope and emperor, elected Conrad of Mainz as his successor. Thereupon Alexander and Frederick wrote separate letters to the clergy and *ministeriales* of Salzburg to inform them of this event. Though the two texts are highly similar, the differences are significant: Where the emperor wrote that Adalbert had resigned his church "into the hands of the lord pope and into our own," the pope wrote simply that the former archbishop had resigned it "into our hands." Alexander remarked that the Salzburg clergy who were present "had received our command" to hold an election, and at the corresponding place in his own letter, Frederick commented that the election was held "by command of the lord pope and by our own." Of Conrad's election, Alexander stated simply, "We . . . have granted our favor and assent"; at the same point, however, Frederick explained, "In any case, the lord pope and the entire Curia ratified and confirmed this election, and we invested him with the *regalia*."[27] Throughout its text, in short, Alexander's letter virtually ignored Frederick's role in the proceedings, and it avoided any reference to the investiture of the archbishop-elect. Frederick's letter, on the other

---

et sacro tenet imperio, ad nos personaliter propter sui corporis debilitatem non possit accedere, . . . sinceritati tue, ut dicto abbati de novo creato, postquam per te canonice fuerit confirmatus, vice et auctoritate regie maiestatis concedas regalia, recepturus ab eodem more consueto fidelitatis nobis debite iuramentum, vices nostras committimus. . . ." Though exceptions were frequently made, imperial custom required prelates-elect to receive their investiture in person.

27 *Chronicon Magni presbiteri Reicherspergensis* anno 1177, *MGH SS* XVII 505f; Wolfram, *Friedrich I.* 91f, quotes the two letters in parallel columns.

hand, not only mentioned Alexander's share in the action but, by citing the pope's name ahead of his own in each context, Frederick accorded to Alexander the primary position of authority and responsibility.

In the crucial differences between these two letters, one can already discern the essential differences between two constitutional theories on the powers of a prelate-elect: In the Church's view, so long as an *electus* had been confirmed, and so long as his subjects and vassals obeyed him, his investiture was a matter of small concern. In the view of the German kings and emperors, the long-standing rule, so firmly stressed by Barbarossa throughout his reign, continued to regard investiture as prerequisite to the exercise of secular governmental and administrative powers. But apparently the German monarchy saw no compelling reason to oppose the Church's requirement of confirmation before acceptance and administration of the *regalia*.

CHAPTER XI

EPILOGUE: BISHOP-ELECT,
CHURCH, AND PAPACY

in ALL Aspects of Europe's history during the twelfth
and thirteenth centuries, organization is the main theme.[1]
Regarded in this way, the English justiciar and the French
court legist, the scholastic philosopher and the Bolognese
canonist, the royal *bailli* and the papal legate were all engaged
in the same enterprise. Politically and ecclesiastically, this
tendency demanded a rational examination and definition (or
redefinition) of the social bonds and institutional relations
which, in an earlier age, had been largely determined by customary usage. For the secular prince as well as for the Church,
this tendency brought increasing centralization. Within the
structure of the Church, this tendency established, almost
without opposition, the effective jurisdictional primacy of the
Roman See. Yet organization and definition had to precede
this centralization. That is to say, systematic organization of
the administrative machinery, and canonical definition of the
various offices and jurisdictions within the Church—these
were two of the major prerequisites to centralization under
the papacy. In this respect, when the papacy came into the
fullness of its power in the thirteenth century, the Roman

---

[1] Marc Bloch, *Feudal Society*, trans. L. A. Manyon (London 1961) 106-
08, views this development as a consequence of the Investiture Struggle,
which provoked men to become more conscious and critical of their society
and its institutions: "Human affairs were newly emerging as subjects for
reflection" (p.107). Also, R. R. Bolgar, *The Classical Heritage and Its
Beneficiaries* (Cambridge 1954) 202.

bishops inherited a legacy which twelfth-century canonists and administrators had arduously assembled.

The most rapid development of the Church's constitutional theory and administrative apparatus belongs to the rich period between Gratian and the Fourth Lateran Council. Before the work of the decretists, in fact, many aspects of ecclesiastical office remained vague and indefinite. After master Rufinus sharpened the distinction between the jurisdictional and the sacramental powers of office, later decretists elaborated his new doctrines. Against this background, a more precise definition of the jurisdictionally constitutive moment in the creation of a prelate became possible and even necessary. The canonical practice of the Early Middle Ages had devised a system in which the critical and constitutive moments were the election and the consecration. Ecclesiastical office was thus, so to speak, elective and sacramental. Finally, by the 1160's the mature concept of *confirmatio* was prescribing that the episcopal jurisdiction of every bishop-elect—with the single exception of a newly elected pope—derives from his confirmation. The first consequence of this new requirement was to diminish the role of the clergy in the elevation of a bishop, while increasing the power and influence of the hierarchical superior, whose consent sanctioned the *electus*'s ecclesiastical jurisdiction. This doctrine was, one might say, hierarchical and sacramental. Hence, the net effects of this development were the tightening of the Church's hierarchy, and the prelate's increasing dependence on the will and approval of his immediate superior.

The new requirement—electoral confirmation as prerequisite to the exercise of jurisdictional powers—could not be uniformly imposed at a single stroke. During the later twelfth and early thirteenth centuries, still following older practice, bishops-elect often administered without waiting for confirmation. Confronted with the accusation of having violated the new regulation, the various prelates directly subject to the Roman See sometimes responded with the plea of

374

customary usage. Yet in the thirteenth-century Church, though custom had a few defenders among the ranks of important churchmen, it had no party, and it provided no banner around which to rally. Roman usage, as defined by canonists, was spreading irresistibly to the entire Latin Church, and in the long run, there could be no effective opposition to this tendency.

Near the end of the twelfth century, a reaction set in against the strict doctrine of electoral confirmation: Master Huguccio drew a brilliant but essentially semantic distinction between the powers of office and the right to exercise those powers—the former being conferred by "mutual consent" to an election, and only the latter being granted through electoral confirmation. A decretal of Innocent III and a constitution of the Fourth Lateran Council recognized the right of an extra-Italian metropolitan or *exemptus* to administer immediately after election. This reaction was, however, more apparent than real. For one thing, subtly reinterpreting Huguccio's compromise, Innocent III restored the original force of the requirement of confirmation. Moreover, in the case of the distant *exempti* and archbishops, the papacy could readily concede an interim right of administration, for these two groups, both of them "immediately under the lord pope," were precisely the categories of officials who must receive *papal* confirmation. And even here, it was not the lower clergy's election which sanctioned these exceptional administrative powers. On the contrary, in the mid-thirteenth century, some regarded the interim administration of these non-Italian metropolitans-elect and exempt prelates-elect as a mere "proctorship," a form of delegated power deriving from papal sanctions.[2] In any case, the contingent character of this right became apparent at the end of the thirteenth century, when Boniface VIII overrode this privilege.

The appearance of this new requirement, electoral con-

[2] Innocent IV, *Apparatus* on *X* 1.6.44 v. *administrent* (above, Ch.VIc n.19).

firmation, was a part of the long, slow process by which the selection and elevation of bishops were largely removed from the sphere of lay control and custom-dominated procedure, and by which episcopal elections were brought under ecclesiastical supervision and under the prescriptions of canon law. In the eleventh century, the Gregorian slogan of *libertas ecclesiae* had aimed at the abolition of lay control over ecclesiastical elections. Essentially vague, however, the program of the Gregorian reformers was clear only in its negative aspects. The Gregorians found it easy enough to recognize the major violations of the Church's liberty, but on its positive side, their program was weak, for it lacked an adequately detailed conception of canonical procedure in the election of bishops. Still, this deficiency soon found effective remedies. During the course of the twelfth century, Gregorian hopes were increasingly fulfilled by two developments in practice: the emergence of the cathedral chapter as the sole competent electors of a bishop, and the gradual exclusion of the laity from everything except a consentaneous acclamation for an already elected bishop.[3] In his massive compilation, Gratian assimilated much of the Gregorian program, and taking his work as a foundation, the decretists began to provide concrete, sharply defined content for the idea of canonical election.[4] Beginning with Alexander III, the Roman pontiffs carried the task further in their decretals. Just as the mid-eleventh-century papacy adopted a reforming ideal which had originated outside of Rome, in the later twelfth century the papacy began to appropriate the subtle theorizing of the masters at Bologna, Paris, and Oxford. In their decretals on problems of election, the popes applied new canonistic concepts to the Church at

[3] In general, see above, Ch.IIA. One should not exaggerate the consistency and effectiveness of the effort to deprive the laity of its right to participate actively. As late as 1321, for example, the *ministeriales* of Hildesheim were still claiming this right—but no longer successfully; O. Franklin, *Sententiae curiae regis* 44 no.94.

[4] At present, there is no systematic study of decretistic and decretalistic doctrines on election.

large, and these new doctrines left little room for lay control over election and over the bishop-elect. It is obvious that for the Church, the new theories were preferable to Gregorian vagueness and, *a fortiori*, to monarchical domination.

Before the Investiture Struggle, the prerogatives of the episcopal office could scarcely be described without constant reference to its secular role and to the powers which monarchs delegated to bishops. Correspondingly, it is impossible to draw a sharp line between the constitutional history of the Church and that of monarchy in the tenth and eleventh centuries: monarchy and Church were indeed inseparable. During the seventy-five years between the *Decretum* and the Fourth Lateran Council, however, a sweeping transformation occurred: by redefining the episcopal office and its jurisdictional competence in purely ecclesiastical terms, by subjecting even the bishop's feudal obligations and prerogatives to canonical criteria, and by ignoring the constitutive significance of regalian investiture, the decretals and the canonists realized in practical fashion the old ideal of *libertas ecclesiae*. Although many bishops continued to hold *regalia* thereafter,[5] one can give a clear—and not seriously misleading—account of the episcopal office during the thirteenth century without mention of the bishops' secular appurtenances.

Along similar lines, the Church's new doctrines on office may even be viewed as a fulfillment to the hopes of the post-Gregorian reformers, disappointed by the compromise of 1122. Indeed, rejecting even the prejudiced term *regalia* in favor of the more neutral expression "ecclesiastical property" (*facultates ecclesiasticae*), Gerhoh of Reichersberg looked forward to the day when all bishops, like the bishop of Rome, would freely possess their property "by right of ancient grant," without any homage or fealty to a secular prince. That is to say, Gerhoh longed to see the very word *regalia* dis-

[5] As they did throughout the rest of the Middle Ages and under the Ancien Régime.

appear in general recognition that the Church enjoyed its holdings unconditionally.[6] Or, which amounted to the same thing, such men preferred not to regard the episcopal *regalia* as the monarch's property, but rather to speak of these temporalities as "the *regalia* of Saint Peter and of the Church," thereby challenging the implication, unavoidable from the traditional terminology, that the *regalia* originated in royal grants and remained subject to royal control.[7] During the thirteenth century, in defense of a French bishopric's exemption from the king's regalian rights, a cleric maintained that "the bishop holds his entire temporalities not from the king, but from God alone and from the Church."[8] Obviously, this claim asserted the privileges of exceptional status, but it was expressive of a larger tendency. In a thoroughly consistent fashion, the Church's new constitutional doctrines increasingly treated all ecclesiastical holdings—including the *regalia*—as subject solely to Church law.[9]

Characteristically, twelfth-century constitutional thought conceived the Church as a pyramidal hierarchy. In the hyperbole of pope Eugene III, the structure of the Church was even an imitation of the heavenly hierarchy:

> The Catholic Church is constructed on earth according to the image . . . of the celestial order. For just as some heavenly spirits are superiors . . . , others are inferiors . . . and rejoice in and humbly obey the command of their superiors, thus in the Catholic Church some are established

[6] *De ordine donorum S. Spiritus*, in *MGH LdL* III 280. But cf. also the view expressed in another of Gerhoh's works (above, Ch. VIIIc n.65).

[7] *Gesta Treverorum* Continuatio c.11, *MGH SS* VIII 184: "Quae utique non sua, sed iuxta Romanam consuetudinem regalia beati Petri vel ecclesie pociori iure possunt appellari." In papal documents the phrase *regalia sancti Petri* referred specifically to the papacy's secular jurisdiction in Central Italy, rather than to the temporal properties or rights of the Church at large (above, Ch.VIIA n.77). In the present context, however, the anonymous chronicler cites the "Roman custom" as the terminological model for the German church.

[8] On behalf of Auxerre: ". . . episcopus suam totam temporalitatem a rege non tenet, sed a solo Deo et ecclesia . . ." (Gaudemet, *Collation par le roi* 38 n.2).

[9] Baethgen, *ZRG KA* 10 (1920) 190 esp. n.3 (= *Mediaevalia* 126 n.52).

Epilogue

as patriarchs or primates, others as archbishops or metropolitans, others as bishops.[10]

In more mundane terms, and with more practical consequences, decretists usually divided this hierarchy into three jurisdictional levels: pope, metropolitan, and bishop. Within this simple schema, like Eugene III, they occasionally inserted the office of patriarch or primate, but in fact, decretal law generally preferred not to recognize any distinct jurisdictional instance between pope and metropolitan.[11] So far as the decretistic theory of ecclesiastical election was concerned, in each case the hierarchical principle pertained, and the new prelate-elect was confirmed by his immediate superior:

> Just as the consent of the archbishop is necessary in the confirmation of the bishop . . . , in the same way the consent of the supreme pontiff is needed in the confirmation of the archbishop.[12]

In practice, moreover, the metropolitan retained the right to confirm and consecrate the newly elected bishops within his province. Since the papacy only began to insist upon confirmation of the metropolitan's election during the last third of the twelfth century, and since jurisdictional consequences were first assigned to electoral confirmation during this same period, in 1200 the practical significance of this hierarchical system was still a new phenomenon within the Church.[13] Indeed, as electoral confirmation achieved its new importance, and as other aspects of the metropolitan's prerogative were already eroding, his role in the episcopal promotions remained briefly as a central part of his power and function.

10 Above, Ch.IIIB n.12. Though the origins of this idea need not concern us here, it derived from a tradition of thought influenced by the writings of Pseudo-Dionysius.

11 For example, *X* 1.31.9 (1199).

12 Simon of Bisignano, *Summa* on D.63 c.10 v. *nostrum spectatur arbitrium* (above, Ch.IVA n.39).

13 See the instructive article by G. Barraclough, "The Making of a Bishop in the Middle Ages: The Part of the Pope in Law and Fact," *CHR* 19 (1933-34) 275-319 at 288ff.

Yet the thirteenth century witnessed a rapid decline in the effectiveness and significance of the metropolitan's right to confirm his suffragans' elections. Throughout the thirteenth century, the papacy steadily extended its influence upon the promotion of new bishops, and thereby papal power virtually destroyed this hierarchical system, in practice as well as in decretal law.[14] During the twelfth century election was still the normal route in the elevation of a bishop, but by 1300 there were several alternatives, all of them involving the exercise of papal power. The translation of a bishop from one see to another had long been an exclusive papal prerogative, but increasingly, where the electors favored a candidate who was not legally qualified for election to the episcopal office, they submitted their "request" (*postulatio*) to the pope for approval, rather than their "election" to the metropolitan for confirmation. At least in part for financial reasons,[15] the

[14] These developments are, needless to say, well known. For a brief summary and voluminous bibliography, consult Feine, *RG* I 300-10.

[15] At least since the 6th century, there had been complaints about—and legislation against—the expectation of "gifts" as payment for services rendered in the elevation of a prelate. During the 13th century, in return for papal confirmation an *electus* was expected to make gifts of money (*servitia communia*)—often a staggeringly large sum—to the pope and the cardinals, and to distribute smaller gifts (*servitia minuta*) to various lesser officials at the Curia. As the number of papal confirmations increased in the 13th and 14th centuries, these donations, theoretically voluntary but in fact compulsory, soon constituted a significant portion of the papacy's income. Understandably, the unfortunate prelates regarded these "gifts" as an oppressive burden, and were often in debt for years afterwards. In general, see William E. Lunt, *Papal Revenues in the Middle Ages* I 82-86, 95; II 219, 234-39, 257-59, 266-70, 273, 283, 286f, 303, 325, 358f, 367f, 385, 497; and for other literature, Feine, *RG* I 305-10.
Hence the question arises: Did the 12th-century papacy originally impose the requirement of electoral confirmation for the sake of its fiscal advantages? To this question, a positive answer might seem attractive, since the earliest restriction on the administrative powers of an *electus* specifically forbade the alienation of church property (C.12 q.2 c.37 [1123]; above, Ch.IIᴀ n.79), and later legislation on the powers of a bishop-elect continued to concentrate on the right to administer property. Nonetheless, two facts suggest that financial motives were not primary: First, electoral confirmation as a general requirement first appeared in the 1160's, long before the papal fiscal system was far developed. Second, at least through the first third of the 13th century, papal decretals firmly and repeatedly insisted on the importance of the metropolitan's confirmation of his suffragans' elections—a requirement in which the papacy obviously had no direct financial interest.

thirteenth-century papacy used its *plenitudo potestatis* in the direct appointment of individual bishops (*provisio*),[16] and beginning in 1265 it "reserved" various categories of episcopal vacancies for direct papal appointment. The net effect of these translations, postulations, provisions, and reservations was to reduce markedly the importance of election as a mode of promotion. Yet even when elections were held during the later thirteenth century and thereafter, the metropolitan's jurisdiction over them had diminished. It was already customary under Innocent III for the Roman pontiff to confirm the election of a metropolitan or an *exemptus*, but if he chose, the pope could, of course, confirm any election whatsoever. Further, the metropolitan's confirmation was little safeguard for an *electus*, since the pope could—and frequently did—quash an episcopal election already confirmed by the competent metropolitan. Indeed, the Fourth Lateran Council provided stern penalties for the prelate who improperly confirmed an election.[17] To be sure, even in the later thirteenth century the popes did not confirm the elections of *all* higher prelates, but the number of elections confirmed at the Roman Curia had steadily multiplied. Contested or disputed elections and procedural irregularities were, practically, an invitation for papal intervention, and the electors often explicitly requested settlement by papal decision. By the fourteenth century, many nonexempt bishops received their electoral confirmation from Rome, and this practice became general in the course of the fifteenth century. In short, it was the papacy which benefited chiefly from the new canonical requirement of electoral confirmation, and from the death of the hierarchical system. In the later thirteenth century, the style of episcopal entitlement began to reflect the bishop's increased dependence on the

---

16 Often the pope quashed an election, but proceeded to appoint the *electus* (or one of the candidates) immediately afterward. Of the older literature on provisions, see: Hinschius, *KR* III 113-18; J. Haller, *Papsttum und Kirchenreform* I (Berlin 1903) 40-44; H. Baier, *Päpstliche Provisionen für niedere Pfründen bis zum Jahre 1304* (Münster 1911); and esp. Barraclough, *Papal Provisions*.

17 *X* 1.6.44.

papacy, for instead of earlier traditional formulas—such as "bishop by the grace of God" (*episcopus Dei gratia*)— episcopal documents occasionally define the bishop as holding his office "by the grace of God and of the Apostolic See" (*Dei et apostolicae sedis gratia*).[18]

As the power and wealth of the Church steadily grew, the interest of canonists shifted from the consecrational aspects of office toward the administrative and jurisdictional, which acquired constantly greater prominence both in theory and in practice. Indeed, before the mid-twelfth century, the core of the episcopal office—the main object of attention, so to speak —could be found in the bishop's sacramental powers. In discussions of the episcopal office during the second quarter of the twelfth century, Hugh of St Victor treated only the sacramental prerogatives,[19] whereas Bernard of Clairvaux concentrated on the bishop's moral qualifications and priestly role.[20] Correspondingly, prior to the papal election decree of 1059, the powers of a Roman pontiff derived from the ceremonies surrounding his consecration, and two generations later, in the same vein the First Lateran Council prescribed that before his consecration, a bishop-elect or abbot-elect is forbidden to alienate church property.[21] In both of these cases, when there was an attempt to limit the competence of an *electus*, the beginning of his full powers was dated from the consecration. Thus the prelate's jurisdictional powers and his right to dispose of church property were linked with his sacramental prerogatives. After 1059, however, the jurisdiction of the papal office—the pope's *plenitudo potestatis*, as it came to be called—was immediately effective through his

[18] Werminghoff, *Verfassungsgeschichte* 139.

[19] See Hugh's disquisition *De ecclesiasticis ordinibus* in his *De sacramentis* 2.3 (and esp. 2.3.13-14), *PL* 176 421-34 (at 430).

[20] *De moribus et officio episcoporum tractatus*, in *PL* 182 809-34. As soon as one focused on the papal office, however, the question of jurisdiction was inevitably far more prominent. Cf. Hugh's brief remarks (*op.cit.* 2.3.15, *PL* 176 430f; above, Ch.IIA n.88), and Bernard's treatise (*De consideratione*, in *PL* 182 727-808).

[21] Above, Ch.IIA n.79.

Epilogue

acceptance of election. It is scarcely surprising that as the theory of the papal "plenitude of power" developed, this unlimited and inexhaustible form of jurisdiction forced the sacramental aspects of the Roman bishop's office into the background.[22] For all lesser bishops after the mid-twelfth century, the consecration similarly had little to do with the acquisition or exercise of jurisdiction; the jurisdictional powers of pope and bishop alike were sanctioned by nonsacramental acts: respectively, by election or by confirmation. So great was the emphasis on the prelate's "power of jurisdiction" that by the beginning of the fourteenth century, a churchman might even rank the *potestas iurisdictionis* above the *potestas ordinis*. Along these lines, James of Viterbo described the Church as a kingdom and Christ as its king:

> A spiritual royal power . . . was entrusted by Christ to the apostles and to their successors. . . . For the power of binding and loosing is a judicial power, which pertains especially to kings.

Consequently, as James explained,

> In the prelates of the Church, the royal power, which is called the power of jurisdiction, is superior to the priestly power, which is called the power of orders.[23]

[22] Both the opponents and the defenders of the papal *plenitudo potestatis* pointed out its purely jurisdictional character, and its theoretical superiority to the pope's sacramental prerogatives. Note the striking critique in Jean Gerson's *De potestate ecclesiastica*: "Et quamvis ex electione possit aliquid iurisdictionis habere, non tamen habet ante consecrationem in episcopum plenitudinem ecclesiasticae potestatis tam ordinis quam iurisdictionis utriusque; quod perspicuum est ex terminis. Hic autem consurgit aequivocatio non modica propter dominos iuristas, qui loquentes de plenitudine potestatis papalis solum loqui videntur de potestate iurisdictionis, ex qua locutione videtur haec absurditas sequi quod pure laicus imo et femina posset esse papa et habere plenitudinem ecclesiasticae potestatis" (quoted by Tierney, *Foundations* 148 n.1).

[23] *De regimine christiano* 2.3, ed. H. X. Arquillière, *Le plus ancien traité de l'Église: Jacques de Viterbe* (Paris 1926) 180: "Potestas autem regia spiritualis . . . est . . . tradita a Christo apostolis et eorum successoribus, tunc scilicet quando dictum est eis: 'quaecumque ligaveritis super terram ligata erunt et in celo.' Potestas enim ligandi et solvendi est potestas iudiciaria, que ad reges utique pertinet." *Id.* 2.4, *ed.cit.* 199: "Quare et in prelatis

Thus, like the purely jurisdictional *plenitudo potestatis* of the pope, the bishop's jurisdiction—that is, the power which makes him "royal"—characterizes his preeminence within the Church more distinctively than his sacramental competence.

Even in the early twelfth century, the same process is visible through the changes in the German monarchy's conception of the episcopal office. Building on an old tradition, the Concordat of Worms had declared the regalian investiture prerequisite to consecration, thus joining the prelate's investiture and his sacramental powers; still, by 1200 this traditional sequence of investiture and consecration had lost its former importance. Through Innocent II's charter of 1133, however, and insistently in twelfth-century imperial thought, investiture gained increasingly widespread recognition as the indispensable prerequisite to the prelate-elect's administration of his *regalia*; here, imperial law explicitly linked the prelate's investiture to his secular jurisdiction. As defined in 1133 at Rome and Würzburg, this juridical concept of regalian investiture anticipated and resembled the post-Rufinian theories of ecclesiastical office, for both sharply distinguished the prelate's sacramental powers from his jurisdiction over property or persons, and both concentrated their attention on the jurisdictional competence.

The newer monarchical concept of regalian investiture and the new ecclesiastical concepts of office were paralleled by yet another contemporary development: during the Investi-

---

ecclesie superior est potestas regalis, que dicitur iurisdictionis, quam sacerdotalis, que dicitur ordinis." In general, see R. Scholz, *Die Publizistik zur Zeit Philipps des Schönen und Bonifaz' VIII.* (Stuttgart 1903) 144f; Carlyle, *Mediaeval Political Theory* V 409-17; M. Grabmann, "Die Lehre des Erzbischofs und Augustinertheologen Jakob von Viterbo," *Episcopus: Festschrift für Kardinal Michael von Faulhaber* (Regensburg 1949) 190f; Kantorowicz, *King's Two Bodies* 56 n.30. One should be aware that most remarks on the bishop's *potestas regalis* referred to powers deriving from regalian investiture (above, Ch.VIIIc). Here, however, it is the essentially ecclesiastical *potestas iurisdictionis* that is termed "royal"; in this passage, James's affinities lie with Geoffrey of Vendôme, who interpreted the bishop's "kingship" as a consequence of his *ecclesiastical* investiture (above, Ch.VIIIc nn.63f).

ture Struggle and its aftermath, the Western European monarchs lost much of the special status which had belonged to them, in theory, through the sacramental effects of the royal anointment.[24] Thereby the prince ceased to be primarily the "vicar of Christ," a "king-priest" with a quasi-clerical status, and the preeminent figure in the all-embracing church of his *regnum*. No longer able (or willing) to base their kingship on this theoretical foundation, the twelfth- and thirteenth-century princes constructed new versions of monarchy, ultimately secular in their roots. In this task, the monarch's most characteristic and effective servants were professional jurists, for the new forms of monarchy were law-centered, stressing the prince's role as supreme judge of the realm. Through their interpretations and applications of Roman, canon, and feudal law, these jurists decisively enlarged and ultimately transformed the royal prerogative.[25]

Thus, in the mid-eleventh century the core of the kingly, imperial, episcopal, and papal offices was the sacramental character gained through consecration, but by the end of the twelfth century or even earlier, through an imperceptible transformation the new interpretation of each of these offices had won general acceptance. Common to the constitutional development of both Church and monarchy, this trend conceived of office primarily in terms of its jurisdiction, rather than of its sacral character. Thereby it created a new center of gravity, a new focus of concern and contention, in the jurisdictional prerogatives of the princely, papal, and episcopal offices.

[24] On anointed kingship see Fritz Kern, *Gottesgnadentum und Widerstandsrecht im früheren Mittelalter*, 2nd ed. rev. R. Buchner (Darmstadt 1954) 46-106 (in English: *Kingship and Law in the Middle Ages* [1914 ed.], trans. S. B. Chrimes [Oxford 1939] 27-61); also, Kantorowicz, *King's Two Bodies* ch.3.

[25] This transition to "law-centered kingship" has been described by Kantorowicz, *King's Two Bodies* esp. ch.4; in addition, see his essay on "Kingship under the Impact of Scientific Jurisprudence," *Twelfth-Century Europe and the Foundations of Modern Society*, ed. M. Clagett et al. (Madison 1961) 89-111 (= *Sel. Studies* 151-66).

APPENDIX 1

A NOTE
ON RECENT STUDIES IN
MEDIEVAL CANON LAW

Within the last two decades, canon law has become a major area of research in medieval studies, and its importance is now beyond dispute. Each year there is a larger outpouring of articles and books on medieval canon law. Moreover, jurisprudence is always inherently technical. To the unfamiliar reader, therefore, recent canonistic literature may seem to present (as Stephen of Tournai remarked of Alexander III's decretals) an "impenetrable forest." This excursus is intended for the nonspecialist needing an introductory guide to some of the principal landmarks.

First, however, a warning: During the century which elapsed between the *Decretum* and the first commentaries on the *Liber extra*, the canonists produced an imposing number of commentaries, treatises, and collections. Few of these have been printed—indeed, a generation ago many of them were utterly unknown. Thus the historian interested in medieval canon law finds himself today roughly in the predicament faced by all medievalists a century and a half ago, before the learned societies and scholarly institutes had begun systematically to edit the sources of medieval history. Recent historical scholarship has been conscientiously exploring canonistic writings in widely scattered manuscripts and has been evalu-

Appendix 1

ating the canonists' contribution.[1] Still, though one encounters ambitious new studies tracing large themes of general importance, such studies cannot be written without constant attention to the countless minute and vexing problems posed by twelfth- and thirteenth-century manuscripts. Necessarily, therefore, most of the recent studies are highly specialized monographs and articles.

As starting points for inquiry, the histories by Fournier and LeBras (on the period before 1140), by Kuttner (1140-1234), and by Schulte (after 1234), remain indispensable.[2] One may supplement these works with A. Van Hove, *Prolegomena* (Commentarium Lovaniense in Codicem iuris canonici I,1: 2nd ed. Malines 1945), and A. Stickler, *Historia iuris canonici latini* I: *Historia fontium* (Turin 1950). On the canonists' lives and writings, on legal doctrines and institutions, and on the technical language of canon law, a useful reference work is the *Dictionnaire de droit canonique* (7 vols. Paris 1935-65). Though its articles vary both in length and in quality, some—especially in the later volumes—are excellent, setting forth the present state of research and indicating the newer scholarly literature.

In 1952 at Bologna, an international congress commemorated the eighth centennial of the *Decretum* and began publication of *Studia Gratiana* (1953ff) with G. Forchielli and A. Stickler as editors; subsequent issues of *Studia Gratiana* contain valuable articles on other aspects of medieval canon law, as well as on Gratian himself.[3] For the systematic development of canonistic studies, however, the most significant event took place in 1955, with the founding of the Institute of Medieval Canon Law under the direction of S. Kuttner.

---

[1] On the value and magnitude of the task still confronting scholars, see S. Kuttner, "The Scientific Investigation of Mediaeval Canon Law: The Need and the Opportunity," *Speculum* 24 (1949) 493-501; *id.*, "Methodological Problems concerning the History of Canon Law," *ibid.* 30 (1955) 539-49.

[2] See the discussion above, Ch.Ib n.1.

[3] Celebrating the same centenary, the 1948 issue of *Apollinaris* was devoted to articles on Gratian.

Appendix 1

Critical editions of the major canonistic works from the eleventh century to the thirteenth are now in progress and will soon begin to appear under the IMCL's auspices. In addition, the IMCL has sponsored two international congresses, at Louvain in 1958 and at Boston in 1963; the articles in their proceedings present a rewarding cross section of canonistic research.[4] A third congress is planned for Strasbourg in 1968.

Published annually in *Traditio* since 1955, the IMCL's Bulletin has become an indispensable reference and source of information about recent work. Bulletins include: regular reports on the editions, meetings, and other projects or activities sponsored by the IMCL; checklists of MSS of canonistic works; descriptions of archival discoveries; analyses of individual MSS; brief articles, frequently on problems emerging in the preparation of editions; and transcriptions of short canonistic texts. Finally, the IMCL Bulletin for 1956 (*Traditio* 12 [1956] 557-622) and subsequent Bulletins contain superb bibliographies, in which the entry is usually accompanied by a brief statement of contents and relevance.

At present, on the classical age of canon law, no single reference work is both reasonably complete and up to date. Moreover, important articles have appeared in a wide variety of publications—in periodicals primarily concerned with modern Church law,[5] as well as in journals of medieval studies or of legal history, in the proceedings of scholarly meetings as well as in Festschriften.[6] In the recent expansion of canonistic studies, many scholars have discussed the writings of the decretists and early decretalists, but the numerous articles by

---

[4] *Congrès de droit canonique médiéval, Louvain et Bruxelles 22-26 juillet 1958* (Bibliothèque de la Revue d'histoire ecclésiastique 33: Louvain 1959); *Proceedings of the Second International Congress of Medieval Canon Law, Boston College 12-16 August 1963*, ed. S. Kuttner and J. J. Ryan (Monumenta iuris canonici, Subsidia 1: Vatican City 1965).

[5] For example: *Apollinaris, Archiv für katholisches Kirchenrecht, Il diritto ecclesiastico, Ephemerides iuris canonici, The Jurist* (and its annual Beiheft, *Seminar*), *Revue de droit canonique*.

[6] Among recent Festschriften, see especially *Études d'histoire du droit canonique dédiées à Gabriel LeBras* (2 vols. Paris 1965).

Appendix 1

S. Kuttner and A. Stickler must be given special attention.[7] Similarly, on the decretal collections of the twelfth and thirteenth centuries, one must consult the studies by the late W. Holtzmann, by C. R. Cheney, and by C. Duggan.[8] Above all, the revised and enlarged edition of Kuttner's *Repertorium der Kanonistik*—scheduled to appear in the near future—will much simplify the tasks of inquiry.

[7] See the Bibliography below, and also the IMCL Bulletins. On the canonistic *quaestiones*, the work by G. Fransen is fundamental.

[8] Detailed bibliographical information in Duggan's *Twelfth-Century Decretal Collections* (London 1963) 1-23, 197-202, supplemented by the IMCL Bulletins.

OECONO'MUS AND LAY PATRON IN
THE RUFINIAN TRADITION

Master Rufinus applied the duality *auctoritas* and *administratio* in two different ways. He had, on the one hand, a static conception of different offices which are principally characterized either by *auctoritas* or by *administratio*, and, on the other hand, a dynamic conception of this duality as the two stages in the acquisition of the full powers pertaining to a single office. Because this study is mainly concerned with the status and powers of prelates-elect, and because Rufinus's successors exploited his terminology and his theoretical schema in order to develop new doctrines on the acquisition of ecclesiastical powers, the dynamic notion of *auctoritas-administratio* has received more attention here. In the period just before and after the Third Lateran Council, however, the static conception was still alive, for decretists of the French school were exploring its possible uses.

Between 1175 and 1178, the *Summa Inperatorie maiestati* differentiated two forms of administrative power over ecclesiastical property: full jurisdiction, which he identified with legislative power (*dispositio promulgande legis*), and a lesser form of jurisdiction, which he explained as the exercise of administrative power (*dispositio exercende dispensationis*).[1]

---

[1] *Summa Inperatorie maiestati* on C.16 q.7 c.24 v. *Laicis*: "Dispensatio uel dispositio alia promulgande legis, alia exercende dispensationis. Que legis est nunquam super re ecclesiastica laico conceditur, ut d. xcvi. c.i., nisi auctoritas ecclesie id fecerit, ut d. xcvii. c. i. et ii. Dispositio autem dispen-

Only exceptionally, he insisted, does the Church grant the full form of jurisdiction to a layman, since it is normally reserved to clerics. Then the anonymous author distinguished among three different levels within the lesser kind of jurisdiction: The bishop has "authority" (*auctoritas*) over his church's property, the *oeconomus* has the power of "ministry" (*ministerium*), and the lay patron of the church has "responsibility" (*diligentia*) and "provision" (*prouisio*). Clearly, this episcopal *auctoritas* is a purely jurisdictional prerogative, without sacramental implications. In decretistic thought, *ministerium* was commonly contrasted with *auctoritas*, and in this particular context, it must refer specifically to the *administratio temporalium*—that is, to general business and to the financial or legal aspects of ecclesiastical administration. This *administratio temporalium* pertains to the *oeconomus*, who (as the anonymous decretist pointed out) is always a cleric. Thus the *oeconomus*'s position resembled the archdeacon's, and one will recall that Rufinus ascribed the *administratio temporalium* to the archdeacon.[2]

By contrasting *auctoritas* and *ministerium* in this way, the *Summa Inperatorie maiestati* added little to the familiar outlines of the Rufinian tradition. Within his theory, however, the appearance of the *patronus* was an innovation. In the realm of practice, although clerics and even ecclesiastical corporations could act as patrons, the *patronus* was usually a layman. The church's maintenance and repair was regarded as his chief duty. Besides certain honorific functions, whenever a vacancy occurred in his church he had the right of presenting a new priest to the bishop for canonical installa-

---

sationis alia est auctoritas ut in persona episcopi, alia ministerii ut in persona yconomi, alia diligentie et prouisionis ut in persona patroni ecclesie. Prima et secunda solum permissum est clericis, tertia autem laicis" (Clm 16084 fol.24rb).

[2] The office of the *oeconomus* has been discussed above, Ch.IIIc nn.18-19. The *oeconomus*, of course, held a special commission with no relation to his ecclesiastical office or rank, whereas the archdeacon's administrative responsibilities belonged inseparably to his office.

tion.[3] Without actually explaining in detail the patron's prerogatives and responsibilities, the anonymous decretist simply summed them up as *diligentia* and *prouisio*. In short, just as master Rufinus had created an essentially ecclesiastical theory but had introduced a layman (that is, the emperor) into it, the *Summa Inperatorie maiestati* appropriated Rufinus's flexible system and made a place in it for the lay patron.

Around 1180, Peter of Blois composed his *Distinctiones*,[4] where he elaborated this system of *auctoritas, ministerium*, and *prouisio* as a more fully developed theory. His discussion begins with the role of laymen in the Church: they should submit to the Church, but never rule or manage it. The rights of lay patrons, however, are not really a form of rule or control, and therefore, he believed, these rights do not actually contradict his general principle. For there are, as he explained, two forms of regulative power within the Church: legislation (*constitutio*) and superintendence (*dispensatio*).[5] The legislative capacity belongs exclusively to the Roman pontiff, and it is the highest expression of the "authority to rule" over the Church (*auctoritas imperandi*), an authority which Peter of Blois denied to all laymen. Like the emperor in the secular

[3] Feine, *RG* I 351. On the *ius patronatus*, see Rufinus, *Summa* on C.16 q.2 dict.p.c.7 v. *tales etsi* etc., on C.16 q.7 c.26 v. *pie mentis* etc., ed. Singer 357f, 368ff; the related *lex diocesiana* is discussed *ibid.* on C.10 q.1 c.1 v. *si ex laicis*, ed. Singer 300f.

[4] Peter was heavily influenced by the *Summa Inperatorie maiestati*. It is worth noting here that in three MSS, Peter's *Distinctiones* (edited by T. A. Reimarus under the title *Speculum iuris canonici* [Berlin 1837]) and Sicard of Cremona's *Summa* appear together; see Kuttner, *Repertorium* 221f.

[5] *Speculum* 48, ed. Reimarus 90f: "Concessa est laicis, imo iniuncta necessitas obsequendi, non auctoritas imperandi, vel aliquid in rebus ecclesiasticis disponendi. Sed his obloqui videntur de ecclesiarum patronis, quibus permissum est rebus ecclesiasticis providere. Notandum ergo, quod dispositio alia est constitutionis, alia dispensationis. Dispositio [*ed.* dispensatio] constitutionis soli summo pontifici permissa est, quia ipse solus potest constituere, i.e. canones condere. Dispositio dispensationis, i.e. secundum quam res ecclesiastice disponantur, alia est auctoritatis, alia ministerii, alia est provisionis. Prima datur episcopo, secunda yconomo, tertia ecclesie patrono. Sola hec ergo datur laicis; prima et secunda solis clericis." For the distinction between the *necessitas obsequendi* and the *auctoritas imperandi*, see above, Ch.IIIc n.10.

sphere, only the pope has the right to issue universally valid and binding laws for the Church, as well as to interpret or abrogate them.[6] On the other hand, the notion of superintendence covers, in a broad fashion, the various administrative tasks within the Church. Indeed, the canonists and their contemporaries alike used the word *dispensatio* as a synonym for *administratio*.[7] This new duality, *constitutio* and *dispensatio*, was thus similar to—and perhaps derivative from—the older dualism of *auctoritas* and *administratio*.

Having distinguished between the supreme authority and the lesser form of ecclesiastical power, Peter then subdivided the notion of *dispensatio*. There are, he asserted, three systems of superintendence,

> according to which the things of the Church should be managed. There is one system with authority, another with ministry, still another with [the right of] provision. The first is given to the bishop, the second to the *oeconomus*, the third to the patron of the church.[8]

Here, Peter has virtually repeated the argument of the *Summa Inperatorie maiestati*. Yet Peter's views emerge more sharply than those of the anonymous decretist. For one thing, Peter's preceding discussion of the Roman pontiff's prerogatives adds an important dimension to this argument, and suggests that the bishop's jurisdictional *auctoritas* is a secondary *auctoritas*

[6] *Speculum* 19, ed. Reimarus 45: ". . . Sicuti enim regulare est, ut is solus possit interpretari leges, qui potest eas condere, scilicet solus imperator, ita et summus pontifex solus canones novos condere et interpretari et dispensare antiquos, cum solus habeat plenitudinem potestatis. . . ." Of course, Peter's conception of *constitutio* can be traced back to the claims of the Reform Papacy. See, for example, Gregory VII, *Dictatus pape* 7 (*Reg.* 2.55a, ed. Caspar 203): "Quod illi [scil. papae] soli licet pro temporis necessitate novas leges condere . . ."; note also the parallel passages quoted by Caspar (*ed.cit.* 203f).

[7] Gratian's and Rufinus's uses of the equation *dispensatio = administratio* are indicated above, Ch.IIB n.15 and Ch.IIIB n.20. Also, Bernard of Pavia, *Summa decretalium* 1.15-20, 1.25.1, ed. Laspeyres 16, 20; van de Kerckhove, *Études franciscaines* 49 (1937) 422; Tierney, *Foundations* 33; Niermeyer, *Mediae Latinitatis lexicon minus* 340f.

[8] *Speculum* 48, ed. Reimarus 90f (above, n.5).

imperandi, under the pope. In addition, more clearly than in the *Summa Inperatorie maiestati*, Peter's analysis brings out the central purpose of both decretists: By stressing that "only" the right of *prouisio* "is given to laymen," both decretists intended to exclude the layman equally from all forms of jurisdiction over ecclesiastical property and from any concrete act of administering a church's properties.

Approximately contemporary with Peter's *Distinctiones*, Sicard of Cremona's *Summa* dealt briefly and simply with the same problem. The bishop is still characterized by *auctoritas*, but Sicard has assigned *ministerium* to the priest.[9] In Sicard's discussion, the priest's *ministerium* corresponds to the *administratio spiritualium* described by Rufinus more than two decades earlier.[10] Like the *Summa Inperatorie maiestati*, Sicard ascribed *prouisio* to the patron—and he hastened to point out that the lay founder of a church has no power over that church.[11]

A further variation of Rufinus's constitutional theory appeared in the French school during the years around 1180, when the author of the *Summa Tractaturus magister* attempted to demonstrate the emperor's juridical subjection to the Roman pontiff:

> There is a right of authority (*auctoritas*), belonging to the pope; a right of power (*potestas*), belonging to the emperor and the bishop; a right of administration (*administratio*), belonging to the *oeconomus*.[12]

The anonymous author's key terms—*auctoritas, potestas,*

---

[9] *Summa* on C.10 q.1: ". . . Est dispensatio uel dispositio uel ordinatio:
—auctoritatis. Hec est episcopi. . . .
—ministerii. Hec est presbiteri. . . .
—prouisionis. Hec est patroni . . ." (Clm 11312 fol.86v).
[10] *Summa* on D.60 pr., on D.21 c.2, ed. Singer 151f, 45 (above, Ch.IIIB nn.5, 20).
[11] *Summa* on C.10 q.1 (Clm 11312 fol.86v).
[12] *Summa Tractaturus magister* on D.22 c.1 v. *terreni simul et celestis*: ". . . Est enim ius auctoritatis in papa, potestatis in imperatore vel episcopo, administrationis in yconomo . . ." (Stickler, *MIÖG* 62 [1954] 201 n.69 on 203).

administratio—differ significantly from those used by Sicard of Cremona and by Peter of Blois. Rufinus himself had used all three of these terms in his analyses of office, but the anonymous decretist assigned new meanings to these familiar terms. Here, in fact, the anonymous decretist has appropriated the terminology from the Gelasian distinction between the pontiff's *auctoritas* and the emperor's *potestas*, and has fused that formula with the Rufinian conception of the bishop and the *oeconomus* as the bearers, respectively, of *auctoritas* (or *potestas*) and *administratio*.[13] The net effect of this fusion is to create a hierarchical structure on three levels, with the pope in the supreme position, with emperor and bishop on the same intermediate level below the pope, and with the *oeconomus* cast in the subordinate role.

[13] On the duality *auctoritas-potestas*, see above, Ch.IIID n.2. Because the political doctrine of the *Summa Tractaturus magister* is woven from so many threads, it deserves a far more extended account—but, unfortunately, one which is not appropriate to this study.

HUGUCCIO, *SUMMA DECRETORUM*
ON D.63 c.10 v. *SUBSCRIPTA RELATIO*

In general, the MSS of Huguccio's *Summa* show surprisingly little textual variation. For the preparation of this text, however, three MSS have been collated:

M = Munich, Staatsbibliothek, Clm 10247 fol. 69rb-va
Va = Vatican, Archivio della Basilica di S. Pietro C.114 fol.81rb-va
Vb = Vatican, Biblioteca Apostolica Vaticana, Cod.lat.2280 fol. 63rb-va

The Munich MS provides the basic transcription; minor scribal slips and orthographic variants are suppressed.

Parts of this gloss have previously been published by Gross, *Recht an der Pfründe* 115ff; Gillmann, *AKKR* 93 (1913) 450ff; and Mochi Onory, *Fonti canonistiche* 151 n.1.

*

subscripta relatio, idest epistola, idest electio per epistolam nobis relata. Videtur innuere quod si esset subscripta, non posset irritari electio nec eligentes possent mutare uoluntatem suam. Set propter subscriptionem nec plus nec minus quam ante, subscriptio enim non fit nisi ad sollempnitatem et cautelam, ut dictum est supra di.lxi. Episcopus dum.[1] De electione mutanda sola uoluntate eligentium uarie sunt opiniones. 5

---

3 possunt Vb

---

[1] D.61 c.11

Dicunt quidam quod usque ad subscriptionem possunt eligentes mutare uoluntatem suam, post subscriptionem nequaquam, arg. hic et cap. Cartaginensis concilii Si quis contra suam[2] et i. q.vii. Saluberrimum[3] et xxvii. q.i. Omnes femine[4] et cap. Affricani concilii Aurelius.[5] Hoc Rufinus, Jo. et Simon.[6] Alii dicunt quod usque ad confirmationem uoluntas eligentium est ambulatoria, idest quotiens uolunt, possunt eam mutare, arg. di.xxviii. De Siracusane[7] et di.xlvii. De Petro[8] et di.lxi. Studii.[9] Hoc idem hic innuitur, et isti et primi in hoc quidem conueniunt, quod ex nuda electione, idest nondum superioris auctoritate confirmata, nil iuris acquiritur electo nec efficitur prelatus illius ecclesie ante confirmationem, arg. hic ut dicunt et di.xl. Sicut uiri[10] et di.xxviii. De Siracusane[11] et di.xxxiiii. Valentino[12] et xxvii. q.ii. Non dubium[13] et in conc. Rom. Cum in cunctis[14] et in extra. Dignum est,[15] Nosti.[16]

Ego autem distinguo: electio dicitur nominatio tam actiua quam passiua, scilicet nominatio eligentium et nominatio eius qui eligitur. Ex hac electione sic simpliciter intellecta nullum ius acquiritur alicui electo nec ob hoc efficitur prelatus. Item electio dicitur uinculum quod ex mutuo consensu, scilicet eligentium et electi, contrahitur inter eos, cum enim isti consentiunt in illum et ille uersa uice in istos, contrahitur inter eos matrimonium spirituale, ut ille iam dicatur sponsus istius ecclesie uel istorum clericorum et hec ecclesia sponsa ipsius. Hec uera sunt nisi ille clericus subsit alii prelato, tunc enim tales consensus tamquam inualidi suspenduntur quousque ille prelatus consentiat, qui si numquam consentit, illi

8 quod *om.* Vb   14 est *om.* Va   16 hic *om.* Vb   17 quidem] quod Va   29-31 cum enim—in istos (illos Vb) contrahitur inter eos VaVb: *om.* M (*homoiotel.*)

2 *Conc. Carthagin. II* c.13 fin., ut in *Dionysiana* (*PL* 67 188D; Hinschius, *Decr. Ps.-Isid.* 296)   3 C.1 q.7 c.21   4 C.27 q.1 c.36   5 C.26 q.6 c.5   6 Johannes Faventinus; Simon de Bisignano   7 D.28 c.13   8 D.47 c.4   9 D.61 c.15   10 D.40 c.8   11 D.28 c.13   12 D.34 c.20   13 C.27 q.2 c.16   14 *Conc. Lat. III* c.2; *Comp.I* 1.4.16 (*X* 1.6.7)   15 *Comp.I* 1.4.19 (*X——*)   16 *Comp.I* 1.4.18 (*X* 1.6.9)

consensus sunt inefficaces, si consentit, statim facti ualidi
generant et faciunt matrimonium inter illos, quod tandem
quasi carnali commixtione perficitur. Ex quo electus post
confirmationem ad concubitum, idest ordinationem illius
ecclesie, accedit, ut vii. q.i. Si quis alterius.[17] Sicut enim in   40
matrimonio carnali precedit matrimonium in desponsatione
per uerba de presenti et postea sequitur carnalis commixtio,
sic et hic in mutuo consensu precedit matrimonium spirituale
et postea sequitur quasi carnalis commixtio, cum iam
ecclesiam disponit et ordinat. Vel potest dici quod clericus   45
alterius episcopi ante consensum episcopi non debet eligi set
postulari, arg. infra eadem Litteras[18] et supra di.lxi. § Set
aliud.[19] Si tamen eligatur, illa electio est inualida ante consensum episcopi, ut dictum est. Ex prima ergo electione,
scilicet antequam electus consentiat, nullum ius acquiritur   50
electo, ex secunda, scilicet cum altrinsecus consensus
accedit, aliquod ius ei acquiritur, scilicet efficitur
prelatus illius ecclesie, et hoc expresse colligitur ex multis
capitulis, ut xvi. q.vii. Contra sanctorum[20] et viii. q.ii. Dilec-
tissimi[21] et xxvii. q.ii. §i. Coniuges[22] et xii. q.i. Expedit[23] et   55
di.xxiii. c.i. et di.lxxii. Placuit[24] et di.lxiii. Si in plebibus[25] et
vii. q.i. Quamuis.[26]
Set numquid administrationem rerum ecclesie inde consequitur? Sic uidetur, arg. di.xxiii. c.i. et di.lxiii. Si in plebibus[27]
et xii. q.i. Expedit,[28] et in quibusdam locis electus ante con-   60
firmationem de consuetudine administrat, set generalis
ecclesie consuetudo tenet in contrarium et in Romano concilio innuitur contrarium, cap. Cum in cunctis,[29] et Alexander
iii. expresse dicit contrarium in extra. Dignum est,[30] Nosti.[31]

---

40 ut] arg. Vb   44 et *om.* Vb   48 electio illa *tr.* Vb   50 acquiritur *om.* Va   51 altrinsecus] utriusque *ex* altrinsecus *corr.* Vb
53 illius] istius Vb   60 quibusdam] quibus Va   62-63 concilio
Romano *tr.* Vb   63 in] de elect. *add.* M *gl. marg.*

---

17 C.7 q.1 c.39 (ed. Friedberg: "Sicut alterius")   18 D.63 c.14
19 D.61 dict.p.c.10   20 C.16 q.7 c.29   21 C.8 q.2 c.2   22 C.27
q.2 c.6   23 C.12 q.1 c.13   24 D.72 c.3   25 D.63 c.20
26 C.7 q.1 c.14   27 D.63 c.20   28 C.12 q.1 c.13   29 supra, n.14
30 supra, n.15   31 supra, n.16

65 Dico ergo quod consequitur inde administrationem quoad ius, idest ius administrandi non statim set postea, set non consequitur actum administrandi, scilicet ut in ipso actu posset administrare statim, quasi: non habet executionem. Idem est in presbitero uel episcopo deposito uel suspenso, qui habet

70 ordinem set non executionem eius. Idem est in marito et uxore tempore menstrui uel partus uel dierum quadragesimalium, et fuit hoc institutum ad cautelam, scilicet ne bona ecclesie dilapidaret corrumpendo alios, quia scit quod factum eius citius posset cassari ante confirmationem quam postea.

75 Preterea dico quod clerici post primam electionem concorditer et legitime factam sua auctoritate nulla alia causa interueniente nisi quia uelint, sine peccato non possunt mutare uoluntatem suam in alium. Si tamen mutauerint et alium elegerint, primus electus nec poterit nec debebit contradicere,

80 cum nil sibi sit acquisitum. Similiter post secundam electionem non possunt mutare. Quid si mutauerint? Irritabitur quicquid fiet. Set pone electus est secundus et ordinatus, numquid primus poterit conuenire eum et repellere? Credo quod sic, nisi auctoritate maioris esset factum ex certa scien-

85 tia. Quidam dicunt quod quamuis de iure posset eum conuenire, non tamen deberet quia presumeretur ambitiosus. Set que ambitio uel quod peccatum si quis utatur iure suo, ut defendat suum ius? Immo non debet quis ius suum indefensum relinquere, ut ff. de pet. hered. Illud,[32] presertim in rebus

90 diuinis, ut vii. q.i. Quam sit,[33] nec dolo uidetur facere si quis utitur iure suo, ut dicit regula iuris. Illis capitulis, scilicet De Siracusane,[34] De Petro,[35] Studii,[36] quibus innuitur quod electio possit mutari, sic respondeo: Illegitime persone erant ibi electe et ideo locus erat irritationi, set nec auctoritate eligen-

---

67 in *om.* Va   possit VaVb   72 et] uel Vb   76 sua *om.*
Va   80 cum] quod Vb   81 mutare quid si *om.* Va (*homoiotel.*)
84 auctoritate—factum Vb: auctoritate maioris M, maioris esset factum
Va   88 ius suum *tr.* VaVb   94 nec] etiam *add.* VaVb

---

[32] *Dig.* 5.3.40 (ed. Mommsen: "De hereditatis petitione"; cf. *Cod.* 3.31)
[33] C.7 q.1 c.8 (ed. Friedberg: "Quam periculosum sit")   [34] D.28 c.13
[35] D.47 c.4   [36] D.61 c.15

tium irritabitur ibi electio, immo auctoritate maioris, qui etiam 95
confirmatam electionem posset irritare. Huic capitulo, scilicet
Quanto,[37] ubi idem innuitur, sic respondeo: Illegitima persona
erat electa, de scientia cuius et uita et moribus papa male
suspicabatur, et ideo cum papa uel non posset uel nollet eum
ita publice reprobare, uoluit saltem hoc modo eis insinuare 100
ut ab ea electione recederent, et hoc dicendo permisit eis
tacite quod alias non liceret, de iure enim non exigebatur ut
illorum absentium consensus inquireretur, cum dicitur ad
cautelam, presertim cum ante consenserant, quod notatur cum
dicitur "perdurare," et cum essent laici, quod innuitur ibi 105
"barbarica" etc.[38] Voluit ergo papa dare eis qualemcumque
occasionem diuertendi ab electione, ut sic quoquo modo
cassaretur.

Quod autem dicunt ante confirmationem nil iuris conferri
electo stare non potest, quia quid est confirmare nisi quod 110
est quasi infirmum firmare et firmius reddere? Quid ergo
confirmat metropolitanus? Non potest dici quod confirmet
primam electionem, idest nominationem, actionem uel passionem, que fuit in eligentibus uel electo, quia illa iam non
est de necessitate. Compellimur dicere quod confirmat uincu- 115
lum illud quod ex mutuo consensu contrahitur et ex quo
electus efficitur prelatus. Preterea quis esset adeo stultus, qui
diceret non esse clericorum sibi facere prelatum et pastorem,
set maioris? Numquid clerici non faciunt sibi prelatum, sicut
principes imperatorem, licet postea confirmetur a papa, ut 120
di.xciii. Legimus?[39]

---

102 non[1] *om.* Vb   106 dare *post* 107 electione *tr.* Vb   108 ces-
saretur M   112 confirmat] confirmet Vb   117-118 adeo—cleri-
corum] qui diceret non clericorum esset Va   119 sicut VaVb: sic M

[37] D.63 c.10   [38] D.63 c.10 (ed. Friedberg, prope nn.119, 118)
[39] D.93 c.24

BIBLIOGRAPHY

MANUSCRIPTS CITED

BAMBERG, Staatsbibliothek
  Canonistische Hs. 42 (P.II.15)
    Summa Animal est substantia (*Summa Bambergensis*)
  Canonistische Hs. 45 (P.II.4)
    Ricardus Anglicus, *Generalia* (*Brocarda*)
  Canonistische Hs. 47 (P.II.22)
    Egidius of Bologna, *Tractatus Ad intelligentiam decretalis Quia propter*
CAMBRIDGE, University Library
  Addit. MS 3321 I
    Summa Cantabrigiensis
ERFURT, Stadtbücherei
  Amplonianische Hs. qu. 117
    Summa Reuerentia sacrorum canonum
LAON, Bibliothèque communale
  MS 371*bis*
    Apparatus Ecce uicit leo
LONDON, British Museum
  Egerton 2901
    Collectio Francofortana
  Royal 15.B.IV
    Royal Collection of Decretals
MONTECASSINO, Biblioteca Abbaziale
  MS 136
    William Naso, *Tractatus Tres sunt forme que fiunt*
MUNICH, Staatsbibliothek
  Codex latinus monacensis 3879
    Alanus Anglicus, *Apparatus decretalium Comp.I*
    Tancred, *Glossa ordinaria ad Comp.II*
    Johannes Galensis (?), Glosses on *Comp.III*
    Johannes Teutonicus, *Summula* on *Comp.III*
  Clm 6352
    Ricardus Anglicus, *Apparatus decretalium Comp.I*
  Clm 10244
    Apparatus Ordinaturus
  Clm 10247
    Huguccio, *Summa decretorum*
  Clm 11312
    Sicard of Cremona, *Summa decretorum*
  Clm 16084
    Summa Inperatorie maiestati

Bibliography

NUREMBERG, Stadtbibliothek
Cent. V. 95
    Ricardus Anglicus, *Generalia* (*Brocarda*)
PARIS, Bibliothèque Mazarine
MS 1318
    Alanus Anglicus, *Apparatus Ius naturale* (recensio longior)
PARIS, Bibliothèque nationale
MS latin 3909
    Alanus Anglicus, *Apparatus Ius naturale* (recensio brevior)
MS latin 3922A
    Collectio Francofortana
MS latin 3934A
    Simon of Bisignano, *Summa decretorum*
MS latin 14320
    Damasus, *Summa decretalium*
    Notabilia Nota per exteriora deprehendi on *Comp.I*
MS latin 15393
    Alanus Anglicus, *Apparatus Ius naturale* (recensio longior)
    Laurentius Hispanus, *Apparatus*
MS 15994
    Summa Tractaturus magister
Nouvelle acquisition latine 1576
    Apparatus Ecce uicit leo
ROUEN, Bibliothèque municipale
MS 710 (E.29)
    Sicard of Cremona, *Summa decretorum*
    Simon of Bisignano, *Summa decretorum*
    Summa Et est sciendum (*Glossae Stuttgardienses*)
MS 743 (E.74)
    Summa Omnis qui iuste iudicat (*Summa Lipsiensis*)
VATICAN CITY, Biblioteca Apostolica Vaticana
Archivio della Basilica di San Pietro C.114
    Huguccio, *Summa decretorum*
Archivio della Basilica di San Pietro H.13
    Boncompagno of Florence, *Rhetorica antiqua*
Codex latinus 2280
    Huguccio, *Summa decretorum*
Codex Palatinus latinus 658
    Glossa Palatina
Codex Reginensis 977
    Glossa Palatina
VIENNA, Nationalbibliothek
MS 2083
    William Naso, *Lectura*
MS 2209
    Hostiensis, *Tractatus Almo ac beatissimo patri*
MS 2238
    Hostiensis, *Tractatus Almo ac beatissimo patri*
WORCESTER, Cathedral Chapter Library
MS Q.70
    Summa Wigorniensis
ZWETTL, Stiftsbibliothek
MS 162
    Honorius, *Summa quaestionum*
    Ricardus Anglicus, *Distinctiones decretorum*

Bibliography

SELECT LIST OF PRINTED WORKS

P. ALDINGER, *Die Neubesetzung der deutschen Bistümer unter Papst Inno-cenz IV. 1243-1254* (Leipzig 1900)

ALEXANDER III, *Die Summa magistri Rolandi nachmals Papstes Alexander III.*, ed. Friedrich Thaner (Innsbruck 1874)

Paul ANCIAUX, *La théologie du sacrement de pénitence au XIIe siècle* (Universitas Catholica Lovaniensis, Dissertationes ad gradum magistri in Facultate Theologica vel in Facultate Iuris Canonici consequendum conscriptae 2nd ser. 41: Louvain 1949)

Michel ANDRIEU, ed., *Les Ordines romani du haut moyen-âge* (5 vols. Spicilegium sacrum Lovaniense, Études et documents 11, 23-24, 28-29: Louvain 1931-61)

————. *Le Pontifical romain au moyen-âge* (4 vols. Studi e testi 86-88, 99: Vatican City 1938-41)

ANSELM of Lucca, *Collectio canonum*, ed. Friedrich Thaner (Innsbruck 1906-15)

Antonius AUGUSTINUS, ed., *Opera omnia IV: Antiquae collectiones decretalium* (Lucca 1769)

Friedrich BAETHGEN, "Der Anspruch des Papsttums auf das Reichsvikariat," *ZRG KA* 10 (1920) 168-268

————. *Mediaevalia: Aufsätze, Nachrufe, Besprechungen* (MGH Schriften 17: Stuttgart 1960)

Geoffrey BARRACLOUGH, "The Making of a Bishop in the Middle Ages," *CHR* 19 (1933-34) 275-319

————, ed., *Mediaeval Germany 911-1250* (2 vols. Oxford 1938)

Franz X. BARTH, *Hildebert von Lavardin (1056-1133) und das kirchliche Stellenbesetzungsrecht* (Kirchenrechtliche Abh. 34-36: Stuttgart 1906)

Johannes BAUERMANN, "Die Frage der Bischofswahlen auf dem Würzburger Reichstag von 1133," *Kritische Beiträge zur Geschichte des Mittelalters: Festschrift für Robert Holtzmann* (Historische Studien 238: Berlin 1933) 103-34

August BAUMHAUER, *Philipp der Schöne und Bonifaz VIII. in ihrer Stellung zur französischen Kirche mit besonderer Berücksichtigung der Bischofswahlen* (Freiburg im Breisgau 1920)

Alfons BECKER, *Studien zum Investiturproblem in Frankreich: Papsttum, Königtum und Episkopat im Zeitalter der gregorianischen Kirchenreform 1049-1119* (Saarbrücken 1955)

Georg von BELOW, *Die Entstehung des ausschliesslichen Wahlrechts der Domkapitel, mit besonderer Rücksicht auf Deutschland* (Historische Studien 11: Leipzig 1883)

Robert L. BENSON, "*Plenitudo potestatis*: Evolution of a Formula from Gregory IV to Gratian," *SGrat* 13 (1968)

BERNARD of Pavia, *Summa decretalium*, ed. E.A.T. Laspeyres (Regensburg 1860)

Ernst BERNHEIM, "Zur Geschichte der kirchlichen Wahlen," *FDG* 20 (1880) 361-81

————. "Investitur und Bischofswahl im 11. und 12. Jahrhundert," *ZKG* 7 (1885) 303-33

————. "Die Praesentia regis im Wormser Konkordat," *Historische Vierteljahrschrift* 10 (1907) 196-212

Robert BOERGER, *Die Belehnungen der deutschen geistlichen Fürsten* (Leipziger Studien aus dem Gebiet der Geschichte VIII 1: Leipzig 1902)

Heinrich BÖHMER, *Kirche und Staat in England und in der Normandie im XI. und XII. Jahrhundert* (Leipzig 1899)

Bibliography

BONIZO of Sutri, *Liber de vita christiana*, ed. Ernst Perels (Texte zur Geschichte des römischen und kanonischen Rechts im Mittelalter 1: Berlin 1930)

Albert BRACKMANN, *Die Kurie und die Salzburger Kirchenprovinz* (Studien und Vorarbeiten zur Germania pontificia 1: Berlin 1912)

Z. N. BROOKE, "Lay Investiture and Its Relation to the Conflict of Empire and Papacy," *PBA* 25 (1939) 217-47

Francesco CALASSO, *I glossatori e la teoria della sovranità* (2nd ed. Milan 1951)

Gerard J. CAMPBELL, "Temporal and Spiritual Regalia during the Reigns of St Louis and Philip III," *Traditio* 20 (1964) 351-83

Norman F. CANTOR, *Church, Kingship, and Lay Investiture in England 1089-1135* (Princeton 1958)

R. W. and A. J. CARLYLE, *A History of Mediaeval Political Theory in the West* (reprint 6 vols. Edinburgh 1950)

Erich CASPAR, *Geschichte des Papsttums von den Anfängen bis zur Höhe der Weltherrschaft* (2 vols. Tübingen 1930-33)

Peter CLASSEN, *Gerhoch von Reichersberg: Eine Biographie* (Wiesbaden 1960)

Codex iuris canonici (Rome 1917)

André DESPRAIRIES, *L'élection des évêques par les chapitres au XIIIe siècle: Théories canoniques* (Paris 1922)

DEUSDEDIT, *Collectio canonum* ed. Victor Wolf von Glanvell, *Die Kanonessammlung des Kardinals Deusdedit* (Paderborn 1905)

Albert DIEGEL, *Der päpstliche Einfluss auf die Bischofswahlen in Deutschland während des 13. Jahrhunderts* (Berlin 1932)

L. DUCHESNE, ed., *Le Liber pontificalis* (3 vols. Paris 1886-1955)

Charles DUGGAN, *Twelfth-Century Decretal Collections and Their Importance in English History* (London 1963)

Karl August ECKHARDT, ed., *Sachsenspiegel Land- und Lehnrecht* (MGH Fontes iuris Germanici antiqui n.s.1: Hanover 1933)

Eduard EICHMANN, *Weihe und Krönung des Papstes im Mittelalter* (Münchener theologische Studien, kanonistische Abteilung 1: Munich 1951)

Arthur ENGEL and Raymond SERRURE, *Traité de numismatique du moyen âge* II (Paris 1894)

Adhémar ESMEIN, *Le mariage en droit canonique*, 2nd ed. rev. R. Génestal (2 vols. Paris 1929-35)

Hans Erich FEINE, *Die Besetzung der Reichsbistümer vom Westfälischen Frieden bis zur Säkularisation 1648-1803* (Kirchenrechtliche Abh. 97-98: Stuttgart 1921)

————. *Kirchliche Rechtsgeschichte* I: *Die Katholische Kirche* (2nd ed. Weimar 1954)

Julius FICKER, *Vom Heerschilde* (Innsbruck 1862)

————. *Forschungen zur Reichs- und Rechtsgeschichte Italiens* (4 vols. Innsbruck 1868-74)

————. "Ueber das Eigenthum des Reichs am Reichskirchengute," *SB Wien* 72 (1872) 55-146, 381-450

————, ed., *Der Spiegel deutscher Leute* (Innsbruck 1859)

Paul FOURNIER and Gabriel LEBRAS, *Histoires des collections canoniques en Occident depuis les fausses décrétales jusqu'au Décret de Gratien* (2 vols. Paris 1931-32)

Emil FRIEDBERG, ed., *Corpus iuris canonici* (2 vols. Leipzig 1879-81)

————, ed., *Quinque compilationes antiquae* (Leipzig 1882)

Vincenz FUCHS, *Der Ordinationstitel von seiner Entstehung bis auf Innocenz III.* (Kanonistische Studien und Texte 4: Bonn 1930)

Bibliography

Horst FUHRMANN, "Studien zur Geschichte mittelalterlicher Patriarchate," *ZRG KA* 39 (1953) 112-76; 40 (1954) 1-84; 41 (1955) 95-183

François Louis GANSHOF, "Note sur l'élection des évêques dans l'empire romain au IVe et pendant la première moitié du Ve siècle," *Revue internationale des droits de l'antiquité* 4 (1950) 467-98

——. *Feudalism*, trans. P. Grierson (London 1952)

Jean GAUDEMET, *La collation par le roi de France des bénéfices vacants en régale des origines à la fin du XIVe siècle* (Bibliothèque de l'École des hautes études, Sciences religieuses 51: Paris 1935)

——. "Les institutions ecclésiastiques en France du milieu du XIIe au début du XIVe siècle," in: F. Lot and R. Fawtier, eds., *Histoire des institutions françaises au moyen-âge* III: *Institutions ecclésiastiques* (Paris 1962) 143-335

Heinrich Gottfried GENGLER, ed., *Des Schwabenspiegels Landrechtsbuch* (2nd ed. Erlangen 1875)

GERHOH of Reichersberg, *Opera inedita*, ed. D. and O. Van den Eynde and P. Rijmersdael (2 vols. Rome 1955-56)

Franz GILLMANN, "Johannes Galensis als Glossator, insbesondere der Compilatio III," *AKKR* 105 (1925) 488-565

——. "Die Dekretglossen des Cod. Stuttgart. hist. f.419," *AKKR* 107 (1927) 192-250

——. "Richardus Anglikus als Glossator der Compilatio I," *AKKR* 107 (1927) 575-655

——. "Der Kommentar des Vincentius Hispanus zu den Kanones des vierten Laterankonzils (1215)," *AKKR* 109 (1929) 223-74

——. "Zum Problem vom Ursprung des ius ad rem," *AKKR* 113 (1933) 463-85

——. *Des Laurentius Hispanus Apparat zur Compilatio III auf der Staatlichen Bibliothek zu Bamberg* (Mainz 1935)

T. GOTTLOB, *Der Kirchliche Amtseid der Bischöfe* (Kanonistische Studien und Texte 9: Bonn 1936)

GREGORY VII, *Das Register Gregors VII.*, ed. Erich Caspar (MGH Epistolae selectae 2: Berlin 1920-23)

Carl GROSS, *Das Recht an der Pfründe, zugleich ein Beitrag zur Ermittlung des Ursprungs des ius ad rem* (Graz 1887)

Curt-Bogislav von HACKE, *Die Palliumverleihungen bis 1143* (Göttingen 1898)

Albert HAUCK, *Kirchengeschichte Deutschlands* (3rd and 4th ed. 5 vols. Leipzig 1911-29)

Joseph HEINRICH, "Kaiser Heinrich VI. und die Besetzung der deutschen Bistümer von seiner Kaiserkrönung bis zur Eroberung Siziliens (April 1191 bis Ende 1194)," *RQSchr* 51 (1956) 189-227

Donald E. HEINTSCHEL, *The Mediaeval Concept of an Ecclesiastical Office* (The Catholic University of America, Canon Law Studies 363: Washington, D.C. 1956)

HENRY of Susa (Henricus de Segusio), *see* Hostiensis

Johanne HEYDENREICH, *Die Metropolitangewalt der Erzbischöfe von Trier bis auf Baldewin* (Marburger Studien zur älteren deutschen Geschichte II 5: Marburg 1938)

Paul HINSCHIUS, *Das Kirchenrecht der Katholiken und Protestanten in Deutschland* (6 vols. Berlin 1869-97)

——, ed., *Decretales Pseudo-Isidorianae et Capitula Angilramni* (Leipzig 1863)

Ludwig HÖDL, *Die Geschichte der scholastischen Literatur und der Theo-*

Bibliography

logie der Schlüsselgewalt I (Beiträge zur Geschichte der Philosophie und Theologie XXXVIII 4: Münster 1960)

Hartmut HOFFMANN, "Ivo von Chartres und die Lösung des Investiturproblems," *DA* 15 (1959) 393-440

Adolf HOFMEISTER, "Zur Erhebung Eberhards I. auf den Salzburger Erzstuhl 1147," *ZKG* 29 (1908) 71-78

――――. "Das Wormser Konkordat: Zum Streit und seine Bedeutung," *Forschungen und Versuche zur Geschichte des Mittelalters und der Neuzeit: Festschrift Dietrich Schäfer zum siebzigsten Geburtstag dargebracht* (Jena 1915) 64-148

Walther HOLTZMANN, "Die Dekretalensammlungen des 12. Jahrhunderts (1): Die Sammlung Tanner," *Festschrift zur Feier des zweihundertjährigen Bestehens der Akademie der Wissenschaften in Göttingen* II, Philologisch-historische Klasse (Berlin 1951) 83-145

――――. "Die Benutzung Gratians in der päpstlichen Kanzlei im 12. Jahrhundert," *SGrat* 1 (1953) 325-49

――――. *Beiträge zur Reichs- und Papstgeschichte des hohen Mittelalters: Ausgewählte Aufsätze* (Bonner historische Forschungen 8: Bonn 1957)

――――. and E. W. KEMP, eds., *Papal Decretals Relating to the Diocese of Lincoln in the Twelfth Century* (Publications of the Lincoln Record Society 47: Hereford 1954)

HOSTIENSIS (Henry of Susa), *Summa aurea* (Venice 1574 [repr. Turin 1965] and other editions)

――――. *Commentaria in decretales Gregorii IX* (Venice 1581 [repr. 2 vols. Turin 1965] and other editions)

Margaret HOWELL, *Regalian Right in Medieval England* (London 1962)

INNOCENT III, *Regestum Innocentii III papae super negotio Romani imperii,* ed. Friedrich Kempf (Miscellanea Historiae Pontificiae 12: Rome 1947)

INNOCENT III, *Selected Letters of Pope Innocent III concerning England,* ed. C. R. Cheney and W. H. Semple (London 1953)

INNOCENT IV, *Apparatus super quinque libris decretalium* (Frankfurt 1570 and other editions)

Josef JUNCKER, "Summen und Glossen: Beiträge zur Literaturgeschichte des kanonischen Rechts im zwölften Jahrhundert," *ZRG KA* 14 (1925) 384-474

――――. "Die Summa des Simon von Bisignano und seine Glossen," *ZRG KA* 15 (1926) 326-500

Ernst H. KANTOROWICZ, *Laudes regiae: A Study in Liturgical Acclamations and Mediaeval Ruler Worship* (University of California Publications in History 33: Berkeley 1946)

――――. *The King's Two Bodies: A Study in Mediaeval Political Theology* (Princeton 1957)

――――. *Selected Studies* (Locust Valley, N.Y. 1965)

Friedrich KEMPF, *Papsttum und Kaisertum bei Innocenz III.: Die geistigen und rechtlichen Grundlagen seiner Thronstreitpolitik* (Miscellanea Historiae Pontificiae 19: Rome 1954)

Fritz KERN, *Die Anfänge der französischen Ausdehnungspolitik bis zum Jahre 1308* (Tübingen 1910)

――――, ed., *Acta imperii, Angliae et Franciae ab a.1267 ad a.1313* (Tübingen 1911)

J. P. KIRSCH, "Das Lütticher Schisma vom Jahre 1238," *RQSchr* 3 (1889) 177-203

Hans-Walter KLEWITZ, "Das Ende des Reformpapsttums," *DA* 3 (1939) 371-412

Bibliography

————. "Die Krönung des Papstes," *ZRG* KA 30 (1941) 96-130

Erich KÖNIG, ed., *Historia Welforum* (Schwäbische Chroniken der Stauferzeit 1: Stuttgart 1938)

Hermann KRABBO, *Die Besetzung der deutschen Bistümer unter der Regierung Kaiser Friedrichs II. 1212-1250* (Historische Studien 25: Berlin 1901)

Hans-Georg KRAUSE, *Das Papstwahldekret von 1059 und seine Rolle im Investiturstreit* (SGreg 7: Rome 1960)

Otto KUHLE, *Die Neubesetzung der deutschen Bistümer unter Papst Innozenz III.* (Berlin 1935)

Stephan KUTTNER, *Repertorium der Kanonistik (1140-1234): Prodromus corporis glossarum* I (Studi e testi 71: Vatican City 1937)

————. "Les débuts de l'école canoniste française," *Studia et documenta historiae et iuris* 4 (1938) 193-204

————. "Bernardus Compostellanus Antiquus: A Study in the Glossators of the Canon Law," *Traditio* 1 (1943) 277-340

————. "Johannes Teutonicus, das vierte Laterankonzil und die Compilatio quarta," *Miscellanea Giovanni Mercati* V (Studi e testi 125: Vatican City 1946) 608-34

————. "Réflexions sur les brocards des glossateurs," *Mélanges Joseph de Ghellinck* II (Gembloux 1951) 767-92

———— and Eleanor RATHBONE, "Anglo-Norman Canonists of the Twelfth Century: An Introductory Study," *Traditio* 7 (1949-51) 279-358

LAURENTIUS de Somercote, *Der Traktat des Laurentius de Somercote, Kanonikus von Chichester, über die Vornahme von Bischofswahlen, entstanden im Jahre 1254*, ed. Alfred von Wretschko (Weimar 1907)

Guillaume LeMAIRE, *Liber Guillelmi Maioris*, ed. Célestin Port, *Mélanges historiques* II (Collection de documents inédits: Paris 1877) 189-569

William E. LUNT, *Papal Revenues in the Middle Ages* (Columbia University, Records of Civilization 19: 2 vols. New York 1934)

Terence P. McLAUGHLIN, ed., *The Summa Parisiensis on the Decretum Gratiani* (Toronto 1952)

E. M. MEIJERS, ed., *Responsa doctorum Tholosanorum* (Rechtshistorisch Instituut 2nd ser. 8: Haarlem 1938)

Erich MEUTHEN, *Kirche und Heilsgeschichte bei Gerhoh von Reichersberg* (Studien und Texte zur Geistesgeschichte des Mittelalters 6: Leiden 1959)

Carl MIRBT, *Die Publizistik im Zeitalter Gregors VII.* (Leipzig 1894)

Heinrich MITTEIS, *Lehnrecht und Staatsgewalt* (Weimar 1933)

Sergio MOCHI ONORY, *Fonti canonistiche dell'idea moderna dello Stato* (Milan 1951)

Bernard MONOD, "La question des investitures à l'entrevue de Châlons (1107)," *Revue historique* 101 (1909) 80-87

Germain MORIN, "Le discours d'ouverture du Concile général de Latran (1179) et l'oeuvre littéraire de maître Rufin, évêque d'Assise," *Atti della Pontificia accademia romana di archeologia* 3rd ser., *Memorie* 2 (1928) 113-33

Engelbert MÜHLBACHER, *Die streitige Papstwahl des Jahres 1130* (Innsbruck 1876)

J. F. NIERMEYER, *Mediae latinitatis lexicon minus* (Leiden 1954ff)

Irene OTT, "Der Regalienbegriff im 12. Jahrhundert," *ZRG* KA 35 (1948) 234-304

OTTO of Freising, *Chronica sive Historia de duobus civitatibus*, 2nd ed. Adolf Hofmeister (MGH SS.rer.Germ. Hanover 1912)

———— and RAHEWIN, *Gesta Friderici I. imperatoris*, 3rd ed. Georg Waitz and B. von Simson (MGH SS.rer.Germ. Hanover 1912)

Bibliography

Marcel PACAUT, *Louis VII et les élections épiscopales dans le royaume de France* (Paris 1957)

——. *Alexandre III: Étude sur la conception du pouvoir pontifical dans sa pensée et dans son oeuvre* (Paris 1956)

Anscar PARSONS, *Canonical Elections: An Historical Synopsis and Commentary* (The Catholic University of America, Canon Law Studies 118: Washington, D.C. 1939)

PAUCAPALEA, *Die Summa des Paucapalea über das Decretum Gratiani*, ed. Johann Friedrich von Schulte (Giessen 1890)

PETER of Blois, *Speculum iuris canonici*, ed. T. A. Reimarus (Berlin 1837)

Charles PETIT-DUTAILLIS, *Étude sur la vie et le règne de Louis VIII (1187-1226)* (Bibliothèque de l'École des hautes études, Sciences philologiques et historiques 101: Paris 1894)

Arnold PÖSCHL, *Die Regalien der mittelalterlichen Kirchen* (Festschrift der Grazer Universität fur 1927: Graz 1928)

Gaines POST, *Studies in Medieval Legal Thought: Public Law and the State 1100-1322* (Princeton 1964)

RAHEWIN, see Otto of Freising

RAYMOND of Peñafort, *Opera omnia* I: *Summa iuris*, ed. José Rius Serra (Barcelona 1945)

Thomas RIED, ed., *Codex diplomatico-chronologicus episcopatus Ratisponensis* (2 vols. Regensburg 1816)

ROLAND Bandinelli, see Alexander III

Eugène de ROZIÈRE, ed., *Liber diurnus Romanorum pontificum: Recueil des formules usitées par la chancellerie pontificale du Ve au XIe siècle* (Paris 1869)

Hermann RUDORFF, *Zur Erklärung des Wormser Konkordats* (Quellen und Studien zur Verfassungsgeschichte des Deutschen Reiches in Mittelalter und Neuzeit I 4: Weimar 1906)

RUFINUS, *Die Summa decretorum des magister Rufinus*, ed. Heinrich Singer (Paderborn 1902)

J. Joseph RYAN, *Saint Peter Damiani and His Canonical Sources: A Preliminary Study in the Antecedents of the Gregorian Reform* (Pontifical Institute of Mediaeval Studies, Studies and Texts 2: Toronto 1956)

Johann Baptist SÄGMÜLLER, *Die Bischofswahl bei Gratian* (Görres-Gesellschaft, Sektion für Rechts- und Sozialwissenschaften 1: Cologne 1908)

Fritz SALOMON, "Der Sachsenspiegel und das Wormser Konkordat," *ZRG GA* 31 (1910) 137-45

Louis SALTET, *Les réordinations: Étude sur le sacrement de l'ordre* (Paris 1907)

Leo SANTIFALLER, *Zur Geschichte des ottonisch-salischen Reichskirchensystems* (SB Wien 229 no.1: Vienna 1954-55)

Dietrich SCHÄFER, *Zur Beurteilung des Wormser Konkordats* (Abh.Berlin 1905 no.1: Berlin 1905)

——. "Consilio vel iudicio = mit minne oder mit rechte," *SB Berlin* (1913) 719-33

——. "Honor, citra, cis im mittelalterlichen Latein," *SB Berlin* (1921) 372-81

Anton SCHARNAGL, *Der Begriff der Investitur in den Quellen und der Literatur des Investiturstreites* (Kirchenrechtliche Abh. 56: Stuttgart 1908)

Franz-Josef SCHMALE, *Studien zum Schisma des Jahres 1130* (Forschungen zur kirchlichen Rechtsgeschichte und zum Kirchenrecht 3: Cologne 1961)

Paul SCHMID, *Der Begriff der kanonischen Wahl in den Anfängen des Investiturstreits* (Stuttgart 1926)

Wilhelm SCHMIDT, "Die Stellung der Erzbischöfe und des Erzstiftes von

Bibliography

Salzburg zu Kirche und Reich unter Kaiser Friedrich I. bis zum Frieden von Venedig (1177)," *Archiv für österreichische Geschichte* 34 (1865) 3-144

Johann Friedrich von SCHULTE, "Zur Geschichte der Literatur über das Dekret Gratians," *SB Wien* 64 (1870) 93-142

———. "Literaturgeschichte der Compilationes antiquae, besonders der drei ersten," *SB Wien* 66 (1870) 51-158

———. "Die Summa Decreti Lipsiensis des Cod. 986 der Leipziger Universitätsbibliothek," *SB Wien* 68 (1871) 37-54

———. *Die Geschichte der Quellen und Literatur des canonischen Rechts von Gratian bis auf die Gegenwart* (3 vols. Stuttgart 1875-80)

Wilhelmine SEIDENSCHNUR, "Die Salzburger Eigenbistümer in ihrer reichs-, kirchen- und landesrechtlichen Stellung," *ZRG KA* 9 (1919) 177-287

T.E.A. SICKEL, ed., *Liber diurnus Romanorum pontificum* (Vienna 1889)

STEPHEN of Tournai, *Die Summa des Stephanus Tornacensis über das Decretum Gratiani*, ed. Johann Friedrich von Schulte (Giessen 1891)

Alfons M. STICKLER, "Magistri Gratiani sententia de potestate Ecclesiae in Statum," *Apollinaris* 21 (1948) 36-111

———. *Historia iuris canonici latini* I: *Historia fontium* (Turin 1950)

———. "Vergessene Bologneser Dekretisten," *Salesianum* 14 (1952) 476-503

———. "Sacerdotium et Regnum nei decretisti e primi decretalisti: Considerazioni metodologiche di ricerca e testi," *Salesianum* 15 (1953) 575-612

———. "Sacerdozio e Regno nelle nuove ricerche attorno ai secoli XII e XIII nei Decretisti e Decretalisti fino alle Decretali di Gregorio IX," *Sacerdozio e Regno da Gregorio VII a Bonifacio VIII* (Miscellanea Historiae Pontificiae 18: Rome 1954) 1-26

———. "Imperator vicarius Papae: Die Lehren der französisch-deutschen Dekretistenschule des 12. und beginnenden 13. Jahrhunderts über die Beziehungen zwischen Papst und Kaiser," *MIÖG* 62 (1954) 165-212

———. "Alanus Anglicus als Verteidiger des monarchischen Papsttums," *Salesianum* 21 (1959) 346-406

William STUBBS, *Select Charters*, 9th ed. rev. H.W.C. Davis (Oxford 1913)

SUGER of St Denis, *Vita Ludovici grossi regis*, ed. Henri Waquet, *Vie de Louis VI le Gros* (Les classiques de l'histoire de France au Moyen Age 11: Paris 1929)

Gerd TELLENBACH, *Church, State, and Christian Society at the Time of the Investiture Contest*, trans. R. F. Bennett (Oxford 1940)

Brian TIERNEY, *Foundations of the Conciliar Theory: The Contribution of the Medieval Canonists from Gratian to the Great Schism* (Cambridge Studies in Medieval Life and Thought n.s.4: Cambridge 1955)

Helene TILLMANN, *Papst Innocenz III.* (Bonner historische Forschungen 3: Bonn 1954)

Josef TRUMMER, "Mystisches im alten Kirchenrecht: Die geistige Ehe zwischen Bischof und Diözese," *Österreichisches Archiv für KR* 2 (1951) 62-75

Walter ULLMANN, *The Growth of Papal Government in the Middle Ages: A Study in the Ideological Relation of Clerical to Lay Power* (London 1955)

Martinien VAN DE KERCKHOVE, "La notion de juridiction chez les Décrétistes et les premiers Décrétalistes (1140-1250)," *Études franciscaines* 49 (1937) 420-55

C. VOLKMAR, "Das Verhältnis Lothars III. zur Investiturfrage," *FDG* 26 (1886) 437-99

Bibliography

Georg WAITZ, *Deutsche Verfassungsgeschichte* (repr. 8 vols. Graz 1955)

Franz WASNER, "De consecratione, inthronizatione, coronatione Summi Pontificis," *Apollinaris* 8 (1935) 86-125, 249-81, 428-39

Albert WERMINGHOFF, *Verfassungsgeschichte der deutschen Kirche im Mittelalter* (Grundriss der Geschichtswissenschaft II 6: 2nd ed. Leipzig 1913)

M. J. WILKS, "*Papa est nomen iurisdictionis*: Augustinus Triumphus and the Papal Vicariate of Christ," *The Journal of Theological Studies* n.s.8 (1957) 71-91, 256-71

WILLIAM of Mandagout, *De iure electionis novorum praelatorum* (Cologne 1602)

George H. WILLIAMS, *The Norman Anonymous of 1100 AD* (Harvard Theological Studies 18: Cambridge, Mass. 1951)

Eduard WINKELMANN, ed., *Acta imperii inedita* (2 vols. Innsbruck 1880-85)

Georg WOLFRAM, *Friedrich I. und das Wormser Konkordat* (Marburg 1883)

Index

Anglo-Norman Anonymous of 1100: 81n; election, 25n; royal anointment, 86n; anointed kingship, 206n; lay investiture, 240; authorship and provenance, 241n; *regale sacerdotium*, 299f; bishop's staff analogous to royal, 358n

Anglo-Norman school, *see*: Oxford

anointment: of emperor, 76, 333; of king, 9n, 86n, 169n, 206, 385

Anonymous of York, *see*: Anglo-Norman Anonymous

Anselm of Lucca: 43f, 73, 211, 264n

apostles: succeeded by bishops, 69f; equality among, 69-71

Apparatus Ecce uicit leo: jurisdiction, 49n; bishop-elect, 139, 192; papal election, 161n; unconfirmed metropolitan-elect, 182; secular jurisdiction of pope and bishop, 323n

Apparatus Ius naturale, see: Alanus Anglicus

Apparatus Ordinaturus: election and jurisdiction, 117n; deposition and jurisdiction, 119n

appeal: by bishop to primate, 68, 183; suspends action, 100, 347f; by vassal of bishop, 321f

approbatio: of bishop-elect, 92f; from election, 94n, 102f; from election and confirmation, 103; requires *subscriptio*, 105; same as election, 128

archbishop: may not use titles of nobility, 7n; title *archiepiscopus* sanctioned only by *pallium*, 171, 175-77; title sanctioned by consecration, 171n; title used by confirmed metropolitans-elect, 176; oath to appear at council, 330f. *See also* metropolitan, *ius metropoliticum, pallium*

archbishop(ric)s: Armagh, 186, 190-93; Besançon, 207n; Braga, 187n; Canterbury, 178, 301, 346n; Capua, 199n; Cologne, 177-79, 182, 285n, 297, 347, 362n; Genoa, 152n; Gnesen, 254n; Lund, 254n; Lyons, 335-37, 364; Magdeburg, 185n, 254; Mainz, 145n, 169n, 185n, 220, 344-46; Ravenna, 206f; Reims, 347-52, 366; Salzburg, 40, 181f, 187n, 289-91, 298n, 356n, 364, 371f; Sens, 207n; Sorrento, 57; Toledo, 26; Trier, 169, 175-78, 182, 234n, 236f, 242f, 270, 344n, 370. *See also* individual archbishops listed by name

archdeacon: eligibility for promotion to, 65; has *administratio secularium*, 66f,

76, 101, 392; supervises clergy and property, 66f; often provost of chapter, 67; has jurisdictional *officium* 209n

archi- as prefix: in titles, 177n

Armagh: double election in archbishopric of, 189-93

Arnold, abp. of Mainz: 171n

Arnold of Brescia: 280, 306, 310, 334

art: fresco publicized Calixtinum, 304

auctoritas and *administratio*: duality formulated by Rufinus, 64-67, 119, 39?, 394; political dimension of, 72, 75, 79-82, 89; origins of duality, 80-89; significance of, 89; applications of, 391

auctoritas and *potestas*: Gelasius I, 80?, 396

Augsburg: Reichstag of 1179 at, 289f

Augustine, bp. of Hippo: sacramental power vs exercise of sacramental power, 49-51; prelate as *procurator*, 84; sacramental powers, 85; imperial law and property rights, 240n, 246n

Augustinus Triumphus: 165

Azo: 83n

Azzo of Acqui: papal legate, 269n

Bandinelli, Roland, *see* Alexander III

banner: investiture of dukes and count? with *vexillum*, 297

baptism: ordination confers power of, 45? "power" and "ministry" of, 85; per formed by layman, 214

Barbarossa, *see*: Frederick Barbarossa

baron: bishop as, 3; English bishops in baronage, 297

Bazianus: bishop's military service, 318n, 324

Becket, Thomas, abp. of Canterbury: 19? 178n

Benedict XV, pope: 6f

benediction of abbot, *see*: abbot

benefice: ordination sanctions claim to income from, 41, 54; deprivation of, 54 linked to sacramental *officium*, 54f *temporalia spiritualibus annexa*, 55; con firmation confers right to grant, 109f 113, 348; confirmed bishop-elect loses former benefice, 112; *beneficia ecclesias-tica* given to vassals, 221f; conferred by monarch *sede vacante*, 365f

Benzo of Alba: *oboedientia* and *militia* 207n; *honor praesulatus*, 242n

Berengar of Tours: 212n

Bernard Balbi, *see*: Bernard of Pavia

Bernard, duke of Saxony: 289n

Index

Bernard of Clairvaux: on papacy, 69, 306, 382n; episcopal office, 82, 313, 382; intervention at Liège (1131), 253, 256n; *plenitudo potestatis*, 306; suspicious of Church's wealth, 306; bishop's duties to king, 313

Bernard of Compostella: 17

Bernard of Constance: 211n

Bernard of Parma: xviii, 188n, 330n

Bernard of Pavia: 19; confirmation and jurisdiction, 99-101, 128f, 142; election and *subscriptio*, 104; bishop-elect's former benefice, 112; influence on Huguccio, 116n, 128f; *ordo* and *iurisdictio*, 131; accepted Huguccio's doctrine, 136; influence, 137, 141n; bishop-elect's rights, 143f; *matrimonium spirituale*, 148; metropolitan and suffragans, 184f, 192; confirmation and ecclesiastical investiture, 358f; *dispensatio*, 394n

Bernold of Constance: universality of papal jurisdiction, 172n; *officium*, 209n; simoniacs' defense, 211n

Berthold IV, duke of Zähringen: 302n

Bertrand de Got, *see*: Clement V

Besançon: Frederick Barbarossa vs papal legates at, 71f, 258

bishop: as baron, 3; as prince, 3, 7, 298, 339, and *passim*; secular jurisdiction of, 3f; place in hierarchy, 3f, 70f, 87f, 107, 182f, 378f, 381f; owes obedience to pope, fealty to emperor, 3f, 207; freely appointed by pope, 6, 116, 348, 350, 381; may not use titles of nobility, 7; created by election and consecration, 24, 96, 231; appointed by king or emperor, 26, 220f, 225, 229, 241f, 275, 285f; comprovincial bishops consent to promotion of, 36f; confirms and installs abbot-elect, 62; subdeacon eligible for election as, 65-67, 90f, 95, 102; *procurator*, not owner of church's property, 84; and cathedral chapter, 85; jurisdiction derived from papacy, 85, 131; confirms inferiors, 107; enacts Christ's role in marriage to church, 123f; deposition of, 129, 361f, 400; deposed or suspended, 129, 400; has bishopric from pope, 131; translation of, 174, 286, 380f; coins of, 176; swears to obey metropolitan, 207n; as *minister curiae regalis*, 245, 247; translation by emperor, 286; holds two swords, 298; as imperial prince, 298, 339, and *passim*; regality of bishop's secular jurisdiction, 299-302, 384n; ac-

quires jurisdiction in ecclesiastical investiture, 300; administers duties of duke, 300, 311; sovereignty of, 302n; dangers in administration of secular offices by, 309, 311f; owes obedience to monarch, 314, 318; delegates secular jurisdiction to lay deputy, 314, 323; with *regalia*, status differs from one without, 317f, 324f, 345; as secular judge, 321-23; conflicting summonses from emperor and pope or metropolitan, 325-30; twofold status as prelate and imperial vassal, 332; kneels before secular lord, 332; analogy with *rex Romanorum*, 356; translation by pope, 380f; royal character of ecclesiastical jurisdiction, 383f; and emperor on same level, 396. *See also*: lay investiture, metropolitan, *potestas iurisdictionis*, *regalia*, regalian investiture, suffragan bishop

bishop-elect: monarchical regulations on, 5f; acclamations to, 29, 36, 370n; enthronement of, 36, 114, 358n, 370n; has power of suspension, 83; *approbatus* by election, 91-93; has claim upon confirmation, 92f, 100f, 128, 143f; appointed as *oeconomus* or *procurator*, 113f; as *procurator*, 113f, 199n; warned not to administer before confirmation, 114f; questioned about preconfirmatory administration, 115; has jurisdiction before confirmation, 120f, 126; consents to election (*nominatio passiva*), 121, 124, 164, 398f, 401; exercises jurisdiction prior to confirmation, 125, 182, 192, 399; jurisdiction from election, exercise from confirmation, 126f, 132, 140; disagreement over rights of, 133; cannot withdraw consent to election, 136; may request confirmation, 140f; when confirmed, has full status of bishop, 144, 146f, 149; when confirmed, removable only by judicial process, 144, 149; coins of, 176; distant from metropolitan, 197; must consent to election within one month, 199n; must request confirmation within three months, 199n; cannot wear episcopal costume, 206. *See also* election, confirmation, *consensus mutuus*, *matrimonium spirituale*

bishop-elect, titles and epithets: *approbatus*, 91-93, 94n, 103; *comprobatus*, 102f; *confirmatus in electione*, 58, 60; *coniunx*, 148; *electus*, 109n, 115, 176,

415

Index

Index

granted *iura terreni et celestis imperii* to Peter, 72; married to Church, 122-24; model for bishop's marriage to church, 123f; owner of Church's property, 212, 248; separation of human and divine natures, 213; both priest and king, 301, 313; model for bishop's *regale sacerdotium*, 301, 313; king of Church, 383

Christian II, abp. of Mainz: 177n, 363

Church and monarchy: compete to control episcopate, 5, 203; relations between, 14, 35n, 203ff, 307f, 343, and *passim*; political authority in, 15f; radical separation of, 229; *regalia* as key issue in relations between, 307f; *sacerdotium* superior to *regnum*, 328; constitutionally indistinguishable, 377

citizenship: invalid if granted by uninvested *electus*, 294f

claves regni caelorum: 47-49, 72-74, 85, 88; *scientia* and *potestas*, 48; given to entire Church, 49n. *See also* St Peter

Clement III, antipope: 225

Clement IV, pope: 366n

Clement V, pope: papal coronation, 166f

clergy: as electors, 29-33, 95f (*see also* election); may not shed blood, 78, 322f; as *regale sacerdotium*, 299; married, 327n

Codex iuris canonici: election, 6-8, 32n; *ordo* and *iurisdictio*, 9; sources, 10; confirmation, 35, 60f, 63, 92; papal coronation, 166n

collections, *see*: decretal collections

Cologne: law school, 12

comprovincial bishops: role in episcopal election, 24, 27; consent to bishop's promotion, 36f. *See also* metropolitan (and comprovincial bishops)

concordat of Rome (1133), *see*: treaty of 1133

Concordat of Worms: 228-35, 237, 251f, 255, 262, 303-06; Gregory VII and, 219n; limited victory for emperor, 232; both parties dissatisfied with, 251f; widely publicized, 303f; publicized as papal victory, 304; read at First Lateran Council, 305; condition of Church after, 308; origin of homage in, 312; ecclesiastical investiture, 357

Calixtinum: *metropolitani et conprovincialium consilio vel iudicio*, 62, 231; valid for Henry V's lifetime, 229f, 233, 257, 272n, 305, 312n; papacy asserted personal character of, 230; recognition

of existing rights, 230, 233; concessions to Henry V, 231f; emperor decides double election, 231f, 285, 364; sequence of investiture and consecration, 231-35, 287n, 292, 367, 384; cited by Otto of Freising, 234; regalian investiture, 237f, 260n; reformers dissatisfied with, 251, 304f, 377; not renewed by Innocent II, 259, 261; office distinct from *regalia*, 279n; "extorted concession," 312

Henricianum: lay investiture abandoned, 229, 252, 255; other concessions, 229; valid in perpetuity, 229; *regalia sancti Petri*, 232n; imperial court dissatisfied with, 251f, 255; general ecclesiastical approval of, 303-05

confirmation: sanctions exercise of jurisdiction, 8, 35, 120, 125-28, 131-33, 137-40, 142f, 148, 335, 346, 375, 399f; letter of, 8, 187n, 200, 369; of bishop-elect by metropolitan, 32, 36f, 95-97, 106f, 168, 379-81; consent differs from *confirmatio*, 35; *confirmatio*, synonyms and cognates, 36n; nonconstitutive, 37f, 60, 62-64, 110; *confirmatio=consecratio*, 38n; decretistic thought on, 58, 60-64, 97-107, 121; meanings of *confirmare* (*confirmatio*), 60, 126f, 401; confers jurisdiction, 60f, 63, 91-94, 97-103, 107-15, 117f, 131, 133f, 137, 165, 180f, 189, 374, 383, 398; pertains to superior, 61, 107; by metropolitan and comprovincial bishops, 61f; "rechtsbekräftigend" or "rechtsbegründend," 63n; confers power of suspension, 91; bishop-elect's claim on, 92f, 100f, 128, 143f; election confers claim upon, 92f, 128, 143f; election ineffective before, 97, 99f, 103, 105, 126-28, 131; confers *approbatio*, 103; renders electors' decision immutable, 104, 138, 398; by chapter of metropolitan church, 106; by primate, 106; by *visitator*, 106; papal policy on, 108, 110-13, 115, 131; confers right to grant benefice, 109f, 113; deprives bishop-elect of former benefice, 112; sanctions disciplinary powers, 112f; confers power of excommunication, 113; sanctions right to receive oaths, 113, 195f, 338f; confers right to confirm elections, 113; warning not to administer before, 114f; *electus* exercises jurisdiction prior to, 125, 182, 192, 398; of *matrimonium spirituale*, 126, 149n, 401; sanctions *ius in re*, 133, 142f; growing importance of, 133; rights

Index

of bishop-elect before, 134f, 141; cannot be denied without cause, 136; requested by bishop-elect, 136f, 140f; creates *prelatus*, 137, 398; confers no new rights, 140; by pope, 144, 198, 380f; protects bishop-elect's right to office, 144; gives *electus* full status of bishop, 146, 149; creates *matrimonium spirituale*, 146; ratifies *matrimonium spirituale*, 147; consummates *matrimonium spirituale*, 148; necessary for *matrimonium spirituale*, 149; by whoever consecrates, 184f; papal letters attesting, 187n; *benedictio* of abbot has effect of, 188; confers *plenitudo officii*, 189; received in Rome, 193f; of extra-Italian *exempti*, 193-96, 200; by papal legate, 196; must be requested within three months, 199n; letter attesting, 200; and ecclesiastical investiture, 358f; and *missio in possessionem*, 359; effective installation in office, 362; patent letter of, 369; improper, 381. *See also* metropolitan, *exempti*

confirmation in relation to feudal rights: confers right to receive fealty, 113, 338f, 346, 348, 352f; confers right to enfeoff vassals, 113, 338f, 346, 352f; sanctions administration of *regalia*, 337, 345, 347, 349; and regalian investiture, 343-53, 356f, 362-64, 370-72; sanctions right to regalian income, 348; prerequisite to regalian investiture, 349, 364; sanctions exercise of feudal jurisdiction, 352f, 356f, 363; simultaneous with regalian investiture, 363; precedes grant of *regalia*, 367-69; precedes fealty, 368; precedes regalian investiture, 370-72

coniugium spirituale, see: *matrimonium spirituale*

Conrad I, abp. of Salzburg: election, 40; and imperial prerogative, 252n; as reformer, 256, 269, 281; and Innocentianum, 261n, 278f, 283; letter to Norbert of Magdeburg, 263-67, 270, 272-74, 277-79, 281f; on *honorati*, 265; indignant over *advocati* in elections, 266, 270; opposed all lay influence, 266f; and Lothar III, 267, 271, 273, 277n, 279-81, 284; consecrated an uninvested bishop, 268f, 271f; and Henry of Regensburg, 268-71, 178f, 283; sequence of investiture and consecration, 272f; disagreed with Norbert of Magdeburg, 277n; *regalia* vs *res ecclesiasticae*, 278-83, 340; *episcopatus*, 279, 340; homage and feal-

ty, 280; and Gerhoh of Reichersberg, 281-83, 311f; refused to relinquish *regalia*, 282; and Church's lands, 311f

Conrad II, abp. of Salzburg: 290

Conrad III, abp. of Salzburg: 289f, 371f

Conrad III, king of the Romans: 280, 283f, 298n

Conrad of Hochstaden, abp. of Cologne: 179

consecration: requires metropolitan's consent, 37, 92, 157, 182; metropolitan's consent and participation, 37, 157; requires primate's consent, 37, 182; alienation of property forbidden before, 41, 54, 380n, 382; confers power of deposition, 58-60, 91, 100; confers *plenitudo auctoritatis*, 58f; confers *dignitas auctoritatis*, 67; creates *prelatus*, 102f; deadline for, 112; marriage between bishop and church, 122, 124 (*see also liturgica*); consummates *matrimonium spirituale*, 124n, 147f; of suffragan by metropolitan, 168-70, 379; by command of confirmed metropolitan-elect, 175; by consecrated metropolitan-elect, 176; metropolitan-elect cannot perform, 176, 180; by whoever confirms, 184f; confers *plenitudo officii*, 189n; authorizes use of episcopal costume, 206; confers right to administer property, 216n; confers no jurisdiction, 239; includes ecclesiastical investiture, 248f; metropolitan acts *vice Christi* in, 249; sanctions exercise of regalian jurisdiction, 272; confers *plenitudo officii in spiritualibus*, 287; should precede regalian investiture, 313, 319; emperor's consent prerequisite to, 316; precedes fealty, 366; homage and fealty precede, 367n; royal permission to receive, 367n. *See also* lay investiture, metropolitan (consecration of), papacy (elevation of pope), *regalia*, regalian investiture

consensus mutuus: of electors and *electus*, 122, 127f, 136, 148, 362, 375, 398f, 400; creates *matrimonium spirituale*, 122, 124, 127, 136, 139-41, 145, 148f, 398f, 401; creates *prelatus*, 122, 140, 399, 401; confers jurisdiction, 126, 375, 399f; renders election irrevocable, 138, 145

Constance, Treaty of: 258n

Constantine the Great, emp.: Donation of Constantine, 152; granted *regalia* to Church, 311

418

Index

constitutions of councils, *see*: decretals and constitutions
Constitutions of Clarendon: 231n, 297n, 367n
coronation, *see*: emperor (coronation), papacy (elevation of pope), king
council: approves election, 158; confirms papal election, 158; general council cannot judge papal election, 164; provincial synod held by metropolitan, 168; cannot be held by metropolitan-elect, 169f, 175, 180; general council should legislate on *regalia*, 308, 315; metropolitan summons bishop to synod, 325; prelates' oath to appear at, 330f
councils and synods: Arles (451), 38n; Carthage II, 398; Chalcedon, 52f, 79n; Lateran I, 35, 41, 305, 382; Lateran II, 23, 31, 35; Lateran III, 57, 85, 111f, 162-64, 391, 398f; Lateran IV, 35, 114n, 189, 193-95, 200, 351, 374f, 381; Lyons II, 113f, 199n, 315; Nicaea, 23, 36; Pavia (1160), 154-56, 158, 164; Poitiers (1078), 223; Roman Synods, (Lent 1075), 218; (Lent 1078), 218, 224; (November 1078), 222, 223n, 225; (Lent 1080), 223n; Toledo IV, 27; Toledo XII, 26
crosier: shown on metropolitan's seal, 178f; investiture with, 239; signifies *dominium terrenarum rerum*, 248f; symbol of jurisdiction and rule, 357f; analogy with royal staff, 358n. *See also* ecclesiastical investiture, lay investiture, ring, ring and crosier

Damasus: 17; accepted Huguccio's doctrine, 136n; use of term *regalia*, 341
Damian, *see*: Peter Damian
Dante: decretalists, 19; papal mantle, 156
David, royal chaplain: 244n
dean: eligibility for promotion to, 65; has *administratio spiritualium*, 66f, 101
decretal: authority of, 12, 48
decretal collections: 13, 390; *Cheltenhamensis*, 109n; *Francofortana*, 109n; *Tanneriana*, 109n; *Lipsiensis*, 110n, 184n; Royal, 111n; Gilbertus Anglicus, 144n; and *passim*
decretals and constitutions: JL 9658, 110n, 184n; JL 13951, 108f, 398f; *X* 1.4.7, 139n, 195; *X* 1.4.8, 139n; *X* 1.6.3, 38n; *X* 1.6.4, 169f; *X* 1.6.6, 162-64, 167; *X* 1.6.7, 111f, 398f; *X* 1.6.9, 109n, 110,

398f; *X* 1.6.11, 175; *X* 1.6.15, 112f, 359n; *X* 1.6.17, 113, 338, 345n; *X* 1.6.19, 199n; *X* 1.6.20, 144, 346n; *X* 1.6.21, 145; *X* 1.6.23, 145n; *X* 1.6.28, 175f, 186-94, 341n, 345n, 375; *X* 1.6.32, 146n, 340; *X* 1.6.33, 145n; *X* 1.6.34, 14; *X* 1.6.39, 285n; *X* 1.6.42, 114n, 146n; *X* 1.6.44, 185, 189, 193-96, 351, 375, 381; *X* 1.6.58, 105; *X* 1.7.1, 174; *X* 1.7.2, 146, 149n; *X* 1.7.4, 146n; *X* 1.8.1, 172n; *X* 1.8.3, 171n; *X* 1.8.4, 172; *X* 1.8.5, 139n, 172n; *X* 1.8.6, 172n, 192n; *X* 1.10.1, 188n; *X* 1.14.9, 65n; *X* 1.31.9, 379; *X* 1.33.6, 332n; *X* 1.33.13, 331n; *X* 2.1.13, 338; *X* 2.24.4, 330f; *X* 3.20.1, 2, 319; *X* 3.24.2, 84; *X* 3.49.4, 319n; *X* 3.49.7, 319n; *X* 5.1.16, 134, 149; *X* 5.7.9, 106; *VI* 1.6.5, 113f; *VI* 1.6.6, 199n; *VI* 1.6.13, 315; *VI* 1.6.16, 199; *VI* 1.6.29, 146n; *VI* 1.6.36, 196n; *VI* 3.23.3, 319n; *Extrav. com.* 1.3.1, 200; *Extrav. com.* 5.10.4, 166f
Decretum, see: Gratian
defectus natalium: 346n
deposition: removes *potestas habilitatis*, 51, 59; consecration confers power of, 58-60, 91, 100; removes *dignitas officii*, 59; *Potestas ordinis* includes power of, 60, 119; *potestas iurisdictionis* includes power of, 60n, 119f; of priest or bishop, 129, 400; of Frederick II, 354; of king or bishop, 361f
Deusdedit, cardinal: 34n, 44n, 73n, 172n, 211, 227n, 264n
Deutschenspiegel: 292
Dialogus de pontificatu sanctae Romanae ecclesiae, 150n, 151n, 153n, 155n, 156n
dignitas: episcopate as, 65, 71, 86-88, 95
diocese: model for papal-imperial relations, 76
Dionysiana: 398
disciples of Christ: prefigured role of priests, 70
dispensation: 166, 194-96
Disputatio vel defensio Paschalis papae: investiture *per sceptrum*, 231n; ecclesiastical investiture, 249n; crosier, 358n
Distinctiones Monacenses: bishop summoned by emperor and metropolitan, 327n; bishop's military service, 331n
Donation of Constantine: papal mantle, 152
Donatists: 49f
duke: archbishop of Cologne as, 297;

Index

Index

(and empire), *regalia*, regalian investiture

imperial election: *Venerabilem*, 14; confirmed by pope, 76, 132, 356, 401; effects of, 77n; analogy with episcopal election, 132, 140, 356, 401; creates emperor, 140; of Lothar III, 272

imperial coronation: confirmation by pope, 76; nonconstitutive, 77; jurisdictionally constitutive, 167, 257f; offered by Innocent II, 252; of Lothar III, 254-57; confers *plenitudo imperatoriae dignitatis*, 257-59; of Frederick Barbarossa, 258; confers *plenitudo dignitatis et honoris*, 258; confers *plenitudo coronae*, 258n; confers *plenitudo imperii*, 258n

terms for imperial jurisdiction: administratio, 81; *auctoritas*, 285; *auctoritas seculares regendi*, 76-78; *officium administrandi*, 76-78; *potestas*, 80, 395; *superabundans ius imperii*, 286n

Engelbert of Altena, abp. of Cologne: 178f, 363

England: decretals addressed to English prelates, 111; force of custom in, 139; unconfirmed metropolitan-elect exercises jurisdiction, 191; election *in capella regis*, 231n; bishops as barons, 297; king as papal legate, 329; king confers benefices *sede vacante* (spiritual *regalia*), 366n; homage and fealty precede consecration, 367n

enthronement: of bishop-elect, 36, 114, 358n, 370n. *See also* papacy (elevation of pope)

episcopal office: acquired by election and consecration, 24, 96, 231; Gratian on theory of office, 45-55; *officium* mainly sacramental, 49f; decretistic theories of office, 64-71, 90ff, 384, 391, and *passim*; as *ordo*, 65; as *dignitas*, 65, 71, 86-88, 95; subdeacon eligible for election to, 65-67, 90f, 95, 102; *ministerium*, not *dominium*, 82; canonical age for election to, 199n; theories of, 203f, 210, and *passim*; ring and crosier as symbols of, 204f, 231n; apparently conferred by monarch, 205; object of lay investiture, 205, 213f, 218, 239; terms for, as object of lay investiture, 205n; *divinum officium* distinguished from *secularia*, 207-09; *episcopale officium* contrasted with *secularia*, 208n, 225f; and property, form indivisible unity, 211-13, 216-18, 248f, 317; layman may not invest bishop

with, 214, 218, 223, 316, 320; (not) distinct from property, 217, 219, 223, 239; separated from *regalia* (1111), 245-47, 361n; *regalia* assigned to, 246n, 286f, 361f; stress on ecclesiastical character of, 331-33, 339. *See also* bishop

episcopatus: object of lay investiture, 205, 210, 223n, 274f, 316; *episcopium* as object of lay investiture, 205n, 275n; meaning of *episcopatus*, 273-76; royal proprietary claim to, 274f; distinct from *regalia*, 275; contrasted with *diocesis* or *parochia*, 276; linked to *ducatus* and *regalia*, 276; *episcopium* equivalent to, 276, *episcopium* as secular office of bishop, 361f

Eucharist: 212n

Eugene III, pope: hierarchy of Church, 68n, 106n, 378f; and St Bernard, 69; confirmation, 110n

Evrard of Ypres: 17; bishop as secular judge, 322n

examination: of bishop-elect, 115

excommunication: ordination confers power of, 45; *claves* and power of, 48; *potestas iurisdictionis* includes power of, 113; confirmation confers power of, 113; of lord suspends vassal's fealty, 129, 360, 362; of Frederick II, 354; no regalian investiture from monarch under, 354f

exempti: consecrated in Rome, 185f, 199; abbot-elect, 186n; confirmed by pope, 186n, 195, 199, 375, 381; receive *plenitudo officii* from confirmation, 189; outside of Italy, administer before confirmation, 193-95, 199f, 375; need no confirmation, 195; before confirmation, cannot alienate property or accept oaths, 195f, 339; outside of Italy, administer as proctors, 196f, 375; oath to appear at council, 331

Fealty, oath of fealty: *potestas iurisdictionis* includes right to receive, 113; unconfirmed bishop-elect cannot receive, 113, 338f, 346, 348, 368; distinction between "obligation" and "execution" of, 129, 362; vassal's duty to excommunicated lord, 129, 362; Norman princes' oath to papacy, 172n, 227n; *fidelitas* distinct from *oboedientia*, 207; owed by bishop to emperor, 207, 321, 326; by vassal-king to emperor, 285n; to uninvested bishop-elect, 288; uninvested *electus* cannot receive, 291, 347; with-

Index

held from uninvested bishop-elect, 295, 297, 357; required for tenure or administration of *regalia*, 308, 333f, 336f, 365f; opposition to, 312, 332f; decretistic thought on, 326, 332f, 360-62; sign of bishop's subjection to emperor, 332f; to confirmed but uninvested *electus*, 348, 353; Church absolves from, 360; to person or to office, 360f; to prelate and to office or church, 361; after consecration, 366; precedes grant of *regalia*, 366; after grant of *regalia*, 369. *See also* homage and fealty

feudal law: 142n; governs tenure of *regalia*, 286f, 320; pope cannot judge *de feudo*, 338; and royal prerogative, 385

fiscal rights: 226, 232n

Flote, Pierre: 352

Foliot, Gilbert, bp. of Hereford: papal election, 162n

Foliot, Robert, bp. of Hereford: 109

Folmar, abp. of Trier: 234n

formulary books: 38n, 103n, 166, 170n

formulas and maxims: *Accipe ecclesiam*, 205, 215, 239; *auctoritas imperandi* vs *necessitas subsequendi*, 75n, 393n; *auxilium et consilium*, 207n; *canonica electio et libera consecratio*, 229, 244n; *consilio vel iudicio*, 62, 231; *electio a clero et populo*, 25, 241, and *passim* (*see also*: election); *Electio clericorum est, consensus plebis*, 33; *electio concors et canonica*, 95n, 144; *Electio et consecratio faciunt episcopum*, 24, 96; *Eligendo confirmatur et confirmando eligitur*, 67n, 98n, 118, 160f; *in partem sollicitudinis, non in plenitudinem potestatis*, 172f; *libertas imperandi* vs *necessitas obediendi*, 29, 75n; *maior et sanior pars*, 145f, 151, 163, 231; *Nullus invitis detur episcopus*, 25; *Nuptias non concubitus sed consensus facit*, 122; *Optima enim est legum interpres consuetudo*, 139n, 333; *Papa a nemine est iudicandus*, 163f; *potestas regendi et iubendi* vs *necessitas obsequendi*, 68, 76n; *Quod omnes tangit, ab omnibus comprobetur*, 25n; *reges a regendo vocati*, 299

forum internum: 48f

forum externum: 49, 240n

France: unconfirmed metropolitan-elect exercises jurisdiction, 191, 351; king's prerogative in royal bishoprics, 219, 276, 325n, 336f; royal consent before election, 244n, 367n; customary procedure

in episcopal promotions, 265n, 366; Lyons's primacy in Church of, 335; annexation of Lyons, 336; confirmation, *regalia*, royal prerogative, 344, 365-69; king confers benefices *sede vacante* (spiritual *regalia*), 365f; consecration precedes grant of *regalia*, 366f; confirmation precedes grant of *regalia*, 367-69

Frederick Barbarossa, emp.: and lawyers, 14; and Hadrian IV, 71, 258; Council of Pavia, 154, 158n; confirmation of Victor IV's election, 158n, 162n; prerogative in episcopal promotions, 232, 235, 284-91; confiscation of *regalia*, 246n, 291, 330, 361; *episcopatus* and *regalia*, 276; imperial episcopate, 284-86, 288-91; regalian investiture, 285-91, 338; enfeoffment by uninvested bishop-elect, 287-91, 338; withheld regalian investiture, 290; confiscated Salzburg's *regalia*, 291; and Alexander III, 371f

Frederick II Hohenstaufen, emp.: confiscation of *regalia*, 246n; regalian investiture, 294; renounced regalian rights, 314f; regalian income *sede vacante*, 315; excommunicated and deposed, 354; Sicilian elections, 370

Frederick of Bogen: 268f

French school, *see*: Paris

Fulbert of Chartres: letter on vassal's duties, 326

Gandulph: 15

Gasparri, Pietro cardinal: 9f

Gelasius I, pope: *auctoritas* and *potestas*, 80, 396; papal-imperial relations, 80f; Gelasian tradition, 217, 360n

Geoffrey Fitzroy, bp. of Lincoln: 110

Geoffrey of Vendôme: election and consecration, 24n, 231; lay investiture, 213n, 238-40; ecclesiastical investiture, 249n, 384n; bishop as king or emperor, 300, 384n

Gerard, abp. of Bremen: 176n, 179

Gerard, abp. of Mainz: 349

Gerard Pucelle: 15, 19

Gerhoh of Reichersberg: election, 34n; *regalia*, 81n, 82, 307-13; papal election of 1159, 154n; *fidelitas* and *oboedientia*, 207n; simoniacs, 211n; consecration before regalian investiture, 236, 313, 319, 363f; and Conrad of Salzburg, 263n, 264n, 265n, 266n, 281-83, 311f; *honorati* in elections, 265n, 266n, 267n; *regalia* and Church's property, 280n, 338n,

Index

Index

Index

Honorius III, pope: election notice, 170n; confirmation and *regalia*, 353; feudal rights of uninvested prelates, 353f

Honorius, emp.: decree on papal election, 158

Honorius: 17; papal *pallium*, 170

Hostiensis: 19; electoral treatise, 115n; papal election, 160, 161n, 164f, 167n; *plenitudo officii*, 189n

Hugh, bp. of Die and abp. of Lyons: 218, 223f

Hugh of Amiens: 50

Hugh of Fleury: papal election decree (1059), 44; investiture before consecration, 233; lay investiture and royal appointment, 241f; *honor praesulatus*, 242; bishop as *rex*, 300

Hugh of St Victor: papal election decree (1059), 44; hierarchy of Church, 86-89; terminology of office, 91, 95; bishop's wedding ring, 123; *regale sacerdotium*, 299; bishop's duties to king, 313f; crosier, 358n; episcopal office, 382; papal jurisdiction, 382n

Huguccio: 13, 17, 19; grammarian and lexicographer, 15, 126; jurisdiction, 49n; *potestas iurisdictionis* includes power of deposition, 60n; metropolitan and suffragans, 63f, 185, 192; papal jurisdiction, 77n, 129, 131f, 173; on decretists, 93, 104n, 398; *subscriptio*, 104n, 121, 124, 397f; election and confirmation, 116-22, 124-29, 131-34, 136f, 139f, 142, 145, 148f, 375, 397-401; bishop-elect's jurisdiction, 117-21, 125-29, 131-34, 136-40, 142, 144, 189, 192f, 375, 398-401; *papa electus*, 117-20; papal election, 117-20, 160, 161n; *iurisdictio* and *ordo*, 120; *matrimonium spirituale*, 122-24, 126-28, 139f, 145, 148f, 398f, 401; unconfirmed *electi* exercise jurisdiction, 125, 182, 192, 399; fealty to excommunicated lord, 129, 362; *potestas ordinis*, 129-31, 400; influence of, 137-42, 144-49, 197n; influence on Alanus, 137f; influence on Johannes Teutonicus, 140; influence on Innocent III, 144-49; bishop-elect's consent, 122, 164, 398f, 401; *plenitudo potestatis*, 173; pope and metropolitan, 173, 186; pope, primate, metropolitan, 183f; regalian investiture, 320; lay investiture, 320, 327n; bishop summoned by emperor and pope or metropolitan, 328-30; monarch as papal legate, 329f; fealty and *regalia*, 333f; *regalia, temporalia*,

spiritualia, 340; oath of fealty, 361f; deposition of king or bishop, 361f

Humbert of Silva Candida, cardinal: election, 32, 34n; papal election decree (1059), 42; lay administration of church, 127n; simoniacs' defense, 210; office and property, 212, 216f; simony and lay investiture, 213; lay investiture, 213f, 238; lay and ecclesiastical investiture, 238

Hungary: king as papal legate, 329

Inalienability: of Church's lands, 282, 309, 311; of tithes, 309; of anything given to Church, 310n. *See also*: alienation, ecclesiastical property

Innocent II, pope: elected by minority, 155n; consecrated an uninvested archbishop, 234n, 236f, 271; and Lothar III, 252-59, 262; Regensburg election, 268, 270. *See also*: Innocentianum

Innocent III, pope: 13, 133; imperial election, 14; subdiaconate, 64f; decretistic influences on, 108, 144-47; confirmation and jurisdiction, 113, 197f, 199n, 381; confirmation and prelates' feudal powers, 113, 338f, 345f, 369n; bishop-elect's rights, 134, 144, 338; custom, 139n; Huguccio's doctrine, 144-47; *matrimonium spirituale*, 145-49; on papal election, 161n, 167n; *pallium*, 171f; pope and metropolitan, 173, 186f, 379n; on confirmed metropolitan-elect, 174f; on consecrated metropolitan-elect, 176n, 181n; papal confirmation, 186f, 198, 381; Armagh election, 189-93; extra-Italian metropolitan-elect, 191-96, 200, 375; extra-Italian *exempti*, 193-96, 200, 375; *plenitudo potestatis* and election, 285n; concern over *regalia*, 314f; and Frederick II, 314f, 370; decretals on fiefs, 319; taxation of clerics, 319n; prelates subject to emperor, 332n; pope cannot judge *de feudo*, 338; *regalia, temporalia, spiritualia*, 340; confirmation before grant of *regalia*, 340n, 369n; use of term *regalia*, 341n; office and *regalia*, 345; confirmation and regalian investiture, 346; royal assent to election, 346n

Innocent IV, pope: *ius ad rem petendam*, 143n; bishop-elect's rights, 146n; confirmation and jurisdiction, 146n, 195n, 196f; *matrimonium spirituale*, 147n; on confirmed metropolitan-elect, 181n; *plenitudo officii*, 187f; abbot-elect, 188, 189n; confirmation at Rome, 194; prel-

426

Index

ates-elect *immediate sub papa*, 195n, 196f, 375n; prelates-elect as proctors, 197, 375n; ordered vassals to obey bishop, 342n, 357; episcopal vacancies, 344n; Halberstadt election, 349; confirmation and regalian investiture, 349, 353, 360; and Frederick II, 354; feudal rights of uninvested prelates, 354f, 357; granted *administratio temporalium*, 356n; confirmation and ecclesiastical investiture, 359

Innocent V, pope: 336

Innocent X, pope: 7n

Innocentianum: regalian investiture, 56, 256, 259-63; bishop-elect's right to administer *regalia*, 56, 259-63, 278, 283, 292, 338, 384; valid for Lothar III's lifetime, 257, 262f, 272n; *plenitudo imperatoriae dignitatis*, 257-59; *debitae et canonicae consuetudines*, 257-59; royal prerogative, 258f, 261-63; did not renew Calixtinum, 259, 261; ignored sequence of investiture and consecration, 260; tested at Würzburg Reichstag, 273; publicized at Würzburg, 278; distinguished office and *regalia*, 279n; value of, 283

Installation (*institutio*): equivalent to *confirmatio*, 62; of abbot-elect, 62; equivalent to ecclesiastical investiture, 358; equivalent to enthronement, 358n; *stallatio* not needed by *electus*, 359

Investiture: of Roman pontiff-elect, 153; *investitura* as term, 208n; with "simple staff," 215f; without constitutive significance, 238; general meaning of, 238f; *investire* vs *instituere*, 240n; of Lothar III by pope, 254; charters of, given by bishops, 289; of dukes and counts with banner, 297. *See also* ecclesiastical investiture, lay investiture, regalian investiture

Investiture Struggle: 53, 203f, 343, 373n, 377, 384f; not ended in 1122, 251; end of, 251, 303; publicists in, 281, 358n, and *passim*; concern over legacy of, 308; in France, 313

Ireland: Armagh election, 189-93; tension between English and Irish, 190

Isidore of Seville: 11; Church's hierarchy, 68n; *reges a regendo vocati*, 298f; crosier, 358n

Italy: *regalia* as fiscal rights, 232n; bishops' obligations to emperor, 246n, 286

Italy and Burgundy: constitutionally different from Germany, 230-32, 237f, 262;

consecration precedes regalian investiture, 231, 253f, 367; regalian investiture a mere formality, 253f

iudex ordinarius: 77n, 341n

iura terreni et celestis imperii: 72-74

ius ad rem petendam: 7n, 8; conferred by election, 133, 142f, 278; origin, 143

ius devolutionis: 173n, 285

ius in re: 8n; from confirmation, 133, 142f; conferred by lay investiture, 205n; by regalian investiture, 278

ius metropoliticum: rights included within, 168, 170n; requires *pallium*, 169-71, 174-76, 180f; partly exercised by confirmed metropolitan-elect, 174; decretistic theories on, 179f; (no) distinction between *ordo* and *iurisdictio* within, 179f; includes *potestas iurisdictionis*, 180; includes power of *ordo vel unctio*, 180. *See also* metropolitan, *pallium*

terms for *ius metropoliticum*: *archiepiscopalia*, 174; *auctoritas pallii*, 169n; *episcopalia officia*, 169n; *iura episcopalia*, 175n; *pars sollicitudinis*, 172f; *plena administratio*, 180f; *plenitudo ecclesiasticae potestatis* (papal), 173; *plenitudo officii pastoralis*, 171; *plenitudo officii pontificalis*, 169-72, 187, 258; other terms, 171n

ius patronatus: 89n, 393n

ius spolii: 270n

ius territorii: 54n

Ivo of Chartres: papal election decrees, 43, 44n; title, 178n; letter on simoniacs, 211; lay investiture with temporalities, 239f, 275f

James of Viterbo: *iurisdictio* and *ordo*, 383f

Jerome, St: 103n, 299n

Joffrid, bp. of Châlons-sur-Marne: 348

Johannes Andreas: papal election, 160n

Johannes Faventinus, *see*: John of Faenza

Johannes Galensis: 17; bishop-elect's rights, 133n; *matrimonium spirituale*, 149n; jurisdiction of *exempti*, 194n, 195n

Johannes Teutonicus: xviii, 12, 17f; Huguccio's doctrine, 134; bishop-elect's rights, 140f, 146n; *matrimonium spirituale*, 149n; *ius metropoliticum*, 175n; pope, primate, metropolitan, 184; pope and metropolitan, 187; *officium* and *iurisdictio*, 188n; metropolitan and suffragans, 192; prelates-elect *immediate*

Index

Index

Index

cal investiture, 358; and confirmation, 359

mitre: signifies pope's episcopal status, 153; on metropolitan's seal, 178; on metropolitan-elect's seal, 179

monarch: relations with episcopate, 3-5, and *passim*; monarchical regulations on bishop-elect, 5f, 56, and *passim*; appoints bishops, 26, 220f, 225, 229, 241f, 275, 285f; approves (confirms) episcopal election, 26-28, 31f, 64, 241, 266f, 346n; as *administrator*, 81; administer sacrament in act of lay investiture, 123; clerical status of, 206, 385; cannot confer sacramental powers, 206; grants secular and ecclesiastical jurisdiction to bishop-elect, 240n; confers *honor praesulatus*, 241f; keeps *regalia* till investiture of bishop-elect, 276, 368; distinction between private and public property of, 310f; receives regalian income *sede vacante*, 314f, 344; bishop owes obedience to, 314, 318; as papal legate, 329f; must grant *regalia* immediately to "legitimate person," 352; consent prerequisite to bishop's enthronement and *laudes*, 370n; vicar of Christ, 385; supreme judge of realm, 385. *See also* bishop, Church and monarchy, emperor, king, lay investiture, regalian investiture, royal prerogative

mysticism: 121

Name: title (*nomen*) distinct from exercise of jurisdiction (*administratio*), 131, 176n; taken by new pope, 154; of Roman pontiff-elect may not appear on bull, 165; of uncrowned pope may not appear on bull, 166; title (*nomen*) virtually identical with office, 176

Nicholas I, pope: 55n

Nicholas II, pope: 72; election of, 42. *See also* papacy (papal election)

Nicholas III, pope: 199

Norbert, abp. of Magdeburg: rewarded by pope, 254; intervened in Rome (1133), 256; and Lothar III, 256, 277n; and Conrad of Salzburg, 264, 267, 277n; *honorati* in election, 265f; royal prerogative, 266; and Henry of Regensburg, 278

Norman Anonymous, *see*: Anglo-Norman Anonymous

Notabilia Nota per exteriora deprehendi: confirmation and jurisdiction, 134

numismatica: coins of bishop, bishop-elect,

176; of metropolitan, 177n; of metropolitan-elect, 177n, 178f; of patriarch, patriarch-elect, 177n; of archbishop of Cologne, 297; of bishop of Würzburg, 297

Oath: confirmation sanctions right to receive, 113, 195f; by metropolitans(-elect) to pope, 169, 330f; of obedience, 195f, 207n; by suffragans to metropolitan, 207n, 331; by exempt bishops-elect, 331; by papal suffragans, 331. *See also* fealty

obedience: owed by bishop to pope, 3f, 207; oath of, 195f, 207n; *oboedientia* distinct from *fidelitas*, 207; sworn by suffragan to metropolitan, 207n; bishop owes *obsequium* to king, 314, 318

Octavian, cardinal, *see*: Victor IV

Odo of Dover: 17

oeconomus: has *administratio*, 75f, 395f; administers property and represents bishop, 79; analogy with emperor, 79, 81; like archdeacon, 79, 392; unconfirmed *electus* appointed as, 113f; always a cleric, 392; has *ministerium*, 392, 394

office, *see*: episcopal office

Oldradus de Ponte: 200n

Omnebene: 15

orders, *see*: *potestas ordinis*

ordination: sanctions claim to income from benefice, 41, 54; confers *potestas baptizandi et excommunicandi*, 45; *ordinatio absoluta*, 51-53

ordines, *see*: *liturgica*

ordo: episcopate as, 65

Ordo iudiciarius Bambergensis: 84n

Otbert, bp. of Liège: 211

Otto, bp. of Bamberg: 267n

Otto, prior of cardinal-deacons: 152

Otto, provost of Aachen: 347f

Otto I, emp.: 39, 205, 298

Otto II, bp. of Freising: 363

Otto IV of Brunswick, emp.: 314f

Otto of Freising: cited Calixtinum, 235; and *passim*

Oxford: law school, 12, 376

Pallium: sanctions exercise of *ius metropoliticum*, 169-71, 174-76, 180f; needed for disciplinary powers, 169; granted by pope, 169, 181, 186; sanctions right to crown and anoint German king, 169n; sanctions right to consecrate suffragans, 169f, 175f, 180; confers *plenitudo officii pontificalis*, 169-72, 187, 258; sanctions

431

Index

right to hold provincial synod, 170, 175, 180; sanctions title *archiepiscopus*, 171, 175-77; sanctions titles *primas* and *patriarcha*, 171n; liturgical garment, 171f; worn only at certain times and places, 171f; signifies metropolitan's *pars sollicitudinis*, 172n, 173; on metropolitan's seal, 178; granted by primate, 183f; grant of, equivalent to confirmation, 186; grant of, linked to confirmation, 187, 191; papal letters attesting possession of, 187n. *See also* metropolitan, *ius metropoliticum*

of pope: conferred after consecration, 166; acquired in election, 170; not needed for jurisdiction, 170; conferred in consecration, 170n; worn always and everywhere, 172; signifies *plenitudo ecclesiasticae potestatis*, 172f

papacy, pope: has no superior, 7, 61, 160, 163f, 189; approves episcopal election, 27n; primacy, 44, 73; grants jurisdiction to bishoprics, 85, 131; confirms metropolitan-elect, 107, 181f, 184-86, 375, 379, 381; policy on confirmation, 108, 110-13, 115, 131; confers bishopric, 131; may confirm any election, 144, 198, 380f; translates bishops, 149, 174, 381; abdication, 153; Rome has no metropolitan over itself, 157; judged only for heresy, 158; judged by no one, 158f, 163f; (not) judged by cardinals, 159; unique prerogative, 163, 167, 189; grants *pallium*, 169, 181, 186; metropolitan's oath to, 169, 330f; wears *pallium* always and everywhere, 172; consecrates metropolitan-elect, 185; prelates-elect directly subject to, 185f, 189, 193-95, 199, 374f; confirms *exempti*, 195, 199, 375, 381; grants jurisdiction without confirming, 198f; consecrates *exempti*, 199; and reform, 203, 376; validates defective elections, 285; primacy based on regality, 300; sovereignty of, 302n; consent to taxation of clergy, 319n; summons bishop, 325-30; preponderance of summons from, 326-30; stressed response to summons, 330f; papal suffragans' oath, 331; grants *administratio temporalium*, 356n; fiscal system, 380f; influence on episcopal promotions, 380f

papal election: in *Codex iuris canonici*, 7; pontiff-elect's consent to, 7f, 164f, 167; confers immediate full jurisdiction, 7f, 42-45, 97f, 118-20, 150n,

160-63, 167, 170, 189, 192f, 374, 382f; emperor's prerogative in, 29, 38n, 60f, 162, 316; freedom of, 30; in *Decretum* 30-32, 41-45; model for episcopal election, 31, 45; decrees of 1059 and 1060, 31f, 35, 41-46, 57, 76n, 92, 119, 150f, 156f, 159, 161f, 167, 382; confirmed or approved by emperor, 60f, 162; need no confirmation, 61, 159f; contrasted with others, 118, 167, 183; equivalent to confirmation, 118, 160; overshadowed by enmantling, 153; majority of votes in, 154; minority, 155n; procedure in, 156, 162f; canonistic thought on, 156-65, 167; problem of double election, 157-59, 162; confirmed by council, 158; acclamatory, 159n; simultaneous election and confirmation, 159f; confers jurisdiction and exercise of jurisdiction, 161; of already consecrated bishop, 161, 166f; origin of two-thirds requirement, 162n; two-thirds majority creates pope, 162f; judged by no one, 163; not judged by council, 164; pontiff-elect's consent equivalent to confirmation, 165; uniqueness, 167; *pe compromissum*, 170n; analogy with metropolitan's election, 183; imperial influence on, 316

papal elections: Nicholas II, 42; schism of 1159, 150f, 153-55, 158, 162, 252, 286, 290; procedure in 1159, 154; schism of 1130, 155n

Roman pontiff-elect: rights, status, powers, 7f, 56, 58, 117, 150, 166 (*see also* papal election); gains jurisdiction from consent to election, 7f, 165, 167; immediately true pope, 160; acclamation to, 162; right to confer prebends, etc., 165; uses *bulla dimidia*, 165f

Roman pontiff-elect, titles and epithets: *electus*, 164; *electus episcopus* 166; *electus episcopus servus servorum Dei*, 166; *electus servus servorum Dei* 165; *nominatus*, 164; *verus papa*, 97f 160

elevation of pope: emperor represented at consecration, 30; enthronement jurisdictionally constitutive, 42f 156, 161, 382; grant of papal ring, 123n 153; enmantling, 151-56, 163f; enmantling as investiture, 153; enmantling overshadows election, 153; grant of mitre, 153; enthronement as part of procedure, 154; assumption of papal name, 154; enmantling merely declara-

Index

tive, 155f, 163; enmantling both declarative and constitutive, 156; consecration by cardinals, 157, 159f; Gratian on enthronement, 158; enthronement no longer important, 162; general procedure, 162f, 166; enthronement merely declarative, 163; enmantling follows pontiff-elect's consent to election, 164; coronation confers jurisdiction, 166f; coronation sanctions use of papal name, 166f; coronation equivalent to consecration, 166f; consecration and jurisdiction, 382. *See also* mantle, *pallium* (of pope)

papal jurisdiction: pope appoints bishops (provisions), 6, 116, 348, 350, 381; over Church and secular world, 74-78; pope judges *ratione peccati*, 77; over clergy, 77n; coercive power, 78, 129, 322f; *claves ligandi et solvendi*, 88; overwhelming superiority, 88, 173, 373f, 383, 393-95; universality, 123n, 172f; dispensations, 166; reservations, 166, 381; regality or sovereign prerogative, 227f, 232n, 300, 302n; *regalia sancti Petri*, 227f, 232n, 310n, 378n; secular jurisdiction in capital cases, 322f; pope cannot judge *de feudo*, 338; unlimited and inexhaustible, 383; legislative power, 393-95

terms for papal jurisdiction: *administratio rerum ecclesiasticarum*, 82n; *auctoritas*, 76, 78, 395f; *auctoritas regendi et disponendi*, 42f, 46, 76n, 119; *constitutio*, 393f; *dispositio temporalium*, 160; *ducatus*, 322; *plena potestas administrandi*, 118; *plenaria potestas*, 84n, 161; *plenitudo ecclesiasticae potestatis*, 173; *plenitudo potestatis*, 77n, 84n, 85n, 167, 172f, 258n, 285, 306, 350, 381-83, 394n; *potestas* (or *ius*) *gladii materialis*, 129, 323; *universalis et principalis potestas*, 172n

papal office: royal or imperial character, 152f, 298, 300, 304; mantle and mitre symbols of, 153; pontiff-elect invested with *papatus Romanus*, 153; mantle symbolizes *dignitas papatus*, 155; sacramental aspects, 382f; emphasis on jurisdictional aspects, 382-85

papacy and empire: relations between, 18f, 61, 71-81, 89; imperial office subject to pope, 75f, 395; pope has *auctoritas* over emperor, 76; confirms, crowns, anoints emperor, 76; pope may not administer *secularia*, 76, 78; emperor as pope's vicar

in *secularia*, 78f; pope confirms emperor, 132, 140, 356, 401; papacy stressed personal character of Calixtinum, 230, 305; emperor as vassal of pope, 254n; pope orders vassals to obey uninvested bishop, 295n, 348, 353-55, 357, 360; papal concern over *regalia*, 314f; papal consent to bishop's military service, 318f, 324; papal consent to regalian duties, 321; pope asks monarch to grant *regalia*, 344, 351f, 355; papal policy on confirmation and regalian investiture, 344-53, 356f, 362f, 371f; papacy denies constitutive significance of regalian investiture, 345-55, 357, 360, 363; papacy recognizes royal assent to election, 346n; concern over prelates' feudal rights, 352-57, 372; pope confirms *rex Romanorum*'s election, 356; absolves subjects from oaths of fealty, 360; papacy ignores regalian investiture, 371f

papal titles and epithets: *archipater*, 177n; *archipontifex*, 177n; *episcopus* (precoronation), 166f; *imperator*, 304; *iudex ordinarius omnium*, 77n; *rex*, 300; *servus servorum Dei*, 178; *universalis*, 172n (cf. 123n); *universalis episcopus*, 172n; *universalis papa*, 172n; *universalis pontifex*, 172n; *vicarius beati Petri*, 74

papal legate: confirms election, 196; summons bishop, 328; monarch as, 329f

Paris: law school, 12, 17, 101n, 376, 391

pars sollicitudinis: metropolitan, 172; suffragan bishop, 173

Paschal II, pope: metropolitan's oath, 169; *pallium*, 169-71; papal-imperial negotiations (1111), 229f, 233, 243-47, 257, 260, 262, 272n, 281, 310n; ordered German bishops to relinquish *regalia*, 229n, 245-47, 260n, 282, 306, 310, 334, 361n; opposed precedence of lay investiture, 233; opposed royal prerogative, 235; imperial coronation, 257; decree against lay investiture, 316

"Paschalis" (or "Paschasius"), pope: 55n, 211

patriarch: may not use title of nobility, 7n; relative rank of patriarchal sees, 44; higher than or same as primate, 88, 183; honorific title, 168; title sanctioned by *pallium*, 171n, 177n; coins of, 177n; patriarch-elect uses title *electus*, 177n; coins of patriarch-elect, 177n. *See also* primate

Index

434

Index

Index

property: *ius territorii*, 54n; rights of, based on human and imperial law, 240n, 246n, 286; distinction between king's private and public property, 310. *See also* ecclesiastical property

provincial synod, *see*: council

provisions: papal, 6, 166, 348, 350, 381; same effect as confirmation, 350

provost: eligibility for promotion to, 65; of chapter, 67

Pseudo-Isidore: 25n, 69, 86n, 127, 183n, 274n

Pseudo-Dionysius: 379n

Quaestio in utramque partem: 301

Radulphus Ardens: 85n, 86n

Rahewin: possibly author of *Dialogus de pontificatu sanctae Romanae ecclesiae*, 150n

Ratherius of Verona: 32n

Ravenna: imperialist forgeries at, 38. *See also* Hadrian I, Leo VIII

Raymond of Peñafort: as canonist, 13, 17; hierarchy and confirmation, 107n; bishop-elect's rights, 141; *pallium*, 173, 180; confirmation and *possessio*, 359

regale sacerdotium: episcopate as, 297-302; archbishop Bruno of Cologne, 298; Biblical, 299; clergy as, 299; eschatological idea, 299; signified by tonsure (*corona*), 299; of Christ, 301, 313; German bishops as, 302

regalia and temporalities: (not) distinct from (other) ecclesiastical property, 53f, 248, 278-81, 320; *potestas iurisdictionis* includes right to administer, 113, 340; term used for ecclesiastical jurisdiction, 191, 341; originated as royal grants, 205, 310f, 378; (not) distinct from spiritualities, 207-09, 222-26, 239, 248, 339f; belong to emperor or imperial dignity, 225f, 228, 243; as fiscal rights, 226, 232n; as technical term, 227; German bishops (1111) ordered to relinquish, 229n, 245-47, 260n, 282, 306, 310, 334, 361n; meanings of, 232f; royal proprietary claim to, 244, 266, 277n, 286; pertain to *servitium regni*, 245, 247; separated from episcopal office (1111), 245-47; imperial (royal) confiscation of, 246, 286f, 330, 339, 361, 367n; assigned to office or church and (not) to prelate, 246n, 286f, 361f; held only *per gratiam regis*, 246f; must be requested by bishop-

elect, 260, 278; distinct from episcopal office, 275, 279n; held by monarch *sede vacante*, 276-81, 286f, 314f, 362n, 368; distinct from *res ecclesiasticae*, 278-82; distinct from ecclesiastical jurisdiction, 279; lands distinct from other forms of, 281; Church should relinquish secular offices, 282, 309, 311f; homage, fealty required for, 286, 308, 333f; held by feudal tenure, 286, 320; make bishops a *regale sacerdotium*, 299-301; diverse opinions on, 306f; key issue in relations of *sacerdotium* and *regnum*, 308; general council should deal with, 308, 315; inextricably mixed with *ecclesiastica*, 309; lands regarded as, 310; secular jurisdiction exercised by lay deputy, 312, 314, 323; bishop owes tribute for, 312, 317f, 321; monarch's right to regalian jurisdiction *sede vacante*, 314f; royal renunciations of regalian rights, 314f; *sede vacante* monarch receives income from, 314f, 344, 368; Gratian on, 315-20; canonistic concepts of, 315-34; possession of, changes bishop's juridical status, 317f, 324f, 345; not Church's property, but for Church's use, 320; jurisdiction (*ius*) distinct from exercise of jurisdiction (*executio iuris*), 323; confiscated for failure to obey imperial summons, 330; cannot be administered prior to fealty, 336f, 365f; confirmation sanctions administration of, 337, 345, 347-49; subject to Church law, 340f, 344, 352f, 378; pope asks monarch to grant, 344, 351f, 355; confirmation entitles *electus* to income from, 348; homage follows grant of, 352; of French royal bishoprics, 365-69; episcopal vacancy ended by grant of, 366; confirmation precedes grant of, 367-69; consecration precedes grant of, 367; administered by chapter *sede vacante*, 368; fealty follows grant of, 369; should be held freely without obligation by Church, 377f. *See also* emperor, monarch, regalian investiture

term for regalia and temporalities: *administratio temporalium*, 294, 342f; *beneficium*, 361; *bona ecclesiastica*, 351; *bona temporalia*, 246n, 341; *castella*, 54n, 243, 317f; *castra*, 248; *civitates*, 54n, 243, 245, 248, 317f; *clers de la citey*, 295f; *comitatus*, 309, 318n, 319n; *corporalia*, 248, 317; *curtes*, 226f, 245, 310n; *dominatio in populum*, 240; *do-*

436

Index

Index

Index

mental power, 130, *administratio* vs *titulus* (or *nomen*), 131, 176n; papal election, 159, 161; bishop's oath of fealty, 326; bishop summoned by emperor and pope or metropolitan, 326, 329

subdeacon: has "holy orders," 64, 71, 91; eligible for election as bishop, 65-67, 90f, 95, 102

subscriptio: of election decree, 33n, 103-05 121, 145, 397f; Huguccio's commentary on, 104, 121, 397-401; renders election irrevocable, 104f, 138, 397f; confirms election, 105; *approbatio* requires, 105; forms part of *substantia electionis*, 105; adds nothing to election, 124, 397f

subscriptio: or *professio* of one entering monastic life, 104n

suffragan bishops: elect metropolitan, 26, 192; confirm metropolitan-elect, 63f, 157n, 184f, 192; consecrate metropolitan-elect, 157n, 184; have *pars sollicitudinis*, 173; consecrate *electus* by order of confirmed metropolitan-elect, 175; oath to appear at provincial council, 331. *See also* bishop, metropolitan

Suger of St Denis: 81n; papal-imperial negotiations (1107), 243f; *honorati* in election, 264n, 265n; elevation of bishop, 366

Summa Animal est substantia: bishop-elect's rights, 142f; *ius ad rem petendam*, 143; *ius metropoliticum*, 180; pope, primate, metropolitan, 183, 192; bishop as secular judge, 322; secular jurisdiction of pope, 323n; bishop's military service, 324n

Summa Antiquitate et tempore: 56n

Summa Bambergensis, see: *Summa Animal est substantia*

Summa Cantabrigiensis: 57n

Summa Conditio ecclesiastice religionis: 57n

Summa De iure naturali: 326n

Summa Elegantius in iure divino: 17, election and confirmation, 94n; *matrimonium spirituale*, 124n, 148n; *pravilegium*, 315n; bishop as secular judge, 322n, 323n; bishop's oath of fealty, 332n; clerical status of emperor, 333n

Summa Et est sciendum: *papa electus* and bishop-elect, 98; vacancy in metropolitan see, 106; influence on Huguccio, 116n; papal election, 160f; *ius metropoliticum*, 180; bishop's military service, 323n;

secular jurisdiction of pope and bishop, 323n; bishop summoned by emperor and pope, 327; bishop as vassal, 332

Summa Inperatorie maiestati: 17; imperial coronation, 77n; office, election, confirmation, 94-97; influence on Huguccio, 116n; council approves election, 158; contrasted papal and episcopal election, 159; clergy may not shed blood, 322n; secular jurisdiction of bishop, 323n; bishop, *oeconomus*, patron, 391-96

Summa Lipsiensis, see: *Summa Omnis qui iuste iudicat*

Summa Monacensis, see: *Summa Inperatorie maiestati*

Summa Omnis qui iuste iudicat: sacramental power, 86n; *papa electus* and bishop-elect, 98f; influence on Huguccio, 116n; confirmation and jurisdiction, 119, 126; papal election, 160f

Summa Parisiensis: 53n, 57n, 74n; *potestas ordinis*, 51, 130n; influence on Huguccio, 116n; secular jurisdiction of bishop, 323n; emperor's consent to election, 325; oath of fealty, 361n

Summa Reginensis: probably composed by Peter of Benevento, 120n; *ordo* and *iurisdictio*, 120n; election, 143n

Summa Reverentia sacrorum canonum: papal election, 160n

Summa Tractaturus magister: *papa electus* and bishop-elect, 97f; papal election, 160; bishop's military service, 323n; absolution from oath of fealty, 360n; pope, bishop, emperor, *oeconomus*, 395f

Summa Wigorniensis: 57n

suspension: removes *usus officii*, 51, 59; power of, 58f, 83, 91; confirmation confers power of, 91; of priest or bishop, 129, 400

sword, see: *gladius*

Symmachus, pope: 75n

synod, *see*: council

Tancred: 17, 19; confirmation and jurisdiction, 113n; bishop-elect's rights, 140; *ius ad rem petendam*, 143n; bishop summoned by emperor and pope or metropolitan, 327-29; fealty and investiture, 338n; *iudex ordinarius*, 341n

taxation: bishop owes tribute for *regalia*, 312, 317f, 321; of clerics needs papal consent, 319n

Te Deum: sung after episcopal election, 114; after papal election, 154

439

Index

temporalities, *see: regalia*

Theobald, abp. of Canterbury: 150n

theology: and canon law, 11, 15f, and *passim*; theologians on *regalia*, 321

tiara, *see:* papacy (elevation of pope)

tithes: 220, 222, 226, 248, 282; clergy should live from, 306; belong inalienably to Church, 309; may not be held by laymen, 309, 316; some bishops live solely from, 317; Gratian on bishops' tithes, 318; part of *spiritualia*, 339

title: *titulus* distinct from exercise of jurisdiction (*administratio*), 131, 176n; *titulus* virtually identical with office, 176

tonsure: 299

Toulouse: *Responsa doctorum Tholosanorum*, 142

Tractatus de investitura episcoporum: papal *regalia*, 227n; investiture before consecration, 233; ecclesiastical and regalian property, 281n

translation: lawful only by pope, 149, 174, 381; of bishop, 174, 286, 380f; by emperor, 286

treaty of 1133: between Lothar III and Innocent II, 254-56, 262; described as *foedus*, 254f

tribute, *see:* taxation

Trier: burgrave of, 274. *See also* archbishoprics

Urban II, pope: on election, 34n; *ordinatio absoluta*, 52f; *beneficium* and *officium*, 54n; *pallium*, 169-71; simoniacs' defense, 211; *episcopatus*, 275n

Urban III, pope: and German church, 234n

Vassals: (un)confirmed bishop-elect may (not) enfeoff, 112, 338f, 346; 352; bishop-elect's right to fealty from, 113; duty to excommunicated lord, 129, 362; owe *auxilium et consilium*, 207n; receive lands from bishop, 222, 308f; refuse fealty to uninvested bishop-elect, 295, 297, 357; must obey confirmed but uninvested bishop-elect, 295n, 348, 353-55, 357, 360; of bishop, appeal to pope or emperor, 321f; Fulbert of Chartres on

duties of, 326; lose fief for disobeying bishop's summons, 330; owe fealty to confirmed *rex Romanorum*, 356; bound to office of deposed king or bishop, 361f

Venice, Peace of: 371

vicarius Christi: clergy as *vicarii Christi* in election, 231; metropolitan in consecration acts as, 231, 249; consecration makes bishop into, 300; monarch as, 385

vicedominus, see: *oeconomus*

Victor IV, antipope: elevation of, 151-56, 161f; enmantling, 151-56; election confirmed by Council of Pavia, 158; enthronement, 161; confirmed by emperor, 162n

Vincentius Hispanus: 17, 19; election confers rights, 133n, 139f; prelates-elect *immediate sub papa*, 195n; confirmation and jurisdiction, 195n, 196n, 197n

visitator: confirms suffragan's election *sede vacante metropolitana*, 106; unconfirmed metropolitan-elect or *exemptus* administers as, 197

Walconinus (Walkelinus): 109n

Wazo of Liège: and Henry III, 3f, 207-09; *secularia* vs *divinum officium*, 207-09; 217; Gelasian, 217

Wenrich of Trier: 221-23

Wibald, abbot of Corvey: 284n

Wichman, abp. of Magdeburg: 234n, 286

Widger, abp. of Ravenna: trial of, 206-09

Wido of Osnabrück: royal anointment, 206n

William LeMaire, *see:* LeMaire

William Naso: election, 114f

William of Holland, king of the Romans: 296, 349, 355

William of Mandagout: confirmation and jurisdiction, 196n

William of Savoy, bp. of Liège: 347f

William of Staufen, bp. of Constance: 198

Würzburg: Reichstag of 1133 at, 261n, 263-68, 270f, 273f, 276-78, 283, 384; *episcopatus* and *ducatus* of, 276n, 297

York, Anonymous of, *see:* Anglo-Norman Anonymous